# Redbrick University Revisited

## The Autobiography of 'Bruce Truscot'

# E. Allison Peers Publications

Editor
ANN L. MACKENZIE
*University of Glasgow*

Assistant Editor
CERI BYRNE
*University of Glasgow*

## Editorial Board

ADRIAN R. ALLAN
  *University of Liverpool*
GRAEME DAVIES
  *University of Glasgow*
R. T. DAVIES
  *University of Liverpool*
ALAN DEYERMOND
  *Queen Mary & Westfield College, London*
VICTOR DIXON
  *Trinity College, Dublin*
P. E. H. HAIR
  *University of Liverpool*
SYLVIA HARROP
  *University of Liverpool*
AUDREY LUMSDEN-KOUVEL
  *University of Illinois, Chicago*
I. L. McCLELLAND
  *University of Glasgow*

KENNETH MUIR
  *University of Liverpool*
†GIOVANNI PONTIERO
  *University of Manchester*
PAUL PRESTON
  *London School of Economics & Political Science*
GEOFFREY RIBBANS
  *Brown University*
J. M. RUANO DE LA HAZA
  *University of Ottawa*
DOROTHY S. SEVERIN
  *University of Liverpool*
HAROLD SILVER
  *The Open University*
ALBERT SLOMAN
  *University of Essex*
JOHN E. VAREY
  *Queen Mary & Westfield College, London*

E. Allison Peers Publications is a scholarly Series which specializes in publishing studies, memoirs and other documents concerned to illuminate the character, history and development of higher education in Great Britain and Ireland. Original contributions to related fields of academic study will also be considered. Scholars wishing to submit manuscripts for assessment may apply for further information to the Editor, to whom they should send a brief summary of their projected book. Manuscripts should not exceed four hundred pages of typescript. Editorial address: Department of Hispanic Studies, Hetherington Building, University of Glasgow, Glasgow, G12 8QQ.

E. Allison Peers Publications
VOLUME 1

E. Allison Peers

# Redbrick University Revisited
## The Autobiography of 'Bruce Truscot'

edited, with introduction, commentary and notes, by
ANN L. MACKENZIE and ADRIAN R. ALLAN

LIVERPOOL UNIVERSITY PRESS

First published 1996 by
Liverpool University Press
PO Box 147, Liverpool, L69 3BX

Copyright © 1996    by Ann L. Mackenzie and Adrian R. Allan

All rights reserved.

No part of this book may be reproduced, stored in a retrieval system, or transmitted in any form or by any means, electronic, mechanical, photocopying, recording or otherwise, without the prior written permission of the publishers.

British Library Cataloguing-in-Publication Data
A British Library CIP Record is available

ISBN  0–85323–397–7  Cased
      0–85323–259–8  Paper

> The authors are gratefully indebted to the University of Liverpool for a subvention from the Vice-Chancellor's Development Fund which has enabled publication of this book.

Printed and bound in the European Community
by Antony Rowe Ltd, Chippenham, Wiltshire

# For

# Professor Sir Graeme Davies

**Principal, University of Glasgow**
(Vice-Chancellor, University of Liverpool, 1986-1991)
(Chief Executive, Universities Funding Council, 1991-1993)
(Chief Executive, Higher Education Funding Council for England, 1993-1995)

## with admiration and gratitude

'A good man from Camford [is] not to be sneezed at'
(*The Autobiography of 'Bruce Truscot'*)

Edgar Allison Peers
('Bruce Truscot')
1891-1952
Gilmour Professor of Spanish 1922-1952
University of Liverpool

# CONTENTS

**INTRODUCTION**　　　Ann L. Mackenzie　　　1

**Editorial Commentary**　　　Ann L. Mackenzie　　　35

**Real Names and False Identities in**
***Redbrick University Revisited***　　　51


**EDITION**

## The Autobiography of E. Allison Peers

### Part I

| | | |
|---|---|---|
| Chapter 1 | School-days and Home Life | 61 |
| Chapter 2 | Cambridge | 75 |
| Chapter 3 | Schoolmastering | 85 |

### Part II

| | | |
|---|---|---|
| Chapter 4 | Probation | 125 |
| Chapter 5 | The 'New Testament' | 139 |
| Chapter 6 | The Gilmour Chair of Spanish | 149 |

# The Autobiography of 'Bruce Truscot'

## Part I

| | | |
|---|---|---|
| Chapter I | School and University, Act I (1885-1907) | 173 |
| Chapter II | School and University, Act II (1907-1918) | 219 |

## Part II

| | | |
|---|---|---|
| Chapter III | Redbrick: The Beginnings | 261 |
| Chapter IV | The Chair of English Literature | 331 |

## Postscript                                                              389

| | |
|---|---|
| Professor E. Allison Peers    Anon. | 395 |
| Allison Peers as a University Teacher    I. L. McClelland | 397 |
| E.A.P. Remembered    Audrey Lumsden-Kouvel | 400 |

## Appendix I
A Chronology of the Filling of the Gilmour Chair of
Spanish, 1919-1922    Adrian R. Allan                         411

Applications by E. Allison Peers for the Gilmour
Chair of Spanish, with related documents                      429

## Appendix II
The 'New Testament': Lipczinski's Painting and
Elton's Poem                                                  459

## Appendix III
Selected Correspondence from and to 'Bruce Truscot'           467

## Appendix IV
**Any Faculty Board**: An Essay by 'Bruce Truscot'            481

## Bibliography                                                            495
## Index                                                                   505

# LIST OF ILLUSTRATIONS

Edgar Allison Peers ('Bruce Truscot'), 1891-1952, Gilmour Professor of Spanish, 1922-1952, University of Liverpool ... ... vii

Letter, dated 8 October 1942, from Allison Peers to Faber and Faber Ltd, inviting them to publish the recently completed manuscript of *Red Brick University*. Reproduced in facsimile by kind permission of Mr John Bodley, Editorial Director, Faber and Faber Ltd, London. Photograph by Suzanne Yee, Photographic Service, Department of Geography, University of Liverpool ... ... ... xv

First page of *The Autobiography of E. Allison Peers* and first page of *The Autobiography of 'Bruce Truscot'* (Archives, University of Liverpool). Originals reproduced in facsimile to illustrate not only Peers' tiny handwriting but his characteristic 'cut and paste' technique. Photographs by Suzanne Yee, Photographic Service, Department of Geography, University of Liverpool ... ... ... 32-33

Letter of reference, dated 10 May 1922, received from Ramón Menéndez Pidal in support of E. Allison Peers' election to the Gilmour Chair of Spanish (Archives, University of Liverpool). Reproduced in facsimile, courtesy of the University, by Suzanne Yee, Photographic Service, Department of Geography, University of Liverpool ... 158

The Victoria Building (1889-1892), designed by Alfred Waterhouse. The water-colour (1950) by Allan P. Tankard is reproduced with permission from Mrs Elizabeth Tankard and the University of Liverpool. The same painting features as the cover illustration of *Redbrick University Revisited* ... ... ... ... ... ... 276

The 'New Testament' (c.1914-1917), an oil painting by Albert Lipczinski (Art Collections, University of Liverpool). Professor John Macdonald Mackay, founder of the group, addresses fellow members of the 'New Testament'. Reproduced, courtesy of the University, by the Central Photographic Service, University of Liverpool ... ... 458

# ACKNOWLEDGEMENTS

We wish to express our profound indebtedness for information and assistance to the following persons and institutions:

A  Professor Audrey Lumsden-Kouvel, University of Illinois at Chicago, who, as literary executor of E. Allison Peers, gave the editors permission to publish his autobiography.

B  The University of Liverpool, for allowing the editors to utilize, without restrictions, the incomparable body of material preserved in its Archives which illuminates the career of E. Allison Peers.

C  Mr John Bodley (Editorial Director, Faber and Faber Ltd, London) for providing copies of early correspondence with E. Allison Peers about the publication by Faber and Faber of *Redbrick University* (1943).

D  Professor David A. Wells, Honorary Secretary of the Modern Humanities Research Association, London, for granting access to the archives of the Association.

E  For information and general assistance:

Mr Stuart Allan (Historical Search Room, Scottish Record Office); Mr Simon Bailey (Archivist, University of Oxford); Mr J. Barrett (Department of Leisure and Libraries, Moray District Council); Mr Keith Barry (formerly Second Master of The Perse School and a member of the School's staff from 1936); Mrs Aimée K. Bass; Mrs J. C. Berry-Richards (Deputy Headmistress, Chelmsford County High School for Girls); Dr Jacqueline Bower (Research Assistant, Centre for Kentish Studies); Mr Henry G. Button (Honorary Archivist of Christ's College, Cambridge); Miss Geraldine M. Cadbury (Headmistress of Chelmsford County High School for Girls, 1935-61); Professor Claude Chauchadis (Director, Institut d'Études Hispaniques et Hispano-Américaines, Université de Toulouse-Le Mirail); Mrs Rosalyn C. Churchman

# ACKNOWLEDGEMENTS

(daughter of the executor of Mrs Julia Fitzmaurice-Kelly); Dr Cecil Clough (Reader in History, University of Liverpool); Mrs Brenda R. Cluer (Regional Archivist, Grampian Regional Council); Jo Currie (Special Collections, Edinburgh University Library); Elinor Fillion (Reference Librarian, University of Toronto Library); Dr Paul Frank (Surgeon of the Hospitals of Strasbourg, Strasbourg); Mr Alastair Graham (Headmaster, Mill Hill School, 1979-92); Mr Timothy B. Groom (Staffordshire County Record Office); Mrs Elizabeth Hall (former postgraduate student of Allison Peers and widow of the late Harold Hall, Gilmour Professor of Spanish [1978-81], University of Liverpool); Professor L. P. Harvey (King's College, London); Professor Alastair Hetherington; Mr Ian Hill (Assistant Registrar, National Register of Archives [Scotland]); Mr Nicholas S. Hinde (Archivist, Felsted School, Dunmow); Mr Steven D. Hobbs (County Archivist, Wiltshire County Record Office); Kate Hutcheson (University Archives, University of Glasgow); Mrs C. Ibrahim (University of London Library); Dr David A. Iredale (District Archivist, Moray District Record Office); Mr Bernard Jubb (Head of Technical Services, Sydney Jones Library, University of Liverpool); Mr Norman J. Lamb (formerly Senior Lecturer in Hispanic Studies, University of Liverpool); Dr Elisabeth Leedham-Green (Assistant Keeper, University Archives, University of Cambridge); the late Professor Derek Lomax (University of Birmingham); Mrs Naomi van Loo (Deputy Librarian, Pembroke College, Oxford); Mr Colin A. McLaren (University Archivist, University of Aberdeen); Dr Peter McNiven (Head of Special Collections, John Rylands University Library of Manchester); Ms Patricia J. Methven (College Archivist, King's College, London); Mr Simon Mills (H.M. Customs and Excise, Personnel Directorate Division 4, Salford); Dorothy E. Mosakowski (Coordinator of Archives and Special Collections, Clark University, Worcester, Mass.); Professor Kenneth Muir (formerly King Alfred Professor of English Literature, University of Liverpool); Mrs Maxine Myerson; Professor Eric Naylor (University of the South, Sewanee); Dr Mark Nicholls (Department of Manuscripts and University Archives,

## ACKNOWLEDGEMENTS

Cambridge University Library); Mr David Patterson (Senior History Teacher, Dartford Grammar School); Mr Roger N. R. Peers (first cousin once removed of E. Allison Peers); the late Professor Pedro Peira (Universidad Complutense de Madrid); Kate Perry (Archivist, Girton College, Cambridge); Mr A. N. Ricketts (formerly member of the senior library staff, University of Liverpool); Eamonn Rodgers (Professor of Spanish and Latin American Studies, University of Strathclyde); Mr Anthony Sampson; Mr M. Seton (Assistant Director [Information and Administration], Department of Leisure and Libraries, Moray District Council); Michael Smallman (Sub-Librarian, Arts/Special Collections, Queen's University of Belfast); Mr Robert C. Sopwith (Archivist, Wellington College); Mrs Anthea Speakman (Chairperson, Chelmsford County High School for Girls Old Girls' Society); Dr Martin Stephen (Headmaster of the Perse School, 1987-1994); Professor Kathleen Tillotson (widow of Professor Geoffrey Tillotson); Lorett Treese (College Archivist, Bryn Mawr College, PA); Mr Jeff Walden (BBC Written Archives Centre, Reading); Mr Geoffrey Waller (Superintendent, Manuscripts Reading Room, Cambridge University Library); Mr Graeme Wilson (Department of Leisure and Libraries, Moray District Council).

### THE UNIVERSITY OF LIVERPOOL

8th October, 1942.

*See as soon as ready*

Dear Sirs,

        I am just concluding a new book on the subject of the modern University, which I should like to submit for your consideration if you thought it was a book which you could advantageously publish.

        I believe it to be the first book of its kind of any length and I am hoping that as it covers a fairly wide ground it will be of interest in connection with post-war reconstruction of the Universities. I am enclosing an analytical Table of Contents which I hope will give you a fair idea of its scope.

        It will have, I am afraid, to be published under a pseudonym, as I have criticised very freely and it would create all kinds of difficulties if my identity were known.

        The approximate length is 75,000 words and I should be very glad to send you the typescript to read if it interests you.

        Believe me to be,

        Yours faithfully,

*Allison Peers*

Letter, dated 8 October 1942, from E. Allison Peers to Faber and Faber Ltd, inviting them to publish the manuscript of *Red Brick University*. Reproduced in facsimile by kind permission of Mr John Bodley, Editorial Director, Faber and Faber Ltd, London.

Photograph by Suzanne Yee, Photographic Service, Department of Geography, University of Liverpool

# INTRODUCTION

## I

*Redbrick University* by 'Bruce Truscot' was published in 1943, together with its sequels, *Redbrick and these Vital Days* (1945) and *First Year at the University* (1946), during what was, indeed, for universities in Britain, a 'vital' period of change into planned development and post-War expansion. Not only within the 'newer' and 'older' institutions of higher learning, but also among educationists, in learned reviews, on the radio, through editorials in newspapers, and even within the inner circles and committees of government, Truscot's books provoked — as their author had wholly intended that they should — spirited and prolonged debates throughout the land.[1] The purposes of a university were discussed and disputed, as were the responsibilities of a university teacher, the priorities in university administration, the nature and importance of research and the requirements of undergraduates. Before long the 'barbarous but convenient' terms, 'Redbrick' and 'Oxbridge', imaginatively publicized by the author of the 'Truscot' books, had entered the British language of education,[2] to be utilized

---

1  A large collection of reviews, in the form of press-cuttings, may be consulted among the Peers Papers, held in the Archives of the University of Liverpool (ref: D.265). Reviewers of the 'Redbrick Books' included: Max Beloff (*Time and Tide*, 11 September 1943 and 7 July 1945); Bonamy Dobrée (*Adult Education*, XVI [December 1943], no.2, 96-98); A. J. P. Taylor (*Oxford Magazine* [10 February 1944]); C. Grant Robertson (*Manchester Guardian*, 13 August 1943); A. V. Murray (*Cambridge Review*, 5 February 1944 and 9 March 1946); W. Burmeister (*Adult Education*, XVIII [March 1946], no. 3, 145-47).

2  See Introduction to Bruce Truscot, *Redbrick University* (London: Faber and Faber Ltd, 1943), 12. Peers coined the term 'Redbrick' but the words 'Oxbridge' and 'Camford' were first used in the nineteenth century by Thackeray (see *The Oxford English Dictionary*; and *cf.*, below, *The Autobiography of 'Bruce Truscot'*, ch. I, p. 182, note 40; Postscript, p. 408). There is no doubt that the popularity and influence of Truscot's books led to the now generalized use of the term 'Oxbridge'. In a review of *The History of the University of Oxford*, Vol. VIII *The Twentieth Century*, which

repeatedly, almost indispensably, in any discussion in which the traditions and attitudes of the ancient seats of learning at Oxford and Cambridge are compared and contrasted with the characteristics and preoccupations of the 'modern' institutions, or 'city' establishments, founded in the late Victorian age, and, therefore, typically housed in Victorian redbrick buildings.

The mysterious question of Truscot's real identity aroused nearly as much intensity of interest as did the issues of which he wrote. In the civic universities especially (Manchester, Leeds, Sheffield, Liverpool...), or so it is said, academics neglected their research, preferring to speculate as to who it was who had accused academics like themselves of neglecting their research. As they walked within buildings usually made of 'hideously cheerful red brick', moved along halls and passages lined with 'harsh and ugly blue or yellow tiles', and ascended 'interminable staircases to corridor upon corridor',[3] they wondered which of their sister-institutions could possibly have been the model for Redbrick University, because, though they could find similarities between themselves and Professors Active and Livewire, only in academics of other establishments did they notice resemblances to Truscot's less reputable colleagues, the disgracefully aloof Professor Inaccessible and the scandalously idle Professor Deadwood. Speculation had intensified in 1945, when *Redbrick and these Vital Days* was published. A report in *The Listener* declared that:

> the common room at Redbrick is already a-buzz with comment and discussion about the new 'Truscot'; speculation as to his identity has stimulated further research into internal evidences, and Professor Livewire brandishes his copy under the nose of Professor Deadwood. Professor Deadwood continues to look down his nose.[4]

---

was published in *The Times Higher Education Supplement* (24 June 1994), entitled ' "Oxbridge" does not exist', Max Beloff began by declaring ' "Oxbridge" is a term freely used by journalists; those who know Oxford and Cambridge from the inside are more impressed by the fact that they do most things differently'.

3  See Introduction, *Redbrick University*, 17. *Cf.* Peers' description, in *The Autobiography of 'Bruce Truscot'* (ch. III, p. 277), of the main buildings at Redbrick University (which is, of course, inspired by his impressions of, especially, the Victoria Building, in the University of Liverpool).

4  See *The Listener*, dated 28 June 1945.

In an appreciative review of 'the new "Truscot" ' in *Adult Education,* W. Burmeister finds the author ('But how entertainingly he writes'):

> regretfully pleased at the 'excited speculation' over his real name... Who done it? Scores of people, some of whom allowed you to infer that they were accessories before the fact, have volunteered an answer to this question.

Burmeister suspects that the hint or two, in the Preface, which the author cannot resist dropping to increase speculation, might prove to be 'his undoing. All power corrupts — even the power to remain anonymous'.[5] Despite these few hints, however, and a huge amount of speculation, the name of the university teacher responsible for the 'Redbrick' books was known only to himself and a tiny number of his close friends and colleagues until the death, in December 1952, at the unexpectedly early age of sixty-one, of E. Allison Peers, Gilmour Professor of Spanish in the University of Liverpool. As Sir James Mountford, then Vice-Chancellor, conceded, in an appreciation published soon after Peers died, 'the identity of "Bruce Truscot" was probably the best kept literary secret of the last half century'.[6]

When the secret of Truscot's real identity was discovered nowhere was there registered a higher degree of astonishment than in the place in which Peers had spent his entire career of

---

    5   See *Adult Education,* XVIII (March 1946), no. 3, 145-47. According to Kenneth Muir, formerly King Alfred Professor of English Literature, University of Liverpool, one of the people suspected of being 'Bruce Truscot' was Bonamy Dobrée, Professor of English Literature, University of Leeds. Dobrée was a logical suspect since he had written upon matters of Higher Education. Indeed, in *Redbrick and these Vital Days* Truscot alludes flatteringly to an 'eloquent lecture' on 'The Universities and Regional Life', which Dobrée had delivered at King's College, Newcastle-upon-Tyne in April 1943 (113). Both Bonamy Dobrée and Bruce Truscot contributed articles to a series on 'The Future of the Universities' which appeared in *The Political Quarterly,* XV (1944). Interestingly, Dobrée's article concerned 'Arts Faculties in Modern Universities'. Truscot's essay was entitled 'The University and its Region'. Dobrée reviewed *Redbrick University* in *Adult Education (cf.* note 1). Letters between Dobrée and Truscot are reproduced in Appendix III.
    6   See J. F. Mountford, 'Bruce Truscot', *Memorial Number* of the *Bulletin of Hispanic Studies,* XXX (1953), no. 117, 10-11, at 10.

more than thirty years as a university teacher.⁷ Had Peers lived to witness the reactions of most of his colleagues at the University of Liverpool he would not have found in the least surprising their extreme surprise. For, as he had commented in the wittily revealing Preface to *Redbrick and these Vital Days*, at the universities with which he was personally acquainted he had never encountered academics prepared to believe that *their* institution could possibly have been the model for an establishment with uninspiring lecturers, non-researching professors and reactionary members of Council.⁸ In fact, however, the shocked feelings of incredulity experienced at Liverpool by many members of staff, particularly within the Faculty of Arts, were caused not so much by their possibly too exalted view of their own university as by their personal opinions and observations of their underestimated colleague, Allison Peers. As complex in character as he was profound in intellect, Peers was a difficult man to know well, and within the University of Liverpool, outside his own department and away from the close circle of his friends, he was not well understood, nor particularly well liked. There were some who were misled or put off by surface-indications of brusqueness or impatience.⁹ Others felt uncomfortable in his company because of perceived differences between what they did at work and how much Peers accomplished — with his students and during his researches. There were also those who considered unseemly the extent to which Peers publicized the activities and projects in Hispanic

---

7   Mountford declares that the guess, made in some quarters prior to 1952, that Allison Peers was the author of the 'Truscot' books, 'was never taken seriously' in Liverpool University (see 'Bruce Truscot', *Bulletin of Hispanic Studies*, XXX [1953], no. 117, 10).

8   See *Redbrick and these Vital Days* (London: Faber and Faber Ltd, 1945), 15. In a letter written to Geoffrey Tillotson (27 December 1943), Peers remarks that Truscot's colleagues never thought to look for themselves in his pages (see letter reproduced in Appendix III, pp. 469-70).

9   Peers, a man with considerable self-knowledge, was aware that he sometimes gave to others misleading impressions of his true nature and attitudes. See his description of Jim Livewire (that is, of himself) in *The Autobiography of 'Bruce Truscot'*, ch. IV, p. 363, and note 86. *Cf.* also Inaccessible's opinion of Livewire: 'a combative, intolerant person who would certainly prove difficult and quite possibly turn out a crank' ('B.T.', ch. IV, p. 366, note 94).

Studies that he inspired and directed. None could deny his indefatigable and thoroughly successful endeavours, during several decades, to promote — not only at Liverpool but in universities, schools and colleges throughout the country — the teaching and the study of the languages, literatures and civilizations of Spain, Portugal and even of Latin America. What many could not understand was how a professor of Spanish who had visited so many schools to talk about the subject, organized so many summer courses in Spain, accepted so many visiting professorships abroad, taught so many students, directed so many gifted postgraduates into university jobs as Hispanists, and — by no means least — written so many different books on diversely important aspects of Hispanic Studies, could possibly have had remaining sufficient professional time in which to accomplish anything besides? When could he have done the considerable reading and research necessary to inform himself about the aims and problems of the modern universities? While seeming so little interested in the affairs and persons of the University which were unconnected with Hispanic Studies, how could he have observed so keenly the functions and malfunctions of faculty boards and senate meetings, the conduct and misconduct of colleagues, the uses, abuses and idiosyncrasies of university regulations? Where on earth, and in heaven's name, did Allison Peers find these 'vital days' or weeks needed to write, as 'Bruce Truscot', the several books about 'Redbrick University'?

Peers was renowned, even revered, widely through the world for the scholarship and influence of his numerous major books and articles on Spain. His works included, among many other contributions, his volumes of *Studies of the Spanish Mystics*, his surveys, analyses and *History of the Romantic Movement in Spain* and his perceptive evaluations of contemporary issues and conflicts — religious, social and political — in an entire series of works about *The Spanish Dilemma*; *Spain, the Church and the Orders*; *Catalonia Infelix*; *The Spanish Tragedy 1930-1936: Dictatorship, Republic, Chaos*; and *Spain in Eclipse 1937-1943*. Nevertheless, this 'man of formidable talent', as he is judiciously described in Thomas Kelly's *For Advancement of Learning. The University of Liverpool 1881-1981,* 'one of the most remarkable men ever to hold a Liverpool Chair',[10] was never remarkable for his popularity within his home-institution. Nearly a decade before *Redbrick University* was pseudonymously composed, the complex and ambiguous attitudes towards Allison Peers evident among other academics at Liverpool University were described in poetry by an acute and admirably objective observer. In a poem written to portray the 'Senate in Laputa' (1934-35), F. J. Routledge, then Senior Lecturer in the Department of History, eloquent in wit and sympathetic through comprehension, conveys at once the acknowledged achievements of Peers, and the resentment which, with admiration, these achievements brought him. Having described 'the Gallic Fire of Eggli', the Professor of French, in Senate, 'when the hated Peers / About some Bursar rashly interferes', Routledge continues, memorably, as follows:

> Should Peers new fields of golden conquest crave,
> He speaks so smoothly that he's thought a knave,
> Or cursed for advertising when he seeks
> To breast, *as scholars should*, some unscaled peaks;[11]

Dislike of 'the hated Peers' reached its height, or depth, at Liverpool in 1952. For when 'the true authorship [of the "Redbrick" books] became known', as Kelly has remarked, 'it was not difficult to trace references, not always complimentary, to the University of Liverpool', and Peers had made 'acid comments on some Arts professors'.[12] As Peers himself had realized, once his own identity was known, the identity of those about whom he wrote was also known.[13] Doubtless, as Peers

---

10 See Thomas Kelly, *For Advancement of Learning. The University of Liverpool 1881-1981* (Liverpool: Liverpool U. P., 1981), 220.

11 My italics. This unpublished poem was lodged by Dr Janet Smellie in the University's Archives (ref. D.498/6/1/1) together with other papers of her father, the late Sir James Mountford (Vice-Chancellor, 1945-63).

12 See Kelly, *For Advancement of Learning*, 221.

13 See his insistence upon anonymity in his letters to Faber and Faber concerning publication of *Red Brick University*; 'It will have, I am afraid, to be published under a pseudonym, as I have criticised very freely and it would create all kinds of difficulties if my identity were known' (letter dated 8 October 1942 — reproduced above in facsimile; *cf.* letter to Faber and Faber, dated 7 December 1942, printed in Appendix III, pp. 467-68). Peers, it will be noticed, originally preferred to write, and have printed, the title of

INTRODUCTION    7

had also suspected, 'a good many identities' were discovered which the author had never put into the books. Personal offence was taken at passages in which personal allusions were absent. As his colleagues went hunting for each other through the pages of *Redbrick University* and *Redbrick and these Vital Days*, resentments which Peers had not wished to provoke were stimulated and aggravated.[14] In Spain and in many other countries the passing of a great scholar was greatly mourned, and masses were said in every Carmelite convent world-wide for the soul of the man of letters and religion who had illuminated, through *Spirit of Flame, Mother of Carmel* and other works, the spiritual profundities within the mystical writings of Saint John of the Cross and Saint Teresa of Ávila. Meanwhile, on Merseyside, during the Requiem Mass for Allison Peers, even when he spoke of Peers with profound admiration as a man who pursued 'the way of interior holiness', the vicar was obliged, in truth, to concede that 'some people did not get on with him very well', because Peers was 'a man of resolute will and strong determination: he knew his own mind and was unswervingly loyal to his own deep-seated convictions'. He was an individual determined never to be pruned 'in the garden of other people's opinions'.[15]

Yet, there were certainly some among Peers' colleagues at Liverpool University who reacted to 'Bruce Truscot' without malice and resentment, giving less importance and attention to

---

Truscot's first book in *three* words (*cf*. 'B.T.', ch. I, p. 216). But the spelling fluctuated, and the term soon entered our language as 'Redbrick' university.

14   See the Preface to *Redbrick and these Vital Days*, and especially, the following passage:

> Once my own identity was known, the identity of those of whom I had written would immediately have been recognized; and not only so, but a good many identities would have been discovered which I had never put there. No good that I could see would be done, and considerable resentment might well be caused, if my colleagues went hunting for each other in the more trenchant of my pages.
>
> (13-14)

15   A copy of this sermon from which I have quoted — which was given at the Requiem Mass for Allison Peers, at St Andrew's Church, West Kirby, on 1 January 1953 — is located among Peers' papers in the Archives of the University of Liverpool (ref. D.265).

the particular institution from which Peers had derived most of his inspiration and material than to the enduring qualities of thoughtful insight into British universities, their aims, problems and attainments, contained within the pages of *Redbrick University, Redbrick and these Vital Days* and *First Year at the University*. The eminent leader of this perceptive group of men, and women, was the Vice-Chancellor himself. In 1953 the *Bulletin of Hispanic Studies* which Peers had founded — and which still continues, as one of the leading journals in its field throughout the world — issued a *Memorial Number* containing an evaluation of the 'Bruce Truscot' books contributed by Sir James Mountford. This respected scholar, educationist, and outstanding vice-chancellor discerned in the author of *Redbrick University* and *Redbrick and these Vital Days* 'a masterly knowledge of the history, organization, ideals, achievements and ethos of the ancient and modern Universities'. In Mountford's good opinion, these are books which

> deal with every aspect of old and new problems from academic freedom, the control allegedly exercised by University Councils, the lecture system, and the residential ideal, to Appointments Boards, athletics and Students' Unions. But what makes them particularly significant is the crusading spirit which underlies them. Peers was desperately anxious that Universities should not be tempted to lose their way or be distracted from their true purposes. First among those purposes he placed research; next he placed hard honest teaching — and how well in both respects he practised what he preached! [...]
>
> In whatever years they had been published, these books would have touched and quickened the academic conscience; issued in 1943 and 1945, they came at a critical juncture in the history of University education and exerted an influence for the good wherever English is understood. As expositor and critic, Peers rendered a service which any professional philosopher of education might well envy. Not everyone will agree with all he wrote; but no one who has read him can fail to have been grateful for his provocative challenge.[16]

---

16 See Mountford, 'Bruce Truscot', *Bulletin of Hispanic Studies*, XXX (1953), no. 117, 11. Peers founded this journal in 1923.

## II

The true identity of 'Bruce Truscot' was not the only unsuspected secret which Allison Peers had kept for years quietly concealed from almost all his colleagues and acquaintances. In the period 1944-1947, when, among British academics and educationists, interest in *Redbrick University* and its sequels was profound and country-wide, Peers had composed a 'Truscot' book which he did not send to his publishers. That book was different from the others because it revealed the author's real name and narrated his life-story. Peers had intended to publish it only after his retirement. 'Truscot' had mentioned his proposed autobiography in more than one letter written in 1945 when he courteously replied, through the discreet offices of his publishers, to the numerous correspondents (writers, reviewers, university teachers and graduates) who wrote to him concerning his views about Redbrick, Oxbridge, Camford and universities in general. A letter written to Bonamy Dobrée, purporting to come from Amelia Truscot, wife of Bruce, mentions that her husband will begin upon his autobiography after his holiday — 'But that will not be published until he retires'.[17] The Professor of Philosophy at Bristol University, G. C. Field, received a letter, dated 11 October 1945, in which the author of *Redbrick University* told him:

> When I retire, I hope to publish my autobiography, which will perhaps make clear that my failure to show professors proper respect is founded on experience.

Field — who like Sir Hector Hetherington, Principal of the University of Glasgow, corresponded with 'Bruce Truscot' without realizing that he was writing to someone who had formerly been his colleague at the University of Liverpool — possibly did not take very seriously this declared intention of his pseudonymous correspondent.[18] In fact, however, by then

---

[17] This letter, dated 23 June 1945, together with other selected correspondence with 'Bruce Truscot' is reproduced in Appendix III, pp. 467-80.

[18] The letter to Field of 11 October 1945 and Hetherington's correspondence with Truscot are printed in Appendix III, pp. 473-74, 479-80.

'Truscot' had already begun work on the book in question. When Allison Peers died and the world of learning at last discovered who was 'Bruce Truscot', his heirs and executors made a much more private discovery of several envelopes in the drawer of his desk. These envelopes contained, in the author's characteristically tiny handwriting, the unpublished autobiographies of Allison Peers and 'Bruce Truscot'.

Had they been published in the early 1950s, when the identity of 'Bruce Truscot' was still a chief talking-point among astonished academics, these autobiographies undoubtedly would have been eagerly purchased and widely read. Their influence and success might even have rivalled that exerted, and achieved, in the previous decade by *Redbrick University* and *Redbrick and these Vital Days*. There were, however, other considerations — not least, bruised resentments of some among Peers' former colleagues at Liverpool University — which made immediate publication of his final 'Redbrick' book seem ill-advised and inappropriate. Admittedly, the manuscript was largely concerned to describe events which had taken place some thirty years previously. Peers narrates, in particular detail, objectively and with discretion, the conflicts and controversies which had divided the Faculty of Arts in 1920-1922, when the semi-secret society of influential academics known as the 'New Testament' had persistently, but, in the end, unsuccessfully, opposed his appointment to the Gilmour Chair of Spanish. Nevertheless, some of the personalities involved in these memorable events were yet living in the early 1950s, and a few of them, in post or not long retired, were even still at or associated with the University of Liverpool. Moreover, Peers' own wishes could not be discounted. Certainly he had wished the manuscript to be published, but he had not intended it to put in an early public appearance. Had he lived, he would have sent it to his publishers only after he had revised and doubtless expanded his recollections of his university career during the unhurried period of retirement, which, as we all do, he had hopefully expected to enjoy.[19] Prudently, Peers' heirs and literary executors decided not to rush the manuscript into print. The autobiographies of Allison

---

19 For further comment upon Peers' intentions, particularly his intention to continue his memoirs, see Editorial Commentary, pp. 39-41.

Peers and 'Bruce Truscot' were allowed to occupy undisturbed a drawer in the desk where their author had left them. There the work remained until times changed, and, in their fullness, became ripe, and right, for publication.

Peers' desk, with its Truscotian contents, remained for a period with his literary executor, Audrey Lumsden,[20] who had been Peers' student and later his colleague at Liverpool University. When Audrey Lumsden moved from England to enjoy married life, and establish a distinguished career as a Hispanist, in the United States, the desk, with the manuscript, passed safely into the keeping of Ivy McClelland, another of Peers' graduates. She had become one of the first women to be appointed to a university post in Hispanic Studies when, in 1930, she obtained a lectureship at the University of Glasgow. She had quickly also acquired an outstanding reputation for the qualities of her research and publications.[21] At Glasgow, during the 1960s, I was privileged to be a student of Ivy McClelland. She had an aptitude for teaching comparable to that which her own exceptionally gifted teacher had possessed: she trained me in Hispanic Studies as Allison Peers had trained her; and she encouraged me, as he had encouraged her, to pursue a university career in teaching and research. As the pupil of his pupil, I regarded myself, academically speaking, as a 'descendant' of Allison Peers, so that when I was appointed to a lectureship in the University of Liverpool, I went with a sense of pleasurable destiny, to join a department in which several of Peers' former colleagues were still teachers. I experienced similarly enjoyable feelings of destiny some twenty years later, when Ivy McClelland gave me the desk which had once belonged to the scholar whose achievements I so much admired — the desk at which he had written many works on Hispanic language, history, literature, and also, indeed, his books about 'Redbrick' universities. Together with the desk

---

20 Now Professor Audrey Lumsden-Kouvel, University of Illinois, Chicago.

21 For information on the career of Ivy McClelland, see my 'Introduction' to *The Eighteenth Century in Spain. Essays in Honour of I. L. McClelland*, edited by Ann L. Mackenzie, *Bulletin of Hispanic Studies*, LXVIII (1991), no. 1, 1-9.

there came into my possession the envelopes containing the still unpublished Peers and 'Truscot' autobiographies.

The autobiographies which were given to me in 1989 were delivered with a request. Would I evaluate the manuscript? Should this text simply be lodged in the University's Archives, to enlarge there the number of unprinted memoirs written by former members of staff, and to form part of the considerable body of papers related to Peers which Liverpool University already possessed? Or, were these autobiographies of sufficiently enduring concern, literary merit and historical importance to justify their publication? Would I make a decision as to whether, more than forty years after 'Bruce Truscot' had ceased to write about his university and his academic colleagues, Redbrick University deserved to be, as it were, revisited?

## III

I read the manuscript with considerable attention, not only because of my genuinely developed interest in Peers, 'Bruce Truscot' and Redbrick University, but because Peers' tiny handwriting, and his numerous changes, corrections and deletions, meant that maximum concentration was required to decipher his text. He had written two narratives, of which the first is a straightforward account of his early life and young manhood. He deals with his childhood and school-days, with his years spent at Cambridge, as a student and student teacher, and with his experiences, during several more years, schoolmastering, for instance at Felsted School. He then describes, in particular detail, his career, his colleagues and his difficulties at Liverpool University between 1920 and 1922 — the period during which a group of senior academics within the Faculty of Arts conspired to prevent his appointment to the Gilmour Chair of Spanish. Peers' opponents, known as the 'New Testament' were led by the Professor of Philosophy, Alexander Mair, and influenced, from London, by the former 'New Testamentarian', Professor James Fitzmaurice-Kelly. He had been previous, and first, holder of the Gilmour Chair at Liverpool, when it was the only Chair of Spanish in Britain. He had resigned to take up the newly established Cervantes

Chair of Spanish Language and Literature at King's College London. His extraordinarily prejudiced views of Peers' character and qualifications are difficult to explain, unless they were caused mainly by envy. While the 'New Testament' manipulated regulations and dominated meetings, Peers' supporters, among whom were E. T. Campagnac, Professor of Education, and the Professor of German, W. E. Collinson, waged a more honourable campaign, which was eventually successful. The first autobiography concludes with the defeat of the 'New Testament' and the confirmation by the University Council of Peers' appointment as professor of Spanish.

The second narrative, which is the autobiography of 'Bruce Truscot', is a fictionalized account of essentially the same conflicts and experiences in Peers' life which he has already described directly, and much more briefly, in the first part of the book. This consciously disguised piece of autobiographical literature assumes many of the characteristics of a masterly *roman à clef* — the keys, or clues, to the understanding of which are to be encountered in Peers' previous narrative. In this autobiography, skilfully disguised as fiction, the narrator and chief character is, to all appearances, Bruce Truscot, renowned author of *Redbrick University* and its sequels. A Camford graduate and former schoolmaster, who supposedly in his youth had been a lecturer at Oxbridge, he is a now elderly scholar of English literature (some years older, so it seems, than Allison Peers), at Redbrick University, where he occupies the Chair of Poetry. Though he does not neglect to describe his early life and career before he came to Redbrick University, Truscot's main concern, like that of the author of the Peers narrative, is to recount the strange history of his conflict, more than twenty years previously, with a group of academics opposed to his principles, and to his appointment to the professorship which he still holds. That group, which was in reality, and also in the Peers narrative, the 'New Testament', are called, in the 'Truscot' account, with witty inappropriateness, the 'Salvation Army'. Prominent among these unholy 'Salvationists' are Professors Wormwood and Inaccessible, figures derived from the real-life characters of Peers' main opponents, Alexander Mair and John Sampson. Fitzmaurice-Kelly is recreated in the form of Professor Upright, whose name accurately describes his bearing but ironically misrepresents his nature. Despite the efforts of Upright and the 'Salvationists', Truscot's election to the Chair of Poetry is confirmed. This victory, however, is not the end of Truscot's story or of the 'Salvation Army'. Truscot and his friends at Redbrick University are obliged to engage subsequently, through concern for justice, in a conflict with Professor Wormwood and his accomplices in intrigue, over the election to the vacant Chair of English Literature. Described in a final chapter, this conflict is a differently fictionalized version of the strange history of strife in the University of Liverpool over Peers' appointment in Spanish to the Gilmour professorship. A Camford graduate with an excellent record of research, by the name of Jim Livewire — which is, of course, another pseudonym of Allison Peers —, is obviously the best candidate. But the 'Salvation Army' are intent upon securing the Chair of English Literature for the internal candidate, Anstruther,[22] a graduate of Redbrick, and, moreover, a 'Salvationist'. Anstruther is a good administrator, and, by all accounts, a reasonably good teacher, but he has done little research, and his list of publications is almost non-existent. Despite the endeavours of Truscot, and of Livewire's other supporters, the 'Salvation Army', through 'blood-and-fire' rhetoric and behind-the-scenes intrigue, nearly succeed in obtaining Anstruther's appointment. If they had done so, they would have saved their damaged reputation, enabling them to convert their previous defeat into final victory. Fortunately, Redbrick University is blessed with an excellent Vice-Chancellor. Sir Archibald Blake — in whose personality the author has combined the best characteristics of two of Liverpool University's vice-chancellors, J. G. Adami and Hector Hetherington — does not believe in appointing unproductive scholars to university Chairs. Fortunately, also, the Senate, most of whose members take the view that 'a good man from Camford was not be sneezed at', votes, justly, against the wishes of the 'Salvationists', and Jim Livewire is appointed to the Chair of English Literature. To conclude his narrative, Truscot remembers a conversation with

---

22 The figure of Anstruther appears mainly to be derived from that of Robert Hope Case (see *The Autobiography of 'Bruce Truscot'*, ch. III, pp. 294-98, and note 94).

his friends about the final downfall of the 'Salvation Army'. During this conversation, amusingly, the victors agree that the activities of that now deceased semi-secret society ought to be recorded in a book — 'as a warning'. Even more amusingly, they decide that their old adversary, Professor Inaccessible ought to be asked to write the book: for, after all, 'isn't he... Professor of Ancient History?'.[23]

In many, though not all, respects the 'Truscot' narrative fits into a peculiarly British literary genre — which is, in Malcolm Bradbury's words, 'something called the University novel', and which 'has become a kind of tradition, now several generations in'.[24] Upon reading Truscot's autobiography one is reminded of the pseudo-autobiographical University novels written by C. P. Snow. In portraying the academic intrigues and personalities at Redbrick University Peers displays qualities of wit, insight and satire not dissimilar to those that characterize Snow's fictionalized recreation — especially in *The Masters* (1951) and *The Affair* (1960) — of the conflicts of lives and between intellects at a purposefully unnamed College at Cambridge University.

If indeed it belongs to the British tradition of the University novel, then *The Autobiography of 'Bruce Truscot'* may legitimately be regarded as a respectable forerunner to Bradbury's *The History Man* (1975) and to other disrespectful satires of academic institutions and attitudes published in more recent, and much more indecorous, times. Bradbury mentioned *The History Man* in the Introduction which he wrote, in 1986, for a published selection of *Professor Lapping Sends his Apologies. The Best of Laurie Taylor* — whose columns, we can be certain, had he lived to read them in *The Times Higher Education Supplement*, the creator of Professor Deadwood, 'the leisured professor at bay', would enjoyably have appreciated. Interestingly, and wittily, Bradbury complains that readers of his novel, instead of concentrating on more important aspects, 'frequently begin trying to find out

---

[23] See *The Autobiography of 'Bruce Truscot'*, ch. IV, p. 386, and note 141.

[24] See Malcolm Bradbury, Introduction to *Professor Lapping Sends his Apologies. The Best of Laurie Taylor* (Trentham, Stoke-on-Trent: Trentham Books, 1986), 3.

what, where, but mostly *whom* it is *about*'. He wishes that scholars would cease thoughtfully endeavouring to discover 'who was *the original Howard Kirk*' — the 'spirited young academic sociologist who appears centrally' in his book — because 'the truth is that the original Howard Kirk is simply a creative thought, a fiction...'.[25] Bradbury's humorous words of meaningful complaint and denial remind one vividly of the protests, comments and denials which were made, equally with thought-provoking humour and emphasis, by the creator of Bruce Truscot in the Preface to *Redbrick and these Vital Days*. To his readers, who were, in his view, over-concerned to discover Truscot's secret identity, Peers insisted that

> the author of *Red Brick University* is a personality created by me and given the name of Bruce Truscot, and he is no-one else.[26]

In his Introduction to *Professor Lapping Sends his Apologies. The Best of Laurie Taylor*, in whose columns he finds 'a great kinship to the genre', Malcolm Bradbury offers a masterly definition of the British University Novel. Bradbury's definition may be applied not only to 'the story of the modern university' as fictionalized in the memoirs of Bruce Truscot but also to that same story as factually narrated in *The Autobiography of E. Allison Peers*. For in recounting developments at the Redbrick University of Liverpool during a critical period of its history, Peers has composed

> the story of a significant part of modern life, of social change, of the rise of new classes and new ways of thinking, of the fate of the arts, sciences and dominant ideas in culture, as well as of the perplexities and comedies of the existence of human kind as a thinking animal in a notoriously unco-operative world.[27]

In regarding the fictionalized autobiography of Bruce Truscot as, on one level, a University novel, we by no means wish to deny or diminish its importance, on another level, as a truthfully informative reconstruction of the social and educational history of Britain during the first decades of the twentieth century. Both narratives, the imaginatively

---

25 Introduction to *Professor Lapping Sends his Apologies*, 1-2.
26 See Preface to *Redbrick and these Vital Days*, 14. In this Preface Peers still uses the original form of the title: *Red Brick University*.
27 Introduction to *Professor Lapping Sends his Apologies*, 3.

INTRODUCTION 17

recounted memoirs of Truscot and the factually accurate autobiography of Peers, jointly consulted, illuminatingly record the shifting standards, preoccupations, conditions and priorities in Britain, as the country moved — politically and socially, emotionally and intellectually — through the last years of uneasy peace into the first turmoil of World War, and then on, to experience the unsettling times and consequences of Amnesty. Moreover, and still more impressively, both autobiographies document reliably in convincing detail the conditions of life and realities of education, during this period, in the schools and universities of Britain: state grammar and expensive public schools; 'modern' universities in industrial cities and ancient seats of higher learning. Peers' and Truscot's recollections of their lives as students at Cambridge and Camford significantly improve our understanding of the University of Cambridge as it was early in the twentieth century: its splendid buildings, and the physical discomforts; its teaching methods, and the educational deficiencies; its subject-preferences, and the academic consequences. What we learn from Peers and Truscot complements admirably the knowledge, necessarily more general and less personalized, with which Christopher Brooke provides us in his fourth volume (1870-1990) — carefully researched and deservedly well-reviewed — of the *History of the University of Cambridge*.[28]

These autobiographies, however, assume particularly noteworthy importance as documents of history because of the original insights which they afford us into influential developments and personalities at the Redbrick University of Liverpool during the decisive period when 'none too soon the New Testament met with its fall'.[29] Peers was not the first, nor was he to be the last, member of staff at Liverpool to write down the story of the 'New Testament' — that controversial chapter in the early history of the University as it endeavoured

---

28 See Christopher N. L. Brooke, *A History of the University of Cambridge*, Vol. IV *1870-1990* (Cambridge: Cambridge U. P., 1993). Brooke is General Editor of the series, besides being author of Vol. IV. Peers was a student at Cambridge in a period when methods of teaching and attitudes to research were about to undergo radical transformations.

29 See *The Autobiobiography of E. Allison Peers*, ch. 5, p. 140.

vitally to grow into academic maturity. In his autobiography, *Scaffolding in the Sky* (1938), a book which Peers knew, and which he mentions in his own memoirs, Charles Reilly describes the group at some length, in a chapter entitled 'The New Testament'. But Reilly, as Peers correctly points out, was himself a member of that semi-secret society of academics. Consequently, he indulges 'in the accomplishment colloquially termed "back-scratching" ', and his description of his fellow 'New Testamentarians' is 'coloured by the rosy tints of hero-worship'.[30] No hint of roses is detectable in Peers' representation of the 'New Testamentarians', who, on the contrary, emerge looking, and smelling, nothing like roses from the full pages of his critical report on their affairs. Nevertheless, his severe criticism of their activities, which had caused him so much professional difficulty and private distress, is made impartially with detachment and almost without animosity. Moreover, the portraits he executes in writing of their personalities lead us to a depth of knowledge about their individual lives which seldom or never is reached through obituary notices and official records. When Thomas Kelly published his outstanding book which documents the extended history of *The University of Liverpool 1881-1981*, he revealed in the Preface what had been the chief aim of his work. More than thirty years previously, Peers, in relating a specific part of that same history, had fulfilled, to his credit, the same aim: he had told the story of the downfall of the 'New Testament' 'in human and not just in constitutional terms'.[31] The autobiographies of Peers demonstrate also the truth of Stanley Dumbell's conviction that

> scenes can be lived again in the imagination as they happened, and men and women who have played their part and passed on can be seen and heard in the mind as they lived and spoke.[32]

---

30 See C. H. Reilly, *Scaffolding in the Sky: A Semi-architectural Autobiography* (London: George Routledge and Sons, 1938); and *cf. The Autobiography of E. Allison Peers*, ch. 5, p. 139.

31 See Preface to *For Advancement of Learning. The University of Liverpool 1881-1981*, v.

32 See Stanley Dumbell, *The University of Liverpool 1903-1953. A Jubilee Book* (Liverpool: University of Liverpool, 1953), [5].

## IV

When I had finished reading the autobiographies of Allison Peers and Bruce Truscot, I was wholly convinced that they deserved publication. The manuscript — to which I had already, notionally, given the title, *Redbrick University Revisited* — was not only an exceptional work of literary art[33] but also, still more importantly, a key-document of history. His understanding and insight improved by observation and deepened through experience, Peers had recorded, personally yet objectively, the events and conflicts, attitudes and prejudices, secret intrigues and public debates, errors of judgement and triumphs of resolution which he witnessed at the University of Liverpool during a critical period of its early development, and which influenced principally its transformation into a major institution of higher learning.

I was considerably less convinced, however, having read the manuscript, of my own abilities to edit and annotate satisfactorily this important literary text and historical document. I had known Peers' name, and work, since, aged twelve, I had begun to learn Spanish as a first foreign language, and had been introduced, perhaps prematurely, to the progressively bitter delights and sweet difficulties of his books of *Graded Passages for Translation from English*. As an undergraduate, I utilized his 'plain-text' editions of Spanish classics; and I read with benefit, and admiration, parts of his *History of the Romantic Movement in Spain*. I also improved more than a little my knowledge of Spain's turbulent history during the early twentieth century, through digesting his opinions on the Spanish Civil War. These were the opinions, expressed in a succession of books, which in the late 1930s and early 1940s had established Peers 'as, on this so controversial topic, the one dispassionate, reliable guide and mentor of the English-speaking world amidst a welter of confusing emotionalisms'.[34] As a scholar, I often consulted, to the

---

33 The literary merits of the autobiographies are discussed further in my Editorial Commentary.

34 See William C. Atkinson, 'In Memoriam', *Memorial Number*, *Bulletin of Hispanic Studies*, XXX (1953), no. 117, 1-5, at 4.

advantage of my own researches, his monumental *Studies of the Spanish Mystics*. Moreover, I had enjoyed, and admired, the 'Truscot' books since 1970, the year in which, as a young lecturer in Spanish at the University of Liverpool, I was given by Ivy McClelland a copy of *Redbrick University*. Years after first reading the 'Redbrick' books, I happened upon the address which Peers had delivered at Liverpool to mark the establishment, in 1934, of the Institute of Hispanic Studies. In this address Peers declares emphatically, on the subject of research, that, 'though its importance is everywhere conceded, there is far too little in the Hispanic Departments of our Universities'.[35] Which public, and published, lecture demonstrates that, even when he was not protected by the Truscotian shield of anonymity, Peers dared to criticize, with thought-provoking frankness, the perceived deficiencies within universities in Britain, and the activities, or inactivities, of his fellow-academics. By the time I read the handwritten autobiographies of Peers and Truscot in 1989, I had been for nearly two decades deeply interested in what Nicholas Round has acutely defined as:

> the rich array of contradictions... in E. Allison Peers: the self-absorbed literary pilgrim who was also a robust and canny publicist for Spanish studies; the political apologist of the Spanish church — and of a free Catalonia; the chronicler of the mystics who — writing as 'Bruce Truscot' — coined the name and defined the initial public image of the 'redbrick university'.[36]

But I was a Hispanist and literary critic, not an educationist or specialist historian. In both parts of the manuscript there were numerous descriptions — direct in the Peers autobiography, disguised in the Truscot narrative — of real places, people, circumstances and events, which would require detailed, accurate elucidation in informative notes. His accounts of conditions at the diverse schools he had himself attended, and his memories of the teachers who had instructed or failed to instruct him, would need to be, as far as possible, verified. Similarly, his remembered experiences of life as a

---

[35] See, for the text of this Inaugural Address, *Bulletin of Spanish Studies*, XI (1934), 186-200; see especially 189.

[36] See Nicholas G. Round, 'The Politics of Hispanism Reconstrued', *Journal of Hispanic Research*, I (1992), no. 1, 134-47, at 136.

schoolmaster in a number of public schools immediately before and during the First World War — memories through which are conveyed his impressions of headmasters he worked for, of teachers he worked with, of working conditions, standards in teaching and many other matters — would require to be compared with other reports about the same institutions. The chapters that recorded Peers' years as an undergraduate at Cambridge University (1909-1912) contained much detailed information about the advantages, and disadvantages — educational, social, practical — for a student, particularly a student of Modern Languages, in that establishment. There were allusions not only to specific dons, their attitudes, styles and deficiencies of teaching, but also to social customs and recreations, and even to the physical discomforts and deprivations of residential life — occasioned, for instance, by the lack of bathrooms and of conveniently placed lavatories. The truthfulness of such information would have to be investigated and confirmed through, if possible, consultation of other eye-witness accounts, and certainly by reference to appropriate records of the University of Cambridge.

Above all, considerable research would have to be conducted into the history of the University of Liverpool. Careful scrutiny not only of reference books and other printed records but of a large quantity of unpublished papers, private and institutional, housed principally in the University's Archives, would have to be undertaken, in order satisfactorily to comment upon, and evaluate, the major sections of both autobiographies in which Peers describes and discusses the controversies and oppositions within the Faculty of Arts in the 1920s, the origins and activities of the 'New Testament', and the personalities of its influential members. Obviously, indispensably, I had to obtain not only advice but also cooperation from an experienced historian or archivist by profession — preferably from a specialist attached to the University of Liverpool, with unlimited access to, and detailed knowledge of, the huge store of its records. Most fortunately, I managed to persuade a respected colleague and knowledgeable specialist, who was Archivist at the University of Liverpool, to be my collaborator in the editing and annotation of *Redbrick University Revisited: The Autobiography of 'Bruce Truscot'*.

My collaborator, Adrian Allan, and I began seriously upon our researches during session 1990-1991. Understandably, while I, to improve my knowledge of 'Bruce Truscot' and the aims and preoccupations of his creator, scrutinized and re-scrutinized the books about *Redbrick University*, Adrian Allan concentrated his attention, in the first place, on the scrutiny of numerous documents housed in the University's Archives. Among the Peers papers, particularly, he discovered many of important relevance to our studies: obituaries, reviews of the 'Redbrick' books, correspondence between 'Bruce Truscot' and a number of prominent scholars, educationists and academics (Bonamy Dobrée, G. C. Field, Hector Hetherington and others). There was even an unpublished 'autobiographical' essay by 'Bruce Truscot' entitled 'Any Faculty Board'.[37] These were, for the most part, documents which had been in the possession of Peers' former colleague, Harold Hall. Ironically, after Harold Hall's death in 1981, I myself had been the person who had deposited the documents in the University's Archives, having at that time not the slightest idea that ten years later I should find them essential for a personal project of research. While I was still concerned to evaluate such sources, Adrian Allan had already extended his researches beyond Liverpool, and was engaged, for instance, in making enquiries of Faber and Faber, the publishers of the original 'Redbrick' books, as to the possibly relevant contents of their files for the period 1940-1950. He had written, for information, to the headmasters of the schools in which, more than seventy years ago, Allison Peers had taught. He had read various wills and several death certificates. He had taken a profound interest in the early twentieth-century records of the University of Cambridge. He had examined, personally, in London, the minutes of the early meetings of the Modern Humanities Research Association, of which now famous and justly influential body the founder, in 1918, had been, as his autobiography reveals, a resourceful young schoolmaster, still only aspiring to a career as a scholar and university teacher, named Edgar Allison Peers. Other libraries, university archives and record offices, too numerous to mention, were also consulted throughout the kingdom by my collaborator. In his indefatigable pursuit of knowledge and

---

37 We have published this essay in Appendix IV.

enlightenment Adrian Allan reminded me of Allison Peers himself. The words which William Atkinson used to sum up, with admiration, the extraordinary industry and persistence of Peers in the conduct of his scholarly investigations might be applied, with equal accuracy, and only minor changes, to describe the dedicated work accomplished, as it were, on Peers' behalf by Adrian Allan:

> His research was genuine research, a patient, resourceful exploration... that involved, among much else, disturbing the dust of archives over the length and breadth of [England], and beyond.[38]

By the Spring of 1991 we had made substantial progress in our different researches. Adrian Allan had gathered a remarkable amount of significant historical and biographical information. Much of that information he was already engaged in converting into factual and explanatory notes. These notes would elucidate for the reader allusions which otherwise would have been imperfectly understood; and — not their least important function — they would assist, so far as possible, identification of the members of the 'New Testament' and other colleagues of Peers at the University of Liverpool, who, within the autobiography of 'Bruce Truscot', appeared in disguise as the narrator's opponents or supporters at Redbrick University. For my part, I had advanced my literary-critical analysis of the autobiographies, and had compared, for instance, the attitudes revealed and opinions expressed in these narratives with the ideas about universities, ancient and modern, and the views about university teachers, frequently critical, which had been previously expounded by 'Bruce Truscot' in *Redbrick University* and *Redbrick and these Vital Days*. Significantly, both books and also *First Year at the University* are specifically mentioned in Truscot's account of remembered events and conflicts at Redbrick University — events in which 'he' had participated at least twenty years before the books, that were to bring notoriety to that institution, were published. I had also, to my

---

38 See Atkinson, 'In Memoriam', *Bulletin of Hispanic Studies*, XXX (1953), no. 117, 2. In describing the extent of Peers' researches, Atkinson had referred to Spain. In applying Atkinson's description to the investigative activities of my colleague, Adrian Allan, I have inserted, instead of 'Spain', in square brackets, 'England'.

further considerable enlightenment, discussed Allison Peers, his personality and his work, particularly his works written as 'Bruce Truscot', with several of his close friends and former colleagues in Hispanic Studies. These included Norman Lamb, Elizabeth Hall, and, most notably, Ivy McClelland and Audrey Lumsden-Kouvel. The latter, at my insistent request, agreed to contribute to this book, in the concise form of essays, their individual memories of Allison Peers as university teacher and colleague.

Adrian Allan and I by this time were also heavily engaged in editing the manuscript — an undertaking which, for reasons more fully explained in the Editorial Commentary, was by no means straightforward. Peers' tiny handwriting presented us with major problems of interpretation. In certain passages his script seemed to me more difficult to read than the seventeenth-century manuscripts of Spanish plays which I had had considerably more practice in deciphering. With this laborious task of textual scrutiny we were given thoroughly competent assistance by my friend and colleague, Ceri Byrne. Using expertise, acquired, or so I suspected, through years spent transforming my ill-defined handwriting into perfect print, Ceri Byrne demonstrated an enviably developed ability to decipher the perplexingly minute, neatly characterized script of E. Allison Peers. As Assistant Editor, Ceri Byrne was additionally responsible for preparing the book technically, in a form 'camera-ready' for press — a major assignment which, with excellent support, in the typing of the lengthy footnotes, from Andrea Owens, she accomplished, as is unfailingly her custom, in creative fashion with irreproachable competence.

As work progressed, we became progressively aware of the large size of the book which we had undertaken. Peers' initially direct account of his early life and career was not particularly extensive. But *The Autobiography of 'Bruce Truscot'* was more than double the length of the first narrative. Together the autobiographies formed over three hundred pages of text. And they were to be published in conjunction with a large amount of secondary and supportive material. A critical Introduction was in detailed preparation. An Editorial Commentary would have to be incorporated. Additionally, there were to be accommodated, in a Conclusion, the essays about Peers written by Ivy McClelland and Audrey Lumsden-Kouvel. A comprehensive Index was necessary. There were to be no fewer than four Appendices, which included: copied testimonials, illuminating letters and other selected papers; the text of a previously unpublished essay of Peers on a Redbrickian topic; and, destined to fill some eighteen printed pages, 'A Chronology of the Filling of the Gilmour Chair of Spanish, 1919-1922', scrupulously compiled by Adrian Allan. Particularly expansive occupiers of printed space were the annotations with which both autobiographies were supplied. Adrian Allan had composed factual and explanatory notes in their hundreds. I had not only enlarged many of his notes, to include, for instance, textual clarifications, but had also provided, in addition, large numbers of literary-critical observations. To publish an academic book of this size, comprising, we estimated, in excess of five-hundred pages, would require a substantial subvention. It was time to approach a potential academic publisher, and to determine a possible source of finance.

## V

> It should be among the chief satisfactions of any academic author to have his books appearing over the imprint of his own university and among the chief glories of the university to bring to light the productions of its graduates and teachers.[39]

Bearing in mind these encouraging observations, made by the very author whose memoirs we wished to publish, I discussed with Robin Bloxsidge, Publisher of Liverpool University Press, the possibility of establishing a new series of scholarly publications, named after E. Allison Peers. After the usual preliminaries, investigations and scholarly assessments had been completed, the series was established: an Editorial Board of specialist advisers was appointed; and it was agreed that the

---

39 See *Redbrick University*, 190.

first volume to be published in the new E. Allison Peers Series, funds permitting, would be *Redbrick University Revisited. The Autobiography of 'Bruce Truscot'*.

Given the subject of the book, it seemed logical to apply for publishing funds to the author's own 'Redbrick University'. I first broached the matter unofficially, in late April 1991, during a luncheon at which the Vice-Chancellor, Graeme Davies, presented to Ivy McClelland a Special Number of the *Bulletin of Hispanic Studies*, published in her honour.[40] Inevitably, in her speech, following the presentation, Ivy McClelland mentioned, with gratitude, her professional indebtedness to her former university teacher, E. Allison Peers. I seized the opportunity to mention the unpublished autobiographies of Allison Peers and 'Bruce Truscot'. I knew already — and was encouraged by my knowledge — that Graeme Davies had a good opinion of Peers' achievements and recognized the importance of Peers' contribution to the history and reputation of Liverpool University. It was at the insistence of Graeme Davies that a photograph of Peers had been obtained to figure prominently in *The University of Liverpool. A Photographic Portrait: Yesterday and Today*, published in 1989.[41] I expressed my hopeful intention to apply for a grant from the Vice-Chancellor's Development Fund. Graeme Davies' response, by no means off-putting, was characteristically direct: 'Better be quick. I'm not here for much longer'. To the considerable benefit of universities throughout the land, but seriously to the disadvantage of the University of Liverpool, Graeme Davies had accepted the principal appointment of Chief Executive of the Universities Funding Council — now the Higher Education Funding Council for England. He was due to resign his vice-chancellorship at the end of June. I could not help remembering, among many soundly based observations made in *The Autobiography of 'Bruce Truscot'*, one comment which, in the circumstances at Liverpool, then seemed particularly truthful:

---

40   For details of the Number, see above, note 21.
41   *The University of Liverpool. A Photographic Portrait: Yesterday and Today* (Liverpool: Liverpool U. P./Ingram Publishing Ltd, 1989).

> As a general rule, Vice-Chancellors at the modern universities resemble popes in the shortness of their reigns: from eight to ten years would probably be a fair average.[42]

My application for a grant to publish Peers' book was acknowledged, and evaluated — a naturally time-consuming process. Further information was requested, and supplied, on such necessarily practical matters as 'anticipated sales flow'. During his final week in office, I received from the Vice-Chancellor a letter generously agreeing to underwrite, by means of a loan from the Vice-Chancellor's Development Fund, the publication of *Redbrick University Revisited: The Autobiography of 'Bruce Truscot'*.

The emotions of regret which the departure of Graeme Davies roused in the University of Liverpool might be compared with those profoundly regretful feelings experienced at the same institution, more than fifty years earlier, when, in 1936, Hector Hetherington resigned to take up the principalship of the University of Glasgow — feelings eloquently recorded by Stanley Dumbell:

> [His] resignation..., coming as it did when the fruits of his administration were ripening so abundantly, was received with disappointment and dismay. Regret at the departure of a strong and wise Vice-Chancellor was underlaid by a deeper emotion at the severance of a comradeship which had counted for much in many lives.[43]

Allison Peers had admired Sir Hector Hetherington[44] — so much so that, in addition to some characteristics taken from J. G. Adami, the latter's predecessor at Liverpool, Peers had borrowed the best qualities observed in Hetherington in order to create the figure of Sir Archibald Blake, Head of Redbrick University, who features, personified as 'an ideal Vice-Chancellor', in *The Autobiography of 'Bruce Truscot'*. In

---

42   See *The Autobiography of 'Bruce Truscot'*, ch. IV, p. 332.
43   See Stanley Dumbell, *The University of Liverpool 1903-1953. A Jubilee Book*, [25].
44   It is clear that Sir Hector Hetherington also admired Allison Peers, for in 1947 Peers was awarded the honorary degree of Doctor of Laws by the University of Glasgow.

Graeme Davies, Peers would have observed, had he known him, the same qualities which he most respected in Hector Hetherington, and which he portrayed in Archibald Blake. It does not seem unsuitable, therefore, to make use of Peers' description of Sir Archibald ['Archie'] Blake in order to describe Sir Graeme Davies, the former Vice-Chancellor of 'Redbrick University' to whom this book is most gratefully dedicated:

> From the first 'Archie' ['Graeme'], as we called him, was... unassuming; and we liked him for that. He was a 'Senate' man, through and through; and we liked him for that too. But he was also extremely energetic and practical, appealing to the City and to the Council; resourceful over problems that demanded a solution wounding no one's susceptibilities; inventive where new ways had to be taken, but always willing to take the old ways if there were any chance that they might be better. I have no wish to appear to be writing him a testimonial, for everybody knows that none is needed.[45]

---

45 See *The Autobiography of 'Bruce Truscot'*, ch. IV, pp. 334-35. For an account of Graeme Davies' years of office as Vice-Chancellor, and an evaluation of his qualities of vision and leadership at Liverpool, see Sylvia Harrop, *Decade of Change. The University of Liverpool 1981-1991* (Liverpool: Liverpool U. P., 1994), especially pp. 40-42, 123-25. Ironically, I had just completed the Introduction to *Redbrick University Revisited*, comparing Graeme Davies and Hector Hetherington, when I was given more grounds for comparison. News broke that Graeme Davies, having been (like Hetherington) Vice-Chancellor at Liverpool University, was to become in 1995 (as Hetherington did in 1936), Principal of the University of Glasgow. The appointment as Principal of Glasgow University nearly coincided, in both cases, with the award of a knighthood (to Hector Hetherington in 1936; to Graeme Davies in 1996).

## VI

During the several years since 1991, through which we have worked to complete this book, I have sensed imaginatively, self-critically, on more than one occasion, the spirit-presence of Allison Peers at my shoulder, lingering to read, as I wrote them down, my impressions of his memoirs. I remembered the ghosts about whom Routledge had speculated in 1934-1935, in his poem describing the Senate at its deliberations in the University of Liverpool. These were, presumably, the spirits of illustrious, deceased past members of that supremely governing body. And, in his concluding stanza, Routledge had asked, in rhetorical wonderment:

> What ghosts are these who flit about the chairs
> To catch new dreams more tenuous than theirs?
> Where men of feeling, full of eager hope,
> Once saw the vision, now successors grope... [46]

I speculated similarly as to what might have been Peers' reactions to *his* successors, the editors of his memoirs, as, with an understanding 'more tenuous' than his, we groped to assess the significances in what he had written. Remembering, however, the final words of 'Bruce Truscot' in *Redbrick University*, I am encouraged to suppose that Peers would not wholly have disapproved of our edition of his autobiography. In his conclusion to that pioneering book, Peers urged the newer universities to keep on 'thinking', to keep on 'experimenting', to keep on 'believing'. For, like Don Quijote — the Spanish knight made world-famous not by success but through endeavour — Peers was convinced that, in any enterprise, what is important is to 'venture boldly', even at risk of failure.[47]

In his poem, 'Kaine Diatheke', written in 1938, to 'chronicle the Great N.T.', Oliver Elton — who was, it will be remembered, one of its members — suspected, regretfully, that

---

46 Quoted from the unpublished poem 'Senate in Laputa', by F. J. Routledge; *cf.* above note 11.

47 See *Redbrick University*, 191.

the activities of that once powerful organization were now largely forgotten:

> What now remains thereof? some pages
> In dusty calendars betray
> The blackened embers of the fray;
> Our triumphs, disappointments, rages
> On that contracted battlefield
> Are there, by legal phrase, concealed.[48]

Peers' main intention, however, in writing his autobiographies, was to ensure that the malpractices and intrigues perpetrated at Liverpool University by that semi-secret society known as the 'New Testament' should not be kept in obscurity, 'by legal phrase, concealed'. He was preoccupied that these should, on the contrary, be vitally laid bare — recorded permanently, with every relevant detail, in the history of that institution. He was determined, through his narratives, to expose the conflicts of personalities, of actions and of opinions which were bitterly waged within the Faculty of Arts over his disputed election to the Gilmour Chair of Spanish — to document, as he perceived it, that heroic 'struggle for fair play against intrigue; for genuine democracy against a hidden oligarchy; for the discrediting of slander and scandal'.[49] In publishing his book, therefore, however much our edition might differ from the one that he would himself have prepared, had he lived, we have enabled him to fulfil the main purpose for which he wrote it. 'So that a younger generation of university teachers may be warned against any such clique as may arise in the future', we have 'made public' the story of the 'decline and fall of the New Testament', in order 'to show to what depths men can descend who have entered a calling which above almost any other should connote the disinterested cultivation of scholarship and love of uprightness and truth'.[50]

---

48 The entire text of Elton's poem is reproduced in Appendix II.
49 See *The Autobiography of 'Bruce Truscot'*, ch. IV, p. 365.
50 See *The Autobiography of E. Allison Peers*, ch. 6, p. 166, and *The Autobiography of 'Bruce Truscot'*, ch. III, p. 320.

First page of *The Autobiography of E. Allison Peers*
(Archives, University of Liverpool)
Reproduced in facsimile

Photograph by Suzanne Yee, Photographic Service,
Department of Geography, University of Liverpool

First page of *The Autobiography of 'Bruce Truscot'*
(Archives, University of Liverpool)
Reproduced in facsimile

Photograph by Suzanne Yee, Photographic Service,
Department of Geography, University of Liverpool

# EDITORIAL COMMENTARY

The autobiographies in manuscript of Peers and Truscot, here published for the first time, as indicated in the Introduction, were discovered in a drawer of Allison Peers' desk after he died in 1952. In that private location they were allowed to remain, for reasons already explained,[1] until 1989, when they came into the possession of Ann L. Mackenzie. The manuscript has now been lodged in the Archives of Liverpool University (ref. D.642), to augment the considerable quantity of documents relating to Peers and Truscot already owned by that institution.

Peers wrote the autobiographies, using his characteristically tiny script, mostly, but not entirely,[2] in ink, and on lined sheets of paper that had originally formed part of note- or exercise-books — of the type commonly in use several decades ago in schools and universities. He kept the manuscript in five used brown envelopes, all of them postmarked, which had been sent to Peers from a variety of places inside and outside England. Not all the postmarks are legible, but the oldest appears to be that dated '15 JAN 1944', and the most recent reads '12 JU 45'.[3] One envelope, the postmark of which is, unfortunately, indecipherable, contains what Peers, on the front of the envelope, called '(E.A.P.) *Auto*': that is, *The Autobiography of E. Allison Peers*. Each of the other envelopes houses one of the four chapters which comprise the 'B.T.' autobiography: *The Autobiography of 'Bruce Truscot'*.

Many pages of the Peers autobiography have been, as it were, deliberately mutilated by the author. He has regularly used scissors to excise passages from the first narrative in order to transfer them, pasting them appropriately into place, to form

---

1 See the Introduction, at p. 10.
2 A significant part of chapter III of *The Autobiography of 'Bruce Truscot'* is written in pencil.
3 Only one other envelope, that containing 'B.T.', ch. IV, has a decipherable postmark, which is '5 AP 45' Another envelope, which contains 'B.T.', ch. III, bears an American stamp, which would have been used only in the War Years, for it carries the slogan 'Win the War'.

part of the story of Bruce Truscot. To facilitate comparison, the first pages of the autobiographies have been reproduced, side by side in facsimile (pp. 32-33), illustrating the typically practical, scissors-and-paste method employed by the author to relocate sections of his work. It will be observed that the gap shown in the page where the Peers narrative begins fits exactly in shape the outline of the piece of paper superimposed upon the first page of the 'Truscot' account. These illustrations serve equally to demonstrate the difficulties presented to the editors by the minuteness of Allison Peers' handwriting.

## Date of composition

There is substantial weight of evidence, external and internal, direct and indirect, which leads to the conclusion that Peers composed both autobiographies during the years 1944-1947.

Particularly informative documents in this respect are two letters (both reproduced in Appendix III),[4] which Peers wrote in 1945 alluding to Truscot's autobiography. One letter, sent to G. C. Field from Truscot, and dated 11 October 1945, declares that Truscot proposes to publish his autobiography after he retires. In the other letter, received more than three months earlier by Bonamy Dobrée, and purportedly composed by Truscot's wife, Amelia Truscot tells Dobrée that 'after his holiday [Bruce] is going to begin on his autobiography'. Interestingly, Amelia's letter bears exactly the same date as is carried on the first page of the manuscript where Peers begins to narrate *The Autobiography of 'Bruce Truscot'*: 23 June 1945.[5] So Bruce, whatever his wife misleadingly says to the contrary, must have begun his autobiography *before* 'his holiday'. Moreover, since Truscot creatively derived his memoirs from *The Autobiography of E. Allison Peers* — to the extent, as we have seen, of borrowing many specific passages — we may confidently assume that some time before Amelia posted her letter to Bonamy Dobrée Peers had completed writing straightforwardly the first narrative.

---

4   See below, pp. 476-77, 479-80.
5   See below, 'B.T.', ch. I, p. 173, note 1.

That Peers should have chosen to write the story of Truscot's life during the mid' 1940s seems wholly understandable, for it was during these years, after all, that he came to know most intimately the author he had created. Truscot completed three major books between 1942 and 1946, as well as the essays describing 'Any Faculty Board' and 'A Redbrick Tea-party'. In the latter piece (1945), Dusty, the Professor of Latin — a disguised name and profession sometimes assumed by Allison Peers — promises a visiting don from Oxbridge that he will tell him 'the story sometime' of Professor Upright and the Chair of Poetry at Redbrick University.[6] Which story Truscot narrates in detail in the third chapter of his autobiography. Allusions made in *The Autobiography of 'Bruce Truscot'* to all three books through which Peers established Truscot's reputation further clarify its date of composition. Each work is mentioned by the author specifically by title: *Redbrick University* (first published, it will be recalled, in 1943); *Redbrick and these Vital Days* (1945); *First Year at the University* (1946).[7] Originally, Peers had not intended to embark Truscot seriously upon his literary activities until after his career as a university teacher had ended. Peers had changed his mind, and had written *Redbrick University* when he did — as his first letters to the publishers reveal — in order that the book 'might play its part in the post-War shakeup', and 'in connection with post-War reconstruction of the Universities'.[8] There was another reason, however, why Peers wrote *Redbrick University*, and its sequels, during the mid' 1940s — which reason also explains the composition in that same period of the autobiographies of Peers and Truscot. Restrictions upon travel imposed by the conditions of War in Europe hindered for years Peers' visits to Spain and the researches in Spanish libraries needed to advance his projects and publications in Hispanic Studies. In the aftermath of the Spanish Civil War, through the Second World War and then during the first years of World Peace, Allison Peers had time at

---

6 See Bruce Truscot, 'A Redbrick Tea-party', in *The Universities Review*, (May 1945), no. 2, 38-40, at p. 39.

7 See *The Autobiography of 'Bruce Truscot'*, ch. I, pp. 190, 196, 217; ch. II, p. 252; ch. IV, p. 337.

8 For the texts of these letters to Faber and Faber Ltd, dated 8 October 1942 and 7 December 1942, see above, illustration at p. 1 and below, Appendix III, pp. 467-68.

his disposal, more than in any other period of his career, to occupy himself in creating the works, and the Life, of Bruce Truscot.

Internal evidence further persuades us that the autobiographies of Peers and Truscot were composed during the period 1944-1947. In the first narrative, when he looks back upon his early career as a schoolmaster (chapter 3), Peers informs us that at the time of writing he has been a university teacher for twenty-five years.[9] Since Peers joined the staff of the University of Liverpool in 1920, he must have written these words in 1945. Precise references to similar matters in the second narrative are equally informative as to date of composition, so long as we always bear in mind that Truscot, allegedly born in 1885, is six years older than his creator, that Truscot became a lecturer at Redbrick University in 1918, and that he was promoted to his professorship in 1920 — that is to say, two years before Peers was appointed to the Gilmour Chair of Spanish at Liverpool. Thus, when Truscot declares, in chapter III, that he has lived happily in Forbridge for twenty-eight years — which information conveys the length of his career to date at Redbrick University — we are able to work out the year in which Truscot wrote these words and therefore, presumably, also the chapter in which they appear. Our calculation is confirmed by a note on the manuscript: in the margin, beside Truscot's reference to 'twenty-eight years', Peers has added in pencil '1919-47'.[10] The year in question was evidently 1947. A similarly revealing comment is made by Truscot in the next chapter of his narrative, when he tells us that, having reached 'the mature age of sixty-two', he has decided to vacate his Chair in the university. Given his date of birth, Truscot would have been aged sixty-two in 1947 — in which same year, therefore, was evidently completed the fourth, final, chapter of *The Autobiography of 'Bruce Truscot'*.[11]

After 1947, as post-War conditions normalized, having resumed regular visits to Spain, Peers concentrated on

---

9  See below '(E.A.P.) *Auto*', ch. 3, p. 101.

10  See below 'B.T.', ch. III, p. 289, and note 80. During his first session at Redbrick University, 1918-19, Truscot, it will be remembered, uncomfortably occupied lodgings near the University.

11  See below 'B.T.', ch. IV, p. 337.

advancing his work, and works, in areas of Hispanic Studies. The autobiographies were evidently set aside, and no further chapters were added. There is no doubt, however, that Peers had intended to write considerably more about his life at Liverpool, and about the career in Redbrick University of Bruce Truscot. The words 'part done' scribbled on the envelope containing the first narrative clearly reveal his plan to continue writing *The Autobiography of E. Allison Peers*. Moreover, the first years of his 'Probation' at Liverpool, ending with his election to the Gilmour Chair in 1922, are described, on the manuscript as 'Part I Liverpool'.[12] Obviously Peers had planned to compose 'Part II Liverpool', in which would have been recounted the significant happenings of his extended career as Professor of Spanish in that institution from the early 1920s, through the 1930s and on into the vital years of the War and of post-War developments. Since Peers had proposed to continue the first narrative in this way, it is difficult to believe that he had not made similar plans to expand the 'Truscot' narrative.[13] The keen enjoyment which Truscot displays as he

---

12  See below, '(E.A.P.) *Auto*', ch. 4, p. 125 and note 1.

13  An interesting letter, written by Peers to Faber and Faber, 7 June 1947, confirms that, in his own view, Peers had not yet completed the 'Truscot' autobiography. In this letter Peers puts forward three proposals for 'the next Truscot' book. His first proposal is a volume of *The Letters of Bruce Truscot*. He says that in this projected book he would 'aim at the further clarification of BT's personality, which would pave the way for the autobiography, *in case at any time it became practical to complete and publish it*' (my italics). In the same letter Peers suggests also writing *A Descriptive Book on Redbrick*, possibly entitled *Redbrick, a Portrait* or *Redbrick as it is*. His third suggestion is to write *Last Year at the University* — as a complementary volume to *First Year at the University*. Peers adds that he will probably 'do nothing before the Autumn', so that Faber and Faber could not expect to receive any manuscript 'earlier than about a year from now. If any urgent commission came along it might be considerably later'. In his reply (letter dated 12 June 1947), Geoffrey Faber, having consulted with colleagues, criticizes the idea of a book of letters, and prefers the third proposal: a book about *Last Year at the University* — if Peers can think of a less 'backward-looking' title. In a letter dated 2 October 1947, however, Geoffrey Faber finally accepts Peers' proposal to write *The Letters of Bruce Truscot*. None of Peers' proposals for 'the next Truscot' was realized doubtless because more 'urgent commission[s]' did come along — which were the numerous books and articles on Hispanic topics completed during the last five years of his life. For copies of the letters cited, and other

reviews, in the late 1940s, his early career at Redbrick in 1918-1924 — observing attitudes and conditions at that university from the perspective changed by the Second World War and through nearly thirty years spent as a professor in the same institution — serves further to persuade us that the author had certainly not intended to leave unnarrated the experiences of the Trevor Professor of Poetry at Redbrick University during the intervening decades. The essay 'Any Faculty Board', as we have suggested elsewhere,[14] might have been written for inclusion in a further book of Truscot's memoirs — in which case this fragment is the only part which Peers survived to compose of the second volume of *The Autobiography of 'Bruce Truscot'*.[15]

In her letter sent to Bonamy Dobrée in June 1945, Amelia Truscot stated categorically with truth that her husband's planned autobiography would 'not be published until he retires'.[16] As we have shown, Peers had indeed never seriously considered publishing his memoirs while he still occupied the Gilmour Chair of Spanish. To have done so would have exposed prematurely, to the world in general, and to his colleagues at Liverpool in particular, the secret of the true identity of Bruce Truscot. With publication not envisaged before 1956, Peers was in no hurry to expand upon the work composed in 1944-1947. He assumed that he would have an extensive run of years in retirement, during which to chronicle more extensively the respective lives of Professors Truscot and Peers at Redbrick University and the University of Liverpool. In fact, as we have seen, Truscot's creator died several years before retirement — before, therefore, he had even the opportunity to revise for press the already completed memoirs. The projected second volumes

---

correspondence between Peers and Faber and Faber 1947-51, consult Liverpool University Archives (ref. D.265).

14   See Appendix IV, p. 482.

15   It is also possible that this sketch of 'Any Faculty Board' — perhaps together with the story of 'A Redbrick Tea-party' — had been intended for inclusion, eventually, in Bruce Truscot, *A Descriptive Book on Redbrick* (*cf.* above, note 13).   That book, if it had been written, after 'a descriptive section', would have consisted of 'a number of sketches and narratives, each complete in itself, and finally some portraits of different types of undergraduates' (cited from Peers' letter of 7 June 1947).

16   See Appendix III, p. 477.

of the autobiographies of Peers and Truscot never materialized into books.

A review, published in the *Sheffield Telegraph* in 1943, in common with many other reviews of *Redbrick University* and its sequels, praised not only this 'thought-stimulating book of great value to those concerned with higher education', but also the narrative style and techniques of the book — 'so well written that the general reader will like it also'.[17] Despite the fact that Peers did not live long enough to turn his manuscript into a typed final version ready for press, the autobiographies of Peers and Truscot are likewise remarkably 'well written'. Always self-critical, as changes and corrections in the manuscript reveal, Peers revised and polished what he wrote even as he wrote it — attending scrupulously to the coherence of his structure and the artistry of his style. A fervent admirer of Cervantes, he adopts measured devices characteristic of the classical methods of narration used by that great Renaissance novelist, in order to unify the themes of his argument, connect up the different parts of his story, shift the pace of the action, and vary the mood or tension of the conflict. Thus, for instance, like Cervantes in *Don Quijote*, Peers uses a recollective technique to tighten the ordered structure of the memoirs: that is, in later parts, he refers us back to incidents recounted earlier. Another favoured, and apparently opposite, technique which fulfils the same structural purpose, in addition to heightening the interested expectations of his readers, obliges us to look not back, but forwards — to a place in the narrative to which the author has not yet conducted us. A good example of this technique may be found in the second narrative, at the point where Truscot has just obtained, after interview, a lectureship at Redbrick University. At this point, therefore, Truscot has not yet begun upon his career at that institution. But he prepares us in advance to expect the difficulties he will encounter: describing 'the atmosphere of self-seeking and intrigue in which [he] was to be plunged soon after [his] arrival', he encourages us to anticipate his account of 'the last of the great disillusionments' of his life. Truscot goes still further, to inform us that the conflict he is about to relate had good effects as well as bad, for

---

17 This review of *Redbrick University*, by Henry Saville, is in the *Sheffield Telegraph*, 7 August 1943.

it allowed him to make firm friendships. That said, he pulls himself up, characteristically conceding that

> to say this is to step considerably in front of my narrative and I must go back to my first term at Redbrick, and describe how I made myself at home there.[18]

An equally classical and Cervantine device of his narrative style is Peers' deliberately occasional employment of a memorable hyperbole, placed to enforce or reinforce the unusual significance of his story. 'The most jealous man in the world' is the phrase used by Cervantes in one of his best exemplary novels to define superlatively in summary the characteristic that principally caused the downfall of his hero.[19] Perhaps Peers had in mind this now famous hyperbole when, to convey its unmatched intensity, he categorized the struggle of Truscot and his allies against the 'Salvation Army' as 'the fiercest conflict in Redbrick History'.[20]

Meticulous craftsman and stylish master of concision, Peers adapts and manipulates admirably such devices of expression and structure in both autobiographies, so as to hold or strengthen our attentive interest in the happenings or characters he describes. In narrating the Peers autobiography he consciously kept under special constraint his literary creativity. By composing a first narrative less than half the length of the disguised autobiography that followed, he successfully avoided, when he came to elaborate creatively upon events and people he had already described, the considerable danger of too much repetition of details, of anecdotes and of traits of character. As a single yet noteworthy example of his self-imposed restraint in the Peers autobiography one might mention his allusion to Vaughan, Master of Wellington College. He would very much have liked, he reveals to us, to have said more about this remarkable person, but he refrains from doing

---

18 See *The Autobiography of 'Bruce Truscot'*, ch. III, pp. 284-85. Peers uses the same technique in *The Autobiography of E. Allison Peers*, ch. 4, p. 129; and ch. 6, pp. 150, 153-54. *Cf.* also 'B.T.', ch. I, p. 208.

19 See, for this short story, Miguel de Cervantes Saavedra, *Exemplary Novels III (Novelas ejemplares). The Jealous Old Man from Extremadura (El celoso extremeño)*, trans., with introduction and notes, by Michael Thacker and Jonathan Thacker (Warminster: Aris & Phillips, 1992).

20 See below, 'B.T.', ch. IV, p. 358.

so, to avoid 'throwing this narrative out of proportion'.[21] Yet even in his first narrative, in which consistently he is obliged to deny himself the artistic satisfaction of expanding his observations, Peers manages to organize the story that he narrates so that it interests us increasingly as it moves increasingly nearer to its conclusion. Nowhere in the first autobiography are his powers as a telling organizer of narrative stronger than they are at the end of that section about the 'New Testament' which we have called chapter 5. Remembering that he had been told that 'distinguished original work was expected from University professors', he observes that he had, therefore, imagined that 'those who expected it had themselves won distinction'. Then he adds a single short sentence; 'I was soon to find out how much I was mistaken'. Curiously, this mildly worded observation, deliberately turned almost into an understatement, works powerfully upon our expectations, leaving us, as this penultimate section finishes, wholly prepared to appreciate the final chapter of conflict over 'The Gilmour Chair'.[22]

In a letter, which, though undated, was obviously sent to Peers in 1945, not long after the publication of *Redbrick and these Vital Days*, Ivy McClelland, reporting upon speculation and rumour at Glasgow University as to the true identity of 'Bruski', commented upon the respective styles of writing of Bruce Truscot and Allison Peers.[23] Dr McClelland, it will be remembered, was at that time one of only a handful of people who knew that Peers had created Truscot and his works. She had, in fact, recognized the style of Peers in the books of Truscot.[24] Even so, as her letter reveals, Ivy McClelland had observed in the writings of both authors not only similarities but also certain differences. Of course, Peers, as he admits in the Preface to *Redbrick and these Vital Days*, had put into Truscot's head some fiercely debatable ideas and attitudes, different from his own, to provoke discussion and startle 'the already over-complacent Redbrickian into serious thought, and

---

21 See '(E.A.P.) *Auto*', ch. 3, p. 117.
22 See '(E.A.P.) *Auto*', ch. 5, p. 148.
23 'Bruski' is Dr McClelland's name for 'Bruce Truscot'. The letter is preserved among the Peers Papers in the Archives, University of Liverpool.
24 *Cf.* Introduction, p. 3; and see also 'B.T.', ch. III, p. 311, note 128.

perhaps even into some form of action'.[25] Almost twenty years after Truscot's books first appeared, James Blackie and Brian Gowenlock, in their revised version of *First Year at the University* (1964), said about Peers: 'It was as though he possessed two personalities. In Bruce Truscot, a rough academic controversialist was revealed, somewhat different from his *alter ego*, the scholar whose studies in the Spanish mystics were responsible for his high reputation'.[26] It seems in no way surprising that when he wrote as Truscot, the 'academic controversialist', Peers should have chosen to assume, together with his 'somewhat different' personality a 'somewhat different' style of literary composition. Peers' natural manner of writing, in the opinion of Ivy McClelland, was 'smoother' than the style he adopted to write Truscot's books about Redbrick University — which Truscotian style was often, in a word, 'terse'.

Interestingly, the stylistic differences perceived by Ivy McClelland in the works of Peers and Truscot are also observable in the autobiographies of Peers and Truscot. Thus, for instance, writing as himself in the first narrative, Peers observes that the masters who taught him when he was a pupil at Dartford Grammar School, 'though nearly all second-rate men, were conscientious and full of interest in their work'. Truscot, however, when he expresses the same opinion about masters at the same institution — now differently named, of course, Chatstone Grammar School — expresses himself less smoothly, more tersely, directly and colloquially, as he describes 'masters, who, poor though their paper qualifications might be, did their job really well'.[27] Despite his autobiographical subject-matter, in his first narrative Peers, using his characteristically objective style, impresses us as a seemingly detached critic-narrator. In *The Autobiography of 'Bruce Truscot'* he consciously changes the manner of his self-expression to accomplish a more vigorously personalized narrative, noteworthy for the creative vitality of its descriptions, as,

---

25 See Preface, *Redbrick and these Vital Days*, 13.

26 See Bruce Truscot, *First Year at the University*, revised by James Blackie and Brian Gowenlock (London: Faber and Faber, 1964), Preface, 9. One might speculate as to whether the lasting popularity enjoyed by this book might have been equalled, had he lived to write it, by Bruce Truscot's projected sequel *Last Year at the University* (see above, p. 39, note 13).

27 See '(E.A.P.) *Auto*', ch. 1, pp. 66-67; and *cf.* 'B.T.', ch. I, p. 180.

equally, for the realism of its key passages in direct speech. In creating, or recreating, conversations Peers displays an enviable talent for adapting the tone and manner of speech to match the character of the speaker. An outstanding example of the author's descriptive imagination — which reveals that Peers, had he wished, could have been, instead of a scholarly critic, a major novelist — is Truscot's first impression, conveyed with wit as well as artistry, of the Victorian Arts Tower and its architectural neighbours at Redbrick University:

> I saw in front of me a vast block of red-brick buildings, ornamented with meaningless scrolls and geometrical figures and tapering here and there into ridiculous little pinnacles looking for all the world like candle-snuffers. At last, standing at the portals of Redbrick University, I was facing my destiny.
>
> The interior... was worse still. Inside the doors was a corridor, running right and left, the lower part of its walls covered with hideous glazed tiles, in blue, yellow and green, of a type once subsequently described to me by a witty colleague as 'Late Lavatory'...
>
> Far away in the distance, someone was yowling about the length of the distance from Redbrick University to Tipperary. I remember reflecting, as I stood wondering which way to go, that it was considerably farther from Redbrick... to Oxbridge.[28]

Both autobiographies, however, in their differently fashioned styles, confirm the comment which 'A Hispanic Scholar' made about Peers in an obituary carried anonymously by a (?Liverpool) newspaper in, or soon after, December 1952:

> He had high literary and artistic standards of composition... Professor Peers from the outset demanded for literary matter a literary expression.[29]

\* \* \* \* \*

---

28  See 'B.T.', ch. III, pp. 277-78.

29  For a copy (undated) of this obituary, published as a letter in an unidentified newspaper, see the Peers Papers, in the Archives, University of Liverpool (ref. D.265).

Inevitably, the manuscript of the autobiographies, despite their excellence in style, form and thought-content, is not by any means free from defects, omissions and textual uncertainties. In a note, scribbled in pencil on the page where *The Autobiography of E. Allison Peers* begins, the author gives himself an important instruction:

> When rest of book done, go thro' this and decide on length of Intr$^{n.}$ and whether things in margin can be put in or not.[30]

As we have seen, however, Peers did not live long enough 'to go thro' ' what he had written and prepare a final version for press. As a result, certain defects, affecting mainly technicalities of presentation and niceties of wording, have not been rectified. Moreover, and most regrettably, passages that he had intended to add were never inserted. The introductory paragraph, for instance, which, as he believed, was 'wanted' to start off the first narrative was not composed. Lacking also is the introductory paragraph on autobiographies and 'whether any point in them', with which, as another marginal note reveals, Peers had fully intended to begin his narration of *The Autobiography of 'Bruce Truscot'*.[31] Another unwritten passage represents a still more significant loss to the contents of the 'Truscot' narrative. 'When more done and length available [could] be determined', Peers had intended to include in the final chapter, to occupy approximately three-and-a-half pages, left blank for the purpose, what surely would have been a fascinating description of a 'Professor's Day'.[32]

As we have indicated, Peers repeatedly made changes, deletions and corrections to the original manuscript to clarify the sense or improve the phraseology and syntax of his narrative. In many cases his changes have been made purposefully in ink, to obliterate the original wording. In almost as many instances, however, he has made alterations and insertions, or has offered alternatives, tentatively in pencil. The editors have usually considered it appropriate to take these

---

30 *Cf.* below '(E.A.P.) *Auto*', ch. 1, p. 61, note 1.
31 See '(E.A.P.) *Auto*', ch. 1, p. 61, note 1; and *cf.* 'B.T.', ch. I, p. 173, note 1.
32 See 'B.T.', ch. IV, p. 339, note 32.

modifications into account, and we have included them — within square brackets — in the body of the text. Words or phrases which, besides being enclosed in square brackets, are preceded by a diagonal line are to be regarded as alternatives — rather than additions — to the original wording. Boldly printed square brackets, used sparingly, signal, on the other hand, minimal additions made by the editors themselves — to correct, for example, punctuation. For the convenience of readers, and to facilitate comparisons, passages which Peers removed from the Peers autobiography and inserted into, particularly, the first two chapters of the 'Truscot' narrative have been printed, for emphasis, in italics. For similar reasons, the editors have subdivided into three chapters that part of the Peers autobiography which its author described simply as the Introduction. The remainder of the first narrative, which Peers called 'Part I. Liverpool', we have divided into three further chapters. With one exception (chapter 4, 'Probation'), we have provided the chapter-headings. We are also responsible for dividing the Peers autobiography into 'Part I' and 'Part II Liverpool'. Peers had himself divided, using Roman numerals, the 'Truscot' narrative into four chapters — which divisions we have, therefore, retained. Only one of these four chapters lacked a title: we have called chapter IV 'The Chair of English Literature'. We have designated the first two chapters 'Part I'; and the remaining chapters form the section that we have called 'Part II Redbrick University'.

The explanatory footnotes which we have provided, including numerous cross-references, contain necessarily detailed information about the condition of the manuscript and the varying characteristics of the text. Footnotes also describe the queries and reminders, often self-critical, not always fully decipherable, that Peers scribbled, usually in the margins, on certain pages of the narratives. Our annotations supply numerous comparisons and analytical comments, to illuminate especially the directions of the author's thought and the objects of his attention. We have endeavoured to be helpfully informative about the actual places and institutions, historical events and circumstances described. In particular, we have done everything that we have considered possible to elucidate the careers and personalities of the real people who figure in both narratives — though we cannot claim to have penetrated completely the elaborate disguises given to members of staff at Redbrick University to conceal the true identities of Allison Peers' colleagues at the University of Liverpool. To assist readers of the second narrative to make plausible connections with *The Autobiography of E. Allison Peers* and, therefore, to comprehend better the true history concealed within the fictionalized story of *The Autobiography of 'Bruce Truscot'*, we have provided, on the pages immediately following, for ease of reference, a list of the **Real Names and False Identities in Redbrick University Revisited**. The titles we have given the two autobiographies are, it should be remembered, simply expanded versions of the abbreviations ('[E.A.P.] *Auto*' and 'B.T.') which Peers himself employed. But we accept wholly responsibility for the title manufactured to describe the contents — both narratives, the Introduction, innumerable footnotes and several appendices, a Postscript, and this Editorial Commentary — which make up the book in its entirety: **Redbrick University Revisited: The Autobiography of 'Bruce Truscot'**.

**EDITORIAL NOTE**

The Editors do not hold themselves responsible for the opinions of the late E. Allison Peers upon any matter or person discussed or portrayed in these Autobiographies.

# REAL NAMES AND FALSE IDENTITIES IN *REDBRICK UNIVERSITY REVISITED*

It should be remembered that some of the characters in Bruce Truscot's *Autobiography* have not been positively identified. It should also be noted that some of Bruce Truscot's teachers and colleagues would appear to derive their personalities from not simply one but at least two of Allison Peers' acquaintances and contemporaries. We have used a (?) to indicate doubtful or partial attributions.

## Places, Institutions etc.

| | |
|---|---|
| Cambridge University | Camford University |
| Christ's College, Cambridge | Trinity College, Camford |
| Dartford Grammar School | Chatstone Grammar School |
| Felsted School | Cranstead School |
| Gilmour Chair of Spanish, University of Liverpool | Trevor Professorship of Poetry, Redbrick University |
| Harchester | Fictitious 'Famous' Public School (Har[row] + [Win]chester) |
| Liverpool | Drabtown |
| Liverpool University | Redbrick University |
| The Maccoll Lectures (Cambridge University) | The Snark Lectures (Camford University) |
| The 'New Testament' Liverpool University | The 'Salvation Army', Redbrick University |
| Oxford University | Oxbridge University |
| The Perse School, Cambridge | Camford Grammar School |
| Victoria Building, University of Liverpool | Arts Tower, Redbrick University |
| West Kirby | Forbridge |

## Characters

Abercrombie, Lascelles, (?)
    Liverpool University

Adami, Dr John George, (?)
    Vice-Chancellor, Liverpool
    University (1919-26)

Bosanquet, Robert Carr, (?)
    Professor of Classical
    Archaeology, Liverpool
    University

Boswell, Professor A. Bruce, (?)
    Dean, Faculty of Arts,
    Liverpool University

Campagnac, Ernest Trafford,
    Professor of Education,
    Liverpool University

Case, Robert Hope,
    Professor of English
    Literature, Liverpool
    University

Collinson, William Edward,
    Professor of German,
    Liverpool University

Collinson , William Edward, (?)
    Professor of German,
    Liverpool University

Eggli, Jean Edmond, (?)
    Professor of French,
    Liverpool University

Eggli, Jean Edmond (?)
    Professor of French,
    Liverpool University

Eggli, Jean Edmond, (?)
    Professor of French,
    Liverpool University

Julius Green,
    Redbrick University

Sir Archibald Blake,
    Vice-Chancellor,
    Redbrick University

Crusty,
    Professor of English
    Language, Redbrick
    University

Fanshawe,
    Dean, Faculty of Arts,
    Redbrick University

Dusty,
    Professor of Latin,
    Redbrick University

Robert Anstruther,
    Lecturer in English
    Literature, Redbrick
    University

Bletherley,
    Professor of Education,
    Redbrick University

Crusty,
    Professor of English
    Language, Redbrick
    University

André,
    Professor of French,
    Redbrick University

Eagles,
    Professor of Economics,
    Redbrick University

Eberhard,
    Professor of German,
    Redbrick University

… REAL NAMES AND FALSE IDENTITIES 53

Elton, Oliver,
  King Alfred Professor of
  English Literature,
  Liverpool University

George Slocombe,
  Professor of
  English Literature,
  Redbrick University

Fitzmaurice-Kelly, James,
  Gilmour Professor of Spanish
  (1909-1916),
  Liverpool University

George Charles
  [or James] Upright,
  Trevor Professor of Poetry,
  Redbrick University

Garmon Jones, Professor William, (?)
  Dean, Faculty of Arts,
  Liverpool University

Dr Dobie,
  Dean, Faculty of Arts,
  Redbrick University

Garmon Jones, Professor William, (?)
  Dean, Faculty of Arts,
  Liverpool University

Fanshawe,
  Dean, Faculty of Arts,
  Redbrick University

Gilmour, Captain George

John Austin Trevor

Glehn, Louis (Camille) de,
  The Perse School

Hopewell,
  Camford Grammar School

Hetherington, Sir Hector, (?)
  Vice-Chancellor (1927-1936),
  Liverpool University

Sir Archibald Blake,
  Vice-Chancellor,
  Redbrick University

Mair, Alexander,
  Professor of Philosophy,
  Liverpool University

Wormwood,
  Professor of Philosophy,
  Redbrick University

Martin, Leonard C., (?)
  Professor of English
  Literature, Liverpool
  University

Robert Anstruther,
  Lecturer in English
  Literature, Redbrick
  University

McClure, Sir John, Headmaster,
  Mill Hill School

Dr Downside, Headmaster,
  Cranstead School

Peers, Edgar Allison,
  Lecturer, then Gilmour
  Professor of Spanish
  (1920-1922; 1922-1952),
  Liverpool University

Bruce Truscot,
  Lecturer, then Trevor
  Professor of Poetry
  (1918-1920; 1920-?1947),
  Redbrick University

Peers, Edgar Allison,
    Gilmour Professor of Spanish
    (1922-1952),
    Liverpool University

Peers, Edgar Allison, (?)
    Gilmour Professor of Spanish,
    Liverpool University

Postgate, J. P., (?)
    Professor of Latin,
    Liverpool University

Praz, Mario, (?)
    Senior Lecturer in Italian,
    Liverpool University

Rébora, Piero, (?)
    Senior Lecturer in Italian,
    Liverpool University

Sampson, John,
    University Librarian,
    Liverpool University

Share Jones, John, (?)
    Professor of Veterinary
    Anatomy, Liverpool University

Skeat, Walter William,
    Professor of Anglo-Saxon,
    Cambridge University

Slater, David Ansell,
    Professor of Latin,
    Liverpool University

Slater, David Ansell, (?)
    Professor of Latin
    Liverpool University

Terracher, Louis Adolphe, (?)
    Professor of French,
    Liverpool University

Jim Livewire,
    successful candidate for
    Chair of English Literature,
    Redbrick University

Dusty,
    Professor of Latin,
    Redbrick University

Crusty,
    Professor of English
    Language, Redbrick
    University

Ratti,
    Lecturer in Italian,
    Redbrick University

Ratti,
    Lecturer in Italian,
    Redbrick University

Inaccessible,
    Professor of Ancient
    History, Redbrick
    University

Loaf,
    Professor of Zoology,
    Redbrick University

Peet,
    Professor of Anglo-
    Saxon, Camford University

Crusty,
    Professor of English
    Language, Redbrick
    University

Bletherley,
    Professor of Education,
    Redbrick University

André,
    Professor of French,
    Redbrick University

# REAL NAMES AND FALSE IDENTITIES

Thomas, Sir Henry, (?)
    Department of
    Printed Books,
    British Museum

Vaughan, Dr William Wyamar,
    Master, Wellington
    College

Verrall, Arthur Woolgar,
    Professor of
    English Literature,
    Cambridge University

Webster, Sir Charles Kingsley, (?)
    Professor of
    Modern History,
    Liverpool University

Josiah Rippon,
    Senior Fellow of
    St Anthony's,
    Camford University

Dr Downside,
    Headmaster, Cranstead
    School

Drake,
    Professor of
    English Literature,
    Camford University

Active,
    Professor of
    International Relations,
    Redbrick University

# THE AUTOBIOGRAPHY OF
# E. ALLISON PEERS

# PART I

# CHAPTER 1[1]

## SCHOOL-DAYS AND HOME LIFE

### I

Few boys can have sampled so many different types of school.[2] My father[3] was an officer of Customs and Excise fated to move

---

1   'When rest of book done, go thro' this and decide on length of Intr$^n$. and whether things in margin can be put in or not': these words, written, in pencil, to serve as a reminder, are found at the top of the first page of his manuscript, where Peers embarks upon what he calls '(E.A.P.) *Auto*' — that is, where he begins to narrate straightforwardly the undisguised 'key' first section of his memoirs. Peers probably regarded as 'Intr$^n$.' ('Introduction') the part of '(E.A.P.) *Auto*' concerned with his school-days, home life, undergraduate years and career as a schoolmaster. We have divided this part (which we have called Part I) to form chapters 1-3, and have provided the chapter-headings. Peers does not use chapter divisions and chapter-headings until he begins to describe his career at Liverpool as a university teacher (see below, Part II LIVERPOOL, CHAPTER 4, 'PROBATION', p. 125, note 1).

Another note, in pencil, in the margin reads: '[Intr. par. wanted]'. This 'introductory paragraph', which might have assisted the reader to understand Peers' reasons for composing both autobiographies, was evidently never inserted (*cf*. 'B.T.', ch. I, p. 173, note 1).

2   Peers begins to describe his 'origins' (this word is in the margin). But, after his initial sentence there is a gap in the manuscript. Peers has carefully excised, with scissors, part of the first page (corresponding to some five lines of text). The section thus removed has been incorporated (using gum) into the first page of the 'Bruce Truscot' narrative (see the italicized passage, ch. I, p. 173). The first pages of both narratives are illustrated in facsimile on pp. 32-33. As explained in the Editorial Commentary, Peers repeatedly trims the text of '(E.A.P.) *Auto*' by this method, transferring the excised material to enlarge *The Autobiography of 'Bruce Truscot'*.

3   John Thomas Peers. He was born at Broad Somerford, Wiltshire, on 31 May 1860, the son of Robert Peers, an Inland Revenue officer, and his wife. He followed in his father's footsteps, being in the employ of Customs and Excise from 26 May 1880 until his retirement on 22 August 1921. (Summary Record of Mr Peers' career amongst the records of the Personnel Directorate Division C4, HM Customs & Excise, London, and Establishment

from one place to another every three or four years; and, as I was a delicate child, it was considered inadvisable to subject me to the supposed rigours of a boarding-school. As the family finances could only have run to a second-rate establishment, this was perhaps not wholly a disaster.

I was born[4] at Leighton Buzzard, a Bedfordshire[5] town

---

Book no. 306 [Supervisors and Officers] relating to Elgin, p. 125, now deposited with the Moray District Archives and formerly deposited in the Scottish Record Office, ref. CE 78/42.)

On 20 January 1887, at the age of 26½ years, John Peers married Jessie Dale Allison, aged twenty-one years, daughter of Charles Allison, an outfitter, of Hampton Hill, Middlesex, at the Congregational Church, High Street, Hampton, Middlesex. Jessie had been born in Hampton in 1865. John Peers retired while Surveyor for the Kingston District, at Croydon. In his retirement he and his wife lived in Worthing, Sussex. John Peers died on 12 February 1944, aged eighty-three years, and Jessie on 18 July 1951 (just seventeen months before their son, E. Allison Peers, himself died).

4   Edgar Allison Peers was born on 7 May 1891, his parents' only son and elder child. Their other child, Winifred Dale Peers, was born three years later, on 9 August 1894, also at Leighton Buzzard; for details of her career, see below, pp. 71-72, note 30. Photographs of E. Allison Peers and of his sister Winifred as children (c.1896-97) have been donated to the University's Archives (ref. D.629) by Mr Roger N. R. Peers, first cousin once removed of Allison Peers.

5   In *Kelly's Directory of Bedfordshire, Hunts and Northamptonshire* (London: Kelly & Co. Ltd, 1894), Leighton Buzzard is described as 'a union town, parish, head of a county court, district and petty sessional division, with a station on the London and North Western railway, 40½ miles from London... in the Southern division of the county... The town stands near the north-western border of the county, and on the eastern bank of the Ousel... it consists of one wide and several smaller streets...' (86). The 1891 Census recorded a population in the parish of 8,814 and in the township of 6,704. The *Directory* records the 'Inland Revenue office, Thomas B. Harmer, supervisor, 29 Lake Street; John Peers, officer, 39 Hockcliffe Road' and John Peers is also listed at 39 Hockcliffe street (*sic*) in the list of commercial residents (87, 91).

According to the staff records of HM Customs and Excise, John Peers was based at Leighton Buzzard from July 1885 until his move to Glasgow in December 1896. The 1891 Census, taken on 5 April, recorded John and Jessie Peers living in Hockcliffe Road together with a domestic servant, Miss Clara Champkins, aged seventeen years, who had been born in Leighton Buzzard (Public Record Office, RG12/1265, Registration District 175/1B f.25d.). Of the seventy-one recorded inhabited houses in Hockcliffe Road, just five households employed servants, these four other households being in close proximity to the Peers' house in what was otherwise a predominantly working class area. It is conceivable that John Peers

which I left at the age of five, and have never seen since except from the window of a London, Midland and Scottish express. My first experience of education was a private school in Glasgow,[6] where we spent less than a year before moving further north still, to a remote village, the sole *raison d'être* of which seemed to be a distillery, a few miles from the Moray Firth.[7] Here the only school for a child aged six was the country elementary school which served a wide district, and to which I tramped a mile and a half daily, ploughing through deep snow in winter and scampering over heather in summer,[8]

---

employed a servant at this time as his wife was expecting their first child.

6    Customs and Excise records reveal that John Peers was appointed to the Glasgow office from 1 December 1896.

7    John Peers was posted by Customs and Excise to the Longmorn 1st Station on 13 December 1897, taking charge on 7 February 1898. During his period at the Station, his salary increased by increments from £195 p.a. to £220 p.a. Longmorn is a village three miles south of Elgin, nowadays in the Moray District of Grampian. The Longmorn-Glenlivet distillery was built in 1894-95 by the Longmorn-Glenlivet Distillery Co. and incorporated in Longmorn-Glenlivet Distilleries Co. Ltd. in 1898 (Michael S. Moss and John R. Hume, *The Making of Scotch Whisky* [Edinburgh: James & James, 1981], 266 and end-paper map of location of distilleries). The distillery was built during a period when investment in whisky became fashionable. In his history of *Dallas Dhu Distillery* (Edinburgh: HMSO, 1988), John R. Hume states that 'between 1894 and 1899 no fewer than 19 distilleries were built in Moray and Banffshire' (3, 5). Under the 1823 Excise Act, distilleries were required to provide separate accommodation for Excise officers, the Board of Excise renting such accommodation. (Moss and Hume, *op. cit.*, 84). Allison Peers' sister, Winifred, is quoted as stating that while in Scotland the family lived 'first in Glasgow and then in Lossiemouth' (see *Cousins' Chronicle: An Account of the Lives of the Grandchildren of Charles Allison and Susanna Bellamy Morris*, ed. Ralph Allison [1976], 16 [copy donated to the University's Archives by Mr Roger N. R. Peers; ref. D.629]). Nevertheless, their father, John T. Peers, as head of the household, is recorded as occupier of a house at the Longmorn-Glenlivet distillery in the Elgin Valuation Rolls for 1898-99, 1899-1900 and 1900-01 (Scottish Record Office, ref. VR 109/44, p. 241; VR 109/45, p. 245; VR 109/46, p. 331). The Valuation Roll for Lossiemouth for 1899-1900 (ref. VR 109/45) does not record any member of the Peers family. The house, which both the predecessor and the successor of John Peers as Customs and Excise Officer also occupied at the distillery, still stands (information supplied by Dr David Iredale, Moray District Archivist, June 1994).

8    As regards Peers' description of his daily journey to school, Mr J. Barrett of the Moray District Department of Leisure and Libraries, writes (March 1993) that it 'squares with local geography only if we allow for the

to be taught exclusively by the dominie,[9] who, for all we laddies and lassies knew (or cared) was an authority on everything. From the said laddies and lassies I learned two accomplishments — to speak the broadest Hielan' [Highland] Scots and to swear like a trooper. Both these, in which I hasten to say I have long since lost my proficiency, I indulged at school only, and my parents were idealistic enough to believe that I conversed with the children of Morayshire farm-hands in their own brand of London-and-home-counties English.

At nine, I was pitchforked from the north of Scotland into the English midlands — at Burton-on-Trent,[10] to be exact, where I spent a further three years at a Higher Grade

---

child making unaccountable diversions from the obvious route and if we allow for the man adding considerable colour from the palette of nostalgia enhanced by romantic reflection'.

9    Schoolmaster. The school in question would appear to have been Clackmarras School, four miles south east of Elgin and about three-quarters of a mile to the east of Longmorn, which, at the time, was a school for pupils aged five to fourteen years of age and was administered under the Elgin Landward School Board; the School's catchment area certainly included Longmorn at a later date (Admission Register 1924-67). The School Board's minutes note that HM Inspectors found the school premises unsatisfactory by 1896 and a new school was built in 1899. The school closed in 1967. Unfortunately no records of the school survive from the period Peers would have been a pupil. The school's headmaster, Alexander Grant, was appointed in 1895 (Minute Book of the School Board 1896-1912) and retired in June 1931 (School Log Book 1931-67). At the time of his appointment he was evidently assistant in Rutherford College, Newcastle-upon-Tyne (*Moray and Nairn Express: Northern Scot*, 23 March 1895). Born at Keith, County Banff, (about a dozen miles to the south east of Clackmarras) on 16 April 1868, Mr Grant (as did Peers' 'dominie' [see p. 65]) graduated M.A. at the University of Aberdeen in 1890 (William Johnston, *Roll of the Graduates of the University of Aberdeen 1860-1900* [Aberdeen, 1906], 206). He died at Rothes, Morayshire on 14 February 1948. (Information supplied by Mrs Brenda R. Cluer, Grampian Regional Archivist, Aberdeen; by Mr Colin A. McLaren, University Archivist, University of Aberdeen; and by Mr Graeme Wilson, Department of Leisure and Libraries, Moray District Council).

10    Customs and Excise records state that John Peers was appointed to the Burton Station on 3 September 1900, leaving the Longmorn Station on 10 September, and spending the next three days in travelling to his new post; he was promoted Assistant Supervisor (12 February 1903) and Supervisor 2nd Class (12 July 1904). Burton was then a municipal borough, and the population of Burton's municipal wards was recorded as 46,254 in the 1891 Census.

school:[11] the greatest mistake of all the mistakes which were made about my education. For from that Morayshire dominie, a Classical graduate of Aberdeen University, I had had a grounding in Latin (think of it, elementary schoolmasters in England!) for which I never ceased to be grateful, and if I had gone thence to a public school which would have built upon this foundation and added first French and then Spanish and German, I should have had some chance as a linguist. Instead of this, for the precious years from nine to twelve in which more progress can be made in language-learning than in any other three years, I ploughed through a higher elementary curriculum and at the end of it still knew no word[12] of any other modern language than my own.

From twelve to fourteen I sampled co-education for a second time at a secondary school for boys and girls in Wiltshire.[13]

---

11 Peers mentions (next paragraph) that the school to which he was sent in Wiltshire was the second co-educational school which he had attended (the first such school being the elementary school in Morayshire); it is clear, therefore, that this school was a boys' school. But *Kelly's Directory of Staffordshire* (1900) lists just one boys (only) school in Burton-on-Trent, besides the Grammar School: Stafford Street School, a Board School, which, according to the Head Teacher of Lansdowne Infants' School (1993), was an infants' school in 1900.

12 Corrected in pencil to: 'hardly a word ('.' Sp.)'. Peers by then evidently knew a few words of Spanish.

13 For the period in question, between the Spring of 1903 and the Spring of 1906 (the outside dates), only one edition (11th) was published of *Kelly's Directory of Hampshire, Wiltshire, Dorsetshire, The Isle of Wight and the Channel Islands*, in 1903, and no Peers is recorded in the listings of the private residents in the Wiltshire section, and no Inland Revenue or Excise staff are listed in the Trades Directory section. The 12th edition, published in 1907, does not record Peers. For that period John Peers was based at the Inland Revenue offices at Burton-upon-Trent and then Dartford; and perhaps his son stayed with relatives while attending school in Wiltshire. Allison Peers' sister, Winifred, is quoted as having stated that she 'first went to school at the age of six in Burton-on-Trent, after that to a boarding school in Trowbridge and, finally, at the age of eleven, to Dartford Grammar School' (*Cousins' Chronicle...*, ed. Ralph Allison [1976], 16). The County Archivist of Wiltshire, Mr Steven D. Hobbs, states that he is unaware of any public or private boarding school for girls only in Trowbridge at the period in question (c.1903-04); that the only secondary school for both boys and girls in Trowbridge at this time was the High School, which became the town's County Secondary Modern School in 1912; and that the High School's admission registers, which survive for the years 1903-12, contain no entry

66    REDBRICK UNIVERSITY REVISITED

Here I resumed Latin and began French — the latter most inadequately, but I loved language-learning enough to rise superior to the method, or lack of method, employed, and it was here, I think, that, through the chance of some relatives' going to live in Peru, I conceived the desire to learn Spanish, which I later indulged clandestinely, since in those days it was considered slightly eccentric to learn any modern language other than French and German.[14]

At fourteen I migrated once more — to Dartford, a market-town in what was then a comparatively rural district [in Kent],[15] where I was allowed to finish my schooldays without further interruption.[16] The school course in itself was quite adequate;[17] the masters, though nearly all second-rate men,

---

for a Peers.

14   'omitted < BT'. This note and other marks in pencil indicate *either* that Peers had taken over this sentence from the 'Bruce Truscot' material; *or* that he had considered transferring it to the 'B.T.' narrative; *or* that he had even thought to omit it altogether — despite the fact that the sentence throws interesting light on the origins of his interest in Spanish.

15   John Peers was transferred to the Dartford District of Customs and Excise from 19 December 1904, being promoted Surveyor in August 1911.

In the 8th edition, 1907, of *Kelly's Directory of Kent, Surrey and Sussex*, Dartford is described as 'a market town and parish and the head of a union, petty sessional division and county court district, lying in one of the valleys of north-west Kent, with a station on the North Kent section of the South Eastern and Chatham railway... 15 miles from London by road... 2 from the Thames' (208). The headmaster of the Grammar School, Mr Mansford (see note 17), also liked to refer to Dartford as a market town, but it was one with a substantial industrial base, as *Kelly's Directory* makes clear. Dartford was not exactly a rural paradise. Amongst 'the extensive manufacturing operations of the place' were chemical works, a gun-cotton manufactory, silk printing works, breweries, malt-houses and brickfields (209). The population in 1901 was recorded as 18,644. The 1907 edition of *Kelly's Directory of Kent...* records John Thomas Peers, supervisor of Inland Revenue, at 10 Miskin Road (216), but the 1909 edition (9th edition) lists him at 30 Miskin Road. The 1909 edition of the 25-inch Ordnance Survey map of Dartford (Kent sheet IX.6) shows the close proximity of Miskin Road to the Grammar School, on West Hill.

16   Originally founded in 1576, Dartford Grammar School, which Peers attended, was then a secondary school, under the Board of Education, with one hundred and twenty boys (*Kelly's Directory of Kent...*, 1907, 212).

17   In his *History of Dartford Grammar School* (Dartford: Dimond & Co. Ltd., 1966), the then headmaster, Mr Ronald L. Hudson, recorded the reorganisation of the School under the headmastership of Mr Charles John Jodrell Mansford, B.A., F.C.S., from his appointment in 1902 until his

SCHOOL-DAYS AND HOME LIFE 67

were conscientious and full of interest in their work;[18] and the headmaster, though disconcertingly temperamental, was a man of ability and imagination.[19] But unfortunately one idea

---

retirement in 1919. Mr Jodrell Mansford 'completely changed the style of education in the School, bringing it into line with the new concept of secondary education and developing it into the style of school we know today' (51); the reorganisation was accompanied by a steady growth in numbers of boys on the register from forty-five to two hundred and eighty-eight during his headmastership. Growth in numbers enabled the staffing to be improved: at the end of 1905 (the year in which Peers entered the School) there were four full-time assistants as well as visiting masters for Art, Drill and Music for the one hundred and nine boys, only ten of whom were boarders. By this date 'Science had begun to take a firm hold and was taught to all forms'; German also now appeared for the first time 'but like Latin, it was "taken only in special cases" ' (47). By 1909, the year in which Peers left the School, the number of boys had increased to one hundred and sixty-two (of whom one hundred and twenty-one paid fees of eight or ten guineas a year according to age, thirty-two were educated free as county scholars, and nine were trainee teachers); they were organised in seven forms, which had mottoes in Latin, French, German, Spanish and English.

Besides E. Allison Peers, two of his fellow pupils at the School, Frank L. Engledow (1904-09) (later Sir Frank Engledow, F.R.S., d.1985) and Percival Gurrey (1902-08) were also to become university professors, of Agriculture and English respectively; Percival Gurrey (b.1890) became Professor of English at the University College of the Gold Coast. F. L. Engledow, in particular, often featured alongside Peers in the School's records — of examination successes, school plays, and the debating society's debates.

18  Appendix II of the *History of Dartford Grammar School* lists the members of staff in 1907 and subsequently; of those eight listed, besides the headmaster, who were on the staff while Peers was a pupil (1905-09), four were graduates, including Mr H. E. Bryant, B.A., who taught English, Mathematics and Science (1906-09), Mr L. J. Oberlé, B.A., who taught French (1906-09), and Mr C. B. Stinson, B.A., who taught English and History (1906-09). The photographic illustrations in the *History* include views of 'staff and boys — about 1907', the exterior of the school 'between 1904 and 1913', and Mr Jodrell Mansford (in army uniform)

19  Mr David Patterson, Senior History Teacher at Dartford Grammar School, comments (in a letter of 16 October 1992) that, in his opinion, Peers is a bit tough in his assessment of Mr Jodrell Mansford, who was highly successful in building up the school from a low point. Mr Mansford was himself an author of over a dozen novels and tales (bearing such titles as *Bully, Fag and Hero; or In Playground and Schoolroom* and *The Adventures of Mark Paton and Other Stories*) and some other publications, including *The Educational Ladder in Kent: Some Considerations* (Maidstone: Kent Messenger, 1906), and was clearly not without a sense of humour. For a list of his publications, see the entry in *The British Library General Catalogue of Printed Books to 1975*.

which his imagination conceived was that of sending in his most promising pupils for every sort and kind of examination[20] so as to be able to present a long list of successes to expectant governors and uncomprehending parents at the annual prize-giving — dignified by the name of 'Speech Day',[21] though the only speeches were that of the celebrity who distributed the

---

20 Mr Mansford's obsession with examinations — which, after 1914, changed to one of involvement in war work to such an extent that he used his private car as an ambulance in France — is documented in his reports to the Governing Body and at Speech Days. The examination successes of Peers were documented as follows:
  a) University Senior Local: 1st Class Honours — E. A. Peers (distinguished in Scripture [8th equal out of 1454 candidates], English, English History [3rd equal out of 1445 candidates], and passed in Spoken French). (Report for Speech Day, 9 April 1907).
  b) London University Intermediate BA Examination — E. A. Peers (1st Class Honours in English); only two other candidates in England obtained the same distinction. (Christmas Term 1908). Then in Form VIa, Peers was awarded a Special Prize by the School for this success. The other subjects he took in this examination were Latin, French, Chemistry, and Pure Mathematics.
  c) Board of Education Examinations — Mathematics Stage III: E. A. Peers (1st Class); Practical Mathematics Stage II: E. A Peers; Practical Chemistry Stage II: E. A. Peers (1909).
  d) Cambridge University Entrance Examination — E. A. Peers (1st Class); Kent County Council Major Scholarship — E. A. Peers (1st in England in English) (Value: £60 p.a. for three years) (report for Speech Day, 12 April 1910).

In their report on an inspection of the School, 16-17 February 1910, the H.M. Inspectors, Mr F. B. Stead and Mr B. W. White-Tomson commented that the 'unusual duplication of examinations of what may be roughly called a Matriculation standard' was:

> somewhat difficult to justify, and the reasons given against making any change were not entirely convincing. In the Report of the former Inspection it was remarked that there was a tendency to direct the teaching on lines indicated by examination questions. There is no doubt that in respect to the pressure of examinations considerable improvement has been effected since 1905: but it is felt that the School is not yet entirely free from the danger of subordinating educational aims to examination requirements. At the same time it is freely recognised, as evidence of the spirit of industry which is characteristic of the place, that in the examinations taken the School has had more than a fair measure of success.

21 Marginal question pencilled here: Peers wonders if he should '?go thro' old [school] programmes'.

prizes and his own.²² It still makes my blood boil to think how, instead of concentrating on preparing me for Cambridge (where eventually I had to go at my father's expense, though I could easily have gained a much-needed College entrance scholarship had I been coached for one)[,] this unspeakable pedagogue sent me in for an innumerable succession of examinations, beginning with the 'Junior Local', which I had already taken in Wiltshire and [...]²³ demanded results; the assistant masters who, as I have said, were good fellows according to their lights had to see that he got them. Hardly a lesson passed, and certainly not a day passed, without our being reminded of the examination next ensuing. Some boys — those of the type who played noughts and crosses in class, and threw ping-pong balls above the head of a dear old [slightly-]deaf master who never *could* understand what the noise was — frankly scoffed at the whole thing and did as little work as possible. A few — the sensible, strong-minded ones, and I wish I had [...]²⁴

[...] a result which I valued considerably less than a chance exclamation of surprise on the part of one of the purple-hooded invigilators (whom I ignorantly supposed must be a person of great distinction) on discovering that the subjects I was taking included Anglo-Saxon and Practical Chemistry.

---

22 Despite the impression given by this account, Peers also took an active part in other School activities — in particular School plays mounted as part of the programme for Speech Days (taking the role of Ebenezer Scrooge in 1907 and Antony, in costume recitals from *Julius Caesar*, in 1909), and the debates of the School's Debating Society (which were chronicled in the School's magazine, *The Dartfordian*). He was Captain of School in 1908-09. At the Prefects' Social on the last day of the winter term 1908, he commenced the proceedings with a pianoforte solo entitled 'Pomp and Circumstances', which *The Dartfordian*, vol. V (1909), no. 2, reported 'he very ably executed'.

23 More than half of page 4 and the entire text on page 5 have been excised. Pencilled in the margin — all that remains of page 5 — there is the query: '?Put in the episode of failing and being "reexam[ined]" '. Most of what has been excised here has been transferred to the 'Bruce Truscot' autobiography (see 'B.T.', ch. I, pp. 185-86, italicized).

24 Occasionally, as in this instance, when cutting pages and transferring parts of them, Peers excised rather more of his text than he had intended. For most of the section excised here (from pp. 6-7) see, in the 'B.T.' text, the lines italicized, ch. I, pp. 188-89. The anecdote involving the invigilator is not, however, told in the 'B.T.' narrative, and, therefore, cannot be completed.

[...] London Intermediate at school, I went up to Cambridge determined to finish the London B.A. during my first year by private study. I achieved my aim and had the satisfaction of being an [Honours] graduate at nineteen; but I nearly wrecked my Cambridge degree, since the syllabuses were very different, and instead of taking a First in each of my languages, as I should have done, I took it only in one.[25]

## II

It is a pleasure to turn from the mishandling of my education by short-sighted schoolmasters to the perfecting of it by home influences for which I can never be sufficiently grateful. In all my personal dealings with individual undergraduates I have found myself unconsciously trying to give them something which my home experiences gave me. Having spent six years as a public-school master,[26] I know something about boarding-schools, and, except in cases where the splitting up of a family or some other cause makes it impracticable or where the home influence is definitely a bad one, I should recommend day-school education every time. If mothers and fathers knew into what mazes of temptation they were driving their children, they would think a long time before sending them away to school 'because it makes them so much more independent'. When Tommy comes home, of course, for his first holidays,

---

25 Peers matriculated in 1907 (while a pupil at Dartford Grammar School) and he graduated B.A. Honours (2nd Class) in English and French in 1910. He contributed an article 'First Impressions of 'Varsity Life' to *The Dartfordian* (vol. VI [Christmas, 1909], no. 1, 15), describing the 'average' student's day 'up' at Cambridge: 'It is a common fallacy that 'Varsity men either work or play; the A. S. [average student] does both, and does them well'.

26 Marginal note in pencil: '?Put in some of the D school correspondence'. Does Peers mean to include correspondence about life at boarding school received — perhaps, during his own Dartford day-school days — from friends unhappily placed in public schools, distant from their families?

SCHOOL-DAYS AND HOME LIFE        71

father takes the opportunity of having a [...]²⁷ happy activity. From my father, for whom fate might have found some more congenial job than that of a civil servant — his father's before him — I derive a passion for knowledge of all kinds, a hatred of unfairness and intolerance, and, above all, an objectivity of outlook which is only one sign of the deep placidity of an interior life with which superficially active persons are not often credited.²⁸ One trait alone has always been a mystery to all who knew my family: where in the world did I derive any proficiency in the learning of languages? Neither my father nor my mother, nor any of their brothers or sisters, appear to have had the slightest interest in such a thing. Many other linguists, however, have told me that the same thing applies to them, so possibly this particular gift normally skips several generations.²⁹

My home life, in all its essential aspects, was as nearly perfect as home life can be. There was little money, yet no parade was ever made of the constant, necessary economies, many of which neither my sister³⁰ nor I ever [...]³¹ we absorbed

---

27  Almost half of page 8, all of page 9 and several lines from page 10 have been removed and transferred to 'B.T.' (ch. I, pp. 191-92 — italicized). In the sentence of which 'happy activity' are the final words, the author declares that from his mother he inherited his business instinct and 'detestation of idleness'.

28  A note pencilled in the margin opposite this sentence reads: '?Priggish? alter'. 'Priggish' or not, the comment illuminates Peers' nature in its two principal and only seemingly contradictory aspects: his indefatigable industry as energetic teacher and productive scholar; and his quietly contemplative 'interior life' as a profoundly spiritual Anglo-Catholic. The very phrase 'interior life' — a term intimately associated with, and wholly familiar to, the great Mystics of Spain — reveals not only Peers' literary familiarity with St Teresa of Ávila and St John of the Cross, but also his deep-reaching sense of affinity with them in their religious endeavours, and his personal insights into their mystic experiences.

29  Peers has bracketed the passage, 'One trait... generations', and has written in the margin: 'Not used'.

30  Miss Winifred Dale Peers (1894-1984) attended the Dartford County Secondary School, 1905-13, and, having passed the Matriculation examination of the University of London in 1913, trained at the Froebel Educational Institute, 1913 — December 1915, being awarded the Higher Certificate of the National Froebel Union. Following teaching posts at a private school at Newcastle, Staffordshire (May-July 1916) and at a private school at Radlett, Hertfordshire (September 1916-July 1917), she was appointed to the teaching staff of the Chelmsford County High School for

quite unconsciously. We enjoyed[32] going to Church because our parents obviously enjoyed it;[33] we had no desire to 'garden' on Sundays, because our father, the keenest of gardeners, always put away his tools on Saturday night. On the few occasions when, either in this or in other respects, we kicked over the traces, my father's method was simply to let us do so and say

---

Girls in September 1917. Miss Peers remained on the staff of the High School until her retirement in July 1956, serving first as Head of the Preparatory Department until it closed in 1947, and then as Mistress in charge of Junior Forms. In his will, Allison Peers provided an annual sum of £100 for his sister, to be paid for the period of her life.

Miss Geraldine M. Cadbury, Headmistress of the County High School from 1935 to 1961 writes (letter of 26 October 1992) of Miss Peers: ' ...Gifted as a teacher, she helped many girls to see and appreciate the world around them, and to love things of beauty. She also quietly took part in many school activities. She helped with the Junior Christian Fellowship, and was a House Mistress... She was a truly wise person, with great love and understanding of girls. Many generations valued her quiet friendliness, support, and encouragement... many of her "Old Girls"... have often told me how much they appreciated her influence and friendship through the years... she talked to me sometimes about her brother. She was proud of him, and obviously very fond of him, and I know she missed him after his death'.

Mrs Aimée K. Bass of Chelmsford, a close friend of Miss Peers, writes of being a guest in the Peers household in Worthing, Sussex (letter of 25 November 1992):

> I now have but two of his [Peers'] books, *Mother of Carmel* and... *Way Up*... I find the meditations on simple things profound, typical of [his] spiritual insight... and clothed in characteristics of the Peers family as a whole. One could not stay amongst them without an enrichment of soul;... It is an honour to be involved with the Peers family however remotely.

31   Peers has transferred this passage, with details about his parents and happy family life, to 'B.T.', ch. I, pp. 192-93 — italicized.

32   Above these words Peers has scribbled, as possibly more accurate or suitable than simply 'enjoy': 'soon began to enjoy', and 'came to enjoy'.

33   It may be presumed that Congregational churches were attended. John and Jessie Peers were married in a Congregational church. Their religious influence on their children is evidenced in a number of legacies in the will of Peers' sister, Winifred (died 27 June 1984), in favour of the Unified Appeal Fund of the United Reformed Church (£300), the British and Foreign Bible Society (£250), the Essex Federation of the Congregational Women's Homes Ltd (£200), the Christian Aid Fund (£150), and the London City Mission (£150).

SCHOOL-DAYS AND HOME LIFE 73

nothing. Almost without exception, we capitulated of our own accord. Only in one respect, as quite a young man, did I feel bound in conscience to take a step which was contrary to my father's wishes. The look in his eyes when I told him of it hurt me as little else has done but he bowed his head and never said a word to [...][34]

[...] character is taking the foremost place[,] and my mother's less dominant, though no less beautiful, is receding into the background.[35] That I always felt to be right: the two were genuine partners, but he was managing director, and even in his last years, as an invalid, when my mother had to act much more on her own initiative, she consulted him whenever it was possible.[36]

Though I have mixed to more than an average extent with men of all classes and of many nationalities, my father still seems to me the most remarkable man I have known: had he had even my own limited opportunities, he would have gone far. Of numerous and quite unrelated subjects he had an

---

34 The words needed to conclude the sentence are 'dissuade me'. In the margin here is written '? omit'; and, indeed, the rest of this paragraph has been excised from this page of the manuscript. For the missing passage, see 'B.T.', ch. I, pp. 194-95 — italicized. The 'B.T.' text reveals that the 'step' which Peers felt 'bound in conscience' to take was to change his religion. Peers' parents were Congregationalists. He became a devout Anglo-Catholic.

35 A reference, evidently, to the fact that his father continued to occupy a particularly vivid and influential place in Peers' thoughts and memories.

36 In his will, dated 11 April 1932, John Peers appointed his 'dearly loved wife' as one of his executors (the others being his son and Sydney Pennington Allison of Hampton Hill, Middlesex) and bequeathed all his estate and effects 'unto my beloved wife Jessie Dale Peers absolutely'. Probate was granted in May 1944, his effects being given a valuation of £2,432/3/10d. In her turn Jessie Peers in her will (which is in the handwriting of E. Allison Peers), signed on 20 March 1944, just over a month after her husband's death, bequeathed all her property to be divided equally between her two children. When probate was granted, in October 1951, her effects were valued at £5,986/12/7d.

extensive knowledge; he was widely read in English literature; he had no mean mastery of theology; he was an expert gardener and carpenter and an excellent electrician.[37] But it was in moral energy that he had most to give [...][38]

---

[37] Peers has written in pencil above 'an excellent': 'a more than adequate' — which possibly describes more accurately his father's prowess as an electrician.

[38] This page of the manuscript, part of which has been neatly removed, is numbered 13; the next page is numbered 18. A lengthy section has been excised. For some of the material excised see 'B.T.', ch. I, pp. 195-96 —italicized.

# CHAPTER 2

# CAMBRIDGE

[...]¹ to be better at history and better still at [chemistry and] mathematics. At the time I could have given no reason, except that my father had had the good sense to send me abroad and I felt drawn to languages in a way I had felt drawn to nothing before. I had wanted to take French and Spanish, but my tutor² seemed to think this was quite preposterous. There was no lecturer in Spanish; but some man from London, it appeared, would come up once a week to coach any undergraduate who insisted on taking the language. But it would hardly be decent to ask him: like everyone else who read modern languages I had 'better do French and German'.

But unfortunately neither my affection for German nor my proficiency in it survived the first term's lectures. The standard was fixed by men who had gained distinctions in the Higher [School] Certificate, spent long vacations in Germany and been taught by Germans. How could I read this on the basis of my grammar-school lessons given me by a man who had only mugged it up as an additional qualification to buttress a London pass degree? Even in French, which I had learned for six years and from at least one capable master, I

---

1 Pages 14-17 of the Allison Peers autobiography — which concern mostly his undergraduate days at Cambridge — have been removed and transferred, renumbered (pp. 27-30) and with necessary changes, to form part of the 'Bruce Truscot' narrative (see especially ch. I, pp. 196-199 — italicized). Peers has changed, for example, his original references to Christ's College, Cambridge, to read Trinity College, Camford — Bruce Truscot's supposed College. (Peers entered Christ's College, Cambridge in October 1909).

2 'gruff old Cartmell' has been deleted between the words 'but' and 'my tutor'. Peers describes Cartmell as 'a gruff old clergyman' further down (79). For the Revd James W. Cartmell, see below, note 13.

had difficulty in keeping up to the required level.³ I decided, then, to play for safety, to concentrate on getting a first class in French, to forget about Spanish till that was done and to take, as my second subject, English, in which, with so much Anglo-Saxon and Middle English already done, I was a head and shoulders above my fellows.⁴

Comparing Cambridge [as it was] then with almost any university to-day, I am appalled at the inefficiency of our instruction.⁵ In neither French or English Literature was there a professor and the only professor to whom I ever spoke in three years, as well as the only one of my lecturers whose house I ever visited, was Skeat, a charming and approachable old man, then at the end of his career as Professor of Anglo-Saxon.⁶ He at least was human; and, though all he ever did for us was to translate and comment upon an Anglo-Saxon anthology as though all our difficulties would disappear at the sound of his voice, he would intersperse delightful little observations upon the style or sentiment and quote parallel passages from more modern authors which were perhaps the only inspiration I got from any of my teachers in three years.

---

3   Peers commenced his study of French at the age of twelve years (see above, p. 66).
4   'All omitted': these words in the margin and other marks, likewise in pencil, indicate that Peers had intended to omit entirely the two preceding paragraphs, and to begin the account of his student-days at Cambridge with the words 'Comparing Cambridge as it was then...'
5   As if to emphasize the point, Peers has written, in pencil, in the margin: 'the ineff. of our instruⁿ. was appalling'.
6   Revd Walter William Skeat, F.B.A. (1835-1912), philologist, Elrington and Bosworth Professor of Anglo-Saxon, University of Cambridge, 1878-1912, and a Fellow, later a Senior Fellow, of Christ's College, Cambridge, 1860-1912. 'Teaching, untiring research, and writing occupied... an evenly happy and full life [as Professor]' (*Dictionary of National Biography*, quoting from Kenneth Sisam's biography of Skeat). The revised and enlarged edition of his *Etymological Dictionary* (1879-82) appeared in 1910. 'Skeat had relatively few pupils, but some of them were eminent; as a scholar he was internationally famous and immensely productive. Some of his Anglo-Saxon editions are still used, and his texts of Chaucer and Langland held the field till the 1950s and 60s' (Brooke, *A History of the University of Cambridge, Vol. IV 1870-1990*, 444). He is listed in vols 1-3 (1906-08) of the *Modern Language Review* as a member of its Advisory Board.

The other English lecturers were A. J. Wyatt,⁷ who was coldly efficient but annoyed many of us with disdainful remarks about Skeat, and G. C. Macaulay,⁸ who was passable when dealing with Middle English but so dreary and soporific on modern literature that in all but the most ardent he must have killed such interest as his hearers had.

In French, matters were little better. Stewart was dull and had hobby-horses which he rode to death: he nearly tired me even of Pascal,⁹ who at that time was easily my favourite

---

7 Alfred John Wyatt (1858-1935) graduated at London and Birmingham Universities before entering Christ's College, Cambridge in 1889, graduating B.A. (Modern Languages Tripos 1st class) in 1891 and M.A. in 1895. He was with the University Correspondence College, Cambridge, for forty-seven years. He does not appear to have held any official university lectureship at Cambridge (though he acted as an examiner for the Medieval and Modern Languages Tripos on several occasions). He proved an energetic lecturer for the Local Lectures Syndicate (later the Extra-Mural Board) at Cambridge; the Cambridge University Archives has copies of syllabuses of courses he gave for the Syndicate/Board between 1899 and 1924, nearly all being on English Literature, on Chaucer and Shakespeare in particular. Dr Venn notes that he was 'a University "Coach" in Modern Languages, 1893' (*sic*) (*Alumni Cantabrigienses*, compiler J. A. Venn [Cambridge: Cambridge U. P., 1954], Part II, Vol. VI, 601).

*The British Library General Catalogue of Printed Books to 1975* lists over sixty works against Wyatt's name, including his editions (in several cases as co-editor) of *Beowulf* and Chaucer's *Canterbury Tales*, and his *Elementary English Grammar: Early West Saxon* (1897) and *An Elementary Old English Reader: Early West Saxon* (1901) and various editions, 1900-65, of his *Tutorial History of English Literature*.

8 George Campbell Macaulay (1852-1915); B.A. 1876, M.A. 1879, Cambridge; elected a Fellow of Trinity College in 1878; University Lecturer in English 1905-15; editor of the *Modern Language Review* (English Department); author, editor, and translator of a number of works which are listed in his entry in *Who Was Who, 1897-1916* and, more fully, in *The British Library General Catalogue of Printed Books to 1975*. He was (first) editor of the English section of the *Modern Language Review* until his death.

9 The Revd Hugh Fraser Stewart (1863-1948); M.A. 1891, B.D. 1906, D.D. 1916, Cambridge; Fellow and Dean of St John's College, Cambridge, 1907-18; Reader in French from 1922 until his resignation in 1944. His published editions and translations of, and extracts from, the works of Blaise Pascal date from after the period of Peers' study at Cambridge. Peers' interest in Pascal is evident, for instance, in *Redbrick University*, in which, considering how to develop the Arts undergraduate's critical faculty, he suggests, as one possible method, a course of twelve lectures on Pascal's

French author. Tilley,[10] though his books were illuminating, was even duller, and he aroused derision by pronouncing all his authors' names English-fashion — as 'Cornale', 'Mohlyare' and so on. Braunholtz,[11] who took us through Historical French Grammar, translated volumes of Chrétien de Troyes and in the summer term provided us with full answers (a popular class, this!) to all the philological questions set in Tripos for the last ten years, was the *pièce de résistance* of what was then, and very rightly, called the 'Mediaeval and Modern' Languages Tripos. For proses and essays we went by night to the rooms of a Frenchman called Chouville,[12] a master at the Perse School

---

*Lettres Provinciales* (138). Stewart's other works include *An Intermediate Book of French Composition* (1891), and (selected and edited with A. A. Tilley) *The Romantic Movement in French Literature Traced by a Series of Texts* (1910). (See, too, entries in *Who Was Who, 1941-1950* and *The British Library General Catalogue of Printed Books to 1975*). See also ch. 3, p. 106, note 79.

In 1916-17 Dr Stewart, the Chairman of the Board of Medieval and Modern Languages, and Professor H. M. Chadwick, Skeat's successor as Professor of Anglo-Saxon, aided Professor Sir Arthur Quiller-Couch to reform the Medieval and Modern Languages Tripos and to devise the English Tripos (Brooke, *A History of the University of Cambridge, Vol. IV 1870-1990*, 432-34, 446).

10 Arthur Augustus Tilley (1851-1942), Renaissance scholar; M.A., Cambridge, 1878; Fellow of King's College, Cambridge, 1876-1942; Lecturer in Modern Languages 1896 onwards; a founder of the Cambridge School of Modern Languages; University Lecturer in Classics, 1887-99. Tilley was a close friend and colleague of the Revd Dr Stewart. For a list of his publications, see entry in *The British Library General Catalogue of Printed Books to 1975* and *Who Was Who, 1941-1950*; for an obituary, see *The Annual Register... for the year 1942*, 452-53.

11 Dr Eugen Gustav Wilhelm Braunholtz (1859-1941); M.A., Cambridge, 1886, Ph.D., Berlin; first holder, 1900-40, of the Readership in Romance, University of Cambridge. He provided testimonials which Peers used in his applications for the Gilmour Chair of Spanish in June 1919 and November 1921. He chaired the meeting on 1 June 1918 which led to the establishment of the Modern Humanities Research Association (as it later became known) and was one of its (first) vice-presidents, appointed later that month. For a list of his publications, see *The British Library General Catalogue of Printed Books to 1975*; and see entry in *Who Was Who, 1941-1950*. See also ch. 3, p. 106, note 82.

12 Mr Léon Chouville, B.ès C., B.ès L., taught French at the Perse School, Cambridge; latterly, 1932-38, he was the School's Second Master, retiring in 1938. In contrast to the more formal methods of Louis de Glehn, head of the School's language department (see ch. 3, pp. 87-88, note 7),

who taught me more than anyone else has ever done of the French language.

To complete this magnificent record I translated a passage of French into English weekly for my first tutor, Cartmell,[13] a [gruff old] clergyman afflicted with some variety of palsy who was said to have been a great man long ago but who retired at about the end of my first year, when I was elected to a College Scholarship. His successor,[14] like himself, a Classical man, had either too many pupils even for a Cambridge tutor or enough sense to admit his lack of qualifications in modern languages. So he farmed us out to a young coach, afterwards a Fellow of Caius, named Bullough,[15] who received us weekly in a hired

---

Chouville adopted live conversational teaching. His 'great contribution to Perse teaching lay in the enthusiasm which he felt, and transmitted to his classes, for French literature and drama' (S. J. D. Mitchell, *Perse, A History of the Perse School 1615-1976* [Cambridge: Oleander Press, 1976], 137; see *op. cit.*, 136-37, 176-77, for further details of Chouville's career and work).

Mr Chouville is listed as one of those present at the meeting on 1 June 1918 which led to the establishment of the Modern Humanities Research Association (see ch. 3, p. 104, note 75); he became a member of the Association's Propaganda (French) Sub-Committee on its formation in January 1919. For a list of his publications, see *The British Library General Catalogue of Printed Books to 1975*. See, too, below, p. 90.

13 In the margin in pencil, referring to Cartmell: 'see last pages'. Revd James William Cartmell (1842-1918); B.A., Christ's College, Cambridge, 1865 (27th Wrangler and 2nd class Classical Tripos), M.A., 1868; Fellow of Christ's College, Cambridge, 1866 onwards, Tutor 1873-1911, and member of the College Council 1882-1911. The *British Library Catalogue* lists four entries against his name, all being in German. *The Times*' obituary, which describes him as Vice-Master of the College, states that during the earlier half of his career he travelled frequently in Central Europe, and became a sound scholar in French and German; notes that he taught these subjects for many years and took an active part in the establishment and development of the Modern Languages Tripos; and states that 'his retentive and accurate memory and his wide reading made him a most interesting companion' (*Biographical Register of Christ's College 1505-1905...*, Vol. II: *1666-1905*, compiler John Peile [Cambridge: Cambridge U. P., 1913], 567-68; *The Times*, 5 June 1918).

14 This was probably Mr Harris Rackham, who is listed as one of the College's three Tutors and also a Lecturer in Classics.

15 Edward Bullough (d.1934); M.A., Cambridge, 1906; he was elected a Fellow of Gonville and Caius College in 1912. In his *A History of Gonville and Caius College* (Woodbridge: The Boydell Press, 1985), Christopher Brooke writes that '...it was Edward Bullough who created modern languages in Caius... Of Lancashire descent but born at Thun in

room in Bridge Street, and, as one of my cynical contemporaries put it, spent the first half-hour in talking about what we had done last time and the second half-hour in predicting what we should do next time. Certainly one never seemed to do very much with him. But he put ideas into one's head, which was what we most needed. Tall, good-looking, and courteously receptive even of one's crudest ideas,[16] interested chiefly (so far as we could gather) in Chinese, Russian, Ibsen, aesthetics and experimental psychology, Bullough was the one and only man among my Cambridge teachers with whom I had any give-and-take of ideas. The remainder took care to lecture from a dais three feet above criticism and professors took the additional precaution of leaving the lecture hall before the undergraduates.

And yet it never occurred to me to complain of this method of instruction: indeed, when anyone else did so, I used to think him rather hyper-critical. It was not that I was without ideas or difficulties, but merely that I supposed the University must know best and therefore accepted with complete docility whatever the University offered me. And, after all, Cambridge gave me so many new and attractive things that I had about as much as I could assimilate. [...][17]

[With the] Dean, Valentine-Richards,[18] I had found interests in common and I grew to know him fairly well,

---

Switzerland, and educated in Germany at Dresden, he brought a European culture to Caius. First he taught German, then Italian; and was remembered by many who were not linguists for his teaching and writing on aesthetics; he died Professor of Italian in 1934...' (243). For a list of his publications, see *The British Library General Catalogue of Printed Books to 1975*.

16 'ideas' — ringed by Peers in pencil, as also is the same word two lines up. For stylistic reasons, Peers liked to avoid this type of repetition.

17 Peers' pages 22 and 23 are missing (extracted on purpose) and transferred to form pp. 42 and 43 of the 'B.T.' autobiography. A passage has been cut from page 24 and incorporated into p. 44 of the second narrative (see our edition, 'B.T.', ch. I, pp. 209-12 — italicized).

18 Revd Alfred Valentine Valentine-Richards (1866-1933); B.A., Cambridge, 1888 (4th Wrangler), 1st class Theological Tripos 1890, M.A., 1892; Fellow of Christ's College, Cambridge, 1904 onwards, and Dean of the College from 1906 for twenty years, serving also as the College's Librarian and Lecturer in Theology. His interests ranged from theology to Alpine climbing and the collection of porcelain, glass and silver. (*Crockford's Clerical Directory for 1915*; *The Cambridge University Calendar for the Year*

though [he was a lackadaisical if well-intentioned creature and] I always thought him a poor choice for what ought to have been a key position. I had been assigned to yet another tutor, easily the best of the three — Norman McLean,[19] the Hebrew scholar, who afterwards became Master. Finally, Shipley[20]

---

*1914-1915*; obituary in *Christ's College Magazine* for the Easter Term of 1933, 41-42).

19 Norman McLean (1865-1947), F.B.A., orientalist; Fellow of Christ's College, Cambridge, 1893 onwards; succeeded Sir Arthur Shipley (see below, note 20) as Master of Christ's College in 1927, retiring in 1936. 'His influence alike in the college and in wider university affairs won him not only respect for his wisdom but a wealth of affection... his friendship was quiet and unvarying... McLean sought honours for his pupils, but not for himself' (W. A. L. Elmslie in *Dictionary of National Biography*). *The Cambridge University Calendar for 1911-1912* lists three Tutors at Christ's College: besides McLean, they were Dr Shipley (the Master) and Mr Harris Rackham. The same edition lists Mr McLean's other College appointments as Lecturer in Hebrew, Director of Studies in Moral Sciences, Director of Studies in Oriental Languages, Steward, and Librarian; he also held the University Lectureship in Aramaic, 1903-31.

As Fellow and Senior Tutor of Christ's College, Mr McLean provided a testimonial in March 1919 which Peers used in his application for the Gilmour Chair of Spanish in June 1919 (see Appendix I, p. 433). He testified 'to the excellent qualifications of my friend and pupil, E. Allison Peers, M.A., for a teaching post or Lectureship in Modern Languages. Mr. Peers proved himself during his four years' course at Cambridge one of the ablest students and hardest workers in this college. He is a man of wide interests and reading and is particularly strong in his knowledge of English and French literatures. His degree was an excellent one... His *Skeleton Spanish Grammar* (1917) shows him alive to the needs of the moment, his introduction to and edition of *Vigny: Poèmes Choisis* (1918) as thoroughly abreast with the latest critical thought and able to take a wide and profound view of literature... Mr. Peers is a man of the highest character and principles, and in every way a gentleman'.

20 Sir Arthur Everett Shipley (1861-1927), G.B.E. (created 1920), F.R.S.; Master of Christ's College, Cambridge, 1910-27 (in succession to John Peile, Litt.D., F.B.A., formerly University Reader in Comparative Philology, who served as Master 1887-1910); Reader in Zoology, University of Cambridge, 1908-27; Vice-Chancellor, University of Cambridge, 1917-19. (*Dictionary of National Biography*) Dr Shipley, as he then was, in April 1919 provided Peers with a testimonial which he used in his application for the Gilmour Chair of Spanish in June (see Appendix I, p. 432). Shipley described Peers as 'a man of wide culture, and, in his way, exceptional learning. His conduct has been exemplary. He is a man with a sense of responsibility, and is thoroughly trustworthy. I have great confidence in recommending him for a post as a University Teacher'.

himself [deigned to] cast his eyes on me, and asked me, not only to a Sunday squash,[21] but to luncheon. About this my intimates were ribald, alleging that I owed the honour to being a member of the House of Peers; for Shipley, universally written down as a snob, was said to have buttonholed a freshman in the front court and exclaimed in the well-known tones which every undergraduate in the college delighted to mimic: 'Oh, —— , I hear you're related to Lord —— . *Do* come to luncheon'.[22]

I cannot remember that I was particularly elated by any of these or other marks of favour: I vaguely supposed that most third-year men probably incurred them. It never occurred to me to connect them with the fact that a Fellow in modern languages was badly needed, and, as the winner of several University prizes and runner-up for a University scholarship,[23]

---

21  To clarify what is meant by 'squash' within the Cambridge context, see 'B.T.', ch. I, pp. 211-12.

22  Dr Rex Salisbury Woods painted a more sympathetic portrait of Shipley, 'a kindly, corpulent old bachelor who spoke in deep grunts' whose 'dislike of exercise was equalled, if not exceeded, by his appreciation of the High Table and the College port'. He noted that 'his enemies voted him a snob because he filled his Lodge with a succession of dignitaries ranging from Russian Grand-Dukes to Smuts of South Africa — a Christ's man, incidentally. But I know of many poor undergraduates whom he took under his roof to convalesce with comfort, food and wine which they themselves could not possibly afford' (*Cambridge Doctor* [London: Robert Hale, 1962], 93-94).

23  Peers won the following *University* prizes:
   (a)  the Winchester Reading Prize, 1912.
   (b)  the Harness Prize, 1913 (see, too, below, ch. 3, p. 91, and note 22).
   (c)  the Members' Prize, 1914 (for an English Essay on some subject connected with British History or Literature)

In 1912 Peers was *proxime accessit* for the Charles Oldham Shakespeare Scholarship; the Scholarship was awarded following an examination directed towards testing the candidates' knowledge of Shakespeare's works.

In addition he won the following awards of *Christ's College*:
   (a)  Skeat Prize (The prize was awarded alternately (1) upon an examination and (2) for an English Essay upon some subject connected with English Literature.)
   (b)  Calverley Prize
   (c)  Dr Porteus Medal

CAMBRIDGE 83

I was[24] being discussed by those in authority. But I certainly supposed, or hoped, in my trusting way, that some of the acquaintanceships I had formed would continue and even grow more intimate. For McLean, in particular, gruff and unapproachable, because slow of speech, as he seemed to some, I developed the keenest affection, and one of my deepest regrets at going down was at no longer seeing him.[25]

The disillusion consisted simply in this: that as I came back on visits to College, after taking my degree, I found that I was no longer wanted. At school, old boys were always welcome, and, [...][26]

[...] that it has affected my whole future career. My own graduates know that for so long as I live, they can come to me for anything I am capable of giving them, and if at any time I found [/find] their numbers too large for this to be possible, I should [shall] assign the outgoing graduates from that time onward to one of my lecturers. This is a subject to which I shall return later[27] but I must say here that this lack of interest in the ordinary graduate, who frequently needs help far more after going down than while at the University, seems to me one of the great disadvantages of an education at Oxford or Cambridge and [again and again] graduates of these universities, who have been taking special[28] courses with me, have frequently asked for the type of advice which there ought to be someone at their own colleges to give them.[29]

---

24 Peers considers inserting an adverb here, before 'was': '? evidently (apparently?)'.
25 Peers enters, in pencil, alternatives which modify the wording here: 'and quite my deepest regret at going down was losing his company (c'pnship?)'.
26 The second half of Peers' p. 25 has been cut out and transferred to the 'B.T.' narrative (see ch. I, p. 216 — italicized).
27 Peers asks himself here, in pencil, in the margin: 'Do I?'
28 Peers suggests, in pencil, instead of 'special': 'holiday'. A reference to his famous Summer Schools in Britain and Spain?
29 The last paragraph on p. 26 of '(E.A.P.) *Auto*' has been excised and transferred to conclude 'B.T.', ch. I, p. 217 — italicized.

# CHAPTER 3

## SCHOOLMASTERING

### I

My degree taken, in 1912, and no opportunity of a University post presenting itself,[1] I decided to stay up for a fourth year, read for the Teachers' Diploma, and, either temporarily or permanently, become a schoolmaster. I think [Probably], in my heart of hearts, I looked upon the [that] decision as final. On the one hand, there were far better men than I in recent Modern Language class-lists, in Cambridge alone: Renfield[2] and Jopson,[3] to take only two, had constellations of stars, denoting distinctions, after their names, whereas I had only one. On the other hand, I had not realized the essential differences between school and university teaching. How should I? None of my own teachers, Skeat and the dilettante Bullough possibly excluded, had seemed more to me than super-schoolmasters. Nobody had so much as whispered the word 'research' to me or suggested that there was anything more that a graduate should do once his examinations were over. Of the university teacher's

---

    1    Peers reminds himself, in a pencilled note, to 'say more of this' — i.e. of the fact that, or reasons why, he was not offered 'a University post'.
    2    Frank Rönnfeldt (Anglicised as Renfield at the end of the First World War) graduated from Christ's College B.A. 1st class in the Mediaeval and Modern Languages Tripos in 1911, M.A. in 1914, and LL.M. in 1920. The University Calendar for 1921-22 notes that he was then a master at Clifton College. *The British Library General Catalogue* lists the translation he and others made of Wilhelm A. von Bode's *Sandro Botticelli* (1925); he also helped edit Paul Quensel's *Der Letzte* (1936).
    3    Norman Brooke Jopson (1890-1969); Scholar of St John's College, Cambridge, Mediaeval and Modern Languages Tripos and Oriental Languages Tripos, 1912 and 1913; later, 1937-55, Professor of Comparative Philology, University of Cambridge. (*Who Was Who, 1961-1970*). Jopson and Peers were among the nine students who were awarded 1st class honours degrees in the Mediaeval and Modern Languages Tripos in 1912.

freedom, the boundless scope which it gives for the most varied activities, the joys of investigation, the thrilling sensation [/sense] of world-comradeship which [successful?] specialization brings — of none of this neither I nor (I honestly believe) the majority of my teachers had the slightest inkling. The choice seemed to be between a school post, comparatively easy to obtain, with longer hours but more scope for climbing and (as a headmaster) a higher salary than a professor ever obtained, and an extremely hypothetical university post, where the work would be more interesting because the pupils would be more mature but there would be poor prospects.

I am sure I could [/I could certainly] never have resigned myself to the thought of returning, even as a headmaster, to any of the schools from which I had myself suffered. I was beginning to realize by now what I had lost through them. But among my Cambridge friends had been men from Rugby, Clifton and Merchant Taylors, and these opened to me a new conception of school life entirely. I would join the Training College, get the best possible preparation for my future vocation, and hope, sooner or later, to get into one of the best possible schools.[4]

[...][5]

---

4   Contrast Peers' comments in chapter 1, when he mentions the disadvantages of boarding-school life. There, of course, he was referring especially to the disadvantages, and even damage, to character, caused by separation from one's family. Here he is conceding the merits of the education provided at the best public schools.

5   Part of p. 28 has been excised and transferred to 'B.T.': see ch. II, p. 219 — italicized. This missing passage shows how much Peers enjoyed teaching practice: 'the joy of giving to counterbalance the satisfaction of getting'. He also experienced for the first time 'an absolutely first-class school'. Peers did his teaching practice at The Perse School and at the Higher Grade School, Paradise Street, teaching totals of seventy-seven days and six and a half days at these schools respectively during the three terms of Session 1912-13 (University Archives, University of Cambridge, ref. EDUC 21/2, pp. 237-38). The University Training College's Secondary Department students had teaching practice at the Perse, Leys and Cambridgeshire County Schools, and usually also at the Higher Grade School in Paradise Street, Cambridge (Peter Searby, *The Training of Teachers in Cambridge University: The First Sixty Years, 1879-1939* [Cambridge: Department of Education, Cambridge University, 1982], 22). Each student was placed for one or more terms in the charge of an experienced master at one or other of the three first named schools (*The Cambridge University Calendar for the*

This was the Cambridge of the Perse School — the equal of which, in modern language teaching, I have never found, nor expect to, again. At that time it was in its heyday. W. H. D. Rouse,[6] whom I had only known from afar, at the Christ's high table, as a podgy little [shuffling] figure in a doctor's gown, was a king reigning supreme, yet a king wise enough [/with the wisdom] to delegate authority to men as able as himself whom he knew he could trust. Foremost amongst those was my immediate chief, Louis de Glehn,[7] the finest modern language

---

*Year 1911-1912*, 195). In the register of teaching practice of students of the University Training College, the 'estimate' of Peers was recorded as follows: 'A man of very great ability and a teacher of unusual power. Is fertile in conception of methods and intelligently sympathetic. Gets the best work out of his boys and spares no pains to put his own best work into the preparation of his lessons'. An alpha mark was recorded for the majority of the various elements of his teaching practice; the only instance when a mark below beta was assigned was in respect of criticism lessons at the Higher Grade School in the Easter Term 1913: '*French* II b (a bad class). Class disorderly and talkative [Whitsun Monday] but held together by firm treatment. Lesson straightforward but not interesting — partly accounting for restlessness of class. β-' (University Archives, Cambridge, ref. EDUC 21/2, pp. 237-38).

6   William Henry Denham Rouse (1863-1950); educated at Christ's College, Cambridge (B.A. Classical Tripos, 1st Class, 1885); Fellow 1888-94 and Honorary Fellow 1933 onwards of Christ's College; Litt.D., Cambridge, 1903; Headmaster, Perse School, Cambridge, 1902-28; University Teacher of Sanskrit, Cambridge, 1903-39; External Examiner in Latin, University of Liverpool, 1908-09 and 1909-10; etc. (*Who Was Who, 1941-1950; Dictionary of National Biography 1941-1950*).

In his previously mentioned *Perse: A History of the Perse School 1615-1976*, S. J. D. Mitchell describes Dr Rouse, 'undoubtedly the greatest Perse Head of all', as 'short of stature and portly of build', but adds that 'he could look impressive, and was especially so on Speech Days, when, resplendent in his scarlet gown, he seemed to outshine the distinguished speakers he had invited down for the occasion' (84, 87).

7   Louis (Camille) de Glehn, who joined the staff of the Perse School with Rouse in 1902, was Head of the School's Language Department and Senior Assistant Master. A first-class linguist, he pioneered the Direct Method in teaching French: 'the results achieved by the French department under this direction were very remarkable, nearly every boy leaving the school with a fluent grasp of the language and its idiom, and an accent far more Gallic than most Englishmen ever attain' (Mitchell, *op. cit*, 136). In 1914 he adopted the surname of 'de Glehn' in place of his original name of 'von Glehn' (Mitchell, *op. cit.*, 133). Louis von Glehn/de Glehn was the editor of *Arnold's French Reading Books* (1899 etc.) and also the joint author of *Cours Français du Lycée Perse* (Cambridge: W. Heffer and Sons &

teacher — and I have heard [in the classroom] the only [/all the] men teach who could [possibly] be considered his rivals — of his generation. I never saw enough of the Direct Method[8] in Classics, under Rouse and Appleton,[9] to be able to form an opinion of it, and it could not fairly be judged by the scholars it produced, since the Perse School had two tremendous advantages — a *clientèle* largely composed of dons' sons and complete freedom from external [...][10]

---

Co./London: Simpkin, Marshall & Co., 1914) (with Léon Chouville and E. R. Wells). He also wrote various novels. For a list of his publications, see *The British Library General Catalogue of Printed Books to 1975.*

8   The reference to the direct method of teaching is to Dr Rouse's conception that Latin should be taught as a spoken language. This method was also taken up by the Modern Language Department at the school. Modern Languages at the time achieved an international reputation at the Perse School.

9   Reginald Bainbridge Appleton. In his history of the Perse School, Mitchell describes W. H. S. Jones (who taught at the School 1902-21) and R. B. Appleton as the two greatest of the masters who assisted Dr Rouse in his classical teaching (*op. cit.*, 116). 'Oral work was, of course, the rule in his [Appleton's] class. He very rarely used English, and pronounced his Latin slowly and clearly... an important part of the method was the introduction into lessons of lively topical comments, which when put in the form of conversation between master and class in a classical language was an admirable way of acquiring familiarity with language and culture... With de Glehn he was one of the strongest personalities on the staff' (*op. cit.*,118, 134). Appleton was the author of a number of books for use in schools, including *Initium: A First Latin Course on the Direct Method* (Cambridge: Cambridge U. P., 1st edition, 1916), written jointly with W. H. S. Jones; *Perse Latin Plays: Original Plays for the Teaching of Latin to Middle Forms...* (Cambridge: W. Heffer & Sons, 2nd edition, 1917); and *Ludi Persici* (Oxford: Oxford U. P., 1921), a new edition of 'Perse Latin Plays'. Together with Dr Rouse, he wrote an account of *Latin on the Direct Method* (London: Univ. of London Press, 1925).

10   The missing word, to complete the sentence, is 'examinations'. A passage has been cut out (at pp. 29-30) and transferred to 'B.T.' (see ch. II, pp. 220-21 — italicized). Dr Rouse disliked the public examination system intensely. He argued that examinations are ' "quite misleading as a guide to comparative merit" and had been designed in the first place for children who would not be going to universities and therefore might require a paper qualification at a lower level... No boy at the Perse in Rouse's time took a School Certificate examination unless his parents absolutely insisted. The only examinations he approved were the University and College Entrance and Scholarship papers' (Mitchell, *op. cit.*, 90). Dr Rouse, however, continued the internal examination system he inherited at the School. As the present Headmaster, Dr Martin Stephen, notes (in a letter of 9

[...] ex-German Fletcher,[11] who died so tragically a year or two later; Psychology with Charles Fox,[12] who inveigled a few of us into the University laboratory on Thursday afternoons [and regaled us with tea and chocolate biscuits in the intervals of using us] to serve as subjects for his experiments; School method with Blandford,[13] to whom I was greatly drawn by his love of phonetics. [...][14] In their lecture rooms, during this fourth year, I began to realize all [/how much] I had missed in

---

September 1991), Dr Rouse's hatred of all public examinations and refusal to allow pupils at the School to sit them allowed a tremendous freedom in the teaching of all subjects in the school, and also allowed him to attract in as staff teachers who would otherwise never have gone near a school.

11 Samuel Sigmund Fechheimer Fletcher (M.A., King's College, Cambridge), Vice-Principal, Lecturer on Education and Master of Method at the Cambridge University Training College for Schoolmasters. Mr Fletcher was general editor of the *Cambridge Handbooks for Teachers*, co-editor of *Macmillan's Manuals for Teachers*; and published a translation of Froebel's chief writings on education in 1912 (Searby, *op. cit.*, 17, 25; and *The Cambridge University Calendar for the Year 1911-1912*, 194)

12 Charles Fox (B.A. 1900, M.A. 1908, Christ's College, Cambridge) was to become Principal of the University Training College after the First World War, resigning in 1937. He is described by Peter Searby as 'an uninspiring teacher' and he quotes a former pupil, Professor W. H. G. Armytage, as regarding Fox as 'deeply reserved and reticent... but if one indicated interest in the periods we spent in the psychology laboratory his defensive mask dropped and he became what he really was, a lonely, but nevertheless dedicated man'. (Searby, *op. cit.*, 34-35). At the time Peers was a student, Fox was a Lecturer and Supervisor of Practice at the College.

13 Francis George Blandford (B.A. 1899, M.A. 1903, Corpus Christi College, Cambridge), Assistant Master of Method at the Day Training College by 1905 (Searby, *op. cit.*, 17). By the time Peers was a student he had become a Lecturer and Supervisor of Practice and also Director of Studies to the College's Secondary Department. Blandford was the joint author, with James Welton, of *Principles and Methods of Moral Training* (1909), and, with Harold E. Palmer, author of *English Pronunciation through Questions and Answers* (1928) and other works on English (and American) phonetics. Peers' first book was *A Phonetic Spanish Reader* (Manchester: Manchester University Press, 1920).

14 Peers used the scissors again elsewhere on p. 30, to cut out what he did not choose to retain. What remains of this page and of page 31, which has been similarly ill-treated, is not coherent. Unfortunately, he did not return to this part of the manuscript to make good its deficiencies. However, we can reconstruct most of the original content by consulting 'B.T.' ch. II, pp. 221, 223— see the passages italicized.

the other three. But my chief love was the Perse School, with its intelligent, [...][15]

[Before long], too, I was not only sitting in De Glehn's classroom during [...][16]

[...] he coached as Chouville[17] did) would turn to me, hand me his book and ask me [/call on me without notice] to finish his lesson.[18]

The free-and-easy state of the Perse School organization, which made such a procedure possible, was the most remarkable tribute to its efficiency under Rouse's wise rule:[19] since he and De Glehn left I have never been inside the building and I have no idea what it is like today.[20] But such was De Glehn's reputation abroad and the confidence reposed [...][21]

---

15 '...friendly staff, who made one forget one was only a student...'. We can complete this passage by consulting 'B.T.', ch. II, p. 221 — italicized.

16 '...the hours prescribed by my timetable, but at any odd hour which I could spare...'. See 'B.T.', ch. II, p. 223 — italicized.

17 For information on Léon Chouville see above, ch. 2, pp. 78-79, note 12.

18 For the context, see 'B.T.', ch. II, pp. 223-24 — passage italicized. The record of Peers' teaching practice reveals — in respect of the twenty-nine and a half days he taught, while under training, at The Perse School in the Michaelmas Term 1912 — that he was 'teaching these two [French and English] chiefly, but also watching (and teaching occasionally) French, German and English throughout the School' (University Archives, Cambridge, ref. EDUC 21/2, p. 237).

19 Nevertheless, rumours began to reach the governing body that Dr Rouse was not good at discipline, and when he came to retirement this was the reason given for not allowing him an extension. Most unwisely the Governors brought in a martinet as his successor and for an extended period thereafter all the staff Dr Rouse had gathered so carefully vanished and the reputation of the School went into decline (letter of 9 September 1991 from Dr Martin Stephen, the present Headmaster).

20 In his 'Epilogue and Prologue for the Future', Mr A. E. Melville, who became Headmaster of the Perse School in 1969, wrote: 'Almost every subject at the Perse is taught with a "modern" syllabus, but our aims remain recognisably the same. The distinctive emphasis falls, as it always has fallen, on academic excellence and the environment that favours it' (Mitchell, op. cit., 253).

21 Page 32 of the manuscript is lacking, which Peers has removed to insert in 'B.T.': see ch. II, pp. 224-25 — italicized. The last sentence of this italicized passage, in which he mentions that, at this time, he began 'in the

The impulse came from the Harness Prize, awarded triennially for an essay, which, if successful, has to be published (I spent [/it cost me] most of the prize-money publishing [/to publish] mine!) on some aspect of Elizabethan literature. The subject set for 1913 was a particularly grisly one — 'Elizabethan drama and its mad folk'[22] — and not perhaps very suitable for young graduates, who could hardly be expected to possess, or acquire, sufficient knowledge of lunacy to produce a satisfactory essay. But we were at least all on the same level here, and, hardly realizing the difficulties of the subject, I plunged into Shakespeare, Beaumont and Fletcher, Massinger, Ford, Middleton, Jonson, Dekker[23] and hosts of other dramatists, determined to pluck all the available mad folk from the plays in which they were hiding by the hair of their head, deposit them in their respective categories and take the measure of each. The jejuneness of the essay, as I reveal it, is as crude as the flimsy rhetoric which I hoped would catch the eyes of the adjudicators (Macaulay[24] and [a later friend] Moore-Smith[25] of Sheffield) but it was at least a genuine attempt to *find out something* not to be gleaned from text-books,[26] it was the first attempt of the kind I had ever made and it stimulated me to make more. In the following year I gained the Members'

---

most modest possible way... the practice of research', provides the link with the paragraph on the Harness prize which follows here.

22 *Elizabethan Drama and its Mad Folk: The Harness Prize Essay for 1913* (Cambridge: W. Heffer & Sons, 1914). The Prize was awarded to the author of the best English Essay upon some subject connected with Shakespearian Literature and was worth about £50 (*The Cambridge University Calendar for the Year 1914-1915*, 132).

23 Francis Beaumont (1584-1616); John Fletcher (1579-1625), Beaumont's collaborator in a number of plays; Philip Massinger (1583-1640); John Ford (fl.1639); Thomas Middleton (?1570-1627); Ben Jonson (?1573-1637); Thomas Dekker (?1570-?1641).

24 G. C. Macaulay (see above, ch. 2, p. 77, note 8).

25 George Charles Moore Smith (1858-1940), Professor of English Language and Literature, Firth College, later University College, Sheffield, later the University of Sheffield, 1896-1924.

26 In his Testimonial in favour of Peers, March 1919 (see above, ch. 2, p. 81, note 19; and Appendix I, p. 433), Norman McLean, Fellow and Senior Tutor of Christ's College, Cambridge, described the work as 'an able work on an exceedingly elusive subject'.

Prize for an English essay on Walt Whitman,[27] but that was quite a different type of composition, and, though commended by Quiller-Couch,[28] who had just been appointed to succeed Verrall[29] as Professor of English literature, I never attempted to publish it and it still lies at the bottom of a drawer.[30] Research — in the sense of investigation, as opposed to creative criticism, of which much will be said hereafter — I was unable for some years to touch again, but when at last leisure for it was given me, I took it up with the firm intention never to drop it till I dropped work, from chronic illness or sheer old age, altogether.

But while revelling in the Direct Method of the Perse School and in the mad folk to be found in the University library, I was also engaged upon the more prosaic but most necessary business of getting a job. When I applied to Shipley and McLean for testimonials they were both anxious to send me abroad. Shipley had heard of a University job in English at Shanghai ('less than a fortnight from home, my deah fellah, and much better paid than anything here') and soon after that McLean wanted me to apply for a lectureship in Canada, writing most persuasively that he 'really felt' I ought to 'abandon this prejudice against going abroad'.[31] I had no such prejudice, as I should have had if a College Fellowship had still been my objective. I had simply decided to be a schoolmaster and said so. Shipley either had no use for schoolmasters or was afraid that if I stayed in England I might come knocking too often at the College door: but he proffered no further arguments

---

27 Awarded in 1914. Of the two Members' Prizes, each of the value of thirty guineas, one was awarded for an English Essay on some subject connected with British History or Literature. A copy of the essay is not held by Cambridge University Library and Peers' copy cannot now be traced.

28 Sir Arthur (Thomas) Quiller-Couch (1863-1944), King Edward VII Professor of English Literature, University of Cambridge, 1912-44; knighted in 1910. (*Who Was Who, 1941-1950*; *Dictionary of National Biography*). Cf. 'B.T.', ch. I, pp. 200-01, note 102. In *Redbrick University* Peers describes Sir Arthur Quiller-Couch as 'one of the greatest of modern lecturers' (186).

29 Arthur Woolgar Verrall, Litt.D., Fellow of Trinity College; in 1911 he was appointed first holder of the King Edward VII Chair of English Literature (*The Cambridge University Calendar for the Year 1914-1915*, 60).

30 The current location of this essay is unknown.

31 Advertisements for these particular posts do not appear in the columns of *The Times Educational Supplement* for 1912 and 1913.

but merely hoped I should 'get out of schoolmastering before it was too late' — in which, at least, I did not disappoint him.

Jobs, in those happy days, were easy enough to get, for men with reasonable degrees, and I was soon fixed up[32] at Mill Hill [, a nonconformist public school just outside London,][33] with a post involving advanced French and elementary German.[34] I had been working hard at German for some time and that summer spent two months or more in intensive reading and constant conversation as a paying guest in the family of an army officer's widow near Berlin. Incidentally, I went out highly optimistic as to future relations between England and Germany, and came back completely convinced that *Der Tag*[35] of Prussian dreams was not far distant.

## II

I stayed at Mill Hill for only a year. In some respects it was a pleasant year. Never having seen [/even been inside] a large

---

32 In a note, pencilled in the margin, Peers adds: 'Surprised at getting £150 resident. out of Gabb. (N.B. mentioned on p. 40, so put him in): "But you're a good man, you know!" '. There is mention of a London agency in 'B.T.', at the corresponding place in the narrative, where a 'cadaverous clerk' encouraged him to apply for a job paying a salary of £150 because he had 'a good degree' (see 'B.T.', ch. II, p. 227). For information on Gabbitas and the agency used by Peers, see below, note 48.

33 Mill Hill School was founded, in 1807, as a Protestant Dissenters' Grammar School. Under Sir John McClure, Headmaster 1891-1922, the School was transformed into one of the great Public Schools. (Norman G. Brett-James, *The History of Mill Hill School 1807-1923* [Reigate: Thomas Malcomson, The Surrey Fine Art Press, n.d. (1923)], 5, 449).

34 Peers served as one of the Assistant Masters, 1913-14 (Ernest Hampden-Cook, *The Register of Mill Hill School 1807-1926* [London: Mill Hill School, 1926], 467). Mill Hill School does not hold bursarial records for the period, Mr Alastair Graham (Headmaster of Mill Hill School, 1979-92) reports, in a letter of 9 September 1991, adding that copies of the School Magazine for 1913-14 show no mention of Peers .

35 There is a note, in pencil, in the margin here: 'Insight into Prussian character'. Peers means that, having visited Berlin personally, his optimism vanished, for he realized that Prussian militaristic and political ambitions (and desires for their 'Fatherland' to have its 'Day') would soon lead Germany into war with England and other countries (*cf.* his more explicit comments in 'B.T.', ch. II, p. 244).

94    REDBRICK UNIVERSITY REVISITED

public school before, I had had no idea of the comfort, not to say luxury, [...][36]

Yet Mill Hill, in those days at least — for I believe it has changed greatly for the better now — was no place for any man to whom work was more important than amenities, still less for a Direct Method enthusiast fresh from the keen and invigorating atmosphere of Persean[37] class-rooms. The boys were for the most part sons of wealthy Nonconformists, many of them with more money than is good for any boy and the prospects of still more when they went to Oxford or Cambridge and of an easy life thereafter. Games were regarded as all-important;[38] scholarship-winners ranked far below members of the elevens or fifteens; most of the masters took a nonchalant, or even a cynical attitude to their work; about modern methods they knew little and cared less. In a journal which I kept at the time I remarked that the methods used in teaching French were inferior to those by which I had learned the language, ten years before, in that little Wiltshire school,[39] where several of the teachers were not even graduates. Yet here were well-paid men, some of them making large incomes by selling their boarders bread and butter, and most of them with [Honours] degrees from Oxford or Cambridge; and all of them within easy reach of the meetings of educational associations and every kind of cultural facility. [Yet they lived the lives of sybaritic and slightly cynical Philistines.] The only theory of education [they understood] was: 'Knock it into them'. The man who got on was the man who could cane hard — and did. Every now and then (it happened only once in my year) the entire school was

---

36   '... in which schoolmasters could live': a passage has been cut from the manuscript, at foot of p. 35 and top of p. 36, and transferred to 'B.T.' (see ch. II, p. 228 — italicized).
37   That is, of the Perse School, Cambridge.
38   Sir John McClure (see below, note 44), the Headmaster, was an enthusiast for athletics; with the end of the First World War, physical training, which had played a big part in the War, was to be made an essential part of the curriculum (Brett-James, *op. cit.*, 437). Brett-James records that 'McClure gathered round him a staff who made it their business to cater for the average boy and the duffer, but also to make it possible for the more brilliant to win scholarships at Oxford and Cambridge' (*op. cit.*, 433).
39   See above, ch. 1, pp. 65-66.

summoned to a special assembly at which [in an atmosphere of tense and animated expectancy][40] the Headmaster administered to some boy [who had been] caught bullying or thieving[41] a public flogging. I am the last person to be sentimental over boys' education, but this, I thought (and still think) was not education at all. By the end of my second term I was depressed beyond endurance; at the beginning of my third, after a vacation spent happily in the Bibliothèque Nationale[42] among Old French epics, I decided that I would see if I could find something more congenial.[43]

Before taking this step, I had an interesting talk with Sir John McClure, the Headmaster, who had built up the school from almost nothing and more than anyone else was responsible for its condition.[44] He was a remarkable man both in appearance and in achievements. Though he was only fifty-three at the time, both boys and masters thought him old [/thought of him as an old scholarly man], and regarded him not only as the personification of muscular Christianity but also as

---

40 After this phrase, inserted in pencil, Peers adds, in brackets: '?Better'. These manuscript emendations demonstrate his keenly critical approach to his style and self-expression.

41 Peers deletes in pencil the reference to 'thieving'.

42 He means, of course, in Paris.

43 At this point, in a pencilled note, Peers wonders whether he should '?say something to suggest disagreement or row'.

44 Sir John David McClure (who was knighted in 1913) served as Headmaster of Mill Hill School from 1891 until his death in February 1922, aged sixty-two years. Educated at Trinity College, Cambridge (B.A. 1885, M.A. 1889, LL.B. 1886, LL.M. 1891, LL.D. 1897), McClure's interests were unusually broad, ranging from Mathematics and Law (in which he graduated) to History and Astronomy. He was called to the Bar (Inner Temple, 1890); his musical ability and interests were recognized by his attainment of a Doctorate of Music of the University of London; as a prominent Nonconformist, he served as Chairman of the Congregational Union of England and Wales in 1919-20. As Headmaster of Mill Hill, he transformed the School's fortunes; when he became Headmaster the School contained just sixty-one boys, but by the time of his death there were more than three hundred and seventy on the roll (Brett-James, *op. cit.*, 270, 431-32, 448; Hampden-Cook, *op. cit.*, 455) (see too entry in *Who Was Who, 1916-1928*; and article by M. L. Jacks in *Dictionary of National Biography 1922-1930*).

an encyclopaedia of learning. They certainly had reason. Tall, powerfully built, with a huge head crowned by [...][45]

[...] McClure in his study on that very morning and he made a remark for which I gladly admit I owe him a debt of gratitude. I was the junior man in a large staff but McClure made it his business to know even his juniors. And when I tried to tell him, as tactfully as might be, what was in my mind, he paused for a moment, and then with one of those charming smiles which so often lit up his magnificent and monumental ugliness, said quietly:

> Well, you know, I think your real success is going to lie in research.

I protested: at that time research was only a side-line [and] nearly all my interest was in teaching. I said as much — and I suppose implied that I might be expected to know best. But you never got the better of McClure in argument. He merely waved my objection aside and with an even sweeter smile remarked even more quietly:

> I didn't say *interest*: I said *success*.

### III

That remark encouraged me amazingly even as long afterwards as 1922 (the year of McClure's untimely death) when Heaven knows I needed encouragement badly enough. What led him to that conclusion I never discovered, or even guessed — unless he had been beguiling his leisure moments, all unknown to me, by reading the *Mad Folk*.[46] Even though disbelieving him at the time I took him so far at his word as to make a fruitless journey

---

45 'a shock of untidy white hair...': Peers has removed most of p. 38, and inserted it in the 'B.T.' narrative (see ch. II, p. 232 — italicized). A photographic portrait of Sir John McClure appears as the frontispiece to Brett-James, *op. cit.*

46 See above, p. 91, and note 22.

to spy out the land at Cambridge and to enter for a lectureship in French at Oxford.[47] The latter I nearly got — I was in a short list of three out of over sixty candidates — but not quite. So, having become thoroughly unsettled in the process, I got into touch once more with Gabbitas[48] and the rest and, after a good deal of hesitation, even withdrawing one application when on the point of [being called to] an interview, I applied for, and was appointed to, a post in French and German at Felsted, in Essex.[49]

This seemed much more satisfactory than Mill Hill — and in every respect proved so. I took the bold but probably wise step of telling the Headmaster — a young clergyman named Stephenson[50] [who had come not long previously from Rossall and Cheltenham] — something of my ideals and disillusionments and of leaving him to judge if I was the man he wanted. He decided that I was and I never had cause to regret the decision. I stayed there for five years and only left because I

---

47 According to his application for the Gilmour Chair of Spanish, June 1919, Peers states that in May 1914 he entered for a Taylorian Lectureship in French at Oxford. There are no records in Oxford University Archives of the unsuccessful applicants for this post in 1914; Mr Dikran Garabedian (M.A. Cambridge, Lic. ès L. Paris) was appointed, to commence in Michaelmas Term 1914, and held the Lectureship until 1920. At this time there were three Taylorian Lecturers in French, Garabedian's contemporaries being Henry E. Berthon (appointed in 1897) and Edwin G. Ross Waters (appointed in 1913) (information kindly provided by Mr Simon Bailey, Oxford University Archivist).

48 Messrs Gabbitas, Thring & Co., Education Agents of Sackville Street, London, advertised in *The Times Educational Supplement* 1912-13 that they assisted parents or guardians seeking information on the choice of schools or tutors for boys or girls in England or abroad.

49 Felsted School, Dunmow, Essex. The School's records for the period, 1914-19, during which Peers was on the staff are rather sparse; there is no record of the terms and conditions of his appointment or his references. Curiously, the *Felstedian Magazine* neither notes his arrival nor his departure (nor is there any mention of his death in its columns) (information supplied by Mr Nicholas S. Hinde, Archivist, Felsted School).

50 Revd Frank Stephenson (1871-1936), Headmaster of Felsted School, 1906-33; late Scholar of Christ's College, Cambridge: B.A. 1st class Classical Tripos 1893, 1st class Theological Tripos 1895, M.A. 1898; Assistant Master at Rossall School, 1895-1900, and then at Cheltenham College, 1901-06 (*Crockford's Clerical Directory for 1923*; Michael Craze, *A History of Felsted School 1564-1947* [Ipswich: Cowell, 1955], chapter xx of which is devoted to the School under Frank Stephenson).

had decided to leave schoolmastering at the first possible moment. I loved every corner of the then rather inadequate buildings.[51] [...][52] I made more friends there than in any other five years of my life: many of them [/these friendships] have since been hallowed by death and some of them thrive still. Briefly, Felsted came to be to me, tossed about from school to school as I had been in my boyhood, a real *alma mater*.[53]

In this pleasant backwater, inconceivably inaccessible and remote at a time when a car was a rare luxury, I spent the entire period of the European War. As I had arranged to go to the Black Forest during the summer vacation after shaking off the dust of Mill Hill, I might easily have spent it in an internment camp; but fortunately when the War broke out I had not yet started, and on the following day, having taken Certificate A of the C.U.O.T.C., I found myself applying for a commission. The news that I was gazetted (one remembers these trivial details) came in the form of a telegram from the

---

51 In his reports to the School's Governors, the Revd Stephenson drew attention to the need for better facilities — in 1912 he had written that 'it is unwise economy to let a school retain quarters which parents must not see'. Though some new accommodation was provided in response in 1913, at the end of the War in 1919 he pointed out the need for new buildings and for the accumulation of funds for that purpose. During the years 1924-29 a number of new buildings were erected and existing buildings extended and improved. Peers appears to have lived at the Old School House at Felsted School. 'The house through which the churchyard [of Holy Cross Church, Felsted] is connected with the main street at its main corner', the Old School House was described by Sir Nikolaus Pevsner as 'a timber-framed and plastered house with an overhanging upper floor' (Nikolaus Pevsner, *The Buildings of England: Essex*, revised by Enid Radcliffe [Harmondsworth: Penguin Books, 1965], 179). Further new buildings were erected in 1930-31, replacing those destroyed in a fire (Craze, *op. cit.*, 256, 268 and 272-87 *passim*).

52 Peers has deleted, at this point on p. 40, the following, still legible sentence which indicates both his interest in botany and his love of the countryside: 'I knew every country walk (it was in the depth of the country) within a radius of five miles and before I left had listed every wild flower that grew within a radius wider still'.

53 In his history of the School, Craze notes that Mr Stephenson tended to appoint men already known to himself and that 'the men who were new to Stephenson as well as to Felsted were soon equally devoted to the place' (*op. cit.*, 250, 251).

War Office at half-past three one August morning.[54] But unfortunately, not only then but on various subsequent occasions, I failed to pass the doctor for active service.[55] [So, although I got my commission, I had to use it in the Felsted O.T.C.].[56] One kindly medical, with whom I chatted during the examination, suggested that with additional linguistic qualifications which I could easily acquire I might get a job as an interpreter.[57] The idea appealed; Stephenson, who was losing his masters more quickly than he liked, gave a rather unwilling consent; and I spent the leisure of six arduous months learning Russian. I had mastered that difficult language well enough to read newspapers with ease and had just acquired a Berlitz-School modicum of fluency in conversation when my hopes were shattered by the Russian Revolution. I have never opened a Russian book since, and, deciding that my stars must have decreed that I should stay at Felsted for the 'duration', made no further effort to leave.

---

54 Peers has ticked this passage and has written in the margin in pencil here: 'In B.T.' (a reference to its inclusion, in substance, in the 'B.T.' narrative? [*cf.* 'B.T.', ch. II, pp. 246-47]).

55 In his 'War Statement', which he appended to his application for the Gilmour Chair of Spanish in June 1919, Peers stated that on 5 August 1914 he applied through the Cambridge University O.T.C. for a Commission in the Army, having previously served in the Corps and taken the War Office Certificate A. Being physically unfit (through a lung weakness and a defect in one eye) for active service, he received a Commission in the Territorial Force and was attached to the Felsted School contingent of the O.T.C. (see Appendix I, p. 432).

Hew Strachan in his *History of the Cambridge University Officers Training Corps* (Tunbridge Wells: Midas Books, 1976) relates that 'The outbreak of war did not find the O.T.C. unprepared... 3 August 1914 was a Monday and hundreds of undergraduates, who had in the past displayed little interest in things military, thronged to the Corps' headquarters in Market Street' (140).

56 Colonel Donald Portway, a pupil at Felsted's Primary School and then at Felsted from 1897 until 1906, makes reference to the School's Cadet Corps in his memoirs, *Militant Don* (London: Robert Hale Ltd., 1964), adding that the claim of the Cadet Corps to be the oldest in the country had sparked considerable controversy in 1959, the centenary year of many units in the auxiliary forces (26).

57 In his 'War Statement', June 1919, Peers wrote 'On several occasions I have applied to go abroad as an Interpreter, but even here I have been unsuccessful'.

To say, as in fairness I must, that Felsted meant for me all the remaining stages of disillusionment but the final and bitterest one[,] which was to come some years later,[58] must not be taken as implying any condemnation of it whatever. The boys were splendid workers; games took something like their proper place; and Stephenson, a scholar, though unfortunately one of those Classical men [now, one hopes, slowly disappearing] who believe themselves qualified *ipso facto* to dogmatize on modern language teaching,[59] gave me as free a hand as he could under war conditions. I evolved a slightly modified form of Direct Method teaching which gave adequate results. I made, over a long period, careful qualitative and quantitative experiments, and recorded their findings in several manuscript volumes intended to form the basis of a book on modern language teaching once the War was over. More, I gave myself (the Russian dream over) to the serious and intensive study of my old love among languages, Spanish; introduced the language into the school curriculum; and published a Spanish grammar as well as a text-book correlating the teaching of French and History and a 'French Accuracy Notebook' applying the results of one series of my educational experiments.[60] Outside the school, I found recreation as well as usefulness in acting as organist[61] at the little church of St Mary, Dunmow Priory,[62]

---

58 An oblique reference, surely, to his treatment, at the hands of the 'New Testament', within the Faculty of Arts, University of Liverpool during the protracted period of his candidacy for the Gilmour Chair.

59 Marginal reminder, in pencil, here: 'enlarge: always know when wrong'. Peers evidently wished to emphasize the importance in a teacher of always recognizing one's own shortcomings in knowledge and understanding.

60 Peers' *A Skeleton Spanish Grammar* was published in 1917 (London: Blackie & Son); *A French Accuracy Notebook, Based upon the Accuracy Chart System* in 1918 (in Dent's Modern Language Series); and his compilation of *French Historical Passages — 1789-1870 — For Reading or Translation* in 1921 (Oxford: Clarendon Press).

61 Peers possessed considerable talents as a musician (*cf.* 'B.T.', ch. II, p. 254).

62 The parish church of Little Dunmow, St Mary's, comprises the South chancel chapel or Lady Chapel of Little Dunmow Priory, a priory of Augustinian canons founded in 1106, the sole part of the Priory to survive above ground. It is described by Sir Nikolaus Pevsner as a building 'of interest wherever one looks, and in addition of great architectural beauty in parts' (Pevsner, *The Buildings of England: Essex*, revised by Enid Radcliffe, *ed. cit.*, 277-78).

where one of my colleagues was incumbent.[63] When the War took him also, I had for some months, as a licensed lay reader,[64] almost entire charge of that parish and the close contacts formed with those sterling Essex country-folk made still another tie which it was bitterly hard to break when the time came. Never was I entirely cut off from London, the British Museum Reading Room, the Modern Language Association, the English Association and other institutions which now I find it [/from the North of England, are] much harder to keep in touch with. No: even after a quarter of a century as a University teacher[65] I can look back on those five years, call them well spent and fruitful in the highest degree, and wish with all my heart, from a knowledge of what they gave me, that every University teacher had to serve an apprenticeship among boys.

In the mellow happiness of that life, the impression made on me by McClure's wise words melted quickly, and it was not until much later that they ever recurred to my memory. Disillusion, not this time with the particular school but with schoolmastering as a profession, crept on me slowly — almost imperceptibly. Boys eager to get the most of their work, as most of these were, proved such pleasant [/the pleasantest of] companions, and the emotions aroused by the War brought them into more intimate contact with masters than in normal times would be possible. One was busy from morning to night: there were extra duties imposed by the absence of men on war service; there was the intensive O.T.C. work speeded up to compensate for the tragic wastage in France and Flanders; there was the evening training of Derby recruits for which we O.T.C. officers were responsible. Even in the holidays, there

---

63 The Revd Edgar Iliff Robson, Vicar of Little Dunmow, 1912-33, and an Assistant Master at Felsted School 1908-31; educated at the University of Melbourne (M.A., 1893) and Christ's College, Cambridge (B.A. 1st class Classical Tripos 1895, M.A. 1906, B.D. 1915); served as an assistant master and as a headmaster of various public schools 1896 onwards. (*Crockford's Clerical Directory for 1915*, and *Crockford's Clerical Directory, 1947*, which lists his biblical, educational and travel-related publications).

64 An early indication of Peers' spirituality and religious convictions, and of the fact that, unlike his parents (see ch. 1, p. 73, note 34) he was an Anglican.

65 An important piece of evidence to indicate that Peers (who began his career at Liverpool University in 1920) wrote his autobiography, or, at any rate, this part of it, c.1945.

were special training courses at Chelsea Barracks which we took in turns.[66] Yet, as my father had taught me so long ago, there was time for everything — [or] for everything [perhaps], that is to say, but reflection. [And it/] It was not until two years had slipped away at Felsted that I began to reflect.

I had little doubt that, after the War, I could build up a thoroughly good three-language curriculum there. Stephenson [, personally,] was quite lukewarm about it, but [he knew what parents were always asking for and] as vacancies arose he would certainly give me two well-trained colleagues and a Classical man's [somewhat detached] blessing. By the time I was thirty the course, if not exactly on De Glehn's lines, would at least be something I should not be ashamed to show him. But — and this was the first of my misgivings — *what then?*

At twenty and twenty-three, I reflected, it had been quite a thrilling adventure to start a [fresh] set of beginners on a course of French, German and Spanish [/language entirely new to them each September]. At twenty-four and twenty-five teaching fresh [/a new batch of] pupils precisely the same thing [as last year] was [still] quite agreeable. But what it would be at thirty-five? And at forty-five? And at fifty-five? [...][67]

[...] Then I looked round the Cranstead[68] Common Room.[69] What sort of men were they? Did I want to grow like them? Some of them — even those in their fifties — were happy enough: they were wrapped up in their boys, [...][70]

---

66 In his War Statement, June 1919, Peers wrote 'During Vacations I have attended Military instructional courses and done clerical and other War work, and I have been responsible in the Corps at Felsted for most of the Military preparation of Candidates for Woolwich and Sandhurst'.

67 p. 45 and most of p. 46 of the manuscript have been removed and transferred to 'B.T.', ch. II, pp. 236-37 — italicized.

68 'Felsted' has been deleted (in error), and replaced by 'Cranstead' — that being the name Peers gives to Felsted in the disguised part of his autobiography, when writing as 'Bruce Truscot'.

69 After 'Common Room' there is a sentence, still legible, which Peers has deleted: 'and my mind went back to the men I had known at Mill Hill'.

70 Between the truncated p. 46 and p. 54, there is only one page, which is numbered '83', in error. Peers has written in the margin of this page, and also in that of p. 54, which follows it: 'for real...' [the word after 'real' is illegible]. Peers has removed these several pages and inserted them in 'B.T.',

[...] The voice of the rotund Shipley ('get out ... too late') echoed unpleasantly in my thoughts. More encouraging was that memory of the words of the wizard McClure.[71] Was academic research capable of bringing me success and happiness? If so, how could I best get into it?

## IV

During the autumn of 1918, when it seemed likely that the War would end in the near future [— though few envisaged the suddenness of its actual collapse —], I made my first real friendship in the academic field, which was destined to go a long way towards solving the problem for me. In the June of that year, in collaboration with Brian Downs,[72] (who had been elected to the modern language fellowship at Christs), Dora Black[73] (who afterwards married Bertrand Russell) and a few

---

ch. II, renumbering the original pp. 47-52, to become pp. 74-79; see pp. 237-42 — italicized.

71 See above, p. 96.

72 Brian Westerdale Downs (1893-1984) was educated at Christ's College, Cambridge (Entrance Scholar 1912 onwards, B.A. 1st class Hons. [with distinction], Medieval and Modern Languages Tripos 1915, M.A. 1919). In 1918 he was made a College Lecturer in Modern and Mediaeval Languages and English, and was elected a Fellow in 1919. From 1919 he lectured for the University in English and in Modern Languages, specializing initially in Dutch and then in the Scandinavian languages. He was first Professor of Scandinavian Studies at Cambridge, from 1950 to 1960, and was Master of Christ's College, 1950-63. He was author of a number of books, including *Richardson* (1928) and studies of modern Norwegian literature, Ibsen, etc. He was elected Treasurer of the Modern Humanities Research Association, 19 February 1919; and he was one of the original members of the Finance Sub-Committee, appointed in October 1918. (Obituary in *The Times*, 13 March 1984; entry in *Who's Who 1984*).

73 Dora Winifred Black (1894-1986), daughter of Sir Frederick Black, former Director-General of Munitions Supply, was educated at Girton College, Cambridge, gaining a Class I in the Mediaeval and Modern Languages Tripos in 1915. She was then successively College Research Student (1916-17), Old Girtonians' Research Student (1917-18), and Pfeiffer Research Fellow (1918-20). Soon after the First World War she took up with Bertrand Russell (1872-1970), who became third Earl Russell in 1931. In 1921 they married but in 1932 parted and finally divorced in 1935; Dora

others[,] I had founded an association, to be referred to again hereafter,[74] which aimed at bringing research workers in the Modern Humanities into touch with one another to their mutual advantage.[75] Though it has done, and still does, good work, partly owing to the interest taken in it by the United States, where modern language specialists take research seriously, it did not at first secure the active support of as many University teachers as we should have liked: we had not realized how few of them ever did any research and how long it would take to educate many of those who did up to the idealistic aim of sharing their discoveries with others.

---

married Gordon Grace in 1940. The author of several books, including *The Right to be Happy* (1927), she collaborated with Bertrand Russell in writing *The Prospects of Industrial Civilization* (1923), etc. Miss Black took an active part in the early work of the M.H.R.A. (see note 75), on whose Committee she sat. She was appointed one of the original members of the Finance Sub-Committee in October 1918. In January 1919 she was appointed Convener of a Propaganda Sub-Committee (French) which was formed to circulate French universities with information about the Association and its work. (For details of Dora Black's life and career up to c.1944, including her political, social and educational work and details of her publications, see the *Girton College Register*, vol. 1, 1869-1946, 676-77).

74  Peers has written, in the margin, the abbreviation 'MHRA'. Perhaps because he was unsure of his intentions, he considered deleting the words 'to be referred to again hereafter'.

75  At a meeting in Christ's College, Cambridge, on 1 June 1918, and convened by Peers, it was decided to form a body which was initially entitled the 'Modern Language Research Students' Association' which, after two later modifications, was changed into the current title, the Modern Humanities Research Association (the M.H.R.A.; *cf*. Peers' abbreviation, p. 105). Present at the 1 June meeting were: Dr. E. G. W. Braunholtz (in the chair), Miss J. P. Strachey (who later became the first Assistant Hon. Secretary), Miss D. W. Black, Miss Steele Smith, Miss K. T. Butler, Miss M. B. Finch, Miss A. Walsh, Miss C. M. Simmins, Miss V. Stockley, the Revd Dr Latimer Jackson, the Revd Dr. H. F. Stewart, and Messrs B. W. Downs, B. J. Hayes, L. Chouville and E. A. Peers. No. 8 of the Association's *Bulletin*, October 1920, states that 'Its main object is the encouragement of advanced study in Modern Languages and Literatures by co-operation, through correspondence, personal intercourse, the interchange of information and counsel, and financial support for students engaged in research'. Peers traces the early ideals and history of the Association in the preliminary remarks of his Presidential Address for 1932 to the Modern Humanities Research Association, 'The Study of Spanish Romanticism'; this address was published in the *M.H.R.A. Annual Bulletin of the Modern Humanities Research Association* (December 1932), no. 11, 1-16.

So far as I can recall [/Idealistic as always], I had flung myself into this venture, without a secretary and without the least [/slightest] financial backing, involving an amount of routine work that I could not now contemplate, from purely unselfish motives [/without a shudder].[76] My time for personal research was extremely small; opportunities were limited to such vacation time as was not absorbed by Chelsea Barracks and the intensive study of Spanish; of instruction and guidance, apart from the picking up of a few crumbs from professors' tables, I had absolutely nothing. But I had contrived to write a thesis[77] which gave me an external M.A. degree at London University and was working on a much wider theme of comparative literature which eventually grew so extensive that it had, in that form, to be abandoned.[78] The M.H.R.A. (as the

---

76 In his Presidential Address for 1918-19 to the Association, on the subject of 'Modern Language Research', Sir Sidney Lee acknowledged that 'Mr. Allison Peers, our honorary secretary, is the virtual founder of the Association'. The minutes of the Association's committee also provide ample evidence that Peers was the driving force behind the Association, putting forward specific proposals to increase the membership — which, after just two years' work numbered six hundred — and to realize the objects of the Association. His proposals were usually accepted by the Committee. It is not thus surprising that in June 1922 Peers intimated that he wished to resign as Honorary Secretary 'the work having grown to an extent entirely beyond his powers' but he was persuaded to continue, the Committee empowering him to appoint a salaried Assistant to take over as much of his work as should be found possible; the appointment of this part-time Assistant Secretary was renewed for an initial three years after the first year. Peers continued as Honorary Secretary for eleven years, until the end of September 1929; he was elected a vice-president and an honorary life member shortly after his resignation was accepted. He served as President in 1931-32.

77 The title of this M.A. thesis, dated May 1915, is 'The Beginnings of French Prose Fiction (down to "L'Astrée") 1608' [sic]; typescript, 7 + 177 pp; copy in the University of London Library. Peers states that 'the main object of the thesis is to trace, wherever possible, development in form, psychology, etc., and this has especially been kept in view when the better known writers have been dealt with' (iv). In chapter 8, 'The Realistic Novel before "L'Astrée" ', he refers to the influence of Spain, crediting Spain in great measure with responsibility for the development of French realistic fiction, and also refers to Spanish fiction in the sixteenth century.

78 This may be a reference to the doctoral thesis 'dealing with Spanish literary relations' which, in his application for the Gilmour Chair of Spanish, June 1919, he states that he was engaged upon (see Appendix I, p. 430). There is apparently no surviving reference to this research for a doctorate

new association was called) did for me what this desultory work, for which there was no hope of publication in the near future, could never have done: it brought me into touch with a few leading men [/scholars] who cared tremendously for scholarship [/research] and were good enough to take an interest in a young man who cared tremendously for it too.

Few of these were found at Cambridge: Stewart[79] and Tilley,[80] of course, who soon afterwards were turned down for the new Chair of French at Cambridge in favour of a Rugby master, Oliver Prior,[81] — because, as the story ran, it was impossible to elect one of them without the other — gave it their joint blessing. Braunholtz,[82] now somewhat ageing, smiled [/beamed] benevolently upon it and was rewarded with [/forthwith elected to] a Vice-Presidency. A new acquaintance whom it brought me, Anna Paues,[83] of Newnham, a great lover

---

among either the archives of the University of London or those of Christ's College, Cambridge. There is nothing among the archives of the University of Cambridge to suggest that he embarked on an official course of postgraduate research. The University of Cambridge (in fact, in common with other British universities) did not award the research degree of Ph.D. until the 1920s.

79  The Revd Hugh Fraser Stewart, D.D., of Trinity College and The Malting House, Cambridge, joined the Committee of the Association and also became its first chairman in July 1918. A French scholar, his publications included editions of Pascal's work; together with A. A. Tilley, he edited an anthology and texts on the Classical and Romantic movements in French Literature. See also above, ch. 2, pp. 77-78, note 9.

80  Arthur Augustus Tilley (1851-1942), M.A., Fellow of King's College, Cambridge, had joined the M.L.R.A. (an earlier name for the M.H.R.A.; see note 75 above) by July 1919; he does not appear on the list of members 'to 15 November 1918'. He was the author of a number of publications on French literature dating from the Middle Ages to the eighteenth century (see *The British Library General Catalogue of Printed Books to 1975* and the entry in *Who Was Who, 1941-1950*). See also above, ch. 2, p. 78, note 10.

81  Oliver Herbert Phelps Prior (1871-1934), D.ès L., Modern Language Master at Rugby School, appears in the list of members of the M.L.R.A. (later M.H.R.A.) 'to 15 November 1918'. He was Drapers' Professor of French, University of Cambridge, 1919-34. (see entry in *Who Was Who, 1929-1940* and *The British Library General Catalogue of Printed Books to 1975*).

82  For Braunholtz, see above, ch. 2, p. 78, note 11. He is listed in vols 1-3 (1906-08) of the *Modern Language Review* as a member of its Advisory Board.

83  Dr Anna Carolina Paues (1867-1945), educated at the University of Uppsala and Newnham College, Cambridge; Research Fellow (1902-06),

of learning, became one of its most stalwart supporters, as, for the short remnant of her life, did the venerable Jane Harrison.[84] But others, whose names are best forgotten, and who, needless to say, neither practised research themselves nor encouraged others to do so, actively, and from obvious motives, resented its foundation. Our staunchest adherents came, as those who knew the University world might have expected, from London and the North. I must mention with gratitude L. E. Kastner,[85] of Manchester, who had done more solid research than all the Cambridge teachers of French put together; Toller[86] and Charlton[87] also of Manchester; Moore-Smith[88] and A. T.

---

Lecturer in English (1906-27), at Newnham College, and University Lecturer in Swedish, 1927-36. She edited five volumes of the Annual Bibliography of English Literature for the Modern Humanities Research Association, 1920-24, and contributed to the *Modern Language Review*, etc. (*Newnham College Register 1871-1950, Vol. I: 1871-1923*, ed. A. B. White n.d. [c.1964], 11).

84 Miss Jane Ellen Harrison (1850-1928), LL.D., D.Litt., Newnham College, Cambridge, was elected a member of the Association, on 24 July 1918. She was a very distinguished Classical scholar and sometime Fellow and Lecturer in Classical Archaeology 1899-1922 at Newnham College, of which she had been a College Scholar as a student. (*Dictionary of National Biography; Who Was Who, 1916-1928*; *Newnham College Register 1871-1950, Vol. I: 1871-1923*, ed. A. B. White n.d. [c.1964], 9). Christopher Brooke describes her as 'a brilliant, flamboyant figure, a very notable student of Greek archaeology and religion, who laid new foundations for the understanding of Greek society...' (Brooke, *A History of the University of Cambridge*, Vol. IV *1870-1990*, 319-20).

85 L. E. Kastner (d.1940), Professor of French Language and Literature, University of Manchester, 1909-33 (*Who Was Who, 1929-1940*). Appointed a vice-president of the M.L.R.A. (later the M.H.R.A.) in July 1918.

86 Thomas Northcote Toller (1844-1930), Smith Professor of English, Owens College, Manchester, 1880-1903; he came to Owens College, Manchester in 1872, immediately after obtaining his Fellowship at Christ's College, Cambridge. An Anglo-Saxon specialist, his reputation was established by his editing and enlargement of Joseph Bosworth's *An Anglo-Saxon Dictionary* (Oxford, 1882, 1898), to which he also produced a *Supplement* (Oxford, 1921) (an appreciation was published in *The Guardian,* 4 March 1930; for an abstract of his will, see *The Times,* 20 June 1930; see also John Peile, *Biographical Register of Christ's College 1505-1905, Vol. II 1666-1905,* 1913, 572).

87 Henry Buckley Charlton (1890-1961), Professor of English Literature, University of Manchester, 1921-57 (*Who Was Who, 1961-1970*).

88 For G. C. Moore Smith, see above, note 25. He became a vice-president of the M.L.R.A. (later, M.H.R.A.) in July 1918, and was editor of the English section of the *Modern Language Review*, vols 11-22 (1916-27).

Baker,[89] of Sheffield, the latter also turned down, though less understandably than Stewart and Tilley, for the Cambridge Chair; W. E. Collinson,[90] of Liverpool; Warren,[91] Craigie[92] and Fiedler[93] from Oxford; Edmund Gardner[94] and Gustave Rudler[95]

89  Alfred Thomas Baker (1873-1936), Professor of French Language and Literature, University of Sheffield, 1901-36 (*Who Was Who, 1929-1940*). Appointed a vice-president of the M.L.R.A. (later, M.H.R.A.) in July 1918.

90  William Edward Collinson (1889-1969), Professor of German, University of Liverpool, 1914-54; also Hon. Lecturer in Comparative Philology, John Buchanan Lecturer in Esperanto, 1931-54 and 1962-64, and Chairman of the Faculty of Arts, 1921-22 and 1943-44. (*Who Was Who, 1961-1970*; Kelly, *For Advancement of Learning. The University of Liverpool 1881-1981*). Collinson served as one of the editors of vols. 29 and 30 (1934-35) of the *Modern Language Review* (by then the organ of the M.H.R.A.). He is listed as the Liverpool correspondent of the M.H.R.A. by October 1920 (*Bulletin* of the Association, no. 8, October 1920); at the suggestion of Peers, made to the Association's Committee in February 1919, 'correspondents' were appointed in university centres and other localities.  In January 1922 Collinson consented to accept the office of Hon. Treasurer of the Association if no other member could be found to undertake it, an offer not taken up because Professor Allen Mawer (see below note 100) expressed his willingness to hold that office.  Collinson later joined the Association's Committee.

91  Sir (Thomas) Herbert Warren, K.C.V.O. (1853-1930); Fellow and Classical Tutor of Magdalen College, Oxford, 1877-85; President of Magdalen College, Oxford, 1885-1928; Vice-Chancellor, University of Oxford, 1906-10; Professor of Poetry, University of Oxford, 1911-16; 'not merely was he a brilliant classical scholar... but he had a wide knowledge of English literature and a genuine passion for it' (*Who Was Who, 1929-1940*; Obituary in *The Times*, 10 June 1930).

92  Sir William A. Craigie, (knighted in 1928), F.B.A. (1867-1957), lexicographer and philologist; Fellow of Oriel College, Oxford, 1917-25; Rawlinson and Bosworth Professor of Anglo-Saxon, University of Oxford, 1916-25; Professor of English, University of Chicago, 1925-36. (*Dictionary of National Biography; Who Was Who, 1951-1960*; Obituary in *Procs. of the British Academy 1961*, 1962).

93  Hermann George Fiedler, M.V.O. (1862-1945), Professor of German Language and Literature in Mason College, Birmingham, 1890-1900 and in the University of Birmingham, 1900-07; Taylor Professor of German Language and Literature, University of Oxford, 1907-37. He is listed in vols 1-3 (1906-08) of the *Modern Language Review* as a member of its Advisory Board. He served as President of the M.H.R.A., 1935-36 (*Who Was Who, 1941-1950*).

94  Edmund Garratt Gardner, F.B.A. (1869-1935); Barlow Lecturer on Dante, University College London, 1910-26; Professor of Italian Studies, University of Manchester, 1919-23; Professor of Early Italian Language and Literature (1923-25) and of Italian (1925-34), University of London; one of

from London; Terracher,[96] now Rector of Bordeaux University, from Liverpool; Grierson,[97] of Edinburgh; Savory[98] and Williams,[99] of Belfast; Allen Mawer,[100] of Newcastle; Saintsbury,[101] from his retirement at Bath; Paget Toynbee,[102]

the editors of vols 16-29 (1921-34) of the *Modern Language Review* (*Who Was Who, 1929-1940*; Obituary in *Procs. of the British Academy 1935*).

95 Gustave Rudler (1872-1953); Professor of French Literature, University of London, 1913-20; Marshal Foch Professor of French Literature, University of Oxford, 1920-49 (*Who Was Who, 1951-1960*).

96 Louis Adolphe Terracher (1881-1955); James Barrow Professor of French, University of Liverpool, 1913-19; Professor of the History of the French Language, University of Strasbourg, 1919-25; Rector of the University of Dijon, 1925-32; Rector of the University of Bordeaux, 1932-38; Rector of the University of Strasbourg, 1938-44 (Kelly, *For Advancement of Learning. The University of Liverpool 1881-1981*, 148, 173, 221, 525; Jean Babin, 'XIII. In Memoriam A. L. [sic] Terracher', *Orbis: Bulletin International de Documentation Linguistique*, [1955], 567-70; *Dernieres nouvelles d'Alsace*, [April 1955], no. 81, 13; Archives de France, Paris, F/17/25295).

97 Sir Herbert John Clifford Grierson (1866-1960), F.B.A., F.R.S.L. (knighted in 1936), Professor of Rhetoric and English Literature, University of Edinburgh, 1915-35. Became a vice-president of the M.L.R.A. (later, M.H.R.A.) in July 1918 (*Who Was Who, 1951-1960*; obituary in *Procs. of the British Academy 1960*, 1961).

98 Sir Douglas (Lloyd) Savory (knighted in 1952) (1878-1969), Professor of French Language and Romance Philology, University of Belfast, 1909-40 (*Who Was Who, 1961-1970*).

99 Robert Allan Williams (1876-1951); Professor of German, Trinity College, Dublin, 1907-15; Professor of German and Teutonic Philology, Queen's University of Belfast, 1915-32; Schröder Professor of German, University of Cambridge, 1932-41 (*Who Was Who, 1951-1960*; T. W. Moody and J. C. Beckett, *Queen's, Belfast 1845-1949, the History of a University*, 2 vols [London: Faber and Faber, 1959]; *The Annual Record of the Queen's University Association 1951*, 52 — which describes Professor Williams as 'one of the most distinguished scholars whom Ulster has produced in recent times').

100 Sir Allen Mawer, Kt (created 1937), F.B.A. (1879-1942); Joseph Cowen Professor of English Language and Literature, Armstrong College, Newcastle, 1908-21; Baines Professor of English Language, University of Liverpool, 1921-29; Provost of University College London, 1930-42. He served as Hon. Treasurer of the M.H.R.A. from 1 October 1922 until 1925 (*Dictionary of National Biography*; *Who Was Who, 1941-1950*; biographical memoir in *Procs. of the British Academy 1943*).

101 George Edward Bateman Saintsbury, F.B.A. (1845-1933); Professor of Rhetoric and English Literature, University of Edinburgh, 1895-1915. Became a vice-president of the M.L.R.A. (later, M.H.R.A.) in July 1918. On 19 November 1919 he was entertained to dinner at the University Club,

110   REDBRICK UNIVERSITY REVISITED

G. G. Coulton,[103] Latimer Jackson,[104] Montague Summers[105] and a number of other scholars independent of, or but loosely attached to universities; Sidney Lee,[106] who became our first

---

Liverpool (*Dictionary of National Biography 1931-1940*; *Who Was Who, 1929-1940*).

102 Dr Paget Jackson Toynbee, F.B.A. (1855-1932); Dante Scholar; Hon. Fellow of Balliol College, Oxford, 1922-32; Hon. Secretary of the Oxford Dante Society, 1916-28; Hon. Vice-President of the London Dante Society, etc. (*Dictionary of National Biography*; obituary in *Procs. of the British Academy 1933*; *Who Was Who, 1929-1940*). He is listed as member of the Advisory Board of the *Modern Language Review* in vols 1-3 (1906-08). He became a vice-president of the M.L.R.A. (later, M.H.R.A.) in July 1918.

103 Dr George Gordon Coulton, F.B.A. (1858-1947); historian of medieval life and thought, and controversialist; in 1918 he began to lecture for the newly founded English tripos as well as for the Historical tripos at Cambridge; in 1919 he was elected University Lecturer in English and Fellow of St John's College, Cambridge (*Dictionary of National Biography*; obituary in *Procs. of the British Academy 1947*; *Who Was Who, 1941-1950*).

104 Revd Henry Latimer Jackson (1851-1926); educated at Christ's College, Cambridge (B.A. 1881; M.A., B.D., D.D.); Lecturer in Modern and Medieval Dutch Literature, University of Cambridge, 1918; Rector of Little Canfield, Dunmow, Essex, 1911-26; Hulsean Lecturer at Cambridge, 1912-13 (*Who Was Who, 1916-1928*; *Crockford's Clerical Directory 1926*; *The British Library General Catalogue of Printed Books to 1975*). A founding member of the Association, he was author of books on the Fourth Gospel (1906, 1918), the National Church, etc. and joint author with Brian W. Downs of *A Manual of the Dutch Language* (1921).

105 Revd Alphonsus Joseph-Mary Augustus Montague Summers, F.R.S.L. (1880-1948); lived largely abroad, particularly in Italy. He founded The Phoenix, a Society for the Production of Old Plays, 1919; his publications are listed in his entry in *Who Was Who, 1941-1950*.

106 Sir Sidney Lee (knighted in 1911), F.B.A. (1859-1926); Shakespearian scholar and editor of the *Dictionary of National Biography*; Professor of English Language and Literature, University of London (East London College), 1913-24. He served as the Association's first President, 1918-19. In his Presidential Address, 'Modern Language Research', published in the Association's *Annual Bulletin*, Lee declared that 'no country of prestige and wealth has hitherto contributed so little to the endowment of research as Great Britain' and laid down what Peers later stated might well have been taken as one of the principles of the new Association:

> In the higher branches the whole spirit of education will be quickened and will be genuinely progressive from generation to generation only if an aptitude for research is recognized as a qualification for the highest appointments.

In his own Presidential Address to the Association in 1932 (see *M.H.R.A. Annual Bulletin of the Modern Humanities Research Association* [December

President (to our sorrow, we could find nobody sufficiently distinguished, Skeat being long since dead, to invite from Cambridge); F. S. Boas,[107] who stood by us nobly for many a year; and the Chief Editor of the *Modern Language Review*, which the M.H.R.A. afterwards took over, J. G. Robertson.[108]

It is Robertson, until his death in...[109] Professor of German at the University of London, whom I must describe as the first real scholar in the modern language field with whom I ever became intimate. His devotion to scholarship for its own sake — a more unselfish man I have never known — first revealed to me the full nobility of that pursuit. His eminently practical nature and scrupulously precise habits of mind disproved the idea which, like so many people, I was inclined to believe, that scholars were myopic and other-worldly dreamers. He told me,

---

1932], no. 11, 1-16), Peers paid tribute to 'the imagination and energy' of Lee, whose 'dominating personality... took hold of us all' and ensured the quick evolution of the M.H.R.A. from the 'M.L.R.S.A' (2). In 1920 the Association inaugurated the *Bibliography of English Language and Literature*, a project which had been advocated by Lee.

107 Frederick Samuel Boas (1862-1957); Inspector, London County Council Education Department, 1905-27; Editor of the English Association's *The Year's Work in English Studies*, 1922-55, and author and editor of many other works, including 'Teachers and Modern Language Research' (M.H.R.A. Publications, no. 2, 1919). He served as chairman of the M.H.R.A. for a period until May 1922, resigning on account of the insertion by the Secretary (Peers) of part of the President's Address in the Association's *Bulletin* (*Who Was Who, 1951-1960*; *The British Library General Catalogue of Printed Books to 1975*).

108 John G. Robertson, F.B.A. (1867-1933); Professor of German Language and Literature, University of London, 1903-33; author of the famous and fundamental *A History of German Literature* (Edinburgh and London: William Blackwood & Sons, 1902; with later editions; 4th ed., revised and enlarged by Edna Purdie *et al.*, 1962); editor of the *Modern Language Review*, vols 1-38, 1906-33, being sole editor of vols 1-4 and one of the joint editors of the subsequent volumes. In 1922 the *Modern Language Review* was taken over by, and henceforth edited for, the Modern Humanities Research Association. Professor Robertson provided a testimonial for Peers when he applied for the Gilmour Chair of Spanish in November 1921 (see Appendix I, p. 441). A member of M.H.R.A. since July 1918, and a member of its committee from October 1918, Robertson served as Chairman of the M.H.R.A. in succession to Dr Stewart and as President in 1924-25 (*Who Was Who, 1929-1940*; obituary in *Procs. of the British Academy 1933*).

109 Peers leaves a space, to insert later the date of Robertson's death (1933).

with the utmost frankness [/candour], though with that well-known [/characteristic] tact which enabled him to call a man a scoundrel without making one feel that he was insulting him, that both McClure and Shipley had been right, that if I wanted to get into University life I had better start at once, as there was considerable prejudice in the Universities against schoolmasters, and finally that as the French field was hopelessly overcrowded, my best outlet was in Spanish, a language which was just coming into the notice of educationists and was likely to be popular in the near future.[110]

For this advice, though it was as nothing by comparison with the kindnesses which this best of friends afterwards did [/showed] me, I was more than grateful. There were only two Chairs of Spanish at that time — at Liverpool, dating from 1908[111] and at London, founded in commemoration of the Cervantes Tercentenary in 1916. But some of the other Universities were founding lectureships and there were practically no qualified candidates for them. At Liverpool, in 1908, as I have since been told, the only possible candidate was the man elected,[112] and there were shoals of applications which

---

110 In 1932 Peers recounted that it was in the summer of 1918 that he 'first began to look rather carefully into the Romantic Movement of the early nineteenth century in Spain with a view to writing its history... I had decided that the origins of Spanish Romanticism looked decidedly more interesting than those of Romanticism in France, and I went to Madrid full of hopes for the investigation...' (*Annual Bulletin of the Modern Humanities Research Association* [December 1932], no. 11, 4).

111 The Gilmour Chair of Spanish, the first such chair to be established in any British university, was endowed, in 1908, by Captain George Gilmour of Birkenhead, a business man with commercial interests in Argentina.

112 Professor James Fitzmaurice-Kelly, F.B.A. (1857-1923) was in fact appointed to the Gilmour Chair of Spanish as from 1 October 1909. Fitzmaurice-Kelly, renowned for various publications (including *A History of Spanish Literature* [London: Heinemann, 1898]), was a member of the Advisory Board of the *Modern Language Review* and was one of the editors of vols 9-14 (1914-19). The Faculty of Arts' Committee on the Chair of Spanish, in recommending Dr Fitzmaurice-Kelly, stated that it had considered one hundred and sixty applications for the Chair:

> the application list has been remarkable in this case both on account of its magnitude and on account of its diversified nature. Applications have been received not only from candidates in this Country but from France, Spain, Portugal, Morocco, the United States and South America. The Committee have observed among the applicants men of letters,

could only be described as grotesque. Business men with little education and underworked Spanish-American consuls seemed to think that a University Chair would be a useful part-time employment for them. Many of the Spanish-speaking candidates sent photographs of themselves surrounded by their numerous progeny, volumes of their poems, newspapers containing their articles and records of municipal employment and military or political distinction.[113]

---

journalists, engineers, school-masters, naval and military officers, barristers, clerics and men engaged in commerce and industry. In the majority of cases the applicants had had a University career and possessed a University degree, but furnished no evidence of having pursued the study of Spanish Language and Literature continuously and systematically, or to such purpose as would render them competent to perform the duties of this Chair.

While stating that 'of all the candidates who have been before them', Dr Fitzmaurice-Kelly was 'most highly qualified for the Chair', the Committee named Mr Fernando de Arteaga (Lecturer in Spanish and Italian, University of Birmingham since 1904) and Mr Milton A. Buchanan (Lecturer in Italian and Spanish, University of Toronto) as the two on the final list of seven candidates 'whose claims, in the view of the Committee, most nearly approximated to those of Dr Fitzmaurice-Kelly'. Besides these two and Dr Fitzmaurice-Kelly, the four other short-listed candidates were Mr Martin Hume, Monsieur C. Pitollet, Mr W. L. A. Poole, and Sr Tomás Navarro. The Committee expressed their thanks to the British Ambassador at Madrid who had 'taken great pains both to make the vacancy known in Spain and to furnish all the information obtainable concerning Spanish candidates'. The Committee's membership was dominated by members of the 'New Testament' group — Professors Bonnier, Elton, Meyer, Mair (Dean of the Faculty of Arts), and Ramsay Muir (Chairman of the Faculty); the Vice-Chancellor, Dr George Adami, was the remaining (*ex officio*) member. For Peers' comments on the applicants for the newly established Gilmour Chair ('there were dozens of candidates, nearly all of the wrong kind') and on the selection of Fitzmaurice-Kelly ('an independent scholar... but without university training or academic experience') see *Spanish — Now* (London: Methuen, 1944), 83.

113 There survive in the University of Liverpool Archives certificates and letters of applicants for the Chair (from Luis García de los Ríos Pedraja, Eduardo M. Moreno, and Amiceto Tapias Navarro) together with a photograph of an unidentified [?Spanish] applicant; the certificates etc. sent in by applicants were generally returned to them by the University Registrar. M. Menéndez y Pelayo wrote a reference on behalf of Luis García de los Ríos Pedraja. Another candidate, whose letter of enquiry and application, unfortunately, has been lost, was the novelist, Ramón Pérez de Ayala.

Already I had been approached as a possible candidate for the new Spanish lectureship at Sheffield,[114] for which I declined to stand out of an unwillingness to leave Felsted at the most difficult period of the War.[115] But, after the Armistice, I decided definitely to cut loose from schoolmastering for good in the following summer and take [/accept/go in for] any kind of University appointment that presented itself with a view to taking up Spanish as my life-work at the first opportunity. So, between January and June 1919, I entered for every kind of University post conceivable.[116] Professorships, readerships and lectureships were advertised in English, French, Spanish and even Education, for I hoped that my first class with double distinction in the Cambridge diploma might stand me in good stead. I even dared to apply for the Gilmour Chair of Spanish at the University of Liverpool,[117] though I had no paper

---

114 The Department of Spanish at the University of Sheffield was established in 1918, opening under the first Herbert Hughes Lecturer in Spanish, J. N. Birch (Arthur W. Chapman, *The Story of a Modern University: A History of the University of Sheffield* [London: Oxford U. P., 1955], 285).

115 Added in pencil here: 'Though I was told that Fisher...'. H. A. L. Fisher, F.B.A., F.R.S., O.M. (1856-1940), while Vice-Chancellor of the University of Sheffield, 1912-16, actively supported the moves to establish a Department of Spanish at the University (Chapman, *op. cit.*, 283-85). Fisher entered the House of Commons in 1916, as M.P. for the Combined English Universities, and, as President of the Board of Education, 1916-22, established state scholarships to universities.

116 In his letters in February 1920 to the Chairman of the Faculty of Arts and to Professor Mair at Liverpool, Professor Fitzmaurice-Kelly stated that Peers was 'recently' interviewed (unsuccessfully) for posts of External Examiner in both French and Spanish at London University.

117 In May 1919 the University of Liverpool advertised the vacant Chair; applications were to be sent to the Registrar not later than 30 June 1919. The appointment was advertised as for life (subject to retirement at the age of sixty-five years) and was to date from 1 October 1919. Peers' application is dated 25 June 1919. Writing from The Old School House, Felsted, he mentioned that his interest in Spanish dated from his boyhood and that since the War began he had taken an active part in the development of Spanish teaching and study in this country. 'For the last three years I have spared no efforts to secure to Spanish a more important place in the University syllabus and the school curriculum'. As previously noted, he was also 'engaged upon a doctorate thesis dealing with Spanish literary relations'. He enclosed testimonials from Dr A. E. Shipley and Mr Norman McLean, both of Christ's College, Cambridge, and from Dr E. G. W. Braunholtz, and gave as his referees Professors Ernest Mérimée (Professor of Spanish,

qualifications in that language — only a vast enthusiasm, a good Spanish accent and a [/some] quite considerable acquaintance with the country's literature. But none of these could be tested except by experts and today I blush for my presumption, though this was prompted by nothing more reprehensible than the feeling that I must make a move now or not at all.

My combined sins of presumption [/ambition] met with their just reward; for, when the summer term of 1919 ended and the final wrench of separation from the friends and the scenes I loved so well [/of five memorable war years] had to be made, I had not only no post to go to in the following September, but, so far as I can remember, I had not even been placed on a short list for one. Again and again during the term it had been in my mind to go to Stephenson and tell him I had changed my mind, but I was so completely convinced [/persuaded] in theory of the wisdom of my projected move that I felt sure something or other would occur in due course to justify it. Further, in the preceding spring, I had made my first long visit to Spain[118] and returned

---

University of Toulouse), L. E. Kastner (Professor of French, University of Manchester), and J. G. Robertson (Professor of German, University of London, and editor of the *Modern Language Review*). See Appendix I, pp. 429-31.

118 In his application for the Gilmour Chair in June 1919, Peers refers to this visit and the motives behind it:

> ...I speak Spanish with fluency and correctness, and desire in a practical way to promote closer relations with Spain, and no less with Spanish America, where I have family connections... Last March I made a special journey to Madrid and other intellectual centres of Northern Spain with the object of investigating at first hand the possibilities of approximation between England and Spain in the immediate future. On my return from this visit, His Excellency the Spanish Ambassador, to whom I am personally known, invited me to attend a Conference of the Anglo-Spanish Society with other corporations for the purpose of setting on foot new movements to further an intercourse with Spain...
>
> (see Appendix I, p. 430).

Peers was to visit Spain regularly, spending several weeks there every year except in the years when the Civil War and the Second World War made his visits impossible. These were visits, of course, for purposes of research in Spanish libraries and archives. But he went also to teach at the summer schools which, from 1921 until 1952, he regularly organized in Santander, and later, for instance, at San Sebastián. And he went to foster, through his many personal contacts with influential Spaniards, intellectual and cultural

with the conviction that my irrational decision of long ago to take up Spanish corresponded to something very deep within me. The Liverpool Chair had not been filled[119] — I had learned indirectly that the election was being indefinitely postponed — and I hoped that, even during the vacation, some new post might be created and that, small as were my qualifications, I might be considered in the filling of it.

But when August came [/arrived], I decided that, for the time being, I should have to go back to teaching, if there was still a school post vacant. I had been given some lecturing for the London and Oxford University Extension Boards and some few inspecting engagements by the Board of Education. But there was not a living wage in all these combined, so, pocketing my pride, I wrote [once again ('promptly yet carefully')] to the obliging Mr Gabbitas[120] and began once more [/again] to receive his attractive little green-ink missives with my breakfast [/at breakfast-time].

In more ways than one I was fortunate to be appointed (for the autumn term only, but with the virtual promise of a permanency after Christmas) to the staff of Wellington College in Berkshire.[121] It introduced me to a school which combined

---

collaboration between Spain and Britain. Among Peers' papers, still unpublished, is a journal which he kept of one of his last visits: 'Diary: Spain, March-April 1950'. This 'Diary', exemplifies both Peers' keen powers of observation, and his deeply affectionate commitment to the study of Spain and its peoples; it illuminates intellectual ideas, cultural preoccupations, social attitudes and characteristically every-day reactions within the country at a critical stage in its post-Civil-War recovery and advancement. The journal was for many years in the possession of Harold Hall, a gifted graduate from Peers' Department, who went on to occupy, for a tragically short period, the Gilmour Chair of Spanish (1978-81). On Harold Hall's death, his widow Elizabeth Hall (see Appendix III, p. 474) gave the journal to the Hispanist and historian, Professor Derek Lomax, University of Birmingham. Before his death, in 1992, Lomax, who had previously been a colleague of Harold Hall in the Department of Hispanic Studies at the University of Liverpool, corresponded with Ann Mackenzie about the possibility of publishing the journal and sent her (to assist her researches into Peers' activities) a photocopy of the text.

119 On 25 June 1919 the Faculty of Arts decided to defer consideration of the applications for the Chair until the Autumn Term.

120 See above, p. 97, note 48.

121 In his *curriculum vitae* submitted to the Faculty of Arts, University of Liverpool, in February 1922, Peers states that from October to December

amenities much superior to those of Mill Hill with a standard of work certainly not lower than that of Felsted. It gave me a comparatively easy time-table, with a chance, not only to fulfil my lecturing engagements but to pursue my Spanish studies at the British Museum. Above all, it won for me the friendship of the Master, W. W. Vaughan[122] — Vaughan of Rugby, as he afterwards became — which [/and that] was a privilege never to be forgotten.

My term at Wellington was in every way [/perhaps] the most placid of my whole career [/in my life down to that time]. Having decided to abandon schoolmastering [at the first opportunity] I was content to follow the methods in vogue, which were reasonably but not devastatingly modern, for what I hoped would be the short period of my stay there. The boys were quiet, gentlemanly, amenable to anyone who knew his job and as easy to get on with in school as out of it. I recall, with pleasure and not without pride, that I had to give not a single punishment or penalty for any form of indiscipline between September and Christmas. I wish that, without throwing this narrative out of proportion, I could say all that is in my mind about Vaughan.[123] He was a remarkable personality: a tall, loose-limbed, hearty giant of a man,[124] rather sentimentally-

---

1919 he was Temporary Master in French and Spanish at Wellington College. Mr Robert Sopwith, the College's Archivist, states that Peers was form master in the Upper School of the Middle First form. His name appears in the Blue Roll for Christmas 1919 but no specific reference to him can be found in the College's Ledgers, nor in the *Wellingtonian* or the *Register* of the College (in the latter cases perhaps because he would not have been an 'appointed' member of staff, since he held a temporary post).

122 Dr William Wyamar Vaughan (1865-1938); Master of Wellington College, 1910-21; Headmaster of Rugby, 1921-31; President of the Modern Language Association, 1915 (see *Dictionary of National Biography*; *Who Was Who, 1921-1940*; R. St C. Talboys, *A Victorian School being the Story of Wellington College* [Oxford: Blackwell, 1943]; David Newsome, *A History of Wellington College 1859-1959* [London: John Murray, 1959], particularly chapter VIII which is devoted to Vaughan's Mastership).

123 Peers reminds himself here, in the margin, to: 'consult my obituary [of Vaughan, apparently] in my red box-file'.

124 Vaughan was described as 'broad-shouldered, broad-minded, large-hearted' by H. C. Bradby in the *Dictionary of National Biography 1931-1940* (880). David Newsome quotes Herbert Fisher's description of Vaughan: 'He was a tall, heavy man...who moved with a kind of clumsy energy...His brow was broad, his light blue eyes keen and penetrating and full of affection and

inclined beneath a general attitude [/thin coating of] of gruffness, apt to come down heavily on either masters or boys ('to bite', the masters called it) and then to feel he had been carried away by impulse and to make something [remarkably/dangerously] like an apology. He had a hatred of slackness or the shirking of duty in any form, and when he went up to London for so much as half a day 'on College business' he would affix a notice describing his errand as such [/in these words] on the Common Room notice-board. But his outstanding characteristics were humanity and interest in the individual. The friendship we began at Wellington was continued when he went to Rugby[125] and later until his tragic death on a visit to India[126] in... .[127] I have always been glad that I ended my career as a schoolmaster with him: it was a fitting crown to these years of almost unspoilt happiness.

It was on one morning late in [/in mid] November when [/that], out of the blue, there came a telegram which changed the whole course of my fortunes. It was from Professor Kastner of Manchester, to whom I had paid a visit in the preceding January to speak at [/address] a meeting of the M.H.R.A. at Manchester University. He knew of my ambitions in the Spanish field; and, having been roped in by Liverpool to give some emergency lectures while a successor in the Chair of

---

benevolence, his rugged countenance eloquent of vitality and human interest and swift to reflect the sunshine and the storm of a nature which felt things deeply and was easily stirred...' (Newsome, *op. cit.*, 277).

125 All those who knew Vaughan testified to his broad humour and deep human sympathy (Newsome, *op. cit.*, 278). One might speculate that additional factors in fostering the friendship between Peers and Vaughan were Vaughan's interest in modern language teaching and his revision of the curriculum of the College, to introduce instruction in German as an alternative to Latin in all but the three lowest forms. He reorganized the Upper School whereby beyond School Certificate form-work was divided so that different groups specialized in a different subject. The list of subjects available included Modern Languages.

126 As a member of the British Association attending the Indian Science Congress in Agra, Vaughan fell and fractured his thigh while visiting the Taj Mahal and died some weeks later, in February 1938, from pneumonia and shock (Newsome, *op. cit.*, 312; biography of Dr Vaughan by H. C. Bradby in *Dictionary of National Biography 1931-1940*).

127 The date of Vaughan's death (1938) is not given by Peers, but a space was left for its insertion. Doubtless Peers meant to look it up in his 'obituary' (see above, note 123).

French was being found to Terracher, who had gone [/been called] to the newly-reorganised University of Strasbourg,[128] had suggested to the Dean of the Faculty that I might be invited temporarily to do this work after Christmas until the election was made.[129] I have no doubt that Kastner, being the good fellow he was, also pressed my claims for the permanent Spanish post upon Liverpool, but if so [/he did] I knew nothing of it at the time. What I had to decide was if I would accept a joint French and Spanish post for one term only — and it was characteristic of my relations with [/the way people regarded] Vaughan that, instead of even attempting to decide by myself what was really my own affair entirely, I took the telegram straight to his study and asked his help [/for his counsel].

He, of course, knew no more than I of the conditions at Liverpool and I doubt if, had I realized what they really were, I should have had the courage to go. But he said that, considering I was young, unmarried and really enthusiastic about Spanish, the risk was worth taking. Further, he said, if I were not given a renewal of the appointment, he would take me back at the end of the spring term.

This was more than I had ever expected; and, full of gratitude, I decided, on his further advice, to go up to Liverpool by the night train on the following Saturday (it would not have done to miss a day's school!) and spy out the land for myself. I well remember the moment of my departure. As I passed the Master's house, which was on the road leading out of the College grounds, I heard coming from somewhere on my left a roar not unlike that of the proverbial bull of Bashan.[130] I turned — and it was Vaughan, who had espied me from a side room, flung up the window and thrust about half his great body through it.

'Good-luck', he roared — 'and don't be late coming back!'

---

128 *Cf.* above, p. 109, note 96. At its meeting on 14 October 1919 the Faculty of Arts was formally informed of Professor Terracher's resignation of the Chair of French. Professor Kastner was appointed to give assistance in the Department of French during the Autumn Term 1919.

129 Peers has deleted the following words, still legible after 'made': 'and at the same time be given the chance to show what I could do at Spanish'.

130 The proverbial comparison, 'to roar like a bull of Bashan' is based on Psalm 22, verses 12-13.

One Sunday morning [/It was on the last Sunday of November], 1919,[131] at six o'clock in the morning, [that] I first made the acquaintance of Liverpool. The city was dingy and grey, as it always is, and deserted, as any city would be at that hour of a Sunday. The Dean of the Faculty [of Arts, it seemed,] lived at Birkenhead on the other side of the Mersey; my appointment with him was for three; and, even after a leisurely toilet and a long breakfast at the old North-Western Hotel, there was more than enough time to [admire the architecture of St George's Hall and to] pace the [empty] streets of the city that was to be my home.[132] Matters were not improved by the fact that the railway which runs under the Mersey was closed till midday on a Sunday and one had to cross to Birkenhead by the Ferry, not easy for a new-comer to find, and then to walk to Birkenhead Park up some of the dingiest streets I have ever seen before or since [/imaginable]. Garmon Jones,[133] the Dean, proved to be a young Welshman of about thirty-five, who lived alone in a big house[134] with his mother, a charming old lady

---

131 Sunday, 30 November 1919.

132 The North Western Hotel, Lime Street, Liverpool, was built in 1868-71 to designs by Alfred Waterhouse and was designed to be integrated with the adjacent Lime Street Station. Nowadays no longer a hotel, it is known as Lime Street Chambers. St George's Hall (completed in 1856 to designs by Harvey Lonsdale Elmes and C. R. Cockerell) has been described by Sir Nikolaus Pevsner as 'the freest neo-Grecian building in England and one of the finest in the world' (*The Buildings of England: Lancashire. I: The Industrial and Commercial North* [Harmondsworth: Penguin, 1969], 155).

133 William Garmon Jones (1884-1937) was born at Birkenhead and studied at the University of Liverpool, where he came under the influence of the Professor of History, J. M. Mackay; he graduated B.A. Hons First Class in History in 1908. After graduating, he held various posts in History, including that of Senior Lecturer. He was appointed Associate Professor of History 1924-37 and University Librarian 1928-37. He was Dean of the Faculty of Arts, 1916-20 and 1926-28. See *The Dictionary of Welsh Biography down to 1940*; Kelly, *For Advancement of Learning. The University of Liverpool 1881-1981*. See too below, ch. 5, p. 146, note 18; 'B.T.', ch. III, p. 279, note 48.

134 Garmon Jones, then a bachelor (he married in 1923), lived at Elm House, Ashville Road, Birkenhead (*The University of Liverpool Students' Handbook*, editions of 1918-19 — 1920-21). W. E. Collinson (see above, p. 108, note 90; below, ch. 5, p. 139, note 1) mentions the Dean's mother in his unpublished autobiographical account, 'Portraits from the Past', as follows: 'His mother, whom many of us met in his home near Birkenhead Park, was from Mold'.

who tried to put me at my ease by asking me to help her choose cushion-covers. I found the Dean extraordinarily pleasant, but also (as well he might be, had I only known it) extraordinarily uncommunicative about the situation at the University. All he told me was that Fitzmaurice-Kelly had accepted the London professorship in 1916 [/three years previously]; [that, in the interval], the [Spanish] Department had more or less lapsed;[135] that a Spaniard from the city engaged to do the work temporarily, had generally failed to come to his classes; and that I should find the teaching light and elementary. The French, on the other hand, was of full Honours standard.[136] As to the future, both the French and the Spanish Professors would be elected in the summer and I should probably be retained till then but not longer.

Viewed in the dim light of the London express on a Sunday evening in November it did not seem exactly promising. But, though little suspecting all that lay ahead, I had not the slightest doubt of the wisdom of accepting it.[137] I told Vaughan

---

[135] Following the resignation of Professor Fitzmaurice-Kelly from the Chair, the only minutes of the Faculty of Arts on the subject of arrangements for teaching Spanish between 1916 and 1919 date from October 1918 (recommending teaching provision for Session 1918-19 to the extent of £100 p.a.); February and June 1919 (empowering the Vice-Chancellor and the Faculty's Officers and Mr Montgomery to make arrangements for the teaching of Spanish to students in the Faculty in Session 1918-19 and in the Autumn Term 1919 respectively); and October 1919 (when Señor J. V. Varela was appointed to conduct the Intermediate and Final classes in Spanish). The only person bearing the surname Varela in *Gore's Directory of Liverpool*, 1920 and 1921 editions, is Gustavo M. Varela, Chilean Consul-General. The University Press Cuttings for the period do not make any reference to Spanish teaching at the University, and no External Examiner in Spanish was appointed for Sessions 1917-18 and 1918-19. In April 1919 the University Registrar wrote to a Dr J. Azurdia of Liverpool, referring to the salary of the latter for 'lectures in Spanish at the University'; the same Dr José Azurdia was one of the applicants for the Gilmour Chair in May 1919. At the date of his application, Dr Azurdia, who had trained as a physician and surgeon in Guatemala, was the master of Spanish at the Liverpool High School of Commerce.

[136] It should be noted that in his last two sessions at Liverpool Professor Fitzmaurice-Kelly had also been responsible for the Department of French (during the absence of Professor Terracher on war service in France).

[137] At its meeting on 16 December 1919, the University's Council approved the recommendation of the Senate that Mr Peers 'be appointed to take charge of the Department of Spanish, and to give assistance in the

of my decision and he congratulated me. 'You will do well there', he said.

I entered the University of Liverpool as a Junior [Ungraded] Lecturer (temporary) in French and Spanish on January [12?][138] 1920. [I have remained at the University of Liverpool ever since.][139]

---

Department of French for the Lent Term, 1920, at a salary of £200'. This was the recommendation made by the Faculty of Arts at its meeting on 3 December; there is no preamble to this recommendation or previous minute referring to the Dean's meeting with Mr Peers. At the same time, Monsieur Renault was appointed to take charge of the Department of French for the Lent Term, 1920, at a salary of £100. Peers' salary was fixed at £600 p.a. in 1920-21 and 1921-22; on appointment to the Chair of Spanish it became £800 p.a., rising to £900 p.a. from 1926-27, and £1,000 p.a. from 1933-34. For some years his salary as professor remained lower than those of some other professors in the Arts Faculty, including those of Professors Campagnac (£1,100 from 1 October 1920) and Collinson (£1,000 from 1 October 1920).

138 The question mark is Peers' own. The Lent Term, in fact, commenced on Thursday, 8 January 1920. Though no record was made of the names of those who attended, Peers might have attended a meeting of the University's teaching staff, chaired by the Vice-Chancellor, on Monday, 12 January, at which it was unanimously decided that a Liverpool Association of University Teachers be formed.

139 As indicated, Peers added, in pencil, the final sentence of this chapter. It is a significant addition, although Peers could not have known when he wrote it that he would die still in post as Gilmour Professor in 1952.

# PART II

# LIVERPOOL

# CHAPTER 4[1]

## PROBATION

When I began work at the University of Liverpool I was completely disillusioned about schoolmastering — that is to say, I had a pretty sound idea of the advantages and disadvantages of the profession and of the weaknesses of the men who engaged in it. But I was not in the least cynical about it: my original idealism had merely been corrected by seven years of the real thing. I loved teaching; I loved [/enjoyed] school life; I loved [/was thoroughly interested in] boys.[2] Even today, I vastly prefer the give-and-take of the classroom to the somewhat statuesque attitude of the lecturer[,] and the stress which I have always laid upon the importance of contact between universities and schools is probably not unconnected with the [/a personal] pleasure which I always get from school visits [/derived from any and every school visit].[3]

---

1   Peers describes this section of his straightforward autobiography (which we have called 'Part II'), as 'Part I. Liverpool'; and, therefore, this fourth chapter, which he entitled 'Probation', in the manuscript is 'Chapter I'. Evidently Peers regarded the preceding section as an 'Introduction' (*cf*. ch. 1, p. 61, note 1). Also, clearly he intended, at a later date, to add a Part II to his undisguised memoirs — an intention which, because of his relatively early death, was never realized (*cf*. Editorial Commentary, pp. 40-41).
2   As indicated, Peers had originally written: 'I loved teaching; I loved school life; I loved boys'. Perhaps, on reflection, he judged that the third comment might be open to misinterpretation.
3   During thirty-two years at the University of Liverpool Peers was indefatigable in his promotion of the teaching of Spanish, to which end he regularly visited, and corresponded with, schools — especially, but not exclusively, schools on Merseyside. He gave talks, held courses, established contacts with schoolteachers, published collections of graded passages for translation and other books to assist language-teaching. Repeatedly he asked and persuasively answered the questions, 'Why Learn Spanish?', and 'How Can We Introduce Spanish?' (an essay published in the *Bulletin of Spanish Studies*, XXII [1945], no. 87, 113-38). See also below note 11.

But during the last months of my career as a schoolmaster there were things I was growing to love [/appreciate] even more. I began to realise [/Introspection showed] that the boys in whom I had been most interested were those in the highest classes and the prospect of having to do with them exclusively [/to do exclusively with young people] between the ages of eighteen and twenty-two was a most attractive one. Writing, investigation, discovery, research — for which it was so hard to find time or opportunity in a county school — were month by month becoming more of a passion with me. Spanish — so tardily begun and so slowly cultivated — was now the only language in which I had any living interest:[4] at a university, one would [/as a university teacher, I should] have a far greater scope for popularizing it and furthering its study than in any school. Most attractive of all was the combination of research with the study of Spanish literature. The field was a vast uncultivated garden, neglected by most horticulturalists and choked with weeds. In whichever direction one looked, there was work [crying out] to be done. I had myself, in what had even then become my own favourite period — the early nineteenth century — several projects in hand: a critical edition of the Catalonian poet Manuel de Cabanyes;[5] a biographical and critical study of the Duque de Rivas;[6] a book on the Unhappy Romantic [in Western European literature] which never materialized; a history of the Romantic Movement in Spain,[7] which saw the light only in 1940.[8] A small edition of selected poems by Alfred

---

[4] Peers altered these words in pencil to read: Spanish 'was the language in which I had by far the greatest interest'.

[5] *The Poems of Manuel de Cabanyes*, ed. E. A. Peers, with critical introduction, notes, and bibliography (Manchester: Manchester U. P./ London: Longmans Green & Co., 1923).

[6] His *Ángel de Saavedra, Duque de Rivas. A Critical Study* was reprinted from vol. LVIII of *Revue Hispanique* (New York and Paris, 1923), 1-600.

[7] In the margin, next to these references, Peers writes: 'Referred to more vaguely in introd$^n$.'

[8] E. Allison Peers, *A History of the Romantic Movement in Spain*, 2 vols (Cambridge: Cambridge U. P., 1940). In the Preface to vol. I, Peers states: 'In one sense this History of the Romantic movement has been in preparation for twenty years; for it was in 1918 that I decided to attempt such a task and drafted the plan of a book which to-day seems illuminatingly unlike this one' (xv). See also above, ch. 3, p. 112, note 110.

de Vigny[9] and a study, [written] in collaboration with a brilliant young London graduate, Margery Finch, on the origins of the Romantic movement in France,[10] were already behind me. The future was to be for Spain.

One of the first enterprises which I undertook at Liverpool was to found the University of Liverpool Summer School of Spanish.[11] It may not be irrelevant to quote here the final

---

9  *Poèmes choisis*, edited, with a critical introduction, was published in the Modern Language Texts series (Manchester: Manchester U. P./London: Longmans Green & Co., 1918). See also below, 'B.T.', ch. I, p. 181, note 33; Appendix I, p. 431.

10  M. B. Finch and E. Allison Peers, *The Origins of French Romanticism* (London: Constable, 1920). Margery Finch was the youngest of the fifteen original members of the Modern Humanities Research Association (as it became entitled). 'When she died, [she] had just begun to work in the field of French Literature' (E. A. Peers in the Association's *Annual Bulletin*, (Dec. 1932), no. 11, 1; see also ch. 3, p. 104, note 75.

11  In a pencilled note in the margin, Peers asks himself: 'Referred to later?'. The Summer School was held at the University for the first time from 30 August to 15 September 1920 and attended by sixty-five students ('largely attended by University students as well as teachers and others in the district', University Annual Report, 1920, 44). In his 'brief statement of my work here since my first appointment', incorporated in his application for the Chair of Spanish, November 1921 (Appendix I), Peers described the chief aims of the Summer School as:

> (1) to raise the standard of work in the Department [of Spanish], and particularly to supply its greatest need, — an intensive pre-Matriculation course, which together with Courses A and B will enable a capable student having learned no Spanish at school to compete successfully with others who have done so; (2) to attract promising students to the University to read for the new Honours School of Spanish or for the School of Modern Languages with Spanish as one language; (3) to encourage and promote the study of Spanish in Liverpool and district; (4) to set on foot active measures of co-operation between the University and Spanish Universities and institutions, in view of possible future developments.

A letter written by the Vice-Chancellor, Dr J. G. Adami [14 November 1920], to His Excellency Don Alfonso Merry del Val, at the Spanish Embassy (clearly at Peers' request) refers to the 'vacation course in Spanish' at Liverpool, 'this last summer', and suggests 'that it might be well to place before your Government the relative advantages of Liverpool, and our University here, for graduate students [from Spain]'. Adami adds 'we have naturally, at the University, a strong Spanish Department, and a large body of persons keenly interested in Spanish life and letters' (from the Vice-Chancellor's Letter Book, vol. 28, 495-96). A similar letter was sent

words[12] of my concluding address to that first summer session as an illustration of the spirit in which I attacked my new work:

> Both in the pursuit of literary research and in our everyday reading and colloquial use of the language, we are continually met by chasms which have never yet been bridged. And if these are obstacles to rapid progress, they are obstacles which we shall gain immeasurably by surmounting. And more than that, they give us that unusual and fascinating sensation of being *the first on the ground*.
>
> ...How much work then remains for us to accomplish! These chasms unbridged — we must bridge them! These fields to be tilled — we are the tillers! These books which no one has written — it is for us, by example or encouragement to be responsible for their production! Why talk only of French and German — of gardens well dug and neatly planted, so crowded with gardeners that there is hardly a corner left to work in, hardly a weed to be up-rooted? Give me the moorland to reclaim, the waste land to dig, the pathless *sierras* to climb, the forest where the way has to be hewn as we go!...
>
> With that charge, to students who are going as explorers — and let us hope as missionaries — to students who have proved themselves prepared for the solid work which the pursuit of this ideal involves, we must bring our class to a close. Our first Summer School of Spanish at Liverpool is over, and our work has come — to a beginning.

I started my Liverpool career, then, almost as idealistically as I had started my career as a schoolmaster. True, [a maturer reflection on] my Cambridge years and the attitude taken to the new Research Association by some of the Cambridge dons had shown me that not all University teachers had the highest conception of their office. But I was young enough — only twenty-eight — to assume that these were rare exceptions; and I certainly believed that [...][13]

---

simultaneously by the Vice-Chancellor to Don José Castillejo, Secretary of the Junta para Ampliación de Estudios. Reference is made to this approach in Peers' application for the Chair of Spanish, 1921 (Appendix I, pp. 435-36).

12 Peers, in a note, in pencil, in the margin, writes: '(Deprecate its language)'. The language of the 'purple' passage quoted is, indeed, excessively, and emotionally, rhetorical. Some twenty-five years after he had written it, not unnaturally, Peers preferred a more restrained style.

13 'men and women who had the highest academic qualifications, who dealt exclusively with things of the mind... might be counted upon to lead the

[...] I contrasted rather wistfully with the [genial] warmth of Felsted and Wellington. But what [/The one thing] I should never have thought it possible to find was an atmosphere of self-seeking, intrigue and entirely unprovoked enmity. Yet it was in this that I found myself unsuspectingly immersed at the end of a few terms at Liverpool. It was the last of the great disillusions that life has up to now had in store for me. I shall always be grateful to the upbringing I had had, which had taught me to rise above even the unspeakable pettinesses of jealous men, and for the good friends who stood by me through a long period of trial which, solely by their efforts, culminated in victory. My enemies — or, more correctly, those who opposed me, for the struggle was more objective than it seemed — always treated me, once the battle was over, with the greatest kindness as both they and the rest of my colleagues have done ever since. I can tell the story of their defeat without a suspicion of either bitterness [/malice] or vainglory: my only feelings have been distress that such a pitiful occurrence was possible at a University and a determination that in any sphere in which I had any power to prevent it, a similar thing should not happen again.

But to say this is to step in front of my story for almost two years and I must first describe those years, which I spent in Liverpool as a lecturer.

No [/Few] more unpleasant contrasts can be imagined, within the limits of Great Britain, than to come from life in a great college standing in its own grounds among the pine forests of Berkshire to a non-resident university, built in the worst Victorian style, and standing in the slums of Liverpool.[14] For

---

lives of scholars'. A large part of page 66 has been excised and transferred to 'B.T.'; see ch. III, p. 284 — italicized.

14 Peers changed the wording, in pencil, to produce a slightly less critical description: standing 'at the outskirts of the Liverpool slums'. The majority of the early buildings of the University, situated at the top of Brownlow Hill, were designed by the leading British architect of the era, Alfred Waterhouse, (and his son, Paul), and erected over the period 1884-1904 — 'Probably the most extensive group of buildings in his best-known style'. Waterhouse's recent biographers concede that appreciation of his work has been slow in coming: 'the aggressiveness of his harsh red terracotta and the relative coarseness of his ornament still sometimes militate against enjoyment' (Colin Cunningham and Prudence Waterhouse, *Alfred Waterhouse 1830-1905: Biography of a Practice* [Oxford: Clarendon Press, 1992], 1, 129).

that, quite frankly, is where our redbrick[15] [/Liverpool] university is. The description of it generally given to strangers is 'behind the Adelphi' — which sounds well, for the Midland Adelphi [, as every American tourist knows,] is one of the finest-looking, as well as one of the most comfortable city hotels in the country.[16] What the stranger actually does is to leave the Adelphi behind and climb Brownlow Hill, a steep street of filthy houses and shops, almost all of which, in a [really] progressive country, would be pulled down [without delay].[17] In those days

---

At Liverpool, general criticism of the University's principal building, Waterhouse's Victoria Building (1889-92) was being voiced in the local press by 1909, possibly by Charles Reilly (Professor of Architecture, 1904-33) who later condemned this 'red and brown brick and terra-cotta building' for 'looking like a less prosperous Prudential Insurance [building]', employing ugly, hard, coarse materials (Reilly, *Scaffolding in the Sky: A Semi-architectural Autobiography*, 68-70).

15 Interestingly, within his straightforwardly autobiographical account, Peers, on second thought, preferred *not* to use the term 'redbrick university' to describe the University of Liverpool.

16 The Midland Adelphi Hotel (nowadays the Britannia Adelphi Hotel), Ranelagh Place, was completed in 1912 to the designs of Frank Atkinson, one of the architects of Selfridges, London. Owned by the London Midland and Scottish Railway Company, the hotel was built to accommodate the wealthy passengers staying the night before and after sailing across the Atlantic — on the liners of the Cunard Steamship Company, which then had its offices in Liverpool. It was the third Adelphi Hotel to be built on the site. For photographs of the exterior and interiors of the hotel, taken in 1912 and 1914, see Priscilla Boniface, *Hotels & Restaurants 1830 to the Present Day* (HMSO for the Royal Commission on Historical Monuments England, 1981), plates 6-11.

17 In his posthumously published autobiography (*Ramsay Muir: An Autobiography and Some Essays*, edited by Stuart Hodgson [London: Lund Humphries & Co. Ltd., 1943]), Ramsay Muir recalls entering University College, Liverpool, as a student in 1889: 'When I entered it, the main part of the college was... in a slum district, with a huge workhouse on one side, and on the other the Royal Infirmary with its medical school... The street [i.e. Brownlow Hill] which climbed the hill from the city to the College — about a quarter of a mile long — contained twenty-two public houses and a number of sordid shops; the pavements were haunted by slatternly women and bare-foot street Arabs...' (23). In June 1903 Professor A. W. W. Dale, Principal of University College, Liverpool, wrote to the chairman of Liverpool Health Committee about access to the College from the centre of the City and from all three railway stations being by 'a thoroughfare that is always squalid and often unsavoury. As a result of this state of affairs, a large proportion of our

there were no trams on the hill,[18] and one would stumble over mangy animals and dirty [/filthy] children performing their natural functions on [/engaged in fouling] the pavement, and pass alluring invitations to 'come down into the cellar for your olive-oil', 'have your hair cut for half price — this morning only' or 'buy our meat and receive one sausage free'. At the top of the hill were the University buildings and across the road was a railway cutting[19] from which the Lime Street expresses belch smoke so that nothing in our academic precincts can be kept clean for so long as a day.[20]

---

citizens never enter the district... and know nothing except by hearsay of the work that is being carried on within its [the College's] walls. This isolation, which I am convinced is largely due to the character of our surroundings, is a serious obstacle to progress and success...' (University Archives, Liverpool, Principal's Letter Book, vol. 7, 341). In a poem 'Impressions of Brownlow Hill, August 1916' published in *The Sphinx* (the Magazine of the Guild of Undergraduates in the University of Liverpool), vol. XXXIII, no. 1, 24 January 1917, 28, 'K.D.T.W.' wrote, in his first verse:

> Oh! Brownlow Hill was never a joke.
> But a gloomy desert of grime and smoke.
> Where Solomon Levi sold his wares.
> And hens rode in prams or even bath chairs.

This poem was reprinted in *Guild Gazette*, vol. 3, no. 9, 6 December 1938, with a postscript: 'Impression in August 1938 — It hasn't changed much'. Professor Louis Rosenhead (Professor of Applied Mathematics, 1933-73) recalled his first visit to Liverpool [in c.1932]: 'I explored Mount Pleasant, Brownlow Hill, and Paddington, on foot, and I saw how down-at-heel the University was, as well as the houses and the people in its immediate environs. For the first time in years I saw boys running barefoot in the streets... Some boys had neither jacket nor overcoat. There were many public houses in the area, but everything was much quieter then than now, I think!' (Louis Rosenhead, *When I Look Back 1933-1973* [Liverpool: Univ. of Liverpool, n.d. (1975)], 2).

18 The *Liverpool Daily Post*, 12 October 1935, reproduced a photograph of 'a new tram track being laid in Brownlow Hill. It forms part of a number of new routes to be opened shortly'.

19 The open railway cuttings on the main line from Lime Street Station which ran through the University precinct were in the main covered (rafted) over in 1961-65. The last steam trains to run on this line ran in 1965.

20 The popular image of 'Victorian' cities like Liverpool at this time, which contemporary novelists both reflected and helped to create, was of places of industrial pollution, unpleasant smells, and dense smoke. That image was accurate in reality in certain parts of urban areas.

In [/During] the last few years Brownlow Hill has acquired the odour of sanctity, since the Roman Catholic Metropolitan Cathedral is being erected on a site immediately opposite the main University building.[21] But at that time there was only the odour! And though, as I was to discover [/one soon discovered], it became worse in summer than in winter, it was quite bad enough to decide me to look for lodgings at the top of the hill, so as to have to climb it as little as possible.

I found them in a long and dismal street called 'Bedford Street South'[22] — the name had a double [/two-fold] suggestion of the pit whence I was [/had been] digged[23] but the suggestion hardly mitigated the drabness of the reality. I occupied the first-floor front; had three large windows, [...][24]

[...] 'Yavent-et-it-all, Mr. Peers!'

Five months of Bedford Street South, even when relieved by a five-weeks visit to Spain during the Easter vacation,[25] were as

---

21 The Catholic Archdiocese of Liverpool in 1930 acquired the site of the Liverpool Workhouse, following its closure. On the majority of the site was erected the Metropolitan Cathedral of Christ the King, commencing with the crypt, designed by Sir Edwin Lutyens, as part of an overall scheme for a vast baroque cathedral. Built 1933-40, the crypt was solemnly opened in 1958; and the remainder of the cathedral was completed, to the designs of Sir Frederick Gibberd, in 1963-67.

22 The University Registrar addressed letters of 4 May and 28 June 1920 to Peers at 160 Bedford Street South. The 1920 and 1921 editions of *Gore's Directory of Liverpool* record a Miss Ellen Marion Randall at this address. On the site of the property, on the west side of Bedford Street South close to the junction with Canning Street, nowadays stands the Deutsche Kirche Liverpool.

23 This word-play provides another example of Peers' gently self-mocking wit. His 'digs' (bed and board) at the top of the hill were an improvement on conditions lower down in the 'pit' of the slums; nevertheless they were drab and depressing.

24 'never clean for more than a few hours'. At this point Peers has removed, as usual with scissors, most of the rest of p. 69. One may assume that he considered that he was providing more detail about Liverpool than was necessary here, to set the scene in which his experiences took place. For the text of the extracted passages see 'B.T.', ch. III, p. 287 — italicized.

25 In a marginal note Peers wonders whether he should '?enlarge' the allusion to that Spanish vacation.

much as I could possibly endure. After the summer term began, therefore, I made [...]²⁶

[...] two districts, reached by train were free from both these reproaches. One was the Formby-Southport region, which had the disadvantage that the train landed you at the Exchange Station,²⁷ a mile and a half from the University. The other was the Hoylake-West Kirby corner of the Dee estuary, where I settled in October 1920, and, except for a two-year interval, have made my home ever since.²⁸ I well remember the keen winter's day on which I first went out in one of the comfortless, unheated trains of the old Wirral Railway, and as I walked along the Hoylake promenade, inhaled pure, clean air for the first time since leaving Berkshire. On my second visit, I walked over the Grange hills in full view of the Dee with the gorse glowing in the spring sunshine. On my third — and it was on the next day but one after the second — I went house-hunting.

It will be gathered that at the end of my first term I had been re-appointed for a second,²⁹ and, after a brief consideration and a week-end consultation with Vaughan, had decided to cut loose from Wellington [and the world of school]. I had not, of course, forgotten that I was still technically a candidate for the Gilmour Chair, and from time to time during my first term used to make discreet enquiries as to when the list of candidates

---

26 'prospecting excursions into the suburbs'. A paragraph has been cut from p. 70 (see 'B.T.', ch. III, pp. 287-88 — italicized). In the margin (which remains) Peers has written 'First class trams' (a reference to the fact that transport in West Kirby was better than in Liverpool?).

27 Exchange Station, Tithebarn Street, erected 1884-86. The Station closed in 1977 and the area was redeveloped; all that remains nowadays of the old buildings is the stone facade of the former Exchange Hotel, now incorporated into a new office block at Mercury Court.

28 22 Shrewsbury Road, West Kirby is the address recorded in the 1921-22, 1922-23, 1923-24, and 1927-28 editions of the *University of Liverpool Students' Handbook*. He is recorded at 16 Mannering Road, Sefton Park, Liverpool in the editions of 1924-25 and 1925-26 (published in 1924 and 1925 respectively), and at 'The University' in the edition of 1926-27. From the edition of 1928-29 (published in 1928) he is recorded at 12 Eddisbury Road, West Kirby, the house he continued to occupy until his death (in the David Lewis Northern Hospital, Liverpool) in December 1952.

29 The University Council, 16 March 1920, accepted the Senate's recommendation that he be [re]appointed for the Summer Term 1920 and that he be paid £200 for his services.

might be expected to come out of cold storage. I did not then know that the indefinite holding up of elections to Chairs was a pastime in which Liverpool University too often indulged (and occasionally, I am afraid, indulges still)[30] and the general reticence caused me great mystification.[31] However, at the beginning of the summer term I received a notification from the Dean of the Faculty that I had been placed on the short list and was required to attend for interview on an afternoon in May.[32] Mystery still hung over the proceedings, for neither before nor after the ordeal did I set eyes on any of my rivals. Some time afterwards I learned that there were two of these, both

---

30 In some (perhaps more than some) instances appointments were indefinitely delayed for reasons of economy. Shortly after Peers' appointment to the Chair of Spanish, the Faculty of Arts in December 1922 agreed unanimously to a motion (moved by Mr Garmon Jones) which recorded the Faculty's grave concern at the suspension of the Andrew Cecil Bradley Chair of English Literature 'whereby one of its most important departments is seriously crippled and its prestige diminished', and urged upon Senate the necessity of making representations to Council against the policy of suspending Chairs without first consulting the academic bodies. The Council had taken this action because of the financial position of the University. In other cases, delays in filling Chairs in the Faculty of Arts probably resulted from divisions of opinion on the candidates, as in the cases of the King Alfred Chair of English Literature and the Brunner Chair of Economics, both in 1926; these departments were placed in the charge of individual lecturers until the Chairs were finally filled, in 1929 (by enquiry and invitation) and 1930 (in effect by invitation) respectively. Consultation of the list of professors, Appendix II, in Kelly, *For Advancement of Learning. The University of Liverpool 1881-1981*, reveals, in the case of Chairs in the Faculty of Arts, vacancies of one or more years in a few Chairs in the mid-late 1940s: they included the Baines Chair of English Language and Philology (vacant during 1943-45), the Andrew Geddes and John Rankin Chair of Modern History (vacant during most of 1943-45), the Chair of Mediaeval History (vacant during most of 1940-45), and the Bowes Chair of Russian (vacant during most of 1949-56).

31 Peers originally wrote, more simply: 'I was really mystified at the general reticence'.

32 Peers is evidently mistaken as to the month; for the interview took place on 9 February 1920 (see Appendix I, p. 417). Peers, in pencil in the margin, writes: 'c'd describe the interview'. There is a description of Jim Livewire's interview for the Chair of English Literature at Redbrick University (presumably based on Peers' own interview for the Gilmour Chair of Spanish), in 'B.T.', ch. IV, pp. 363-64.

considerably older than myself — Baldomero Sanín Cano,[33] a Colombian journalist then aged [60+?],[34] and reputed to be a [personal] friend of [the late Professor,] Fitzmaurice-Kelly, and Salvador de Madariaga,[35] author of the then recently published *Shelley and Calderon*, who, some years after being rejected at Liverpool,[36] was elected to the Chair at Oxford. Still later

---

33 Baldomero Sanín Cano (1861-1957) was born in Colombia: essayist, critic and philologist; Chief Editor of the *Revista Contemporánea* (Bogotá) 1905-06; London correspondent of *La Nación* (of Buenos Aires) 1915 onwards; in charge of the section of literary criticism in *Hispania*, the monthly Spanish review published in London, 1912-16; Lecturer in Spanish, University of Edinburgh, 1919-20. His Spanish translation of Professor J. Fitzmaurice-Kelly's book on Cervantes was published in 1917 by the Clarendon Press, Oxford, which also published his *An Elementary Spanish Grammar* (1918) and *Spanish Reader* (1920), both in The Oxford Spanish Series which Professor Fitzmaurice-Kelly edited 1918-23. By the time of his application (1919) for the Gilmour Chair Sanín Cano had also had several articles published in *The Modern Language Review* (brief biographical details etc. in *Diccionario de la Literatura Latinoamericana: Colombia* [Washington, U.S.A.: Unión Panamericana, 1959]; also in José A. Nuñez Segura, *Literatura Colombiana: sinopsis y comentarios de autores representativos* [10th ed., Medellín: Editorial Bedout, 1967]; and in *History of the University of Edinburgh 1883-1933*, ed. A. Logan Turner [London: Oliver and Boyd, 1933]). For a list of his publications see *The British Library General Catalogue of Printed Books to 1975*). Sanín Cano acted as the University of Liverpool's External Examiner in Spanish for the July and September 1910 examinations and for Session 1914-15.

34 Peers reminds himself to verify details about Sanín Cano in 'Sp. Am. Lit. or *Who Was Who*', though, in fact, Sanín Cano outlived Peers (note 33).

35 Salvador de Madariaga y Rojo (1886-1978), Spanish essayist, historian, and diplomat. Having given up his profession as an engineer (1916) to go to England, he became head of the Disarmament Section of the League of Nations from 1921 to 1927. In that year he was appointed (first) Professor of Spanish Literature at the University of Oxford. He was Spanish Ambassador to the USA 1931-32 and to France 1932-36. His first book of essays was *Shelley and Calderon, and Other Essays on English and Spanish Poetry* (London: Constable, 1920). See G. G. Brown, *A Literary History of Spain: The Twentieth Century* (London: Benn, 1972); Richard E. Chandler and Kessel Schwartz, *A New History of Spanish Literature* (Louisiana State Univ. Press, 1961); *A Dictionary of Twentieth Century World Biography*, consultant editor Asa Briggs (Oxford: Oxford U. P., 1992); and entries in *Who's Who in Spain* (1st ed., Barcelona, 1963) and *The Oxford Companion to Spanish Literature*, ed. Philip Ward (Oxford, 1978).

36 Madariaga was in fact rejected by the Chair Selection Committee in February 1920. But the new Chair Selection Committee, appointed in October 1921, evidently briefly reconsidered his candidature (28 October

(these elections seemed to take a portentous time!) I was officially informed that, though not considered suitable for the Chair, I could have charge of the Spanish Department (dropping the French) for a further year with the status of a lecturer and three-quarters of [what was then] a Professor's salary.[37] It was not a satisfactory position, for peace of mind is necessary to the production of original work and the selection committee, I was told, required original work of [/from] would-be professors.[38] But I still felt [/realized] my youth; I still loved my [/was still attracted by the] work; and above all I still saw[39] unlimited possibilities for it. So I accepted, reflecting that it was better to be out of work in a year's time than in a term's time, and settled down to a Long Vacation which included a week's lecturing at Oxford, a month's lecturing at Dublin and the organization, at Liverpool, of my first Summer School of Spanish.[40]

[Little idea had I of the clouds that were already dark over my head.] But one day shortly before that summer term came to a close, a very curious thing happened. I was walking down Brownlow Hill to our usual rendez-vous for lunch, the University Club,[41] with a young lecturer of little more than my

---

1921) and, upon later enquiry, were informed (in May 1922) that he had stated he was no longer available (see Appendix I, p. 425).

37   At its meeting on 6 July 1920, the University Council appointed Mr Peers to take charge of the Department of Spanish and to give assistance in the Department of French for the Session 1920-21, at a salary of £600.

38   In the margin Peers wonders whether to '? enlarge' on this point. *Cf.* '(E.A.P.) *Auto*', ch. 5, p. 148, ch. 6, p. 161; 'B.T.', ch. IV, pp. 345-46.

39   In pencil Peers asks: 'Better? Was still conscious of?'

40   See above, note 11.

41   The University Club occupied the upper floors of no. 2, Mount Pleasant, from 1905 until the Club's closure in 1973. The Club had been formed in 1896 to provide a common meeting place for people from the University College and people from the city. Its first Chairman and President was Professor J. M. Mackay, leader of the 'New Testament' group of members of the Faculty of Arts; the 'N.T.' generally met after lunch in the Club's committee room or in one of the member's private rooms at the University. At a meeting of the Club's Committee on 15 January 1920, Peers was elected a member for three months on payment of one guinea; his nomination was supported by the University Registrar, Mr Edward Carey, and by Mr J. Montgomery, Lecturer in Commercial Theory and Practice. When Peers' membership was renewed a year later, the proposer of his nomination was Mr W. Garmon Jones, who was to feature prominently in the debate on Peers' appointment to the Chair of Spanish. Peers continued as a

own age who had done [/seen] some seven years' service at Liverpool. During a momentary pause in our conversation, he suddenly turned to me and said in a low voice [, apparently apropos of absolutely nothing]:

'Have you ever heard of the New Testament?'

If he had said: 'Are you saved, brother?' — I could hardly have been more astounded. I [stared at him and] made no reply.

'All right!' he went on. 'Never mind'.

But I did puzzle during the Vacation as to what he could mean.

---

member of the Club, certainly up to 1932-33. It is ironic, in the light of this debate, that Professor Fitzmaurice-Kelly's candidature for membership of the Club, in October 1909, which had been proposed by Professor Kuno Meyer, was seconded by Professor Campagnac; Professor Reilly, another member, as we shall see, of the 'New Testament', supported the candidature, as did Professor (later Sir) John L. Myres and Mr Edward Carey.

# CHAPTER 5

## THE 'NEW TESTAMENT'

The story of the 'New Testament', which I did not learn till long after the events [just] described in the last chapter, has been skilfully told, from the special angle of the group of people concerned, whose members have always been experts in the accomplishment colloquially termed 'back-scratching', by one of themselves — my former colleague and New Testamentarian, C. H. Reilly.[1] His description of it, however, besides being coloured by the rosy tints of hero-worship, refers, no doubt for good reasons, almost exclusively to its palmy days, before and during the War. My narrative, therefore, which may be taken

---

1   Reilly, *Scaffolding in the Sky: A Semi-architectural Autobiography*, chapter VIII, 'The New Testament'. Amongst the papers of Sir Charles Reilly which his son, the late Lord Reilly, deposited with the University Archives, Liverpool, is a volume of reviews and letters received following publication of his autobiography, which was inaccurate in parts, and 'gossipy', as Sir Charles himself admitted it to be. The majority of his correspondents echoed the sentiments of (later Sir) Robert E. Kelly (Professor of Surgery, 1922-39) who expressed the pleasure which the book had given him but added 'distance *does* lend enchantment — or perhaps it is that age always puts on rose tinted specs' (University Archives, Liverpool, D.207/7/1). An alternative view of the 'New Testament' group is provided by W. E. Collinson (Assistant Lecturer in German, 1913-14; Professor of German, 1914-54; see also ch. 3, p. 108, note 90). See his unpublished essay 'Portraits from the Past', n.d. [written after 1946], concerning the 'New Testament' group portrayed in Albert Lipczinski's painting, c.1914-17, and also their associates (University Archives, Liverpool, D.5/3/). For a poetic description of the characters in this famous painting, see Oliver Elton's poem 'Kaine Diatheke' (reproduced in Appendix II, pp. 460-65). In *Ramsay Muir: An Autobiography and Some Essays* (already mentioned in ch. 4, p. 130, note 17), Ramsay Muir makes reference to the origins of the 'New Testament' in the years before the establishment, in 1903, of the University. Muir, former student and colleague of J. M. Mackay, the first leader of the 'New Testament', provides a description of those we know to have been members (as he himself was for some time) (see *op. cit.*, especially pp. 65, 78-79, 82-83). Peers mentions 'the late Ramsay Muir' in *Redbrick University* (161).

as supplementary to his, will describe how, none too soon, the New Testament met with its fall.

In defence of the group it can be recalled that many prospectors and colonizers have had, for practical reasons, to use methods which, given perfect freedom, they would probably have preferred to leave to others.[2] And the makers of a new University — Liverpool had only received its charter in 1903 — are in many ways like the makers of a nation. The New Testament — 'N.T.' as it called itself — might be condemned, perhaps, not so much for the use of those methods as for the lofty morality with which they cloaked their intrigues; I like to think that some of them even persuaded themselves (or perhaps each other) that the undoubted[3] crookedness of their methods was made up for by the excellence of their intentions.

The University is, of course, a democratic body, the academic business of which is done by the Senate, consisting of the Vice-Chancellor, the Professorial body, the Deans of the five Faculties[4] and the Librarian. The New Testament was a group of members of the Faculty of Arts, most of whom had also seats on the Senate, and who met periodically in secret in order to decide how they would like things done and to see that things were done as they would like them. Quite apart from the influence which individuals of the group could, and did, use on others in favour of whatever they had decided upon, they nearly always got their way for the simple reason that they were united. Like all large committees, a University Faculty is at the mercy of any group with a definite policy except in the rare eventuality of there being a second group with a definite policy as well. This occasionally, but rarely, happened in the Faculty, though one or two of the senior men, who loathed the N.T. and its methods, had the courage to stand out against them and sometimes attracted supporters.

In other words, the aim of the N.T. was to stifle free discussion and prevent a free vote upon any subject upon which they had their collective opinion. 'This caucus', for that is what

---

    2   As a marginal note reveals, Peers is reminded at this point of the conduct of the Spaniards in the New World.
    3   Peers deletes this adjective in pencil.
    4   Faculties of Arts, Engineering, Law, Medicine, and Science.

THE 'NEW TESTAMENT' 141

it was[,] as Reilly naively puts it, was 'careful to hide its identity', for the chief element in its deceptions was to produce at the actual meetings the impression of spontaneity and absence of collusion.* I have myself seen the group in action, and, even when I knew who its members were (for I was a member of the Faculty from October 1920 onwards)[5] I could easily have been deceived by them. One of the seniors would rise — [...][6]

And all this was done, so Reilly tells us, from 'highly honourable' motives, of which he mentions only one — 'to promote the great ideal of academic freedom'. Freedom, forsooth — the freedom to do as I like! [/get my own way!] The forcing of the Faculty into a groove of N.T. manufacture! Only regulations with which the N.T. agreed to be passed. Only professors whom the N.T. approved to be appointed. And who were its members? What claim had they to safeguard the traditions of scholarship which men like Sir Oliver Lodge, Andrew Cecil Bradley, and Sir Walter Raleigh had created?[7] Let us see.

---

\* This, too, Reilly freely avows: 'The secrecy may seem a little childish, but it made any action decided on for the next meeting of the Faculty or Senate seem more spontaneous and consequently more effective' (*Scaffolding in the Sky*, London, 1938, p. 162). [\* denotes Peers' own footnote].

5 At its meeting on 23 June 1920 the Faculty of Arts agreed that Peers be recognised as a member of Faculty for the period during which he was in charge of the Department of Spanish. The record of attendances reveals that he attended almost all of the Faculty's meetings in Sessions 1920-21 and 1921-22.

6 'tall, reverend and unbelievably upright in stature'. Peers has excised most of p. 76 and the first half of p. 77, and, in consequence, his description of the incident at Faculty illustrating the 'N.T.' in action. For the excised piece of description — and additional information on the clique's collusion at meetings of the Faculty — see 'B.T.', ch. III, pp. 320-23 — italicized. The 'upright' stature of the person described indicates that the speaker whom Peers has in mind is Fitzmaurice-Kelly (Professor Upright in 'B.T.').

7 Sir Oliver J. Lodge (knighted in 1902) was the first holder of the Lyon Jones Chair of Experimental Physics at University College, Liverpool, 1881-1900. Professor A. C. Bradley was the first holder of the King Alfred Chair of Modern Literature and English Language (as it was latterly entitled) at the College, 1881-89, his successor in the Chair (1890-1900) being Sir Walter A. Raleigh (knighted in 1911). There are entries for all three of

The founder and leading spirit of the group, J. M. Mackay,[8] had retired from the Chair of Ancient History in 1914 and I knew him only in London, where he came during the War, presumably through the influence of Fitzmaurice-Kelly, to attempt to organize the Anglo-Spanish Society.[9] About his work

---

these renowned scholars in the *Dictionary of National Biography*; an assessment of their work is also provided in Kelly, *For Advancement of Learning. The University of Liverpool 1881-1981*.

8   John Macdonald Mackay (1856-1931), Rathbone Professor of History, 1884-1914; the title of the Chair was changed to that of Ancient History following his retirement in 1914. As Kelly has noted 'as a historian Mackay never made much of a mark' (*For Advancement of Learning*, 118), but his influence on the development of the University College and its transformation into an independent University of Liverpool was very considerable. Ramsay Muir, who himself was a member of the 'New Testament' caucus before he fell out with Mackay, later wrote that 'over the members of this group Mackay exercised an extraordinary domination. Men who were immeasurably his superior in scholarship and achievement, impressed by his masterful personality, regarded him almost as an inspired prophet — as I had done... I have never seen any parallel to the kind of spell he was able to cast' (*Ramsay Muir: An Autobiography and Some Essays*, 65). Mackay retired early from his Chair, perhaps in part recognising his waning influence. In a letter of 19 February 1911 Kuno Meyer (whose resignation from his Chairs of Celtic and German had recently been accepted by the University Council on his appointment as Professor of Celtic Philology in the University of Berlin) wrote to his friend, Mr J. Glyn Davies, Lecturer in Welsh at the University of Liverpool, referring to an unspecified 'tremendous crisis in the Univ... I am in the thick of it and to show you what it all means I may tell you that I have already resigned my seat on the German Chair Committee and am going to resign from the Celtic and Greek Committee as well... As to your future, I now also believe that Liverpool after I am gone is no place for you. The most pathetic thing about it all is to me that Mackay is no longer of any account in the affairs of the University. I believe that quite a number of the staff will clear out as soon as any opportunity offers' (University Archives, Liverpool, ref. Box 159).   That same month the University Council 'willingly' assented to Professor Mackay's application for leave of absence for Session 1911-12.

9   In its obituary of Professor Mackay, the *Liverpool Post and Mercury*, 12 March 1931, stated that 'Professor Mackay left Liverpool soon after his retirement. During the war he was associated with Intelligence work so far as it related to Spain'. D. S. MacColl states that Mackay 'had a doctor brother in Spain' (D. S. MacColl, 'A Batch of Memories VI — A Tender Thistle', *The Week-end Review*, 11 April 1931, 534). In a letter to the editor, published in *The Times*, 5 September 1917, Professor Mackay, as 'Hon. Organising Secretary of the Anglo-Spanish Society, London Chamber of Commerce, 97 Cannon Street', London, refers to the recently held first

THE 'NEW TESTAMENT'    143

in that capacity, the less said the better: he was an elderly man and must have [completely] lost his grip, for at Liverpool his was a name to conjure with. Another most able man, who had left before I came, was Sir Bernard Pares.[10] Fitzmaurice-Kelly[11] had been a journalist who had written nothing of

---

meeting of the general council of the Society; mentions the existence of branches of the Society, established at Oxford, Cambridge, Liverpool, and London; and states that 'this international society is, on our part, a demonstration and a lasting recognition of the friendly sympathy of Spanish lands, as welcome to our own people resident there as are its existence and objects to our Spanish friends who are supporting the common cause against incessant hostile propaganda'. Appended to the letter is a list of the Society's main objects and its principal vice-presidents (who included the Prime Minister), its honorary president (the Spanish Ambassador in London) and president (the British Ambassador at Madrid), and supporters (who included Professor Fitzmaurice-Kelly, Lord Leverhulme, and the Directors of Intelligence of the Foreign Office and the War Office). Among the main objects were 'to stimulate reciprocal study of language, literature, art, and history, and to promote historical research' and 'to advocate, and, if possible, to provide for the endowment of professorships and lectureships in the Spanish language and literature, and the foundation of travelling scholarships'. Most of Mackay's letter and also the appendix were published in *The Times Educational Supplement*, no. 125, 6 September 1917, 348. Some records of the Anglo-Spanish Society survive in the Archives of King's College London, in files relating to the Cervantes Chair of Spanish Language and Literature (KAS/AC2/F344).

10 Peers asked, in the margin, in a pencilled note: 'Was BP a N.T.?'. Professor Sir Bernard Pares (1870-1945), the first holder of the Bowes Chair of Russian History, Language and Literature at the University of Liverpool, 1908-17, was indeed a member of the 'New Testament' group. He features in Lipczinski's painting of the group, and is described by Reilly as 'another eager member' (*Scaffolding in the Sky*, 177). Pares, who previously had been Reader in Modern Russian History at the University (1906-08), left 'a vivid impression' on W. E. Collinson. Collinson describes him as a 'born journalist' who took 'immense trouble in assembling his facts' and wrote with authority and insight on Russia ('Portraits from the Past', 13). Pares served as President of the Modern Humanities Research Association, 1932-33, in succession to Allison Peers. In *Redbrick University* (34) Peers refers with admiration to the achievements of both Pares and Charles Reilly (see below, note 16).

11 Professor James Fitzmaurice-Kelly (1857-1923) was the first holder of the Gilmour Chair of Spanish, 1909-16; he resigned the Chair to take up the newly established Cervantes Chair of Spanish Language and Literature at King's College London. He became a member of the Modern Humanities Research Association in 1919, later becoming a Life Member. Illness prevented him attending, by invitation, a meeting of the Association's

permanent value till he was nearly forty but since that time had acquired a tremendous reputation as a Hispanist from the fact that till late in the War [/chiefly because for many years] he was the only Briton with the slightest claim to Hispanic scholarship. A much finer scholar, and a greater man than any of the rest, was the Romany expert, John Sampson,[12] University Librarian.

---

Committee on 1 March 1919 at which relations between the Association and the *Modern Language Review* were discussed. See too above, ch. 3, pp. 112-13, note 112.   Fitzmaurice-Kelly resigned in 1920, before the age of retirement, from the Cervantes Chair. Fitzmaurice-Kelly was reputed to have been unhappy at King's College, 'constantly grumbling about the other professors' (letter, dated 24 August 1993, from Rosalyn C. Churchman, daughter of the executor of Mrs Julia Fitzmaurice-Kelly, widow of the Hispanist).   No appointment was made to the Cervantes Chair after Fitzmaurice-Kelly's resignation. Owing to an insufficiency of funds, the post was suspended. Instead, a Cervantes *Readership* in Spanish Language and Literature was constituted (King's College Archives PB/M5).   Dr Antonio Ruiz Pastor, who was appointed to this Readership in 1920, finally became Professor (but not *Cervantes* Professor) in 1930.

12   Peers writes in the margin: 'date of Sampson's death not known (not in *Who's Who*).  He retired in 1928'.  Dr John Sampson (1862-1931) was Librarian of University College Liverpool, later the University of Liverpool, 1892-1928. '...He possessed a semi-divine inspiration being endowed with a fertile imagination and a robust constitution. A forbidding exterior concealed a kind heart and witty conversation relieved an aloof bearing. A cultivated man about town, he loved the country for the wind on the heath and talks with his friends as they wandered together. The Gypsies accepted him as one of their own for his skill in searching out their language and literature and named him RAI.   Indeed he became a veritable treasure-house of knowledge on their manners and ways...' (translation by Mr A. N. Ricketts of part of the Latin tribute to Dr Sampson, written by Professor E. T. Campagnac, which is incised on a tablet in the Harold Cohen Library, University of Liverpool).  As Collinson noted ('Portraits from the Past'), Sampson was a man of wide learning, whose interests extended beyond the Welsh Gypsies to William Blake, comparative philology, etc. For brief details of his career, see, too, Kelly, *For Advancement of Learning. The University of Liverpool 1881-1981*, with its references to publications by and about Sampson. Dr Sampson himself contributed some recollections of 'the New Dispensation or the New Testament' which 'stood for a sound constitution and academic rights, on the model of the great Continental Universities' in his valedictory speech at the University Club in 1928 (reported in *The Sphinx*, vol. XXXV, no. 2, 22 November 1928, 40-42). He stated that 'the New Testament, though it lingered on for a time, having achieved its main objects, seems to have perished by its very successes. But though there was perhaps less left to fight for, still something may be said in favour of a body which encouraged due regard for method among those who were already

The remainder can be dealt with very briefly. Oliver Elton,[13] Professor of English Literature, who was in his sixtieth year when I first met him, had built up a reputation largely on personality and a 'Survey' of English Literature, of which only a small part had then been produced. Alexander Mair,[14] Professor of Philosophy, from whose slighting article on research I shall presently quote,[15] was an ex-Dean and an expert in university business, but a nonentity in the world of scholarship. Reilly,[16] Professor of Architecture, was an organizer, who would

---

agreed as to principle. It at least served to restrain the flow of Bright Ideas, often (as the speaker explained) "just thrown out on the spur of the moment" ' (*ibid.*, 40).

13 Oliver Elton F.B.A. (1861-1945) held the King Alfred Chair of English Literature at Liverpool 1901-25. His *Survey of English Literature from 1730 to 1880* was published in six volumes over the period 1912-28. Described by Collinson (in 'Portraits from the Past') as an 'Olympian figure... intellectual he certainly was, deliberate in speech and sparing of words... Elton enjoyed a... well-founded reputation as a literary critic and historian'.

14 Peers comments in the margin: 'Mair died in 1927 (v. below)'. Alexander Mair (1870-1927); Assistant Lecturer, later Lecturer, in Philosophy, 1900-10, and Professor of Philosophy, University of Liverpool, 1910-27; Dean of the Faculty of Arts, 1908-11; President of the University Club, Liverpool, 1921; President of the Association of University Teachers, 1925 (*Who Was Who, 1916-1928*). 'His manner was gentle and at times he seemed to take a serene view of life, though he could be roused to strong emotion... Mair became one of the leaders of the depleted 'New Testament', kept in touch with Fitzmaurice-Kelly and took a leading part in the debates on the Spanish Chair in 1922' (Collinson, 'Portraits from the Past', 19). 'He was fragile physically and died of a weak heart, with his death, we thought, hastened by the fights he felt it his duty to put up' (Reilly, *Scaffolding in the Sky*, 173). In 'An Appreciation' of his friend, Oliver Elton wrote that after joining the staff at Liverpool Mair 'soon joined the "forward" group (as I suppose it may now be fairly called), who were active in the policy of the still new University... I also thought him pre-eminent for ease and address in Senates and places where they talk business. Mair served on every possible kind of academic "body", including the Council, and could never be ignored... He was indeed, a born idealist, in every good sense of that word...' (*The Sphinx*, vol. XXXIV, no. 1, 27 October 1927, 5-6).

15 Peers considered deleting this foregoing clause which he enclosed, in pencil, in square brackets. He does not, in fact, quote from any article by Mair.

16 Sir Charles H. Reilly (1874-1948) (knighted in 1944) was Roscoe Professor of Architecture, 1904-33. Described as 'the father of modern architectural education in Britain' (Gordon E. Cherry and Leith Penny, *Holford, a Study in Architecture, Planning and Civic Design* [London/New York: Mansell, 1986], 10), Reilly established a national and international

have made no claim to be heard on matters of scholarship.[17] Garmon Jones [, Lecturer in History, long Dean and later Librarian,][18] was a cultivated and charming Welshman, who would have made a good Vice-Chancellor, but when he died, all too soon, at fifty-two, had made all too few contributions to learning. The remainder — Case,[19] a delightful but

---

reputation for the Liverpool School of Architecture. 'He made no claim to scholarship... He was a man of action... and made it [the School] during the 1920s into one of the best and easily the most publicized schools of architecture in the world' (Myles Wright, *Lord Leverhulme's Unknown Venture: The Lever Chair and the Beginnings of Town and Regional Planning 1908-48* [London: Hutchinson Benham, 1982], 49). As noted above, Chapter VIII of Reilly's *Scaffolding in the Sky*, is devoted to 'The New Testament'.

17  Before 'scholarship' Peers considered inserting: '?humanistic'.

18  For W. Garmon Jones (1884-1937), see above, ch. 3, p. 120, note 133. Inscribed on a memorial tablet in the University's Harold Cohen Library is a Latin tribute to him which was probably composed by E. T. Campagnac who, upon its unveiling in 1938, provided a (loose) translation:

> William Garmon Jones was... loving guardian of our books: he fostered all the arts with learned care, but gave his mind with supreme devotion to illumine the letters and monuments of his native land. He was a skilful interpreter of our academic laws and regulations, a champion and defender of our liberties, full of wise counsel in all our undertakings. He shewed himself a charming companion, a staunch and true friend...
> 
> (*William Garmon Jones*, University of Liverpool [1938])

In a testimonial provided in May 1919 when Garmon Jones was an applicant for the Principalship of a University College in Wales (probably Aberystwyth), the Vice-Chancellor, Sir Alfred Dale, refers to his scholarship, etc.: '...since he became Dean of our Arts Faculty, I have been impressed by his aptitude for business; by his grasp of principle and his methodical handling of details. He has a clean stroke, and leaves no loose ends or ragged edges. In dealing with his colleagues in the Faculty he has shewn courage, wisdom, and tact. He can bring an awkward team round a dangerous corner as skillfully as any of the men with whom I have had to work... His influence grows steadily, and has met with no set-back... he has the gifts of leadership...' (University Archives, Liverpool, Vice-Chancellor's Letter Book, vol. 27, 679-80). In 1926 Garmon Jones was short-listed for the Principalship of the University College of North Wales, Bangor; in the particular circumstances he preferred to withdraw, rather than compete against another candidate (J. Gwynn Williams, *The University College of North Wales: Foundations 1884-1927* [Cardiff: University of Wales Press, 1985], 425).

19  Robert Hope Case (1857-1944) was Lecturer in Elizabethan Literature, 1906-19, Associate Professor of English Literature, 1907-1919, Andrew Cecil Bradley Professor of English Literature, 1919-23; Dean of the

unproductive person who late in life was given a Professorship which lapsed on his retirement; Newberry,[20] and Bosanquet,[21] archaeologists; and Norman Wyld,[22] secretary of the Extension Board, were, as far as politics were concerned, minor figures. Two more members should perhaps be mentioned: Kuno Meyer, a German professor of German, who was deprived of his Chair during the War,[23] and Cecil Wyld,[24] Professor of English

---

Faculty of Arts, 1913-16. A specialist in Elizabethan studies, he was General Editor from 1909 of the Arden edition of Shakespeare (*Who Was Who, 1941-1950*). As Peers says, the Andrew Cecil Bradley Chair of English Literature lapsed when Case retired. The Chair was later reinstated as a Chair of Modern English Literature, of which, in 1964, Kenneth Allott became the first holder (see Kelly, *For Advancement of Learning. The University of Liverpool 1881-1981*, 347).

20 Percy Edward Newberry (1869-1949), Brunner Professor of Egyptology, 1907-19; 'a quiet, unassuming scholar' (Collinson, 'Portraits from the Past', 5).

21 Robert Carr Bosanquet (1871-1935), Professor of Classical Archaeology, 1906-20; a 'tall, reserved and balanced Northumbrian' (Collinson, 'Portraits from the Past', 6).

22 Norman Wyld, General Secretary of the Society for University Extension in Liverpool and District, 1902-10, Secretary of the University Extension Board, 1910-17.

23 Peers comments, in pencil, in the margin: 'so Reilly says (p. 174) but I thought he [i.e. Meyer] retired in 1911' (Peers adds a note to try the [University] Calendar). Kuno Meyer (1858-1919) was Lecturer in Teutonic Languages and Literature 1884-94, Professor of Teutonic Studies (later German) 1894-1911, Honorary Professor of Celtic 1908-11 and 1913-14. Meyer, in fact, resigned the Chair of German in 1911 to accept the Chair of Celtic Philology at Berlin. It was his Honorary Chair of Celtic of which he was, in effect, deprived in December 1914 (see Kelly, *For Advancement of Learning. The University of Liverpool 1881-1981*, 174-76). 'He was one of the greatest Celtic scholars of his day... His fertility in publication was absolutely outstanding, and most of his work is as important today as it ever was' (the late Professor Kenneth Jackson, quoted in Seán Ó. Lúing, *Kuno Meyer 1858-1919, a Biography* [Dublin: Geography Publications, 1991], 222).

24 Henry Cecil Kennedy Wyld (1870-1945) was Lecturer in English Language, 1899-1904, Baines Professor of English Language and Philology, 1904-20; Merton Professor of English Language and Literature, Oxford University, 1920-45. 'He was Liverpool's best all-round philologist after Kuno Meyer's departure in 1911... a keen member of the N.T. and progressive in his academic views... During term he shared rooms with the aristocratic looking professor of Spanish, Fitzmaurice-Kelly... After I returned in 1919 he [Wyld] seemed to have fallen out with some of his, I dare not say, "comrades" of the N.T. for he was consorting with Professor Campagnac, one of its opponents' (Collinson, 'Portraits from the Past', 9-10).

Language, who, as Reilly blandly puts it, left the N.T. to go 'into the wilderness'. The phrase unconsciously betrays N.T. mentality, though it was used sixteen years after the group fell from power.

Not a word of [all] this had I heard when I walked 'down the hill' (as we say) on that June day of 1920. I had supposed that the proceedings of University bodies were as straight and aboveboard as could be; and, when I had been told that distinguished original work was expected from University professors, I imagined in my simplicity that those who expected it had themselves won distinction. I was soon to find how much I was mistaken.[25]

---

See also *Who Was Who, 1941-1950*; *Dictionary of National Biography 1941-1950*.

25 Concern about the progress of research in various Faculties (particularly the Faculty of Engineering) was voiced by Benjamin Moore (Johnston Professor of Biochemistry, 1902-14) in the Senate in 1913 — a concern which ultimately led the Senate, in 1914, to establish a Committee to consider and report upon research undertaken in the different Faculties. As a result, lists of books and articles published by members of staff were published from 1914 onwards, the ancestors of the University's more recent *Research Supplement to the Annual Report* and the various compilations on research activities and publications submitted to the Universities Funding Council, and now to the Higher Education Funding Council for England.

# CHAPTER 6

# THE GILMOUR CHAIR OF SPANISH

The session 1920-21 passed, and at its conclusion, instead of another interview for the Chair of Spanish, I received an invitation to do the work of the Chair for a further session, with three quarters of a professor's salary and with none of his status.[1] But at the beginning of this new session, things began to move. [In October 1921] a new Committee was appointed to elect a professor: I was the only candidate considered [/on the final list] and the result of the election was made known in the following July. It was hardly the atmosphere (for the election of someone else would have meant the losing of my job [/unemployment]) in which to organise and teach successfully, let alone to produce 'original work of distinction'!

Long before the Committee reported to the Faculty (of which, as I said, I was a member, though [for reasons of etiquette] I did not of course attend the meeting which discussed the report) I became aware of a certain constraint among some of my colleagues both in the University and at the Club: conversations ceased when I approached and professors to whom I had hardly spoken manifested sudden interest in my Departmental or personal activities. In more than eighteen months, I had of course come to know several members of the N.T., though with none of them, except Case, who had showed me real personal kindness, had I become in the least friendly. But it was not so much they whose interest in me I began to notice as a number of other colleagues about which something ought now to be said.

---

1 Peers deleted, in pencil, after 'session', the last part of this sentence. The University Council, 7 June 1921, accepted the Senate's recommendation that he be reappointed 'to take charge of the Department of Spanish for the Session 1921-22, on the same terms and conditions as before'.

Reilly, set upon eulogizing his New Testament heroes, has said hardly anything of the other leading spirits in the Faculty, whose names were at least as distinguished as those of the others and far more worthy of perpetuation. In a moment I am going to describe how some of these — a few of them old adversaries of the N.T. but the majority comparative newcomers who prized independence of honesty[2] and would have no truck with the evil thing — made a determined onslaught upon the caucus — unhappily for me, over my unfortunate body — and routed them for good and all. But first I will try to present them quite irrespectively of the part they played in this battle, merely in order to show how small, in 1921-22, was the academic importance of the caucus (now shorn of Mackay, Pares, Newberry, Wyld and Fitzmaurice-Kelly) by comparison with the Faculty as a whole.

The protagonist in this last battle was E. T. Campagnac,[3] who, everything considered, is perhaps the greatest man the Faculty of Arts has had in this generation. After a brilliant Classical career and a short period spent as an inspector under

---

2  Peers writes 'of honesty' but probably meant to write 'and honesty'.
3  Ernest Trafford Campagnac (1872-1952), Professor of Education, 1908-38; Dean of the Faculty of Arts, 1911-13; Public Orator, 1927-31. 'He was admired for his dignified bearing, his precise classical scholarship, his wit, and his gift of graceful and polished speech... but his wit had an acid quality about it... His aim was not to teach method but to give his students a liberal education' (Kelly, *For Advancement of Learning. The University of Liverpool 1881-1981*, 232, 233); '...a brilliant speaker... Scholarly, cynical and always so hard up that his gas and water were in daily danger of being cut off, he was a thorn in the flesh of slower minds and incompetent colleagues' (P. G. H. Boswell, Professor of Geology, 1917-30, in his unpublished autobiography, University Archives, Liverpool, D4/1, 137). 'Campagnac's conception of education, as shown in his teaching and his writings, was in the best sense of the word humane' (obituary in *The Times*, 14 June 1952). Campagnac had originally been a member of the 'New Testament', but turned against the group when he realized its true nature and function. He was a powerful supporter of Peers, and through his opposition to the 'New Testament' did much to bring about Peers' appointment to the Gilmour Chair of Spanish. For evidence of his support of Peers see, for instance, his letter to the Dean, dated 9 January 1922, passing on the opinion of Professor Milton A. Buchanan that Peers should be given the Chair (mentioned in Appendix I, p. 422). According to Peers, Campagnac delivered in Senate 'a magnificent speech' in Peers' favour (see below, p. 163).

the Board of Education, he came to Liverpool as Professor of Education in 1908 and remained in that post for exactly thirty years. His original work, despite an enormous burden of administrative duties, was both considerable in volume and exquisite in quality. But it was as a man that Campagnac wielded the greatest influence. He had presence and he had power. I have never seen anyone, other than a professed contemplative, who gave such clear signs that he lived in a world known to too few. His idealism was overpowering. He could love and he could hate magnificently. What he hated was what he believed with his whole soul to be evil and against it he would do battle with all his might, even if he knew that every single man in the room was against him. And yet, strange to say, his *rôle* in debate was again and again that of the peacemaker. For if he thought, as he often did, that compromise was the right solution he would plead for it as winningly as he would have opposed it fiercely had he believed it to be wrong. Incidentally, he had the finest command of English that I have ever heard in a University speaker. His short term as Public Orator of the University was a joy; and when he rose in his deliberate way to speak in Faculty or Senate, the whole company, however dull the debate had been, was at once electrified into attention. I am proud that he fought for me and I have always felt it an inspiration [in my work] that he thought me worth fighting for.

Three men, all much younger than Campagnac, but appointed to their Chairs only six years after him, also refused to bow the knee to Baal and scorned any but straightforward politics. C. K. Webster,[4] who unhappily left us, while still young, for Aberystwyth and then for London, is one of the best-known modern historians in the country. A tall, hearty,

---

4   Sir Charles Kingsley Webster, F.B.A. (1886-1961) (knighted in 1946), Andrew Geddes and John Rankin Professor of Modern History, 1914-22; Professor of International Relations, University College of Wales at Aberystwyth, 1922-32; Professor of International History, London School of Economics, 1932-53. 'His temperament was sanguine; he was optimistic, appreciative, and friendly... Sometimes impatient or tactless, he was not sensitive to the impression made by his outspoken opinions; but he was so transparently a man of good will that he had no enemies' (G. N. Clark, 'Sir Charles Kingsley Webster', in *Dictionary of National Biography 1961-1970* [Oxford: Oxford U. P, 1981], 1064-65).

outspoken man in his middle thirties, he loathed underhand methods in any shape or form and never hesitated to express his contempt of them. W. R. Halliday,[5] Mackay's successor in the Chair of Ancient History, who at forty-two [/later] went as Principal to King's College, London, was less approachable and sometimes even a little difficult in University matters, but at bottom thoroughly sound.[6] The youngest of this group was W. E. Collinson,[7] Professor of German and once a pupil of my friend J. G. Robertson.[8] He, more than anyone else except Campagnac, was responsible for my election to the Gilmour Chair. Our temperaments are very dissimilar; and, had not Robertson brought us into [close] contact, I doubt if we should ever have known one another well [/achieved it naturally]. The alliance which Collinson made with Campagnac and his sturdy and unflinching opposition to the New Testament in this last battle was the more remarkable because, eight years earlier, it was the New Testament that had secured his own election, and Campagnac who had resolutely opposed it. Collinson is no great organizer and has no oratorical graces. But he is a scholar to his finger-tips, an indefatigable worker in any cause he espouses and an influence for good in the very deepest sense wherever he goes. Would that every university had more like

---

5 Sir William Reginald Halliday (1886-1966) (knighted in 1946), Rathbone Professor of Ancient History, 1914-27; Principal of King's College, London, 1927-52. 'By nature shy and retiring, Halliday was not at his best on formal occasions, and to strangers he often seemed aloof and rather forbidding. Among his friends, however — and he was essentially a clubable man — he was good company, appreciated for his shrewd wisdom and dry humour... in his dealings with his colleagues and with the students under his authority he was respected for his fair dealing, sympathetic understanding and tolerance, and his profound common sense' (obituary in *The Times*, 28 November 1966).

6 Peers wields his correcting pencil here, to bracket the phrase after 'matters', proposing to exclude it because it 'sounds patronizing'.

7 William Edward Collinson (1889-1969), Professor of German, 1914-54. 'In the modern languages departments... [between the wars]... the outstanding figures were W. E. Collinson... and Allison Peers... Collinson, solid, dependable, benevolent, was a comparative philologist, with a wide and exact knowledge ranging over a dozen or more European languages' (Kelly, *For Advancement of Learning. The University of Liverpool 1881-1981*, 219). See too above, ch. 3, p. 108, note 90.

8 For Professor J. G. Robertson, see above, ch. 3, p. 111, note 108. See also below, p. 161.

him![9]

In the two years following the end of the War a great deal of new blood came into the Faculty — men of all ages, with the most diverse experience; men on the whole excellent scholars, thoroughly enthusiastic for their work and caring nothing for this old gang which still thought it was the new gang, and liked to get its own way everywhere. But the gang had the great advantage of being organized, which the newcomers were not, and when men of ten or fifteen years' seniority get up solemnly and propose each other as members of committees, each of them as if the idea had only just occurred to them, new men [/newcomers], however clearly they see through the game, cannot immediately set themselves up in opposition. Some of them, indeed, preoccupied with the difficult task of post-War departmental organization, probably failed to penetrate the inflexible façade erected by the N.T. Others were wiser, and wilier, as will be seen.

Among these newcomers were Eric Peet,[10] a young Egyptologist who died tragically in his prime soon after his election to a post at Oxford; Edmond Eggli,[11] a rather retiring Frenchman who for years has upheld a rigid ideal of scholarship for which we who prize it cannot be too grateful; J. P. Droop,[12] a Classical Archaeologist from Cambridge, most charming and courteous of colleagues; A. C. Pearson,[13] another Cambridge man who left us too soon for the Cambridge Regius

---

9 Wondering whether to '?omit' them, Peers brackets in pencil the three final sentences of his description of Collinson.

10 Thomas Eric Peet (1882-1934), Brunner Professor of Egyptology, 1920-33; Reader in Egyptology, University of Oxford, 1933-34 (*Dictionary of National Biography 1931-40*). He was 'one of the leading figures in British Egyptology' (Kelly, *For Advancement of Learning. The University of Liverpool 1881-1981*, 224).

11 Jean Edmond Eggli (1881-1956), James Barrow Professor of French, 1920-46.

12 John Percival Droop (1882-1963), Charles W. Jones Professor of Classical Archaeology, 1921-48 (*Who Was Who, 1961-1970*).

13 Alfred Chilton Pearson, F.B.A. (1861-1935), Gladstone Professor of Greek, 1919-21; Regius Professor of Greek, University of Cambridge, 1921-28 (obituary notice in *Dictionary of National Biography*; *Procs.* of the British Academy, vol. XXI [1936]).

Chair of Greek; and Mawer,[14] who became Provost of University College, London, [and died in 1942], a giant in size and a giant in scholarship, as well as an organizer of the first water.

But the most significant actor in the scenes that were to come was the last man one would have expected to find in a fight. David Slater,[15] a close friend of Pearson's, came to Liverpool as Professor of Latin, from Bedford College, London.[16] He was not much over fifty but he seemed to us an old man: a rather tired though meticulous scholar, a poet, a dreamer, a recluse. He was known to take periodic solitary walks of inconceivable length from his Cheshire home and reputed to lose his way in Liverpool whenever he strayed beyond the route from the Central Station to the University. He was the kindliest, gentlest person save when he had made up his mind to do something in face of opposition. Personally, I saw only the gentle side of him, except on this one occasion now to be described — and I must say I am glad I was never on the wrong side when he was moved to anger.

Though several others had put me wise to the N.T.'s intentions soon after the Committee, well packed with N.T., had been formed, it was Slater who first discovered the extent of their intrigues and revealed them to me. I have been told that Slater was originally put on the Committee (at a private N.T. meeting, of course) because he was believed to be a harmless nonentity. [If that was true] the caucus had for once miscalculated, as will be seen.

The unpleasant fact at the bottom of the trouble — which

---

14 For Sir Allen Mawer (Baines Professor of English Language and Philology, 1921-29), see above, ch. 3, p. 109, note 100.

15 David Ansell Slater, F.B.A. (1866-1938), Professor of Latin, 1920-32; he celebrated his fifty-fourth birthday within six days of taking up the Chair. 'Slater was a gentle and rather shy scholar... He worthily maintained the Latin Department's reputation for textual criticism with an edition of Ovid's *Metamorphoses* (1927), which brought him the Fellowship of the British Academy' (Kelly, *For Advancement of Learning. The University of Liverpool 1881-1981*, 218). On his resignation (to take early retirement), the Faculty of Arts (of which Peers was then chairman, for Session 1931-32) paid tribute to Professor Slater's '...wide learning... his modesty and humour, his Horatian urbanity, his kindness'.

16 Peers reminds himself, in a note pencilled in the margin, to 'use the Slater necrology matter'.

some, with high ideals of university life, might think incredible — was that Fitzmaurice-Kelly, who had left Liverpool for the Cervantes Chair at King's College, London was determined that no-one should succeed him at Liverpool [/Liverpool should remain without a successor to him]. He had always been the only British Hispanist and he would remain so. His reputation as a scholar, today greatly reduced, derived largely from the fact that it was unchallenged.[17] As a teacher he had no reputation at all, for in all his eight years at Liverpool he had only a handful of pupils and no Honours School, nor have I ever found that he [/and he seems never to have] made any very serious attempts to get any.[18] As a public lecturer he was poor in the extreme: Charles Carroll Marden[19] used to tell an

---

17 Peers, correctly, reminds himself in the margin that this has already been 'said above, p. 78'.

18 When Fitzmaurice-Kelly arrived in Liverpool he found just seventy-one Spanish books in the University's Tate Library. Within a year he had obtained a grant from the University to permit the purchase of seven hundred and fourteen volumes of Spanish publications (principally classical texts of the sixteenth and seventeenth centuries) and sought further funds and again recommended the formation of a separate Class Library. One of the justifications generally advanced for the establishment of Class Libraries, physically separate from the University Library, was to foster research; the system of Departmental Libraries was formally established in 1908. There are no reports on the Department of Spanish in the Faculty of Arts section of the University's Annual Reports during Fitzmaurice-Kelly's period (1909-16). But the Annual Reports record attendances in classes, the total entries for Spanish during these sessions being: 1909-10, 25; 1910-11, 11; 1911-12, 7; 1912-13, 11; 1913-14, 5; 1914-15, 8; 1915-16, 5. In the absence of Professor Terracher and the Lecturer in French on War service, Professor Fitzmaurice-Kelly carried on the work of the large Department of French, with some assistance, from 1914-15 onwards. The salary of the Gilmour Chair during Fitzmaurice-Kelly's tenure was £500 p.a., together with one-third share of the fees — the total emoluments being guaranteed to amount to not less than £600 p.a., with a maximum of £1,000. The University had to make up the guaranteed total of £600 p.a., the share of fees and of examination fees earned evidently turning out to be very low (totals, for instance, of just £15/3/4d in 1909-10 and £5/13/4d in both 1910-11 and 1911-12).

19 Charles Carroll Marden, a Hispanist who specialized in Romance philology and medieval Spanish literature, held the Chair of Spanish at Princeton, New Jersey. He completed erudite editions of key medieval texts (*Fernán González*, and the *Libro de Apolonio*), and took a particular interest in the works of Gonzalo de Berceo (see the article 'Charles Carroll Marden', signed ASIM [A Student in Madrid] in the series, 'Hispanists Past

excellent story of how he confessed complacently to a belief that he was not audible beyond the second row of his audience — 'which', Marden would add with a twinkle, 'was perfectly true'. To any such man, if he put self before scholarship, it would be galling in the extreme to find younger men springing up, not only at Liverpool, but at Manchester, Edinburgh, Belfast, and in half-a-dozen other cities, who might well outshine him as scholars, and as lecturers and teachers could hardly fail to do so. With Mackay temporarily at his side in London, and the remnants of the N.T. to support him at Liverpool, he exerted his utmost influence, without appearing to do so, to keep his old Chair unfilled.[20]

The chief intriguer at Liverpool was Mair, who, knowing nothing about Spanish himself, had to be coached by Fitzmaurice-Kelly in methods of driving out the intruder. But this was an awkward procedure, because one of our Liverpool traditions [subscribed to by the N.T. itself] has always been that the outgoing professor shall take no part, direct or indirect, in the election of his successor. However, a second Hispanist was found who could be represented as unprejudiced and into whose mouth could be put the words of Fitzmaurice-Kelly, as well as a few of his own. He was no great authority on anything but [/His speciality was] a very brief epoch of Spanish literature, some centuries removed from my own special period; of lecturing and teaching he had no practical experience, still less of a modern University.[21] His name I

---

and Present', *Bulletin of Spanish Studies*, VI [1929], 63-64).

20  It is worth remembering, in this connection, that, since there were at this time still only two Chairs of Spanish in Britain, while the Gilmour Chair of Spanish remained vacant Fitzmaurice-Kelly continued to be the sole Hispanist of professorial status throughout the land.

21  This Hispanist is presumably Dr (later Sir) Henry Thomas. Sir Henry Thomas F.B.A. (1878-1952) was educated at Mason College, Birmingham (later the University of Birmingham) and spent his whole career in the Department of Printed Books, British Museum, 1903-47. In his obituary, Dr Victor Scholderer displays a different opinion from that held by Allison Peers. Scholderer wrote of Sir Henry Thomas that the 'integrity [of Thomas] was absolute... His ordinary manner was calm and self-possessed, but it... masked an extremely kind heart and great delicacy of feeling... He combined sound judgement with determination and presence of mind to an exceptional degree and those who challenged him risked a defeat which was the more impressive for being so quietly inflicted'

THE GILMOUR CHAIR OF SPANISH        157

suppress; it is best forgotten; and indeed, but for the lesson it teaches I would gladly be silent on this entire episode.[22]

The few unprejudiced members of the Selection Committee had been puzzled by Mair's apparent omniscience in Hispanic matters, especially as the source of them seemed not to be entirely Fitzmaurice-Kelly. It was Slater who discovered their immediate *provenance*. Being on a visit to the British Museum, he went into a neighbouring hotel and there found Mair in close collusion with Mr X — a new version of the eternal triangle. From what passed, he knew enough to come straight back to Liverpool and ask me to give him the fullest possible set of testimonials which he could read at the Committee's next meeting.

Fortunately, having some knowledge of what was happening, I had already been amassing testimonials and had collected a much larger number than is generally considered necessary for such a purpose.[23] Since there was not a single Hispanist in Great Britain, other than Fitzmaurice-Kelly, whose name commanded respect, they had all to come from abroad. They included a long letter from Menéndez Pidal, undoubtedly the greatest living Spanish scholar,[24] in the

---

(*Proceedings of the British Academy 1954*, 245). As a Hispanist Henry Thomas is best remembered for his short-title catalogues of books in the British Museum printed in Spain and Portugal before 1601; and for his still useful book on *Spanish and Portuguese Romances of Chivalry* (Cambridge: Cambridge U. P., 1920).

22  Peers, in pencil, indicates an inclination to delete what follows after 'indeed', and to finish the sentence simply, with the words: 'Mr X will serve'.

23  Peers' letter of 30 November 1921 in which he applies for the Chair, is supported by testimonials from E. G. W. Braunholtz (slightly updated version of his March 1919 testimonial), E. Mérimée, Professor J. G. Robertson, Mr J. N. Birch, Miguel Artigas, P. H. Churchman, T. B. Rudmose Brown, and Fernando González. The report of the Selection Committee quotes extracts from several testimonials. See Appendix I, especially pp. 439-45.

24  Ramón Menéndez Pidal (1869-1968). The extract from the testimonial which the Chair Selection Committee incorporated (in translation) in their report, June 1922, is, in fact, taken from the letter of 10 May 1922 which he wrote to Mr [Professor] A. Bruce Boswell, [Dean of the Faculty of Arts]. The report of the Selection Committee quoted almost a complete translation of the letter, but omitting reference to Navarro Tomás' published opinion of Peers.

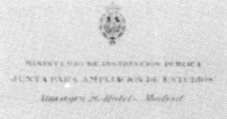

10 de Mayo de 1922

Mr. A. Bruce Boswell.

Muy señor mío:

Recibo su segunda carta del 6 del corriente,(habiéndose extraviado la primera), y me apresuro a contestarle acerca de la pregunta relativa al Sr. Peers, candidato a la cátedra de Español de la Faculty of Arts de la Universidad de Liverpool.

Conozco algunos de los trabajos publicados por el Sr. Peers, los cuales demuestran que el autor ha estudiado detalladamente el movimiento romántico en España. Las cuidadosas investigaciones del Sr. Peers en los periodos de esa época, no solo de Madrid sino hasta en los menos conocidos de provincias, sus estudios en las bibliotecas provinciales y particulares, sobre todo en Barcelona y Cádiz, han sido fructuosos, pues aclaran y rectifican muchos puntos hasta ahora confusos o inexactos de este periodo de la Literatura Española.

En el libro de Lecturas fonéticas, demuestra el Sr. Peers un conocimiento suficiente de la lengua española, proporcionando de este modo un instrumento útil para la enseñanza de este idioma, en un aspecto que carece casi por completo de biblografía y de elementos utilizables. Me remito a la autorizada opinión del Sr. Navarro Tomás, expuesta en la REVISTA DE FILOLOGIA ESPAÑOLA, tomo VII, pag. 392, que elogia las buenas cualidades de las obras del Sr. Peers.

Me es muy grato manifestarle esto, y ofrecerme de usted atentamente

*Menéndez Pidal*

Letter of reference, dated 10 May 1922, received from R. Menéndez Pidal in support of E. Allison Peers' election to the Gilmour Chair of Spanish (Archives, University of Liverpool)

Reproduced in facsimile, courtesy of the University, by Suzanne Yee, Photographic Service, Department of Geography, University of Liverpool

A translation of the letter is provided in Appendix I, p. 448.

linguistic and literary field,[25] and another from Don Miguel Artigas,[26] who soon afterwards was elected Director of the National Library of Spain. From France, the *doyen* of Spanish

---

25 Understandably, Peers had an enormous admiration for this outstanding Spanish scholar, critic, editor and philologist. Peers published, in the *Bulletin of Spanish Studies* (III [1926], no. 11, 105-11), a lengthy commentary wholly concerning Ramón Menéndez Pidal. This commentary was occasioned by the latter's election to the presidency of the Royal Spanish Academy (Real Academia Española) and by the publication of a three-volume *Homenaje ofrecido a Menéndez Pidal* (1925), issued to celebrate Menéndez Pidal's twenty-fifth year as a professor in the University of Madrid. Writing in eloquent praise of the great man, Peers does not fail to mention, almost in his first paragraph, Menéndez Pidal's presidency of the M.H.R.A. (1926-27), the learned body which Peers, as we have seen, had founded:

> Sr Menéndez Pidal is well known by name to all our readers: to some, as the author of half a score of books which are on their shelves; to others, as editor-in-chief of the *Revista de Filología Española*; to others, again, as director of the Centro de Estudios Históricos in Madrid, where so many foreigners study Spanish; to others, as the recently elected president of the Modern Humanities Research Association... In these, and in many other spheres, the reputation of Sr Menéndez Pidal has during the last decade become pre-eminent. He has not gone out to seek fame: rather he has stayed at home and thrust it from him, the ideal man of letters and man of science, the ideal combination of scholar and organizer in one.
> But his work has gone out into every land, and the renown it has brought him has come back to Spain, as is but just, and to himself.

In 1928 Peers published, in the *Bulletin of Spanish Studies*, another tribute to Ramón Menéndez Pidal (V [1928], no. 19, 127-31) as the third in a series of articles on 'Hispanists Past and Present', in which he praises the great man's 'spirit of unselfish and unfaltering search for truth' and 'his rigidly scientific method' (130). For further information on the career of Menéndez Pidal see, for instance, *Columbia Dictionary of Modern European Literature*, ed. Jean-Albert Bédé and William B. Edgerton (New York: Columbia U. P. [2nd ed.], 1980).

26 Miguel Artigas (1887-1947), Spanish scholar and bibliographer, was then Director of the Biblioteca Menéndez y Pelayo, Santander, and Editor of the *Boletín de la Biblioteca Menéndez y Pelayo*. He published important studies on Luis de Góngora and on Marcelino Menéndez y Pelayo. He became, as Peers states, Head of the Biblioteca Nacional, Madrid. See Appendix I, pp. 442-43, for a translation of the testimonial given by Artigas, dated 16 November 1921; just the final sentence was quoted in the report of the Selection Committee.

studies, Ernest Mérimée,[27] wrote warmly in my favour. To the United States, I had called for a testimonial to Philip Churchman,[28] one of Harvard's best scholars in the field, with whom I had conducted some investigations on the influence in Spain of Sir Walter Scott.[29] Canada's leading Hispanist, Milton Buchanan,[30] had written from Toronto, and one of the

---

27 M. Ernest Mérimée (1846-1924), Professor of Spanish at the University of Toulouse and Dean of the Faculty of Letters; Director of the Institut Français en Espagne, Madrid. The Chair of Spanish Language and Literature, the first such Chair in France, was created for Mérimée at the University of Toulouse in 1886 (see *Chaire Ernest Mérimée, Toulouse 1886-1986* [Toulouse: France-Ibérie Recherche, Université de Toulouse-Le Mirail, 1986]). See Appendix I, p. 440, for Mérimée's testimonial, dated 7 September 1920, which was not quoted in the Selection Committee's report.

28 Philip H. Churchman (1874-1954), then (1920-44) Professor of Romance Languages at Clark University, Worcester, Massachusetts, U.S.A., on whose staff he served 1908-44. Besides his work on Scott's influence in Spain, his publications included *Beginnings of Byronism in Spain* (1910) and *French Literature in Outline* (1928). (*Who's Who in America*, vol. 24, 1946-1947 [Chicago, 1946], 426); obituary in *The Worcester Daily Telegram*, 15 April 1954). See Appendix I, p. 443, for his testimonial, dated 8 November 1921; except for the preface, this testimonial was quoted in full in the report of the Selection Committee.

29 Published later: Philip H. Churchman and E. Allison Peers, 'A Survey of the Influence of Sir Walter Scott in Spain', *Revue Hispanique*, LV (1922), 227-310.

30 Milton A. Buchanan (1878-1952), Professor in the Department of Italian and Spanish, University of Toronto, 1916-46, wrote to Mr Garmon Jones [lately Dean of the Faculty of Arts] on 6 December 1921. A brief extract from his letter was quoted in the Selection Committee's report. See Appendix I, pp. 445-46, for the text of the letter. Buchanan was a candidate for the Chair in 1909 (see above ch. 3, pp. 112-13, note 112). In March 1920 the Dean of the Faculty (Mr Garmon Jones), having consulted the Vice-Chancellor, approached Buchanan, offering to consider him as a candidate for the Chair, but Buchanan replied that 'unfortunately for me, circumstances prevent my entertaining the thought of leaving my present position' (letter of 10 May 1920). In a letter of 12 December 1921 to Professor Bruce Boswell, Dean of the Faculty of Arts, Buchanan wrote that though he did not know Peers personally, he had considerable correspondence with him about Spanish matters and the Modern Humanities Research Association; though Peers had not had the leisure as yet to publish very much, he seemed 'to be a man of extraordinary energy and with fine endowments for investigation and criticism'; Peers seemed to have succeeded as a teacher and as to his standing as a scholar 'you need have no fear'; and concluded by observing that 'the study of Spanish has had such an extraordinary development in Canada and the United States that

British scholars in other fields whose scholarly interests touched mine, my old friend J. G. Robertson,[31] was good enough to say that I seemed to 'stand alone among the younger generation of scholars in England'. 'I know of no other', he added, 'who is making so determined an effort to maintain the standard of Spanish scholarship and to win respect for English research in the subject in Spain'.[32]

The actual bulk of my original work in the Hispanic field presented to the Committee, though considerably greater than that of a number of the men on the Committee itself, was not large, even for so comparatively young a man, since I had so recently been freed from work which had made research almost impossible. It amounted in all to three books and twelve articles in [professional] learned reviews.[33] But the opinions of so many scholars of different nationalities were hard to get over, as the New Testament was to find. When the Committee met, Mair, in his usual jaunty tones, proceeded to present the picture painted by his confederates of a young schoolmaster, with no pretensions to scholarship, lured into University work

---

there is a dearth of teachers and I know of no one at present who would be accessible to your Committee'. On his death, in 1952, Buchanan was mourned as 'not only her [Canada's] only Hispanist with an international reputation, but one of her very few scholars in the whole modern language field who were known outside their national borders' (A. F. B. Clark, 'Milton Alexander Buchanan, 1878-1952', *Royal Society of Canada: Proceedings and Transactions*, 3rd series, XLIX (1955), 69-73, at p. 69).

31 For the full text of J. G. Robertson's testimonial, dated 11 November 1921, see Appendix I, p. 441; an extract was included in the report of the Selection Committee.

32 The query 'shorten', written in the margin, indicates that Peers (for reasons of modesty perhaps) considered cutting part of this paragraph. Yet, to understand the injustice of his treatment at the hands of the 'New Testament', the reader must appreciate Peers' exceptional merits as a Hispanist and his considerable reputation abroad.

33 In his letter applying for the Chair, of 30 November 1921, Peers lists three books published or completed during his period at Liverpool — *A Phonetic Spanish Reader* (Manchester: Manchester U. P./London: Longmans Green & Co., 1920); *The Origins of French Romanticism* (with M. B. Finch) (London: Constable, 1920); and *The Poems of Manuel de Cabanyes*. His large book on *Ángel Saavedra, Duque de Rivas* was more than half finished. He lists twelve articles (of which four had been published, five had been accepted for publication, and three had been completed). See Appendix I, pp. 436-39.

by the prospect of an easily acquired Chair, who should be sent back to his proper place as soon as possible. Then it was the turn of Slater. One after another he read the verdicts of scholars whose fame none of my detractors could deny. The unfortunate Mair (narrates the eye witness who described the scene to me soon afterwards) grew glummer and glummer as the recital proceeded, now burying his face in his hands, now drumming his fingers with impatience. When the reading was over, and Slater had added a few [pungent] comments of his own, one thing was clear to everybody — the N.T. had been fairly challenged by a new group which was determined to see its underhand methods brought to an end. The challenge was taken up, it was to be a fight to the death.

From October to May the Committee thrashed out the question. [Vain] attempts were made by would-be compromisers to find other candidates. Mair [even] endeavoured to persuade his confederate from London to stand, but without success:[34] he then had the effrontery to propose that he should be co-opted to the Committee. All sorts of insinuations were started to prejudice opinion against a young ex-schoolmaster. I will refer only to one of them: the [entirely baseless] suggestion that I was (or had been) a Jew. This falsehood I had actually to be asked to deny, which I did; but it is interesting to add, as an example of how difficult malicious rumours are to kill, that to my knowledge it was still being repeated twelve years later.[35]

It was early in June when the Committee made its final report to the Faculty. The N.T. had been driven back to its last defences but beyond these — the violently expressed opinions

---

34 An allusion to Henry Thomas. See Appendix I, pp. 420-24 — the entries from 21 November 1921 to 12 April 1922; and *cf.* above, pp. 156-57, note 21.

35 As pencilled marks reveal, Peers considered cutting out entirely his chosen example of the 'insinuations' made 'to prejudice opinions' against him. Colleagues of Allison Peers have confirmed that the rumour that Peers 'was (or had been) a Jew' was indeed circulated by his opponents, to create prejudice against him, and, as Peers says, the rumour, despite his denials, persisted. This rumour is also mentioned in the 'Bruce Truscot' narrative (see 'B.T.', ch. IV, p. 356, and — for evidence of Peers' own wholly unprejudiced attitude in this matter of race or religion — see also p. 369, and note 101).

of Fitzmaurice-Kelly — their opponents were unable to penetrate. On the other hand, the N.T. was forced to yield everything but the last vital point — tenure of the Chair. The report proposed to promote me from a lectureship on a single-year tenure at three-quarters of a professor's salary, to a Senior Lectureship on a three years' tenure at seven-eighths that salary.[36] It was almost victory but not quite. Grave dissatisfaction was felt with the report by many members of the Faculty — but in the end, true to their former colleague (for whose reputation, it must be remembered, everybody at that time had an exaggerated respect),[37] they agreed to it by a small majority.

But they had yet to reckon with the Senate. In this full body of professors the N.T. had always had less power than in the Faculty, and when the Faculty report came up in the middle of June, it was only too clear to the robust minds of the scientists and medicals that the campaign, inspired ostensibly by such lofty motives, was in reality a put-up job engineered by a clique now rapidly losing power. Some of the more outspoken communications produced by the N.T. were received with ridicule and scorn. They might have convinced the converted[,] but the unprejudiced men, who knew nothing of the conflict till they came to the meeting, made no difficulty about describing them as ill-tempered and ungentlemanly. They certainly did nothing but harm to their cause. A magnificent speech by Campagnac (which I only wish I could have heard) and a carefully reasoned statement by Collinson, were sufficient to complete the rout. Though the N.T. and one or two of its satellites voted for the report, it was lost by a large majority and I was elected to the Chair.

At Oxford and Cambridge there would have been no appeal from this decision. At Liverpool there is just one, and no greater condemnation of the N.T.'s lack of principle can be

---

36 In fact, as a result of an amendment, moved by Professor Mair, the Faculty rejected the recommendation of its Committee to make Peers a 'Senior Lecturer', and recommended (7 June 1922) that he should be appointed merely 'Lecturer in Charge' (see Appendix I, p. 426). Just one week later Senate overruled the recommendation of the Faculty and appointed Peers to the Gilmour Chair (which appointment Council in due course ratified despite the worst endeavours of the 'N.T.').

37 He means, of course, Fitzmaurice-Kelly.

imagined than the fact that they took it. Above the Senate sits the Council, an elected [lay] body, composed for the most part of successful business men,[38] with a very small academic representation. Most of the Senate's legislation has to be approved by the Council before being carried into effect, but, the Council's most important function is to control the purse-strings, the only objection which it normally makes to any Senate resolution is on grounds of finance [/and it seldom objects to any Senate resolution for academic motives]. If excellent relations prevail (as they nearly always do) between Senate and Council, this is due to the Council's readiness to let Senate manage purely academic affairs and Senate's readiness to meet Council in financial affairs, particularly in making necessary economies, whenever possible.

Now the N.T. had again and again defended the rights of Senate against hypothetical or actual encroachments on that right by Council. Reilly, in fact, cites a particular case (casting himself for the part of the hero) in which he censures Council for its attempt to reject a candidate for a Chair who had been approved, by a majority, by Senate. 'It would have been a very bad precedent', he remarks, 'to have had the laymen overrule the Senate's judgment on an important academic matter like the filling of a Chair'.

Yet this is precisely what the N.T., rather than lose a battle on which it had staked its prestige, tried to persuade the laymen to do. Having failed with Senate, Mair and his friends began to canvass members of Council, who were to vote on the question at the very last meeting of the session, on July 4. Adami,[39] the Vice-Chancellor, who had enquired into the antecedents of the N.T. and viewed their present activities with unmitigated disgust, was seriously concerned at this almost unprecedented method of approach to Council. After a discussion between the leaders of that body, it was thought best to force the N.T. into the open and hear what it had to say.

---

38 These words, after 'body', are marked by Peers for deletion.

39 In the margin Peers writes in pencil: '1st mention of Adami ?Say more'. Dr J. George Adami was Vice-Chancellor of the University 1919-26. He was succeeded by Sir Hector Hetherington. In the 'Bruce Truscot' autobiography the figure of Sir Archibald Blake, Vice-Chancellor of Redbrick University (see ch. IV), combines characteristics observed in both Adami and Hetherington.

Accordingly representatives of each side were summoned to a special meeting and agreed to state their case in full.[40] The result was that Council confirmed the verdict of Senate and that, just two and a half years after coming to Liverpool, I was elected to the Gilmour Chair.[41]

'That's the end of the N.T.', Sampson was heard to remark to Mair, who nodded gloomy assent. It had been fated since the end of the War to disappear before long, though but for this knock-out blow it might have retained power for some years. In the years immediately succeeding its great fall it suffered serious losses. Case, one of its lesser lights, retired in 1923. Elton went in 1925. Mair died in 192.. Sampson retired in... and died... years later:[42] I recall that it fell to my lot, as Chairman of the Faculty at that time, to make the usual necrological oration before that body. Reilly, whose health began to fail, decided to retire, six years before his time, in 1933. Garmon Jones, the youngest of the caucus, succeeded Sampson as University Librarian, and died prematurely and to everybody's grief (for, in spite of his temperamental defects,[43] we all loved him) in 1937.

As I have already said, my colleagues, even those who had fought most bitterly against me, received me as a member of

---

40 In fact, a special committee was set up by Council to consider the debated question of the Gilmour Chair: the report from Senate, the documentation submitted, the deliberations of the Faculty of Arts etc. (see the entries 20 June—4 July 1922, Appendix I, pp. 426-28).

41 In the margin Peers has pencilled: '?majority ?almost unanim.'. In fact, Council agreed to confirm Peers' election to the Gilmour Chair by twelve votes to six (see Appendix I, p. 428). Given the delays, complications and controversies before Peers was finally appointed to the Gilmour Chair of Spanish we should not be surprised that Bruce Truscot criticizes the cumbersome machinery used at Redbrick University in appointments to Chairs, where 'a multiplicity of meetings are needed for the election of a single professor' (see *Redbrick University*, ch. 3, 57-66, especially p. 66).

42 Peers left spaces to complete the dates when he had verified them. Professor Mair died in 1927; Dr Sampson retired in 1928 and died three years later, in 1931.

43 Peers deletes, in pencil, this phrase which modifies his praise of Garmon Jones. For confirmation that Garmon Jones was universally liked see Collinson, 'Portraits from the Past': 'I have seldom seen such universal sorrow in the University as was caused by his death from a stroke he suffered as his train was approaching Birkenhead on his return from a visit to Elton'.

Senate generously and kindly; and, though repercussions of the conflict were felt elsewhere,[44] in Liverpool I have never received anything but kindness. I have told the story of the decline and fall of the New Testament without the slightest rancour, solely in order to show to what depths men can descend who have entered a calling which above almost any other should connote the disinterested cultivation of scholarship and love of uprightness and truth. This lesson I learned myself at the cost of distress which all but caused me [/brought me to the verge of] a physical breakdown and of which I have deliberately given no inkling so that my narrative might have the greatest possible objectivity.[45] In the summer following that memorable session, I made two vows, which I have rigidly kept. First, if in my University career I ever saw another group attempting to control power (fortunately this has never happened)[46] as the N.T. did, I would do my utmost to create an opposition party pledged to true freedom and never rest till their power was destroyed. Secondly, in any and every academic question on which I might be called to act or to judge, I would be guided solely by my conscience and never by attachment to, or friendship with, anyone, however close my relations with him might be. This resolution steadily maintained, has more than once brought me, as it often brought Campagnac, into opposition with majorities, sometimes even into a minority of one. But only once have I broken it — and then only because, in a matter on which strong feelings were aroused, I was very strongly urged to take the line which I believed to be wrong by no less a person than Collinson [/by one of those who had supported me in 1922].[47] The result was disastrous and I often wish that I had

---

44 An indirect reference, perhaps, to Fitzmaurice-Kelly's bitter disappointment? Fitzmaurice-Kelly was, by this time, in poor health. He died of pneumonia in 1923 — possibly as an end-result of Parkinson's Disease, from which, according to his death certificate, he had suffered for four years.

45 Peers has deleted, in pencil, after 'breakdown' the remainder of this sentence.

46 Peers considered deleting ('? omit') the words in parentheses.

47 As indicated, Peers deleted, in pencil, the reference to Collinson, preferring, on reflection (and probably rightly) not to identify the supporter who had persuaded him to 'take the line' which he 'believed to be wrong'.

continued in opposition to my friend; but at least I can be glad it has been an isolated occasion; and I sincerely trust that my telling of the unpleasant story of intrigue which I should prefer to forget may lead others, both in university circles and outside them, to make similar resolutions.[48]

---

48 Opposite this final half-sentence of the undisguised section of his memoirs, Peers, consistently the self-critical writer, has written: 'Priggish [he underlines this word twice]. Different ending'.

# THE AUTOBIOGRAPHY OF 'BRUCE TRUSCOT'

# PART I

# CHAPTER I

## SCHOOL AND UNIVERSITY, ACT I (1885-1907)[1]

### I

I was born, on June 23, 1885, at a little town a few miles out of London,[2] which I left at the age of five and have never seen since except from the window of a London, Midland and Scottish express.[3] Few boys can have sampled so many types of education *as I had the privilege of doing before the age of eighteen — a privilege which I would gladly have forgone for that of spending the whole of my school life at one of the first-class London day schools, whence I have since come to believe that, all things considered, a boy can obtain the best education. The remarkable thing is that I picked up any continuous [/adequate?] knowledge at all.*

---

1  The title of this chapter is that added to the manuscript, in pencil, by Peers himself. Immediately below this inserted title, Peers has written, also in pencil, a reminder to himself to write as a preamble (which evidently he never did), an 'Introd[uctory] par[agraph] on autobiog[raphie]s in g[ener]al and whether [there is] any point in them'. As we have noted, Peers added a similar message to himself at the beginning of the '(E.A.P.) Auto' (see above, ch. 1, p. 61, note 1).

In the top left-hand margin of this first page of the 'B.T.' narrative, Peers has written — showing a considerate interest in the requirements of future readers for which the present editors are grateful — the date on which 'Bruce Truscot' began to compose his autobiography. That date (Truscot's sixtieth birthday) was: '23/6/[19]45'. For further information on date of composition see the Editorial Commentary, pp. 36-40.

2  While 'Truscot' s' character is in many respects that of Peers, his background, home life, the circumstances of his university career, etc., though often similar or comparable, are rarely identical. Truscot's narrative is composed of truth and invention, realistically, convincingly, intermingled. Allison Peers, in fact, was born on 7 May 1891 at Leighton Buzzard, which is just over forty miles from London: see '(E.A.P.) *Auto*', ch. 1, p. 62, and note 4.

3  *Cf.* Peers' identically-worded remark in '(E.A.P.) *Auto*', ch. 1, p. 63.

My father was a Methodist minister, who, according to the extraordinary practice of that denomination, was destined [/compelled/fated] to spend the greater part of his life in moving about the country.⁴ Normally, he spent three years in one circuit, and then, just as my mother was getting used to the place and the people, off he would be sent to another. I never took to Methodism from any point of view, and one of the first things I had against it was its lack of consideration for its ministers. When I think of those endless moves in those hot Septembers and of my gentle, delicate little mother needlessly wearing herself out with the physical effort of uprooting us from the old place and the mental strain of accommodating herself to the new one, my heart (as the Psalmist says) grows hot within me. As a little boy I loved the moves, however, for we had about five thousand books and I was allowed to take them from their shelves and arrange them in neat piles beside the packing-cases. That was the great attraction, though second to it came the thought of going to a new school: so accustomed did I become to changing my school every three years that I should have thought it strange to stay at one for longer. It might have been expected that I should be sent, like other ministers' sons, to one of the large Methodist boarding-schools. But I was too delicate for that: constant illnesses kept me at home for short periods or for long, and, before I had grown out of my delicate boyhood, as I did, a cycling smash lamed me and left me for life with a limp of which other people are now more conscious than I am.⁵

---

4     John T. Peers was a member of staff of HM Customs and Excise (the Excise Department, to which he was appointed, being transferred from the Commissioners of Inland Revenue to the Commissioners of Customs in 1909 to become the Board of Customs and Excise). No doubt he was obliged to move in order to gain promotion in the service. The 'base and villainous system of "General Removes" is now an atrocity of the past', the Secretary of a campaigning Excise officers organization stated, following reform of the removal system (Graham Smith, *Something to Declare: 1000 Years of Customs and Excise* [London: Harrap, 1980], 119).

5     In his War Statement, in applying for the Chair of Spanish in 1919, Peers stated that he was physically unfit for active service because of a lung weakness and a defect in one eye. Peers, therefore, has given his 'other' self a different (but in its effects perhaps roughly equivalent) physical disability. Because of his limp, Truscot is unfit for military service (see below, p. 246). Truscot mentions his limp more than once (see also below, pp. 181, 196-97,

SCHOOL AND UNIVERSITY (1885-1907)     175

My first experience of education was being taught by a girl in the Nottinghamshire village who came to us for that purpose for a couple of hours daily.[6] Thence we moved to an isolated spot in Yorkshire[7] where it was decided that I might be sent to the country elementary school which served a wide district, and to which, at the tender age of seven, I tramped a mile and a half daily, ploughing through deep snow in winter and scampering over the heather in summer:[8] not, one might have supposed, a very suitable life for a child thought too weakly to leave home. But I heard later that the doctor who had pulled me through a bad bout of pneumonia had recommended it: the regular exercise in the open air, he had said, would be better for me than anything else.[9]

I learned a good deal at that country school: the classes were relatively small and the master and mistress who took nearly all the classes were genuinely interested in me. The master[10] even went so far as to spend some of his own time in teaching me Latin, which in an elementary school must be rare. But I also picked up some accomplishments myself — notably to speak the broadest dialect and to swear like a trooper. Both these, in which I have long since lost my proficiency, I indulged at school only, and my parents were apparently idealistic enough to believe that I conversed with the children of Yorkshire farm-hands in their own brand of London-and-home-counties English.[11]

---

248, 303).

6   Peers' formal education commenced in a private school in Glasgow in 1897; see '(E.A.P.) *Auto*', ch. 1, p. 63, note 6.

7   In fact to Longmorn in Morayshire, in 1898, and attending Clackmarras School: see '(E.A.P.) *Auto*', ch. 1, pp. 63-64, and notes 7-9.

8   Peers uses virtually the same words to describe his daily tramp to school in '(E.A.P.) *Auto*' (see ch. 1, p. 63).

9   Given the lung weakness from which he suffered (see above, note 5), Peers probably did suffer as a child from the 'bad bout of pneumonia' here described though he does not refer to it in the other autobiography. It will be observed that, in order to avoid excessive, tedious repetitions, Peers consciously excludes from one autobiography anecdotes or reminiscences inserted in the other narrative.

10   The headmaster he has in mind is Alexander Grant, who had graduated M.A. at the University of Aberdeen (see '[E.A.P.] *Auto*', ch. 1, pp. 64-65, and note 9).

11   The phraseology in these two sentences is closely related to that

At ten, I was pitchforked from my Yorkshire village into a large manufacturing town in the Midlands,[12] where my father went as junior minister in a large circuit. Here I found more congenial companionship among neighbours, but not at school, for by some extraordinarily perverse fate I was sent, not to the preparatory division of the local Grammar School,[13] which was quite a good one and situated not far from our house, but to an immense Higher Grade School in the very centre of the town where the conditions of instruction were surely as bad as they have been anywhere in the country.[14] During the three years I was there, I was only once in a class of less than sixty; and I remember this very well because, ridiculous as it may sound, we boys took a pride in the size of the class we were in and used to boast to boys in other standards that ours were bigger than theirs: the thing we most dreaded was that our numbers would fall below sixty, and, on the one occasion when they fell to fifty-eight, I got mixed up in quite a sanguinary playground scrimmage between my standard and another.

In classes of such dimensions, little individual attention was possible. The master would come round and look over your shoulder while you did your written work; often the first indication you had of his presence behind you was a stinging blow on the cheek which meant that he had detected some careless error in what you had written. This we took quite as a matter of course, as much so as the bi-weekly visits of the headmaster, armed with a cane, to administer, *coram populo*, such punishments as had accumulated since his last visit. The master would enter the offence in an exercise book, and the headmaster, after scanning it, would call on the offenders in turn, and, the castigations being completed, would enter their nature — thus, 3B, 6H: a notation, I suppose, easily interpretable — and pass on to the next form. Except on what might be described as 12B occasions, when the victim yelled, nobody thought anything of these cold-blooded, semi-automatic

---

found in '(E.A.P.) *Auto*' (see ch. 1, p. 64).

12 In fact Peers was 'pitchforked' into Burton-on-Trent, in 1900, when he was aged nine years (see '[E.A.P.] *Auto*', ch. 1, pp. 64-65, notes 10 and 11).

13 The Grammar School in Burton-on-Trent was situated in Lichfield Street.

14 See '(E.A.P.) *Auto*', pp. 64-65, and note 11.

proceedings. Once, I remember, a boy with whom I often walked home, was asked by the headmaster what he was about to punish him for, and for the life of him he couldn't remember. Saying nothing, he was given two additional strokes for sulkiness. I remember asking him, as we went home that evening, why he didn't say he had forgotten, to which he replied that, in that case, he would undoubtedly have got four strokes extra for telling a lie.

I began life at that school in Standard IV and finished up just as I had attained Standard VII. This meant that I spent almost the whole of those three years in the same assembly hall, which every morning, after prayers, was divided into three by partitions. The partition between Standards V and VI was a very flimsy one; and, as Mr Hurley, who taught Standard V, had a reed-like voice, while that of the Standard VI master, Mr Cumper, was loud and thunderous, the unfortunates in the lower standard who sat next to the partition heard more of the lessons of the higher standard than of their own.

My father, who was a well-educated man, must often have been shocked by the episodes of school life which I would narrate in all innocence; and I feel sure that it can only have been financial stringency which kept me there. Not that I ever thought it a cheap school; indeed, our masters, in rebuking us for careless work, continually reminded us that we were not like primary school boys, since our parents contributed the sum of sixpence per week to our education. These sixpences had to be brought every Monday morning and laid on the desk, at the left-hand side of the inkwell, whence the monitors retrieved them. On that morning, instead of saying 'Here, sir', when your name was called from the register, you said 'Here, sir; money, sir' — unless, of course, the coin had been forgotten, in which case you said it on Tuesday. If it was forgotten on Tuesday as well, the matter was generally attended to at the next headmagisterial visit.

I lost two things by going to this wretched school. The first was friendships. Though my command of bad language and a considerable skill at imitating masters won me a certain notoriety,[15] I was generally disliked by my companions as being

---

15 Peers retained his gift for mimicry in later life. In his obituary of Peers, Atkinson recalls that 'for the foibles of his fellows he had a keen eye

in some vague way superior to them, and, being weakly and of very little use in a fight, I suffered from intermittent bullying. On dark evenings, a favourite practice of some of the bullies was to run ahead of the younger boys, hide behind a large urinal at the corner of the street, dart out upon them, to the accompaniment of loud cries, and chase them till they got tired of the fun. I sometimes used to evade this ordeal by attaching myself to a much bigger boy who lived near us, and this was the nearest approach I made to a friendship. I recall this particularly because I lost sight of him altogether until, after more than forty years, he walked unannounced into my room at Redbrick some little time ago — and I immediately recognized him. An elderly and tired-looking commercial traveller, he had seen my name on a lecture-poster outside the university and had come in on the off-chance of my being the Truscot he had known.[16]

A more serious loss was in the content of my knowledge. Had I gone from my Yorkshire village to a first-class school, or even to the Grammar School near my home, I should undoubtedly have become a linguist, or even a Classic. But the Latin which I had so eagerly assimilated lay for five years untouched and forgotten; I learned no modern language till I was thirteen, and then only French;[17] and I spent unconscionable periods marking time in the subjects I did learn, the pace of a class of sixty being the pace of the slowest member of it. By the time my interest in languages really awakened, I was too old to take them up seriously; and though the ability to read about a dozen has stood my special studies in good stead, I should have probably have been a greater success had I specialized in two or three.[18] Still, I may be deluding myself

---

and a gift of mimicry which in the intimacy of the fireside made him always good company' ('In Memoriam', *Bulletin of Hispanic Studies*, XXX [1953], no. 117, 1-5, at p. 4).

    16 The re-encounter with his school-friend — without doubt a true event — is not mentioned in '(E.A.P.) *Auto*'.

    17 See '(E.A.P.) *Auto*', ch. 1, pp. 65-66, where Peers refers to 'a secondary school... in Wiltshire', where, from twelve to fourteen, he 'resumed Latin and began French'.

    18 As the 'Redbrick' books indicate, Peers enjoyed adeptly leaving false, though plausible, clues as to the specialist career-interests of Professor 'Bruce Truscot'. Clearly, it amused the Gilmour Professor of Spanish at

here: if so, I am far from being the first person who has omitted to thank Providence for preventing him from following his own fancies.

From the Midlands, in the October of 1898 (the move had been delayed a few weeks by my father's illness) we moved to a small town in Somerset,[19] where till the age of fifteen I sampled co-education in its crudest form. We only stayed there for two years — I forget exactly why — and it was just as well, for the school was a poor one. Recently created, and temporarily housed in the local Technical Institute, it had the misfortune to begin its existence under a headmaster who was not only a weak character and a bad disciplinarian but also a man of little judgment. Looking back on incidents that happened at that school — some scandalous, some comic — I can see what a tragedy it is when the wrong person gets a headship.[20] Just because of that unfortunate experience, I have never liked to express an opinion on co-education in schools, to which in general I am opposed. The one thing it undeniably does is to promote natural relations between the sexes; and of this I had no need, since I had no brothers, but two younger sisters,[21] and so saw more of girls than of boys.

Fortunately, my second experience of Secondary education was much better than my first. It was in the September of 1900 that we moved to a market-town in the heart of Kent,[22] where my father went as senior minister of the circuit; and, as he stayed there for five years instead of the usual three, I was able to finish my schooling without further interruptions. Despite its defects — and, after all, most schools have defects of some kind

---

Liverpool to suggest to the reader of his narrative that he had never taken up languages seriously. The redundant 'have' in this sentence is present in the original manuscript.

19 Peers' family evidently remained in Burton-on-Trent, until late 1904 (see '[E.A.P.] *Auto*', ch. 1, pp. 64-66). But, as we recalled above (note 17), Peers states that he was at a (co-educational) school in Wiltshire from the age of twelve years to fourteen years.

20 In the margin, Peers has written, in pencil, opposite this observation: 'could enlarge'.

21 Peers in fact had one younger sister, Winifred (see '[E.A.P.] *Auto*', ch. 1, pp. 71-72, and note 30).

22 In fact in late 1904 (or, more probably, early 1905) to Dartford, Kent (see '[E.A.P.] *Auto*', ch. 1, p. 66, and note 15).

— I shall always look back upon Chatstone Grammar School[23] with admiration as well as with affection. The headmaster, though disconcertingly temperamental and in some respects unwise, was a man of ability and imagination;[24] and, unlike the head of my Somerset school, he had the gift of picking masters who, poor though their paper qualifications might be,[25] did their job really well.

There were only eight of them when I went, including the music-master,[26] whom I seldom saw, and a lad of eighteen,[27] who worked by night for a London pass degree, and by day taught the lowest form. The other six, though not one of them would have been short-listed for a 'good' school, were all heaven-sent teachers. Take the man to whom I owed most — who captured my imagination for English literature and fired me with a love for poetry: his degree was a London External,[28] Third-class Honours in English and French, and he taught Form Three.[29] But he was the master who lived in the

---

23 Chatstone Grammar School is Dartford Grammar School in the 'real' autobiography.

24 Mr C. J. Jodrell Mansford (see '[E.A.P.] *Auto*', ch. 1, pp. 66-67, and notes 17 and 19). Peers uses almost these same words to describe Mr Mansford in the other narrative.

25 *Cf*. Peers' description of the masters at Dartford Grammar school in '(E.A.P.) *Auto*': 'though nearly all second-rate men, [they] were conscientious and full of interest in their work' (pp. 66-67).

26 Mr D. Mackenzie (born in 1871) was the part-time music master at the School, teaching only 2¾ hours weekly, later 4½ hours.

27 The 'lad of eighteen' is Mr Josiah Davies (born in 1885, and so in his early twenties when Peers encountered him). An old boy of the School, he taught general subjects at the School, 1900-14, leaving to study for a degree. He does not, however, appear as a student in the records of the University of London.

28 In *Redbrick University*, Peers expresses his admiration for the University of London and its 'external' system: 'which has brought a university degree within the reach of thousands to whom it would otherwise have been inaccessible'. He describes himself as 'among the most ardent of its apologists and would be proud if he could claim it for his Alma Mater' (see his Introduction, 13-14). In fact, Peers had taken a London B.A. in English and French in 1910 (see below, pp. 189-90, note 61; and *cf*. 'E.A.P [*Auto*]', ch. 1, p. 70, note 25).

29 This is believed to be Mr Charles Bertram Stinson (born in 1880) who graduated at the University of London in 1905 with 3rd class Honours in English and French, and was appointed to the School's staff in 1906. According to the School's Register, he had 'Boarding House Duties'. His

## SCHOOL AND UNIVERSITY (1885-1907)   181

Headmaster's house and looked after the dozen or so weedy boarders. He had only an attic bed-sitting-room, but there he used to take me and sit on the bed while I browsed among his books. He knew them all like children and would tell me where he bought them, and what he paid for them, and how the Swinburne[30] had a marmalade stain on the cover because he used to read it at breakfast, and the Henley[31] had a marker at a lyric which he had once set to music; and how Sully-Prudhomme[32] was difficult, but well worth learning French in order to master; and would I take down the Alfred de Vigny,[33] because he wanted to read me the last stanza of 'La Mort du loup', which, according to him, was the finest quatrain in modern literature. That sort of thing was repeated day after day, till I knew those books as well as he did, and continued at all sorts of times — after boarders' prep., which I sometimes attended, as I lived near the school;[34] on half-holidays, as we sat out cricket matches after my accident prevented me from playing;[35] at home, where he often came to tea and my father used to try to draw him out, but without the least success — he never quite discovered what I saw in him. That was perhaps the best part of my education, though I never realized it at the time, and only thought of it as amazing and thrilling fun. Once he took me up to London for the day to hear some poetry readings. Half-a-century afterwards every detail of that day lives in my memory. No visit that I ever made to the

---

teaching subjects were English Language, English Literature, History, French, and Classics. Mr. David Patterson (Senior History Teacher) states (letter of 31 March 1993) that both Stinson and H. E. Bryant (see below, p. 183, note 43) were highly regarded by at least one other pupil of this era, who returned to the school in about 1970 and gave a sum of money to establish a prize in their name, and also one in honour of Mr Jodrell Mansford.

30 Algernon C. Swinburne (1837-1909), English poet and critic, associated with Rossetti and the Pre-Raphaelite circle.

31 William E. Henley (1849-1903), poet, critic and dramatist.

32 Sully Prudhomme (pseudonym of René F. Prudhomme) (1839-1907), French poet and essayist.

33 Alfred Victor, Comte de Vigny (1797-1863), French poet, novelist and playwright. Peers published a critical edition of his poems (1918), which he mentions in the 'real' autobiography (see ch. 4, pp. 126-27, and note 9; and *cf.* Appendix I, p. 431).

34 In Miskin Road (see '[E.A.P.] *Auto*', ch. 1, p. 66, note 15).

35 See above, p. 174, and note 5.

pantomime, to His Majesty's,[36] to Covent Garden, to the Houses of Parliament, can even approach it. After the readings, we walked up Charing Cross Road — the first time I had ever seen more than a single second-hand bookshop. And, after we had dipped into the twopenny boxes and extracted a treasure or two, my companion led me along Great Russell St, past the British Museum, 'where', he explained, 'there's the greatest reading room in the world. And', he added, 'you'll be able to go and read there whenever you like, after you're twenty-one'.

Poor fellow! He stayed for twenty years at Chatstone, before he finally rebelled against being the boarders' Nanny (that was his nickname) and went to another school of much the same type where there were none.[37] He lived and died an assistant master. So, as far as I know, did the rest, for they had no paper qualifications which, as we say, would 'get them looked at'.[38] But to every one of them I owe something. The French master,[39] for example, was a Camford[40] ne'er-do-well, who was

---

36 His Majesty's (now Her Majesty's) Theatre, Haymarket.

37 Mr Stinson in fact left the School in April 1909, after *three* years' service. He went to Skerry's College, Ireland, and then to Lord Williams's School, Thame, in 1912.

38 Peers has ringed, in pencil, the words '[no] paper qualifications', probably realizing these were not strictly accurate, given that his English teacher, for instance, had an External degree from London University (see above, p. 180).

39 Mr Lucien Joseph Oberlé, the French master, was appointed in 1906 and left in 1909 and is said to have purchased a school. He was born on Jersey in 1883, the first son of Armand Oberlé, whose profession is listed as secretary. He was educated in France, at Rennes, then at Victoria College on Jersey, and at Pembroke College, Oxford. See also pp. 186, 199, and note 94 below.

40 Peers' creative term for Cambridge, which he sometimes also uses to denote Oxford, or to mean both institutions. Peers uses with the same meanings the similarly hybrid term 'Oxbridge'. This word, now a commonplace, in the 1940s was as unusual as its equivalent 'Camford' — so much so that reviewers of the 'Redbrick' books believed that 'Bruce Truscot' (whoever he was) had invented, as surely as he had coined the phrase 'Redbrick University', 'the barbarous but convenient term "Oxbridge" ' (see *Redbrick University*, 12). In fact, the words 'Oxbridge' and 'Camford' were evidently first used in the nineteenth century. The earliest reference to 'Oxbridge' (1849) recorded by *The Oxford English Dictionary* (2nd ed., 1989) is in W. M. Thackeray, *Pendennis* I, xxix. 286; the earliest reference to 'Camford' (1850), recorded by the same dictionary, is also in Thackeray, *Pendennis* II, xiv. 135.

all but sent down for being drunk and disorderly, and, though a French-speaking Guernsey man, came out of his Finals with only a Third. But to me he was a romantic figure in Harris tweeds, with a genuine French 'r', like no other master I had ever known — and what hours we spent with a map of France while he advised me what district to visit first. Then there was the English language man, who coached me, in my last days, in Anglo-Saxon.[41] Even at my age I knew that he had forgotten most of what he had known, but he made no pretence to omniscience, and if he was occasionally stumped that only spurred me on to try to solve the problem first: hours spent with him were my first experience of the collaboration between teacher and taught.[42]

The fourth man taught me Latin[43] — and other things too, for he was the Fifth Form master, but he was the only man with a degree in Classics and in my last year he also taught me the required Oxbridge[44] minimum of Greek. He was a sound, rather than a brilliant teacher, but in class his abilities never got full play, for he was the butt of all. Tall and imposing to the sight, he was hesitant in speech, vacillating in resolution, and — worst defect of all — more than a little deaf. Noughts and crosses could be played in his class, *ad nauseam* and with impunity. The bolder spirits raised the lids of the desks and

---

41 This is perhaps Mr C. B. Stinson again (see above, notes 29 and 37), rather than Mr S. J. Woodall, B.A. (Manchester) who taught at the School for one term, September-December 1908.

42 Peers' comment here reminds one of the views he expressed on the art and profession of teaching in *Redbrick University*, and especially of the following statement: '...the most important, yet most difficult, idea to impart to the undergraduate is that his teachers at the university — his fellow members — are not so much teachers as collaborators: learners like himself...' (143).

43 This is probably Mr Herbert Edward Bryant, Form Master of Form V, who taught Latin. He also taught Mathematics and Science, and English Language and Literature to the lower forms. Born in 1866, Mr Bryant graduated B.A. (First Class) of the University of London in 1885, and passed the Intermediate Science Examination in 1890; he was fifth in the 2nd Class in Latin; but he did not take honours in any subject. He left the School in December 1909 to become Head of Brigg Grammar School. The latter appointment is difficult to equate with his apparent lack of discipline as portrayed by Peers. See too above note 29.

44 For comments on Peers' use of the term 'Oxbridge', and on its origins, see above, note 40.

consumed odorous oranges there, pretending not to hear, when ordered to close their desks, until they had finished. Some, as he stood at his high desk, head in hands, construing a knotty passage, would throw a ping-pong ball at the wall behind him, catching it as it came down and looking as surprised as anybody when he raised his head and enquired pathetically what the noise was.[45] The incident about him that I remember best was connected with a class examination. He had ordered some boy, for making an obscene noise, to stand on the form. As we wrote, he paced about the room; and, each time he turned his back on the class, another boy mounted the form and the one previously there sat down. Believe it or not, *he never noticed*! And yet, if you gave him a chance, he *could* teach. And he *did* teach me.

The other two men, who taught Maths. and Science respectively, had no degrees,[46] though the latter, a repulsive-looking creature suggestively nicknamed 'Meaty', had an F.C.S., which caused him to be looked upon with great awe, the boys confusing it with F.R.S. — perhaps the confusion was inspired by authority! The Maths. man was young, and eventually went to Camford, having earned enough money to live on by teaching at a starvation wage from seventeen to twenty-five. I never heard what happened to him, but I am sure he did well.

The Headmaster, as I have implied, was a man of

---

45 Peers refers also to the misconduct of boys during the classes of the deaf Mr Bryant in '(E.A.P.) *Auto*', ch. 1, p. 69.

46 The Science master is possibly Mr Charles Percy Hines (born in 1880), who, in fact, graduated B.Sc. of the University of London in 1905. He taught Science, Maths, Geography, and Rifle Shooting. Later he became a Major in the Territorial Force, and trained six thousand cadets during World War I. He left the School in 1910.

The Maths master is probably not to be identified with Mr Sidney James Jennings (born in 1884) inasmuch as he taught Science and Maths for such a brief period, being appointed in January 1909 and leaving the School in April 1909. He also had a London B.Sc. degree. The master in question may be Mr Josiah Davies again (see above, note 27), who taught Science, Maths, and English and whose salary was the lowest of the regular teachers.

As Peers indicates, to be an F.C.S. was entirely different from being a Fellow of the Royal Society. No teacher had an F.C.S. (Fellow of the Chemical Society) qualification except Mr Jodrell Mansford, the Headmaster. (The Chemical Society merged with the Royal Institute of Chemistry in 1980 to form The Royal Society of Chemistry.)

considerable initiative, but unfortunately his initiative occupied itself principally in sending in his most promising pupils for every conceivable kind of examination. The idea of this, of course, was to be able to present a long list of successes to expectant governors and uncomprehending but admiring parents at the annual prize-giving — dignified by the name of 'Speech Day', though the only speeches made were that of the local celebrity who distributed the prizes and his own. It still makes my blood boil to think how, whenever he found a bright boy, this unspeakable pedagogue sacrificed his education to examination results. And unfortunately he found one in me.[47]

First of all, he sent me in for the 'Junior Local', which I had already taken in Somerset,[48] and *in which I was fool enough to play into his hands by gaining first-class honours with three distinctions. This, of course, merely made him worse: in the following December it had to be the 'Senior Local', which brought his miserable 'Honour List' first-class honours and five distinctions;*[49] *then it was the London Matriculation; and finally — the greatest scandal of all, for there was no question of my going to London University — the London Intermediate B.A., in which I regret to say I rewarded him by obtaining first-class honours in English.*[50]

*This is by no means the full tale of the examinations that I was dragooned into taking for the honour and glory of* Chatstone.[51] *There were a whole series of certificates awarded by the Board of Education for scientific subjects — theoretical chemistry, practical chemistry, heat, light and sound, electricity and magnetism, pure mathematics, applied mathematics, and Heaven knows what beside. I have them all — a heap of them, witnessing to things which I once knew and have long since forgotten and to the craving of a myopically minded educator*[52]

---

47  Peers makes the same complaint about this headmaster, using, for the most part, the same words in '(E.A.P.) *Auto*' (see above, ch. 1, pp. 68-69).
48  In fact in Wiltshire (see '[E.A.P.] *Auto*', ch. 1, p. 65).
49  See '(E.A.P.) *Auto*', p. 68, note 20.
50  *Cf.* pp. 189-90, and note 61, below.
51  In fact, Dartford (Grammar School).
52  The phrase 'myopically minded educator', applied here to the headmaster (in reality Mr Jodrell Mansford), provides a possible clue to the character and short-sighted attitudes of the predecessor of Jim Livewire in the Chair of English Literature at Redbrick University. That professor is

*for cheap success.*

Even in the holidays I was not allowed to rest: after I had been learning French for three years I was sent, partly at the expense of a school fund, to take a holiday course in Normandy.[53] My Guernsey master had been all against this. He wanted to take me to Paris, and give me what he described as a 'good time' there, speaking French exclusively, or to send me *en pension* to some friends of his in Savoy. But the Head was adamant; and, as the Head had the funds, he also had the last word. So I spent that August in a poky little Norman town, my lameness debarring me from most of the excursions of the Course and my love of the country[54] making me grudge the four hours spent daily on the hard benches of the local primary school listening to lectures impeccably delivered in somewhat florid French on the dullest subjects.

All the thirty of us who took the Course were farmed out as paying guests to local families, and I was fortunate to be allotted to the Director — the 'Professor', as his wife and the other lecturers encouraged us to call him — who in real life was just the master of the primary school where we had our classes. Monsieur Fouquet was a stout, good-humoured little man of about forty, who ate and drank voraciously, with napkin wound round his neck in French fashion, and talked somewhat explosively, continually making little jokes which not even his sad-faced little wife seemed to take in but at which he himself always laughed heartily.

Somehow I suspected at the time that M. Fouquet had more than an intellectual or pastoral interest in the success of the Course, and I have little doubt now, from what I know of the world[,] that it was run, either largely or entirely, for his own private profit. He was continually asking us for the names and addresses of people to whom he might write about the Course, exhorting us to induce others to attend it, and expatiating on

---

referred to as Professor Miope (?another pseudonym for Oliver Elton ['Professor Slocombe']) in the essay 'Any Faculty Board' — of which the text is printed in Appendix IV.

53 Dartford Grammar School no longer possesses records which might substantiate or document this holiday course.

54 Peers' authentic delight in the countryside is evident also in '(E.A.P.) *Auto*' (see ch. 3 'Schoolmastering', p. 98, note 52; and *cf.* 'B.T.', ch. I, p. 197, and note 85).

the wonderful Certificate of Proficiency which, he hoped, we should be awarded on the results of an examination on the last day of the month, and which, as no doubt he also hoped, would be a potent inducement to others to come next summer.

Two or three days before the examination, M. Fouquet underwent an alarming transformation. His appetite failed him. The corners of his mouth turned down. He said little. Instead of making jokes, he sighed [at intervals] voluminously. His wife, who invariably talked to us at the rate of about twenty words per minute, seemed quite familiar with the symptoms and mingled exhortations with her diagnosis.

'The poor man!', she would exclaim. 'See him, how he worries, how he frets. The cause, it is the examination. The visiting examiner, he who comes from Caen, he is the strictest in the world. My husband, he fears lest you all fail. So you must work, *hein*? So you must redouble the efforts. There will be no more excursions till the day of the examination is over'.

The day came. The morning we spent scratching out answers to a written paper; the afternoon, in groups of two, being oralled by M. Fouquet and the visiting 'Professor' (no doubt a fellow-headmaster) from Caen. The visitor was the most perfect stage Frenchman — moustached, gesturing and shoulder-shrugging — I have ever seen. The ordeal of each [of us] over, we retired, as directed, to the parlour of the little schoolhouse, to await the declaration of the results. In about half-an-hour, we saw the door of the school open and the visitor depart for his train. Then the rotund little figure of M. Fouquet, beaming once more, bounced across the asphalt playground and burst into the parlour.

'*Mes enfants*', he cried, with visible emotion. 'It is good news, splendid news, that I have for you. You have *all* passed! All! All!'

And so saying, he went to the cupboard, brought out a pile of certificates and proceeded to inscribe them with our names and sign them.

Oh, but it was a wonderful certificate — about four feet by three, and adorned with scrolls, flourishes and, in the corners, atrociously engraved pictures symbolic of various branches of learning. But it impressed my Headmaster at the Grammar

School[55] all right — and from that time forward one or more of his boys visited M. Fouquet every summer.[56]

'I should frame it if I were you', was his first comment to me, 'and hang it in my bedroom'.

My father, however, to whom I passed on the suggestion, smiled tolerantly.

'I should wait a bit before you do that', he said.[57]

The Chatstone examination-cult had only one advantage *that I can think of: it prevented that unduly early specialization which is so much decried to-day.*[58] *I am grateful, for example, to that school for inducing me to work hard at sciences for which I have never had the least aptitude, as well as at French for which I had a good deal. It must be admitted that any boy who in four years studied all the sciences enumerated above, together with English Literature, Scripture, Geography, English and Roman History, Latin, French, Anglo-Saxon, a modicum of German and rather more than a modicum of Greek, enjoyed a broad, if somewhat superficial, education. But the harm done to me by this particular form of training much more than outweighed this [/the] advantage. Being of a docile temperament — even now, after decades of disillusionment, I am still rather too much inclined to trust the man who ought to know his own job — I accepted unquestioningly the insidiously conveyed idea that the*

---

55   Chatstone, but, in reality, Dartford Grammar School.

56   This amusing account is clearly derived from Peers' own memories of his schooldays. Yet, despite his educationally less than valuable experiences at this vacation course in France, Peers was to become, during his tenure of the Gilmour Chair of Spanish at Liverpool University, an enthusiastic advocate and tireless organizer of regular Summer courses and educational excursions for students and teachers in Spain (see, for instance, his second application for the Gilmour Chair, 1921 [Appendix I, p. 436]; and, in the Postscript, Audrey Lumsden-Kouvel's essay, 'E.A.P. Remembered', pp. 401-02).

57   At this point in the narrative, Peers has written, in pencil: 'space' — to indicate the conclusion of the first section of 'Bruce Truscot''s opening chapter.

58   In *Redbrick University* Peers is critical of excessive specialization both at school and in universities. But he also warns against the opposite extreme — too little specialization: 'The fear of premature specialization is a bogy which has haunted educationalists far too long' (see *op. cit.*, ch. 5, 128-41, and especially 141).

*chief end of education was the passing of examinations.*[59] The Headmaster demanded results; the assistant masters had to see that he got them. Hardly a lesson passed, and certainly not a day passed, without our being reminded of the examination next ensuing. Some boys frankly scoffed at the whole thing and did as little work as possible: at the time I thought they were mere lazy cynics, but years afterwards I began to wonder. A few — the sensible, strong-minded ones and I wish I had *been one of them* — scorned 'pot-hunting' as they scorned 'mark-grubbing' (we had weekly 'mark-sheets' and a maximum of ten marks for every lesson!), worked for the sake of working and took examinations in their stride. But the 'good boys', not in the least because they wanted to curry favour but because they believed implicitly that the master was always right, allowed this pernicious conception of education to permeate their whole attitude to work, with disastrous consequences. When I went up to Camford,[60] the idea firmly fixed in the centre of my consciousness was how to get the highest possible class in the greatest possible number of examinations. Scholarships only interested me to the extent that I knew they would be a help to my father; prizes, though I got quite a number, interested me hardly at all, I had the most ardent desire to educate myself to the highest degree possible: the mistake I made was to suppose that the examination was the one and only test of education and that by some miraculous means everything one learned would 'come out' in that brief final test which I looked upon as being only less infallible than the ultimate examination of mankind on Judgment Day. This misconception it took me quite ten years to eradicate, and eventually I reacted from it so violently that to this day I have a horror of men who pile up university degrees. It nearly defeated its own ideals; for, having taken the London Intermediate at school, I went up to Camford determined to finish the London B.A. during my first year without any further tuition. By dint of strenuous and (as I later realized) misplaced efforts, I achieved my aim, and had the satisfaction of being a

---

59 One recalls Bruce Truscot's observation in *Redbrick University* that blame must 'be attributed to schools which think too much of examination results, honours boards and future university distinctions and too little of their boys' or girls' personal welfare' (131).

60 That is to say, Cambridge (see above note 40).

graduate of London University, with Second Class Honours in English[61] at nineteen; but I nearly wrecked my Camford degree, since the syllabuses for the two examinations were very different and I got so far behind with my Camford work that I was lucky to get a First there at all.

## II

It is a pleasure to turn from the misplanning and mishandling of my education at school to the perfecting of it by home influences for which I can never be sufficiently grateful. Again and again, in thinking retrospectively over my personal relations with undergraduates, I have realized how much of my unconscious aim has been to try to give them something which my home experiences gave me.[62] It would be pointless here to enter into a discussion on the relative merits of day schools and boarding schools, especially as I tried to put the case for each, as fairly as I could, in *Redbrick and these vital days*.[63] But here, having seen both types of education from the inside — twelve years as a boy at day-school and seven years as master at a boarding-school[64] — I may perhaps be allowed to say that, for the large majority of boys, I should advise a day school without the least hesitation. There are, of course, cases where all sensible people would recommend a boarding school: a family with a long boarding-school tradition; parents living abroad; a boy needing Spartan discipline; a home with bad influences; and so on. But those are exceptional cases. If the average mother and father realised what they were depriving their son of, and what they were sending him into, when they packed him off to

---

61 In fact in English and French, in 1910: *cf.* what he writes in '(E.A.P.) *Auto*', ch. 1, p. 70, and see note 25.

62 Peers begins the corresponding part of his 'real' autobiography with the same observations, phrased in nearly identical terms.

63 Chapters 8 and 9 of *Redbrick and these Vital Days* are devoted respectively to 'The Public School Problem: (I) Synthesis' and 'The Public School Problem: (II) Some Solutions'.

64 Peers taught in three boarding schools over the period 1913-19 (Mill Hill School, 1913-14; Felsted School, May 1914-July 1919; Wellington College, October-December 1919).

his boarding-school, they would do it far less complacently.⁶⁵ When the son comes home for his first holidays, of course, father takes the opportunity of having a *serious talk with him and is vastly relieved to find that the boy can still look him in the face — with that fine manly gaze,* as he expresses it to mother — *and assure him that all is well with him, father, so you needn't bother, really you needn't. If only he knew — what every public-schoolmaster knows — that almost any boy can look you straight in the face and lie to you without blinking an eyelid, he might feel rather differently.*

*But the case for day-schools is built upon something much more positive than misgivings. No headmaster, no house-master, no big-boy hero and no contemporary can ever have as profound an influence on a boy as his own father, from whom he has inherited so much already. And to absorb this influence it is not sufficient for him to meet his father occasionally every few weeks: he must live with him, grow up with him and be able unconsciously to take the measure of him in all the frequent minor crises of his life. What is true of the boy is true, though perhaps to a lesser extent, of the girl: on the whole, and for many reasons, I should feel safer in sending a girl away to school than a boy.*⁶⁶ *It applies less, however, to the mother's influence than to the father's: so far as my experience goes, the former, as well as being absorbed at a much earlier age, is as a rule the more easily recaptured. My advice, then, to parents who are unfortunate enough not to live near a good day school would be to avoid the resident 'prep. school', and when public-school age comes, or earlier if necessary, to send their boy, if they can, to live with someone, such as one's brother, or old friend, who will stand genuinely in loco parentis to him rather than commit him to the care of a house-master who cannot possibly know the individual members of a family from six to eight times as large as one of even maximum Victorian size.*⁶⁷

---

65  Peers makes similar comments in '(E.A.P.) *Auto*', ch. 1, p. 70.

66  Here, as in the imagined conversation between a new boarding-school boy and his father, Peers is apparently referring discreetly to the homosexual practices prevalent in public schools. Peers addresses the subject of 'sexual vice' in public schools — which he thinks can never be wholly avoided — in *Redbrick and these Vital Days* (164-65).

67  Peers, therefore, is clearly not so much against public schools as against the loss of family life and influence which results for schoolboys, from

*Everyone, I suppose, who has known his parents, can trace the majority of his temperamental traits to one of them. From my mother,*[68] *one of a large family, composed mainly of boys who in monotonous succession became 'something in the City'[,] I inherit a business instinct which has stood me in remarkably good stead and an agility, a quickness of movement and a detestation of idleness which have ensured for me a life of happy activity. From my father, and from his father before him,*[69] *I derive a passion for all kinds of knowledge, a love of writing, a hatred of unfairness and intolerance, and above all an objectivity of outlook which, in him, as I found when I grew to know him better, was one sign of the deep placidity of his interior life.*[70]

My home life, in all its essential aspects, was as nearly perfect as home life can be.[71] That is not merely a pious phrase: looking back upon it, as one often does when the home has been broken up, I have been unable to think of one single way in which, given the material conditions of my family, it could have been bettered. There was little money, yet no parade was ever made of the constant necessary economies, of many of which neither my sisters[72] nor I were *ever conscious — largely, no doubt, because we had no well-to-do friends as we should if we had been to more expensive schools. Though simple, everything*

---

residential education. He makes very similar observations in *Redbrick and these Vital Days*: 'Any kind of boarding-school life, by comparison with it [home life], is artificial. There may be a minority of boys for whom it is better — those, for example, of certain antecedents or temperaments, orphans, only children, those with no home or whose parents live abroad or in the depths of the country' (173). Interestingly, however — for instance, in *Redbrick University* — Peers strongly believes in the advantages, for students in general, of attending a residential university: 'one of the primary future aims of the modern university will be to have more of its students, both men and women, in residence' (see chapter 1, 20-22, 26, 39-41).

    68  Jessie Dale Peers (née Allison) (see '[E.A.P.] *Auto*', ch. 1, p. 62, note 3).

    69  John Thomas Peers and his father, Robert Peers (see '[E.A.P.] *Auto*', ch. 1, pp. 61-62, note 3).

    70  Peers describes his father in notably similar terms in '(E.A.P.) *Auto*', ch. 1, p. 71 (and see note 28).

    71  Peers uses exactly the same sentence in his 'real' autobiography (see ch. 1, p. 71).

    72  As previously noted, unlike Truscot, Peers had only one sister (see above, note 21).

*bought and used in the house was good, and dislike for the cheap and pretentious was reflected in the studied care with which everything thought worth doing was done. The table was as carefully and neatly laid for a meal* **en famille** *as when there were strangers and the spare room was always ready for an unexpected visitor, though few visitors, in fact, came without due notice. My mother's health, over a period of my ten most impressionable years, was extremely precarious, and my father's almost womanly care for her afforded constant object-lessons in considerateness and practical affection. In later life, she grew rather stronger, while my father, after his retirement, developed a heart weakness which turned her into the nurse and him into the patient. Among the many joys which have fallen to my lot one of the greatest has been the privilege of visiting them constantly during their old age. For nearly sixty years they lived as perfect partners and I never hope to see a lovelier picture of happy and contented old age than in the country cottage which until a few years ago was for me a place of pilgrimage.*[73]

*We were taught, as children, far more by example than by precept. Religion, with the various somewhat puritanical restrictions usual in the homes of religiously-minded Victorians,* we absorbed quite unconsciously. As our father preached only occasionally in the church which we attended,[74] it was not because it pleased us to see and hear him that we went to Church willingly. We went because we enjoyed it; and we enjoyed it because father and mother enjoyed it — in fact we never enjoyed it as much as in the summer, when we all went away to 'rooms' at the seaside, and father would smile at mother over the Sunday breakfast-table, and say: 'Well, dears, how nice it is to be able to go to church all together again!'

In the same way, we had no desire to 'garden' on Sundays, not because we thought it was wrong, or had ever so much as considered whether it was right or wrong, but because our father, the keenest of gardeners, always put away his tools on

---

73 The first version, which Peers changed, is still visible and reads 'little south coast retreat', and in fact the Peers lived at Worthing on the south coast after John Peers' retirement (see '[E.A.P.] *Auto*', ch. 1, p. 62, note 3).

74 The Peers family attended Congregational churches, but Allison Peers was later in life a member of the Church of England (*cf.* '[E.A.P.] *Auto*', ch. 1, pp. 72-73, notes 33-34).

Saturday night.⁷⁵ We were never allowed to use paints, though we could use crayons if we liked, on Sundays, and this restriction we accepted as perfectly natural, because with paints you generally make a mess, whereas with crayons you didn't, and part of the ethos of our upbringing was that Sunday was a day when messes were not made.

On the few occasions when we kicked over the traces my father's method was simply to let us have our way without comment. Almost without exception, we capitulated of our own accord.⁷⁶ I can recall only a single occasion when I knowingly persisted in acting against my father's wishes, and that was when, as a very young man, I felt bound in conscience to tell him that Methodism, which in most ways I found unsympathetic and in a few quite revolting, was not for me. That was a worse blow for him than I, who have never had much understanding of exclusiveness in religion, can possibly realize. A convert himself from the Church of England, he loved the denomination which he had embraced as a man loves his bride. I have little doubt, though he never said so, that he had set his heart upon my entering the Methodist ministry. Few things have hurt me as much as the look in his eyes when I told him of my decision, but he bowed his head in silence, and never then nor afterwards said a word to *dissuade me. He knew that, if anything less than conscience had driven me to it, the community between us was too close to make any continued recalcitrance possible. Perhaps he remembered a scene that took place when I was only seven years old — I can still see every detail of it — just outside the garden gate of our little house in Yorkshire.*⁷⁷ *'I hate you', I had cried in a fit of passion; 'I shall bite you'. 'Very well', he had replied, quietly, extending his hand, with its back toward me. I can see that hand now, browned by the sun, but not hardened, with its long sensitive fingers; and again and again I have seen it since, when momentarily blinded by anger. But I had felt then as if I were seeing it for the first time. And I had paused a moment, stupefied, all my passion*

---

75 *Cf.* the similar passage, about his father's conduct on Sundays, in '(E.A.P.) *Auto*', ch. 1, p. 72.

76 The two initial sentences of this paragraph occur, almost word for word, in '(E.A.P.) *Auto*', ch. 1, pp. 72-73.

77 In fact, in Morayshire.

*gone, and covered the beloved hand with tears and kisses.*

*Little by little, I see, in this picture of home, my father's character is taking the foremost place, and my mother's, less dominant, though no less fine, is receding into the background. That I always felt to be right.* The two were partners in the work of organizing the household, and to a large extent they had each their self-delimited spheres so that neither interfered with the other. Mother would no more have suggested modifying the time-table for the garden than father the time-table of spring-cleaning. But, genuine though the partnership was, he took his natural place as managing director, and even in his last years, when he was a semi-invalid and my mother had to act much more on her own initiative, she sought his opinion whenever it was possible.[78]

Though I have mixed to more than an average extent with men of various classes and nationalities, my father still seems to me the most remarkable man I have known. Had he had even my own limited opportunities, he would have gone much farther. His sermons were simple, and he had an unusual power of vivid appeal to unlettered people, but his ministerial friends have often told me that he was more than a competent theologian. (As a schoolboy, I remember wondering why, if he knew all there was in those rows and rows of books, he did not put it into his sermons). But of other subjects, too, he had an extensive knowledge. He was widely read in English literature, in translations of foreign literature and in European history. He was, as I have said, an expert gardener, an excellent carpenter and a very useful electrician. But it was in moral, rather than in intellectual, energy that he had most to give.[79] *To the disciplinary value of his own personality I have already alluded; and, as a schoolmaster, I found his methods effective when all the maxims of the education text-books failed. He was the sweetest tempered of men: in all my life I can never recall an occasion when he either lost his temper or raised his voice, however slightly, in anger. He taught us tolerance by always insisting on hearing, and giving due weight, to both sides of every question. He taught us to prize exactness and to avoid exaggeration: even now when I get up to consult a dictionary I*

---

78  *Cf.* '(E.A.P.) *Auto*', ch. 1, p. 73.
79  *Cf.* '(E.A.P.) *Auto*', ch. 1, pp 73-74.

*can see him rising from table, as he often did, in the middle of a meal, to do the same. He taught us to make good use of scraps of time. 'It is a strange but a true thing that the busiest people have the most time' is a maxim which experience has made axiomatic to me and on which I have laid great stress in my little book written for freshmen,* **First Year at the University**.[80] *That maxim has its source in a letter which I received from my father at the age of nine. He taught us to practise initiative, concentration, perseverance, mental gymnastics and much more which I have tried to teach others. He taught us an idealism to which I shall refer later. No teacher I have ever had can for a moment be compared with him; nearly every moral quality I may possess I can trace to him; and it is one of my greatest satisfactions that, though I have never been able to repay him directly for what he has done for me, there are many men and women in the world who, without having known him,*[81] *are unconsciously indebted to him through what I have been able to teach them of his character and example.*

### III

*It was in October 1904 that the peregrinations which made up my school life came to an end and I matriculated as a freshman at Trinity College, Camford.*[82]

*So far I have said little about myself, as distinct from my actions, though, having been blessed all my life with close and candid friends, I have a fair idea of what I was like at this time. I was a queer, rather gauche individual, keenly sensitive of my*

---

80 The clause containing the specific reference to *First Year at the University* did not originally figure in, but has been added to, this passage transferred from the Peers autobiography. Published by Faber and Faber, London, in 1946, the book was still thought useful to, and by, undergraduates in the 1960s; because a revised version, by James Blackie and Brian Gowenlock, was issued in 1964.

81 In the manuscript the words 'but who' follow here, which the editors have removed, since clearly Peers intended to delete them.

82 As previously indicated, Peers entered Christ's College, Cambridge, in October 1909. Bruce Truscot, born, supposedly, in 1885, is some six years older than his creator.

*physical disabilities, rather shy with people whom I felt to be outside my previous limited experience, a good talker once I was at my ease,*[83] *and on the whole, I think, a fairly good companion, though it was years before I lost the habit of doing erratic things for no reason that I could myself explain, which were most disconcerting for my friends. I used to say that I hated all kinds of games, from football to spillikins,*[84] *and I was certainly relieved when, except for exercise or Christmas-party relaxation, I had to play them no more. But probably what I really hated was the desire to win: to this day it annoys me to hear a full-grown man or woman speak of a game as if it were in itself of the slightest importance and to see someone lose his temper over a game makes me feel physically ill. My chief delights were walking, bird-watching, reading, and playing or listening to music.*[85]

*The most important characteristic in my moral make-up, however, was idealism. Perhaps it still is; but, ever since it received its first rude shocks at Camford,*[86] *it has been increasingly tempered by practical common sense; I hope that, as a result of subsequent shocks at Cranstead, Oxbridge and Redbrick,*[87] *these two ingredients are now mingled with it in a more suitable proportion.*

*In the summer before I went up to Camford my idealism, created at home and fostered by Chatstone Grammar School,*[88] *was probably at its height. I worked like a Trojan for my*

---

83 Peers has deleted, in pencil, the adjective 'limited', and bracketed (also for deletion) the words 'I was'.

84 Spillikins is 'a game played with a heap of slips or small rods of wood, bone, or the like, the object being to pull off each by means of a hook without disturbing the rest' (*The Oxford English Dictionary*, 2nd ed., 1989).

85 Peers' authentic delight in country walks and bird-watching is also revealed later, as are his fondness and aptitude for music (see below, ch. II, pp. 227-28, 253-54, and note 92; and *cf.* above, '[E.A.P.] *Auto*', ch. 3, p. 100). Norman Lamb, former student of Peers at Liverpool, and later (from 1946) his colleague in the Department of Hispanic Studies there, vividly remembers Peers' exceptional talents as a musician. See also, in the Postscript, Ivy L. McClelland, 'Allison Peers as a University Teacher', pp. 398-99.

86 That is to say, Cambridge.

87 In Peers' case, the 'shocks' to his idealism were suffered, after Cambridge, at Felsted (School), and then at Liverpool.

88 That is, Dartford Grammar School.

London B.A. while allowing myself at intervals to dream happily of Trinity.[89] I had seen it for the first time, only a few weeks before, in all the beauty of late June and I thought there could not be another place so beautiful. Not having a Camford scholarship, but only a County one, I had been able to choose my college; and my father, having ascertained from a brother-minister who had been there that none of the colleges was 'specifically Methodist in its spirit and life', had wisely allowed me a free choice. And I had chosen Trinity — oh, how characteristically! — because two of my heroes in English literature had been educated there.[90] So I dreamed, in that heavenly last vacation, of a career of unadulterated first-classes, of earning more in scholarships than it would cost my father to educate me, of a brilliant career at the Union — the only form of distinction I ever coveted —, of becoming in some way 'Captain' of my college (I had the vaguest ideas of what forms of leadership there might be) as I had been Captain of my school, and finally, of becoming a don,[91] if not indeed Master of the College, and in some magnificent set of Fellows' Rooms (perhaps even a set with a bathroom, if such existed)[92] living happily every after.

All this is trite enough, no doubt: presumably such ambitions fire a large proportion of the breasts that are encased every October in brand-new freshmen's blazers. But I think I went much farther than most; certainly, much farther than I have yet said. The majority of freshmen, when they come up to the University, were then, and are still, fairly sophisticated. Old boys from their schools already in residence see to this: they coach them beforehand in Freshers' 'Don'ts' and receive them into their

---

89 In fact, of Christ's College.

90 Famous former members of Christ's College, Cambridge, include John Milton (1608-74). Trinity College, Cambridge, boasts a number of famous poets, playwrights and novelists among its former members, including John Dryden, Lord Byron, Alfred, Lord Tennyson and W. M. Thackeray.

91 It is interesting that when still scarcely more than a schoolboy, before his undergraduate studies had begun, Peers should intuitively have desired to become a university teacher and scholar.

92 Peers' pre-university desire for the luxury of a private bathroom is worth remembering, with amusement, when reading his account of the primitive conditions he experienced within College, without bathroom or lavatory ('except across a wind-swept quadrangle') (see below, p. 209; and *cf.* p. 217).

## SCHOOL AND UNIVERSITY (1885-1907) 199

*habitations for a short period on their arrival. Fathers, uncles or schoolmasters supply any deficiencies and much good advice. I had had none of this. Not a single boy from Chatstone Grammar School*[93] *had ever been either to Camford or to Oxbridge. Not a single master at that time, so far as I remember, had graduated there, except the vivacious Guernseyman*[94] *— who, it might be added here, had taken too much to drink on the night of my last breaking-up party, and, after chasing the Headmaster round his house with a carving knife, had been summarily dismissed. Neither my father nor any of my relatives had been to a resident university. I had hardly even met anyone who had. So I felt extraordinarily lonely as I threaded my way through groups of hearty, loud-voiced young men at the London terminus*[95] *looking for a corner seat (third class and non-smoking!) in the Camford train. My father had driven with me from the house to Chatstone station in a particularly malodorous provincial horsecab: I can smell it still! I remember that drive as one of the very rare occasions when, somewhat in the best Tom Brown manner, he endeavoured to give me some 'good advice': Bless him! He needn't have troubled! His own example, over nineteen years of continuous contact, had taught me and inspired me far more than anything he could ever say.*

*Behold, then, an insignificant undergraduate member of Trinity College, Camford,*[96] *embarked upon a course of study leading to the examination for a degree in Honours in English Language and Literature.*[97]

By the present-day standards of almost any university, ancient or modern, the inefficiency of the instruction given us at

---

93 That is to say, Dartford Grammar School.

94 Mr L. J. Oberlé was King Charles I Exhibitioner at Pembroke College (a scholarship associated with Channel Island students), matriculating in 1902. He began to study Mathematics, but after obtaining a 3rd class in Moderations changed to Modern Languages and gained a 3rd class B.A. in 1906 and his M.A. in 1909. He died in 1948. See too above, p. 182, and note 39.

95 Liverpool Street Station. Peers' memories of his own emotions and difficulties as a freshman doubtless assisted him when he wrote *First Year at the University*, and certain parts of *Redbrick University* (see, for instance, ch. 1, section I).

96 In reality, Christ's College, Cambridge.

97 In fact, Peers studied for a degree with Honours in the Mediaeval and Modern Languages Tripos.

Camford was appalling. Being an ambitious man, I had secretly determined, while taking a degree in the School of English, to go through at least part of the course in French as well, and for my first term, even with the incubus of the London examination upon me, I stuck to this intention religiously. At the beginning of my second term, however, my tutor told me one day that my work in English seemed to him unusually good and that if I went on at this rate I should be in the running for a fellowship: was it really worth my while, then, to take all these lectures in French, which could not possibly help my degree and might very possibly harm it. As I had only entered for the French lectures because I was interested in them, I readily agreed, for, to tell the truth, I was already bored stiff with them. The nineteenth-century lecturer[98] was dull in manner and had hobby-horses which he rode to death. The sixteenth-century man[99] aroused derision by pronouncing the names of all his authors English-fashion: 'Cornale', 'Mohlyere', and so on. The unspeakable don[100] who lectured on Old French spent two terms dictating an unintelligent construe of Chrétien de Troyes and in the third dictated model answers to all the questions on Historical French Grammar set during the last ten years in the examinations for Final Honours. Add that Camford (and, for that matter, Oxbridge) had at that time no professorship of French[101] and you will see why I was glad to shake the dust of France off my feet at the age of nineteen. I have never taken an examination in the language since, though I have read in it widely.

Not that the English Language and Literature School at that time was a great deal better. There were two professors, but I never addressed, or was addressed by, either of them. Of Drake, the Professor of English Literature,[102] I should

---

98 The Revd Hugh F. Stewart (see '[E.A.P.] *Auto*', ch. 2, pp. 77-78, and note 9).

99 Arthur A. Tilley (see '[E.A.P.] *Auto*', ch. 2, p. 78, and note 10).

100 Dr E. G. W. Braunholtz (see '[E.A.P.] *Auto*', ch. 2, p. 78, and note 11).

101 The Drapers Professorship in French at Cambridge was not established until 1919. In *Redbrick University* Peers remembers that Cambridge only forty years ago 'had no English Tripos, and no professorships of French, Italian, Spanish or English Literature' (32-33).

102 Professor A. W. Verrall was first holder (1911) of the King Edward VII Chair of English Literature (see '[E.A.P.] *Auto*', ch. 3, p. 92, and note 29). But probably Peers is portraying Verrall's successor in the Chair, Sir Arthur

undoubtedly have made a hero if he had not been so completely unapproachable. He was a tall man, with the stoop of a scholar, a humorous mouth and interesting, rather dreamy eyes — a good lecturer, too, as Camford standards went, and a fascinating writer. He was, I suppose, the ablest man who has ever taught me, if you can call a man never less than ten feet away from you a teacher. Peet, the Professor of Anglo-Saxon[103] — an old man, who died shortly after I went down — was said to be much more approachable; he lived about three miles out, on the Woodchester Road, and the story went that, if you called on him any evening after dinner, he would give you coffee, and talk to you about *Beowolf* [so long] that you wouldn't get home until after midnight, which meant a gating for the rest of the term. As the prospect sounded very dubiously attractive, and the story may in any case have been apocryphal, I never tested its truth, but remained at the statutory distance of ten feet while he translated and commented upon an Anglo-Saxon reader as though all our difficulties would disappear at the sound of his voice. But it is only fair to add that he was human. He would intersperse delightful little observations upon style or sentiment and his quotations of parallel passages from modern authors comprised perhaps the only inspiration which I got in three years from any of my regular teachers. I still have that reader, with the notes from his lectures in the margin, and his photograph, which I bought when I went down, still hangs in my study. I wish I had known him; but in my day etiquette protected professors from hypothetically presumptuous undergraduates (I don't know if it does still) by ruling that, while you might quit the lecture-room of a mere lecturer as soon as his discourse was ended, you must allow a professor to leave

---

Quiller-Couch, whom he admired (see '[E.A.P.] *Auto*', ch. 3, p. 92 and note 28). Dr Rex Salisbury Woods recollects that Quiller-Couch was 'outstanding, not only in appearance but also for the respect and affection he inspired... Tall and rugged... he looked far more an outdoor man than the second holder of the Chair... He usually wore a rough tweed suit, a single white starched collar and bow tie, but for lecturing he put on full morning dress. He was beloved of the undergraduates and "Q" to everyone' (*Cambridge Doctor*, [London: Robert Hale, 1962], 95).

103 Professor W. W. Skeat (d.1912). He lived at 2 Salisbury Villas, Cambridge. For Peers' comments on Skeat, which are very similar to those made here of 'Peet', see '(E.A.P.) *Auto*', ch. 2, p. 76; see also note 6.

the room before you stirred.[104]

Such were my two professors. The lecturers were much worse — so bad that I had better not name them. One, whose field was Old English grammar,[105] was coldly efficient, but everyone disliked him because he used to make veiled attacks on poor old Peet.[106] Middle English texts were taken by the worst of all the bunch,[107] who drearily translated page after page of Chaucer and Langland[108] into modern English, adding notes which often differed little from those in the annotated editions which we had before us. But it was when this same man lectured on eighteenth- and nineteenth-century poetry that the English School sank to its lowest depths of all. For he was cursed with the most foully monotonous voice, and apparently also with a complete unawareness of the fact. And he would quote poem after poem, without a semblance of expressiveness, in that soporific sing-song which must have killed the interest of all but the most ardent of his hearers.

There were others, but, perhaps mercifully, I have forgotten them. At that time I was by way of being a specialist in Shakespeare, but whose lectures on Shakespeare I went to I cannot for the life of me remember. Perhaps I abandoned them in disgust. I remember, too, a course on the Victorian novel, but again I forget who gave it. Only of one man besides those I have mentioned have I preserved any vivid recollection, and he was no lecturer, but only a supervisor of studies. In fairness, however, I ought to say something about him.

My first tutor at Camford was a feeble old clergyman of nearly eighty[109] afflicted with some variety of palsy which made

---

104 In *Redbrick University*, referring to Oxbridge more than thirty years later than the period here described, Peers still felt obliged to complain about the teaching system there: 'the undergraduate has the minimum of contact with those whom he most needs to know' (24).

105 A. J. Wyatt (see '[E.A.P.] *Auto*', ch. 2, p. 77, and note 7).

106 That is to say, Skeat.

107 Evidently this was G. C. Macaulay (see '[E.A.P.] *Auto*', ch. 2, p. 77, and note 8).

108 Presumably the work of Geoffrey Chaucer (*c.*1342-1400) that was translated so drearily was *The Canterbury Tales*; William Langland (*c.*1330-*c.*1386) is best remembered for his great allegorical poem, *Piers Plowman*. Skeat was a specialist on Chaucer and Langland. But since Peers admired Skeat, he must here be criticizing Macaulay, whom he probably disliked.

109 Revd J. W. Cartmell (see '[E.A.P.] *Auto*', ch. 2, p. 79, and note 13).

the weekly ordeal of reading an essay to him perfectly terrifying. At the end of my first year, his speech became so incoherent that he had to retire. In the following October, the numbers reading English became so large that his successor farmed a bunch of us out to a young man of under thirty,[110] who, like a good many brilliant young men of that age, was living in a cheap set of rooms over a shop in a noisy street, and indulging in [/existing on] plain living, high thinking and as much coaching as he could lay hands on. He preferred discussions to formal essays; or, as one of my cynical contemporaries put it, he would spend the first half-hour in talking about what we had talked about last time and the second half-hour in predicting what we should talk about next time. Certainly, one never seemed to get very much farther with him. But he put ideas into our head, which was what we most needed. His intellectual interests were immensely wide — among them, to my knowledge, were Chinese, Russian, Ibsen (in those days a terrible person!), aesthetics and experimental psychology. And the best thing about him was that, despite his own wide range and intensively modern outlook, he would be as courteously receptive of the ideas of a boy of twenty from a provincial grammar school as he could be of those of a world-famed scholar at the High Table.[111] Heaven knows what he must have thought of some of mine! But the fact remains that he was the only one of my Camford teachers with whom I had any give-and-take of ideas, and for that, I shall always remember him with gratitude.

There was just one more source of inspiration which I found in lecture-rooms — the discourses of occasional visiting professors. These were so much superior to our home products both in delivery and in content that I was sometimes tempted to wish I had gone to another university: it never occurred to me to suspect that our own people could be equally good *if they liked*.

---

110 Edward Bullough (see '[E.A.P.] *Auto*', ch. 2, pp. 79-80, and note 15).

111 Bullough, for whom, clearly, Peers had a profound admiration, is characterized in markedly similar, and comparably favourable, terms in both autobiographies. Bullough's courteously receptive responses to the opinions of his students evidently influenced Peers, during his own career as a university teacher; for he adopted a similar approach in his seminars, to develop the confidence of diffident undergraduates (see below, Ivy L. McClelland, 'Allison Peers as a University Teacher', p. 398).

I will refer only to one of these, who happened to make a particular impression on me, and I do so because, though I never imagined it at the time, he was to exercise a great influence on my own fortunes.

The Snark Lectures, as they are popularly called, were founded in memory of Lewis Carroll, and are delivered on a subject connected with lyric poetry, or, in alternate years, with prose fiction.[112] Though forty years have passed, and in the interval, I have twice given the Snark lectures myself,[113] I can recall as vividly as though it were yesterday the announcement in the *University Gazette* that the lecturer for 1906 would be George Charles Upright, Litt.D. (Oxbridge), Professor of Poetry in the University of Redbrick.[114]

I can recall, too, that the announcement gave me a slight

---

112 The Snark Lectures are the famous Norman Maccoll Lectures, wittily disguised. The disguise chosen reveals Peers' fondness and admiration for the writings of Lewis Carroll: not only the 'Alice' books, but Carroll's nonsense verse, for instance, *The Hunting of the Snark* (1876). In choosing to re-name the Maccoll Lectures as The Snark Lectures Peers might have remembered, among others, the line: 'What I tell you three times is true' (in *Hunting of the Snark*, Fit I *The Landing*).

Another indication of Peers' interest in Lewis Carroll is Bruce Truscot's essay, 'A Redbrick Tea-party', published in *The Universities Review*, XVII (May 1945), no. 2, 38-40 — an amusing piece, for which the author's source of literary inspiration was 'A Mad Tea-Party' in *Alice's Adventures in Wonderland*. The Norman Maccoll Lectureship in the Language or Literature of Spain or Portugal was established at the University of Cambridge in 1905 through a bequest from Norman Maccoll (1843-1905), M.A., of Downing College, and a former editor of the *Athenaeum*; the Lecturer was appointed in every fourth year. Maccoll, who spent three terms at Christ's College, Cambridge, 1862-63, before moving to Downing College, published editions of Calderón and Cervantes.

113 In reality, Peers was never a Norman Maccoll Lecturer. Besides Fitzmaurice-Kelly (see note 114), Dr Henry Thomas, who also features in both narratives (see '[E.A.P.] *Auto*', ch. 6, pp. 156-57, and note 21; and 'B.T.', ch. IV, pp. 353-57, and note 66), gave the Maccoll Lectures (1916). A more recent Norman Maccoll Lecturer (1985), Geoffrey Ribbans — now William R. Kenan Jr Professor of Hispanic Studies, Brown University — was formerly Gilmour Professor of Spanish at Liverpool University (1963-78).

114 The Lecturer for 1912 was James Fitzmaurice-Kelly, Litt.D., F.B.A., Gilmour Professor of Spanish, University of Liverpool; he had also been the first Maccoll Lecturer, in 1908. As noted below, his Maccoll Lectures for 1912 were in fact delivered in 1913. For more information on Fitzmaurice-Kelly, see '(E.A.P.) *Auto*', ch. 3, pp. 112-13, and note 112.

SCHOOL AND UNIVERSITY (1885-1907)    205

shock. The name of Upright, of course, was well known to me, for it was only a year or two since he had published his monumental *History of Elizabethan Poetry*.[115] But that he was Professor of Poetry at Redbrick University I had not realized, and perhaps the greatest shock was that Redbrick should have a Chair of Poetry at all.[116] The only one of its graduates I had ever known was the egregious chemistry master, Meaty.[117] So I associated it subconsciously with the odour of sulphuretted hydrogen, and an uncultured, slightly bloated face bending over a porcelain crucible, with the recitation of a string of formulae in a crude northern accent, and with a succession of loud sniffs followed by the brandishing of a green and yellow silk handkerchief and the blowing of a nose of unusual dimensions with a shattering sonority.

But these first associations were quickly forgotten, and from the time of those Snark Lectures for 1906 onwards, Redbrick was ineradicably associated in my mind with the personality of George Charles Upright. Never was man more appropriately named; for Upright was as tall as Drake and as straight as a die into the bargain. But it was neither his height nor his erectness that took possession of me, but his dominating presence.[118] The

---

115 Fitzmaurice-Kelly's *A History of Spanish Literature* (ix + 423 pp.) was published in 1898; it was translated into French by H. D. Davray, Paris, 1904, and a 2nd revised edition, in French, was published in 1913; a Spanish edition was published in Madrid in 1901 (2nd edition, 1916; 3rd ed., 1921; 4th ed., 1926); a German edition was published in 1925.

116 The Chair of Poetry at Redbrick is, of course, in reality, the Gilmour Chair of Spanish at Liverpool University. The fact that Liverpool had a Chair of Spanish surprised most academics at this time, for until the Cervantes Chair of Spanish Language and Literature was established at King's College London in 1916, the Gilmour Chair was the only professorship of Spanish in the country (see '[E.A.P.] *Auto*', ch. 3, pp. 112-13, and notes 111 and 112).

117 For 'Meaty', who taught science at Chatstone Grammar School, see p. 184, where Peers states — thinking back, perhaps, to the time in Dartford, when he was 'Meaty' 's pupil — that the latter was *not* a graduate. If 'Meaty' was, in reality, Charles Percy Hines, then he obtained his degree in 1905 (see above, note 46).

118 'Fitzmaurice-Kelly was a man of goodly presence and distinguished bearing, marked by a certain courteous aloofness to mere acquaintance' (Oliver Elton, 'James Fitzmaurice-Kelly', *Revue Hispanique*, LX [1924], 1-11, 10).

lectures, by tradition, were given in my [/Trinity] College;[119] and, when the President had concluded his introduction, and Upright very slowly rose, you had the feeling that he was never going to stop rising. He drew himself up to his full height and *took possession of* his audience — I can use no less emphatic phrase — in a way that I have never experienced before or since. 'Just imagine', I remember saying to myself in my unsophisticated way, 'having a man like that for your own professor!'

The subject of the course was 'British Balladry'[120] and none could have been chosen which was likely to impress me more. For in my last year at Chatstone[121] I had learned some German, and after finishing off my London degree I had taught myself to read first Italian and then Spanish. Now both German and Spanish have remarkable ballad literatures, and, drawn to them by a love of popular poetry which has always been strong in me, I found that I could read both with comparative ease. Therefore, as undergraduates went, I was unusually well prepared for the course, which was by far the finest that I had ever heard.

Upright's material, as I should have expected from his *History*, was original and well arranged: one could sit through each lecture without taking a note and then go back to one's rooms and write a précis of it. But it was by his delivery, as arresting as his presence, that one remembered him. He was an exquisite reader.[122] I recall the extraordinarily penetrating

---

119 The lectures were, in fact, given by Professor Fitzmaurice-Kelly in the 'New Lecture Rooms Building' in Bene't Street (i.e. in the 'Arts School' where the Scientific Periodicals Library now is) on five successive days, Monday 21-Friday 25 April 1913. It is possible that Peers, who, it will be remembered, was still in Cambridge in 1913, attended at least some of these lectures.

120 The subject of Fitzmaurice-Kelly's lectures was 'The Lyric Poetry of Spain', and doubtless included commentary on early Spanish ballads.

121 That is, in Dartford Grammar School.

122 In reality, according to Peers, 'as a public lecturer he [Fitzmaurice-Kelly] was poor in the extreme'. Peers even emphasizes Fitzmaurice-Kelly's deficiencies in this respect with an anecdote (see '[E.A.P.] *Auto*', ch. 6, pp. 155-56). Possibly it was Peers' interestingly idiosyncratic sense of humour which caused him to give Upright an ability in which Fitzmaurice-Kelly was, it would seem, notoriously lacking. Peers omits to say whether Fitzmaurice-Kelly's lectures, though badly delivered, were good in substance (*cf.* note

force with which he read the description of 'Fair Rosamond':

> Her crispèd lockes like threads of golde
> Appeard to each mans sight;
> Her sparkling eyes, like Orient pearles,
> Did cast a heavenlye light.
>
> The blood within her crystal cheekes
> Did such a colour drive,
> As though the lillye and the rose
> For mastership did strive.[123]

And the restrained pathos of his rendering of one of the ballads of Spain:

> Gentle river, gentle river,
> Lo, thy streams are stain'd with gore,
> Many a brave and noble captain
> Floats along thy willow'd shore.[124]

And yet, though there was restraint in all he read, and said, the primary impression which he left was one of power. You felt, in a way that even now I cannot explain, that these ballads meant something to him which was inexpressible in words. The reader will gather that, in my usual way, I had over-idealized Upright, and he will be perfectly right. I had. But, even when years afterwards, the ideal I had gradually built up of him was completely shattered, I could still listen to his masterly lectures and be thrilled by their power and charm. Right down to his death, a few years ago, at the age of eighty-five,[125] he retained

---

126).

123 The third and fourth stanzas of 'Fair Rosamond'. Peers used Percy's *Reliques* for his text of 'Fair Rosamond', as also for his text of 'Gentle River, Gentle River' — as notes he made in the margin of his manuscript reveal (PR2²²; 'PR1²⁸¹').

124 The first stanza of 'Gentle River, Gentle River' (a translation of 'Río verde, río verde', which was, for instance, published in Madrid, 1694). The original text accompanies the translation in Percy's *Reliques*, vol. I (*cf.* above, note 123). This ballad is also included in *Ancient Songs, chiefly on Moorish subjects. Translated from the Spanish. By the editor of the Hermit of Warkworth* [i.e. Bishop Thomas Percy] (London, 1775), 27. It seems reasonable to assume that, for his lectures, Fitzmaurice-Kelly indeed chose this ballad, as one of his examples of early Spanish poetry, and recited it (for his largely non-Spanish speaking audience) in English translation.

125 In fact, Fitzmaurice-Kelly died in 1923 at the age of sixty-six years.

his majestic presence, his superb delivery[126] and a great deal of those gifts of literary architecture by which he will always be known.

In 1906, he could have been little over fifty.[127] His hair was greying but his features and mien were still those of a young man. On the evening of his last lecture the President invited the Scholars (of whom I had been once since the end of my first year) to take coffee with him at the Lodge, where for the first time — and the last time for twelve years — I met my hero. He had been reading the current *Grisis*,[128] which had printed some trivial verses of mine, and, recognizing the name, asked me what else I had written. Greatly daring, and not realizing into what an embarrassing position I was putting him, I asked him if I might copy out some of my verses to send him. He smiled encouragingly...

I sat up till midnight copying verses. Then I spent another hour writing to my father and to Nanny. I knew such elation that night as I had never known before and have seldom experienced since. Alas, I had much to unlearn ...!

## IV

These last pages will have given some idea of the way we were dragged up at the Camford[129] of the beginning of the century. Yet, disgraceful as it was, we never did more than grouse at an

---

[126] Upright's presentation and exquisite delivery of his material impressed Truscot exceedingly, in his impressionable youth. Years later, however, as a mature and experienced university professor, when he wrote *Redbrick University*, Truscot thought it important to remind us that an undistinguished lecture could be delivered superbly, and *vice versa*: a lecture delivered atrociously in monotonous tones could be challenging and give 'food for thought', could be 'life disguised as death', and much better, therefore, 'than that terrible kind of intellectual death which simulates vivaciousness and vitality' (144).

[127] In 1913, when he delivered the lectures, Fitzmaurice-Kelly was in his mid-fifties.

[128] There is no known periodical of this title. Presumably a corruption of Isis, the name of the upper part of the river Thames which flows by Oxford to its confluence with the Thame, Oxfordshire.

[129] That is to say, Cambridge. The comments which make up the rest of this paragraph are very similar to the author's observations in '(E.A.P.) *Auto*'; see ch. 2, p. 80.

occasional professor or apply to our tutors to be allowed to give up someone's lectures. To me, at least, it certainly never occurred to complain of the whole system: indeed, when anybody did so, I used to think him rather hypercritical. It was not that I was without either ideas or difficulties, but merely that I supposed the University might know best, and therefore accepted with complete docility whatever the University offered me. After all, lectures are only a small part of one's education; and Camford gave me so many new and attractive things that I had about as much as I could assimilate.

A brave new world, and a strange new world, it will always be to the freshman who comes up without a friend in it. Perhaps he feels bolder now that he dismounts at the college gate from a taxi than he did when he crept from the interior of a horse-drawn cab. But the basic sensation is still the same — the sensation of wonder. Only the thrill of the unknown could have blinded one to the considerable inconveniences and discomforts to which the boy coming from home, or from a superior type of boarding school, had to accustom himself.[130]

*For example, you may think it incredible, but, excepting for the period of his residence when an undergraduate was in residence, he could never take a full-length bath.*[131] *For college had no bathroom — only a large tin saucer pulled out daily by one's servant from under one's bed with the sour reminder 'Arparsate!';*[132] *no lavatory, either by day or by night, except across [/at the other side of] a wind-swept quadrangle; no communal meals except dinner, so that poverty-stricken undergraduates would breakfast off an interminable calf's tongue*[133] *and lunch all the term long on bread and marmalade*

---

130 Peers contributed an article on 'First Impressions of 'Varsity Life' to the Christmas 1909 issue of *The Dartfordian* (vol. VI, no.1, 15).

131 Peers did not, but probably intended to, delete the words 'excepting for the period of his residence'.

On 3 June 1913, the Baths Committee of Christ's College, Cambridge was given authority for the construction of baths 'at a cost of not more than £1,370'. Peers would, indeed, therefore not have enjoyed these amenities.

132 Presumably a phonetic transcription of the servant's 'Half past eight' [a.m.].

133 ' "Brekker" is quite an institution and is often the occasion for hospitality on a three-course scale, probably because it is followed by nothing more serious than "lekkers" — the technical term for one's lectures... dinner in the College Hall is not regarded either as a pleasure or a penance by our

*and pretend they liked it.*[134] *But against that — the delight of having rooms all one's own, after the choice at home between the family sitting-room and a cold bedroom (there were no gas fires then); the thrill of those heart-to-heart conversations in which one discussed one's lectures, or more often hypothetical moral problems, till three o'clock in the morning: the jostling and clashing of dissimilar minds the like of which my grammar school had never suspected; the cosy little College library, the comfortable Union library, and the vast University library whose dusty shelves any of us might explore; the glories of mediaeval architecture, the sleek loveliness of the Fellows' Gardens, the long afternoon walks over the countryside*[135] *and the unlimited buttered toast when one returned.*[136] *These were the things that made Camford memorable to me. Lectures and dons were extras which hardly entered into one's real life; while as for professors, one supposed they all lived on Poore's Hill*[137] *or somewhere on the way to Woodchester and spent their time doing something vague called research which was no concern of undergraduates anyway.*

---

A. S. [average student]. He finds there the opportunity of meeting men with whom he would not otherwise come in contact; on the other hand, well, the best cooks occasionally make mistakes and College cooks are no exception to the rule' (Peers, *op.cit.*, in *The Dartfordian*, 1909).

134 Peers is describing the conditions which undergraduates endured at Cambridge (and doubtless also Oxford) in the period before the First World War. More than thirty years later, as Peers comments in *Redbrick University* (1943), the financial strain of life at Oxbridge for the ex-council-school boy on a scholarship is still heavy: 'Far from lunching off venison in the Master's Lodgings, he is too often engaged in calculating over how many meals he can spread a piece of dry cheese or a pot of marmalade' (27).

135 Peers' fondness for walks in the countryside is again revealed in this narrative (*cf.* above, p. 197; '[E.A.P.] *Auto*', ch. 3, p. 98, note 52).

136 'The average student, be it understood, does not (as a general rule) begin his day at 2 a.m. by going to bed... The evening is spent, even by Average Students, in many different ways. Most men find time for social duties — "squashes", debates, socials and the like — and a certain amount of "reading" in addition. A quiet smoke and talk after Hall [dinner], followed by a few hours' steady work, is appreciated by the great majority of Cambridge men. It is a common fallacy that 'Varsity men either work or play; the A. S. [average student] does both, and does them well' (Peers, *op.cit.*, in *The Dartfordian*, 1909).

137 Perhaps reference is intended to such areas as Boar's Hill, south west of Oxford, and Grantchester, south west of Cambridge.

*It was not until after taking my degree that I first began to be thoroughly disillusioned about the University. In my first two years I had seen no more and no less of my College dons than the average man. At the outset of your career the Dean and your tutor asked you to breakfast, the principal difference between these two functions being that before the first you had to keep an early chapel and before the second you had not. Your table companions were generally selected according to the alphabet, or more rarely according to the schools they came from or the subject they read. Now and then there were disasters, as when a scion of an old Trinity*[138] *family called Sing*[139] *(who later changed his name to Synge) found himself at the Dean's breakfast-table beside a Japanese and opposite two Chinamen. Evidently the Dean had mistaken him for a member of that happy family Uno-Sum-Sing of our nursery days.*

*Besides these rare functions, there were weekly 'squashes' at the Dean's on Sunday nights, which it was 'done' for everybody to attend once a term (on the last Sunday there was generally a shortage of chairs and coffee).*[140] *There was also a Sunday night squash at the President's Lodge, which, however, could be attended only by invitation. That was the extent of donnish hospitality which the ordinary man enjoyed: if the undergraduates had been divided among the whole body of*

---

138 That is to say, Christ's College.

139 Revd Edward Joshua Sing (later Synge), who was educated at Uppingham School and Clifton College before entering Christ's College (B.A. 1883, M.A. 1886) was father of two Christ's College students (Martin Millington Sing, later Synge, B.A. 1913, M.A. 1917, and Charles Millington Sing, later Synge, B.A. 1910); three of the Revd Synge's brothers were also students at Christ's College. See John Peile (compiler), *Biographical Register of Christ's College 1505-1905...Vol. II: 1666-1905* (Cambridge: Cambridge U. P., 1913).

140 At this point Peers has deleted the following lines (still decipherable), no doubt because the real people to whom they directly refer do not belong in 'Bruce Truscot' 's narrative: 'and in Shipley's (the aged and almost invisible John Peile had died at the beginning of my second year)'. Though Peers makes only passing reference to Dr Peile (1837-1910), in the view of Christopher Brooke he was 'a remarkable man who combined the love of the old and the new to a quite exceptional extent... he was a classical scholar, oarsman, much loved tutor, and leader in liberal causes' (Brooke, *A History of the University of Cambridge*, Vol. IV *1870-1990*, 59). (On Sir Arthur Everett Shipley and John Peile, see '[E.A.P.] *Auto*', ch. 2, pp. 81-82, note 20).

*Fellows more of them might perhaps have made friends of their seniors as well as being more efficiently tutored. But this would have made tutorships less lucrative appointments and the other Fellows might not have thought the comparatively small additions to the stipends worthwhile.*

A few months before completing my degree course I found myself becoming more intimate with the Senior Fellows. With the Dean, and with my own tutor,[141] I had several interests in common, but most of the others I hardly knew even by sight. It did strike me, therefore, as a little peculiar when the President[142] invited me, for no apparent reason, not to a squash or a perfunctory breakfast, but to a luncheon at which the only other guest was one Gilkes,[143] a fellow-Scholar in my year who was also reading English. Two or three days later, I received a similar invitation from the Senior Tutor,[144] and again Gilkes was there. On the afternoon of that same day I was hailed by the Professor of German,[145] a Fellow of Trinity, who walked me round and round the quad discussing — or rather lecturing to me on — German balladry. These and other marks of favour were a great puzzle to me. At first I vaguely supposed that most third-year men probably received them. Then they became too pointed to admit of such an explanation. I remember putting it to Gilkes one day, as we walked to a lecture. Gilkes had come from one of the finest Public Schools and was much more knowledgeable and more sophisticated than I. He was fully equal to the occasion.

'Oh', he said, 'Don't you know? They're discussing us both for a fellowship'.[146]

That proved in fact to be the case. Some of the larger

---

141 The Revd A. V. Valentine-Richards, Dean of the College, and Mr Norman McLean, one of the College's Tutors. For information on these individuals see '(E.A.P.) *Auto*', ch. 2, pp. 80-81, especially notes 18 and 19.

142 Arthur E. Shipley, Master of Christ's College; see above note 140 and '(E.A.P.) *Auto*', ch. 2, p. 81, note 20.

143 Frank Rönnfeldt (later Renfield). See '(E.A.P.) *Auto*', ch. 3, p. 85, note 2.

144 Mr Norman McLean presumably.

145 The Schröder Professor of German, Dr Karl H. Breul, was attached to King's College, Cambridge.

146 A Fellow in Modern Languages *was* being sought: see '(E.A.P.) *Auto*', ch. 2, p. 82.

colleges at Camford throw their Junior fellowships open to competition, competitors submitting dissertations on subjects of their choice. But at Trinity, a college of moderate size, the elections are made privately, and the candidate selected is often apprised of the fact only a day or two beforehand. I knew that a Fellow in English literature was badly needed to stop the transference of undergraduates to supervisors from other colleges. I ought to have realized that, having won a University Essay prize and a Shakespeare scholarship, and, despite my early flirtation with London, taken a first in each of my College examinations, I was very much in the running for a fellowship.[147] My post-graduation plans were still very vague. I had won sufficient scholarship money to enable me to stay on for a fourth year and I had simply hoped that during that time something would turn up. Any possibility of being elected to a fellowship on graduation had never occurred to me. But, once I realized that it existed, I could think of nothing else. The inscrutable Gilkes made no further reference to the matter — indeed, he seemed to me to be choosing other' subjects of conversation with studied care. I found it difficult to follow him. Debarred from discussing my hopes and dreams, I gave vent to them in letters. Yet nothing happened. The final examinations came and went; my First was announced; the College awarded me a graduate scholarship; I took my degree; my tutor discussed what I should read in my fourth year, saying not a word as to the prospects of a fellowship. I had packed my trunks and was about to go down for the vacation, when, passing the College Boards on my last afternoon up, I caught sight of a half-sheet of notepaper with an announcement in the spidery hand of the President:

Trinity College<br>
Camford

Elected this day into a College Fellowship<br>
MAURICE WEBSTER GILKES, B.A.<br>
June 23 1907.[148]

---

[147] For Peers' University prizes, etc., see '(E.A.P.) *Auto*', ch. 2, p. 82, note 23.

[148] Frank Renfield (*cf.* above, note 143) did not obtain a College fellowship. Peers possibly has in mind Brian W. Downs, also a student at

It was my twenty-second birthday, and the thought of the delight which my father and mother would have felt had I been able to telegraph them my own success made the cup of failure doubly bitter. It was the first time I had failed to get something I had badly wanted, and in the life of any ambitious young man that salutary event is a very chastening one. I could, of course, stay up as I had planned, and begin work either for a higher degree or perhaps submit a dissertation for a fellowship at another College. But after these weeks during which I had imagined myself migrating to the Fellows' Block and spending the rest of my life (there were no age limits in those days) at my beloved Camford, the reaction was tremendous. Neither then nor later did I cherish the slightest rancour against the electors, nor think it unfair that Gilkes had been preferred to me: he had much the maturer mind and a suave, urbane manner which would make the process of fossilization which every don has to undergo much more painless than it would be to me. No, the thing was purely personal. I had a problem to solve: what should I do when I went down? For some weeks I had nursed the hope that it was going to be solved for me in the way I should have liked above all others [/best]. Now I suddenly found that it was not. Within a few hours of reading that notice I had decided not to return to Camford in the following October and to take up some other profession.

During the vacation, and chiefly by correspondence, I discussed my future with more people than I had ever done before. Gilkes, to whom I had sent a line of congratulation, wrote me a long and characteristically charming letter, in which

---

Christ's College, (B.A. 1915, M.A. 1919). Downs was not elected a Fellow until 1919; but in 1918 he had become the College's Lecturer in Modern and Mediaeval Languages and English, a position previously held by the Revd J. W. Cartmell (d.1918). For details of Downs' career, see also '(E.A.P.) *Auto*', ch. 3, p. 103, note 72. The only Fellow of the College elected in 1912 was Mr John Tennant Saunders (1888-1965). Contemporary with Peers at Cambridge, he was educated at Tonbridge before entering Christ's College, graduating First Class in the Natural Sciences Tripos, Part I, in 1910, and Part II in Zoology in 1911. At Cambridge he was Demonstrator of Animal Morphology, 1914-26 and University Lecturer in Zoology, 1926-34. He served as Tutor, 1923-35, and Vice-Master, 1950-53, of Christ's College (*Who Was Who, 1961-1970*).

There is, one scarcely needs to add, no record of a 'Maurice Webster Gilkes' studying or graduating at Cambridge.

he urged me to come back and go in for a fellowship elsewhere and prophesised my certain success. The Dean,[149] with whom some time previously I had discussed taking Orders, invited me to stay for a week with him in Cornwall[150] — but that phase was over, so I declined.[151] My old headmaster, who had no great opinion of fellowships, advised me to go into a school and study for an External London doctorate, so as to get a headship early. My father, too, rather to my surprise, seemed to think that I was lucky to have escaped the deadening existence of dondom. The most curious advice, however, came from the President and the Senior Tutor.[152] They had evidently put their heads together and decided that I should be a dreadful nuisance if I remained at Camford, so they decided to do their best to send me abroad. The President wrote to say that he had heard of a University job in English at Shanghai — 'less than a fortnight from home, you know, and much better paid than anything here'. The Senior Tutor pressed me to apply for a lectureship which was going in Canada, and, when I wrote saying that I had no intention of leaving England, replied rather tartly that, if I wanted to get on, I must really 'abandon this foolish prejudice against going abroad'. I had no such prejudice, as I should have had if a College Fellowship had still been my objective. I had simply decided, during these restless weeks, that I had a vocation for teaching, and that, if I could not be a don as I had hoped, I would be a schoolmaster. And such, I had decided before the end of August 1907,[153] I would live and die.

---

149 The Revd A. V. Valentine-Richards (*cf.* above, p. 212; and see note 141).

150 *Crockford's Clerical Directory* records only one address for the Revd Valentine-Richards, that of Christ's College, Cambridge.

151 Peers' interest, at this stage in his life, in taking (Anglican) orders is not surprising. He was a profoundly religious man. See also below, 'B.T.', ch. II, pp. 253-54, and note 92. Peers became a lay reader (*cf.* 'E.A.P [*Auto*]', ch. 3, p. 101). And he often preached in St Andrew's church, West Kirby, the Church, at which, on 1 January 1953, a requiem mass was said for the repose of his soul.

152 Dr A. E. Shipley, Master, and Mr Norman McLean, Senior Tutor, of Christ's College, Cambridge: see too '(E.A.P.) *Auto*', ch. 3, p. 92, for an account of this episode, which evidently took place in 1912-13.

153 Presumably, in fact, the end of August 1912.

Neither the President nor the Senior Tutor reacted at all kindly to this decision. In their letters of advice I thought I had detected the note valedictory, but in their final communications they positively slammed the door upon me. The President, in particular, thought that I should be 'throwing myself away' upon schoolboys — whom he evidently considered inferior to Shanghaians — and sincerely hoped that, if I was determined to sample schoolmastering, I should 'get out of it before it was too late'. In that, at least, I did not disappoint him, though the opportunity to get out was not to come from Camford.

Since my undergraduate days, as will be seen, I have suffered, as all idealists must, repeated disillusionments, and, as the first of these came from Camford, it will be convenient to anticipate a little and refer to it now. It consisted in this: that, as I came back to College on visits, after going down, I began to realize that I was no longer wanted. At school, Old Boys were always welcome, *and, one's old masters, with all their limitations, were only too anxious to give such advice and help as might be at their command. In joining a Camford College I had assumed, with my usual idealism, that I was joining a society, on which I could always depend. When I found I was wrong, I accepted the situation quite philosophically, but it made such an impression upon me* that it has affected my whole career. My own graduates know that they are mine for life, and that they can come to me at any time for whatever I am capable of giving them.[154] If at any time I had found their numbers too large for this to be possible I should [have] assigned the outgoing graduates from that time onward to one of my lecturers. As I hinted in *Red Brick University*, it seems to me a great

---

154 As convincing evidence of Peers' profound and enduring concern for his graduates, there is, for example, the testimony of Ivy L. McClelland, in 'Allison Peers as a University Teacher' (see below, p. 399). Obituaries and letters written when he died confirm Dr McClelland's testimony. See the unsigned letter (reproduced in the Postscript) from a university teacher, and former student, who, referring to the fact that Peers never lost touch with any of his Honours graduates, said: 'each one of them knew that at any moment of intellectual or professional crisis his far-sighted and judicious advice was at their disposal' (396). Further evidence is provided by the *University of Liverpool Hispanic Honour Society Newsletter* which he produced to ensure graduates kept in touch with him and his Department, and, indeed, with each other. A copy of this *Newsletter* (one of the War-time issues [October 1944]) has been lodged in the University's Archives.

disadvantage of education at Camford and Oxbridge that so little interest is taken in the young graduate, who, for some time after going down, frequently needs help far more than while at the university.[155]

*I ought to add that I have never ceased to look upon my Camford days with gratitude and affection. Until I went to live the other side of England [/some hundreds of miles away] I visited Trinity several times yearly. It is not so distinguished a College as in my innocence I once believed, but it does good work and it has better men now than it had then. If I could retire on a research fellowship tomorrow and go where I liked, it would be to Trinity that I should go without the slightest hesitation.*[156] *But I must say that [I] hope I should find a staircase with a bathroom and lavatory.*

---

155 See, for instance, the following comment in *Redbrick University* which, though Peers makes it when discussing the welfare of undergraduates, also indicates his concern for them after they graduate: 'A second, and perhaps the principal, advantage of the modern over the ancient university is the greater care with which the former looks after its alumni' (23). See also, in the same book, the following comment: 'the head of a School... will cultivate each of his students; be a guide, philosopher and friend to them as no-one else in the university can; and keep in touch with them after graduation' (76); see also 150-53.

156 Peers, as we know, never enjoyed a research fellowship of this kind, for he died before his retirement, aged only sixty-one, in 1952.

## CHAPTER II

## SCHOOL AND UNIVERSITY, ACT II (1907-1918)[1]

### I

It is not in my temperament to do things by halves, or to toy with two irreconcilable ideals without endeavouring to decide between them. For this reason alone, I am quite sure that, when I decided to turn my back upon the life of a don, and to become a schoolmaster, I looked upon that decision as final. So my subsequent resolve to make use of my graduate scholarship, and of the County Scholarship, which had been extended for a fourth year, must not in any way be interpreted as a weakening of purpose. For, instead of returning to College and engaging in higher study, I went into lodgings, joined the Camford University Training College[2] and spent the year reading for the Teachers' Diploma.

*That year was undoubtedly, though quite unexpectedly, the happiest of the four. As practically all my friends had gone down I had not looked forward to it: I had not realized how many were the compensations. There was a complete change of subject — itself a relief after three years' cramming. All fear of failing to get a First was gone — one either got the Diploma or one failed to, and apparently few failed. There was, in the teaching practice, the joy of giving to counterbalance the satisfaction of getting. And there was the discovery of* what I had never known before — an absolutely first-class school.

I am quite sure that, if I had had only the prospect of going to a school like Chatstone Grammar School[3] — and that was the best of the five I had myself known — I could never have

---

1 The author's own title, added in pencil
2 That is to say, the University Training College, Cambridge.
3 That is, Dartford Grammar School.

resigned myself to schoolmastering as a profession. In fact, I was only just beginning to realize what I had lost through them. But among my Camford friends had been men from Rugby, Clifton and Merchant Taylors, and these opened to me a new conception of school life entirely.[4] What was my surprise, on going to Camford Grammar School[5] for my school practice, to discover that here, almost at the door of my own college, was a school as good as any of these — as vital and progressive a place as I could wish for.

Since my time Camford Grammar School has gone through numerous vicissitudes and I have no idea what it is like now; but in 1907 it was in its heyday. The headmaster,[6] whom I had seen several times at meetings and lectures, was a podgy, undistinguished looking little man who struck the onlooker as slightly comical. But in his own domain he was looked up to with something like reverence — a king reigning supreme, yet a king with the wisdom to delegate authority to men as able as himself whom he knew he could trust.[7] In three fields — Classics, Modern Languages and English Literature — he had made the school famous, not only throughout the country but in many other parts in the world. It is only right to say that it had two other great advantages — a *clientèle* well leavened by the sons of dons and complete freedom from external *examinations below the standard of University scholarships.*[8] *Brought up, as I had been, on a diet of continual examinations,*[9] *I was astounded that any school could be found where they were simply not taken. A very few weeks [were]*[10] *sufficient to convince me that,* in English literature *at least, they were nothing but an impediment to progress. Since then I have learned that, by regarding them rationally, it is possible to minimize their ill effects, but I could never again consider them as anything better than a necessary*

---

4 Peers uses the same sentence in '(E.A.P.) *Auto*', ch. 3, p. 86.
5 The Perse School, Cambridge. See '(E.A.P.) *Auto*', ch. 3, pp. 87-90.
6 Dr W. H. D. Rouse (see '[E.A.P.] *Auto*', ch. 3, pp. 87-88, and note 6).
7 Peers makes almost the same observation about Dr Rouse in '(E.A.P.) *Auto*', ch. 3, p. 87.
8 For information on Dr Rouse's dislike of examinations, see '(E.A.P.) *Auto*', pp. 88-89, especially note 10.
9 See '(E.A.P.) *Auto*', ch. 1, pp. 67-70.
10 Peers inadvertently omitted the verb which the editors have inserted.

evil.¹¹

*Into my work for the Teachers' Diploma I threw myself with an energy and an eagerness which nothing whatever had previously inspired in me. I liked my lectures — Philosophy and History of Education with a whimsical* cynic¹² whose technique surpassed that of anyone in the English School of the University; Psychology with a man who was busy with experimental investigations¹³ and in whose laboratory I met my former supervisor in English; Teaching Method with an ex-schoolmaster¹⁴ who had a most comprehensive knowledge of various kinds of school — again quite a fresh type to me. But the thing *I liked best about all these people was that one could talk to them, discuss one's difficulties with them and get to know them.* Just as during my three years at the University I gradually began to realize what I had lost by going to inferior schools,¹⁵ so during my fourth year I discovered what I had lost by the inferior system which had dominated the other three.¹⁶ But my chief delight during that year was Camford Grammar School, with its intelligent, *friendly staff, who made one forget one was only a 'student', and its no less companionable boys, who lived on much more intimate terms with their masters than any boys I had previously known. Before long, when I arrived at school on the ubiquitous bicycle, it was with some small boy, picked up en route, on my step, his arms resting on my shoulders.*

I must not stop to talk about the remarkable staff of that school, with the exception of Hopewell,¹⁷ the English Literature

---

11 For Peers' views on university examinations, and methods of assessment, see *Redbrick University*, ch. 3, section VIII ('The Examination System'), where Peers asks, and sensibly answers, the wholly reasonable question: 'What do we want the class which we award, the indelible seal which we set on our student, to represent? Surely the whole of his career, from beginning to end, and not one hectic week in his last June' (102).

12 Peers has in mind S. S. F. Fletcher (see '[E.A.P.] *Auto*', ch. 3, p. 89, and note 11).

13 Charles Fox (see '[E.A.P.] *Auto*', ch. 3, p. 89, note 12).

14 F. G. Blandford (see '[E.A.P.] *Auto*', ch. 3, p. 89, and note 13).

15 At Camford [Cambridge], despite 'the inefficiency of the instruction', he had come to appreciate, for instance, *'the jostling and clashing of dissimilar minds the like of which my grammar school had never suspected'* (see 'B.T.', ch. I, pp. 199, 210).

16 In the margin, opposite this sentence, Peers has written: '?alter'.

17 Hopewell is Louis de Glehn, head of the Perse School's Language

man, in whose classes I did my practice. He was only in his early thirties — a teacher of tremendous power, who, in a different sphere, affected me as Professor Upright had done twelve months before.[18] 'If only I had been taught like that', — I would say to myself, 'what might I not have done?'

Hopewell's teaching was inspired by two leading ideas, both of which he held with a conviction that amounted to passion. One was that far more English literature could, and should, be read at school, if we forgot about archaisms and freak constructions and concentrated upon an understanding and appreciation of each work as a whole. The other was that, with teaching of the right kind, children could be taught, or, more properly, encouraged and induced, to write prose and verse which was of real artistic value. Amazed by the quality of the

---

department (see '[E.A.P.] *Auto*', ch. 3, pp. 87-88, and note 7). In a letter of 24 March 1993 commenting on this and the following three paragraphs, Mr Keith Barry (who retired as the Second Master of The Perse School) writes that 'De Glehn taught me at the University [of Cambridge] in the early thirties (as did Chouville), but he had retired from the Perse before I went there in 1936. He had taught French and German (not English) and was a formidable and much respected figure. Dr Rouse allowed his staff very considerable latitude, and the picture given of "Hopewell" rings true. Certainly De Glehn and Chouville came and went more or less as they pleased, being heavily involved in University work as well, and De Glehn particularly seldom spent much time in the staff room. He would go straight to his lesson(s) and then back to his University teaching. Both he and Chouville (who was still there when I joined the Perse) were inspiring teachers, wholly involved in the direct method. The great English teacher, however, was Caldwell Cook, though he was never in charge of the English, as he was part-time, and interested only in teaching the younger boys, through the "play way"... I suspect that the portrait of Hopewell may well, therefore, be an amalgam of De Glehn and Caldwell Cook, both of whom — but especially the latter — gave the kind of inspirational teaching that Prof. Peers obviously admired; and it would be quite like De Glehn to hand over his work to a trusted lieutenant without troubling about the formalities...'. Henry Caldwell Cook (1886-1939) 'as English Master at the Perse School, Cambridge, 1911-15 and 1919-33, constructed experiments designed to convert school-work into organised play, resulting chiefly in the conviction that true education is hampered by the class-room system and the teaching of subjects' (*Who Was Who, 1929-1940*). His publications included *The Play Way, an Essay in Educational Method* (1917) and (as editor) *Perse Playbooks*, nos 1-6 — being poems, ballads, prose studies, and plays by boys of the School, 1911-21.

18  *Cf.* above, 'B.T.', ch. I, pp. 205-08, and notes 118-19.

prose appreciations, verses and even plays which his boys turned out, I embraced this second idea with characteristic enthusiasm, and I remember having a long argument with my External examiner, who demurred to the idea that such productions could, save in exceptional cases, have more than an extrinsic value.

So enthralled was I by Hopewell that before long I would be sitting in his classroom, not only during *the hours prescribed by my time-table, but at any odd hour which I could spare, drinking in his marvellous technique till I knew his methods almost by heart. By my side would be young Pierre Legouis, son of the great Émile,*[19] *who had sent him [/come] over from France to study the teaching of English from its most capable exponent, and there were generally one or two other auditors — students from the Womens Training College, visiting Americans, teachers from other parts of England.*[20] *All were [/Any of them was] welcome to [find] a chair [where he could and retire on it] in the [/into a] corner of the room but neither boys nor master took the slightest notice of them, and this complete lack of self-consciousness was a great help to the more nervous of the student-teachers. For my own part, I never was, and never have been, in the slightest degree nervous in front of any class, and my happiest moments were when Hopewell, having for some reason*

---

19 Professor Émile Legouis and his son, Pierre, were both distinguished professors of English Literature. Émile Legouis (d.1937), professor at the University of Lyon and later Professor of English Literature at The Sorbonne, Paris, was the author of books on the early life of William Wordsworth (published in French in 1896 and in English in 1897, with later editions), on Chaucer, Edmund Spencer, etc. and co-author of a History of English Literature (Macmillan, 1929). His son Pierre's doctoral thesis (University of Paris) on Andrew Marvell was dedicated to his father and was published initially in French in 1928; Pierre was latterly Professor of English Language and Literature at the University of Lyon. Mr Keith Barry (see above, note 17), however, wonders whether 'Pierre Legouis, son of the great "Émile" ' might not be a son of Léon Chouville. Léon Chouville's sons were at The Perse.

20 Mr Barry (see above note 17) writes that 'it is certainly true that many students — and, indeed, eminent people — came from many areas to watch Rouse, De Glehn, Chouville and Caldwell Cook at work, and the boys were quite accustomed to this, taking it in their stride. By the time I came Wootton [Mr H. A. Wootton, Headmaster, 1928-45, in succession to Dr Rouse] had virtually killed this kind of thing, though Chouville remained, rather sadly, until 1938, when he retired to live at Bihorel, near Rouen'.

*to go away before a class was over* (for the Camford staff were allowed unusual liberty to engage in other activities), would suddenly hand me his book and call on me without notice to finish his lesson.

*During the summer term of 1908 Hopewell was invited, and given leave of absence, to go on a lecturing tour in the United States. To my amazement and delight, he offered me the whole of his work, with the Headmaster's concurrence, for the period between the Diploma examination in late May and the end of the term. I accepted the invitation, did the work as well as I knew how; and, much to my surprise, when the end of the school term came, found that it cost me about ten times as* much to *part with my friends of one year as twelve months previously it had cost me to part with those of three.*

*At the same time, I had in no way remained aloof from University and College life during this period. I started going to Union debates again:*[21] *as an undergraduate I had had*

---

21  The Record of Debates of the Cambridge Union Society reveals that Allison Peers was quite a frequent contributor to debates, speaking at no fewer than fourteen debates over the period 9 November 1909 to 5 November 1912 (six in 1909-10, four in 1910-11 and two each in 1911-12 and 1912-13). Though it is not possible to state whether he argued propositions in which he did not, in fact, believe, the motions which he *supported* included ones advocating the disestablishment and disendowment of the Church of England (23 November 1909); the reduction in the number of licensed houses as a genuine measure of temperance reform (17 May 1910); identification with the cause of Democracy as against the claims of the House of Peers (22 November 1910); preference of Orthodoxy to Eccentricity (5 March 1912); and opposition to a government inquiry into the affairs of the University with a view to Educational Reform (5 November 1912). Motions which he *opposed* included ones that declared that the censorship of plays is perverse and harmful, and should be abolished (9 November 1909); that 'this House would view with alarm any advance towards Socialistic principles' (8 February 1910); that the Government's schemes of defence are inadequate to the needs of the country (31 January 1911); and that 'this House regards as disastrous to the Country the principles and tactics of the Liberal Party' (9 May 1911). With the exception of the debate of 22 November 1910, when a majority voted against the motion, and the debate of 31 January 1911, when the voting figures were not recorded, all these motions were approved on division (Cambridge University Library, ref. Cambridge Union Society Record of Debates, 1902-09 and 1910-19). The only other member of Christ's College who took a particularly active part in the Union Society's debates during Peers' period was Frank Rönnfeldt (see '[E.A.P.] *Auto*', ch. 3, p. 85, note 2), who also acted as a (principal) proposer and opposer of motions, and served

*ambitions as a speaker, but a low place in the Committee elections and some pointed remarks by my tutor had caused me to take a vow of total abstinence from participation in debates. I dined in College more frequently than was usual for Bachelors and struck up acquaintances with several men [/younger Fellows] only a few years my senior. More significantly still, I began in the most modest possible way, and without any kind of help, instruction or encouragement, the practice of research, a love for which was eventually to carry me back into University life again.*

Looking back upon my four years at Camford, I think the most surprising thing about them is my utter unawareness of research. Nobody had ever whispered the word to me, or suggested that there was anything a graduate should do once his examinations were over. Of the thrill of creation and discovery, of the boundless scope given by the university teacher's freedom for the most varied activities of the world-comradeship engendered by successful specialization — of none of these things had I the slightest inkling. My tutor had on various occasions suggested that I should write a dissertation in order to get a fellowship at some other college; my Chatstone headmaster had suggested that I should write one to get a Doctor's degree which in turn would procure me a headmastership: what no one had even hinted at was that I might undertake research for its own sake or that the pursual of research is the essential function of a university.[22]

So when, at the age of twenty-three, I took up literary research of a kind which I have hardly laid down since, I did it solely from an ulterior motive. Once every five years the University offered a prize for an essay on some aspect of Elizabethan literature. The value of the prize was one hundred

---

as an active member of the Society's Standing Committee.

22 Peers' enduring passion for research, which turned him into an extraordinarily productive Hispanist, the author of numerous books and articles, is clearly revealed through his enthusiastic words in this paragraph. His comments here are wholly consistent with the importance which Peers attaches to research in *Redbrick University*. See especially ch. 4, in which Peers declares, 'the promotion of research... is (or, more correctly, should be) the chief part of the aim of every university... [T]hough in any university of to-day there will in practice always be teaching, it suffices for the ideal university that there should be research' (*op. cit.*, 105).

pounds, though this was greatly reduced by a provision that the essay must be published at the author's expense: it cost me more than half that sum to publish mine.[23] The jejuneness of the essay, as I now re-read it, is as crude as the flimsy rhetoric which I hoped would impress the adjudicators. But it was at least a genuine attempt to *find out something* not be gathered from text books — a process which, during all my three years as an undergraduate, I had not attempted —[24] and from the long afternoons which I spent delving into the works of the Elizabethans in the University library I derived a new stimulus, complementary, as it were, to that afforded by teaching. The university teacher's twofold function, the incessant taking in and the incessant giving out, is the most fascinating aspect of his activity,[25] and of this I obtained the first inkling during that winter and spring, though at that time I could not have expressed my reactions to the experience in words.

## II

In the summer of 1908 I obtained the Teachers' Diploma, with distinction both in the theory of teaching and in the practice[26] (the standard in neither branch was high) and then set out, through the intermediary of the usual agents, to obtain my first post in a school.

After applying promptly yet carefully to a number of schools, I received a summons for interview at a large Public school

---

23 Allison Peers' essay was, in fact, *Elizabethan Drama and its Mad Folk: The Harness Prize Essay for 1913* (1914) (see '[E.A.P.] *Auto*', ch. 3, p. 91, and note 22).

24 Peers makes the same observatons, in the same, or similar, words in '(E.A.P.) *Auto*', ch. 3, p. 91.

25 *Cf.* this comment in *Redbrick University*: 'Research and teaching form one twofold aim... the spirit of research must permeate all genuine university teaching' (105).

26 Peers obtained a First Class with double distinction in the examination for the Teacher's Diploma at Cambridge in 1913.

attractively situated in the heart of Sussex.[27] I had not seriously aspired so high as this, for I was curiously modest about my prospects as a teacher — probably this was the result of an inferiority complex deriving from my own inferior education. In these days of high salaries and crushing taxation, the reader will probably be amused to know that I asked the cadaverous clerk in the London agency if he thought it was of any use my applying for a job with so high a salary as £150 resident.

'Oh, I don't know', said the clerk, with just the ghost of a smile, 'I think I should. After all, you've got a good degree, you know'.[28]

His optimism was justified. Whether any other candidates were interviewed or not I cannot say, but after a stroll round the playing-fields and a pleasant half-hour over a cup of tea the Headmaster gave me the job. I stayed there for six years,[29] during which my salary rose to the height of £180, by three instalments of ten pounds each. Considering that Cranstead was in the first dozen or so schools in England, the salary was certainly not excessive.

But there were numerous compensations. The situation was perfect. Cranstead village, one of the most charming I know, lies in the heart of the country, yet is only three miles from a station on the Brighton line, about half an hour from London.[30] By catching the right bus one could be in the City three quarters of an hour after leaving one's study. And yet, by taking the right footpaths, one could roam for miles and see nothing more like a town than a single red roof or cottage chimney. I soon knew every footpath within a five mile radius of the school. I was able to pursue my hobby of bird-watching

---

27 Cranstead, but, in fact, Felsted School, Dunmow, Essex.

28 *Cf.* '(E.A.P.) *Auto*', ch. 3, p. 93, and note 32; see also p. 97, and note 48.

29 Peers served on Felsted School's staff for *five* years, from 1914 until 1919 (see '[E.A.P.] *Auto*', ch. 3, especially pp. 97-103). In the 'Bruce Truscot' narrative Peers omits separate reference to his previous service, of one year, at Mill Hill School, blending his experiences of both schools.

30 Felsted is about seven miles from Braintree station. Nowadays the journey time for the (direct) train from Braintree to London's Liverpool Street Station is one hour.

more vigorously than ever before: and, by sharing my knowledge of birds with a colleague who was a specialist in botany, I gave him a new interest and in exchange acquired another. The best walks were over Ashdown Forest,[31] that magnificent expanse of the most varied beauty. In one place, dense fir woods or glades of oak and birch. In another, undulating moorland, glowing with gorse, ling and heather, and diversified with vast tracts of bracken coming up to one's waist or shoulder. And the whole swept at intervals by keen wind or refreshing breeze, five hundred feet above sea-level.[32] A grand playground, to which even now I return with zest at every opportunity.[33]

The amenities of Cranstead itself came as a great surprise to me, Never having even been inside a large Public School, I had had no conception of the comfort (or, as I should then have said, luxury) in *which schoolmasters could live. I had delightful quarters, with bedroom and sitting-room, in a picturesque little house, opposite the main school buildings.*[34] *There was a good deal of entertaining and both the Headmaster and the men who had their own boarding-houses were given to hospitality. Hours were not heavy; no time was lost, as in a non-resident post, getting to and from one's work; and week-ends in London, were quite practicable. 'You see, we are not without our amenities', the Headmaster had remarked when he had interviewed me; and he had been right.*

Yet Cranstead,[35] when I went there first, was no place for any man to whom work was more important than amenities, still less for an enthusiast fresh from the invigorating

---

31 Ashdown Forest, an ancient forest now mainly heath, is in East Sussex, in The Weald and, being not too far distant from Worthing, his parents' home, would no doubt be familiar to Peers.

32 For evidence of Peers' interest in the countryside see also above, 'B.T.', ch. I, pp. 186, 197; and *cf.* '(E.A.P.) *Auto*', ch. 4, p. 133.

33 Peers indicates, in pencil, a space here, where he moves to the next stage in his narrative.

34 The Old School House, Felsted (see '[E.A.P.] *Auto*', ch. 3, p. 98, and note 51).

35 Peers is referring, in the sentences which follow, to Mill Hill School, which he describes in very similar terms, in '(E.A.P.) *Auto*'; see ch. 3, pp. 94-95.

atmosphere of Hopewell's classroom at Camford. The boys were for the most part sons of wealthy business men, many of them with more pocket-money than is good for any boy and the prospects of still more when they went to Camford or Oxbridge, and of an easy life thereafter. Games were not only compulsory but regarded as all-important; scholarship-winners ranked far below members of the elevens or fifteens; most of the masters took a nonchalant, or even a cynical attitude to their work; about modern methods they knew little and cared less. The methods used in teaching English language and literature[36] were inferior [even] to those of my little co-educational school in Somerset.[37] Yet here were highly educated men, most of them with Camford or Oxbridge Honours degrees and some of them making large incomes by keeping boarding-houses: all of them were within easy reach of the meetings of educational associations and every kind of cultural facility. Yet they lived the lives of sybaritic and slightly cynical Philistines.[38]

The only theory of education they understood was 'knock it into them'. When a new man came who was more than mildly interested in education, the tacit understanding was: 'We must knock it out of him'.

'Where's Roberts?' a canary-waistcoated tennis blue would drawl, on a Saturday afternoon when the young master in question was absent from common-room tea.

'Must have gone into London to get a book to improve his teaching!' his opposite number would reply, and the witticism, none too obvious, perhaps, to the outsider, would never fail to elicit appreciation.

Books on education, to these men, were fantastic absurdities. Teaching meant, first, giving your boys something to learn, and second, seeing they learned it. If they didn't, you beat them; and if that didn't work, you beat them again. 'Hit hard and hit in the same place' was the infallible recipe of the School House master. Perhaps the thing that most shocked me

---

36 Peers is, in fact, alluding to his experiences in teaching French (see '[E.A.P.] *Auto*', ch. 3, p. 94).

37 Peers means his school in Wiltshire (see above, 'B.T.', ch. I, p. 178, note 17; and 'E.A.P. [*Auto*]', ch. 1, p. 65; ch. 3, p. 94).

38 Peers uses exactly the same sentence in '(E.A.P.) *Auto*' in describing his colleagues at Mill Hill School (see above, ch. 3, p. 94).

230  REDBRICK UNIVERSITY REVISITED

in my first term was the barbarous emphasis laid on corporal punishment. At the least, in a highly educated community, one would expect it to be treated as a regrettable necessity; but here it was a common-place. I had never expected to see the methods of my Higher Grade school here. To smack a boy viciously across the cheek was as usual as to reprove him. The man who got on was the man who could cane hard — and did. Every now and then, the entire school, boys and masters, would be summoned to a special assembly, at which, in an atmosphere of tense and animated expectancy, the Headmaster (or, in my first year, the somewhat brawnier senior housemaster) administered to some boy who had been caught bullying or thieving a public flogging. I am the last person to be sentimental over boys' education, but this, I thought (and still think), was not education at all.[39]

In most Public Schools, so far as my considerable experience goes, there is a tendency to exalt games at the expense of work, to despise modern methods in education and to resort with unnecessary speed to the short and easy method of discipline. It was the length to which this tendency had been carried at Cranstead that was unusual, and this was indirectly attributable to the Headmaster.[40]

It was nearly fifteen years since he had been appointed, while still in his thirties, a scholar to the finger-tips, straight from the Sixth Form at Harchester[41] which he had given such a reputation for scholarship-winning that his name was current in every Common Room at Camford and Oxbridge. The Governors

---

39  These passages in fact relate to Mill Hill School. Almost identical comments are made in '(E.A.P.) *Auto*', ch. 3, pp. 94-95.

40  Peers is alluding to Sir John McClure, who was appointed Headmaster of Mill Hill School in 1891, while in his early thirties (see '[E.A.P.] *Auto*', ch. 3, pp. 95-96). Born at Wigan in 1860, Sir John McClure was educated at Holly Mount College, near Bury (1874-76), Owens College, Manchester (1876-77), and Trinity College, Cambridge (1882-86). At the time of his appointment McClure was an Extension Lecturer and also (from 1889-94) Professor of Astronomy at Queen's College, London; he had previous experience as a schoolmaster, at Holly Mount College, Lancashire (1877-78) and at Hinckley Grammar School, Leicestershire (1878-82).

41  Another hybrid coinage (*cf.* 'Oxbridge'; 'Camford'), which Peers creates by combining Harrow and Winchester to suggest: any one of the top class public schools. Peers used the word, with this meaning, in, for example, *Redbrick and these Vital Days* (169).

had appointed him precisely because they were aware of the direction in which the school was heading and were anxious to arrest the decline. It seemed natural to choose the man with the finest name for scholarship in the Sixth Forms of the country. Being in Orders,[42] a respectable athlete and an impressive personality, he seemed the very man for the job.

But it soon became clear that he was not. The Sixth Form master at Cranstead, being well dug in, had no mind for the new Head to take over any large part of his work — and said so. And the new Head proved to be no great organizer: his strength had been in teaching. Again, his intellectual ambitions were almost entirely limited to the Classics: of modern methods in the teaching of English, French and Science, for example, he knew little and recked less. Finally, he was unfortunate with his staff. When he came he battered heroically but vainly against the indifference and cynicism of men who had been at Cranstead for donkeys' years and had every intention of playing out time there. One by one, with exasperating slowness, they retired, and it was then that the Headmaster's greatest weakness became apparent: he was a poor judge of men. So his new appointments turned out to be very little better than the old ones, and had the supreme disadvantage of being from thirty to forty years younger.

At the end of my first year, he resigned,[43] and accepted the clerical headmaster's very present help in trouble — a country living. This time, possibly on the principle of setting a thief to catch a thief, the Governors appointed an athlete with small academic pretensions, but with a remarkable range of accomplishments, and above all with an unerring knowledge of human nature. Dr Downside[44] was nearly fifty when he came

---

42 Though not, in fact, in Holy Orders, Sir John McClure was a prominent Congregationalist (see '[E.A.P.] *Auto*', ch. 3, pp. 95-96, and note 44).

43 In reality, Sir John McClure died in office. The figure of 'Dr Downside', known as 'The Owl', and the 'successor' to the headmaster who 'resigned', is evidently also based on Sir John McClure (see '[E.A.P.] *Auto*', ch. 3, p. 95, and below, note 44).

44 Most of the physical and psychological description of 'Dr Downside' which follows fits both the portrait of Sir John McClure published in the history of the school, and the article on him in the *Dictionary of National Biography* (see '[E.A.P.] *Auto*', ch. 3, pp. 95-96, notes 44 and 45).

to us from a smaller Public School which he had found on the verge of collapse and turned into a model of prosperous efficiency. Tall, powerfully built, monumentally ugly, with a huge head crowned by *a shock of untidy white hair, a humorous mouth and piercing eyes framed in large round glasses, he was universally and appropriately known as 'The Owl'[,]* but [/though] no [other] ornithological specimen [extant] was ever [/can ever have been] *so respectfully treated. He was a self-made northerner who had begun his teaching career in an obscure grammar school at the age of sixteen and had then sent himself to my* own college at Camford — a man among boys little younger in years than himself. At Camford he gained a blue for cricket and a half-blue for swimming and took Second-class Honours in Law, proceeding to a Doctorate in Law some years later. By means of travel he had learned to speak French and German fluently; he wrote frequently in the reviews on what we should call to-day Social Science; his hobbies were an unusual combination — astronomy and music. At the school which he had resuscitated he was regarded as the personification of muscular Christianity[45] and as an encyclopaedia of learning. Yet his greatest qualities were those imponderable ones *which make a successful headmaster. He could quell a mutiny with his eye, pulverize even [/silence] a captain of games with a word, pacify the most cantankerous of parents, play off one domineering housemaster against another, and sense what was going on anywhere, at any time, without leaving his study. If one has to find a single word for all this, I suppose the word is 'shrewdness', but any word falls short of the reality.*

My own attitude to Downside was that of a good many of my colleagues. I began by being slightly repelled by him; I ended by worshipping him. He was not in the least the kind of person

---

45  Peers employs this identical phrase to describe Sir John McClure in '(E.A.P.) *Auto*', ch. 3, p. 95. Interestingly, in his review of Christopher Brooke's *A History of the University of Cambridge*, Vol. IV *1870-1990*, John Marenbon uses the same phrase to describe the 'Camford' way of life which Sir John McClure evidently personified: 'Muscular Christianity was as dominant in the university as at the public schools, and for many students college life centred on rowing and the chapel' ('Echoes in the Studious Cloister', *The Times*, 11 February 1993, 34).

SCHOOL AND UNIVERSITY (1907-1918) 233

I had ever wanted to be — as, for example, Upright[46] or Hopewell was, but he was so altogether admirable as the sort of person he was. And during the five years I served under him[47] he pulled Cranstead out of what to me was a Slough of Despond and made sufficient new appointments of the right type to ensure its becoming what it is to-day, a school that gives as good an education as any in the country.

Those who were slack — whether masters or boys — because slackness was the line of least resistance he pulled up partly by sharp rebukes ('bites', the boys called them) and partly by his own example of extreme conscientiousness and efficiency. When he went up to London during term on school business he would post a notice describing his business in these words in the Common Room. Of such small matters as punctuality he said little — but he had an uncanny way of knowing when a man was late for class and an unfailing habit of sending him a note about it. And yet, automaton-like as he might seem on paper, no one was ever more human. Beneath his gruffness there was a sympathetic, even sentimental streak which endeared him to one: he would deliver one of his 'bites' in the morning, and before luncheon, feel that he had perhaps been carried away by the impulse of the moment and come round to make something dangerously like an apology. Or was that all part of his technique? Did he realize that when one has been justly rebuked, and the rebuker shows generosity, the delinquent feels more of a worm than before and is much less likely to need rebuking again?[48]

I was never anything but happy at Cranstead. In the first year, I could do little good work, but there was compensation for that in the amenities and the countryside. In the second year

---

46 A reference to George Charles Upright (i.e. to James Fitzmaurice-Kelly), who had delivered the Snark (i.e. Maccoll) Lectures at Camford (Cambridge) which had so much impressed the author in his youth (see above, 'B.T.', ch. I, pp. 205-08). Peers deliberately brings in Upright at this point in the interests of the structure of his narrative. He wishes to remind the reader of the person, and personality, of Upright, in preparation for the re-entry of this character to play a key-role in the rest of the autobiography.

47 Peers served, in fact, only one year, 1913-14, at Mill Hill School.

48 This passage clearly refers to Dr W. W. Vaughan, Master of Wellington College, on whose staff Peers served from October to December 1919 (see '[E.A.P.] *Auto*', ch. 3, pp. 117-19).

the invigorating wind of Downside's innovations freshened things academically, some of the worst masters vanished, and thenceforward the standard grew gradually higher. I began to see that, if in this sophisticated atmosphere I could not become a Hopewell, I might at least in time produce results of which he would not be ashamed.[49]

Again, not only in vacations, but for one week-end out of every three, I was able to go to London, to read in the British Museum, to attend meetings of that admirable body, the English Association and to keep in touch with other interests centred in the capital in a way I have never been able to since.[50] Then I gained immeasurably as a university teacher by the valuable experience of learning to handle boys: even after thirty years spent continuously in a university[51] I can look back on those six years, call them well spent and fruitful in the highest degree, and wish with all my heart, from a knowledge of what they gave me, that every university teacher had to serve an apprenticeship among boys.[52]

---

49 As indicated, Hopewell is, in reality, de Glehn. This part of the narrative relates to Peers' period at Felsted School (see '[E.A.P.] *Auto*', ch. 3, especially pp. 101-02).

50 This corresponds to Peers' comments in '(E.A.P.) *Auto*', ch. 3, pp. 101, 103-06.

51 Bruce Truscot is several years older than his creator. Peers joined the staff of the University of Liverpool in January 1920, and when he wrote these words had been a university teacher for twenty-five years. As indicated in the Introduction, in a letter of 23 June 1945 to Professor Bonamy Dobrée, the 'wife' of 'Bruce Truscot' wrote that 'after his holiday [Bruce] is going to begin on his autobiography. But that will not be published until he retires which, unfortunately[,] as I expect you have discovered with all your critical faculties, is going to be quite soon' (for the complete text of this letter, see Appendix III, pp. 476-77). Peers was only fifty-four in 1945, but Truscot, supposedly born on 23 June 1885, was (that is to say, would have been, if he had existed) exactly sixty.

52 Peers expresses the same desire, in identical words, in '(E.A.P.) *Auto*', ch. 3, p. 101. Far from considering Peers' years as a schoolmaster to be useful training, the opponents of his appointment to the Gilmour Chair of Spanish at Liverpool regarded them as a good reason for rejecting Peers' application. Evidently, resentment and prejudice against schoolmasters who became university teachers were particularly strong in British universities in the years immediately following the First World War. This was because, in part, of continuing anti-German attitudes, for in Germany academics normally taught for a period in schools before taking up posts in universities. We are indebted for this insight to Norman Lamb.

## SCHOOL AND UNIVERSITY (1907-1918)

But Cranstead meant chiefly personal ties and personal friendships. Because I felt that the success or failure of my teaching depended largely on establishing individual contacts I laboured to establish as many of these contacts as possible. Some of them loosened quickly when the boys left; others were rudely snapped by the murderous war of 1914-18; but many others remained and have lasted for a generation. Undoubtedly I made more friends, in the true sense, at Cranstead than in any other six years of my life; and both for that reason and because I loved every field-path and lane of the place, I have always thought of it as most men feel about the school at which they were educated. Tossed about as I was in my boyhood from school to school, Cranstead, with Trinity, became to me a real *alma mater*.[53]


### III

In the mellow happiness of that life, any lingering disappointment that I might still have felt at my unachieved fellowship melted quickly, and it was not till some years had passed that I began to be conscious of it again. But I had not been at Cranstead very long when I did begin to feel some misgivings — or, to put it more exactly, when some disconcerting reflections would from time to time invade my complacency. It is when one has passed the half-decade that one first thinks on toward the next and it was soon after my twenty-fifth birthday that I began to wonder how I should feel about schoolmastering when I was thirty.

---

In *Redbrick University*, Peers strongly believes that new lecturers should be trained in how to teach (see, for instance, p. 83). In the same book, remembering his own hard work as a schoolteacher, he exhorts university professors, who claim they have insufficient time for their research, to 'think of the schoolmaster engaged in the wearing task of teaching — and, what is more, controlling — classes of lively boys, from nine o'clock till four, who has then to mark a pile of exercises, and perhaps, in a boarding-school, supervise "prep" ' (113).

53 *Cf.* the similar sentiments which Peers expresses about Felsted in '(E.A.P.) *Auto*', ch. 3, p. 98.

At twenty-three and twenty-four, I reflected, it had been quite a thrilling adventure to start a fresh set of beginners on a programme new to them each September. At twenty-five teaching new batches of pupils precisely the same thing as last year was still quite agreeable. But what would it be at thirty-five? And at forty-five? And at fifty-five?[54] *And in those last uphill years between fifty-five and sixty-five, at the end of which one would retire, after doing almost exactly the same routine for forty-two years in succession? The prospect became rather a nightmare to the imagination. The amount of variation possible in the programme of a school, even assuming that one were sufficiently in command of affairs to have the power to vary it, was negligible. What were the alternatives?*

*There was [/If one remained at a school there would be] only one: to become a headmaster. The idea of a [purely] administrative post I rejected because it would rob me of the thing I most valued [/most valuable thing/best thing] in school work — contact with the immature but rapidly growing mind. Administration under a local authority I found even less attractive. The inspectorate, of which I knew next to nothing, seemed to me (wrongly, as I afterwards found) insufficiently constructive. A headmastership, on the other hand, would* give *all the personal contact one could require, a chance to combine administrative work with it and (if one were fortunate) a more than adequate salary and pension.*

*But [in that case] what chance was there of teaching? And after all it was a teacher I had set out to be — not a flogger of boys, a pacifier of parents, or a diplomat in [/among] the masters' common-room [/boarding-houses]. I looked at the headmasters I had known. How much teaching did they do? Two or three periods weekly with the Sixth — from any one of which they might be called out at any [/a] moment['s] notice to receive a Governor who had called or to speak on the telephone to the parent of a boy who had just developed whooping-cough. Scripture for a term or so with some form which seemed not to be making the progress it should. An occasional lesson on a subject of which one knew nothing when the staff was suffering from an epidemic of influenza and no one else could be found to do it. No, this [/that] was distinctly not what I had bargained for.* I

---

54  Peers asks himself the same question in '(E.A.P.) *Auto*', ch. 3, p. 102.

*should have to remain an assistant master or change my occupation altogether.*

Then, one day when I felt in a critical mood, I looked critically around the Cranstead Common Room. What sort of men were these? Did I really want to grow like them?

Some were happy enough: they were wrapped up in their boys,[55] *knew all the names, ages, tastes and accomplishments of the members of their form or house, to say nothing of the cricket averages for the last few [/half-dozen] seasons.* But they had entirely lost their intellectual interests — read nothing, except novels and occasional biographies or memoirs, and neither knew nor cared about the progress made in their special subjects. Their vacations they appeared to spend either with relatives (most of them were unmarried) or with the parents of their favourite boys. In the summer vacation they generally went abroad — *preferably to Switzerland,* where there was no trouble with the language.[56]

*Little by little I discovered what would have been an alarming and shocking fact if the discovery had not come so gradually — [that,] as a result of constant immersion in the petty details of school life, and their inability to embrace any other type of interest, they were becoming like the very boys around whom their lives centred.* Whether the first eleven would beat St Edmunds or not, whether Richards' or Stokes'[57] would be cock house meant as much to them as to their pupils. Fiercely, day after day, they would argue the merits of this and that half-back or wicket-keeper across the Common Room table. Sometimes they openly quarrelled.

'Why does A⎯⎯ never seem to speak to B⎯⎯', I enquired innocently in my first term of two men who sat [/took their meals] in opposite corners of the [masters'] dining-room?

'Oh they had a feud last year over the house matches', was the answer.

*I am afraid I expressed incredulity; but a short time*

---

55 The author makes almost the same remarks in '(E.A.P.) *Auto*', ch. 3, p. 102.

56 Two versions of this sentence are repeated in the manuscript. In the second version, instead of 'where there was no trouble with the language', Peers adds the comment (of a master): '*where [ — so much more convenient:]* "English will get you anywhere" '.

57 Peers originally wrote 'whether Stokes' or Montgomery's'.

*afterwards, over Common Room tea, I heard C— complaining heatedly to B— about some act of insubordination which a boy in B—'s house had committed in C—'s Latin class. It appeared that B— had refused to 'speak to him' as requested.*

*'Some housemasters would be only too glad to', grumbled the Latin master.*

*'So I don't run my house properly, do I?' retorted the other. 'Well, suppose we don't speak to each other in future'.*

*And, incredible to relate, they cut each other for a year or more, at the end of which time the hatchet was buried — characteristically over a boy who was seriously ill in the infirmary.*

*Some of the boyish [/puerile] idiosyncrasies of these pedagogues were more amusing. There was one man — he could hardly have been less than fifty — who had an insatiable appetite for afternoon tea and always timed himself to be in the Common Room before anyone else, even if it meant leaving a cricket match before the interval. There were two more, older men still,*[58] *the very thought of whom still induces a chuckle. One was a rotund old bachelor, possessed of considerable means, charmingly generous and mawkishly sentimental, but with a tremendous sense of his own dignity, which the boys soon discovered and played up to. The other was a lame and ascetic widower, reputed to be forbiddingly religious, who used occasionally to embarass some of the younger bachelors by dilating upon the culpable childlessness of the few married men on the staff: he had done his duty, in his time, by his own wife, and what was the world coming to? These two hated each other like poison, and as they sat opposite each other, on either side of the President of Common Room, at all meals except lunch, which we took with the boys, they had ample opportunity of indulging their animosities.*

*'Pass the sugar, please, Wright', Hay would say, gruffly.*

*'I'm afraid there is none left', Wright would reply as though explaining the situation to a child.*

---

58 After 'older men still' Peers had originally written (the words are still decipherable): '— *"dug-outs", in fact, who had retired from headmasterships in different schools before the War and came as substitutes for men who had gone on active service. I still chuckle inwardly when I think of those two*'.

*'Huh, eaten it all?' (Wright was known to have a sweet tooth, despite his general frugality).*

*I may like sugar',* Wright would retort in dulcet tones which almost justified his greed, *'but at least I do not gorge myself with sausages'.*

And so breakfast after breakfast, for term after term, wore on. It was about this time, in one Long Vacation, that I first read **Mr. Perrin and Mr. Traill.**[59] I remember assuring my father, who had been rather shocked by it, that the characters were not overdrawn, and that, if a similar tragedy had not already taken place at Cranstead, it would soon.

Besides the men who had reverted to schoolboys, there were the cranks. One I remember particularly well — the efficiency crank. He used to sit in a back seat at daily chapel, wait till the Headmaster had emerged, and then stride swiftly after him with head thrust forward and gown flying and engage him in earnest conversation until they reached the Head's study which they would enter together unless there happened to be a boy outside waiting to be flogged — the close of Divine worship being the usual time for that ceremony. No one ever knew what the Crank found to talk about but subsequent happenings often inspired deductions highly unflattering to him. And it was universally believed — among the staff, at least — that the conversations invariably started with the words:

'Oh, Headmaster, I think you ought to know....!'

Lastly, there was the man with the perpetual grievance.

He was nearly always elderly — counting the Septembers, no doubt, until he would be able to cease starting to teach the same thing to a new generation of vipers and retire to share a cottage with an elder sister on an inadequate pension. Since leaving Cranstead, I have come to know scores of secondary schools of an inferior type, in each of which there are men or women of this kind, with far fewer grievances and far more excuse for them than some of the public-school masters I have referred to. Pity them, young schoolmaster or schoolmarm, but look at them very

---

59 A reference to (Sir) Hugh (S.) Walpole, *Mr Perrin and Mr Traill. A Tragi-comedy* (London: Mills & Boon, 1911); later editions also appeared. Walpole's work, based on his own short experience as a schoolmaster, set a vogue for novels and plays about schoolmasters.

*carefully, for some day you may be like them. They were happy and hopeful idealists in their twenties. In their thirties they were thinking pleasantly of headships to which they would soon be elected and which would enable them to exchange an income of four hundred a year for one of a thousand, give their wives that little extra summer holiday, send Johnny away to some other school instead of having to expose him to the indignity of attending one where his father was designated as 'Old Stinker', begin to save regularly and buy an annuity to supplement one's pension... but all that was in one's thirties. Now one is fifty-five, fifty-six, fifty-seven... All joy has gone from one's work; one is just a **little** hard of hearing and one suspects an ominous ring in the laugh which greets one's well-worn classroom jokes; one no longer seems to enjoy having boys to tea; unsettling young men, fresh from the university, smile condescendingly when one stands with one's back to the Common Room fire and expounds one's theories of teaching. Besides, the Head is just a **little** short with one when one has to make quite minor complaints nowadays. If only a single one of those headships of past years had materialized...! From thirty-five to somewhere near fifty, one application after another, sheaves of testimonials, myriads of castles in the air ('Of course, if I go to Birmingham...' 'Well, when I get to a school in the country...' 'Oh, I shall probably get that post at Worcester...'). How in the early years one's heart used to leap when one read on the last page of the **Times Educational Supplement**: 'Preference will be given to a man under forty-five' ('Ah, they want a go-ahead man! That should suit you, dear!'). How, in the latter years, before hope so often deferred made one desist from the unequal struggle, did the same words induce that sinking feeling in the pit of the stomach ('Ah, they want another of those young fellows! I wonder if — no, it's no good: they wouldn't consider a man of forty-eight'). Well, there will never be headships for more than a small minority, but let teachers, while still in their twenties, ask themselves if they are sure they will have the resilience of mind, the equanimity of temperament, the love of their work for its own sake, to come back each September for thirty-five or forty more years, on a salary mounting only microscopically if at all, with perhaps a wife and family, or possibly as a bachelor or a spinster in lodgings the door of which fewer and fewer of one's colleagues or* *pupils seem to want to enter.*⁶⁰

*There was one old bachelor of this type at Cranstead.*⁶¹ *He lived in the village —*⁶² *an embittered and disappointed man, at loggerheads with everybody but new masters, whom during their first term he would invariably invite to tea with him. Unsuspectingly, I went, as others had done before me, and listened to a tirade against the Headmaster, the housemasters, the curriculum, the time-table, the Governors, the chapel services and much more that I have since forgotten. I was not a little impressed, for he was a patriarchal old man and I suppose I was subconsciously flattered at being singled out as the recipient of these confidences. That night at dinner in the Common Room, however, I was regaled with a hilarious reproduction, by all and sundry, of the very criticisms to which I had been listening.*⁶³ *I have never forgotten the text of a letter which the man in question was alleged to have written to the Owl*⁶⁴ *during [/in the latter stages of] some more than usually acrimonious controversy:*

Dear Headmaster,

*I hear you have thought it consistent with your dignity to make opprobrious remarks about me in the course of a masters' meeting.*
**I wish I could say it surprised me.**
Yours sincerely,

——— .

---

60 This imaginative commentary on the life of a disappointed schoolmaster reveals Peers' acute powers of observation and perception; and, simultaneously, identifies the profound misgivings which caused him to resolve to give up his first profession.

61 It appears that here Peers has deleted 'Mill Hill' and inserted 'Cranstead'.

62 Peers has deleted two lines here, which are, however still decipherable: '*and, morning after morning, with automaton-like tread, he climbed the hill which led to his day's duties. In some ways he was better than the average of his kind but none the less he was*'...

63 Deleted but still decipherable here are the words: '*It was my first introduction to this type of elderly, disappointed schoolmaster. None the less,*'...

64 It appears that Peers has deleted 'McClure' and substituted 'the Owl'.

*Much of my leisure during the Cranstead years was filled with these imaginings of a very distant future. Fortunately I had tackled the problem in ample time, as I am exhorting others to do,*[65] *and I soon realized that, though I believed I had [/myself to have] sufficient flexibility and breadth of interests to enable me to support and alleviate such conditions as I have [/those just] described, neither the prospect of forty years as an assistant master nor that of rising to a hypothetical headship corresponded with the kind of life I knew I wanted for my own.*

But it was not till late in 1913, when I was twenty-eight that I got as far as going to see the Owl. So completely accustomed had I become to the idea of remaining a schoolmaster that the idea of returning to university work never occurred to me. I continued to write — but simply for writing's own sake; and my thoughts were turning in the direction of a headmastership while still young, with the idea of saving enough (I was still unmarried) to retire in the fifties and devote the rest of my working life to study. The other idea which I was pursuing with some vigour was entering the inspectorate. These were the two alternatives which I went to lay before Dr Downside in an interview which, trivial as it may seem, was in fact the turning point in my life.[66]

It was a brilliant November morning — and in that lovely Sussex climate November seldom fails to provide a St Martin's summer. Dr Downside's study opened right on to his rose-garden, at the gate of which he was in the habit of standing and gazing musingly into space at the moment when we were due to go into first school. I remember that, as he sat at his desk, the sun shone on his mop of white hair, giving it the appearance of a woolly halo. One remembers these things at such times.

He let me talk on. No doubt he was making deductions which I never dreamed of: the young seldom realize how much more their elders know of them than they tell them.

When I had finished, he said nothing at first, but toyed with

---

65 Peers has marked these words for deletion. Perhaps, on reflection, he thought it unsuitable, off-putting, or unnecessary, to state openly to those schoolmasters among his readers his didactic intention.

66 This interview with McClure probably took place in 1913, when Peers was aged twenty-two. See '(E.A.P.) *Auto*', ch. 3, pp. 95-96, for a briefer, though otherwise similar, account of this interview.

a paper-knife as though he were thinking it all over. Then [he][67] looked up at me with one of those charming smiles which so often lit up his ugliness.

'Well, you know', he said, slowly, 'I think your real success is going to lie in research'.

My first reaction was astonishment. How did he know I cared for research? I had not yet written a book: could he have seen my articles in the *Modern Language Review*[68] or in the *Year's Work in English Studies*? My second reaction was protest. Research, after all, had never been more than a sideline to me: nearly all my interest was in teaching. I said as much — and I suppose implied that I might be expected to know best. But you never got the better of the Owl in argument. He only waved my objections aside, and, with an even sweeter smile, remarked even more gently:

'I didn't say *interest*: I said *success*'.[69]

## IV

That simple remark gave me quite a disproportionate amount of encouragement. It did more: looking back on those years, I can see now that it started to change the direction of my whole career.

The War of 1914 — the 'Great War', we used to call it till we experienced a Greater — came to more people with the shock of complete surprise than is now generally realized. A large proportion of our countrymen — people who held aloof from

---

[67] Peers missed out 'he' at this point, which pronoun the editors have inserted.

[68] Peers indeed contributed two early articles to the *Modern Language Review*, but they did not appear in that journal until 1920 and 1921 (see 'Some Provincial Periodicals in Spain during the Romantic Movement', *MLR*, XV [1920], 374-91; and 'Some Spanish Conceptions of Romanticism', *MLR*, XVI [1921], 281-96).

[69] The words reportedly spoken by McClure (Dr Downside) are exactly the same in both accounts and the same emphasis is given, to distinguish *success* from *interest*.

party politics as well as supporters of the Liberal and Labour parties — refused to entertain the idea that Germany had designs on the peace of Europe, and even a great many followers of the statesmen who were most instant in warning us against the Kaiser's aggressiveness hardly thought the danger as imminent as they proclaimed it to be. Brought up myself as an Asquithian Liberal[70] and an idealist about party politics as about everything else, I scouted alarmism and talked scathingly of Tory scaremongerers till I was twenty-five. But from 1911 to 1913 I spent the whole of each summer vacation on the Continent, for I had determined to make a hobby of Comparative Literature and was labouring to perfect my French and German and to read as much as I could in Italian and Spanish. I revised my ideas a good deal while wandering about France and Italy in 1911 — the summer of the Algeciras Conference [/crisis].[71] And in the two following summers I realized the whole truth, for I spent them as a paying guest in the family of an officer's widow in Berlin.[72] There were three boys — two in the Army and one about to enter it. They taught me a tremendous amount of colloquial German but a tremendous amount also about Prussian militarism. Once I grasped what the ruling passion in Germany really was I knew that most of those whom I had called scaremongerers were actually underestimating the danger, I marvelled at our national blindness and reconciled myself to the certainty that soon the longed-for *Tag* must dawn and with it the bloodiest war that the world would ever have seen.

How well I remember those early August days of 1914 and the critical weeks that followed them! We had broken up on July 29 and I had intended to go off two days later for a walking holiday in the Black Forest. Had I done so, I might well have

---

70 Herbert Henry Asquith (1852-1928) was Liberal leader and Prime Minister in the years before the First World War. In late 1916, he was replaced by Lloyd George.

71 The Conference at Algeciras over Morocco was in 1906; but there was a crisis in the summer of 1911, which represented the so-called 'second phase' of the Morocco Question, culminating in the Agadir incident.

72 In '(E.A.P.) *Auto*', ch. 3, p. 93, and note 35, Peers indicates that he spent part of the summer of 1913 with this German family. In the 'B.T.' narrative Peers is more explicit, than he is in the 'real' autobiography, as to his feelings and apprehensions at this period.

passed the next four years in an internment camp; but, by one of those strange chances that we are apt to think providential, I was invited to spend a few days with some friends at Camford before leaving England, so I postponed my departure for a week. Pacifism has always been strong in what someone has dubbed Lost Cause University, and I well recall the sandwich-men parading the streets before that fateful Fourth with boards bearing the legend 'England — keep out'. On the very eve of the outbreak of war, the wives of progressive dons were planning mass meetings to advocate British neutrality. Then came Germany's violation of the 'scrap of paper' treaty — and, as by a miracle, the whole neutrality movement collapsed. To me those days mark one of the high-points of psychological interest in the history of the country during my lifetime. Only three others that I have experienced are comparable with them: the reception by the nation of the Hoare-Laval agreement,[73] the revulsion of popular opinion after the conversations at Munich and the British reaction to the fall of France. In 1914, as in 1935, 1938 and 1940, the conscience of the nation was aroused; its characteristically defensive and protective covering was thrown off; its sensitiveness was bared.[74] I cannot say I always approve of my countrymen when they are gripped by strong feelings — the promiscuous tendering of white feathers to apparently fit males of military age was a characteristic indecency — but they always give me a queer feeling of pride. I was much prouder of being an Englishman on August 4 1914 than on November 11, 1918, though never so much so as in the summer of 1940.

On the night of August 4 it happened that I was dining at Trinity Lodge,[75] and after dinner our host brought out a giant atlas, laid it on an occasional table and invited us all to forecast the course of the coming struggle. Most of us chased the Germans back into their own country; one, however, foretold the

---

[73] The Hoare-Laval proposals on Abyssinia, which favoured Italy, were wrecked by public indignation in Britain and France, December 1935.

[74] Peers reveals here his profound interest in history and contemporary affairs. It should be remembered that several of his most influential publications (for instance, *The Spanish Tragedy 1930-1936: Dictatorship, Republic, Chaos*, and *Spain in Eclipse 1937-1943*), are concerned with the Civil War in Spain.

[75] In fact, at the Master's Lodge, Christ's College, Cambridge.

early capture of Paris and an attempt to invade England; nobody, so far as I recollect, ever imagined that for over four years the armies would remain all but stationary. Nor, for that matter, did anyone believe that a war between the chief European Powers could possibly last for four years. The President, I remember, had his daughter, with her twin sons, aged fourteen, staying with him[76] and at dinner she remarked to me how thankful she was that they, at least, would be too young to play a part in the struggle. Alas, they were both out in Flanders by the spring of 1918: one was killed in action three months before the Armistice and the other contracted an illness from which he died in 1920.

As to what my own duty was I had no hesitation whatever. Long before my eyes had been opened to the designs of Germany, I had been an enthusiastic advocate of Officers' Training Corps; even at school, before my accident, I had been a sergeant in the old Cadet Corps.[77] Despite my lameness, I determined to apply for a commission, for I knew that at least two of the Cranstead masters who ran the School O.T.C. would join up when war broke out, and it seemed to me that, if I could not fight in the trenches, I could at least step into the puttees of someone who could. My application was backed up by the Owl, who was spending an unenviable August receiving the resignations of his masters and scraping up a scratch staff to carry on, and, amazing as it may seem in an age when such things are done so differently, I was gazetted Second Lieutenant without the slightest question on August 25.[78] The intimation (another trivial detail indelibly graven upon the memory)

---

76 Dr Shipley, the Master, was a bachelor. If this account is based on fact, as it certainly seems to be, it may concern relations of Dr Shipley.

77 At this point in his narrative Peers has written, in pencil, in the margin, a reminder: 'Check this'. Though it was in February 1909 (shortly before Peers left) that Dartford Grammar School was given permission to establish a unit of the Officers Training Corps, the School arranged rifle classes from 1903 onwards and teams were sent to Bisley from 1907 (Hudson, *History of Dartford Grammar School*, 47).

78 Peers served in Felsted School's O.T.C. In fact it was in *The London Gazette* of Tuesday, 13 October 1914 (p. 8148) that it was gazetted that Peers had on 25 September 1914 been appointed 'to be Second Lieutenant for service with the Felsted School Contingent, Junior Division, Officers Training Corps' in the 'Unattached List for the Territorial Force' (see '[E.A.P.] *Auto*', ch. 3, pp. 98-99).

arrived in the form of a telegram from the War Office which my father took in at half-past-three in the morning.

All that August I spent at home, helping my father and mother pack up for another of those interminable moves.[79] I had no heart to go away for a holiday.[80]

By the time I went back to Cranstead, [what was happening?] It was a curiously bereft place that we returned to. The scratch staff included a dozen of the old hands, a mistress or two, an ex-headmaster patriotically re-donning the harness, three men who had retired from Cranstead years before under the age limit — dug-outs, the boys called them — and a few fresh appointments: elderly men who had never previously taught at a Public School, a younger man with a game leg like myself, another in whom short-sightedness reached a pitch which I have never seen equalled.

The boys were different, too. The Soccer Captain and three of last year's Hockey colours had got commissions. The Army Sixth had been spirited off in a body to Woolwich or Sandhurst. The new Monitors' list was larger than it had ever been before. Apropos of this, a good story went the rounds which is probably true. On the first Sunday of term, the Head invited half-a-dozen seniors to lunch. They came at one. At a quarter-to-two, they repaired with their host for the usual polite half-hour in his drawing-room. At a quarter-to-three, they were still sitting there, discussing the War. Soon after three, the resourceful old Owl, anxious for his Sunday nap, attempted to get them on the move by taking them into his study to show them photographs of Belgium. At half-past-three, they were still in the study, though looking, now this way, now that, and manifestly uneasy. At a quarter-to-four, the Head, who had another party coming to tea, saw no other way out of his difficulty than to break the unwritten law of hospitality by exclaiming in a bluff and breezy voice: 'Well, well, I suppose you'll be wanting to get back to your studies!' No doubt he puzzled over their unwonted reluctance to move earlier, but the other side of the story came back to the

---

79 Mr John T. Peers was 'admitted' Surveyor, Kingston District, Croydon, 17 November 1915 and presumably it was about then that he moved from Dartford.

80 A note, in pencil, indicates that Peers had planned to insert a passage here to: 'Describe course of War in August'.

Common Room via a housemaster, who had it from the Head of his house, who had been one of the party. The invariable rule at Cranstead, it seemed, which no one must ever break, was that it is for the senior man of a party to proffer the 'I think we must be going now, Sir'; and as all these unfortunates had been given their monitorships on the same day, there was no way of deciding which of them was senior. Naturally, they could not discuss the matter in the Head's presence and none of them would risk incurring the censure of the rest by speaking out of turn. How typically and ineradicably public-schoolish!

For the whole of that autumn term I laboured with the O.T.C. as well as in the classroom and in various departments of out-of-school activity for which substitutes were needed. I was of no use, of course, at parades, but I did a lot of instructional work with the seniors, for the Corps worked feverishly, since everyone was anxious to gain Certificate A as soon as possible so as not to serve in the ranks when he was called up. Being a good shot, I also made myself useful at the rifle range and in the evening I took my share in training village lads, and even grown men, to do what we should describe to-day as 'Home Guard' duties. It was a hard term's work; but, when one looked back, it was surprising how days which one had previously thought full to capacity could bear more stuffed into them. 'It is the busiest people', my father had written to me long ago, 'who have the most time'.[81] And so, once more, it proved — though I think the additional work was the more welcome because it deprived us of time which otherwise we might have spent in reflection.

The event of the term for me, however, was a letter which I received out of the blue — and a different blue than I had previously known — in the middle of October. It contained nothing less than an invitation to leave Cranstead for Oxbridge. Somehow, even when frustrated in my hope of a Camford

---

81 *Cf.* Truscot's similar observations above, ch. I, p. 196. Peers was renowned for his energetic and methodical use of time and refusal to waste it. In *Redbrick University*, he points out that the odd free hour between lectures should be utilized for 'clearing up odd pieces of routine', thus freeing a day that 'research will then be able to claim' (112). In *Redbrick and these Vital Days*, he makes the same observation as he makes here — namely that it is the hard-worked people who can always 'make more time if necessary' (96).

fellowship, I had never even considered the possibility of going to what we disrespectfully referred to as 'the other place'.[82] But for the 'Great' War, the idea would probably not have occurred to me to this day.

The letter was from one of the tutors of St Dunstan's, who had heard of me from my old friend ___[83] of Trinity, and was writing, not as a Fellow of his own college but as secretary of what we should call at Redbrick the 'Board of English Studies'. At Oxbridge, they designate this body the 'Faculty of English'.

The Faculty of English, it appeared, had been particularly unfortunate since the outbreak in losing nearly all its junior members. It was in urgent need of a University lecturer in Anglo-Saxon, of another in Middle English and of a third in Literature from 1579 onwards. Would I present myself as a candidate for the last of these posts? If I would, there were no other candidates and my election would be a formality. The post was a permanent one, to begin as soon as I could come, and, though no fellowship was attached to it, I should be morally certain to get one before long.

In ordinary circumstances I should not have hesitated for a moment. But then, I reflected, in ordinary circumstances I should not have received the invitation. As Oxbridge would never do anything so vulgar as to advertise a lectureship in the Press, I should have heard of the appointment only after it had been made. It seemed to me clear that I must decline it. Both Camford and Oxbridge had lost a large proportion of their undergraduates whereas Cranstead had lost most of its staff but had more boys than ever. It would be unkind — even unpatriotic — to go at short notice just for the sake of a more congenial job.

All this I said to myself, again and again, for days on end. But somehow I knew that I was fated to go.

In the end I found myself knocking at the door of the Headmaster's study. I suppose it was because I had decided to go that I determined to pacify my conscience by asking his

---

82 By 'Oxbridge' Peers, in this case, clearly means Oxford. This account of the offer and acceptance of a University Lectureship at Oxford is, of course, though plausibly written, fictional.

83 Peers left a space here to insert the name of his friend 'of Trinity', but omitted to make the insertion.

advice, though at the time I told myself that it was to justify myself for declining the offer. The Head, I argued, would put the case for my staying so unanswerably that he would dispose of all my objections. I believe, when I entered the well-known room on that October morning, that I really expected him to do so. But, as I stood there, I suddenly had that curious sensation of having already done what I was going to do now. The French window that led into the rose garden was open.[84] Outside, the last blooms were full-blown and petals were swirling in the wind. Inside, the bright sunshine lit up the desk...

Before the Head had said a word, I knew that I was saying good-bye.

I explained the unusual position... My natural inclinations... My scruples... My unwillingness to desert Cranstead...

The Owl's reply was almost explosive in its decisiveness. He might have been scolding me — 'biting'.

'But of *course* you must go, man. It's the chance of a lifetime. What did I say to you when you came to see me before? I said your real success would lie in research.[85] No, no, you're not a bad schoolmaster, but schoolmastering's not your real job. You go to Oxbridge, Truscot, and, mark my word, you'll climb to the top of the tree... What's that? Oh, *we* shall manage all right. I've lost so many that one more won't matter much. You'll stay till Christmas, hey? Good, then that's settled'.

And that was the end. I left Cranstead for good at the end of 1914,[86] fully conscious that, whatever might happen to me after the War, I should never be a schoolmaster again.

---

[84] In a note, made in pencil, in the margin, Peers reminds himself to 'check details'.

[85] It was, in fact, McClure who had made that observation, and it was McClure's study which opened on to his rose garden (see above pp. 242-43, and note 69). But it was Dr Vaughan, Master of Wellington College, who in November 1919 encouraged Peers to take up the offer of a temporary lectureship at the University of Liverpool (see '[E.A.P.] *Auto*', ch. 3, p. 119).

[86] In fact, Peers left Wellington College in December 1919.

## V

I was not, of course, elected to my Oxbridge post merely on the strength of a letter. After writing the letter, I had still to make formal application for the vacancy. At the end of a decorous interval, a letter came from the Registrary, summoning me to an interview. And in those days (it may not be so to-day [/now]) an interview at Oxbridge was a much dreaded ordeal. For one not only had to meet the electors as a body, but also to spend the preceding day calling upon them individually in their homes.

This extraordinary procedure meant [/involved me in] a two-day absence from school and the days were well filled at that. I stayed at the Golden Hind, the oldest of Oxbridge's hotels, planted in the very centre of the Haymarket, from which point, so the map in the coffee room informed me, my routes would radiate in all directions. At half past ten on the next morning I began my visits, and, with a generous interval for lunch, they continued until half past four. My first ordeal was with the Professor of English Literature,[87] who inhabited a large house in the residential hinterland beyond the river: to him the interview was a kind of super-viva and he led me up and down the ages as though he were trying to discover the limits of my knowledge. Near him lived my second inquisitor — a renowned philologist,[88] no more than a name to me, who turned out to have an atrocious Bradford accent and treated my irruption as nothing more than a social call. Thence I returned to the town, and took a bus to East Oxbridge, past streets of Council houses, to the humble lodgings of a young Fellow who seemed more nervous than I was. My remaining visits were to the Colleges, or to the side streets and alleys which run between them. Last of all came the Dunstan's man who had written to me, and who was content to talk about mutual friends over a cup of tea.

---

87 Though these events are not based on fact, Peers possibly modelled this professor of English Literature on Sir Arthur Quiller-Couch, King Edward VII Professor of English Literature, University of Cambridge, 1912-44 (*cf.* above, ch. I, pp. 200-01, and note 102; see also [E.A.P.] *Auto*, ch. 3, p. 92, note 28).

88 Peers might have had vaguely in mind Professor W. W. Skeat, the renowned philologist, but Skeat was born in London, and educated in London and at Christ's College, Cambridge (see '[E.A.P.] *Auto*', ch. 2, p. 76, note 6).

## 252 REDBRICK UNIVERSITY REVISITED

After all this, the formal interview on the next morning was pure bathos: a quarter of an hour's questioning, a wait of barely two minutes and finally a return summons to hear the news of my election. As there had been no other candidates I could hardly manifest any surprise, but I hope at least that I contrived to register pleasure. The emotion uppermost within me, however, was mild disgust at meaningless and time-wasting formalities, natural to anyone accustomed to the more direct methods of the world of school. To-day I should probably be a good deal more tolerant.

I stayed at Oxbridge for close upon four years,[89] about which I propose here to say very little. Though not the least enjoyable years of my life, they were certainly the least significant. I saw something of the inner workings of College life for in the summer of 1915 I was elected to a fellowship at Queen's. But both at College and in the University conditions were abnormal. There were many difficult, and sometimes absorbing, problems, but they were special problems created by the War. I lectured comparatively little and to mere skeletons of audiences. Contacts of all kinds were fewer than in peace-time. Opportunities for indulging outside interests were small. Travel abroad was impossible. So it would be unfair for me to draw any conclusions as to the advantages and drawbacks of a don's life at Oxbridge from my own experience of it. When I was thinking over these, I remember, with a view to writing the first chapter of *Red Brick University*, I found myself relying rather on what I had been told by Camford and Oxbridge dons at one time or another during the intervening quarter of a century.[90]

None the less, that fallow period played an important part in

---

89 As noted, Peers, in reality, spent the years 1914-19 as a schoolmaster — at Felsted School and then, very briefly, at Wellington College. He never held a post at Oxford or at Cambridge. Not surprisingly, therefore, he passes quickly over his supposed experiences as a don at Oxbridge.

90 The observation reveals Peers' individually developed sense of humour. He makes this remark knowing that his own direct experience of a 'don's life at Oxbridge' is non-existent. In writing the first chapter of *Redbrick University* (which is entitled 'The Battle of the Ancients and the Moderns') he was, therefore, obliged to depend heavily on what he 'had been told by Camford and Oxbridge dons', about life as teacher and scholar in these institutions.

my development. I needed a period of transition before plunging into full academic activity. I needed to throw off classroom methods and reaccustom myself to the atmosphere of the lecture-room and the study. I needed an opportunity for extensive reading, which enabled me, as it proved, to plan the writing that, from one point of view, was to be my life-work.[91] In those four years I laid foundations without which the modest edifice that I was to rear would have tumbled to the ground.

Again, those four years gave me a chance to think about my future. People say that the four years from eighteen to twenty-two are the most important in a professional man's life. In my own, the years from twenty-nine to thirty-three were very much more so. I was conscious of very little psychological change as an undergraduate; of considerably more at Cranstead; and of most of all at Oxbridge. Without undergoing any particularly formative experiences I seemed to be maturing rapidly. I thought a great deal about my future and came to the conclusion that the career for which I had a clear vocation was one which embodied three activities — investigation, teaching and the cure of souls.

The last of these three was by no means the least important. No doubt I had inherited the pastoral instinct from my father, who was always more of a pastor than of a scholar or a preacher; and I realized that it had developed in me a great deal during the years at Cranstead. At one point in the Oxbridge period I had been tremendously attracted by the country parson's life, through having struck up an acquaintance with the holder of a Queen's living in the College library. I used to notice that this other-worldly-looking clergyman would be working there every Tuesday and Wednesday and never on any other day of the week, either in term or in vacation.[92] After a

---

91 Another indication of the importance which, during his career, Peers attached to research.

92 It should be noted that all of the older Cambridge and Oxford Colleges were patrons of a number of Anglican benefices: in the case of Christ's College, Cambridge, eighteen benefices in all were held in 1911 by sixteen individual clergymen who had graduated from Christ's College (*The Cambridge University Calendar for the Year 1911-1912*, p. 1069). The clergyman mentioned by Peers may be partly modelled on his colleague and friend at Felsted School, the Revd Edgar Iliff Robson, who was, like Peers, a graduate of Christ's College, Cambridge (see '[E.A.P.] *Auto*', ch. 3, p. 101, and

time we got to know each other quite well, and I would go down to spend week-ends with him at Denham, twenty miles away. I could not fail to notice how intensely he enjoyed his varied life: his weekly two days of intensive research at Oxbridge; the long evenings in his study at Denham; his Sunday services at which he came down to earth and preached in his parishioners' vernacular; his regular excursions into the parish school; his intercourse with the simple country folk, who never ceased to marvel how the 'Raverund', so learned as he was and all, could talk simple with the likes o' we. He was a musician, too, and on summer evenings he would stroll over to the church and play the more than adequate organ, accompanied perhaps by one of the private pupils whom the College used to send him in the vacation for coaching. He was a bachelor, of course, but, at that time, so was I, and his life seemed to me absolutely ideal. But when I came to contemplate taking Orders, I realized that I could not. I had become an Anglican — partly, I think, as a reaction from the Methodism in which I had been brought up, and partly because I admired its comprehensiveness.[93] But as soon as I began to consider Anglican Orders, I realized that I was too much of a cosmopolitan in religion to become a professional exponent of any one of its denominations. Niceties of dogma have always seemed trivial by comparison with the ideal of unity, which is a passion with me.[94] Of all this I hope to

---

note 63). It is possible also that the clergyman personifies certain aspects and inclinations of the author himself at this period in his life and development. It will be remembered that, while at Felsted School during the War, for several months Peers took charge, as a licensed lay reader, of Robson's parish and that, like the unnamed clergyman here, he used to play the church organ, and enjoy talking to the country folk (*cf.* '[E.A.P.] *Auto*', ch. 3, pp. 100-01, and notes 61-64). There is no doubt that, before he became a university professor, Peers, as he reveals here, seriously considered becoming an Anglican priest (*cf.* also above, ch. I, p. 215, and note 151).

[93] In reality, as we have seen, Peers was brought up as a Congregationalist, then became an Anglican (see '[E.A.P.] *Auto*', ch. 1, p. 73, note 34. *Cf.* also 'B.T.' ch. I, pp. 193-94, and note 74).

[94] *Cf.* Peers' admission in ch. I of the 'Bruce Truscot' autobiography that he had 'never had much understanding of exclusiveness in religion' (p. 194). Though an Anglican, throughout his adult life Peers had an extraordinarily profound understanding of, and affinity with, the Roman Catholic faith. Peers' translations into English of Saint Teresa of Ávila and Saint John of the Cross received the *imprimatur* of the Roman Catholic Church. In the obituary, 'Edgar Allison Peers. A Tribute', which appeared in

SCHOOL AND UNIVERSITY (1907-1918)     255

say a good deal in the future.⁹⁵

After a term, too, I found that, quite apart from my religious convictions, the scholar-parson's life would not satisfy my desire for teaching.  Catechizing village children and coaching occasional undergraduates was no job for a man whose vocation was teaching. At the same time, a thirty-hour teaching week in a Secondary or Public School would completely frustrate my instinct for investigation. So, by a process of checks and balances, I was driven to the conclusion that all three elements in my vocation would be satisfied by a University career, and by that alone.⁹⁶

And yet I never once considered 'settling down' at Oxbridge. Should I have done so, I wonder, if I had stayed on there for a year or two after the end of the War? I doubt it. I was always keenly conscious, and even slightly and quite unreasoningly resentful, of its artificiality. We seemed, at Queen's, in a way that it had never occurred to me was being done at my own Trinity (though no doubt it was) to be fencing off our little community and from behind our gilded fence getting a warped

---

*The Tablet*, Robert Sencourt wrote that Peers 'combined an authority no Catholic could disdain with an art which made him a master of the spiritual life for not only Anglicans, but certain extreme Protestants. For it is through mystical theology that we come closest to Church Unity' (January 10, 1953, 29).

95  Peers published a number of works of a religious and devotional, yet non-denominational, character, and doubtless had planned to write further books of this nature, but death prevented their completion.  He left completed, but unpublished, the manuscript of a work, written in the early 1940s, which he provisionally entitled *Mysticism and Modern Christianity*. The manuscript was read and highly praised by John Stirling (letter to Peers dated 15 October 1941 [University Archives, Liverpool]).  It is hoped to publish this manuscript as a volume in the E. Allison Peers Series.  This book is important for reasons now of its historical perspectives as well as for its undated insights into faith, life and worship.

96  Peers' expressed belief that his vocation as university teacher embodied 'three elements', or 'three activities — investigation, teaching and the cure of souls' (*cf*. above, p. 253) confirms his commitment to the welfare (personal and spiritual, not purely academic) of his students and graduates. One remembers his earlier affirmaton that 'My own graduates know that they are mine for life, and that they can come to me at any time for whatever I am capable of giving them' (see above 'B.T.', ch. I, pp. 216-17, and note 155). *First Year at the University* and the other two 'Redbrick' books reveal the importance which Peers attached to the 'pastoral' functions (which he saw as moral obligations) of the University Teacher.

view of the world outside. We talked, even of the momentous current events that were making history, in a detached, donnish way which I accepted, and even relished, in the Senior Common Room, but which, as soon as I rubbed up against the real world in London, or among my hard-living, bread-earning friends at home, sounded quite intolerable.

That, in one form or another, was the chief reason why I never thought of staying at Oxbridge for life. There were others: the dislike of a man trained at Camford for certain varieties of Oxbridge pose; the unsatisfactory financial position of a Senior Fellow as he grows older when he neither wishes to accumulate offices (each with its stipend) nor aspires to a Headship; the unpleasantness of having to teach youths of whom so large a proportion have no intention of putting forth more than fifty per cent (if even so much) of their ability.[97] But my main objection to becoming a Don for life was simply that I had no desire to become a Don for life, and I rather hoped that, in some way or other, I might shake myself free from Oxbridge,[98] before the first thin layer of donnishness formed over me.

Precisely what my programme for getting away was I cannot now remember. Intensive cultivation of Camford, I know, was one item of it, and, even as early as 1917, I used to spend apparently aimless week-ends at Trinity in order to get myself known again. Again, I had the idea of going abroad for a considerable time, perhaps as a visiting lecturer to some Dominion university. Then there was London: though I had

---

97 *Cf.* Peers' comments in *Redbrick University*, especially in ch. 1, 'The Battle of the Ancients and the Moderns', 29-31: 'how heartbreaking it can become to watch good material continually going to seed' (30).

98 Peers' attitude to the don's life at Oxbridge was, however, ambiguous. He could perceive its disadvantages, yet was attracted by its amenities. His career at Liverpool clearly brought him a whole measure of personal and professional fulfilment that he could not have achieved at Oxford or Cambridge. In this respect, see below, in 'B.T.', ch. III, his declaration: 'faced with the possibility of returning to the comfortable, easygoing life of an ancient university,... I realized that, in spite of all its advantages, *I did not want to go*' (325). But what he says at the end of chapter I probably comes near to expressing his true feelings: 'If I could retire on a research fellowship tomorrow and go where I liked, it would be to Trinity [i.e. to Christ's College, Cambridge] that I should go without the slightest hesitation' (217).

graduated externally, I had made a number of contacts with the two chief London Colleges and for many reasons should have welcomed a life spent at either of them. What I did actually do in the summer of 1918, however, was something which I had not only never contemplated, but should probably have turned down with scorn had anyone suggested it to me. It was a thoroughly prejudiced Camfordian[99] who took a single ticket from Oxbridge to Redbrick University.

---

99 There is, in the final sentence of this chapter, an endearingly frank admission that the prejudices against the modern universities of which he has complained — and which he has tried to abolish, or at least reduce, through books like *Redbrick University* — are preconceptions and misconceptions which he himself once shared.

# PART II

# REDBRICK UNIVERSITY

## CHAPTER III

## REDBRICK: THE BEGINNINGS[1]

REDBRICK UNIVERSITY — Applications are invited for the post of LECTURER IN POETRY (Grade II B), the appointment to date from October 1, 1918. The lecturer appointed will work under the direction of Professor James [/G.J.?][2] Upright, within the Department of English Literature, and, if not already a member, will be required to join the Federated Superannuation Scheme for Universities. Candidates should give particulars of their War Service (if any). Further details may be obtained from the Registrar, to whom fifteen copies of the application should be sent not later than August 15, 1918.[3]

---

1   Peers' own choice of chapter-heading has been used.
2   Peers has forgotten that he gave Upright the first names of George Charles (initials, therefore, G. C.) (see 'B.T.', ch. I, p. 205; and *cf.* notes 21 and 50 below). One might regard his lapse of memory almost as a 'Freudian' slip: for the real name of Peers' chief adversary and predecessor in the Gilmour Chair at Liverpool was, of course, **James** Fitzmaurice-Kelly.
3   The text of the press advertisement of the Gilmour Chair of Spanish, May 1919 (of which this is a disguised version) reads:

The University of Liverpool.

---

Gilmour Chair of Spanish.

---

The Council invite Applications for this Chair. The appointment will date from 1st October, 1919. Candidates are invited to state whether they would be prepared to teach Portuguese if required. Full particulars as to emoluments and duties can be obtained on application to the Registrar.
   Applications, together with the names of at least three scholars of recognized standing, to whom reference may be made, and (if the

That was the text of the advertisement which completed the transformation of my career begun when I had left Cranstead for Oxbridge. It caught my eye on the back page of a *Times Educational Supplement* which the newsagent's boy had thrown outside my door one Saturday afternoon in June, and which I retrieved as I came in with Shoebridge after a turn round the Westchester Grind in weather that was less like June than February. Shoebridge was the young Fellow with digs in East Oxbridge whom I had first met on that famous day of interviews.[4] Too unlike ever to become real friends, we had nevertheless for long been close companions. He, too, was a University Lecturer in English Literature, and soon after our first meeting I had discovered that he was only a term my senior. In many ways we were completely antithetical. He was a product of Harchester[5] and some expensive prep. school whose name I forget. After taking his degree, he had stayed on in the hope of getting a fellowship and for five years had eked out a livelihood in cheap lodgings by coaching undergraduates until the War gave him his opportunity as it had given me mine. Lung trouble and a weak heart relegated him at once to Grade C and left him free to step into his lectureship when it presented itself.

Shoebridge was the first example of a scholar endowed with the complete set of Public School and Ancient University prejudices that I had had the opportunity of studying at close quarters. At Cranstead, the men of his type (and there were not many of them) had been nothing but overgrown schoolboys.[6] But Shoebridge had shed his interest in batting averages and what one might describe as the Cock House

---

Candidate so desires) 12 copies of testimonials should be sent to the Registrar not later than 30th June, 1919.

Edward Carey, Registrar.

On Saturday, 17 May 1919, the Registrar acknowledged receipt of a letter from Peers of 16 May, and stated, referring to the statement of particulars of the Chair, that the last day on which applications for the Chair would be received was 30 June.

    4   See above, ch. II, p. 251.
    5   *Cf.* above, 'B.T.', ch. II, p. 230, note 41.
    6   *Cf.* Peers' comments above, in the 'Bruce Truscot' narrative, ch. II, especially pp. 237-38.

mentality:⁷ indeed, being a typical intellectual, he may even never have had any. Certainly he had very little interest in boys and their pursuits and he would probably have been a great deal less in his element as a schoolmaster than I was. But the belief that education equalled Harchester plus Oxbridge was only less ingrained in him than the belief that twice two equalled four. Every school that was ever spoke of I felt that he was mentally comparing with his own. There were about half a dozen to which he would refer as though they were [/might be] on a level with it: the rest were nowhere. He professed particular disdain for what he called the 'smaller public schools', lumping them with municipal secondary schools and other kinds of institution which he believed to exist, though he could not have named them. As for universities, he would admit, for the sake of politeness, that there were two, but in his heart of hearts he recognized only one. Camford methods, the Camford mentality, the Camford manner and the Camford accent were things which he never mentioned but which one felt caused him real grief. 'Oh, he's a Camford man!' he would say and nod understandingly. I sometimes wished he would master his courteous inhibitions sufficiently to tell me what he really thought of us; and I often wondered if there are any Camford people who feel quite as deeply about Oxbridge as he did about Camford. If there are, I have never met them.⁸

It was a capricious fate which decreed that Shoebridge of all people should have been with me when I first read that advertisement. I came upon it so suddenly that I was quite unable to restrain my surprise. For, as I stooped to pick it up from the mat, one name leapt out at me: a name which evoked a never-to-be-forgotten occasion — the name of my first academic hero, Professor Upright.⁹

'By Jove!' I exclaimed as I read the advertisement.

---

7   That is to say, the mentality of those Public School products, who concentrate competitively, on being top, or making their House top, usually at games. *Cf.* Peers' use of the same term, 'B.T.', ch. II, p. 237.

8   In making this remark, the author, doubtless with intentional irony and self-mockery, is revealing the 'Camford' prejudices and superior feelings of Bruce Truscot — revealing, that is to say, the Cambridge preferences and prejudices of E. Allison Peers.

9   As indicated, Peers' pseudonym for James Fitzmaurice-Kelly (see above, note 2).

Shoebridge raised his eyes queryingly.

'Here's a lectureship going at Redbrick under Upright', I explained, handing him the paper.

'My dear Bob', he retorted, giving it a cursory glance (I ought to say here that I have always been known as Bob to my intimates), 'Why will you take in these low newspapers? Just imagine an Oxbridge don reading columns of stuff about local authorities and workers' educational associations![10] As for old Upright — will you never get rid of that childish habit of hero-worship? You know perfectly well I have always deprecated it in you. Really, you are more like a boy of thirteen than a full-grown man of thirty-three'.

This was a battle we had fought out over and over again, the result invariably being a stalemate.

'You inform me', he went on, solemnly, 'that some unfortunate creature is going to be lured into spending several years in the insalubrious and smoke-laden atmosphere of Drabtown,[11] the prize being the opportunity of working for a Camford man who sold himself to a municipal institution misnamed a university[12] so that he might be able to flaunt the title of professor before he was forty. I am aware', he went on, checking my attempt at protest, 'that long years ago you sat at this gentleman's feet and were even honoured by being permitted to shake his hand.[13] But what possible interest you

---

10 To his credit, Peers had the greatest respect for workers' educational associations. At Liverpool, Peers gave lectures for the University's Extension Board (see below, pp. 324-25, and note 160). See also his comments in *Redbrick University*, ch. 7, in which he pays 'tribute to the magnificent work done by the Workers' Educational Association and the Tutorial Classes' scheme' (187).

11 Liverpool. Peers uses the same pseudonym for Liverpool, and for any industrial town in the provinces, in *Redbrick University* and *Redbrick and these Vital Days*. No doubt Peers had in mind Charles Dickens' 'Coketown' (*Hard Times*, 1854) 'a town of red brick, or of brick that would have been red if the smoke and ashes had allowed it'. 'Coketown' was largely inspired by Preston, the county town of Lancashire. Peers' predilection for Dickens is evident, for example, in *Redbrick University* (see p. 11).

12 For Shoebridge, of course, with his extreme prejudices, to work for a 'Camford man' was a fate equally as undesirable as to take a job teaching in Redbrick — an institution 'misnamed a university'.

13 See above, 'B.T.', ch. I, pp. 206-08. In the next sentence Peers again wrongly gives Professor George Charles Upright the same first name as James Fitzmaurice-Kelly.

can find in the fact that James Upright requires a valet or a bottle-washer I cannot conceive'.

'Yes', I replied lamely, and rather inconsequently, 'I suppose Redbrick is a bit of a hole'.

Bit of a hole!' cried Shoebridge, *'Bit of a hole!* My dear Bob, it is a hole without qualification. It is a glorified Council School set in the Drabtown slums. It is in fact the abomination of desolation standing where it ought not. It is...'

'Have you ever been there?' I enquired, coldly — not that I had any desire to defend Redbrick, about which I should have spoken in much the same way myself, in other circumstances, but that I was nettled at the terms in which he had spoken about a man for whom I still had such great admiration.

'Been there?' he retorted. 'Of course not. But what I say's perfectly true. Ask old Binns: he's examined there. The place is actually built in the slums. From the Senate House, or whatever they have, you can see the washing hanging out. The air is heavy with the perfume of fried fish.[14] Children of tender years commit nuisances in the streets. Oh, my dear Bob, let us leave this painful subject and betake ourselves to the task of toasting muffins. Just think of it! Muffins toasted at a real English fire — in a real English June!'

So we toasted, and talked — about everything in the world but Redbrick. After his serio-comic tirade I did begin to feel the least bit ashamed. I might almost have conveyed the impression that I was interested in the post myself. People did, of course, occasionally leave Oxbridge for the newer universities, but they always went to Chairs there. And even then they sacrificed a lot — Hall, Common Room, libraries, contacts, amenities, perquisites...[15]

---

14 Bruce Truscot, on his first visit to Drabtown and Redbrick University, which is indeed 'built in the slums', discovers the accuracy of Shoebridge's physical description of both place and institution (*cf.* below, pp. 272-77).

15 In the 'Redbrick' books, written in the 1940s, Peers admits that the buildings at the 'new' universities are still usually unprepossessing, and that there is a lack or shortage of huge lecture theatres — and, also, therefore of halls spacious enough for social activities like dances. Peers concedes, however that some 'really striking and beautiful buildings' have been added, among which he mentions 'the new libraries at Leeds and Liverpool' [a reference to the Brotherton Library, University of Leeds, and

None the less, after Shoebridge had gone, I took up the paper again and re-read the advertisement. Had I any pupil who could apply for it? A fine thing to start one's academic career under a man like Upright!...[16] What did 'Grade II B' mean? What did a lecturer in poetry have to do? Would they consider a man newly graduated if I could think of one? What was this Federated Superannuation Scheme?[17] — it sounded ominous! Well, perhaps one might write to the Registrar and find out...

[So] I wrote a brief note on the spot and went down to the Porter's Lodge to post it...

After Hall I went back to my rooms earlier than usual and sat regarding the remains of the fire in a way no young man should. For thirty-three is no age [/not an age] to conjure [/for conjuring] up pictures of the past and wonder [/wondering] where one would be if certain things had happened and other things had not. I remembered so vividly those Snark Lectures,[18] the corner of that Trinity lecture-room where I sat, the way Professor Upright seemed to rise and rise as though he would never stop,[19] his shining bald head, his tiny dapper grey

---

the Harold Cohen Library, University of Liverpool, which were opened in 1936 and 1938 respectively] (*Redbrick University*, 17-18). In Peers' opinion, of course, Redbrick University, Drabtown, offers both the university teacher and the undergraduate advantages which are more important than buildings and amenities. One of these advantages — as the youthful Bruce Truscot, hero of this narrative, will soon discover — is the opportunity which young members of staff are given to be pioneers in their discipline and in their profession (see, for instance, *Redbrick University*, 31-32).

16  This exclamation is deliberately ironical and ambiguous. The youthful and inexperienced Bruce Truscot, at this stage, sincerely regarded the possibility of working under Upright as indeed 'a fine thing'. The much older Bruce Truscot who is writing these memoirs, however, knows the truth about Upright's character and has suffered as a result of Upright's jealousy, and of the influence unjustly wielded by the older man to damage the career of his talented young colleague: 'A fine thing' indeed to start one's career under such difficulties.

17  Peers has written, in pencil, a query in the margin: '?not at Oxbr.?'

18  Peers' name for the Norman Maccoll Lectures (see above, 'B.T.', ch. I, pp. 204-05, and notes 112, 114).

19  See Bruce Truscot's earlier description of Upright on that same occasion: 'you had the feeling that he was never going to stop rising' (ch. I, p. 206). Peers repeats this observation, deliberately, in the structural interests of narrative unity. The reader is encouraged to remember

beard, his...[20]

'Good gracious', I though to myself, 'he must be getting on in years by now. Something like seventy, surely?'

I reached for my *Who's Who* — a second-hand one, a few years old: I had picked it up quite recently in Pepper's. There he was... Upright, James, M.A., D.Litt., Hon LL.D... Born London, May 15, 1855...[21]

Sixty-three, that would make him. Yes, of course, he couldn't be seventy. Didn't these modern universities retire their professors at sixty-five? There had even been talk of the same thing happening at Oxbridge...

Sixty-three... That meant he would be retiring in two years' time... Sixty-three... Two years' time... Who would succeed him?... Professor of Poetry: there was only one other such professorship in the whole country...[22] Two years' time...

---

Truscot's earlier description, and thus to connect the first encounter and immediate admiration for Upright with Truscot's present interest in a post as Upright's assistant at Redbrick University.

20 Photographs reveal that Fitzmaurice-Kelly was, as Peers suggests, both balding and bearded (regarding Fitzmaurice-Kelly's appearance, see also 'B.T.', ch. I, p. 205, note 118).

21 Again Peers wrongly gives Upright the first name of Fitzmaurice-Kelly (*cf*., above, note 2, and also below, note 50). After 'James' Peers uses here, in pencil, the sign ∧ (i.e. an insertion sign): doubtless he meant to check and insert the correct names which he had previously given to George Charles Upright. Professor James Fitzmaurice-Kelly, Litt.D., F.B.A., was, in fact, born at Glasgow on 20 June 1857 (see also '[E.A.P.] *Auto*', ch. 3, pp. 112-13, note 112). 'Pepper's', the bookshop where Truscot supposedly bought the *Who's Who* he consults for information on Upright, is probably a deliberate corruption of the name of the Cambridge booksellers, Heffers.

22 As previously indicated, the Professorship of Poetry at Redbrick University corresponds to the Gilmour Chair of Spanish at Liverpool University, which was the oldest such Chair in the country, there being, at this time, only one other (the Cervantes Chair of Spanish Language and Literature, King's College London [see also 'B.T.', ch. I, p. 205, note 116]). It is not surprising that, to provide a professorship of sufficient extraordinariness, Peers should give Upright a Chair of Poetry. In Bruce Truscot's 'A Redbrick Tea-party' (1945), a visiting scholar from Oxbridge expresses surprise that a place like Redbrick has a Professorship of Poetry. Even nowadays, more than seventy years after the events here remembered, and about fifty years since Peers composed his autobiography, Chairs of Poetry, of the type occupied by Upright, are almost unknown in British universities. The Professorship of Poetry at Oxford (founded in 1708) was described as recently as 1986 as 'a unique institution in any university' (see

Was it a practical proposition?... Of course, if it didn't come off, it would be awkward. One could hardly go from Oxbridge to Redbrick and expect to get back to Oxbridge again...

And the fried-fish shops... And the washing...

But, after all, Upright was Upright; and, whatever happened, one would learn an awful lot from him.[23]

And I had already decided not to spend my whole life at Oxbridge... ...

I slept very little that night. The next morning, I went to see the Master.

By the time the Registrar's reply reached me, my mind was made up. I would go in for that lectureship on the chance of succeeding to Upright's Chair in two years' time. It was a risk, but a risk well worth taking. And, if the worst came to the worst, there were Chairs of English Literature in more than one of the grimmer spots in the wilderness of the world outside Oxbridge.

II

One day, late in August, I received a note from the Dean of Redbrick's Faculty of Arts asking me to attend for interview by the Faculty Board's Vacation Emergency Committee in ten days' time.[24]

It sounded extremely formal and I wondered if I was in for

---

*The History of the University of Oxford*, Vol. V *The Eighteenth Century*, ed. L. S. Sutherland and L. G. Mitchell [Oxford: Clarendon Press, 1986], 474). Fortunately, thanks largely to Peers' activities in the development of teaching and research in the subject, Chairs of Spanish are now numerous and well established.

23 More deliberate irony: Truscot was to learn a great deal about academic life and human nature from Upright, including the truth about Upright's professional and personal character, which belied the trust-inspiring implications of his name.

24 Peers states that it was in November 1919, while he was at Wellington College, that he was informed of the possible opening at the University of Liverpool and subsequently arranged an informal interview with the Dean of the Faculty of Arts (see '[E.A.P.] *Auto*', ch. 3, pp. 118-21).

a worse ordeal than I had had at Oxbridge.²⁵ Once more, I was at home when the summons came, but it was a permanent home now, for my father had retired from active work to a modest bungalow in Surrey,²⁶ and, except for occasional preaching engagements within the local circuit, he devoted himself exclusively to his books and his garden.

I have said little about him in these last pages, but that does not mean that he failed to follow every step I took with interest and critical comment. Throughout my Camford career, he had observed, and occasionally criticized, my tendency to excessive idealism.²⁷ Both then and during my Cranstead years, he had warned me against taking what people said at its face value. I would tell him how some of the elder men ran down the school and everything to do with it. 'But you will notice', he would remark, 'that they stay there'. He had a poor opinion of schoolmasters: 'they live a narrow life and they seem to care very little about broadening it'. He was frankly concerned, when I moved to Oxbridge, lest I should attach overmuch importance to superficial amenities and settle down to a life governed by ease and comfort.²⁸

---

25 An encouragement to the reader — serving as a unifying technique of structure — to remember the interviews Truscot had had for the Oxbridge post (described above, 'B.T.', ch. II, pp. 251-52).

26 Peers deletes, in pencil, the word 'modest'; and he considers changing Surrey into 'Sussex?'. Mr John T. Peers did not, in fact, retire until 1921 and, in his retirement, lived at Worthing, Sussex (see '[E.A.P.] *Auto*', ch. 1, pp. 61-62, note 3). It would appear, from letters sent by the University Registrar to Peers during the Christmas 1919 and Summer 1920 Vacations, that his parents were, at that time, (still) living at 24 Beaufort Road, Kingston-on-Thames.

27 By no means all the traits of character and attitudes of mind observable in Bruce Truscot are necessarily those of Allison Peers. One remembers that, in the 'Preface' to *Redbrick and these Vital Days*, he indicates that some of the views of Truscot are not necessarily his own: he gave them to Truscot deliberately to provoke discussion (14-15). Nevertheless, we may reasonably assume that the 'excessive idealism' of the youthful Bruce Truscot to which the author refers in more than one passage (*cf.* above, 'B.T.', ch. I, p. 197) was a significant characteristic which Peers, in his maturity, had correctly identified among the authentic attitudes of his younger self. It will be remembered that he attributes to himself this same characteristic in '(E.A.P.) *Auto*' (see, e.g., ch. 4, pp. 125, 128).

28 *Cf.* his father's reactions to Truscot's failure to win a fellowship at Camford reported above (ch. I, p. 215).

I was not altogether surprised, then, when he warmly commended my decision to leave Oxbridge for [/go in for the post at] Redbrick.²⁹ To be perfectly honest, as I can afford to be after so many years, I had not told him of my ulterior motive, and thus [I] got more credit than I deserved. But I felt I deserved a little additional encouragement to compensate for the frigid surprise of my colleagues at Queens and the absolute speechlessness of Shoebridge. In the Common Room I had made no attempt to justify my action, leaving it to be interpreted as an exhibition of sheer eccentricity. But at home I told them that, though I should be forfeiting a hundred a year and living in conditions very much less pleasant than those of Oxbridge, I felt that I had been living in a world too good to be altogether true and that I preferred a spell of truth to an overdose of somewhat cloying good-ness.

'A brave decision, my boy', was my father's comment. 'You've more courage and initiative than I gave you credit for. I'm very proud of you'.

I hope I had the grace to blush at this commendation. I would only too gladly have confessed my real motive, but I knew how deeply my father would be disappointed if the Chair failed to come off. So it was not only original sin that was responsible for my silence.

As a matter of fact, the Registrar's letter, a subsequent communication from the Dean and a perusal of the Redbrick University Calendar showed that I was not going to do so badly after all. Though the salary in Grade II B [/A] was, as I have said, a hundred pounds less than I was getting, I found that examining and extension-lecturing³⁰ would make up a good

---

29 In reality, of course, Peers abandoned Public Schoolmastering, not 'dondom' at Oxbridge, for Redbrick. However, he clearly perceived the comfortable life and amenities which he had enjoyed as a schoolmaster at Felsted School, and, briefly, also at Wellington College — and of which he had not wished to become too fond — as by no means dissimilar to the life of a don at Oxbridge, 'governed by ease and comfort'. It will be remembered that the boys, whom Peers describes in *Redbrick University,* who come from public school to Oxbridge regard the move as 'a natural stage of evolution' (19). Certainly they find at the Ancient University many of the attitudes and familiar customs which directed their occupations as public schoolboys.

30 As previously noted, Peers lectured for the Extension Board at Liverpool University (see above, p. 264, note 10, and below, p. 325, and note 160).

part of this and also that, if I were promoted to Grade II[/I] A, I should be earning more than now.[31] But my principal surprise was the discovery of how little work had to be done. At Oxbridge I had six weekly lectures, covering a much wider field than I could claim to be a specialist in, interviews with undergraduates, college meetings, certain duties as sub-librarian and a host of obligations, chiefly social but quite unavoidable, attaching to my fellowship. At Redbrick, if I were elected to the post, I should have five lectures a week, all within my special field of poetry, and apparently nothing more.

This was puzzling in the extreme. I knew very little of the modern universities, and, as will have been gathered, a large part of what I did know came from unsympathetic and none too well informed sources. But one thing I had believed incontrovertible: that the professors and lecturers at these places were incredibly over-worked — rather like schoolmasters, in fact — and for that reason had no time to do original work, which was the reason why so few of them ever went any farther. I had imagined myself lecturing for about twenty hours a week all the term long and spending the vacations in recovering from the effects of overwork. And now I found that the person appointed to this post would be expected to lecture for only five hours weekly. He would have no supervision of students, for that was the work of the Professor; and, the Professorship of Poetry being attached, as it were, to the English Literature Department, this particular Professor had less than usual. There would be no meetings to attend, for the lecturer in Poetry was not a member of the Faculty Board. There would be no social duties, for lectures ended at four, and, with the exception of the University Library, the buildings then closed.[32]

---

31 In July 1920 the University Council fixed the salaries of members of the non-professorial teaching staff as from 1 October 1920: Grade I: not less than £500 p.a.; Grade II: £400 to £500 p.a., by annual increments of £25; and Grade III: £300 to £400 p.a., by annual increments of £50.

32 Of the Day Classes in the Faculty of Arts in Session 1919-20, it would appear that very few indeed were programmed to end after 4.00 p.m. (though the hours of a number of classes were described as 'to be arranged'). The University Library (the Tate Library, in the Victoria Building) was open during the term between 9.30 a.m. and 5.00 p.m. on every weekday, except Saturday, when it closed at 1.00 p.m.; Class Libraries in the Faculty had

So, as I sat in the train, passing through the most attractive scenery of the Home Counties, I felt a good deal less pessimistic about my hypothetical future than I might have expected. Only when hills and woods gave place to chimneys and oceans of slate roofs did my misgivings attack me again. A few miles before journey's end, my spirits sank as the sun disappeared and a smoky pall obscured the blue sky. Before we drew into the gloom of Drabtown station[33] I was already a prey to depression.

It was nearly three in the afternoon when I arrived; and, as my interview was at four, I left my suit-case in the Station Hotel,[34] where I was to stay, and set out almost immediately in search of the University. The porter's direction was simple: the front door of the hotel opened into the principal thoroughfare of Drabtown. I was to turn to the right and take the first turning on the right, after which a quarter of an hour's walk would take me to my destination.

And it did. But it took me through the very depths of depression first.

For no sooner had I turned to the right, away from the trams and the shops, than I turned literally into slumland. A long, straight street, it was named — one might almost have guessed it — Paradise Street.[35] And, having neither trams nor buses, it had to be traversed in all its grisly length of a mile and a quarter by everyone who came from that quarter of the town every day. That such a neighbourhood could exist so near the centre of a great city seemed incredible.

The houses were mean, filthy, blackened with age — some of them, homes of the poorest type; others, tumbledown shops or dingy 'publics' [/public houses]. Women, with tousled hair, or wearing men's caps on their heads, sat on the unwashed steps of their houses, exchanging raucous arguments or screaming to half-naked children running about the pavements

---

similar opening hours. (*Faculty of Arts Prospectus of Courses for the Session 1919-1920; Calendar 1919-20*). It would appear that the Students' Union remained open until later, for debates and for various meetings of student societies.

33  In reality, Lime Street Station, Liverpool.
34  That is The North Western Hotel, Lime Street (*cf.* '[E.A.P.] *Auto*', ch. 3, p. 120, note 132).
35  Peers' ironic name for Brownlow Hill.

— their only playground. Every detail of that first view of Drabtown is engraven on my memory. Two urchins of nine or ten were riding on the tail of a lorry, each trying to maintain his own position while dislodging the other. One child, who could hardly have been more than three, was gleefully investigating the contents of a garbage tin and throwing any of the contents which made no appeal to him about the street. Indescribable odours, such as I had never before experienced, mounted in the hot August air. And that was the road that led to Redbrick University.[36]

I tried not to think of the busy Haymarket, the cool lawns behind the river, the mediaeval buildings, the courts and gardens of Oxbridge.[37] To distract my thoughts, I glanced carelessly at the shops I was passing. Their wares, in the main, were composite: heaps of green apples, bottles of coloured sweets, cigarette cartons, revolting-looking buns and what seemed to be uncooked fish-cakes covered with bright orange bread-crumbs, were a fair sample of the contents of any one of them. There were tailors, mainly with Jewish names; there was a Chinese laundry; there were shops which appeared to sell nothing but olive-oil, bottles of which were stacked in profusion in their windows. One window was unlike all the rest: it contained dog-eared books of Catholic devotion, and, as

---

36 For Peers' corresponding description, in his straightforward autobiography, of Brownlow Hill, its shops and inhabitants, see '(E.A.P.) *Auto*', ch. 4, pp. 130-31, and notes 17-20. One is reminded of comments about the slums in Liverpool made by Olaf Stapledon and Agnes Miller in their letters to each other, 1913-1919. In a letter from Rouen dated 3 February 1914, Agnes Miller declares: 'These slums [in Rouen] are very dirty, but Liverpool slums are more depressing'. On 7 February 1914, Stapledon, who was a tutor in the Adult Education Movement, referred to his adult pupils in Liverpool as follows: 'Their houses are miserable, — dirty, pokey and full of broken down rubbish'; 'they are overcrowded and have no privacy, and therefore no chance of thinking' (see *Talking across the World. The Love Letters of Olaf Stapledon and Agnes Miller, 1913-1919*, ed. Robert Crossley [Hanover and London: Univ. Press of New England, 1987], 30-31). Stapledon, like Peers, lived in West Kirby, and, in fact, was a close friend of Peers whose involvement in Adult Education has already been noted (see above, note 10).

37 One remembers Peers' descriptions of Oxbridge in the 'Redbrick' books — for instance, his reference to 'the medieval courts and quadrangles, the storied windows, the congenial, cultured society' (*Redbrick University*, 11).

a background, a vile representation, in cheap colour, of the reigning Pontiff, and below it in large letters, the legend 'God bless our Pope'.

But the majority of the shops catered for the needs of the body.[38] One, larger and more prosperous-looking than the rest, was a butcher's, which was to afford me grim amusement for decades. The butcher evidently believed in the power of advertisements and also in that of appeal to the patriotic instincts of his potential customers. Continually changed, and plastered all over his shop windows, his notices were hand-drawn, in red and blue on a dead-white paper, with a Union Jack in the top left hand corner.

<u>BUY</u> Jenkins' beef,

they proclaimed, or alternatively,

Buy <u>JENKINS'</u> beef

or again,

Buy Jenkins' <u>BEEF</u>

And, below this guileless exhortation, was an irresistible offer:

---

[38] An analysis of the occupations of the residents of both sides of Brownlow Hill between the Adelphi Hotel (at the foot of the hill) and the University, as recorded in *Gore's Directory of Liverpool and its Environs...*, 1921, reveals nine public houses and three hotels; seven boot repairers; seven drapers, five tailors, and three (tailors') trimmings dealers; six butchers; four grocers and six greengrocers; six tobacconists; five hairdressers; four confectioners; three fried fish dealers and two fishmongers; three cabinet makers; three 'shopkeepers'; three bakers and nine bakers and flour dealers; three chandlers; and two or less of other trades and occupations, including two booksellers (one a secondhand bookseller), and two pawnbrokers. There were two laundries, one run by Sun Kwong Lee, at No. 227 Brownlow Hill, further up the hill, beyond the University, and the other run by Sang Lee, at No. 89, about midway up the hill on the way to the University. No butchers of the surname Jenkins are listed in the 1921 Directory, and those of this surname who appear later in the 1920s and 1930s are found elsewhere in Liverpool (e.g. Abraham W. Jenkins at 212 and 213 Kensington, and elsewhere, in the 1924 Directory). Jewish names are found not only among the tailors in the *Directory*; they are also to be found among the butchers, boot repairers, etc.

Buy a shilling's worth of prime beef from
Pa Jenkins and receive ONE SAUSAGE — FREE.[39]

I particularly remember the emporium of Mr Jenkins because it stood at the junction of Paradise Street and a so-called 'Pleasant Grove'[40] — crossing which, I caught sight of something that almost brought me to a full-stop with horror. On the opposite corner of the street was a fried-fish shop: in front of it, high on a ladder was perched a sign-painter. And the words which he was repainting, in vivid green, were:

VARSITY SUPPER BAR[41]

Good God! I exclaimed to myself, we have now reached the University precincts.

And we had. The next shock was a 'Leibschutz: Varsity Hairdresser', bearing a large notice diagonally pasted across the window, 'Have your hair cut for half price — this week only', and a smaller one, on the door, 'Closed on Saturdays'.[42] Then we became more rigidly academic: no less than three second-hand bookshops with twopenny boxes competed for what they would no doubt have termed 'Varsity custom'. At this point the street bore sharply to the left and I saw in front

---

39   Peers recalls this same special offer in '(E.A.P.) *Auto*', ch. 4, p. 131.

40   A reference to Mount Pleasant which was, despite its name, by no means a pleasant slope.

41   It will be remembered that the University Club, a higher class establishment than the 'Varsity Supper Bar' here mentioned, was located at No. 2, Mount Pleasant (see '[E.A.P.] *Auto*', ch. 4, pp. 136-37, and note 41).

42   The 1921 Liverpool Directory records Soloman (*sic*) Liebschutz, a tailor, at 87 Brownlow Hill; no other person bearing this surname is recorded. The only hairdresser with a Jewish-sounding name recorded in the 1921 Directory is David Bernstein, at No. 85 (next to Soloman Liebschutz). At 159 Brownlow Hill [to the west of, and relatively close to, the Walker Engineering Laboratories] was a hairdresser, John Watson Robinson. The University's *Calendar* carried advertisements but none for the Brownlow Hill residents except those for a pharmacy and a supplier of scientific instruments etc. However, in several issues of *The Sphinx*, the magazine of the Guild of Undergraduates of the University of Liverpool, dating from 6 March 1912 onwards (at least until January 1917) appeared an advertisement of J. Beere ('33 years Hairdresser of the Adelphi Hotel'). Beere (sometimes spelt Beeré) advertised that he had 'now opened the Premises No. 2, Brownlow Hill, as High-Class Ladies' and Gentlemen's Hairdressing Saloons', also offering, as a speciality 'The 'Varsitee Hair Dressing, 2/6 per bottle'.

The Victoria Building (1889-92), University of Liverpool
Architect: Alfred Waterhouse
from the water-colour by Allan P. Tankard (1950)
(Art Collections, University of Liverpool)

of me a vast block of red-brick buildings, ornamented with meaningless scrolls and geometrical figures and tapering here and there into ridiculous little pinnacles looking for all the world like miniature candle-snuffers.[43] At last, standing at the portals of Redbrick University, I was facing my destiny.

## III

The interior, at the initial attack, was worse still. Passing through the swing-doors which appeared to constitute the main entrance, one would at least have expected to have been met by some kind of hall, however modest. But there was nothing of the kind. Inside the doors was a corridor, running right and left, the lower part of its walls covered with hideous glazed tiles, in blue, yellow and green, of a type once subsequently described to me by a witty colleague as 'Late Lavatory'.[44] The upper part, on either side, almost as far as I could see, was hidden by notice-boards, from which hung, droopingly and disconsolately, the faded and tattered announcements of the preceding term. The corridor was bisected by another running at right angles to it, and, as this faced me as I entered, I naturally walked straight down it. On either side of me were dark class-rooms. I retraced my steps and reached the front door again.

Far away in the distance, someone was yowling about the length of the distance from Redbrick University to

---

43 Bruce Truscot saw, and Peers describes, the Walker Engineering Laboratories and the adjoining Victoria Building, both designed by Alfred Waterhouse and both fronting Brownlow Hill.

44 In fact, the Victoria Building has an impressive entrance hall, with Italian mosaic paving, with the walls and balustrades of the hall and the principal staircase faced in faience and terracotta. '...The double-height hall on the ground floor...still retains its drama as a space... It was faced in Waterhouse's favourite buff and blue terracotta, set off by treacly brown faience for the dado and fireplace. The mixture presents a startling originality, and it is as typical of the man as the splendid space it decorates' (Cunningham and Waterhouse, *Alfred Waterhouse 1830-1905: Biography of a Practice*, 130). Regarding the Victoria Building, see '(E.A.P.) *Auto*', ch. 4, p. 129, note 14.

Tipperary.⁴⁵ I remember reflecting, as I stood wondering which way to go, that it was considerably farther from Redbrick to Queen's College, Oxbridge. The yowling drew nearer till round a corner came a youth in navy-blue uniform the tunic of which, unbuttoned, revealed a shirt open at the neck — no doubt some sort of porter.

'You the gent I was to take to the Dean?' he enquired, sharply.

Resignedly I replied that I probably was.

'This way', he said, and led me along the corridor, still humming reminiscences of Tipperary.

We ascended a stone staircase with iron railings. On the first floor was a corridor as dark as the one below.⁴⁶ We went along it, past large rooms which seemed to be partitioned off into long narrow ones, with the title of a professor painted on each. At the end was a larger room, marked 'Dean: Faculty of

---

45 This reference to a popular First World War song, besides enabling the author (in the next sentence) to emphasize wittily the differences separating Redbrick and Oxbridge/Camford, serves to remind the reader that Bruce Truscot begins his career of conflict at Redbrick just when the World Conflict of the Great War is ending.

The contrasts between the Universities of Oxford and Cambridge and the University of Liverpool are referred to in 'Our Alma Mater on the Hill' and 'The Liverpool 'Varsitee' — two songs which were published in the *Liverpool Students' Song Book* (1906). In the first verse of 'The Liverpool 'Varsitee', Ramsay Muir wrote:

> I've seen Oxford's spires and gardens
>   All sleeping 'neath the moon,
> And Cambridge with her chapels fair,
>   And her gyps and her wooden spoon.
> They've proctors there to fine them;
>   They've caps and gowns to wear;
> But those 'Varsities! What a farce it is,
>   If you've not much cash to spare!
> But — the Liverpool 'Varsitee!
>   Oh, that is the place for me!
> Be you poor, be you rich, why it matters not which
>   In the Liverpool 'Varsitee.

(In the next edition of the *Song Book*, published in 1913, this text was to appear in a modified and less critical version.)

46 One remembers Peers' comment in *Redbrick University*, that Oxbridge men who come to work at the 'new universities' consider them 'at first positively sepulchral in their gloom' (17).

Arts'.⁴⁷ The porter knocked and I went in. A girl typist rose and conducted me into an inner sanctum. There, at a kneehole desk, in a room of which the walls were covered from ceiling to floor with box-files and copies of the Redbrick University Calendar sat Dr Dobie, the Dean.⁴⁸

Strange to say, this first of the Redbrick Arts Deans I have known was never much more than a lay figure to me. He retired in my second year at Redbrick and soon afterwards died. He was a short, thickset man of about sixty, rather undistinguished in appearance, with a brusque but business-like manner: vaguely he always reminded me of a successful and rather preoccupied tradesman. He was a good, hard-working Dean with a gift for effacing himself and letting other people do the talking while keeping the business in hand all the time under control.

'Come along to see Professor Upright', he said, after a word of greeting.

We went a few doors down the passage and turned into a room marked 'Professor of English Literature'. It was a barely furnished room, containing a writing-table, four hard chairs, one small bookcase, a cupboard — I really believe that was all. The walls, once primrose-yellow, were grimy with age. The window, one would say, had not been cleaned for years.

Sitting at the writing-table were old George Slocombe⁴⁹ (who made his name, you will remember, in the nineties, with

---

47 The large room which was occupied (certainly latterly and probably since 1914) by the Dean of the Faculty of Arts was off the central corridor on the first floor of the new Arts Building (nowadays known as the Ashton Building), Room 1.03 (now a Seminar Room), which overlooks the Quadrangle.

48 At the date to which the narrative purports to refer, Mr W. Garmon Jones was Dean of the Faculty of Arts (1916-20); he died in office (as University Librarian and Associate Professor of History) in 1937, aged fifty-two years. Some of the characteristics of 'Dr Dobie' are similar to those which Mr Garmon Jones evidently possessed (see '[E.A.P.] *Auto*', ch. 3, p. 120, note 133; and especially, ch. 5, p. 146, note 18).

49 'George Slocombe', Professor of English Literature, is presumably modelled on Oliver Elton, King Alfred Professor of English Literature, 1901-25 (see Peers' comments on Elton in '[E.A.P.] *Auto*', ch. 5, p. 145; and see note 13). In the essay, 'Any Faculty Board', Peers would appear to give Elton a different pseudonym: that of Professor Miope (see Appendix IV, p. 489, note 26; and *cf.* 'B.T.', ch. I, pp. 185-86, note 52).

his critical biography of Wordsworth, and then gave up writing altogether as if once were enough) and James Upright.[50] Both rose as we entered. The Dean introduced me to each in turn.

'But I need no introduction to Mr Truscot', cried Upright, beaming down upon me. 'We met at Trinity twelve years ago, did we not, and I have followed his career with great interest ever since. At one time I was afraid he was going to be lost to scholarship altogether'.

This was indeed a surprise. I am not unduly modest, but it had never occurred to me that a Visiting Professor ever remembered a chance meeting with an undergraduate. Afterwards, I realized that the President might very well have consulted Upright on the subject of the Trinity fellowship, though I never discovered if that guess was correct.[51]

What I did notice, however, even then, was the way in which Upright took possession of the meeting. Slocombe and the Dean, as it were, fell into their places at his feet. It was always like that wherever he went and whatever he might be doing. If he lectured, he kept the eyes of his audience intent upon him. If he spoke at a meeting, everyone listened. If he rose — whether to speak or to leave — he became the centre of attraction until it was clear which he was going to do.

He stood up now, while the rest of us sat down around him. His immense height, his poise, his erectness made him as fascinating a figure as ever.[52] Twelve years had done nothing to age him: it seemed impossible that he could be sixty-three.

---

50 Peers, deliberately or unconsciously, continues to give George Charles Upright the first name of James Fitzmaurice-Kelly (see above, notes 2 and 21).

51 If Upright *was* consulted on that subject, he could not have supported Truscot with much conviction, since the post, it will be remembered, went to Maurice Gilkes (see above 'B.T.', ch. I, p. 213). The latter might well have been a friend of Upright's, for, as we shall see, in the next chapter, Gilkes' misinformation nearly costs Jim Livewire the Chair of English Literature at Redbrick University (ch. IV, pp. 357, 369).

52 As regards Fitzmaurice-Kelly's physical appearance, *cf.*, above, pp. 266-67, note 19; and also 'B.T.', ch. I, p. 205, and note 118. Peers' allusions to Upright's 'erectness' of bearing, like his frequent references to Upright's misleading surname, are intended to encourage the reader to see through Fitzmaurice-Kelly's surface-characteristics — suggestive of good intentions, straight dealing and honest judgement —, and perceive his essential lack of integrity.

'This is really a sub-committee of our Vacation Emergency Committee, Truscot', he explained, in a friendly tone, 'but we have power to recommend an appointment precisely as if we were the Faculty Board. That is to say, the person we recommend can come into residence in October, though neither of the Higher Bodies will have cognisance of the appointment until about the end of that month. Do I make myself clear to you?'

I told him he did, though I had not the foggiest idea what the Higher Bodies might be. It sounded frightfully occult, I thought, flippantly.

Again, what would happen if the Higher Bodies were not pleased with the appointment when they eventually acquired cognisance of it? If I were elected (or 'recommended') now, I should have been in residence for a month before they had the chance to object. It seemed a queer way of doing things.

'Now I will be perfectly frank with you', Upright went on. 'Yours is by far the best application we have received and on academic grounds alone your election is certain. The President [/Provost] of Trinity — *our* Trinity', he emended, smilingly — 'and the Master of Queens, Oxbridge[,] have written very warmly about you. But what we are uncertain about is the reasons for your wanting to come here. What consideration induced you to apply?'

This [/That] was an awkward question — and a most unpleasantly direct one. I might, of course, have foreseen it. These people knew perfectly well that I should be forfeiting good money, leaving a congenial atmosphere, and sacrificing a life crowded with amenities for no good reason that they could think of. I suppose, if I had given the matter a thought, I should have decided that Upright would have tumbled to what I was after. And if he had, he would have said nothing, but probably thought the more. It was disconcerting to find that the idea of an ulterior motive had evidently not occurred to him.[53]

However, I had to say something quickly, so I said some of

---

53 The author expects us to be more perceptive than is young Truscot, hindered by inexperience, and to conclude that Upright is wholly aware of the main reason why Truscot has applied for the lectureship at Redbrick University.

the things that had been passing through my mind since that cold afternoon in June. How I wanted to escape for a time from a life stiff with amenities. How I wanted experience of another type of university. And so on. I hinted vaguely that such experience might be valuable to me when I was older and ended by as delicate a reference as I could muster at short notice to the advantages that I should gain by working under Upright himself.

The answer was evidently considered satisfactory.[54] Upright raised his eyebrows towards the other two in turn and each nodded emphatically. Then he turned his head to me.

'Well, that sounds quite reasonable — though I doubt if you'd find many people at Oxbridge to agree with you. Can you be here by the second of October? Rather earlier than Oxbridge: we have ten-week terms, you know'.[55]

I intimated that I thought I could manage it.

'The teaching work will be very light', went on Upright. 'That will give you time for the research which I see from the *Modern Language Review*[56] you are going at pretty steadily. Nominally, you see, you are in the English Literature Department: that's to say, you examine in their Honours School and advise students when a special subject is some aspect of poetry. But really the Professor and Lecturer in Poetry are semi-independent and do pretty much what they like. Oh, by the way, you won't mind giving a course of public lectures every Lent Term, will you? I do feel we ought to do some missionary work and I always give a short course in the Autumn Term myself'.

I said I should have no possible objection — mentally registering a determination to be in the front row for Upright's lectures in October.

'Then I think that's everything', he concluded. 'Oh, could you dine with me to-night? [Business suit] — half-past-seven?

---

54 Peers has written in the margin here, in pencil, the question: 'Could it really be settled as quickly as that?'.

55 The Autumn Term 1918 in fact commenced on 8 October. In reality, Peers commenced his duties at Liverpool at the beginning of the Lent Term, in January, 1920.

56 See Truscot's earlier reference to his articles in this journal ('B.T.', ch. II, p. 243; and, for Peers' contributions to the *Modern Language Review*, see note 68).

Then we can talk shop. I live some way out.[57] Look here, where are you staying? I'll pick you up in my car... Well, till then, and I hope you will be very happy here'.[58]

'We all hope so', echoed Slocombe, in a tired voice.

'And you'll let me know what your expenses are?' put in the Dean.

Only when [/Not till] I got outside did I realize that those were the only words those [/the] two had spoken since the interview began.

## IV

Looking back on my life now, I can see that I was extraordinarily immature for thirty-three when I came to Redbrick. Both at Cranstead and at Oxbridge I had lived for the greater part of each year in an enclosed and sheltered community, absorbed, first of all, in the multifarious interests of a boarding school, and then with my own reading and research. I had never had any experience of life in a large city. Except as a boy,[59] I had never been in contact with education other than that enjoyed by the privileged classes. I had shed a few illusions, but more had to go yet.

At Cranstead I had discovered that men could dedicate their lives to the noble calling of educating youth in its most impressionable years and yet could be quite content to remain

---

57 Professor Fitzmaurice-Kelly ('Upright') lived at 16 Mersey Road, Aigburth, Liverpool. Oliver Elton in his biographical memoir of Fitzmaurice-Kelly — which Peers would appear to have used in his account — describes 'the little house, called "The Old Hall", an oasis in a suburb, which he shared with his friend Professor Wyld the philologist, was a cheerful resort for talk and company' (*Revue Hispanique*, LX, [1924], 7-8). See too below, pp. 305-06, note 116.

58 A hope not very sincerely felt, but which, despite Upright's worst endeavours, in due course was wholly to be fulfilled. Bruce Truscot (Allison Peers) was to enjoy many years of personal and professional happiness at Redbrick University.

59 See, for instance, Truscot's description of his early schooldays in ch. I, pp. 175-78 (and *cf.* Peers' authentic account — for instance, of his school near Longmorn ['(E.A.P.) *Auto*', ch. 1, pp. 63-64]).

incredibly narrow in outlook and petty in conduct.[60] At Camford I had dimly suspected, and at Oxbridge I had fully realized, that not all university teachers had the highest conception of their office. But I was immature enough to cherish the illusion that these were only exceptions;[61] and I certainly believed that *men and women who had the highest academic qualifications, who dealt exclusively with things of the mind, who had ample leisure for their own reading, who were completely free from those innumerable little pettinesses which go so far to excuse any shortcomings of the school-teacher might be counted upon to lead scholars' lives [/the lives of scholars]. I think (for the old idea of the professor dies hard and I had already met several 'professors of fiction') that I rather expected my new colleagues to be of the absent-minded, otherworldly type, living in complete aloofness from their students as my Camford professors had done, and I vaguely dreaded [/had vague fears of] a coldness and inhospitableness contrasting pitifully* with the genial warmth I had always known. I was certainly quite unprepared for the atmosphere of self-seeking and intrigue in which I was to be plunged soon after my arrival,[62] and the realization that it could exist was the last of the great disillusionments that life has up to now had in store for me. Often, in retrospect, I have been grateful for the kind of upbringing I had, which enabled me to rise above pettinesses far more despicable than those of the world of school — pettinesses that feed on jealousy and conceit.[63] Often, too, I have reflected happily upon the firm friendships I made in the course of the conflict into which they led me: my life at Redbrick would have been much more placid, but also much less rich, without them.

But to say this is to step considerably in front of my

---

60 See above B.T., ch. II, especially pp. 237-39.

61 At the time of writing his autobiography, Bruce Truscot has been enlightened, or disillusioned, upon this point. In *Redbrick and these Vital Days*, he declares, in his view, that 'a *large number* of idle professors are ruining the traditions of their calling' (105).

62 Peers, as Bruce Truscot, is preparing the reader for his account of the machinations at Redbrick of the 'Salvation Army' (that is to say, of the 'New Testament' in Liverpool University).

63 Jealousy and conceit are, as we shall soon discover, two of the principal character-defects of Professor James Upright.

narrative and I must go back to my first term at Redbrick and describe how I made myself at home there.

My first care was to look for lodgings — and, as I had had no experience of lodging-houses save for the refined and academically controlled ones of Camford, this was an unwelcome task. I found to my horror that the University not only exercised no sort of control or oversight upon the houses in which many of its students lived, but had officially no knowledge of such houses at all.[64] When I consulted the Office[65] — a large room with rows of clerks at desks where one learned to apply for any kind of academic information — I was handed a typed paper containing about a hundred addresses with a warning in capitals at the top that the University took no responsibility for any of them.[66] Knowing not a soul in the place, I went out into the highways and byways of Drabtown oppressed by a vast loneliness and resolved only upon one thing — that, whatever rooms I took, I would not take them for long.

The most important consideration seemed to me at the time to be to avoid a daily walk along Paradise Street,[67] and, so far as I could see from the map, this meant that I should have to find lodgings on the far side of it. That seemed not impossible; for, though Redbrick is separated from Drabtown's main railway station and city centre by slum land, a short walk beyond it takes one to the fringe of a district which is still highly respectable and was once the main professional quarter

---

64 'There is no accommodation for the residence of students within the University precincts. Students not living at home or with relatives are recommended to reside at one of the Halls of Residence, or in lodgings which are on the list kept by the Registrar' (*The University of Liverpool Calendar 1920-21*, 1920, 150).

65 The University's central administrative staff had offices in the Victoria Building.

66 His early experience of the lack of interest taken by the University in the provision and supervision of suitable lodgings for its students and staff doubtless contributed to Peers' strong conviction, expressed in the 'Redbrick' books, of the advantages of residential universities (see, e.g., *Redbrick University*, ch. 1, 39-41).

67 That is to say, Brownlow Hill. Peers expresses a similar desire to avoid a daily walk through this area in '(E.A.P.) *Auto*', ch. 4, p. 132.

of the city.[68]

The names of the streets — Prince Albert Street, Gladstone Street, Beaconsfield Terrace — indicate the period when this district was built up,[69] conveniently far from the centre of the city in days when traction was exclusively the work of horses. The rows of tall, dignified houses, with their well-worn steps, their roomy basements, the marks left by the removal of the brass plates which once lent them tone[,] were formerly inhabited by doctors, dentists, solicitors, and the ministers of the gloomy and forbidding churches and chapels which met the eye in all directions. Then came the motor-car; the professional life of Drabtown migrated to the suburbs; and upon their former abodes descended a host of lodging-house keepers who rented them at low rates and let them to undergraduates and bachelor members of the staff in the conveniently adjacent university.[70]

---

68 Peers is referring here to the area principally to the south of Oxford Street (including Abercromby Square, which the University began to colonize in the 1920s) and Mount Pleasant (including Rodney Street, 'the Harley Street of Liverpool'). These were areas to which the professional (and other) classes moved, leaving the centre of Liverpool, from the late eighteenth century onwards.

69 Much of the area, beyond the principal streets, was developed in the 1830s-1870s, a bit earlier than Peers implies. It should be noted that no Prince Albert Street is recorded in *Gore's Directory of Liverpool and its Environs*, 1921; and the only streets, roads and terraces named after Queen Victoria's Prime Ministers, W. E. Gladstone and his rival and Conservative opposite number, the Earl of Beaconsfield, (i.e. Benjamin Disraeli), were in other areas of Liverpool and in Wirral.

70 A perusal of successive editions of *Gore's* (later *Kelly's*) *Directory of Liverpool and its Environs* helps to document this migration and record the change in use of residential properties. As regards Abercromby Square, this had been a select area developed for superior residences, principally in the 1820s and 1830s, but migration by residents further out of the heart of Liverpool had begun by the 1840s (to Princes Park and elsewhere) and was pronounced by the turn of the century; the University began its colonization of the Square in 1920. As Richard Lawton has written, 'The middle classes had begun to desert the centre of the city from the early nineteenth century. One notable line of advance was along a sector from the merchant quarter of central Liverpool through the Mount Pleasant-Abercromby area towards Princes Park, one of the first of a great belt of parks which ring mid-Victorian Liverpool. Land for villa development was set aside around Sefton Park, Newsham Park and Stanley Park... "Carriage folk" had already moved further afield... Their mansions, sheltered behind sandstone walls in

I soon discovered that while most of the married staff had houses between two and ten miles from the University, the bachelors saved themselves time, money and the odour of the Varsity Supper Bar by taking rooms in this genteel environment. After investigating some stale-smelling houses in Beaconsfield Terrace, I picked upon a thoroughfare named New Gladstone Street, and took the first-floor front of No. 60.[71] In the winter months — and that [first] winter was [/happened to be] a severe one — I might have been much worse off. I had three large windows *never clean for more than a few hours; an enormous arm-chair perpetually set in front of an old-fashioned fireplace which sent the heat straight up the chimney; and a little, wizened, kindly old landlady*[72] *who gave me my first close-up of a* Drabtonian. She ran all her words together; misplaced her vowels; flung my name at me whenever she spoke; prefaced any suggestion she might make with a shrill 'Nah, see here...'; and never, at any meal, produced less *than two and a half times as much as I could eat. When after a meal I would ring the bell, the poor creature would tiptoe into the room, stand nursing her arms, survey the remnants of the repast and finally, eyeing me with the utmost reproachfulness, exclaim sadly:*

'Y'aint-ate-it-all, Mr Truscot'.

Two terms of New Gladstone Street, even though bisected by a blissful Christmas vacation in which I engaged myself to be married,[73] were as much as I could possibly endure. So, towards the end of the Lent Term I began to make *prospecting excursions into the suburbs.* Several of these, such as Denesholm and Esmond, had modern houses, extensive parks

---

estates at Allerton, Childwall, Crosby, Mossley Hill or Oxton or behind the lodge gates of private residential parks, became a feature of upper middle-class Merseyside' (see his chapter 1, 'From the Port of Liverpool to the Merseyside Conurbation', in *The Resources of Merseyside*, ed. William T. S. Gould and Alan G. Hodgkiss [Liverpool: Liverpool U. P., 1982], 7-8).

71 Peers' first accommodation in Liverpool was at No. 160 Bedford Street South (on the first floor) (see '[E.A.P.] *Auto*', ch. 4, p. 132).

72 This was Miss Ellen M. Randall (see '[E.A.P.] *Auto*', p. 132, note 22).

73 Peers married Miss Marion Young in 1924.

and comparatively little smoke.[74] *Their chief disadvantages seemed to be that, to get to any of them you had to take endless journeys in trams full of the most [/highly] repulsive people, and that, once there, if you penetrated only a little way farther, you found yourself within sight of some other town which seemed to consist chiefly of smoky chimneys.* Only one district was free from both these reproaches and this had the disadvantage of being accessible only by railway and the walk up Paradise Street. But its situation was so ideal that I could not hesitate. The river on which Drabtown stands runs eastwards, through industrial districts, to the distant sea.[75] But track it westwards to its source and you have another story. Five miles out, houses end[,] the road rises, woods and fields appear; ten miles out, you are in what seems the depths of the country. Forbridge, the village where I first lodged in a honeysuckle-covered cottage and later bought a small house with a large garden, is two miles farther on still — think of it, only five-and-twenty minutes by train from Drabtown[76] and yet only a handful of us live there.[77]

I well remember the March afternoon when I discovered Forbridge. The river twisted and turned, and I could have shouted for joy as I inhaled the pure, keen air of the mountains. I climbed up by a steep path, through woods spangled with the year's first primroses, to a bare, grassy hill,

---

74 It is probable that Peers has in mind the residential areas in the southern suburbs of Liverpool, including the Sefton and Princes Parks area, Calderstones Park, and Grassendale and Cressington Parks; nineteenth-century residential developments fringed all of these parks.

75 The River Mersey — which, however, in reality, runs north westwards to the sea, past Birkenhead to New Brighton on the west and Bootle on the east.

76 Peers lived initially (c.1921 onwards) at 22 Shrewsbury Road and later (c.1928 onwards) at 12 Eddisbury Road; both houses are in West Kirby, Wirral (cf. '[E.A.P.] *Auto*', ch. 4, p. 133, note 28). Nowadays West Kirby Station may be reached by train from Central Station, Liverpool, in twenty-six minutes.

77 'live there': Peers refers, presumably, to the mid' 1940s, at the time when he is composing his autobiography. In fact, of the members of the academic staff whose addresses are given in *The University of Liverpool Diary 1946-47*, no fewer than ten members of the Senate (which comprised a total of fifty-five persons) lived at West Kirby. In 1933-34, however, the number of Senate members living at West Kirby had been only four out of a total of sixty members.

and there I sat down and surveyed the village with its square Norman church-tower;[78] its picturesque bridge built centuries ago as a substitute for the old ford; its cross roads leading — one [of them] to the mountains, one to the sea, one to a great Roman road and one to a mining area; its houses quaintly perched among the hills, or, like a row of untrained recruits, raggedly guarding the [long] village street. I went back to Drabtown by the evening train to think things over — and even Paradise Street seemed more tolerable when one remembered whither it would lead. On the next day — a June-like day, with the gorse glowing in the tenuous spring sunshine[79] — I went back again, and this time I went house-hunting.

My landlady viewed me pityingly when I gave her notice.

'Now, see here, Mr Truscot', she observed, 'You'll find it damp-like out there, I shouldn't wonder. Besides, whatever will you find to do with yourself?'

I told her what I should find to do with myself. But she was quite unconvinced.

'Well', she remarked, finally, 'there's them as likes those parts and there's them as don't, and I can't say as I care much for them meself'.

Undeterred by which frigid warning, I duly moved into my cottage at Forbridge, and at Forbridge, perhaps the place I love most in the world, I have remained for twenty-eight years.[80]

---

78 The parish church of St Bridget, Church Road, West Kirby, was almost completely rebuilt in 1869-70 (Nikolaus Pevsner and Edward Hubbard, *The Buildings of England: Cheshire* [Harmondsworth: Penguin Books 1971], 378-79).

79 Peers refers similarly to 'the gorse glowing' in the corresponding passage of '(E.A.P.) *Auto*' (ch. 4, p. 133). This paragraph further demonstrates Peers' sensitivity to the beauties of nature (*cf.* above 'B.T.', ch. II, pp. 227-28, and note 32; and also '[E.A.P.] *Auto*', ch. 3, p. 98, and note 52).

80 At this point in the MS. there is a marginal note, in pencil, '1919-47' — which might imply that Peers was still engaged in writing this pseudo-autobiography in 1947. Concerning the date of composition of Peers' autobiographies, see the Editorial Commentary, pp. 36-38.

## V

One of the first discoveries I made about Redbrick was the extent to which the junior staff lived in departmentalized seclusion. At Oxbridge, on any evening in Common Room, the youngest member would find himself among mixed assortment of chemists, medicals, linguists, engineers, historians and theologians. At Redbrick, there was no such salutary promiscuity. All the lecturers functioned within the confines of the Faculty and rarely went outside it. The lecture-rooms and common rooms of the Arts Faculty were housed in one building,[81] where alone you could obtain midday coffee and afternoon tea.[82] Even in the Refectory, where a mix-up at the High Table would have been simple, tradition ruled that Arts people should sit at one end, Science people at the other and members of smaller [/other] faculties in the middle.[83] This narrowness was quite new to me and I felt it very keenly. Not till I became a professor, and found myself on inter-faculty committees, did I develop a really wide circle of acquaintances. Of recent years, in the Refectory and elsewhere, I have made several attempts to mix up the faculties, but I cannot say that they have been very successful.

The first people I became intimate with were naturally those in the Department of English Literature. With old Slocombe — known inevitably to the undergraduate world as Slowcoach — I had six years of the pleasantest relations before the age limit of sixty-five sent him into retirement; but, if I am to be candid, I must say that there should have been some way of retiring him much earlier.[84] He was a sad example of

---

81 The Arts Building, opened in 1914, provided most of the Faculty of Arts' accommodation until, between the Wars and particularly in the 1950s and 1960s, departments gradually migrated to the area of Abercromby Square.

82 In the Arts Building, for many years, until c.1966-67, a coffee club was provided for male staff on the ground floor (Room G.04); women staff could use a separate common room, also on the ground floor.

83 Even within the Faculty of Arts there were unwritten rules about seating arrangements. Cf. Truscot's description of 'Any Faculty Board' meeting, in which all the members sit in specified places and all the seats are 'sacrosanct' (see Appendix IV, p. 486).

84 In *Redbrick University*, Truscot favours short-term appointments, to facilitate the removal of unproductive academics (119-20).

academic degeneration caused by prosperity. He had made his name before he was forty, with the book I have already referred to, which won him his Chair. For a short time he was in request everywhere. Then, as he wrote no more, and younger men came along, he became forgotten, but not before he had feathered his nest comfortably for life. Besides his Chair, he had a position as staff reviewer on the best literary periodical in the country, and another as general editor of school books in English for one of our leading publishers. He did a good deal of occasional work and an incredible deal of examining: he once told me, in a burst of confidence, that his stipend represented only about a quarter of his earned income, and I could quite believe it. In his way, he led a busy life, and it must certainly have been a congenial one, but he was anything but an asset to the University.[85]

He was fifty-nine when I first met him, and for at least ten years, I gathered, he had ceased to take any serious interest in his Department. His method was to have one good man under him, who, partly from keenness and partly with an eye to future favours, would do the bulk of the work which he himself ought to have done, and a number of yes-men who could be relied upon to give him no trouble. On the Faculty Board he was an obstructionist, and his mulishness simply enraged the progressives, especially as his personal popularity invariably won him support. Towards the end of his time, one continually heard the remark: 'Well, we must get that done when old Slocombe goes'; and during the last year or two his Department

---

85 This assessment of 'Slocombe' can only loosely (and unfairly) be applied to Professor Oliver Elton, who was appointed to his Chair of English Literature eleven years before the first of the six volumes of his 'massive and magisterial *Survey of English Literature from 1730 to 1880*' was published. This is the work upon which, in the view of Kelly, his reputation as a scholar mainly rests (*For Advancement of Learning. The University of Liverpool 1881-1981*, 111). Elton's successor, Leonard C. Martin, wrote that, during his tenure of the Chair (1901-1925), Elton 'was mainly absorbed in teaching and administrative duties, and in the writing of the three two-volumed surveys of English Literature which appeared in 1912, 1920, and 1928, respectively' (*Proceedings of the British Academy 1945*, 321). Elton was responsible for vols 5-11 of the English Association's Essays and Studies; and edited Milton's minor poems for the Clarendon Press (1891-93) (see also above, note 49; and '[E.A.P.] *Auto*', ch. 5, p. 145; and see note 13).

got into the worst state in which I have ever seen one, since there was a general feeling that nothing less than pulling it down and building it up again would be of any use.[86]

None the less, I liked old Slocombe — not only because he and Upright were almost the only people who ever showed me any hospitality, but because, with all his faults, he was a thoroughly nice person. In a world which, as in due course I shall show, was one of jealousy, back-biting and scandal, I never heard him say an unkind word of anyone. His graduates came back to him, not because he ever took much interest in them or did anything for them, but simply because he made them welcome and manifestly enjoyed their company.[87] The most amusing thing about him was his skill in creating legends about himself — by what means I have no idea — and securing their circulation in precisely the places where he would find them useful. All the more knowledgeable of the undergraduates, for example, were aware that he had written nothing of importance for something like a quarter of a century, but they all implicitly shared in the current belief that his study harboured some vast unfinished masterpiece. Among students and staff in general, he had built up a most convenient reputation for absent-mindedness: the abstracted air which he habitually wore, the untidiness of his dress, and, in his last years, a slight hesitancy of speech all combined to give a vague impression of other-worldliness, and to obscure the fact that, wherever his own interests were involved, he was the most wide-awake and practical person alive. But his greatest achievement was the creation of an impression in other universities that his Department was one of top-notch efficiency. Ths was done principally by means of the yes-men, who, it was tacitly understood, were engaged as strictly

---

[86] Though Peers, as Truscot, exaggerates the defects of Slocombe, the English Department was evidently run down by the time Elton retired, and indeed required some careful re-building up by his successor.

[87] *Cf.* Bruce Truscot's complaints about his former teachers, who discouraged him from returning to visit them at Camford (see 'B.T.', ch. I, pp. 215-16). At least Slocombe, though of little practical assistance to his graduates, did not 'slam the door' upon them. As already observed, Peers believed a university teacher's obligations to his students should continue after their graduation and endure 'for life'; he consistently practised what he preached.

confidential trumpeters. It was also helped a good deal by the technique of external examining, an institution which can have more uses than the one for which it was invented, if you know what they are. When Slocombe examined elsewhere, he did so with the utmost efficiency, combined with the maximum of considerateness for his internal colleague and [(at the viva)] an old-world courtesy towards his victims which won him golden opinions everywhere. On the other hand, he was careful to pick for his own Externals either former yes-men of his own who had been promoted to headships elsewhere or persons of similar type who could be relied upon to overlook obvious deficiencies and swell the chorus of praise.[88]

Though Slocombe so soon disappeared from the Redbrick scene, I have said a good deal about him because his type still exists and will have to be uprooted and brought into discredit before the modern universities do the work that they should.[89] Had I been one of his own lecturers, we should undoubtedly have engaged in [frequent] pitched battles; but, being little more than an onlooker, I saw no reason to interfere.

The other English Literature people, all of whom I knew well, can be dismissed more briefly. Two of the three yes-men were in fact women. Betty Bumpkin[90] was one of Slocombe's own products — a hearty creature, in her early thirties, much in demand at tennis parties, with no originality of mind and an academic creed of which the first article seemed to be that Professor Slocombe was the personification of perfection in every respect whatsoever. Completely unlike her was Beatrice Doolittle,[91] a languid, rather decorative Oxbridge girl of

---

88 This description of Slocombe is an evidently shrewd assessment of Oliver Elton, based on Peers' personal knowledge and observation.

89 These comments on Slocombe and 'his type' remind one vividly of Peers' vigorous criticisms of 'the leisured professor' in *Redbrick University* and *Redbrick and these Vital Days*.

90 Could this be modelled on Miss Grace R. Trenery (B.A., 1912, M.A., 1913, University of Liverpool)? She was Assistant Lecturer, later Lecturer, in English Literature 1918-38, and Lecturer in Education, 1939-43?

91 There were no long-serving women Lecturers in the Department of English Literature 1918-43 besides Miss Trenery. The only other women members of the academic staff of the Department within the period 1918-43 served for very brief periods, as temporary lecturers, tutors or fellows, except for Dorothy C. Jones who is recorded in the *Calendar* as tutor for session 1924-25, and from session 1928-29 through to that of 1934-35. The

twenty-seven who stayed at Redbrick for over twenty years, when she retired on a convenient legacy, and managed [/after contriving] to do less work than anyone else I ever knew there. An outsider would think it inconceivable that anyone should be paid four hundred pounds a year for giving seven lectures a week, doing no research, undertaking no supervision, attending no meetings, but merely spending the rest of each day in amusing herself and perhaps doing a little desultory reading. Yet Redbrick is a breeding place for such idlers; year after year they stay on, drawing their increments of pay and receiving periodical promotion. And why, it may be asked, does the Senate allow such a thing? Chiefly, it is to be feared, because the record of so many Arts professors will itself hardly bear examination.[92]

Of the two men on Slocombe's staff, one, Julius Green,[93] calls for no comment and would certainly desire none: he was by way of being a modern poet, and, provided he was left alone to write modern poetry, he asked nothing further. But the second, Robert Anstruther,[94] plays a prominent part in this

---

only female lecturers in the Faculty of Arts to be found in *both* the 1922-23 *and* 1941-42 *Calendars* were Miss Aenid Picton (Assistant Lecturer, later Lecturer, in German, 1922-53) and Miss Marjorie P. Howden (later Mrs. Marjorie P. Roxby), (M.A. 1920, University of Liverpool). Miss Howden was Junior Lecturer, later Lecturer, in Mediaeval History, 1919-27, and Lecturer in Modern History, 1927-44.

92 In the margin here Peers has written in pencil: '?alter or enlarge?' For information on the research productivity of professors within the Faculty of Arts at Liverpool University in 1946-49, see below, 'B.T.', ch. IV, p. 345, note 45.

93 Green might be modelled on Lascelles Abercrombie who was the first holder of the Lectureship in Poetry, 1919-23; under the terms of his appointment, he had to reside and offer courses in the University during the Autumn and Lent terms of each Session. The courses were to include lectures of a public or semi-public character and lectures devised principally for students in the Faculty's Honours Schools (especially that of English Literature).

94 Anstruther may be modelled on two persons, especially Professor Robert Hope Case (see '[E.A.P.] *Auto*', ch. 5, pp. 146-47, and note 19) and, to some extent, Mr (later Professor) Leonard C. Martin. Case (1857-1944) was educated at Birkenhead School and at University College, Liverpool, graduating B.A. of the University of London in 1888 (students of University College, Liverpool generally graduated of the federal Victoria University [of which the College was a constituent 1884-1903] or of the University of London). Following graduation, Case acted in 1899 as deputy professor of

story and must be introduced a little more fully.

In so far as any work was done by the staff of the English Literature Department, it was Anstruther who did it. But how

---

English Literature and Language at Cardiff. For two years he was Assistant Lecturer in Latin at Liverpool. In 1900 he took over work and responsibility in English Literature at Liverpool during the term after Professor Walter Raleigh's resignation; since 1900 he taught university students privately. He was appointed Lecturer in Elizabethan Literature in 1906 and remained on the University's staff until his retirement in 1923; latterly, 1919-23, he was Andrew Cecil Bradley Professor of English. In the request which he made for the Lectureship to which Mr Case was appointed, Professor Elton stressed the need to relieve the pressure on existing staff (eleven hours of lecturing per week, apart from interviews for tuition, covered by the professor and an Assistant Lecturer); and suggested that the hours of service required of the Lecturer requested should be two or three per week. Elton stressed Case's abilities as a teacher and tutor, who had an exceptional knowledge of sixteenth- and seventeenth-century literature. In the report submitted in 1907, in favour of making Case's post permanent and of giving him the title of Associate Professor, it is stated that Mr Case 'shares already in the teaching (both lecturing and tutorials) of students of every grade... He gives instruction in almost every part of the curriculum... He works so intimately with the Professor [Elton]... that in respect of the work he undertakes and of its quality and value, he is already in fact an associate professor. He has become indispensable to the Department as lecturer, tutor, and examiner'.

Leonard Martin was educated at Chigwall (Essex) and Keble College, Oxford, graduating B.A. Honours (Class II) in English Language and Literature, M.A. in 1911, and B.Litt. in 1913 (for which he presented a dissertation on the works of Henry Vaughan, published by the Clarendon Press in 1914). Following varied experience as a teacher at Oxford, Toronto, Lund, Reading, and Paris, from October 1923 he was appointed Senior Lecturer in English Literature at Liverpool, for an initial period of two years. Martin was one of five persons who were interviewed for the King Alfred Chair of English Literature, vacant upon Oliver Elton's retirement in 1925. In the Report of the Faculty of Arts' Committee on candidates for the Chair, February 1926, the success of Mr Martin as a teacher was noted, it being added that his published work was mainly that of an editor and textual critic. The Committee was unable to present an agreed report, a minority supporting Mr Martin's candidature, against a majority in favour of Professor W. L. Renwick of Armstrong College, Newcastle. The Faculty was divided but agreed by a majority to the amendment moved by Professor Garmon Jones recommending that, in view of the divergence of opinion and evidence, no appointment be made to the Chair for the forthcoming Session, the Faculty being prepared to make further temporary arrangements. Mr Martin remained in charge of the Department until finally appointed to the Chair in 1929; the procedure adopted for filling the Chair on that occasion was, after debate in the Faculty, by enquiry and invitation.

in the world Anstruther [/he] ever got into a University at all passed my imagination.

His University was Redbrick, but his home, as an undergraduate, had been in the country, and he had first made his mark, not in the Schools, but as a back-bench member of Student Union assemblies and as a personality in the Men's Hall of Residence. Before coming up, he had been at a small Public School in the Midlands and he had absorbed a good deal of the Public School outlook on life and tried to infuse some of it into Redbrick. Contemporaries of his on the staff (and there were quite a number of them, for he was only twenty-eight) painted an extraordinarily attractive picture of him as an undergraduate. With an outstanding First in English Literature he combined excellence at both cricket and football. He was the finest public speaker of his year, and, as President of the Students Union in his last year, he showed real talent as an administrator. All that would suggest a man likely to be in every way an ornament, as well as an acquisition, to the Redbrick staff.

And yet one had only to be his colleague for a short time to realize that he was quite out of place on it. To begin with, he was no scholar. [Precisely] how he got his First I cannot say — but the standards of Slocombe's School were so low that the classes attained by his graduates meant very little. I should say that it was largely attributable to a good memory, for he had little critical judgment, and, of the few things he has written, I have seen nothing that was [/is] more than ordinary. He stayed on after graduating and took an M.A. by research, but his thesis was not published and I have never seen it. Graduates who have talked to me about him say that his lectures were well-planned, slickly delivered and easy to remember, but that as a director of research students he was devoid of ideas, uninspiring and generally [/altogether] unhelpful. No doubt he did his best, and without him the Department would certainly have gone to pieces, but he was hardly the man to be the chief lieutenant of an unconscientious professor.

His second defect was inbreeding. In a Department notorious for it he was its most conspicuous example. He had never spent a term away from Redbrick since he came to it as an undergraduate of eighteen.⁹⁵ After taking his two degrees he had been appointed to a junior lectureship and had moved up the ladder rather more rapidly than was usual on account of the more than usually responsible work entrusted to him. Not only had he neither studied nor taught at any other university, but he had hardly even visited one. More amazing still, apart from two visits to Switzerland for winter sports, he had never been abroad, and except for a schoolboy acquaintance with Latin and French I believe he knew no other [/foreign] language.

But the most striking thing about him was the immaturity of his mentality. His proper vocation was the headmastership of a prep. school. He was a 'boys' man' all over — the sort of character I thought I had left behind at Cranstead.⁹⁶ The first remark he ever made to me was about County cricket. Somebody, he said, had told him of my connection with Cranstead. Then I must often have gone to 'see Sussex'. And what did I think of Sussex? Did I suppose it would ever be as great a side as it had been ten or twelve years ago? And so on. This was the kind of subject on which he talked best. If one liked that particular type of conversation, he was a pleasant fellow to go for a walk with, provided one had no objection to the little short-haired terrier which he invariably took with him. But it was hopeless trying to discuss anything else. Anything in the remotest degree intellectual he always shied at. As to politics (and we talked a good deal of politics in my first year at Redbrick: (it was the period of the 'Hang the Kaiser' election) he never got beyond reproducing, or making

---

95 A Cambridge man and former public schoolmaster, Peers was, and was regarded at Liverpool as, an incomer or outsider. His different academic education and experience, as well as the prejudices which he encountered, sharpened his sensitivity to the dangers of 'inbreeding' within the newer universities.

96 One recalls that the type of schoolmaster Peers knew at Cranstead and now recognizes personified in Anstruther, also used to go to Switzerland for holidays (because they spoke English there) and took an excessive interest in cricket scores (see above, 'B.T.', ch. II, p. 237). One remembers that in *Redbrick University and these Vital Days* Truscot complains about the type of professor — personified here in Anstruther — who was or became like 'a caricature of a schoolmaster... teaching hard all the term, engaging in outside activities during all the vacations and doing nothing whatsoever to advance knowledge' (97).

the most superficial comments on, the views of the *Daily Tale*, which he read in the bus every morning. He was highly popular with the students, who mimicked his precise little walk and nicknamed him 'Strutty', but made him a vice-president of most of their games clubs, honorary chairman of their debating society, staff editor (which in practice means censor) of their magazine, and any number of things more. A highly useful member of any staff, in fact, in every respect but the one which matters most[97] — and in that respect he was a disaster.

At the same time, he has been a colleague for nearly thirty years, and it is only right to say this. As regards promotion, he has had one disappointment after another. First Redbrick turned him down for a Chair and then other universities followed its example. He has had none too happy a family life. He has suffered financially from being still a lecturer and from the hard conditions brought about by two major wars. And yet, though he displays exactly the same immature prep-school mentality as he did in 1918, he is also the same pleasant companion, the same genial, easy colleague, with greying hair and wrinkled forehead but with a boyish figure which many of us envy and a happy chuckle which few of us have attained. Though to my mind he has always been a square peg in a round hole, I would not be supposed for a moment to be despising him. To none of my colleagues shall I more regret saying good-bye when the time comes; to none do I wish a longer life or a happier retirement.[98]

Outside the English Literature department my first close contacts were with two men only a little older than myself — Crusty, the Professor of English Language and Dusty, the Professor of Latin.[99]

---

[97] In Peers' opinion, which he consistently expresses in the 'Redbrick' books, a university teacher who does not dedicate himself principally to research is not fulfilling that part of his professional obligations 'which matters most'.

[98] One may infer, from his expressed desire for his colleague's happiness, that Peers wished also for himself, what, in fact, he did not attain: a long life in happy retirement.

[99] In fashioning the figure of Crusty, Peers may have used as his principal model David A. Slater, Professor of Latin, 1920-32 (see also '[E.A.P.] *Auto*', ch. 6, p. 154, and note 15. The model for Dusty appears to be E. T. Campagnac, Professor of Education, 1908-38 (see '[E.A.P.] *Auto*', ch. 6,

Now the reader will certainly accuse me of inventing these two names, but, as many people know, surnames are very curious things and there were a number of unusually curious ones at Redbrick. Miss Doolittle's, for example, was often commented upon by her critics as being cruelly apt, but she once told me, in casual conversation, that her father, a provincial doctor, had a partner called Dally: one can hardly imagine Drs Doolittle and Dally having a successful practice, but apparently this was the case, even when they took on a young man called Dr Sicker. Whenever reviewers[100] have cited our Redbrick names in order to cast doubts upon the veracity of my narratives, I have recalled an incident which happened in

---

p. 150, and note 3). Both Slater (b.1866) and Campagnac (b.1872) were, in reality, considerably older than Peers. In Crusty's character there are also elements reminiscent of W. E. Collinson, Professor of German and Comparative Philologist, though he figures in the narrative mainly through the character of Bletherley (for Collinson see '[E.A.P.] *Auto*', ch. 6, p. 152, note 7). Collinson (b.1889) was a contemporary of Peers being 'only a little older' and his colleague for years. Crusty, Professor of English Language, is mentioned in *Redbrick and these Vital Days* (57). Crusty, the Professor of Anglo-Saxon, and Dusty, the Latinist, both figure in Truscot's essay 'A Redbrick Tea-party' (1945). Crusty, again as Professor of English Language, and Dusty, 'an energetic but rather hide-bound professor of Latin', are also characters in Truscot's 'Any Faculty Board' (1945). In the same essay Truscot describes Professor Vapid, 'also a Classic, our Professor of Education'. Vapid might be another figure through whom Peers means to recall E. T. Campagnac. David Slater and W. E. Collinson are, however, more probable models for Professor Vapid. For Slater could give the wholly false impression that he was a characterless person — 'a harmless nonentity' (*cf.* '[E.A.P.] *Auto*', ch. 6, p. 154). Moreover, the figure of Bletherley, who probably incorporates elements of Slater though he personifies mostly Collinson, is said by Truscot to have a deceptively 'half-childish, half-vacant smile'. In another passage, Truscot uses the very adjective 'vapid' to describe Bletherley's smile, when, during the Committee's arguments over the election to the Chair of English Literature, Bletherley breaks in, 'the vapid smile, the inane expression gone, and in his voice a note of resolution, of indignation' (see 'B.T.', ch. IV, pp. 351-52, 367). In 'Any Faculty Board' Truscot says Vapid is someone 'about whom I hope to write a good deal some day' (see Appendix IV, pp. 487-88).

100 Peers took a lively interest in academic reactions to his books and the comments made by reviewers and correspondents. In *Redbrick and these Vital Days* (see especially the Preface) he responds wittily to some of their observations concerning Truscot's identity. He also considers, in the same book, their reactions to his opinions expressed in *Redbrick University* (see, for instance, pp. 94-95).

the Queens Common Room over thirty years ago. We were talking idly over our port about surnames and I put forward the opinion that there was no actual or invented name of English origin which would not be found in the London Telephone Directory. My right-hand neighbour took me up and challenged me to find anyone answering to the name of Corneure. As we had no London Telephone Directory on the premises I undertook to consult one at the public library the next morning. But I need not have troubled; for, on emerging into my living-room for breakfast, I took up my *Times* to read that a Mrs Corneure, of Digby Mansions, S.W. 7, had two days previously given birth to twins.

The reader, then, must accept both Dusty and Crusty, who, in fact, dwelt together in comparative unity for over a quarter of a century.[101] Crusty, I never got to know very well socially, but I came across him a great deal in the way of business since we dealt with so many of the same students.[102] But Dusty, from my first term until his retirement two years ago, I knew very well indeed. He was very good to me — in fact, in my early days at Redbrick, he was the best friend I had. And, both for the interest of his personality and because he enters into the early part of this story, I must say a good deal about him.

He was a Northerner, educated at Durham, with the faintest hint of a Northumbrian accent. What sort of a Latinist he was I hardly know: he seemed interested chiefly in the minutiae of criticism, and I fancy, though this is little more than a guess, that he had developed in a way that had rather disappointed his teachers.[103] Before getting his Redbrick Chair, at the age of thirty-three, he had had experience in places as far apart as London and Aberdeen, and he certainly

---

101 Slater and Campagnac were colleagues only for some twelve years; Collinson and Campagnac, in fact, 'dwelt together in comparative unity' for *almost* a quarter of a century. Does Peers use 'comparative' here wittily in two senses, remembering Collinson's interests in comparative philology?

102 Given that Collinson was Professor of German, he and Peers would indeed have shared 'many of the same students'.

103 This might have been said of Campagnac, who, 'after a brilliant Classical career', became a Professor of Education (not of Classics) at Liverpool University: Peers is more positively admiring of Campagnac's research in the real autobiography (see '[E.A.P.] *Auto*', ch. 6, pp. 150-51, and note 3).

justified his appointment. In Classical scholarship, Redbrick will never be able to rival Camford and Oxbridge, but there is good work in Classics to be done there, especially in Latin, and Dusty, a fine natural teacher, who retained his keenness to the day of his retirement, certainly did it. Quite apart from that, he was a striking personality: Upright, I suppose, on the Arts side, and perhaps Wormwood, our Professor of Philosophy,[104] might have rivalled him, but, not till Slocombe was succeeded by Livewire,[105] and young Active[106] was appointed, at a ridiculously early age, to the new Chair of International Relations, was there anyone else to touch him. And even with Upright, who, as I shall explain, was anything but the man he seemed, and with Wormwood, whose strength lay chiefly in his tongue, he could more than hold his own.

The two things I liked best about Dusty, even more than his keenness, were his essential kindness, completely devoid of anything like sentimentality, and his remarkable objectivity. Again and again, on the Faculty Board and on Senate, I have heard him intervene in debates where passions have run high, and the level tone of his voice has never altered.[107] Giving, as he did, the impression of bluntness, even of brusqueness, he was the last man to invite confidences, and it was a long time before even I (who, after all, was almost his equal in age) could bring myself to confide in him. Yet, as I slowly discovered, both

---

104 For Professor Wormwood (Alexander Mair) see below p. 308, note 120.

105 As previously stated, Jim Livewire is another identity adopted by E. Allison Peers (see also below, ch. IV, especially p. 346, and note 48). Livewire is a member of 'Any Faculty Board' (see Appendix IV, pp. 484-85).

106 Active might well be Professor (later Sir) Charles K. Webster (1886-1951), who in 1922 left his Liverpool Chair of Modern History for a Chair of International Relations (see '[E.A.P.] *Auto*', ch. 6, p. 151, note 4). Professor Active figures as Professor of International Affairs, and as a close friend of Jim Livewire, in Truscot's essay, 'Any Faculty Board'. At 'Any Faculty Board', Professor Active seeks leave of absence to give a series of lectures 'at International Forums throughout the country' — which proposal provokes a lively debate (see Appendix IV, p. 490). Professor Active also appears, in a similar connection, in *Redbrick and these Vital Days*: keen to give lectures in another institution, he is refused permission by his University Council (75).

107 Peers' profound admiration for Campagnac is eloquently expressed in '(E.A.P.) *Auto*', ch. 6, pp. 150-51.

undergraduates and junior colleagues would come to him in difficulties, simply because his judgment was so good, his knowledge of our academic world so profound and his counsel so tactfully administered. He had also the knack of being interested in you, and making you feel that he was interested in you, without in the very least appearing to be curious about your business.[108] Quite apart from the help he gave me at the University, I owe him a tremendous debt for his personal kindness. For he lived not far from my first lodgings at Forbridge, and, when I married and settled down there, he and his wife became our closest acquaintances.

But at the time I am speaking of, I had still much to learn about him and I thought him, as many other people thought him, a forbidding and rather cynical person given to making disconcerting remarks without notice.[109] Because we both lived at Forbridge we used often to travel up in the same train or he would overtake me in Paradise Street [on the way home].[110] The first thing I noticed about him, I remember, was how unostentatiously he slowed his pace so that, in spite of my

---

108 These particular characteristics, so much admired by Truscot in Dusty, were traits and qualities not only valued but also possessed by Allison Peers himself (see, in the Postscript, the essays of Ivy L. McClelland and Audrey Lumsden-Kouvel, and also the memorial letter, written in appreciation of Peers, from a grateful graduate and Hispanist, pp. 395-96). It would be wholly in keeping with Peers' subtlety of humour for him deliberately to give 'Dusty' some elements of his own nature — not all of them, incidentally, virtues. Peers, like Dusty, could be forbidding and seem cynical, and he had a brusqueness of manner which people found off-putting if they did not know him well (see Introduction, p. 4). If Peers has, in fact, put parts of himself into Dusty then what Peers says in the same paragraph is certainly true: Dusty and his wife did not live far from him and were, indeed, the 'closest acquaintances' of Allison Peers and his wife, Marion.

109 These characteristics appear to reflect contemporary views of Professor Campagnac. Kelly (*For Advancement of Learning. The University of Liverpool 1881-1981*) noted that Campagnac 'was admired rather than liked... for his dignified bearing, his precise classical scholarship, his wit, and his gift of graceful and polished speech... but his wit had an acid quality about it...' (*op.cit.*, 232).

110 If we are right in assuming that Dusty, in part, represents Peers, i.e., that part of Peers' nature is in Dusty (*cf.* note 108), then, naturally, in reality, both professors would often travel to work together. Professor Campagnac lived at Green Gate, Dingle Lane, Liverpool (*The University of Liverpool Students' Handbook*, editions of 1921-22 to 1933-34). Professor Slater (Crusty), however, lived at Hoylake, Wirral, not far from Peers.

slight limp,[111] I could keep up with him. He spoke little, questioning me about life at Oxbridge as diffidently as though he were an undergraduate addressing a don. Realizing how little I knew about modern universities, he might have given me a good deal of information about politics and customs at Redbrick — I wish he had! — but it was not his way to vouchsafe information, and it was only when I began to ask him questions that he demonstrated his readiness to reply.

And yet he used at times to make me feel strangely uncomfortable and I sometimes wondered if he were holding some secret from me. When I talked to him, as I sometimes did, of the contrasts I found between Oxbridge and Redbrick, he would become extraordinarily quiet, as though he were brooding over something. I would put a question to him and he would remain silent, as though he had not heard. Once, quite a long time after my appointment — the ex-service influx was at its height, it must have been in the session 1919-20 — we were talking in the train about some matter of university politics on which I was giving him, perhaps over-fully, my particular views, when suddenly he cut me short, and, turning towards me, demanded, in his brusquest voice:

'Tell me — why did you come here?'

It was so long since anyone had asked me this that I had almost forgotten the conventional reply. My real reason I had never told anyone at Redbrick and I was not going to begin now. So I stammered something, no doubt unconvincingly, about experience and administrative posts, though that could hardly have deceived him, for he must have known I should never be attracted by administration. However, my reply appeared to satisfy him, and, as at that moment the train steamed into Drabtown, the subject dropped.

Still, it stuck in my mind. I wondered if some of my colleagues had guessed my real motive and were regarding me with suspicion, having candidates of their own for Upright's Chair when he went. My imaginings went even farther; so crude and immature was I that I am not even going to put them on paper. It was not that I had, or have ever had,

---

111 *Cf.* above 'B.T.', ch. I, p. 174, note 5. As previously indicated, Peers had no limp in reality, but was unfit for war service 'through a lung weakness and a defect in one eye'.

anything approaching persecution mania, but merely that Dusty's blunt speech had a habit of affecting people like that.

But the effect which that question had upon me was nothing as compared with the astonishment produced by another, which I can date as exactly as anything in this book. The incident happened on the second of February 1920; and I remember the date by an alarming episode which took place on the very next day. It was a Monday, and, as Dusty and I both had our first lecture at half-past ten on Mondays, we invariably came up by the same [/9-30] train. It had snowed heavily in the night and begun to thaw at sunrise, so to the joys of Paradise Street were added the delight of squelching through an inch of dirty slush and the prospect of doing so for a day or two more, as, whatever the municipality might do in the main thoroughfares, it never gave a thought to the slums. Dusty was telling me of a trivial incident which had taken place on the Faculty Board a few days earlier and which in an indirect way affected the Department of English Literature.[112] Before the meeting Slocombe had told me that judging from appearances he had expected the matter to be settled in our favour, but on the following morning, without giving any reason, he reported with some acerbity that it had gone against us. I had sensed some mystery, and deliberately brought up the matter in the rather remote hope that Dusty might throw some light upon it. As I had feared, he did not; indeed, he increased my surprise by telling me that Upright, who usually got on very well with Slocombe, had spoken against him.

I made no reply: there seemed nothing more to say. We had just cornered Pleasant Grove and passed the Varsity Supper Bar. There was silence for a moment. Then, with that same almost terrifying directness as he had used before, Dusty turned right round to me, and, in a low voice, said slowly and deliberately:

---

[112] In the margin here, in pencil, Peers has written: '?specify'. The meeting of the Faculty of Arts prior to 2 February 1920 was held on 21 January. The minutes of that meeting (attended by Professor Campagnac — but not, of course, by Professor Fitzmaurice-Kelly who had left Liverpool in 1916) do not record any division of opinion besides that on the salaries for the vacant Chairs of Latin and French (which the Faculty had recommended should be £1,000 p.a., whereas the Council had substituted the figure of £800 p.a.).

'Have you ever heard of the Salvation Army?'[113]

If he had enquired after my own salvation I could not have been more completely mystified. Presumably the question had some occult significance and was not referring to the religious sect which had its 'Citadel' at the other end of Paradise Street not far from the station.[114] So I told him that I had not heard of that body and asked him what he meant.

'Oh, never mind', he said lightly, as we turned in at Redbrick's main entrance.

But I did mind quite a lot, and for the next forty-eight hours I pondered about it considerably.

## VI

The first stage in my initial disillusionment with Redbrick was accomplished on the following evening, the first of February,[115] when I was dining with Professor Upright.

Upright, as I may not have remembered to say, was a bachelor, who had a villa in Drabtown's best residential suburb, which was much too large for his household — a niece and two maids — but much too small for his immense and continually growing library.[116] From that first [August] night,

---

[113] The name given to the 'New Testament' in the 'Bruce Truscot' narrative. In the Peers autobiography, the author makes clear that the colleague with whom he had this conversation and who asked him: 'Have you ever heard of the New Testament?', was not a professor, but a young lecturer (see '[E.A.P.] *Auto*', ch. 4, pp. 136-37).

[114] The Salvation Army's Divisional Headquarters were at 12 Pembroke Place and its halls included one in Pembroke Place (near the Liverpool School of Tropical Medicine); there was no hall (citadel) in the immediate vicinity of Brownlow Hill. (*Gore's Directory of Liverpool and its Environs*, 1921).

[115] Peers writes 'first of February', but must have intended to write 'third of February', for the day before — the Monday of Truscot's conversation with Dusty about the 'Salvation Army' — was the second of February (*cf.* above, p. 304). The second of February 1920 was, indeed, a Monday.

[116] Fitzmaurice-Kelly married Miss Julia H. Sanders, third daughter of the Revd W. H. Sanders, curate of St Nicholas's Church, Nottingham in 1918, two years after leaving Liverpool. *The University of Liverpool Students' Handbook*, in the editions from 1910-11 to 1915-16, records his

when the hours after dinner had passed like magic, he had been extraordinarily hospitable to me, not only inviting me to dinner several times in each term, but allowing me to come and consult his books whenever I liked. In return, I would do things for him such as proof-reading, which fell outside the scope of my official duties, and these in turn brought me more closely into contact with him than I should otherwise have come. During almost the whole of 1919 I had helped to see the third volume of his *History of English Poetry* through the press, an experience which proved invaluable to me in later years, when I took up this work where he had left it and was able to bring the work [/it] down to the end of the nineteenth century.

But Upright's invitations to dine were not mere preludes to evenings in which I did routine work for him. They were quite *sui generis*. To begin with, I was nearly always the only guest, and, when after dinner we repaired to the study, we talked shop unashamedly all the time. And then, as I noticed from the first, my host seemed thoroughly to enjoy himself. On any one occasion, he might have been feigning to be so out of courtesy, but he could hardly have kept up such a pretence over a long period; and yet I failed to see what interest he could take in the views of a colleague so much younger than himself whose field of study was moving farther and farther from his own. I noticed, too, that our talk almost invariably centred in the pre-1700 period,[117] which was his, rather than on the moderns,[118] with whom I was increasingly occupying myself.

---

address — which he shared with a fellow 'New Testamentarian', Professor H. C. K. Wyld, Baines Professor of English Language and Philology — as 16 Mersey Road, Aigburth, Liverpool. For information on Cecil Wyld see '(E.A.P.) *Auto*', ch. 5, pp. 147-48, and note 24. Collinson ('Portraits from the Past') recollects attending a dinner party both professors gave in 1914 at this property, 'the Old Hall, now demolished but once standing near the corner of Mersey Road and Aigburth Road... I thought at the time that he [Fitzmaurice-Kelly] was an elegant bachelor of impeccable taste...' See also above, p. 283, note 57.

117 Besides his *History of Spanish Literature*, Fitzmaurice-Kelly made his reputation mainly through his book on the life of Cervantes. He also edited *Don Quijote* (see also '[E.A.P.] *Auto*', ch. 3, pp. 112-13, note 112).

118 A reference, one may suppose, to Peers' extending research and comparative interests in writers of the Romantic Movement in Spain, and elsewhere in Europe.

At first, however, I thought little about this. I only knew that I enjoyed those evenings more than I had enjoyed anything of the kind since I had left Camford. In fact, they were in some curious way like a return to Camford — the return, after a long absence, of an alumnus with a deeper experience and an enhanced capacity for appreciation, in the company of one more mature and mellowed still. Sometimes, especially at the dinner-table (for Helen, Upright's niece, was also a Camford girl) he would tell stories of personalities well known to us, though only by name, and re-create the Trinity he had known in the past.[119] Often I stayed until after the last tram had gone, when he would take out his car and make short work of the twelve miles from Drabtown home.

But as the months passed, I became conscious of a change in my attitude to Upright so subtle that for a long time I was unable to define it. I could not help noticing that no one whatever had anything like my own admiration for him. Of his books everybody spoke with admiration — that was inevitable, for his scholarship was undisputed. To his teaching, lecturing

---

[119] Fitzmaurice-Kelly was in fact privately educated and did not study at any university: his doctorate of letters (Litt.D.) was awarded by Columbia University during his 1907 tour of American universities. We know little about Fitzmaurice-Kelly's family relationships. Upright's supposed niece 'Helen' may, in reality, have been his wife Julia, a Cambridge graduate, who was some twenty-one years younger than her husband. In his one-line will, signed on 26 March 1922, Fitzmaurice-Kelly makes reference only to his wife, to whom he left 'everything' that he possessed. Mrs Julia Henrietta Fitzmaurice-Kelly (1878-1964), the third daughter of the Revd William H. Sanders, was educated in England and Switzerland before studying at Newnham College, Cambridge, where in 1902 she obtained a First Class (with special distinction in French) in the Mediaeval and Modern Language Tripos (French and German); in 1917 she obtained a First Class with Distinction in Spanish in the Cambridge Higher Local examination, her tutor having been her future husband. Prior to her marriage in 1918 she taught, mainly at Girls' Public Day School Trust schools at Blackheath, Sydenham, and Clapham. In 1920, when her husband was unable through illness to lecture at King's College, she was allowed to take his place. Her published work was principally on Spanish literature (studies on [El Inca] Garcilaso de la Vega and on Antonio Pérez in 1921-22), work which she continued after her husband's death. She was British Editor, from 1924 to 1925, of the Hispanic Notes and Monographs series of the Hispanic Society of America, and undertook literary research abroad.

and directing of research everyone also referred with respect, though, I sometimes thought, a little grudgingly. It was with regard to Upright the man that there was cold silence. He seemed to be on good terms with the Dean, with Wormwood the philosopher,[120] with Inaccessible, the professor of Ancient History,[121] with Eagles, the professor of Economics,[122] and, as I

---

120 The model for Wormwood appears to be Professor Alexander Mair (Professor of Philosophy). C. S. Lewis' *The Screwtape Letters*, an imaginary correspondence between an experienced devil (Screwtape) and a subordinate (his nephew, Wormwood), was published in 1942 and perhaps influenced Peers in his choice of name for Mair. The Dictionary gives as one definition of wormwood: 'bitter mortification or its cause'. Mair was certainly the cause of Peers' mortification, but eventually also suffered bitter humiliation himself. Because of the similarity in names, it is tempting, but probably simplistic and inaccurate, to equate Professor Wormwood (and, therefore Alexander Mair) with Cuthbert Deadwood, Professor of Mediaeval History who appears in 'A Redbrick Tea-party' and 'Any Faculty Board' (see Appendix IV, p. 486). Interestingly, in 'A Redbrick Tea-party', it is suggested that the author of the 'Redbrick' books is of a mind to mention Deadwood 'by name' in his next book. Professor Deadwood indeed figures as the disreputably leisured professor in *Redbrick and these Vital Days* (see, for instance, 93-97). In 'Any Faculty Board', rather than by Deadwood, Mair is probably represented by Professor Lovewit, 'our Philosopher, a typical Greats man and a cynic who gives us some of our finest moments' (Appendix IV, p. 487). It is true, however, that Peers regarded Mair as 'a nonentity in the world of scholarship' (for this comment and more information on Alexander Mair, see '[E.A.P.] *Auto*', ch. 5, p. 145, and note 14).

121 Professor Inaccessible is probably Dr John Sampson, the University Librarian, whom Peers admired for his scholarship (see '[E.A.P.] *Auto*', ch. 5, pp. 144-45, and note 12). Professor Inaccessible is remembered in *Redbrick and these Vital Days*, as the type of Professor who, in Truscot's opinion, would benefit from teaching in a school, to learn how to get 'nearer to the minds of his own freshmen' (213). Inaccessible takes part, as Professor of Ancient History, in 'Any Faculty Board'. In this essay Truscot describes him as a professor of the Old School '— or shall we say a professor of fiction? — if there ever was one' (see Appendix IV, p. 487). *Cf.* Truscot's disparaging reference, above, to 'professors of fiction' — professors, that is, who live inaccessibly, 'in complete aloofness from their students'(ch. III, p. 284).

122 Eagles is clearly a member of the 'Salvation Army', and presumably, therefore, has his counterpart in the 'New Testament'. The role he plays in the events narrated is insignificant, and his true identity is uncertain (*cf.*, however, ch. IV, p. 373, note 111). Professor Sir Edward C. K. Gonner, who held the Brunner Chair of Economic Science, 1891-1922, and was knighted in 1921, may be eliminated as a possible model for Eagles, because, as Reilly noted, 'he belonged to the wrong party in

thought for a long time, with Slocombe.[123] At one corner of the main building was a ridiculous little turret,[124] and at the top of it, reached by a spiral staircase, a large octagonal room which belonged to Wormwood. Upright, I knew, spent long periods there, and I knew too that Wormwood, Inaccessible and Eagles often spent evenings with him at his home. But there seemed to be nobody else who would do anything more charitable than keep silence about him. Dusty, with whom I had discussed almost everyone, shut up whenever his name was mentioned, like an oyster. I had not been at Redbrick a year before I sensed that there was something wrong.

And then, less quickly than I should have done had I not been blinded by admiration, I made a discovery for myself. Scholar though he was, Upright suffered from a pitiful and incurable vanity. If our conversations turned on his field rather than on mine, it was because his self-esteem was flattered by the deference with which I listened to him. Once I realised this, I observed how often he took the opportunity of showing me fulsome reviews of his books, admiring letters from foreign scholars, and the like: he was too much of an artist to dwell on them, but he would enjoy the effect they produced on me. He was gratified, I afterwards learned, because I came regularly to his public lectures, which none of my predecessors had done. He saw only a compliment to himself in my desire, at which I sometimes hinted, to continue his *History* if he were unable to do so himself. In fact, after I had become completely disillusioned with him, it dawned upon me that the reason he had wanted me (and my appointment had in effect been his sole doing) was no merit of my own, but the obvious admiration

---

university politics' (*Scaffolding in the Sky* [1938], 75).

123 Apparently, Professor Oliver Elton (see above, note 85). In the margin, opposite the sentence which identifies the colleagues with whom Upright 'seemed to be on good terms', Peers has written '= S.A.' — an indication that all those named here are members of the 'Salvation Army' (i.e., in reality, 'New Testamentarians').

124 A small turret does indeed decorate the east corner of the Victoria Building, at the junction of Brownlow Hill with Ashton Street. In June 1914 the New Arts Building (nowadays known as the Ashton Building) was officially opened and came into use in Session 1914-15 and gave 'great relief to the various departments [of the Faculty of Arts] formerly crowded within insufficient space' (*Annual Report* of the University, 1915, p. 31); Common Rooms were also 'now first provided for the use of the staff' in the building.

for him which I had manifested, both in my application and in the subsequent interview.

Still, it must not be imagined either that I realized all this at once, or that, when at last I had begun to take it in, it had any great effect upon my attitude to him. After all, I reflected, no man is a hero to his valet — and had not the superior Shoebridge compared me to Upright's valet or bottle-washer? To me, as I had said at Oxbridge, Upright was Upright, and, even had he been haughty and overbearing to me, I should no doubt still have idealized him. I only felt vaguely disappointed that so great a man could have so childish a weakness, and subconsciously perhaps[,] I tried to give him fewer opportunities of displaying it.

So, although on that fateful third of February I had known him intimately for nearly eighteen months, I spent as enjoyable an evening with him as I had ever done. We talked of a remarkable new edition of Percy's *Reliques*,[125] which brought back to my mind once more that first course of lectures which I had heard him give at Trinity. Thence we passed on to discuss Lockhart[126] and Southey,[127] in the middle of which he remembered a new notice of his Volume III which I had not seen. In this notice there was some criticism of a reference to the projected scope of Volume IV and this led me to ask him some questions about that volume, which I knew he intended to get to work upon as soon as he retired in the following June. And then a very strange thing happened. I was sitting in an arm-chair, reading the review, while he had risen to take down

---

125 Bishop Thomas Percy's *Reliques of Ancient English Poetry: consisting of old heroic ballads, songs, and other pieces of our earlier poets...* [which he edited], was first published in London in 1765. A number of later editions and reissues of editions appeared in subsequent centuries, including ones published in 1893, ?1900, and 1906. *Cf.* above, ch. I, p. 207, notes 123 and 124.

126 John Gibson Lockhart (1794-1854), editor of the *Quarterly Review* (1825-53), author of lives of Robert Burns and Sir Walter Scott and of several novels, and, as a poet, author of a translation of *Ancient Spanish Ballads Historical and Romantic* (1st ed., 1823).

127 Robert Southey (1774-1843), English poet and prose writer. Southey (like Lockhart) took an interest in Spanish literature. He translated the *Chronicle of the Cid* from the Spanish (a translation first published in 1808). Truscot's literary concerns reveal Peers' own main area of scholarship: Spain, and the Romantic Period.

the large interleaved copy of Volume III from a bookshelf. Suddenly, as though on impulse, he put down the book on the table which separated us, and shot a question at me in an unwontedly brusque tone which would have come more naturally from Dusty:

'Tell me, Truscot, what are your plans for the future?'

Long afterwards when I came to think the whole thing over, I was astonished that the question — a very natural one in the circumstances — should have caused me any surprise, and equally so that, in all the four terms of our association, he should never have put it to me before. After all, he had certainly a moral responsibility for his only lecturer. But the fact is that I was getting on very well at Redbrick and I had come to take my succession to Upright's professorship almost for granted.[128] So, although the brusqueness of the question came as a shock to me, I was in no way alarmed; in fact it seemed rather a good moment to sound him on the possibilities of my succeeding him. So I replied that I had no very definite plans at present and that I supposed when his Chair was advertised next term I should be among the candidates.

Then [/And then] I saw what I have never seen in a man before or since — the transformation of one personality into another.

First, the gracious, benevolent look which he habitually wore vanished, and, as I looked at him, he seemed to freeze into immobility. Hours seemed to pass before he moved — indeed, the whole experience gave me the [/a queer] impression of timelessness — and, when his expression changed, he became someone new to me [/I had never seen before]. Instead of kindness and consideration, I read in his face frustration, annoyance, thwarted pride. In everything that concerned me, I

---

[128] At this point, Peers has written, in the margin, several words of self-instruction, self-criticism even: 'Ivy: why should he? Make him reflect'. 'Ivy' is Ivy McClelland (see Editorial Commentary, pp. 43-44; and Postscript, p. 397). She is one of the few people who knew, before Peers' death, the identity of Bruce Truscot. He had given her *Redbrick University* as a present, and then asked her opinion. She recognized in the book the style of Allison Peers. She was often invited to comment on early drafts of his books. Sometimes Peers added notes to his manuscript, to remind himself of points she had made, or (as, perhaps, in this case) to draw her attention to specific passages concerning which he wanted her advice.

knew from that moment I was dealing with a different person. When he spoke, it was with a coldness and hardness which he appeared to be trying to disguise under his normal manner. But the first few seconds told me that relations between us would never be quite the same again.

What he said, too, surprised me almost as much as the tone in which he said it.

'My dear man, don't you know that my professorship disappears with me? The money for it was given merely for the period of my tenure'.[129]

That was indeed news to me,[130] and even at that moment it occurred to me to wonder why he had not told me before. The obvious answer came into my mind on the heels of the question,[131] but I rejected it instinctively as imputing unworthy motives to a great man.

I managed to reply that I had had no idea of such a thing.

Upright turned, and took down from a shelf a maroon volume which I now know from cover to cover, but at that time had studied very little — the *Redbrick University Calendar*.

'Look', he said, 'at the top of page 463'.

I looked at the place which he indicated. 'John Austin Trevor Professorship of Poetry', I read. 'Unendowed. Income provided for the tenure of the holder only'.[132]

---

[129] Besides the endowed Chairs of which, in reality, the Chair of Spanish was one, there were, at Liverpool, a number of unendowed Chairs founded (a) 'by guarantee for a term of years' or (b) 'in recognition of the scholarship of the holder'. Examples of (b) include the (Honorary) Chair of Social Anthropology (held by Sir James Frazer, 1907-22), the (Honorary) Chair of Mediaeval Archaeology (held by F. P. Barnard, 1908-15), the (Honorary) Chair of Celtic (held by Kuno Meyer, 1908-11, 1913-14), and the (Honorary) Chair of International Law (held by A. P. Thomas, 1910-31).

[130] Peers, always self-critical, asks himself in the margin: 'Why didn't other people talk of it?'. That is, he found it unconvincing that Truscot should not have learned before now, from other people, of the conditions attached to the Chair of Poetry.

[131] The 'obvious answer' is that Truscot was a highly efficient and flatteringly deferential subordinate, and Upright, therefore, had not wished him to resign — as Truscot might well have done, had he realized that Upright's chair, though soon to be vacated, was unendowed. This is the explanation — for Upright's long silence on the matter of the Chair — which Dusty gives Truscot (see below, p. 319).

[132] The University of Liverpool *Calendar 1919-20* records that the Gilmour Chair of Spanish was 'founded in the year 1908 by Captain George

I felt vexed with myself for never having seen this before. Then I reflected that I could hardly have been expected to see it before applying for my lectureship, and that it would have done me no good to have learned of it once I was here. My feelings changed to mortification at having been placed in this position. After all, I had been intimate with this man for nearly eighteen months: why had he given me no hint of the unusual conditions on which he had been appointed? Then my sense of justice re-asserted itself. I had deliberately deceived everyone, hadn't I, with my talk of wanting experience and my hints of applying for administrative appointments? So I could hardly blame anyone but myself for what had happened. If I had confided my hopes to Upright a year ago he could not have failed to tell me of the position then.

But as I raised my eyes and looked up at him again I saw once more what I had dreaded to see. The old Upright was gone: I should have to learn to know another one now.

'Oh, well', I said lightly, 'I shall have to look in some other direction, then'.[133]

---

Gilmour'. Several other Chairs, in contrast, are, as the *Calendar* states, 'unendowed', and are founded 'for a term of years' only, or 'in recognition of the scholarship of the present holder'. Peers makes the Trevor Professorship of Poetry, as distinct from the Gilmour Chair, an unendowed Chair, in order conveniently to assist the partially fictionalized development of plot in Bruce Truscot's autobiography. Interestingly, it would seem that he had already decided upon this principally complicating feature of Truscot's account when he wrote 'A Redbrick Tea-party' (1945). In that story when a visiting don from Oxbridge expresses surprise that Redbrick has a Professor of Poetry (*cf.* above, p. 267, note 22), Dusty explains that the Chair was established as a 'special foundation': 'The money was given for the lifetime of Professor Upright, the man who held it first'. Dusty adds significantly: 'I must tell you the story sometime'. Which comment encourages us in our belief that there are, indeed, elements of the author of *The Autobiography of 'Bruce Truscot'* in the figure of Dusty (*cf.* above, p. 302, note 108).

133 Peers indicates a 'space' here — to denote, presumably, a new subsection. It is not impossible that Peers and Fitzmaurice-Kelly once had, in reality, a conversation of which this meeting is a fictionalized version. Given Peers' regular visits to London (to the British Museum, and to attend meetings of the Modern Humanities Research Association — see '[E.A.P.] *Auto*', ch. 3, p. 101) he might have met Fitzmaurice-Kelly there, and made known his interest in becoming the second holder of the Chair of Spanish at Liverpool, vacant since Fitzmaurice-Kelly's acceptance, in 1916, of the Cervantes Chair at King's College London. We know (from Fitzmaurice-

Two evenings later, I was sitting in Dusty's study at Forbridge. Like so many others in perplexity, I had turned to him instinctively. The more I thought of all this, the surer I felt that there must be more in it than met the eye. Vaguely I connected it with the mysterious questions that Dusty had been putting to me.

'Well', he said, after I had told him my story, 'I think I'd better tell you just how I feel about it. There's a good deal of past history you ought to know. Only, of course, none of us have felt we were the proper people to tell you.[134] Upright was your boss and it was for him to put you wise about it. Though, personally, I felt pretty sure he wouldn't'.

I sensed the beginning of a long narrative and composed myself to listen.

'Well, to begin with, you've presumably discovered that Upright's most inordinately vain.[135] Some people don't see it, but I imagine that everybody must who has much to do with him. You wouldn't think that scholarship could co-exist with such vanity. I can't explain that. I can only say that he'd be a much greater scholar than he is without it, and I could give you examples of how it's led him up the garden path in search of bouquets when he ought to have been doing something quite different'.[136]

---

Kelly's letter of 14 February 1920 to Alexander Mair (Appendix I, p. 453) that the former had 'come across him [Peers] in connexion with the *Modern Language Review*'. The M.H.R.A. took over responsibility for this journal in 1922, after discussions which were initiated as early as March 1919. Peers might have hoped for Fitzmaurice-Kelly's support. Instead, presumably, he had aroused, or aggravated, the senior man's jealousy and antagonism.

134 Through this comment of Dusty, Peers answers the question he self-critically asked himself earlier (see note 130): 'Why didn't other people talk of it?'.

135 Peers, at this point, has written the one word 'vanity' in the margin.

136 Through Dusty Peers is expressing his own rather critical opinion of Fitzmaurice-Kelly's contribution to Hispanic Studies. It is worth remembering that an appreciation of 'James Fitzmaurice-Kelly', written by John D. Fitz-Gerald, was published in the *Bulletin of Spanish Studies*, VII (1930), no. 27, 129-35, as part of a series of articles on 'Hispanists Past and Present'. Fitz-Gerald describes Fitzmaurice-Kelly as 'the most brilliant of contemporary English-speaking Hispanists', and adds: 'By his death the cause of Hispanic Studies throughout the world was deprived of an

'You mean he likes to hear himself praised?' I queried. 'Isn't that a very common and superficial weakness in a man of his reputation?'

'Oh, I mean much more than that', was the reply. 'Now let me tell you about the Trevor Chair. Trevor[137] was a Camford man who was elected to the Council when the University was founded. He was in a big way of business here: made braces I believe — he's dead now. Upright had been up at Camford with Trevor's son, who thought no end of him. The majestic presence, don't you know, the fastidious tailoring, the mellifluous voice, and all the other things that take people in'.[138]

'Yes', I assented, humbly. 'I know'.

'Well, at this time there was a kind of competition between the rich men of Drabtown as to who could endow the most Chairs best — or do I mean the best Chairs most?[139] Well

---

indefatigable champion and a great refined soul that it could never replace and could ill afford to lose' (129). Fitz-Gerald ends by proclaiming Fitzmaurice-Kelly's most marked characteristics: 'his tolerance, his courtesy, his consideration of others, his gentleness. To him may appropriately be applied the Spanish phrase describing the perfect knight: "cristiano valiente y comedido" ' (135). As editor of the journal in which it appeared, Peers must have felt when he published this eulogy no small degree of ironical amusement. Doubtless for mixed reasons, and with intentional irony, Peers dedicated one of his own books: 'To the memory of James Fitzmaurice-Kelly 1858-1923' (see *Spain: A Companion to Spanish Studies*, ed. [and contrib.] E. Allison Peers [London: Methuen, 1929; 4th, revised, ed., 1948]).

137 That is to say, Captain George Gilmour (1839-1925). A Birkenhead businessman with interests in Argentina, he became a member of the University Court by virtue of his gift permitting the establishment, in 1908, of the Gilmour Chair of Spanish. He was formerly a Captain in the Twenty First Royal Scots Fusiliers. In his will (8 June 1922) he refers to his late wife, his late brother (who also had business interests in the Argentine), his married daughter and a married granddaughter and their children, but makes no reference to a son or late son. For probate purposes, his estate was valued at £445,048/16s/7d. See also below, note 144.

138 'The majestic presence' etc. mentioned by Dusty had greatly impressed Truscot as an undergraduate (*cf.* 'B.T.', ch. I, pp. 205-07; and see note 118).

139 The Preface to the editions of the *Calendar* of University College, Liverpool, chronicles the benefactions of the citizens of Liverpool. A stimulus to the fund-raising was an address by Canon J. B. Lightfoot in 1879 following which (in 1880 and subsequently):

anyway, Trevor senior was leading in the race. He'd given the Chair of Economics (named after his wife, you recall?) and filled in his time by building us a gymnasium and founding the Rome and Athens scholarships. But he still wanted to endow another Chair: I've heard this story myself from the son'.

'Isn't the son on the Council, too?' I enquired.[140]

'Was till recently' replied Dusty. 'But he's retired from business now and gone to live in the south — Hampshire, I believe. Well, as you'll gather, he made braces too. And one day he suggested to Papa that it would be a good thing to get Upright here. Upright was a Fellow at Camford — about forty I suppose — just beginning to get known.[141] Of course a man

---

Mr. W. Rathbone, with his brothers, Mr. S. G. Rathbone and Mr. P. H. Rathbone, offered £10,000 for the permanent endowment of a Professorship; Colonel A. H. Brown, in conjunction with Messrs. Crosfield and Barrow, did the same; Mrs. Grant, of Rock Ferry, sister of the late Mr. Rayner, gave another £10,000 for a similar purpose. Mr. Edward Whitley and his co-trustee assigned from the Roger Lyon Jones Trust Fund a sum of £10,000 to the School of Medicine, with which that body endowed another Chair. By the energy of Mr. Samuel Smith and Mr. Alexander Balfour, a fifth Professorship was endowed with a similar sum, contributed by Scotch firms carrying on business in Liverpool. A number of ladies and gentlemen, desirous of perpetuating the illustrious name of Roscoe in connection with an institution with whose objects he would most assuredly have sympathised, raised £10,000 to endow a Roscoe Professorship of Art. Another Professorship was founded by Lord Derby, who generously and not inappropriately followed up his father's gift to Liverpool of a Natural History Museum, by endowing a Chair of Natural History with a sum of £10,000. Through the instrumentality of Mr. Thomas Cope and Mr. Malcolm Guthrie, a number of manufacturers and traders were induced to contribute to a fund for the the erection of Chemical Laboratories; while the shipbuilders, the members of both branches of the legal profession, and other gentlemen contributed large sums for various purposes, special or general, connected with the College (*Calendar for the Session 1895-96*, v-vi).

140 Though Gilmour had no son who was a member of the University Council or University Court (of which latter, as stated, Captain Gilmour was a member), the near relatives of a number of the University's benefactors have served on the Council and/or Court and also held the various lay officer posts with distinction.

141 In reality, as Oliver Elton noted in his obituary of the first Gilmour Professor of Spanish, Fitzmaurice-Kelly at the time of his appointment 'had not held a regular post before' and was 'self-trained'. He received his (honorary) Doctorate of Letters from Columbia University while on his

on the Council can't just write a cheque and get a friend of his a job, so it had to be done rather carefully'.

'You mean the Senate would object?' I enquired.

'Of course. It's for the Senate, acting with the Faculty, to make permanent appointments. So they had Upright up [/here] for a week-end and hatched this scheme. Old Trevor was to offer a thousand or two to have Upright as a visiting professor for a couple of sessions — the Senate would hardly raise any objection to that. Once he was [/they'd got him] here, the old man was going to offer twenty thousand to endow a Chair of Poetry — without conditions, of course, but it was pretty certain that the man on the spot would get it — probably without the formality of a competition. But, believe it or not, Upright refused to agree'.

'Refused to agree?' I cried, 'Then how does he come to be here?'

'Refused to agree to an endowment', explained Dusty. 'The condition he made was that the income of the Chair, if there were to be one, should be provided for the period of his tenure only. To be Professor of Poetry at Redbrick was not [/wasn't] good enough for James Upright.[142] He must be Redbrick's one and only Professor of Poetry. Whenever he went, the dynasty must come to an end. The impression created among people not in the know must be that there was nobody in the country eminent enough to take his place'.[143]

'What astounding vanity!' I exclaimed, 'I should never have thought it!'

'Of course not', observed Dusty. 'You have joined the number of those who have been taken in. The majestic

---

lecture tour of American universities in 1907 (*cf.* also '[E.A.P.] *Auto*', ch. 5, pp. 143-44).

142 As regards Professor Upright's first name, which, changed from George Charles to James, now coincides with that of Professor Fitzmaurice-Kelly, see our comments above, in notes 2, 21 and 50.

143 The motives ascribed to Upright are, as Peers understood them, essentially the same reasons which inspired Fitzmaurice-Kelly to oppose Peers' appointment to the Chair of Spanish at Liverpool (see '[E.A.P.] *Auto*', ch. 6, pp. 154-55). Moreover, Fitzmaurice-Kelly was evidently envious and fearful of Peers' talent. He suspected, consciously or unconsciously, that Peers' achievements at Liverpool might eclipse the memory of his own tenure of the Gilmour Chair.

presence, the flashing eye — but there, you know it all! Well, the Trevors agreed — I suppose Upright didn't put it quite as crudely to them as I've done to you, though the son had no illusions about his motives. The scheme worked. Nobody had an inkling of what was going to happen till old Trevor came down to a Finance Meeting and said he was prepared to continue the Professorship of Poetry for the lifetime of the holder provided the present holder were elected. The Vice-Chancellor pointed out that he would have to retire at sixty-five and Trevor said that was what he meant. There was some hesitancy about it on Senate, but the Faculty was unanimous, and even enthusiastic, so there was really nothing more to be said'[144].

---

144 The true facts regarding the establishment of the Gilmour Chair of Spanish are as follows: in a letter of 13 July 1908, Captain George Gilmour wrote to the Vice-Chancellor, 'As one who for upwards of thirty years has been connected with Argentina, as Merchant and Estanciero, I desire to establish a chair of Spanish in the University of Liverpool. Among the objects present to my mind is the wish to direct attention to the language of Spain as used in Argentina and the other Spanish-speaking countries of South America, and to promote an effective interest in such modifications of the original idiom. For this purpose I offer a sum of £*10,000* (ten thousand pounds) to the University for the endowment of the aforesaid chair. I should wish the name of Gilmour to be attached to the Chair'. From a letter which the Vice-Chancellor wrote to Capt. Gilmour on 10 July, it would appear that they met [earlier] on 13 July and no doubt discussed this gift and the amount required to endow a Chair. The Vice-Chancellor wrote to Capt. Gilmour on 14 July stating that he would receive an official communication on behalf of the University Council accepting his offer and stating personally 'how greatly we are indebted to you for this most valuable addition to our equipment. It will enable us to do well what we should otherwise have done badly, and to get a first-rate instead of a second-rate man'. The Vice-Chancellor in February 1909 informed Capt. Gilmour that applications for the Chair were coming in and that he believed the field would be strong in quality as well as numbers. In sending him a copy of the report, dated March 1909, recommending to the Senate Dr Fitzmaurice-Kelly's appointment, the Vice-Chancellor wrote implying that Capt. Gilmour did not know Dr Fitzmaurice-Kelly: '...as you will see, [he] is a scholar of the very highest reputation, thoroughly competent in every way. He comes to us prepared to undertake the ordinary work of the teacher, and does not wish to restrict himself to study of research. His appointment will be an immense accession to the strength of the University, and we have reason to congratulate ourselves on securing him'. Capt. Gilmour acknowledged this communication, expressing his appreciation of the care the Committee had taken in selecting Dr Fitzmaurice-Kelly out of one hundred and sixty

'And where do I come in?' I asked. 'Why couldn't he have told me about the tenure of the Chair when I came here? Surely it would have been the natural thing to do?'

'Ah, there', remarked Dusty, sagely, 'we can only conjecture. If I were one of the Upright fans, I should say that it probably never occurred to [one of] his single-minded nature what you were after. (It occurred to *me*, by the way: you remember I asked you the other day why you came here?) Being a suspicious person, I suspect that he tumbled to it perfectly, and guessed that, if he told you, you'd go. And he must have found you pretty useful, from all I hear — just the sort of assistant a man likes to have in his declining years. But there's another thing you ought to know. A year ago the Faculty Board considered a Dean's resolution — do you know what that is, by the way?'

I said I didn't, not being a member of the Faculty Board.

'Well, the Dean is Chairman of the Board,[145] and a Dean's resolution is one supported by the key members, as we call them, which normally goes through without opposition. And Dobie put up a resolution asking the Council to continue the Chair of Poetry for another ten years — "as a tribute to the scholarship of the present holder", was the priceless phrase he used. But the resolution never got to Senate, let alone to Council'.

'You mean it was defeated?'

'I do', assented Dusty. 'Good heavens, what an amazing

---

candidates. The Vice-Chancellor's Letter Books for the period up to 21 July 1919 contain copies of a few further letters to Capt. Gilmour but all of them on other subjects (his gift of funds for the Gilmour Hall of the Students' Union [1911]; an appeal for funds for equipment for the Liverpool University contingent of Manchester University OTC [1915]; and an appeal for funds to endow the Chair of Geography [1917]).

145 The University's Ordinances provided that the Deans of the Faculties should each 'be the executive officer and public representative of the Faculty', responsible for summoning meetings of the Faculty, preparing business for and recording the minutes of such meetings, etc. The office of Chairman of the Faculty was separate from that of Dean. In February 1926 a Committee of the Faculty of Arts, appointed to consider the duties and emoluments of the Dean, reported that it had considered (and dismissed) the 'suggestion of conforming to the practice of all other Universities by abolishing the separate office of Chairman, the Dean to act as Chairman and public representative of the Faculty'.

thing it is that you should be living in a nest of intrigues like this and be blissfully ignorant of things that concern you more than anyone else! I mean that it was defeated, wholly and exclusively, through the machinations of the Salvation Army, of which Upright is a leading member'.[146]

'Oh!' I said, blankly, that other question of Dusty's recurring to my mind.

'Yes', he remarked 'and I suppose I'd better tell you all about that too. There ought to be a course of information for non-members of the Faculty Board in Redbrick politics'.

So he told me the most extraordinary story I had heard since I came to Redbrick of how in a would-be democratic community a determined and unprincipled clique can usurp power. Quite apart from its relevance to my narrative, it ought to be made public so that a younger generation of university teachers may be warned against any such clique as may arise in the future.[147] The difficulty in telling the story is that it sounds entirely fantastic — and yet it did happen.

Soon after the foundation of Redbrick University, it

---

[146] Though, perhaps naturally, no records of the 'New Testament' caucus of the Faculty of Arts survive (apart from an album of photographs — 'N.T.'; Liverpool University Archives, ref. S.34), the origins of the 'N.T.' can be traced to the period before the University received its charter in 1903. The album of photographs of 'N.T.' members is incompletely captioned but thirteen of the fifteen portraits may be identified as those of Professors J. M. Mackay, Kuno Meyer, Oliver Elton, Alexander Mair, Charles Bonnier (Professor of French, 1905-13), Ramsay Muir, Bernard Pares, E. T. Campagnac, Fitzmaurice-Kelly, Charles Reilly, and John Garstang, Dr John Sampson, and Mr Norman Wyld. It seems likely that most of the photographs were taken at the same time, very possibly in 1911. Is it possible that this album is the set of beautiful portraits, probably photographic, of his Arts colleagues which Seán Ó. Lúing records was presented to Kuno Meyer at a farewell dinner (held at the University Club) on 5 July 1911 (Seán Ó. Lúing, *Kuno Meyer 1858-1919* [Dublin: Geography Publications, 1991], 99)? The *Liverpool Daily Post and Liverpool Mercury* did not carry an account of this dinner; nor is it reported upon in the Club's archives.

[147] *Cf.* essentially the same reasons which Peers gives in his straightforward autobiography for telling the story of the Gilmour Chair and the downfall of the 'New Testament': 'I have told the story... solely in order to show to what depths men can descend... I sincerely trust that my telling of the unpleasant story of intrigue... may lead others... to make similar resolutions' (see '[E.A.P.] *Auto*', ch. 6, pp. 166-67).

appears, five members of the Faculty of Arts came together and resolved to attempt to seize power. There might, said Dusty, have been some excuse for them at that time, when the Faculty Board was small and inexperienced. The first members of the clique were among its most forceful members and they no doubt led it in the right direction: further, everyone knew about them and they were recognized as a kind of unofficial General Purposes Committee. It was all quite honest and above-board, and the nickname given to the clique was inspired, not by irony, but by admiration.

But then the Board grew in members, from ten to fifteen, from fifteen to twenty and eventually to its present strength of twenty-five. It elected its own General Purposes Committee and most people supposed that the Salvation Army had gone into dissolution. But it had not. It remained in being as a secret society, with a tradition behind it of nearly twenty years, and, on the February day of 1920 when Dusty revealed its methods to me, it was in its hey-day.

Its members, so far as were known, were Upright, who was believed to be Chairman, Wormwood, Inaccessible, Eagles, ___.[148] It was not known if Dobie was a member or not: the general belief was that he had revolted against it. Its meetings were held between the issue of the agenda for a Faculty Board meeting and the holding of that meeting, in Wormwood's private room in the Arts Tower. The members would go through the items of the agenda one by one, decide on the policy they wished to be adopted with respect to each of the important ones, and plan means by which they could implement their intentions.[149] When any of the members left the University, a successor was elected from a list of those believed to be 'safe'. Every member, on election, was pledged to the strictest secrecy.

What I found difficult to understand, I told Dusty, was why, if it was known they were acting in collusion, the Faculty Board paid any heed to them: intrigues of that kind, in my limited experience, generally collapsed as soon as their

---

148 Peers leaves a space and adds a '?' after Eagles' name. His intention evidently was to add at least one other name to the list.

149 *Cf.* Peers' description of the methods of the 'New Testament', '(E.A.P.) *Auto*', ch. 5, pp. 140-41.

existence was known.

'But it's not known', was his reply. 'At least, so little is known about it as to make no matter. Even Slocombe, who has been here for donkeys' years, couldn't tell you exactly who they are. And, when one of them speaks at a Board meeting, even if he's known to be in the S.A., he may be speaking on his own account and not for the S.A. at all. Besides, as you see, they're among our senior people. They *can't* be disregarded'.

He went on to describe a Faculty Board meeting when some burning question is under discussion. Not having then seen the group in action, I thought it fantastic; but, when later I became a member of the Board[150] I realized how completely, had I not been forewarned, I should have been taken in. Dusty named no names, but I was soon able to supply them. One of the group, he said, would rise — *tall, reverend and unbelievably upright in stature, with the reputation also of being upright in character*[151] — *and tell his colleagues that he had really been thinking very seriously about this and had come at last to the conclusion that... Some criticism outside the group would follow, after which a jovial and somewhat boisterous Salvationist,*[152] *who always put the Faculty [/Board] in a good humour, would back up his revered colleague with a jovial, boisterous speech — of course quite 'spontaneous'. Then, if the opposition seemed to be at all serious the wiliest and one of the youngest of the group, respected by all but trusted by very few,*[153] *would half-rise, as though doubtful if his opinion was worth being heard at all, and in an apologetic voice murmur: 'Well, sir, I* **do** *hope that the Faculty will not be influenced by this criticism. I* **do** *feel that what Professor Upright has said is right*

---

150 As a member of the Board of the Faculty of Arts, Peers became a keen observer, at its meetings, of the wiles and idiosyncrasies of those who were its leaders, who manipulated the procedures, or who influenced its decisions (see Bruce Truscot, 'Any Faculty Board', Appendix IV).

151 Obviously, from the description, the member in question can be none other than James Upright.

152 Peers had originally written 'New Testamentarian', for this passage, as our italics indicate, had formed, initially, part of the 'real' autobiography. The jovial and boisterous 'New Testamentarian' might conceivably have been, in reality, Charles Reilly or Garmon Jones.

153 Probably Wormwood (Alexander Mair) was 'the wiliest' of the group. Peers regarded him as 'the chief intriguer at Liverpool' ('[E.A.P.] *Auto*', ch. 6, p. 156).

*[/correct/true]*.[154]

'Well there you are', Dusty went on 'and that's the sort of thing that happened when we debated the proposal to continue the Chair of Poetry. You never heard such a display of hypocrisy. Wormwood led the attack: there was no place for a Chair of Poetry at Redbrick; everyone was aware of the distinction of the present holder (with a deferential side-glance at Upright); but for his own part he did feel that the subject was better served by a lectureship. Then came old Inaccessible; and his line was concern for University finances: we couldn't afford luxuries; there were so many more urgent things for the Council to spend its money on that we should only prejudice these if we pressed them to continue the Chair. Then the S.A. kindly allowed two or three of us to speak on the other side, including our friend, Crusty, who was pretty good, and completely smashed the finances argument; but when they judged the right moment had come, up gets old Honest-and-Upright, rolls his eyes and in a voice broken with emotion says what a grief it is to him to have to oppose this motion [/resolution], but he has given the subject long and anxious thought, and he really doesn't feel that the experiment has justified itself. Of course, he went on, it may have been his fault — he's so conscious of his own deficiencies; but he wouldn't be acting as his conscience dictated if he didn't confess that the time had come — and so on. That settled it: the motion was defeated by 13 votes to 7, and the proposal will never be put up to the Council at all'.

'But what about Slocombe?' I enquired in bewilderment, 'Surely he could make a case for the continuance of the professorship'.

'Oh, Slocombe!' exclaimed Dusty with a dry laugh, 'He never comes to Faculty Board meetings now.[155] He wasn't there'.

---

154 Peers leaves a space here, in case, as he writes, he wishes to add: '?more'.

155 Because, we may suppose, of his previous defeat at the Board of Faculty, over another matter affecting the Department of English Literature — a defeat brought about through the opposition of Slocombe's supposed friend and fellow 'Salvationist', Upright (see above, p. 304). In reality, during this period, Professor Elton attended most of the meetings of the Faculty of Arts.

## VII

The rest of the term dragged wearily and I went home for the Easter vacation more depressed than I had been since I first came — depressed, I reflected ironically, at the prospect, not of coming to Redbrick, but of leaving it.[156] For I didn't doubt that I should leave it. Slocombe had four years still to go[157] and I was not prepared to wait till I was nearly forty on the chance of getting his Chair. If I was to go in for an English Literature Chair at all I must get busy before that.

The alternative would be to attempt a return to Camford or Oxbridge. That, I realized, would be very difficult. To start with, not only had my own former lectureship been permanently filled, but the glut of other post-war appointments had ceased and the most I could hope for would be a fellowship at one of the smaller colleges.

Besides, to go back to Camford or Oxbridge after only two or three years at Redbrick would look like an admission of failure, and I did not feel in the least that the experiment had been a failure. On the contrary, it had been a great success. Once you got used to the hideous tiles,[158] the cramped and sordid surroundings, the Drabtown accent, and the indifference of the material you often had to work upon, there was a vitality, a sense of urgency, a tang of real life about Redbrick which Oxbridge, with all its amenities, had never provided.[159] As yet I had penetrated very little into the inner workings of Redbrick, nor had I investigated more than a few of the inspiring possibilities of life in a civic university. But I had seen something of its Extension work, made contacts with the

---

[156] Truscot's previously negative and prejudiced attitudes to Redbrick are already radically altered (contrast his last words in 'B.T.', ch. II: 'It was a thoroughly prejudiced Camfordian who took a single ticket from Oxbridge to Redbrick University'[p. 257]).

[157] Oliver Elton, in fact, retired from his Chair in 1925 (*cf.* below, ch. IV, p. 344, note 44).

[158] An allusion to the 'Late Lavatory' tiles within the Arts Tower at Redbrick (the Victoria Building of Liverpool University), of which Bruce Truscot expressed his low opinion earlier in this chapter (see above, p. 277).

[159] Bruce Truscot's keenly approving words memorably define the profoundly developed respect and affection within Allison Peers for the vitality of Liverpool: the city and the University.

Workers Educational Association,[160] been elected to the Committee of the University Press,[161] visited some of Drabtown's large municipal schools and held the attention of a thousand boys or girls — some of them my undergraduates of the future —[162] as I talked to them of contemporary English poetry. And now, for the first time, I was faced with the possibility of returning to the comfortable, easy-going life of an ancient university, and I realized that, in spite of all its advantages, *I did not want to go.*[163]

There was, I supposed, no immediate urgency. Early in the summer term, presumably, the Faculty Board would meet and recommend that I should be incorporated in Slocombe's Department and there were still three more years to run of the quinquennium for which I had been originally appointed. But, when one sees the forties approaching, one begins to think of a permanent post, and I realized, as I returned to Drabtown at the end of April, that I could not expect to find another for some time to come.

And yet, within a month, the whole of my problems

---

160 Peers' name does not appear in the lists of those who gave lectures for the University's Extension Board in the Board's reports for sessions 1919-20 to 1924-25, but he is listed as having delivered Extension Lectures (on various aspects of Spain, its history and geography), and also a Holiday Lecture for schoolchildren, in Lancashire, Merseyside and Wirral, in sessions 1927-28, 1928-29, 1930-31, and 1932-33. See also above, p. 264, and note 10. For further evidence of Peers' commitment to such activities, see *Redbrick and these Vital Days*, chapter 5, 'The University and its Region'.

161 The minutes of the Liverpool University Press Committee do not survive for the inter-Wars period, but Peers' name does not appear amongst the Senate's recommendations for membership of the Committee for the period 1929-40. In respect of the period up to 1946, Liverpool University Press published just one of his many books, *Rivas and Romanticism in Spain* (1923). For Peers' opinions on the importance of a University Press, see *Redbrick University*, in which he affirms: 'Every university should put the establishment of a Press in the forefront of its post-War programme' (190).

162 As previously noted, Peers was an indefatigable publicist for his subject, and regularly visited schools throughout and beyond Merseyside, advocating to schoolchildren the merits of learning Spanish and of taking a degree in Hispanic Studies (see Postscript, pp. 390, 392-93, 403-04; and Appendix I, in his application (1921) for the Chair of Spanish, p. 435).

163 Through the forceful brevity of this emphatic statement of feeling Peers conveys the full strength of his commitment to Liverpool University.

disappeared in a way which seemed almost miraculous.

One evening at the end of May, Dusty told me, as we walked along Paradise Street, that my position was going, as he put it, to be 'regularized', and, when I pressed him to elucidate this hint, he went so far as to say that I was likely before long to hear of something to my advantage. More than that he would not tell me.

But on the following Tuesday morning, the Dean sent a message that he wanted to see me urgently as soon as possible. Knowing that the Faculty Board met on Mondays, I lost no time in going to his room. It was his last term in office: I remember thinking how tired and even ill he looked. But he greeted me with more than his usual geniality.

'Sit down Truscot, I've some news for you. I hope you'll think it good news'.

I waited, curiously expectant, though I had no kind of idea what good news he could possibly have.

'Rather a strange thing has happened', he said. 'Certainly a very unexpected thing. During the Vacation the Vice-Chancellor had a letter from the solicitors of Austin Trevor — that's the son of the founder of the professorship of Poetry — putting £25,000 at the disposal of the University for the endowment of the Chair'.[164]

'But I thought he had decided not to endow it', I objected.

'That was certainly the original decision', said the Dean. 'It's past history and I've no idea how much you know about it, if anything. But the father wanted to endow the Chair from the start, only he took the advice of a certain person and was persuaded into giving the money yearly instead'.

'Yes', I nodded. 'I knew that'.

'Well', Dobie went on, 'What nobody whatever knew was that the old man had never really been persuaded at all. He'd determined that Redbrick should have a Chair of Poetry because Oxbridge had one, but he didn't want to cross a certain person, who was a great friend of his son, so he agreed to provide the money yearly. But, without telling anyone except his lawyers, he created a trust fund of £25,000, and instructed them to pay the interest to Redbrick every year until Upright

---

[164] In fact, the amount given by Captain Gilmour to endow the Chair of Spanish was £10,000.

resigned or retired and then to offer them the principal to endow the Chair. If the offer was refused, it was to be made to Camford, and, if Camford refused, to the other universities of the country in the order of the seniority of their foundation'.[165]

'And Upright knew nothing about this?' I asked.

'No, but he does now', answered the Dean, with a broad smile. 'And I haven't asked for his views on it either. The Faculty Board received a communication from the Council on the subject yesterday and decided unanimously — or, strictly speaking, *nem. con.*, as two or three people didn't vote — to accept the offer'.

'Was Upright at the meeting?' I asked.

'No', said the Dean, smiling still more broadly, 'He had important private business in London. But', he continued, answering my unspoken question, 'if he *had* been there, he couldn't have done anything. The only real argument against the continuance of the Chair was that the University couldn't afford it. And if it once became known that we were turning down cheques for £25,000, we should soon stop receiving them'.

'Then will the Chair be advertised?' I enquired.

'I don't think so', said the Dean. 'We appointed a Committee which will examine the situation, make some preliminary investigations as to the field of candidates, and report to the Board, which will report to Senate. But we had a considerable preliminary discussion on the question and the view expressed was that you were the obvious person for the

---

165 There is one known instance at the University of Liverpool where the donor of funds for a Chair made provision for the funds to be offered to another university if Liverpool did not accept his offer. In his will, J. Campbell Brown (Grant Professor of Chemistry, 1881-1910, d.1910) made provision for the endowment of a Campbell Brown Chair of Chemistry upon certain conditions (relating to the salary and duties of the holder of the Chair and provision of adequate accommodation and equipment etc.). In the event of the University of Liverpool declining or failing to accept this bequest with the attached conditions, Professor Campbell Brown provided for the funds to be transferred to the University of Manchester as an endowment of a Campbell Brown Chair of Music in that university. It might be worth noting that in his will (holograph, dated 16 March 1948) Peers left monies in trust to promote the teaching of Spanish at Liverpool University, with an instruction that, should Liverpool cease to teach Spanish, the funds should be transferred, for the same purpose, to Glasgow University.

Chair, not merely on your own merits, but because you are still young and because, as everybody knows, you have been in such close touch with Upright and will continue the tradition which he has created. And I think there's not the slightest doubt that that will be the view of the Committee. I will even go so far as to ask if I might be the first to congratulate you.'

'Thank you', I replied. 'Then the thing was unanimous?'

'Well', smiled the Dean once more, 'Shall we say *nem. con.*?'

That was how I became the second Trevor Professor of Poetry at Redbrick University, a position which at the time of writing I still hold.[166] Everything turned out as Dobie had predicted. The proposal went, unopposed, from the Committee to the Board and thence to Senate and Council. I never exchanged a word about it with Upright, who, on the day after the Council meeting which made the formal appointment, sent me his congratulations in an elegantly worded letter. He may never have known that I was aware of the part which he had played in the matter: indeed I am pretty sure he did not, for only Dusty and Dobie knew it and neither would have dreamed of telling him.

Immediately on leaving Redbrick, Upright moved to a country house not far from Camford,[167] where he lived until his death in 1928. We parted the best of friends: it fell to me to make the principal speech at the parting dinner we gave him, and I was able, without the slightest mental reservation,[168] to

---

[166] Peers' appointment, in 1922, to the Gilmour Chair of Spanish was confirmed only after considerable opposition (see '[E.A.P.] *Auto*', ch. 6). Truscot's account, given in the next chapter, of the trials of Jim Livewire, candidate for the Chair of English Literature at Redbrick University, is a disguised version of the difficulties which Peers encountered at the University of Liverpool until he and his supporters defeated the 'New Testament' and secured his election to the Gilmour Chair.

[167] In fact, Fitzmaurice-Kelly lived in London (at 1, Longton Avenue, Sydenham, S.E.26) for several years before his death in November 1923. In the details of the grant of probate (1924) the address is noted as ...Sydenham, *Kent*. Letters, dated December 1915 and June 1917, from the University Registrar, were addressed to him at the Savile Club, 107 Piccadilly, London.

[168] Having read Truscot's account of Upright's anything but upright conduct, we must receive this comment as the author humorously intended: that is, with amusement and disbelief. Moreover, compare, and contrast, Truscot's frank condemnation of Upright for his malicious criticism of

REDBRICK: THE BEGINNINGS      329

speak warmly, not only of his scholarship and of his devotion to the subject which he professed, but of his great personal kindness to younger men, including myself. Yet a gulf between us had sprung up on that February night in his house which was never bridged, and I could never feel towards the new Upright as I had felt towards the old. Fortunately there was no [/never any] risk of personal feeling on my part, for he had done me no kind of injury. But I felt an intense bitterness, which at bottom may have been mainly chagrin at the discovery of my idol's feet of clay, when I thought of how, through his miserable, petty vanity, he had nearly done so great a wrong to the University. And it gave me a feeling of insecurity, such as I had never previously experienced, when I realized how, over so long a period of years, he had taken nearly everybody in. 'Old Honest-and-Upright', Dusty had called him ironically, but so successful had been his pose that the majority [/many] of his colleagues could have applied the phrase to him in sober earnest. Were there many other such people at Redbrick? I wondered; and then I began to realize one of the disadvantages of a non-resident university.[169] At either Camford or Oxbridge, a man of that type would inevitably have been found out.

However, in professional and academic matters we remained colleagues. After succeeding to his Chair I continued to collaborate with him in his *History of English Poetry* and after his death I carried it to its close, so that to this day everybody in our particular field thinks of me as Upright's admirer and principal disciple. But I think that, unaware though he probably was that I knew the Trevor story, he must have guessed that I had penetrated his armour and discovered [/bared] the vanity that lay beneath it. For, though I often went down for the day to visit him at Little Camfield Manor, I never spent a single night there.[170] And I cannot recall any

---

Livewire (see below, ch. IV, pp. 383-84).

169 As previously indicated (see above, p. 285, note 66), Peers believed firmly in the special advantages offered by residential universities.

170 There is no evidence that Peers ever visited Fitzmaurice-Kelly at his home. Given the latter's ill health since, at least, February 1922, and Peers' knowledge of Fitzmaurice-Kelly's prejudices and intrigues against him, it is unlikely that the two Hispanists met following Peers' appointment to the Chair.

occasion when we devoted more than a passing moment to discussing Redbrick.

As I went down at the end of June I felt in a very different mood from that of three months earlier. A professor at thirty-five,[171] I had exactly thirty years of pleasurable activity stretching before me.[172] Now I could make long-term plans for reading and writing, with no risk, as in the past, of their being brought to nothing by the termination of my appointment. Now I could work for the creation of a Department of Poetry dissociated from the Department of English Literature. Now, as a member of the Faculty Board and of the Senate, I could get to know more of the workings of the University and play my part in its government.

And that last thought recalled the Salvation Army. What would become of it, now that old Honest-and-Upright was no more? No doubt its ranks would be closed by the election of some other anonymous intriguer: well at least they would not elect *me*! Presumably, as the innocent cause of its most recent defeat, I should not be exactly *persona grata* to it, but could I help to bring about its fall? Though as yet I had not come to grips with it, I could not fail to do so before long; and if in due course I could gather together a group of people pledged to oppose intrigue in any shape or form, it might be possible to deal it a death-blow.

But it was early to be thinking of that. I was still a junior; and, even in modern universities, the junior professor is not encouraged to push himself. None the less, at every debate on the Faculty Board, I kept my ears open, and the Salvation Army was continually in my mind.

---

171 Peers was, in fact, aged thirty-one years when he was appointed to the Gilmour Chair.

172 Characteristically, Bruce Truscot, unlike 'the leisured professor' he describes in the 'Redbrick' books, does not regard his Chair, once awarded, as an excuse to reduce his professional labours. On the contrary, he looks forward to three decades of dedicated work undertaken for the benefit of his subject, his department and his university. Strangely, Peers himself was to enjoy tenure of the Gilmour Chair during 'exactly [the] thirty years of pleasurable activity', which Bruce Truscot here predicts will be the entire length of his professorial career. Appointed from 1 October 1922, Peers remained Gilmour Professor of Spanish at Liverpool University until his death, preceded by several months of illness, on 21 December 1952.

# CHAPTER IV

## THE CHAIR OF ENGLISH LITERATURE

### I

The session of 1919-20, during which the events related in the last chapter took place, witnessed the maximum influx of ex-Service students and the growth of the University to the maximum [/largest] size which it ever reached.[1]

Again and again, while our ranks were depleted during the Second World War, I used to indulge in curious reminiscence upon those days of plenty. Walking along the ground-floor corridor when crowds were debouching from lecture-rooms, one would be caught in the human whirlpool with movement as difficult as in a London tube-train at rush hour. Almost anywhere about the buildings, in fact, it was advisable to wear a gown to ensure oneself a passage, for at peak periods every corridor and every landing were thick with men and women — and [blue] with smoke! For the first time, we became conscious of the smallness of our lecture rooms, the largest of which seated barely one hundred. As the first year English Literature class alone numbered two hundred and eighty and the figures for French and Modern History were hardly less, it became necessary to duplicate or triplicate many of the classes, a procedure agreeable neither to staff nor to students.[2]

---

1  In Session 1919-20 the number of full-time and part-time students in residence was 2,605 (1,522 in Session 1918-19), a total not exceeded until Session 1946-47 (3,276). In his report on Session 1919-20, the Vice-Chancellor, J. G. Adami, wrote that 'the first full session after the Great War has seen a University transformed, teeming and pulsating with life, crowded with students to its utmost capacity, and those students, as a body, filled with a spirit of work and eagerness to learn, only paralleled by the student spirit of the Renaissance'.

2  In Session 1919-20 undergraduates preparing for degrees in the *Honours Schools* of English Literature, French, and Modern History

Not less troublesome than the congestion of undergraduate life was its variety. Ex-service scholarships were given in great numbers and boys and girls of eighteen had to be taught by the side of mature freshmen of twenty-eight or even thirty.[3] I remember Anstruther reporting that in one tutorial class he had found three people older than himself. Such conditions are inevitable after a World War; and in 1919 they were very much worse than in 1945 because the whole of the conflict ended at once and demobilization was very much more rapid.[4]

The same session that brought us such an influx of students brought us also a new Vice-Chancellor.[5]

As a general rule, Vice-Chancellors at the modern universities resemble popes in the shortness of their reigns: from eight to ten years would probably be a fair average.[6] But Redbrick is happy in having had an efficient and active Vice-Chancellor for nearly thirty years, who will have held office for precisely that time when he retires in 1950.[7]

Sir Archibald Blake (he received a knighthood, it will be remembered, in the year of the Coronation)[8] succeeded a gentle

---

numbered twenty-four, nine and nine respectively; the only other Honours Schools in the Arts Faculty with greater numbers were Mediaeval History and Geography with eleven each (see the University's *Annual Report* for the period November 1919 to November 1920 [University Press of Liverpool, 1920], 38). Students studying these subjects for the First Year *Ordinary* B.A. would, however, have considerably boosted these figures. 'The existing class rooms and laboratories were not built for such numbers; and to meet the needs courses have had to be repeated two, three, and four times' (the Vice-Chancellor in his *Report* on Session 1919-20, 17).

3   More than 1,100 ex-service officers and men receiving grants from the Government through the Board of Education were admitted to the University in Session 1919-20.

4   After this passage Peers has written in pencil, and left a half page space unfilled for, 'any more on this'.

5   Colonel J. G. Adami, M.D., F.R.S., was appointed Vice-Chancellor as from 1 October 1919. He died in office on 29 August 1926, aged 64.

6   An amusing comparison, which, some fifty years later, might still be made with confidence, and without risk of contradiction.

7   Some further evidence that Bruce Truscot is writing his memoirs in the second half of the 1940s.

8   A nice touch of realism.   Vice-chancellors, as Peers was aware, usually receive knighthoods after a suitable period in office. The Coronation, to which Bruce Truscot refers is, of course, that of George VI, in 1937.

old man with a beard[9] which, even in the early nineteen-hundreds, was unfashionably long[,] and a voice which was embarrassingly low and husky. He had been at Redbrick ever since it received its Charter; and it was as difficult to imagine the place without him as without the Arts Tower or the tiles in the corridors.[10] But even harder was it to get used to his successor, a dapper little man of thirty-five, five foot three inches in height, with a singularly youthful face and bland expression, but the bearer of a great reputation from Oxbridge, where he had spent all his graduate life, both as an economist and as an administrator.[11]

---

9 Dr Adami succeeded Sir Alfred Dale, who was last Principal of University College, Liverpool (1900-03) and first Vice-Chancellor of the University of Liverpool (1903-19). Writing in 1953, the Registrar of the University, Stanley Dumbell (B.A. Liverpool, 1920), remembered Dale as a great Vice-Chancellor who had 'the quick smile and the sometimes abrupt manner of a man who... was still shy at heart. To him, the path of duty was always plainly defined, and the difference between right and wrong never obscured by circumstance. Although his decisions were firm they were never harsh... ; more than any other individual he shaped and guided [the University's] early destiny and none could have been better fitted for the task' (*The University of Liverpool 1903-1953. A Jubilee Book*, [8]).
10 Cf. 'B.T.', ch. III, p. 277, and notes 43, 44; p. 324, and note 158.
11 It is possible that, for his portrait of Sir Archibald Blake, Peers has drawn upon the characters of both Dr Adami (Vice-Chancellor, 1919-26) and Dr (later Sir) Hector J. W. Hetherington (Vice-Chancellor, 1927-36). Adami was described as 'ruddy, of medium height, prosperous, having kindly eyes that sometimes wake up with an astonishing fire' by 'Altair' in *The Sphinx* — the magazine of the Guild of Undergraduates — in November 1919. He was 'a stout and tubby round-faced jolly looking creature', remembered P. G. H. Boswell (Professor of Geology, 1917-30). According to Boswell, Adami compared unfavourably as an administrator with his predecessor, Dale: 'Probably by Army standards he was very capable, but we were to suffer from his incapacity for years'. See Boswell's unpublished autobiography, University Archives, Liverpool, D.4/1/, especially p. 149. John Share Jones (Lecturer in the Veterinary School, 1904-19, and Professor of Veterinary Anatomy, 1919-38) also recollected that 'Dale and Adami were as unlike as it was possible for two men to be'. A 'very short and very stout' man, Adami 'was not the young vigorous man that the work ahead demanded. He was most affable and ready to agree to and promise most things to most people... He had little regard for constitutional procedure which was such a pronounced feature in Dale'. See Share Jones' unpublished autobiography, 'University Vet', University Archives, Liverpool, D.161, at p. 68. On the other hand, Hetherington, formerly Professor of Moral Philosophy at the University of Glasgow, was just thirty-eight years old on appointment and

All sorts of tales were told about his youthful appearance, some of them probably apocryphal, but I did witness one encounter over which I have often chuckled. We had an emeritus professor, now long forgotten, who combined kindness of heart with an incredibly pompous manner. Dining in the refectory, as he did every Wednesday, he espied this little man sitting by himself at the High Table. It was early and few people had arrived, so he went and sat by him to make him feel at home.

'New here, I see', he remarked to the little man.

The little man assented.

'And what Department do you belong to?' he continued, as one might to a third-grade lecturer.

'Oh, I'm the Vice-Chancellor', said the little man, humbly.

He [/From the first 'Archie', as we called him,] was modest and unassuming; and we liked him for that. He was a 'Senate man', through and through; and we liked him for that too. But he was also extremely energetic and practical, appealing to the City and to the Council;[12] resourceful over problems that demanded a solution wounding no one's susceptibilities; inventive where new ways had to be taken, but always willing

---

soon established a reputation as a great administrator. Like Adami, he was friendly and approachable and took a deep interest in the wider life of Liverpool. In his biography, *University Statesman: Sir Hector Hetherington* (Glasgow: Outram, 1971), Sir Charles Illingworth wrote that 'Hetherington's occupancy of the Vice-Chancellorship in Liverpool is to be reckoned as one of the busiest and most effective phases of his life' (42). Share Jones recollected that Hetherington 'took an active part in the conduct of the affairs of most branches of university education and especially in matters of finance... Although Hetherington's actions were regarded by many as those of the village schoolmaster it was also said of him that he got people working'. At the time when 'Bruce Truscot' was writing this autobiography Sir James Mountford was Vice-Chancellor of Liverpool University (1945-63).

12  It was Dr Adami who persuaded the University's Council in 1920 to launch an appeal for £1m. to meet the urgent need for new buildings and equipment and additional staff; despite the general economic situation, just over £350,000 was raised. During Sir Hector Hetherington's period as Vice-Chancellor several other new or converted buildings, or extensions to buildings, were added to the University's estate. These were financed mainly through private benefactions — not least those from prominent lay officers such as Sir Sydney Jones, who served the University successively as Treasurer (1918-30), President of Council (1930-36) and Pro-Chancellor (1936-42).

to take the old ways if there were any chance that they might be better. I have no wish to appear to be writing him a testimonial, for [everybody knows that] none is needed. Redbrick has been fortunate for close on a generation in having an ideal Vice-Chancellor.

I settled remarkably quickly into my position as professor. For this I have largely to thank Upright, who left me so free academically to go my own way. Certainly at the end of a few weeks I found it difficult to believe that I was a newcomer to the professoriate. My marriage, which also took place in this year, was considerably more upsetting.[13] A honeymoon spent abroad — as long a break as I could contrive to make it — piled up arrears of work for me when I got home. A period of several months spent in looking all around Drabtown for a home made havoc with evenings previously spent in work. Finally, we decided to settle at Forbridge, after which still more time had to be spent in establishing new social contacts; for, so completely wedded to the town and its immediate suburbs were the huge majority of my colleagues that we found few 'Faculty wives', as they call them in the United States,[14] for my own wife to make friends of. I was well into my third year as professor before I saw any possibility of getting that independence for the Department of Poetry which had long been one of my ambitions, and not for six years was that goal actually accomplished.[15]

---

13 Peers married Marion, daughter of James Frederic Young, Director of Education for Devon, in 1924 (*cf*. 'B.T.', ch. III, p. 287, and note 73).

14 Peers speaks from personal knowledge, for he went to the United States as visiting professor, and on lecturing tours, on several occasions. He held, for instance, a visiting professorship in modern comparative literature at Columbia University (1929-30), and was Centennial Lecturer at New York University (1932). See Postscript, p. 392, and note 8.

15 In fact the Department of Spanish was independent of and not subsidiary to any other department; in common with most of the other departments of the Faculty of Arts, it had its own Class Library (established at least by November 1911). It is probable, however, that, particularly in his first years, Peers felt his Department to be overshadowed by the larger and better established Department of French. Certainly he worked indefatigably throughout his career to develop the range of languages and courses the Department offered, and to expand the numbers of its undergraduates (see his application (1921) for the Chair, Appendix I, p. 435). See also Postscript,

It had always seemed wrong to me that a Professor of Poetry should in effect be a Professor of English Poetry and that he should work almost wholly in the Department of English Literature. An independent Department, as I saw it, could work in with many others and my aim was to have a professor and two lecturers,[16] covering between them four fields: poetics including... ;[17] English poetry — by which I mean all poetry written in the English language; Classical poetry; and the post-Renaissance poetry of Western Europe.[18] I have not actually accomplished this, though I was on the point of getting a second lecturer when the World War of 1939 burst upon us; but, having a good knowledge of French, German, Italian and Spanish literatures,[19] I have myself consistently lectured on this as well as upon English, and for my lecturer I have tried, where possible, to get a Classical scholar with a marked interest in poetics. I can say without exaggeration that for nearly twenty years I have lectured every session to students of either French, German and Italian, and now that, as a result of the War, Redbrick has taken up Russian,[20] I should presumably be

---

especially, p. 390.

16 The *Calendar 1938-39* records, that in the Department of Hispanic Studies, besides Peers, there were a Lecturer and an Assistant Lecturer in Spanish and a vacancy in the Lectureship in Portuguese; the *Calendar 1946-47* records, besides Peers, a Lecturer and an Assistant Lecturer (previously Part-Time Temporary Lecturer) in Spanish and a Lecturer and a Temporary Lecturer in Portuguese. Before Peers died, in 1952, the total number of staff had increased by one: there were two Lecturers in Spanish and two in Portuguese and Catalan, an Assistant Lecturer in Spanish, and, of course, Peers himself.

17 Peers has left a space for an insertion, which he never made, explaining the type of poetics to be studied.

18 Peers had a considerable and informative understanding of European poetry of the post-Renaissance and Romantic periods. Two of his early publications, for example, discussed 'The Fortunes of Lamartine in Spain', *Modern Language Notes*, XXXVII (1922), 458-65, and 'The Influence of Ossian in Spain', *Philological Quarterly*, IV (1925), 121-38.

19 Peers had studied French and some German (for a term) at Cambridge. After graduating, he worked hard at German in order to teach it (at an elementary level) at Mill Hill School (see '[E.A.P.] *Auto*', ch. 2, p. 75; ch. 3, p. 93).

20 In fact, Liverpool University had had a Chair and Department of Russian since 1908. Also Peers, despite Truscot's declared ignorance of Russian, had spent six months learning Russian while at Felsted School (see '[E.A.P.] *Auto*', ch. 3, p. 99). The first holder of the Chair of Russian was Sir

THE CHAIR OF ENGLISH LITERATURE    337

taking up that language at the mature age of sixty-two[21] if I had not decided to leave the University.[22]

This is not the place to amplify the general observations on university life which I have made in *Red Brick University*, but I should like to digress to the extent of recording my conviction that our Arts departments do not make nearly enough use of each other's services.[23] Every Arts Faculty should have a Department of Comparative Philology and another of Comparative Literature, each with a skeleton staff augmented by short-period secondments from other Departments. Our Department of Poetry as it exists to-day does part of the work which would fall to one of Comparative Literature.[24] My French and German colleagues tell me that their students' knowledge is greatly broadened by the lecture courses which have been given in my Department on European balladry, the Renaissance in Western Europe, foreign influences on Elizabethan and Jacobean poetry, the Romantic Revival in England, France and Germany, and so on.[25] Normally one, sometimes two, of these courses will be given yearly, after consultation with the

---

Bernard Pares (who was a member of the 'New Testament') (see '[E.A.P.] *Auto*', ch. 5, p. 143, note 10).

21 Yet another indication of the year in which Truscot is engaged in writing this part of his autobiography: 1947; for Truscot was born in 1885 (see above 'B.T.', ch. I, p. 173).

22 There is no evidence that Peers had decided to leave the University before the usual age of retirement at sixty-five years. The last entry he contributed to the University's Annual Report, for Session 1951-52, refers to his work in the press and to the revised and enlarged edition of his *Complete Works of St John of the Cross*, a collection of lectures and essays and the third volume of his *Studies of the Spanish Mystics* which he intended to publish during the Session 1952-53. This volume, edited by I. L. McClelland, was published (1960) after Peers' death.

23 Educationalists nowadays who advocate interdepartmental courses and cooperation suppose (and suppose wrongly) that they are proposing 'modern' and innovative developments.

24 The breadth of the courses provided in the Department of Hispanic Studies at Liverpool University, during Peers' tenure of the Gilmour Chair, is demonstrated in the Faculty of Arts' Prospectus for each Session between 1922 and 1952. See also the description of Peers' department contained in the report of the Chairs Committee of the Faculty, January 1953 — which report is cited in the Postscript (p. 390).

25 As previously indicated, Peers had major research interests in the Romantic Period in Spain and the rest of Europe (see '[E.A.P.] *Auto*', ch. 3, p. 112, note 110; and especially ch. 4, pp. 126-27, and notes 5-10).

Departmental Heads concerned. Except where the course covers some special subject prescribed for a certain school, attendance is entirely voluntary, though a register of attendances is kept and students are told that they are expected to be present or to send a written excuse if they are not. The average of attendances is as high as for any compulsory lectures that I have ever given.

Before I could establish a Department of this kind, I had both to win the co-operation of my colleagues in those which I wished to enter and also to contract out of the Department of Literature.

The former of these two tasks was the easier. No Italian was taught at Redbrick when I came,[26] and, as the Redbrick tradition (a mistaken one, I think, in principle, though it has worked well here) has been to appoint foreigners to the professorships of French and German,[27] the approach there was simple, for neither André nor Eberhard had any personal ambitions in the sphere of Comparative Literature which an Englishman might have had. Within two years I had established myself in both these Departments and when the enthusiastic little Ratti[28] came from Florence to teach us all Italian I was gratified to discover that the Faculty Board took it for granted that the Department of Poetry would be represented in his School as well.

---

26 In fact Dr Piero Rébora was Lecturer, later Senior Lecturer, in Italian, 1914-23. He held a Doctorate of Letters of the University of Turin. He was succeeded by Dr Mario Praz who resigned as from the end of the 1931-32 Session. Though a successor was appointed for the Lent and Summer Terms 1933, Professor Peers was asked by the Faculty in January 1933 'to continue in general supervision of the department of Italian, and to represent the department on Faculty'.

27 The James Barrow Chair of French was held by Frenchmen until 1946 (L. A. Terracher, 1913-19, and J. E. Eggli, 1920-46), and the Chair of German by an Englishman, W. E. Collinson (1914-54), friend and supporter of Allison Peers, and opponent of the 'New Testament' (see '[E.A.P.] *Auto*', ch. 6, p. 152 and note 7).

28 In characterizing 'the enthusiastic little Ratti', Peers may have been influenced to some extent by the personality of Dr Rébora. Ratti, 'a dark, explosive little man', features as Professor of Italian in 'Any Faculty Board'. Ratti was the family name of Pope Pius XI, who reigned 1922-39. But Peers' reason for calling the lecturer in Italian by this name was probably more lighthearted (see Appendix IV, p. 485, and note 15).

## THE CHAIR OF ENGLISH LITERATURE 339

To persuade the Faculty Board to free me and my lecturer from our obligations to English Literature was, until Slocombe[29] went, a much harder task; it was accomplished without much difficulty, however, in the year after his departure. Slocombe's attitude seemed to be that, as the only poetry worthy of the name was English poetry, the Professor belonged to him, and it was extremely generous of him to allow all the gadding about to other Departments which went on as it was.[30] The root of his objection was disinclination for change, for we did as much for English Literature after the divorce as we had done before. No doubt I could have forced a separation earlier had I been inclined for a pitched battle about it, but I had more than enough work to do as it was and I guessed that a younger man would be more amenable.

As I have always held that teaching and research should go together, not only within every Department, but also in the activities of each individual teacher, I spent as much of my time as I could spare from balladry and Upright's *History* in research within the field of Comparative Literature. The special subject which attracted me, and on which, as some readers may know, I have published a good deal, is that of 'pessimism'[31] in European literature of the nineteenth century.[32]

---

29 That is to say, Professor Oliver Elton (see especially above, ch. III, pp. 290-93).

30 Slocombe's attitude is markedly similar to that displayed by members of the reactionary University Council criticized by Truscot in *Redbrick and these Vital Days*, who refused Professor Active permission to give lectures in another institution.

31 Peers' researches into the nineteenth century in Spain, and into the Romantic Movement generally, indeed led him to study ' "pessimism" in European literature'. He published, for instance, an article on 'The "Pessimism" of Manuel de Cabanyes', *Modern Philology*, XXI (1923), 49-52. See also '(E.A.P.) *Auto*', ch. 4, where he mentions that he had begun a book on 'the Unhappy Romantic [in Western European literature] which never materialized' (see p. 126).

32 After this paragraph, Peers leaves blank approximately three and a half pages for additions. He has scribbled, in pencil, in the margin, the following note to himself: 'Write this when more done and length available can be determined'. He then adds: 'Go on to a "Professor's day" '. Regrettably, Peers' impressions and experiences of a 'Professor's day' were never inserted.

## II

So far as university politics were concerned my principal desire was to put a stop to the activities of the Salvation Army and I devoted a good deal of attention to its methods. Notwithstanding what Dusty had said, I found it hard to understand why in a body with an average attendance of over twenty, no more than five people should be able to do more or less as they liked.[33] When I had some experience of Faculty Board meetings, however, the reason became clearer.

When a committee of eight or ten meets for some specific purpose, such as the allocation of a library grant or the choice of a lecturer, the attention of all its members is concentrated upon the task in hand, and any group of two or three would need to exercise a good deal of planning and guile before they could mould it to their own intentions. But a Faculty Board of twenty-five is a different matter. It deals with a great variety of business, much of it routine, and much more so departmental that only one or two persons are competent to express an opinion on it. The meetings are long — from two to three hours — and come at the end of the day when many people are tired.[34]

---

33 The average attendance at the seventeen meetings of the Faculty of Arts held in 1920 works out at 24.47, with a minimum of twenty and a maximum of twenty-nine at any one meeting.

34 The University's *Calendar*, in its Almanac section, gives the time of commencement of Faculty of Arts meetings as 4.00 p.m. in those issues, of the 1920s, when such information is given for this Faculty. The Minutes of the Faculty of Arts record the time of commencement (generally at 4.00 p.m., but very occasionally earlier or slightly later in the afternoon) of meetings but not the time they terminated. Most of the meetings were held in the Senate Room (in the Victoria Building) but on occasion they were held in the Staff Common Room or in the Dean's Room. It is worth comparing Truscot's description of the conduct of the 'Salvation Army' at meetings of the Faculty Board, with his essay portraying 'Any Faculty Board' (Appendix IV, pp. 484-93). Truscot describes above a typical meeting of the Faculty in the early 1920s, whereas in his essay he is Truscot, twenty, or more, years later, writing about 'Any Faculty Board' in the 1940s. There are, however, interesting similarities noticeable in the conduct of both meetings. Certain aspects of academic life at Redbrick University did not change much in the intervening years. Fifty years after Bruce Truscot ceased to be a university teacher, those of us who follow the same profession, were we to be honest, should have to admit to having observed colleagues at meetings of the

What happens, therefore, is that the Secretary's reading of lengthy minutes, of a stack of letters most of which are either trivial or formal, and of a string of Dean's motions that (for example) So-and-so shall be given an additional year for his M.A. thesis, or that someone else shall be examined in French as a three-year, instead of a two-year, subject has such a soporific effect that, at the end of the first hour, everybody is mentally stagnant.[35] Then comes, let us say, the election of some special lecturer. No one has any views about it, but someone vaguely suggests one Jones. The S.A., however, has already decided upon Brown, and Inaccessible at once makes the counter-proposal. Someone out of the blue (which is [obligingly] provided by the smoke-haze of many pipes) supports this, and someone else languidly suggests one Robinson. This is the moment at which Eagles gets up, remarks lightly that time is getting on, and that in his view Brown is easily the best qualified person. Wormwood then reinforces these remarks with a graceful flourish of words rounded off with an epigram. Everybody, amused rather than convinced, and impatient to be getting on with the business, then votes for Brown. If by any chance the opposition develops farther, Inaccessible rises solemnly (the *rôle*, I gather, was formerly Upright's) and suggests that, as there is evidently a serious cleavage of opinion, the choice should be left to a small committee. In the same breath he proposes that the committee consist of the Dean, Eagles, Wormwood and someone who can be relied upon to have no very marked opinion — one of 'the good boys', as Wormwood once termed them in an unguarded moment. The Dean then plays the S.A. card by making the obvious suggestion that, as Inaccessible called for the committee he should be on it, and so it is duly appointed, with three of its five members vowed to blood and fire.[36]

---

Faculty behaving in ways reminiscent of Professors Wormwood and Inaccessible.

35 *Cf.* the concern of the members at 'Any Faculty Board', with an undergraduate beginning her second year, who wishes to be allowed to take Mediaeval History as a three-year subject and German as a two-year subject, instead of the other way round, 'notwithstanding Regulation 72, Section 3 (a) which declares this procedure to be illegal' (see Appendix IV, p. 490).

36 An amusingly deliberate misapplication of the motto of the throughly well-intentioned, good-doing Christian organization, to describe

Another of the tricks of the clique was to get an item in which they were interested postponed to the end of the meeting,[37] either by introducing it themselves under 'Other business' or by asking for a rearrangement of the agenda in the supposed interest of one of them who had to leave early. In either case, the members were jaded and weary by the time the matter came up, and prepared to agree to almost anything.

When some problem came up on which there was certain to be a fight, and to their solution of which the S.A. attached extreme importance, they would plan their campaign and arrange the order of their speeches much in the way that Dusty had described to me. On the other hand, when a matter seemed to them of no great moment, they not only allowed a 'free vote' but made a point of taking opposite sides, and even of simulating heat, in order to dispel any idea that they invariably worked in collusion. I used sometimes to think that they even created contention when there was none. A famous debate, for example, once took place on whether Eagles' external examiner should be paid £25 or £30.[38] Eagles himself thought £25 enough, but Inaccessible remarked that he had observed a tendency to underpay external examiners and proposed £30. This led to a detailed explanation of the amount and nature of the work involved and a comparison of it with the work in other Departments. After Eagles had fought Wormwood and Inaccessible for half-an-hour, the Dean suggested a revision of the whole scale of payments by means of a special committee, to which suggestion Eagles demurred, though the other two gave it their hearty support. Who could suspect these honest fellows of collusion after that?

---

the misconduct of the unworthy body of academic self-seekers, which had usurped its name.

37 Truscot describes the same trick as it is used in 'Any Faculty Board' (Appendix IV, p. 492).

38 Peers became a member of the Board of the Faculty of Arts at the start of the Session 1920-21 and at an early meeting which he attended, on 19 January 1921, the Dean reported that he had received a letter from Professor Gonner (Professor of Economic Science, 1891-1922) requesting that the fee of the External Examiner in Economics be increased from £25 to £35. It was agreed that the matter be deferred until the next meeting of Faculty and that the Dean be asked to prepare a schedule of the fees of all External Examiners in the Faculty.

I have said that, in Upright's time, nobody knew for certain who was the fifth member of the S.A., and, so far as I am aware, his identity never became public, though a good many of us had our suspicions. But Upright's place as Chairman, and his *rôle* of Honest John, were both taken by Inaccessible, while the vacancy he left was filled by Anstruther.

This I really regretted, for, negligible though he was as a scholar, I had a great respect for little Strutty as a man — indeed, I had hoped that his energy and his skill in the practical conduct of affairs might win him a Vice-Chancellorship.[39] I have little doubt that he was influenced, if not actually bribed to join the clique, by the promise of its support in his candidature for the Chair of English Literature. As he was a man of some influence on the Board, to which he had been elected, though not a Departmental Head, for his own merits, he became a great accession to the clique and was also their most active member — in effect, if not in name, their secretary. He always seemed to be running up the spiral staircase to the Arts Tower, and that alone would have caused us to smell a rat, even if his activities on the Faculty Board had not, for previously he had been no friend of Wormwood who had found him an easy target for his mordant wit.

The prestige of the S.A., however, had suffered a good deal from its defeat over the Chair of Poetry: in their anxiety to win a last victory for Upright, they had gone a little too far,[40] and from that time forward more members of the Board were wise to their methods than had been so earlier. At the beginning of my second term on the Faculty Board, Dusty, Crusty and I held a counter-meeting on a matter in which we guessed they would intervene and were successful in defeating their intervention when it came. A little later, Dusty challenged the election of Wormwood to a committee on some contentious matter on the

---

39 A characteristically Peersian observation made partly for amusement, partly to provoke discussion and disagreement. Truscot displays here a seemingly inadequate conception of the qualities required of a university leader. Yet previously, in describing Archie, Vice-Chancellor of Redbrick University, he appeared wholly to appreciate the exceptional insight, diplomacy and resourcefulness needed to fulfil supremely this supreme university office (*cf.* above, pp. 334-35).

40 In the margin, Peers asks himself in pencil: 'is this fact clear above?'.

ground that he was an interested party. The Dean allowed the objection and this was said to be the first occasion on which the S.A. had been thwarted of a representation which it had angled for. It is rather important to say something about this here, for otherwise the sudden and complete collapse of the clique four years later would seem unnatural.[41]

I am inclined to think that the biggest mistake which the S.A. ever made (for they could not conceivably have foreseen [/suspected/guessed at] the foresight of old Trevor) was the election of Anstruther. He had not the natural finesse of Upright and Wormwood. His intervention in debate had always been of the direct and spontaneous kind: he would jump up, emit a not very subtle [but generally common-sense] opinion, and sit down again.[42] Now he changed his tactics and tried to imitate the Honest-and-Upright technique of Inaccessible. But he was too young to make much impression by this and so obviously was he doing it to order that even the least experienced member of the Board saw in him an object lesson of a good man spoiled by an unprincipled party.[43]

## III

At the beginning of 1924 the Faculty Board received formal notice from the Registrar that in the following September[44] Professor Slocombe would be retiring under the age limit and that the Board should recommend to Senate at its early convenience the name of a successor. It was generally known that Anstruther, though only thirty-two, aspired to the succession and a good many of those who knew him, not as a scholar, but only as a man, were of the opinion that he would be elected.

---

41 Instead of simply one adjective 'unnatural', Peers considers writing here: '?melodramatic and unnatural'.

42 There is persuasive evidence here that Anstruther would not have made a good vice-chancellor (*cf.* note 39).

43 At the end of this section, Peers considers whether to add further comment, asking himself: '?Any more in this'.

44 Oliver Elton indeed resigned, 'under the age limit' for retirement (aged sixty-four, as from 31 December 1925).

For myself, I never took this view: even before I knew the name of a single candidate, I failed to see how even a *prima facie* case could be made out for a man who had so consistently thrust research into a corner. It is true — and even truer, I fear, to-day than it was twenty years ago — that a vast proportion of our professors in the Arts Faculty fail to produce the research they should,[45] but that seems to be due solely to the facts that life has been made too easy for them and that they are safely seated [/immovably ensconced] in their comfortable Chairs till the age of sixty-five.[46] Redbrick has always made an effort to see that the candidates for its Chairs have a reasonable body of work either published or ready for publication: one of the most solemn farces it ever stages, in fact, is the turning-down of a candidate for insufficiency of research

---

45 Reference, for instance, to the Reports of the University's Joint Committee on Research upon Research and other Original Work published during the Sessions 1946-47 to 1948-49, reveals, in crude numbers, the total publications credited to professors in the Arts Faculty: Greek (eight articles), Latin (one book, contribution to a book, four articles, five reviews), French (joint author of two books, general editor of a series, five articles, and three reviews), Spanish (six books, twenty articles, forty reviews), German (three articles, 'articles' contributed to an encyclopaedia, and eight reviews), English Language and Philology (two books, joint author of one book, two articles, nine reviews), English Literature (two books, four articles, two reviews), Egyptology (three articles), Mediaeval History (-), Modern History (one article, one review), Geography (four articles, and contributions to a book), Economic Science (two articles), Economics (three articles, and contributions to a book), Social Science (one book, nine articles, one joint article, four reviews), Classical Archaeology (one article, one review), Philosophy (-), Education ('contributions' to a dictionary and to an encylopaedia), Architecture (one article), Civic Design (three articles), Music (four books, one article) and Psychology (two articles). Different professors had differing workloads of teaching, administration, etc. Nevertheless, these figures demonstrate Peers' outstanding record of productivity in research publications.

46 Truscot expresses similar opinions in discussing 'the leisured professor' in the 'Redbrick' books: 'The life of a well-established, middle-aged professor in the Arts Faculty of a modern university can, if he likes to make it so, be one of the safest jobs to be found on the earth's surface' (*Redbrick University*, 71). He believes professors should be obliged to work harder, and particularly to do more research by, for instance, giving them short-term appointments, which would be renewed only if the quality and productivity of their publications, on assessment, were considered satisfactory (see *op. cit.*, 119-20).

by a selection committee of professors of whom not more than one or two have published anything substantial for a quarter of a century.[47] I knew, better than anyone else, what the external experts whom we consulted would say about Strutty's research, or lack of it, and in face of such evidence it was hard to believe that he would be given the Chair as a prize for exceptional industry and good behaviour.

But as soon as I heard that Jim Livewire[48] was a candidate for the Chair I gave Anstruther's chances no further thought, nor had I the slightest doubt as to the result of the election. Livewire was a Trinity man, a very old friend of mine and very nearly a contemporary. He had come up in the October after I had gone down — that is, during my year at Camford Grammar School. I had made his acquaintance [/come to know him] because he was an old boy of the school, and I had also had some dealings with his father, who was a don at St Anthony's, and president of an inter-collegiate society of which for a short time I had been secretary. When I came to the school as a student-teacher, the Headmaster suggested that I might look him up when I was at college, and soon after I had first called

---

[47] Peers is recollecting, not without a certain bitterness, his own experience: when his election to the Gilmour Chair was opposed by members of the 'New Testament', who had, nevertheless, with one or two exceptions, published little of importance. See, for instance, his comments on Mair ('a nonentity in the world of scholarship'), Reilly ('made no claim to be heard on matters of scholarship') and Garmon Jones ('made all too few contributions to learning') ('[E.A.P.] *Auto*', ch. 5, pp. 145-46). See also Peers' remark that his 'original work in the Hispanic field' was 'considerably greater than that of a number of the men on the [Appointing] Committee itself' ('[E.A.P.] *Auto*', ch. 6, p. 161).

[48] In this autobiographical novel of Redbrickian intrigue, Peers adopts, for the purposes of his argument, an additional identity. He continues to 'be' 'Bob' Truscot, (see above, ch. III, p. 264), Professor of Poetry, but, from now on, is at the same time Jim Livewire. This talented candidate for the Chair of English Literature is opposed, like Truscot, by the inappropriately named 'Salvation Army'. With characteristic wit, the author introduces Livewire as 'a very old friend' of Truscot and 'very nearly a contemporary'. Jim Livewire is a character, together with his friend, Truscot, in 'Any Faculty Board' (see Appendix IV, pp. 484-85). He also appears, as Professor of English Literature at Redbrick University in 'A Redbrick Tea-party', and in *Redbrick and these Vital Days* (76). In 'A Redbrick Tea-party' Livewire expresses some of Peers' favourite opinions — on, for instance, research, and the proper use of vacation-time.

on him the father invited me to dine in order to consult me about a rather unusual combination of options which Jim was proposing to take for his degree. I formed the idea that he had been badly advised by his tutor and offered to take the matter up with him and see if the proposal could be altered. A series of three-cornered discussions settled it to everyone's satisfaction and the quite disproportionate gratitude of father and son led to our forming a close friendship.

From Cranstead,[49] where he often visited me when the Camford vacation overlapped ours, I watched his brilliant career — an outstanding First Class, three University prizes, and a fellowship, awarded immediately upon graduation, at one of the smaller colleges.[50] This fellowship he was still holding in 1914, when, at the age of twenty-six, he volunteered for the Army: after four years in France he had risen from Second Lieutenant to Colonel. On demobilization, he obtained a university lectureship of precisely the same type as I had held at Oxbridge,[51] together with a Fellowship at Trinity. There he settled down to the work which he had long since mapped out as his own: a study of certain Elizabethan dramatists.[52] In his pre-war days, he had got a considerable distance with an edition of Massinger; now, though only thirty-six, he had completed this and was hard at work on Dekker.[53] It was generally believed that, if he cared to wait ten years for it, he would succeed to the English Literature Chair at Camford, unless he preferred a research fellowship which would lighten a burden of teaching so heavy that most men who bore it would consider themselves

---

49 Cranstead School, it will be remembered, is, in the Truscot narrative, equivalent to Felsted School in the Peers autobiography.

50 Peers has written in the margin here: 'What size is Trinity?'.

51 Since Truscot and Livewire are both characterized projections of Professor E. Allison Peers, it does not seem surprising that each obtained 'precisely the same type' of university lectureship.

52 Peers himself had undertaken 'a study of certain Elizabethan dramatists' for an essay which brought him the Harness Prize. Among the dramatists he had studied were both Massinger and Dekker. See '(E.A.P.) *Auto*', ch. 3, p. 91, and notes 22 and 23.

53 Editions of the plays (or of some of the plays) of Philip Massinger (1583-1640) were produced by A. Symons and by Lucius A. Sherman before the First World War. Editions of the collected dramatic and non-dramatic works of Thomas Dekker (?1570-1632) were published in the late nineteenth century and again in the mid-twentieth century.

348  REDBRICK UNIVERSITY REVISITED

absolved from doing any research at all.

But if Upright was Upright, so, in a very different sense, Livewire was Livewire,[54] and I cannot say that I was in the least surprised when he wrote to tell me of his aspiration to succeed Slocombe. An immense lover of hard work, and even of uphill work, he knew all about our Augean stables and was prepared to undertake the cleaning of them. He asked me what I thought of his chances: I replied that, on paper, they were excellent, and that, though then I knew the names of only two other candidates, I found it difficult to foresee any accident that would prevent his winning.

But, in writing so optimistically, I had not realized how much kick the S.A. had still left in it, nor the lengths to which its more unprincipled members would go. They had managed to get two of themselves — Inaccessible and Wormwood — elected to the Committee: the other Faculty members were Fanshawe, the recently elected Dean, Dusty, André, Crusty, a new man named Bletherley and myself. To these were added, of necessity, two members of Senate, nominated by the Faculty, whose duty was to see fair play, and two members of Council, chosen by Council, who were supposed to watch the financial aspect of the affair, but frequently did a great deal more. The Vice-Chancellor, who was an ex-*officio* member, though the Dean acted as Chairman, brought the number of the Committee to the unlucky thirteen.[55]

---

54  And, Peers invites us to think, 'if Fitzmaurice-Kelly was Fitzmaurice-Kelly, so, in a very different sense, Allison Peers was Allison Peers'.

55  The Faculty of Arts' Committee to report on the qualifications of the applicants for the Gilmour Chair of Spanish did indeed number thirteen in all and included the Vice-Chancellor, the Dean of the Faculty and two members of the Council (Mr Charles Booth and Miss Emma G. Holt); the 'two members of Senate' were not identified as such when the Faculty appointed the Committee. For the Committee's membership see 'A Chronology of the Filling of the Gilmour Chair of Spanish, 1919-22', Appendix I: entries of 28 May and 14 October 1919 (p. 413). 'Wormwood', as previously suggested, would appear to be modelled on Professor Alexander Mair, a member of the 'New Testament' group who *was* also a member of the Committee. André might be the Professor of French: L. A. Terracher (see '[E.A.P.] *Auto*', ch. 3, p. 109, note 96), or J. E. Eggli; or Dr Rébora, Senior Lecturer in Italian (see above, note 26). Bletherley is probably W. E. Collinson (see '[E.A.P.] *Auto*', ch. 6, p. 152, and note 7). The Dean of the

THE CHAIR OF ENGLISH LITERATURE    349

The first stages of the Committee's work were easy. [The] Twenty-nine applications [/applicants] were reduced [/thinned down] to five.⁵⁶ One of these, the holder of a Chair in Tasmania [/Canada],⁵⁷ was turned down because of the impossibility of interviewing him [before the summer vacation]. Another, an eminent Oxbridge don, was considered with some care but rejected without interview because of his age, which was fifty-

---

Faculty of Arts at the time (1916-20) was Mr W. Garmon Jones (a member of the 'New Testament'). Dusty has hitherto been identified as Professor Campagnac but the latter was not a member of the Committee (see above, 'B.T.', ch. III, pp. 298-99, note 99). So, in this instance, Dusty might be Professor R. C. Bosanquet. He was on the first Committee appointed to report on the Chair. Bosanquet was a member of the 'New Testament', but a minor figure, 'as far as politics were concerned' (see '[E.A.P.] *Auto*', ch. 5, p. 147). It is worth remembering that Dusty, as described by Truscot, was 'a Northerner, educated at Durham, with the faintest hint of a Northumbrian accent' ('B.T.', ch. III, p. 300), and that Bosanquet was, according to Collinson, a 'tall, reserved and balanced Northumbrian' (quoted p. 147, note 21). Moreover, Dusty, according to Truscot (ch. III, p. 298), was Professor of Latin, and Bosanquet was a classical archaeologist. Peers might have mixed a few characteristics of Bosanquet into the characterization of Campagnac, represented by the figure of Dusty. It will be remembered that Campagnac himself was formerly a member of the 'New Testament'. Crusty has been previously identified with D. A. Slater and linked also with W. E. Collinson ('B.T.', ch. III, pp. 298-99, and note 99), but, in this instance, he might be J. P. Postgate, Professor of Latin, 1909-20. We have suggested previously that Inaccessible — who elsewhere (p. 343) is stated to have succeeded Upright as chairman of the 'New Testament' group on the latter's retirement — represents Dr John Sampson (see 'B.T.', ch. III, p. 308, and note 121; and see '[E.A.P.] *Auto*', ch. 5, p. 144, and note 12). However Sampson was not a member of the committee. On the other hand, Professor R. H. Case, a known member of the 'New Testament' group (see '[E.A.P.] *Auto*', ch. 5, pp. 146-47, note 19), *was* a member of the Committee. At first glance Case does not appear to fit the role of Inaccessible. But it should be remembered that earlier in this same chapter Truscot has described how Anstruther (who is principally modelled on Robert Hope Case) once he was elected to the 'New Testament', 'changed his tactics' in the debates of Faculty, and, though not very convincingly, 'tried to imitate the Honest-and-Upright technique of Inaccessible' (see above, p. 344).

56 Twenty-three applicants for the Gilmour Chair are listed. The Committee decided initially to consider three of the applicants (Appendix I; see entries for 30 October and [*c*.November] 1919, p. 414).

57 Professor Milton Buchanan of the University of Toronto was later approached but informed the Dean of the Faculty of Arts that circumstances prevented him from leaving his present post (Appendix I; see entries for 24 & 26 November 1919 and 29 March and 10 May 1920, pp. 415, 419).

nine.[58] That left three for interview: Anstruther, Livewire and a professor from a University College in Yorkshire. Before the summonses were sent out, however, the Yorkshireman was elected to a Chair at a university in his own locality and retired from the contest.[59]

By this time it was the end of March and the interview was fixed for the beginning of May, immediately after the Easter vacation. The issue was at least a clear-cut one: two men of nearly the same age and each with experience of only one university: one from Camford and one from Redbrick; the one a teacher and a researcher, the other a teacher only; the one unknown, with no backing in the Committee but mine, the other, generally popular, and supported by a powerful organization.[60]

---

58 The oldest of the three selected applicants was Baldomero Sanín Cano, who, being born in 1861, was in his late fifties and who was ruled out through not being able to devote all his time to the Chair (see Appendix I; see entries for 9 Feb.—[?10] March 1920, pp. 417-19).

59 In reality, Sanín Cano, Madariaga and Peers were interviewed on 9 February 1920. By the time the new Selection Committee was advised by Dr Henry Thomas to reconsider Madariaga, the latter had accepted a post with the League of Nations (Appendix I; see entries for 2 & 4 May 1922, pp. 424-25).

60 This was not the issue in reality, for Sanín Cano, besides being much older than Peers, was **not** the internal candidate. On the other hand, it is true that Sanín Cano's candidacy, thanks to the influence of Fitzmaurice-Kelly, was internally 'supported by a powerful organization'.

As is clearly revealed in the 'Redbrick' books, Peers had a particular interest in analysing 'The Battle of the Ancients and the Moderns' (*cf. Redbrick University*, ch. 1). A Cambridge man himself, he had known, even shared, Oxbridge attitudes towards the Modern Institutions. As a Cambridge man teaching in a provincial university, he had observed, even suffered from, the prejudices and resentment felt against the Ancient Seats of Learning by the graduates and university teachers of the newer universities. Peers refers to 'Redbrick' prejudices against other universities (Camford and Oxbridge?) in *Redbrick University* (see p. 62). It is not surprising, in his fictionalized account of the conflict over the Gilmour Chair, that Peers should have introduced, as rival to the Camfordian Livewire for the professorship vacated by Slocombe, the thoroughly Redbrickian candidate, Anstruther. Neither is it surprising that, though he is good at teaching and in administration, Anstruther is shown to have, in contrast to the productive and talented Livewire, almost a non-existent record of research. Through portraying the inferiority of Anstruther as a scholar, on the one hand, and the achievements of Jim Livewire as a scholar, on the other, Peers is able to insist repeatedly — as he insists equally in the

One of the difficulties about getting things done in the university world is that, at the end of every eight or ten weeks, life comes to a standstill during that phenomenon known as vacation. But to some extent, even in vacation, life sometimes moves on.

Just after Easter, I was spending a fortnight in the British Museum Reading Room when one afternoon I ran into Professor Bletherley.[61] Now, as a rule, it is etiquette among readers in the Museum not to show more than the faintest sign of recognition when they meet: silence is so important, and one is so loath to spend longer in that well-known atmosphere than one need, that anything like prolonged conversation is frowned upon [rather] as though it were obscene. But seeing Bletherley consulting the catalogue at the central desk, I broke the conventions to the extent of asking him to dine with me. He had been appointed, in the previous year, as Professor of Education, which meant that his work lay, not in the Arts Building, but in the Training College over the way.[62] I had had very little to do with him, therefore, and the English Literature Committee was the first we had been on together, so the opportunity of seeing a little more of him was not one to be lost.

I had already decided he was a curious fellow and nobody knew quite what to make of him. Thirty-three years of age (one always knows the ages of one's recently appointed colleagues from the Senate reports), he was a graduate in English (whence his presence on the Committee) of [the University of] London, and had been a schoolmaster from his graduation till his appointment as lecturer at a Training College two years before his coming to us. He had a boyish face, a queer, half-childish,

---

'Redbrick' books — that the primary function of universities (ancient or modern), and of university teachers (from Camford or Redbrick), is to conduct research for the advancement of learning.

61 We have identified Bletherley, Professor of Education, with W. E. Collinson. But he is apparently modelled also to some extent on David A. Slater, Professor of Latin, 1920-32. Peers shows some inclination to mix characteristics from Collinson and Slater, to form not only Bletherley, but also Crusty (see E.A.P [Auto], ch. 6, pp. 152 and 154, and notes 7 and 15; and cf. 'B.T.', ch. III, pp. 298-99, and note 99).

62 The University's Education Department was from 1921 housed at Nos. 20-22 Abercromby Square. In 1920 the Department took over direct responsibility for the work previously done by the University Training College, which was then closed.

half-vacant smile, and a clearly-marked vein of sentimentality which was always coming out at Faculty Board and Senate. Either [,I had decided,] he was totally devoid of judgment and could be worked upon by any tale of woe, or he fancied himself cast for the *rôle* of protector of the helpless student. For the last year, we had noticed, whenever some particularly preposterous application was made to the Board — some student asking to be excused a year's residence, to be admitted to a course for which he was not qualified [/manifestly unqualified] or to be allowed part of an examination in which he had failed — Bletherley would get up and plead for the 'poor fellow', painting his woes in such pathetic detail that we used to think he must have some inside information about him until we discovered that the circumstances he would describe were entirely imaginary. The cases he made out, however, were always remarkably convincing, and again and again he overcame the Board's better judgment and got his way.

Even at this time Bletherley was quite popular, and, in succeeding years he became still more so, for he was pleasant, hospitable, generous to a fault, completely devoid of guile and always anxious, when no principle was involved, to fall in with others' opinions.[63] For me he had the further attraction of being a good scholar;[64] [as a schoolmaster he had kept up his research under great difficulties] and, though his duties in the Education Department were both exacting and absorbing, he showed every intention of continuing the work on nineteenth-century poetic theory which he had begun for his London M.A.

The British Museum Reading Room, it will be recalled, yields up its dead, amid the clanging of metal book-rests by employees eager to escape, at precisely six o'clock in the

---

63 As a person, according to Kelly, Collinson was 'solid, dependable, benevolent' (*For the Advancement of Learning. The University of Liverpool 1881-1981*, 219). Peers speaks of him with admiration — as a man with a temperament very different from his own, as 'an influence for good in the very deepest sense wherever he goes' (see '[E.A.P.] *Auto*', ch. 6, p. 152). Slater was also admired by Allison Peers, for being 'the kindliest, gentlest person save when he had made up his mind to do something in face of opposition' ('[E.A.P.] *Auto*', ch. 6, p. 154).

64 *Cf.* Peers' comments on Collinson: 'he is a scholar to his finger-tips' ('[E.A.P.] *Auto*', ch. 6, p. 152); and on Slater: 'a rather tired though meticulous scholar ('[E.A.P.] *Auto*', ch. 6, p. 154).

evening.[65] The little restaurant round the corner, which every reader at the BM knows so well, starts to serve dinners at six-thirty. So, before we went in, Bletherley and I had time to stroll round the Bloomsbury squares and talk a deal of shop, and even then we found ourselves almost the first-comers.

But at the far table on the left hand side I was surprised to see another colleague, Professor Wormwood, in earnest conversation with a man whom for the moment I could not place, and then hesitatingly recognized as Josiah Rippon,[66] a Senior Fellow of St Anthony's, Camford. I gravitated towards them, almost unthinkingly, and, raising my eyes enquiringly, was met with a response none too cordial but quite definitely affirmative. So we sat down at the table and made up the four.

Rippon was apparently in the middle of some narrative, for, after a pause as we took our seats, he looked at Wormwood, who nodded and said:

'Oh, yes, I think so. Truscot and Bletherley are both comparative newcomers, but they're on the Committee and they really ought to know'.

'Well, then, Wormwood, as I was saying', went on Rippon, when we had duly been introduced to him, 'you'd find him a very unpleasant colleague. Quite apart from his uncertain temper, he's a conceited young pup. High rank in the army and

---

65 Peers writes in the margin, in pencil, a reminder to 'enlarge'.

66 Dr Josiah Rippon corresponds to the 'Mr X' whom Professor Slater found in conversation with Professor Mair in a hotel near the British Museum (see '[E.A.P.] *Auto*', ch. 6, p. 157). The evidence of the surviving correspondence, suggests that 'Mr X' was Dr (later Sir) Henry Thomas — see the entries for 16-24 June 1920, Appendix I, p. 419. A Hispanist but not a university teacher, Thomas was a senior member of staff at the British Museum's Department of Printed Books (see pp. 156-57, note 21). Peers had a low opinion of Thomas, both as a scholar and as a human being. Dickens was one of Peers' favourite writers, and we have found in Drabtown reminiscences of Coketown in Dickens' *Hard Times* (see above, 'B.T.', ch. III, p. 264, note 11). When he gave Henry Thomas the pseudonym of 'Josiah Rippon', Peers might have had in mind the name of one of the least attractive characters in *Hard Times*: Josiah Bounderby, the ruthless manufacturer and self-made man, memorable for his false displays of humility and his lack of compassion. One recalls that it was another principal character (Gradgrind) in Dickens' *Hard Times*, who declared: 'Facts alone are wanted in life'. As a bibliographer, Henry Thomas dealt mostly with facts; yet in his adverse comments on the work of Allison Peers he ignored concrete evidence of Peers' abilities.

all that sort of thing. Spoilt in his early twenties. Never recovered and never will'.[67]

'This is that fellow Livewire we're talking about', explained Wormwood. 'Rippon knows him well'.

'You're not from his college, Dr. Rippon?' I enquired, thinking hard as I spoke.

'No, but I'm a Fellow of his father's college', said Rippon, 'and I've seen a good deal of him. Besides, he's well known among the younger men at Camford — notorious, one might almost say'. And he chuckled disagreeably, as though some malicious reminiscence had just occurred to him.

At this moment the waitress came for our orders, and, as our dissimilar and complicated wants took some few minutes to convey to her, I did some more thinking and decided upon a line of action.

Rippon, I remembered perfectly now, had had a long-standing feud with Livewire's father. He was a disappointed man: between fifty and sixty, turned down for the Readership in Moral Philosophy at Camford [and, I fancied having heard, for some professorship elsewhere as well].[68] I hardly knew him by sight and I couldn't remember what the trouble with Jim's father had been about, but I distinctly recalled him telling me about it when I was staying with them one vacation.

So the S.A. were making good use of the vacation! Determined to push Anstruther into Slocombe's Chair, they were setting to work to undermine the candidature of his only rival. Wormwood had contacted Rippon, who was in his own line of business — or had Rippon made the first move? — and

---

67 In his comments about the three candidates who were interviewed for the Gilmour Chair, Fitzmaurice-Kelly wrote 'A. P. seems to be very "pushful". I see he applied to be appointed [as External Examiner] at London University in *both* French and Spanish. He was not, apparently, thought well of by either the French or the Spaniards... who were foaming at the mouth because of his assurance in coming forward...' (see Fitzmaurice-Kelly's letter to Mair, dated 14 February 1920, reproduced in Appendix I, p. 453).

68 The published biographical essays on Sir Henry Thomas do not suggest that he was a 'a disappointed man', but imply, rather, that he was absorbed in his work at the British Museum and satisfied with his career. Had Thomas been interested in the Gilmour Chair of Spanish in 1921-22, it appears likely that the post would have been offered to him. See entries for 21 and 28 November 1921, and for 24 and 25 February, 12 April and 2 and 4 May 1922, Appendix I, pp. 420-21, 423-25.

Wormwood was going to get a mass of adverse testimony to produce at the meeting in May. Strange that it had never occurred to him that I might also know Livewire! And yet [, I reflected,] it was not so strange, for everyone thought of me as an Oxbridge man since it was from Oxbridge that I came to Redbrick.

And then another thought struck me. Was this apparently casual meeting quite so casual after all? I hadn't seen Wormwood in the B.M., but he might very well have seen me. Could he even have overheard my invitation to Bletherley and seen an unexpected opportunity of increasing the size of Rippon's audience? His next remark, conventional though it was, answered one of my questions.

'You know, Truscot, I often wonder why you sit so far from the catalogue. You always arrive early and yet I saw you this morning almost at the far end of the row. I always think the second seat from the catalogue circle is the best. You're almost as near to it as you can be and yet you're a little way from the [main] line of traffic'.

'Oh', I replied lightly, 'I don't use the catalogue much during the day. I prefer to be near the book-stacks on the outer wall: I find them much more useful'.

But inwardly I was thinking:

'So that's the game. And they don't suspect I know him. Well, for once the Salvation Army will find itself outwitted'.

[So] When Rippon resumed his harangue, I set myself to draw him out, and I laughed inwardly at the reflection that Wormwood probably imagined I was lapping up the information in order to use it in favour of my old friend Anstruther and against this stranger.

'And a dreadful pusher',[69] he went on. 'Gets himself into everything. Got his lectureship by sheer push — and his father's influence, of course', he added, almost apologetically, as though that [influence] were the normal way of obtaining lectureships. 'They say, you know', he went on, and then stopped, 'However, that's scandal'.

'Well, what do they say?' asked Bletherley, who so far had said not a word.

---

69 One is reminded of Fitzmaurice-Kelly's word for Peers: 'pushful' (*cf.* note 67).

'Oh, they say he's got some Jewish blood,[70] you know', explained Rippon, 'but I don't believe that. Mere talk'.

It might be worth recording here that, whether he believed it or not, the story was so effectively repeated at Redbrick that eventually it came to Livewire's own ears, and, as long as ten years afterwards, he had to refute it publicly [/was having to refute it]. So much harm can malicious scandal do even in a community devoted to the pursuit of the noblest ideals.

'However', Rippon continued. 'The real point is that Livewire's a very poor scholar. Believe me, that Massinger of his[71] is very largely modelled on some work done by a group of people at Princeton. It's been mainly published in the form of articles in learned reviews, so it's very little known. But I have it on the authority of an American professor who was over here last summer'.

'Really?' I interpolated. 'Who was he? Thorndike? I remember hearing he was in England. And he's an Elizabethan specialist'.

'Ye-es, I think [/fancy] that was the name', replied Rippon, rather doubtfully.

'Oh, no, of course not', I exclaimed. 'How stupid of me! It's next summer that Thorndike's coming. I remember seeing it in

---

70   Peers comments on this same enduring rumour, and the malicious intentions of those who started it, in his straightforward autobiography (see '[E.A.P.] *Auto*', ch. 6, p. 162; and consult note 35). For further insight into Peers' indignant, but racially unprejudiced, reactions to this untruth, see below, p. 369, and note 101.

71   Livewire's specialist interests in Elizabethan drama were explained previously (*cf.* p. 347; and see note 52). In reality, the merits of Peers' publications were indeed questioned by Fitzmaurice-Kelly and Henry Thomas. In particular, both these Hispanists attacked Peers' *A Skeleton Spanish Grammar* (London: Blackie and Son, 1917). In his letter to Professor Mair, 14 February 1920, Fitzmaurice-Kelly declared: 'He has written a *Spanish Grammar* which we tried at King's. It had to be dropped as not up to the mark'. Henry Thomas, in his letter to the Dean of the Faculty, 2 May 1922, was also scathing in alluding to the 'grammar from which his [Peers'] reputation may in time recover; but the adoption of this particular book as a medium of instruction in Liverpool University is not calculated to hasten that end...' (see Appendix I, pp. 424, 453). It is also not unlikely that, in his conversation with Mair in London, Thomas insinuated, in his criticisms of Peers, that the youthful scholar's first literary-critical articles, on Romanticism etc., were excessively dependent upon the opinions and researches of other Hispanists.

the *Times*'.

'Well, I'm not sure of the name', confessed Rippon. 'I didn't see the man myself. But he told Gilkes, whom he was dining with at Trinity. By the way', he added suspiciously, 'aren't you a Trinity man?'

'I am', I replied. And I could see from Wormwood's expression that my guess about his believing me to be an Oxbridge man was [/had been] a correct one.

'Then you'll know him?' enquired Rippon. 'You must be much of an age'.

'Yes, I know him', I replied, simply. And said nothing further.

With unusual rapidity the subject was changed. Soon after Bletherley and I took our leave.

'This sounds a bit fishy', he said, when we got outside.

'Yes', I replied. 'Come back to my hotel and I'll tell you a thing or two'.

He came; and I told him about the Salvation Army; about Upright; and about the Trevor Chair.

'I wonder', hazarded Bletherley, stroking his chin as he spoke, 'if Upright's at the bottom of all this. He lives near Camford, doesn't he? Depend upon it, it was he who put Rippon into touch with Wormwood'.[72]

'It might be', I replied.

'It certainly might', agreed Bletherly, with emphasis. ' "Old soldiers never die", you know, and from all you say Upright seems to have been the Salvation Army's Brigadier-General!'

---

72 Fitzmaurice-Kelly evidently did put Mair, and through him the Faculty Committee of which Mair was a member, in touch with Thomas. Peers refers to Fitzmaurice-Kelly, Mair and Thomas in collusion, as 'a new version of the eternal triangle' (see [E.A.P.] Auto, ch. 6, p. 157; see also, in 'A Chronology of the Filling of the Gilmour Chair of Spanish, University of Liverpool, 1919-22', the entries of 16 and 21 June 1920, and of 28 November 1921, Appendix I, pp. 419, 421).

358  REDBRICK UNIVERSITY REVISITED

## IV

Ten days after the start of the Summer Term, the English Literature Committee gathered once more round the table in the Dean's consulting-room, ready to interview the two candidates who were waiting, in separate rooms, outside.[73]

An academic enough group, I thought, as I looked round at them while the Dean was marking them off on the attendance list.[74] Who, gazing on those placid, almost cow-like, countenances, would ever have supposed that they included the principals in the fiercest conflict in Redbrick history? For, on that evening in London, Bletherley and I had sat up late discussing how the machinations of the Salvation Army could best be circumvented — Bletherley, with his passion — it was nothing less — for fair play and I, with my determination to destroy the power of this miserable clique and my conviction that Livewire was the best man for our job. Our principal decision had been to take Dusty[75] into our confidence, for he, too, loathed the Salvation Army, and besides having more influence than either of us, was a very much better tactician. Hearing the story of our encounter with Wormwood and Rippon, he emphatically endorsed Bletherley's view that Upright was at the bottom of it. For, he told us, there had been other cases in which a member of the S.A., after his retirement, had remained in close communication with it and continued his intriguing, as opportunity offered, from his new home in Oxbridge or London.[76] There had been one case, in fact, where the Chair of

---

73  In reality the Faculty Committee met in the Dean's room on 9 February 1920 to interview the three candidates (see Appendix I, p. 417).

74  The only attendance list to survive is that of the reconstituted Committee, which met from October 1921 until May 1922.

75  Dusty is clearly, in this context, Professor Campagnac.

76  One of the former members of the 'New Testament' who remained, after retirement, in closest contact with the group was Professor J. M. Mackay. The latter (who retired in 1914), being a particular friend of Fitzmaurice-Kelly, wrote a letter in support of Fitzmaurice-Kelly's protegé, Sanín Cano (see, in 'A Chronology of the Filling of the Gilmour Chair', entry for 26 January 1920, Appendix I, p. 416). P. G. H. Boswell (appointed Professor of Geology in 1917), who was a member of the University Club, mentions that he got to know and like Mackay 'on his occasional return visits to Liverpool' (unpublished autobiography, at p. 135). See also Peers'

an S.A. man had remained unfilled, and the man had carried on a campaign in Drabtown itself to secure the election of one of his own pupils: he had actually postponed moving to a house he had bought on the South coast until he had brought the matter to a successful conclusion.

So we discussed tactics with Dusty, and decided to tell no one but Crusty, whose vote we could then count upon, though he would be of little use as a fighter, and at the meeting to continue the line which I had taken in London — hold our hand entirely, and, in fact, encourage the enemy until we judged him to have done his worst, and then make a concerted attack on him which we hoped would carry the bulk of the Committee with us. If we could get a large majority for Livewire — say ten to three — there was little fear that it would be reversed by the Faculty Board, for, of the five members of the S.A., one was a candidate, and would not be present, two would have done their worst at the Committee and it was unlikely that the other two could produce any arguments to which we did not already know the answer.

My great fear was that Wormwood had realized in London that I was pro-Livewire and rout out some other evidence which I could not refute without notice. One could, of course, always ask for an adjournment so that it might be investigated, but adjournments were never popular with the four Senate and Council members, who naturally took much less interest in the election than the Arts people did, and it would never do to antagonize four members out of a Committee of thirteen. However, I need not have troubled. Whatever he may have suspected, Wormwood did nothing about it. The truth is that all his strength lay in argument: as a strategist he was worse than useless.

When the brief preliminaries of the interview meeting were completed, then, and the Dean's secretary went to call in Anstruther, whom we were to see first, the strength of the parties was as follows. For Livewire: four. For Anstruther: two. Uncertain: seven. At least the position was promising.

The interviews were exceptionally long — the longest of

---

comments on Mackay, founder of the 'New Testament', in '(E.A.P.) *Auto*', ch. 5, pp. 142-43. For a poetic portrait of Mackay, see Oliver Elton's poem, 'Kaine Diatheke', reproduced in Appendix II, pp. 460-65.

their kind that I can ever remember.[77] Both candidates had a good deal to say, and, as English Literature was a subject which even the Council representatives thought they knew something about, the Committee contrived to ask a good many more questions than it would had it been interviewing for the Chair of Greek or of Egyptology.[78]

Anstruther had evidently decided that his trump card was his familiarity with the Department. He had evidently thought a good deal about what he was going to say, and I was amused at the skill with which he hinted that Slocombe had neglected the Department, and that, but for himself, it would have collapsed altogether, without saying anything that could be construed as open criticism of his retiring chief. With equal skill he steered away from the dangerous subject of research, saying, when the question was put to him, that his particular interests lay in this and that epoch or author, but going on to suggest that for years he had been nobly sacrificing these interests for the sake of Redbrick. Once he got the Department into proper shape, was the assumption, he would at last have time to do some writing. How often have I heard that said of or by candidates for Chairs since that time, and how seldom has the prediction been fulfilled![79]

Pleasant, unassuming and completely at home with people whom he had the great advantage of knowing, Strutty made an excellent impression. Some time had to be spent, before Livewire was called, in explaining to the Senate and Council members the present position of the Department. So highly departmentalized is Redbrick, and so little do the Faculties mix,

---

77 In fact, the interviews were timed to last not more than thirty minutes each (see, in 'A Chronology of the Filling of the Gilmour Chair', the entry for 9 February 1920, Appendix I, p. 417); but it is more than likely, given the circumstances, that the candidates were each interviewed for a longer period than had been intended.

78 Peers' second example is an understandable choice, given that Liverpool University had one of the few Chairs of Egyptology in the country. The Brunner Chair of Egyptology was vacant at the same time as the Gilmour Chair. The person appointed to the Brunner Chair, from 1920, was Thomas Eric Peet (see '[E.A.P.] *Auto*', ch. 6, p. 153, and note 10).

79 The author displays the same critical attitude in the 'Redbrick' books, towards non-researchers and their excuses for their lack, or shortage, of publications. One recalls how, in *Redbrick and these Vital Days*, Truscot urges all his fellow academics, to develop a 'conscience about research' (101).

that no Science department knows anything about the condition of any Arts department, or vice versa.[80] The two Senate nominees, if I remember rightly, were an elderly pharmacologist and an ex-Dean of the Faculty of Engineering.[81] The Council men were the Treasurer — a high-up in the insurance[82] world — and a director of the firm already alluded to which manufactured braces.[83] The braces-man, who had never been to a university, wasted a lot of valuable time through being unable

---

80 This observation is probably accurate. On the other hand, 'although there were caucuses on the University Senate, apparently persisting from early times, and almost continuous friendly feuds between the various Faculties (undoubtedly intensified by the scramble for funds), the grouping never seemed to have had a political basis' (P. G. H. Boswell, unpublished autobiography, at p. 140). It should be noted that, in the Senate, Professor Loaf, the Zoologist, intervenes in the discussions over the Chair of English Literature, in the cause of justice (see below, pp. 382, 384).

81 In fact, in the case of both Selection Committees for the Gilmour Chair, all the members who were members of the Senate (besides the Vice-Chancellor) were drawn from the Faculty of Arts.

82 Peers has indicated, in pencil, his intention to 'alter' the profession of this Council member.

83 The founder of the Trevor Chair of Poetry — now occupied by Bruce Truscot — was a Camford man who 'made braces' and was elected to the Council. Trevor's son, also a Camford man, also made braces (see above, ch. III, pp. 315-16). The member of Council here, who, unlike the Trevors, 'had never been to a university', was evidently a director of their firm.

On the first Selection Committee for the Gilmour Chair of Spanish (1919-20), the two University Council representatives were Mr Charles Booth (1868-1938) and Miss Emma G. Holt (1862-1944). Educated at Malvern College and at University College, Oxford, Charles Booth was a Director of the Midland Railway, 1898-1923 (Chairman 1919-22), and Chairman of the Booth Steamship Co. Ltd., etc. Miss Holt was the daughter of George Holt, a founder of the shipping firm of Lamport and Holt of Liverpool, and a local benefactress (particularly of the University).

On the second Selection Committee for the chair (1921-22), the two Council representatives were Mr (later Sir) Henry Wade Deacon (1852-1932) and Mr J. Arthur Smith (1872-1931). Mr Wade Deacon was the son of a partner in the firm of Messrs Gaskell, Deacon & Co., alkali manufacturers of Widnes. Educated privately and at King's College London, he entered his father's firm but, later, retired from the business and engaged in public and philanthropic works. He served as the University's President of Council (1924-30) and Pro-Chancellor (1930-32). Mr Smith, a Liverpool cotton broker, was educated at Loretto School and at Trinity College, Oxford; his firm closed in 1916 and thereafter he served as a director of numerous companies; he was a member of the University's Finance Committee, and Vice-President of the University Council 1930-31.

to understand how a man could be paid Slocombe's salary to do a certain job and yet spend all his time but a few hours weekly making a comparatively large income in other ways. When it was made clear to him, he was tactless enough to say it was immoral[84] and it took all the Chairman's tact to suppress an incipient harangue on what would happen if a chap like that were in *his* business and to lead him back to the matter in hand.

All this rambling discussion did Anstruther a lot of good, since it concentrated attention on teaching and organization, in which he was strong, and ignored the question of research altogether. Before we saw Livewire, however, I managed to say a good deal about Anstruther's weakness in research, and to Wormwood's repeated attempts to sidetrack this issue I opposed nothing less than the reputation of Upright, which he could not, nor would, gainsay. What the English Literature Department wanted was a man who, besides doing his job well within these walls, as either of the two would, might be relied upon to reach a far wider circle through his writings. There were no grounds, I submitted, for supposing that Anstruther would do any writing at all. His M.A. thesis had been consigned to oblivion; such reviews as he had published were superficial; all his testimonials stressed his organizing and teaching ability and said ominously little of his scholarship; not one of the referees to whom we had written on the subject had a good word to say of him [/that].

'No', remarked the Dean, obligingly, at this point, and so apposite was the observation that I was deluded into believing him to be on our side. 'I might remind the Committee of the testimony sent us by the Professor of English at Durham. "As to Mr Anstruther's research", he asks, "I have never seen any. What is it and where can it be found?"'

Strange to say, neither Wormwood nor Inaccessible had much to say about this, and I concluded, rightly, that their attitude was going to be, not so much pro-Anstruther, as anti-Livewire. So I felt that my remarks, having gone unchallenged, would form an excellent preparation for Livewire's appearance, for he would at once give the impression of being a practical man and a scholar at the same time. But I was disappointed.

---

84 The author, as we know, shares the opinion of the outspoken 'bracesman' (see his comments on Professor Slocombe, ch. III, pp. 290-91).

It was with Livewire's appearance that our troubles really began. He will not mind my saying, as an old friend,[85] that he has always had rather a quick, clipped manner of speech, which, under the strain of nervousness, or any other emotion, is apt to convey an impression of impatience or pugnacity.[86] To-day he had been waiting alone in an ante-room for nearly an hour; it was the first important [academic] interview he had ever had; and he was aware that his rival was a local candidate who would have strong backing.

Then, again, nearly all the questions he was asked turned upon practical issues. Had he had experience of a modern university? No, he had not. Had he never even visited one to lecture or examined in one? No. How would he propose to remedy the unfortunate state into which the Department had fallen? Well, as he didn't know it was in an unfortunate state, it was difficult to answer that question straight away. And so on.

Once or twice the discussion grew slightly warm and several questions were flung at him at once. His quick, eager replies, I felt, were doing him no good, but only intensifying the undercurrent of feeling against him. Worse still, the issue I had dreaded — the ancient university *versus* the modern[87] — was coming forward. Counting heads rapidly, I decided that if the voting was going to be on that issue, we were unlikely to get more than five out of the thirteen. So, with a meaning look at Bletherley, I turned the conversation into a safer channel. First I alluded to Livewire's achievements as an undergraduate and asked him to amplify what I had said of them. Then, speaking slowly and quietly so as to change the tone of the discussion, I drew him out on his Elizabethan studies. Bletherley joined me

---

85 A typically humorous reminder from author to reader of the identity in real life of Jim Livewire, candidate for the Chair of English Literature at Redbrick University.

86 Peers, a self-perceptive man, is clearly aware that he did not do himself justice at the interview. People who knew him well are agreed that he has aptly described how his manner of speech — on first acquaintance, or when he was 'under the strain of nervousness' — might have given others a false impression of his mood or character. *Cf.* above pp. 353-55 and notes 67, 69. On Peers' individual manner and mannerisms, see also Introduction, p. 4. According to Collinson, Peers made a diffident impression on the Committee (see, in 'A Chronology of the Filling of the Gilmour Chair', the entry for 9 February 1920, Appendix I, p. 417).

87 *Cf.* above p. 350, and see note 60.

here, and we got some information about his Massinger which I knew would be valuable in the subsequent pitched battle; about his Dekker,[88] which apparently was farther advanced than I had supposed; and about his relations with certain well-known scholars, some of whom had written about him to us privately in the highest terms.[89] By the time the position was restored, however, the meeting had gone on for two hours. At least, I had played at time. The few remaining questions were quite perfunctory. When at length Livewire withdrew, it was five minutes to five.

It was clear to me that no decision would be reached at that meeting. The S.A. had hardly begun. But the proposal for an adjournment, I was determined, should not come from our side, and it was certain not to come from Senate or Council. Inaccessible or Wormwood must be manoeuvred into suggesting it, and I took a step which proved more successful than I could have hoped.

'It seems to me', I said, briskly, when the door had hardly closed upon this candidate, 'that this man is quite an outstanding scholar. So before we go any farther I want the Committee to survey the whole range of his scholarship'.

There was an awkward pause, during which the University clock was good enough to render the Westminster chimes, and then, slowly and deliberately, to strike five.[90] Two and a half hours! Would anyone bite...?[91]

---

88 *Cf.* above p. 347, and note 52. In *Redbrick and these Vital Days*, Professor Livewire, of the Department of English Literature at Redbrick University is said to be working on his forthcoming edition of Dekker — which explains his initial reluctance to address meetings, in various parts of the country, on behalf of the English Association (76).

89 For the opinions of 'certain well-known scholars' about Allison Peers and his research, see the testimonials and references reproduced in Appendix I, especially pp. 439-48.

90 The chimes of the clock in the Victoria Building's clock tower are indeed the same as those at Westminster (and at St Mary's, Cambridge) (Reginald Bushell, 'The New Clock and Bells at University College', *University College Magazine*, New Issue, I [December 1892], no. 5, 67-68). The same clock strikes several times during 'Any Faculty Board' meeting, as described by Bruce Truscot (see Appendix IV, pp. 488, 490, 492-93).

91 The author here describes, no doubt with conscious irony, his use, for a worthy cause, of the same subtle tactics of manipulated delay and persuasive psychology which his adversaries, the members of the 'New

Fortunately someone did. The Vice-Chancellor. For all that time he had been sitting at the Dean's right-hand, an insignificant little figure, looking meditatively at the candidates, saying almost nothing and thinking, no doubt, the more. Now he raised his head.

'Might we postpone this till next time?' he asked, rather plaintively. 'I've got a meeting in the town at half-past five. Could we meet again, say, at half-past two next Monday?'

With no great enthusiasm we nodded assent, the braces-merchant groaning heavily.

'I don't know how you get anything done at all in this place', he exclaimed. 'Now, in *my* business...!'

## V

The next meeting, as both sides knew, would be the pitched battle. Four-two, was the [close-of-play] score [to date]: who would get the remaining seven? But I realized — and Dusty realized even more clearly — that there was more at stake than the identity of Slocombe's successor: if, with Upright gone, the S.A. were defeated again, and one of its own members turned down for a Chair, its influence and prestige would be over.

So, as the discussion warmed up, I forgot that I had known Livewire for seventeen years; I almost forgot that I had ever known him at all. For me, as for Dusty and Bletherley,[92] this was a struggle for fair play against intrigue; for genuine democracy against a hidden oligarchy; for the discrediting of slander and scandal.

As I had expected, the limelight was on Livewire all the time. The question at issue was whether or no he was the man for Slocombe's Chair. If he were not, it was tacitly agreed that Anstruther was the second best [/would do (there were no

---

Testament', are accustomed to employ to achieve their less scrupulous purposes at committees of the Faculty (see above, pp. 319-23, 340-42). *Cf.* the similar methods utilized by Truscot and his colleagues in 'Any Faculty Board' (see Appendix IV).

92 Here, and in several other passages, Peers writes 'Bretherley', having forgotten, perhaps, the exact form of surname which he had decided upon. We have regularized the word to spell Bletherley in every case.

others)]. To put the question in another way, it was for Livewire's supporters to show cause why this stranger from Camford should be preferred to the man of Redbrick. I was determined that it should be well and truly shown.

The S.A. went in first, Wormwood and Inaccessible (as Anstruther would have said)[93] batting from opposite ends and giving every indication of remaining together for a considerable time. Inaccessible led off cautiously, scoring a few singles as he dilated upon Slocombe's well-known preoccupation with outside interests; the importance of English Literature as a 'key Department', the necessity for some years of spade-work before the Department could be satisfactory; the value of continuity and the man on the spot. Then he began to hit out. Who was the other candidate? A Camford man of thirty-six who confessed that [except for the War] he had never been outside Camford. He knew nothing of the Redbrick type of student; nothing of our system of government; nothing of our departmental organisation. Again, he would be a difficult man to get on with. They had seen him and heard him themselves: a combative, intolerant person, who would certainly prove difficult and quite possibly turn out a crank.[94] He, Inaccessible, had information from Camford which bore out that view. No doubt he was a good scholar, but....

At this point the two crossed over and the bowling fell to Wormwood, who started to lay about him with some ferocity. *Was* he a good scholar? He, Wormwood, had a letter from their old colleague, Professor Upright, about that...[95]

(Bletherley and I exchanged significant glances.)

He would not read the whole letter but merely give some extracts and then lay it on the table. The views of Professor Upright ought surely to weigh heavily with the Committee: he was a Camford man himself, living near Camford now and in touch with Camford opinion. There could be no more valuable

---

93 A humorous reminder of Anstruther's 'schoolmasterly' interests and (in Truscot's view) limited intellect (*cf.* above, ch. III, pp. 296-97; and note 96).

94 More evidence, in this sentence, of Peers' unusually keen abilities ('the giftie', as Robert Burns calls it [in 'To a Louse']) to see himself as some among his colleagues were disposed to see him.

95 Professor Fitzmaurice-Kelly wrote to Professor Mair (14 February 1920) dismissing Peers as a candidate (for this letter see Appendix I, p. 453).

testimony than their old friend Upright's...[96]

(That one certainly went to the boundary — and I had an uncomfortable feeling that it had managed to hit me on the way.)[97]

Now, pursued Wormwood, he would come to that famous Massinger. He didn't want to say anything uncharitable, but it was common knowledge among specialists in the period that a great deal of that work was not original.

(The battle was joined now, with a vengeance. I waited for a moment, anxious for Dusty to take up the challenge, for he would fence more skilfully than I. But, to my surprise, it was Bletherley who broke in — a Bletherley I had neither seen nor heard before, the vapid smile, the inane expression gone,[98] and in his voice a note of resolution, of indignation.)

'As we're not specialists here', he said, 'will Professor Wormwood tell us some more about this. After all, he's less of a specialist than either Truscot or I'.

'Well', replied Wormwood, with the air of one anxious to say as little as possible — as he certainly must have been, 'The fact is that a considerable proportion of the material in Livewire's Massinger has been lifted from America'.

'Lifted from America!' exclaimed Bletherley, with all the incredulity that he could put into his voice. 'What a preposterous suggestion! Do you mean to say that he could do that without the knowledge of any of the specialists who have written to us in his favour?'

---

96 There had been a motion (proposed by members of the 'New Testament'?) to appoint Fitzmaurice-Kelly officially to the Committee, which was not accepted. But it was agreed to consult him about the candidates (see, in 'A Chronology of the Filling of the Gilmour Chair', the entry for 28 May 1919, Appendix I, p. 413). The influence exerted by Fitzmaurice-Kelly, with his personal prejudices and unprofessional resentments, upon the opinions of the Committee concerned to fill the vacancy created by his departure, clearly demonstrates how much more just and prudent is the present-day practice in universities wholly to exclude the previous holder of a Chair from assisting in the selection of a successor.

97 Truscot recollects that Upright had done his best (that is to say his worst) to prevent the appointment of Truscot as his successor to the Trevor Professorship of Poetry.

98 *Cf.* Truscot's description, above, of Bletherley, with his 'queer, half-childish, half-vacant smile' (pp. 351-52) (*cf.* also, 'B.T.', ch. III, pp. 298-99, note 99).

'It was largely unpublished work', explained Wormwood, 'or work that had appeared only in learned reviews. That's how it's escaped people's notice'.

'It hasn't apparently escaped yours', returned Bletherley. 'Pray how did you come to hear of it? Who is the person that vouches for its accuracy?'

'An American professor who was over here last summer'.

'What was his name?' I put in, suddenly.

'I'm afraid I don't remember that', replied Wormwood, 'but I could find out'.

'Oh, he didn't tell you himself, then?' enquired Bletherley.

'No, he told a man named Gilkes, a Fellow of Trinity.[99] He gave him the fullest information, I can assure you'.

'Do you know Gilkes, then?' I asked, with apparent casualness. 'He was at Trinity with me; I didn't know he was a friend of yours'.

'No, I can't say I do', answered Wormwood, now growing manifestly uncomfortable.

'Oh', put in Bletherley, 'so you didn't even get it at second hand! Whom did Gilkes tell, may I ask?'

There was no answer, and after a moment's silence, Dusty took a hand.

'Professor Wormwood has made a serious accusation against a candidate for this post', he said. 'We have surely a right to know the source of that information. Will you ask him to divulge it, sir?'

'I think you'd better, you know', said the Dean, mildly.

'Well', replied Wormwood, 'it doesn't seem very important to me, but it was a Camford don, a Fellow of St Anthony's, named Rippon'.

'A specialist in Elizabethan literature?' enquired Bletherley, caustically.

'No', I said, 'a philosopher — like Wormwood'.

There was a general laugh at that, which relieved the growing tension. Then Bletherley, seeing his opportunity, took a deep breath and began.

'This story', he said, 'was repeated to Truscot and me in the

---

[99] Maurice Gilkes was the man who was awarded, probably because of support from Upright, the fellowship at Trinity which Truscot had hoped for (see above, 'B.T.', ch. I, p. 213; and see also ch. III, p. 280, note 51).

vacation by Professor Wormwood, who got it from Rippon, who apparently got it from Gilkes, who in turn seems to have got it from some unknown American professor, whose name I have been unable to trace. In fact', he continued, 'we don't even know that the American professor told the story from his own knowledge; he may himself have got it at third or fourth hand across the Atlantic'.

'We could find out pretty quickly through Gilkes', suggested the Vice-Chancellor. 'The accusation is a very serious one and it ought to be investigated'.

'I have already investigated it, sir', answered Bletherley, quietly.

At that unexpected statement both Wormwood and Inaccessible looked up quickly. The atmosphere of the Committee grew tense again.

'But before I tell the Committee the results of my investigations, I should like to describe how the original information came to me. At a chance meeting in London' — 'at least', he corrected himself, 'I took it to be a chance meeting' —[100] 'Professor Wormwood made a deliberate attempt to prejudice Professor Truscot and myself against this candidate. He first of all attacked his character, said he was conceited, quick-tempered, and generally unpleasant as a colleague. He told us he had gained his fellowship though undue influence. He then went on — '

'It was a private and confidential conversation', alleged Wormwood, 'and as such was privileged'.

'Privileged my foot!' exclaimed Dusty, impatiently. 'It sounds to me extraordinarily like slander'.

'He went on', pursued Bletherley, 'to repeat a story that Livewire was a Jew — which is neither here nor there, but the remark was clearly intended to create prejudice against him.[101] He then launched this ridiculous tale, which I couldn't have exploded but for one detail which gave me the key to the whole situation'.

---

100 Cf. above, pp. 353-57.

101 With this observation Peers clearly dissociates himself from the racially prejudiced attitudes of certain academics at Redbrick who would have considered his Jewish blood (had he actually had any) good reason for opposing his election to the Gilmour Chair.

'What was that?' asked the Dean, as Bletherley paused, presumably for effect. Wormwood, who had been growing glummer and glummer, began to drum his fingers on the table with impatience.[102]

'Why, he told us that the group of American scholars whose work Livewire is alleged to have lifted was from Princeton. Now, I have a close friend — an Englishman — teaching in the English Literature Department at Princeton. His name's Harkness. He was in my year at the University. So I wrote him a long letter, telling him the whole story — and some related stories', he added, glancing across at Wormwood, who had now buried his head in his hands in an attitude of deep dejection.[103] 'I asked him to investigate the whole thing as quickly as possible and cable me a night-letter in reply. I received the reply on the day after our last meeting. May I read it to the Committee, sir'.

'By all means', said the Dean. Wormwood remained with head in hands, motionless.

'It says this', announced Bletherley. 'WHOLE STORY MALICIOUS FABRICATION STOP BEFORE HIS MASSINGER PUBLISHED LIVEWIRE GENEROUSLY ALLOWED PRINCETON GROUP USE HIS MATERIAL IN INTERESTS OF SCHOLARSHIP STOP THIS GENEROSITY FULLY ACKNOWLEDGED IN ARTICLES MENTIONED STOP PRINCETON GROUP WISHES ADD CONSIDERS LIVEWIRE OUTSTANDING ELIZABETHAN SCHOLAR YOUR COUNTRY.[104] HARKNESS'.[105]

---

102 Wormwood's glum and impatient reactions here correspond closely to those of Mair, in reality — which reactions an eyewitness had narrated to Peers soon after the meeting: 'the unfortunate Mair... grew glummer and glummer... now burying his face in his hands, now drumming his fingers with impatience' (see '[E.A.P.] *Auto*', ch. 6, p. 162).

103 *Cf.*, regarding Mair's conduct in reality, note 102.

104 Peers indicates in pencil, in the margin, that the telegram should be in capitals ('Tel. in caps').

105 In reality, Peers had a testimonial from 'one of Harvard's best scholars in the field', Philip Churchman, who was, doubtless, the model for Harkness. In 1922 Peers and Churchman collaborated in an article about the influence of Walter Scott in Spain (see '[E.A.P.] *Auto*', ch. 6, p. 160, and notes 28 and 29). Additionally, from North America, Professor Milton Buchanan, at the University of Toronto, wrote in strong support of Peers' candidature at a later stage in the discussions (see, in 'A Chronology of the Filling of the Gilmour Chair', the entries for 6 & 12 December 1921, and 24 February 1922, Appendix I, pp. 421-23; and *cf.* ch. 6, pp. 160-61, note 30).

THE CHAIR OF ENGLISH LITERATURE   371

There was a long pause. Several members of the Committee straightened themselves, as though shaking off a disagreeable incident. The Dean looked at Wormwood, whose turn it seemed to be next.

'I must regret', he said, frigidly, 'that I have apparently been misinformed. I can only say that the information was given me in good faith and that I thought it my duty, however unpleasant, to bring it to the notice of the Committee. None the less, with your permission, sir, I will abstain from taking any further part in the Committee's deliberations'.

Saying which, he got up and left the room.

His departure did not entirely end the proceedings, for the discussion returned to the practical issue and the state of the Department, which both the Senate and one of the Council members thought could best be tackled by the man from Redbrick. These three, with Inaccessible and (to my surprise) the Dean voted for Anstruther. The rest of us, including the Vice-Chancellor, went for Livewire. The figures, seven to five, were duly reported to the Faculty Board at its next meeting.[106] There was an almost hundred-per-cent attendance,[107] for everybody wanted to see what the Salvation Army would do next.

## VI

In the interval, one fact had leaked out, which I had never even suspected: the fifth member of the S.A. was Fanshawe, the Dean.[108] He was seen mounting the turret staircase on the

---

106 In reality, the Committee met for the final time on 22 May 1922 and eventually voted by seven to two, with one abstention, to recommend Peers' appointment to a Senior Lectureship in Spanish for three years (see, in 'A Chronology of the Filling of the Gilmour Chair', the entry for 22 May 1922, Appendix I, pp. 425-26).

107 The meeting of the Faculty of Arts on 7 June 1922 was attended by thirty-one members. Excluding Sir James Frazer, whose resignation of his honorary chair of Social Anthropology was shortly afterwards accepted, there were, in all, forty-one members of the Faculty.

108 Peers would seem to have Garmon Jones in mind. The Dean at the time in question, however, was Professor Bruce Boswell who, unlike his predecessor, Garmon Jones, appears *not* to have been a 'New Testament' member and indeed to have supported Peers (see, in 'A Chronology of the Filling of the Gilmour Chair', the entry for 26 June 1922, Appendix I, pp.

afternoon following the Committee's last meeting, at which the clique evidently determined on new tactics so as to reverse the decision before it went up for confirmation to Senate. His subsequent intervention in the Faculty Board debate left no doubt as to his affiliation, and thoughtful people recalled that his election to the Deanship had been due in large measure to an earnest speech in his favour made by Inaccessible. Soon after the fall of the S.A. pressure of opinion led him to resign that office; it was generally felt that a Dean should in no circumstances belong to a party — least of all to such a party as that. Fanshawe, in passing, was succeeded by Dusty, who held the office for ten years and then became a kind of elder statesman, in which rôle he has been respected as no one else in the Faculty has that I can remember. He was undoubtedly the best Dean we ever had.[109]

These reminiscences[,] however, carry us far beyond the long- remembered meeting of the Faculty Board at the end of May 1924,[110] when, after an hour of dreary routine business,

---

427-28). Bruce Boswell was succeeded as Dean, in 1923, by G. C. Field, the philosopher. Associate Professor (as he had become) Garmon Jones returned to the Deanship in 1926, following Mr Field. G. C. Field, as noted in the Introduction, who was by then Professor Field, and at the University of Bristol, corresponded with Bruce Truscot about the 'Redbrick' books, unaware that their true author was his former colleague at Liverpool. One of Peers' letters of reply to Field is printed in Appendix III (pp. 479-80). Field's lengthy but extremely interesting letters to Peers can be consulted in the University Archives, Liverpool (ref. D.265).

[109] Dusty has been previously, and principally, identified with Professor E. T. Campagnac. Campagnac served as Dean of the Faculty of Arts 1911-13, and at no other time. Nevertheless, the qualities attributed to Dusty, and the position of respect which he attained as 'elder statesman', are in keeping with the character of Campagnac as portrayed by Peers. For Peers' assessment of Campagnac, see '(E.A.P.) *Auto*', ch. 6, pp. 150-51.

[110] The Faculty of Arts, in fact, met on 7 June 1922 to consider the Committee's report (see, in 'A Chronology of the Filling of the Gilmour Chair', the entry for that date, Appendix I, p. 426). The Chairman of the Faculty in Session 1921-22 was Professor Collinson; besides Collinson, as Chairman, and the Dean (Professor Bruce Boswell), there were twenty-nine members present including Professors Abercrombie, Campagnac, Case, Dewsnup, Droop, Eggli, Elton, Halliday, Mair, Mawer, Peet, Reilly, Slater, and Webster, Dr Veitch, Mr Garmon Jones, and **Mr Peers**; Dr Sampson, the Librarian, was not present. The presence of Peers, at this Faculty Board meeting, indicates that he did not show the 'natural reticence' which, according to Eagles (p. 374), kept Anstruther from attending the Faculty

THE CHAIR OF ENGLISH LITERATURE    373

the Dean, unable to move the Committee's report because he himself had opposed it, asked Dusty to do so in his place. He complied, and, without any attempt at elaboration, briefly set out the grounds on which a majority of the Committee had recommended Livewire. He could undoubtedly have gained much-needed votes by speaking at greater length and quoting from the various referees, but, as nine committee reports out of ten are endorsed by Faculty Board and Senate without more ado, he had asked me if I did not think it savoured of protesting too much to press the case more than was usual.

But if we supposed that the S.A. was going to take its defeat by the Committee lying down we were greatly mistaken. Wormwood, it is true, contributed not a word to the debate, but, no sooner had Dusty sat down than the murmur of conversation was cut short by the voice of Eagles.

The strong suit of Eagles was suavity.[111] He rose, he said, with real reluctance. He had not been on the Selection Committee. He knew nothing about English Literature. But he knew a good deal about the English Literature Department (*Mild laughter*). Well, all Departments had their ups and downs, and English Literature just now was in the downs and

---

Board at Redbrick University when the Chair of English Literature was discussed.

111 As previously stated (see 'B.T.', ch. III, p. 308, note 122), we do not know the identity of the colleague whom Peers had in mind when he created Eagles. One might be tempted (by the similar names, for instance) to think of J. E. Eggli (possibly also André [see p. 348, note 55]), who was appointed to the Chair of French in 1920. In the first autobiography, Peers describes Eggli (whose scholarship he admires) as 'a rather retiring Frenchman' ('[E.A.P.] *Auto*', ch. 6, p. 153), a description which does not seem to fit the suave figure of Eagles. On the other hand, Eggli, who was a member of the Selection Committee (though Eagles declares that he was not), wrote opposing Peers' appointment to the Chair (letter in French dated 27 June 1922). Also, there is evidence to suggest that Eggli had a personal dislike of Peers. Routledge, in his poem, *Senate in Laputa* (1934-35) alludes to: 'The Gallic fire of Eggli, curbed by notes, / And only igneous when the hated Peers / About some Bursar rashly interferes' (University Archives, Liverpool, D.498/6/1/1); and *cf.* above, Introduction, p. 6. We have no evidence that Eggli was a member of the 'New Testament'. But the 'New Testament' caucus had supported and secured Eggli's election to the Chair of French, despite opposition from Campagnac, Bruce Boswell and others (see below, note 124). So Eggli might have been one of the new men deceived (as Peers put it) by that group's 'inflexible façade' ('[E.A.P.] *Auto*', ch. 6, p. 153).

the problem was to get the best man to pull it together again. And, in his view, they had that man in their colleague whom a natural reticence had kept away that afternoon (*Here two or three members tapped with their knuckles on the table*). He understood there had been some division of opinion on the Committee on the question of scholarship. Well, nobody felt more strongly than he did about scholarship, but what the Department needed at this moment was an organizer and a teacher. What reason was there to suppose that this Camford man, without a grain of experience of a modern university, would do what their colleague Anstruther was already doing, and doing well?

It was a most skilful speech, simple, persuasive, pitched in just the right key, and wisely avoiding all mention of the Wormwood fiasco, since it was obvious that the other side, for the sake of peace, would avoid mentioning it too if that were possible. It killed the Livewire cause, for it represented the issue as one of efficiency pure and simple, and, despite our efforts, neither Bletherley nor myself were able to raise the debate to the level of scholarship at all.

We spoke next, he first, I second, but we were both speaking to a dead house. Yet Inaccessible, who followed us, aroused it immediately by a return to personalities. He had never — *never*, he repeated — addressed the Board with as much feeling as he did now. Here was a man — one of themselves: they all knew him — who quite manifestly was the proper successor for the colleague whom all deeply respected, but who, of late years, had perhaps — well, been losing touch a little, who had let things slide as one does at times when retirement draws near, and who, during this period, had been ably, indeed magnificently — yes, *magnificently* — supported by their colleague Anstruther. To elect Anstruther, a Redbrick man through and through, to the [Chair of][112] English Literature, was a piece of the most elementary justice. There had been talk about the other man's superior scholarship. Nonsense: their own man was as good a scholar as the man from Camford, and, once he had got his Department in order, he would show them so. But[,] of course, no one could do two things at once.

---

[112] The Editors have made this insertion, the need for which Peers had indicated, in pencil, through an insertion mark (∧).

THE CHAIR OF ENGLISH LITERATURE      375

Anstruther knew as well as anyone that, unless he published, he would stand small chance of promotion. And in spite of that, out of sheer devotion to Redbrick, he had filled his days with teaching and with administration, just because that work was there to be done and there was no one else to do it.[113] Nor had he ever shirked all the multifarious duties placed upon him by his interest in the students. They all knew that he was indispensable. Did not such devotion deserve — nay, *demand* — a reward? Let them register an act of simple justice and turn down this report.

Towards the end of this harangue, which was delivered with great feeling, and drew the first outright applause of the afternoon, those facing the door of the Board Room saw it gently open to admit the unassuming figure of the Vice-Chancellor. By the Redbrick Ordinances the Vice-Chancellor is an *ex-officio* member of every board and committee in the University,[114] though he seldom comes to Faculty Board meetings, and it must have been an unpleasant surprise to the S.A. when he next rose to speak. By this time he had made his influence felt everywhere, and as he never spoke unless he had something to say, no one was listened to with greater respect.[115]

He apologized for his late arrival — this was his third

---

[113] When such arguments are used to excuse an inadequate record of publications, Peers' reactions (as seen, for instance in the 'Redbrick' books) are scorn and disbelief (*cf.* above, pp. 345-46, and note 46; and, below, pp. 376-77, and note 119).

[114] The original Statutes of the University of Liverpool provided that the Vice-Chancellor was a member of the Court, Council, and the Senate and of each Faculty, of every Committee of the Court and of the Council and of every joint Committee of the Court and Council (*The University of Liverpool Calendar, 1903-04*). Under the Statutes of the University appended to the Supplemental Charter of 1961 (which revoked most of the Charter of 1903), the Vice-Chancellor is *ex officio* a member of the Court, the Council, and the Senate, and of all Committees of the Court, the Council, the Senate and the Boards of the Faculties and of all bar one of the Joint Committees of these bodies (*The University of Liverpool Calendar Session 1961-62*). The Vice-Chancellor did not, in fact, attend the meeting of the Faculty on 7 June 1922. Unlike his predecessor, Sir Alfred Dale, Dr Adami very rarely attended meetings of the Faculty. During his first two sessions as Vice-Chancellor (1927-1929) Hetherington often attended meetings of the Faculty of Arts (possibly to assert his position). Thereafter, his attendance was infrequent.

[115] *Cf.* Truscot's praise of the Vice-Chancellor of Redbrick, above, pp. 332-35.

meeting since luncheon — and for intervening in what at this stage was still a Faculty matter. But he was very anxious, he said, that the Committee's resolution should go to Senate with a much larger majority. And he wanted to put the position to the Board as it really was — not as, with all respect, Professor Inaccessible, in the goodness of his heart and the generosity of his nature, had made it out to be. Would they try to look at it afresh?

'First', he said, 'there is the question of efficiency. It is common ground that a teacher and an administrator is needed. The mistake some of us are making is to assume that Anstruther is superior here to Livewire. On the contrary, we have the strongest written eulogies of Livewire as a teacher, as a member of the English Faculty at Camford, as a Fellow of his college and as a valuable member of several University committees. Admirably as Anstruther has done his work, and no doubt will continue to do it under Livewire, I cannot agree that a Redbrick graduate is the proper person for this task. There has been too much inbreeding in the English Literature Department. The first step towards the cleansing of the Augean stables[116] is to open a window and let in the fresh air'.[117]

'Secondly, there is the question of scholarship. Now here there is simply no comparison. The written testimony of all our external experts reveals Livewire as a man in the very first class; Anstruther, according to those who have heard of him (and two referees knew nothing of his work at all) stands not very high in the second. I am sorry to have to put it so bluntly, but at a time like this all personal feelings must be set aside. We want the best man for a very difficult and responsible job.

'It has been said that Anstruther, if we elect him, will cleanse his stables[118] first and do his research afterwards. No:

---

116 Peers reminds himself that this was an expression he had already 'used above' which indicates he intended to change it. It is indeed not the first time that the state of the English Department has been compared to the filthy condition of the Augean stables before Hercules had laboured successfully to cleanse them (see above, p. 348; *cf.* also below).

117 In Bruce Truscot's essay 'Any Faculty Board', the meeting concludes when Professor Inaccessible (of all people!), can stand the fetid atmosphere of the Committee Room no longer and asks if he might 'open a window?' (see Appendix IV, p. 493).

118 Peers wonders whether to insert again the adjective before 'stables':

research is not done like that. A man who has research in his blood is like a man who has teaching in his blood: he will do it, under any conditions, good or bad.[119] If you send forward Anstruther's name, you will be recommending a schoolmaster, not a scholar.[120] I devoutly hope you will not'.

For the second time there was applause. Then came an awkward silence. The discussion seemed to be over. The Dean rose. We all thought he was going to take a vote. But instead he pronounced a formula not heard on the Faculty Board once in five years.

'With your permission', he said 'the senior member of the Board will take the Chair'.

So the Dean was going to speak against a Committee's motion. That was obvious. But only when he began did the tactics of the S.A. become evident. They had planned that, unless Dusty claimed the right of reply, the debate should be ended by Inaccessible: hence the fervour and sentimentality of his peroration. But probably the Vice-Chancellor had indicated to Fanshawe, in his capacity of Dean, that he proposed to support Livewire, and the S.A. had agreed that, in this case, the Dean should vacate the Chair and give him battle. But it was not so much the fact of his speaking, as the outrageousness of what he said, that took my breath away.

'I want', he explained, 'as an impartial observer of all this, to suggest a practical solution. We are deeply divided. There is no hope, on either side, of anything but a small majority. It is a pity to fill a Chair in that way. I suggest a course for which we can vote unanimously. Let the Chair be declared vacant for two years.[121] Let Anstruther be given two additional lecturers to

---

'Aug?'.

119 The Vice-Chancellor is expressing Peers' own opinion.

120 Opponents of Peers' appointment to the Gilmour Chair had argued that he was not really a proper scholar, merely an ex-schoolmaster — an argument of which Peers was aware (see '[E.A.P.] *Auto*', ch. 6, p. 162 ). What Peers is saying, through the mouth of the Vice-Chancellor, with conscious irony and truthful bluntness, is that the typical (or mythical) schoolmaster is not a person who fulfils, or has fulfilled, a particular occupation, but an individual who is possessed of a certain attitude of mind. Anstruther, who, unlike Peers, or Bletherley (*cf.* 'B.T.', ch. IV, p. 352), had never taught in a school, was in character and mentality 'a schoolmaster, not a scholar' (*cf.* also 'B.T.', ch. III, p. 297, and note 96).

121 Between receipt of applications for the Gilmour Chair and its

relieve him of much of his burden. In two years he will show if he is capable of combining research with administration. Let the Department be represented on this Board by Anstruther, as its Acting Head, and on Senate by one who is closely in touch with it, Professor Truscot. I do trust that this solution of a difficult problem will commend itself to you... I am not a party man...'

And so on. I was aghast at the cleverness of it. In two years Strutty would no doubt put something together for publication — and, once elected to the Chair, would never publish again.[122] In those same two years the S.A. would seize every possible opportunity of advancing his eventual candidature. With his skill in organization, bolstered up by a modicum of published work, he would probably slip into the Chair without opposition.[123] If the amendment were carried, the S.A. had

---

ultimate filling there was an interval of three years (see Appendix I).

[122] In *Redbrick and these Vital Days*, Peers criticizes those professors and senior lecturers, who do useful research until they obtain their high positions, but then produce little or nothing more (95-97).

[123] Concern at the procedures by which Chairs were filled was expressed in the Faculty of Arts in 1929. Professors Campagnac and Dewsnup unsuccessfully proposed amendments to the report of the Selection Committee on the King Alfred Chair of English Literature in order that the vacancy in the Chair should be advertised. Shortly afterwards Professor Ormerod unsuccessfully moved a resolution that in future all Selection Committees appointed by the Faculty should submit for Faculty's approval a statement of the procedure to be followed. In 1928 the University Council had agreed to Senate's recommendation that Chair Selection Committees be **not** required to report on the method of procedure to be adopted, a decision which Professor Ormerod and others had deplored.

Concern over procedures used for the filling of senior academic appointments was by no means new. In her life of her husband, James Alsop, Mrs Constance Alsop relates how in 1902-03, in the months during which Mr Alsop helped to draft the University's Charter, Professor Mackay regularly visited him and emphasised his wish that 'when it came to the government of the business of the University' he wanted 'power vested in the Academic Staff and not merely power over academic questions' — something which Mr Alsop would not countenance (*The Life of James W. Alsop LL.D., B.A.* [Liverpool: Liverpool U. P., 1926], 77). In 1905 Professor Oliver Elton, a member of the 'New Testament', gave notice of a motion (which it seems he later withdrew) criticising the University Council for themselves deciding to advertise the vacant Chair of French against the desire of the Senate and the Faculty of Arts, which was that the Chair be filled by invitation. The convention that the Council should not interfere in Senate decisions on

turned defeat into virtual victory.

A buzz of voices greeted the end of Fanshawe's speech and the discussion became brisk and informal. But it soon became clear that each side had hopes of victory and after a quarter of an hour Fanshawe withdrew his motion. But it had served its real purpose, which was to destroy the effectiveness of the Vice-Chancellor's speech. By the time that a vote was taken, it had almost been forgotten.

A show of hands, three times counted in an atmosphere electric with tension, gave Anstruther eleven votes and Livewire ten.[124]

The Committee's report was negatived and the next move lay with the Senate.

---

academic appointments took a number of years to establish. It will be remembered that, in 1922, the 'New Testament' endeavoured to persuade Council to overturn Senate's decision, in respect of the Gilmour Chair, but Council ratified the appointment of Allison Peers (see '[E.A.P.] *Auto*', ch. 6, p. 165; and see below, p. 385, note 139).

124 An amendment to appoint Peers to the Gilmour Chair was lost by thirteen votes to fourteen (see the entry for 7 June 1922, Appendix I, p. 426).

By no means all Chair Selection Committee Reports were accepted by the Faculty of Arts in the 1920s without amendments being moved. In June 1920 the Faculty was divided on the appointment to the Chair of French. Those who might be identified as 'New Testament' caucus members and supporters, and others, including Professor Collinson, mustered fourteen votes for Monsieur E. Eggli (who *was* appointed to the Chair) as against eight votes mustered for Monsieur F. J. Tanquery by Professor Bruce Boswell and colleagues (amongst them Professors Campagnac, Dewsnup, Halliday, Pearson, and Postgate, and Mr [as he then was] H. A. Ormerod). The Faculty's Committee which had reported on applications for the Chair had been split, seven (including the President of the Council, the Vice-Chancellor, Dr Adami, and Professors Bruce Boswell and H. C. Wyld) supporting M. Tanquery, and five (Professors Collinson, Elton and Mair, Mr Garmon Jones, and Dr Veitch) supporting M. Eggli. In May 1923 Professors Campagnac and Halliday moved and seconded an unsuccessful amendment to recommend Professor W. Alison Phillips to the Andrew Geddes and John Rankin Chair of Modern History, rather than Dr. G. S. Veitch. Kelly has discussed this latter debate and its significance in *For Advancement of Learning. The University of Liverpool 1881-1981* (199-200). In February 1926 Professor Dewsnup's amendment to the report of the Committee on the King Alfred Chair of English Literature (in effect to ascertain which of the three short-listed candidates was most suitable), was lost. Instead, Faculty agreed to Associate Professor Garmon Jones' motion that no appointment be made for the forthcoming Session.

## VII

It was a fortnight before the final debate in the Livewire controversy could take place and the milieu was very different from that of the last one.  Normally, the Senate merely nods approval to reports from the Faculty Boards, and, had the issue been merely a domestic one, it might have done so even now. But the Wormwood-Rippon plot, the association of Anstruther with the S.A. and the intervention of Fanshawe soon became topics of conversation far beyond the bounds of the Faculty, and they were being freely discussed by the fifty-seven professors, who, with the Vice-Chancellor, the Librarian, and non-professorial Deans make up the Senate,[125] before the Board's recommendation came up for discussion in the middle of June.[126]

Redbrick is stronger in the Sciences than in Arts,[127] and, partly for this reason, though partly also as a result of long-forgotten controversies, the Arts Faculty is somewhat despised by the rest.  As a proof of its degeneracy, the Scientists, the Engineers and the Technologists — and occasionally, when they were not too busy, even the Medicals — would point to the existence of a domineering Arts caucus, which, they said, no right-minded Faculty would allow.  Few of them knew who the members of the S.A. were — and, if they had known their names, not all of them would have known them by sight.  But they were perfectly clear on the main lines of the controversy.

---

125 In 1922, the Senate of Liverpool University comprised the Vice-Chancellor, the University Librarian, and fifty-seven professors; all the Faculty Deans were, at the time, professors.

126 Senate met on 14 June 1922. This particular meeting of the Senate was attended by thirty-seven members; besides the Vice-Chancellor and the Librarian, twenty of those attending were drawn from the Faculties of Engineering (4), Law (1) Medicine (7), and Science (8), the remainder (15) from the Faculty of Arts.

127 The statistics of percentages of full-time students in the various faculties in Sessions 1938-39, 1951-52, 1956-57 and 1961-62, 'reveal Liverpool as quite definitely a scientifically oriented University' (Kelly, *For Advancement of Learning. The University of Liverpool 1881-1981*, 298). This pattern was long-standing: at Liverpool in the Session 1921-22, to which this narrative, in reality, relates, of a total of 2,296 full-time students, 1,630 were in the Faculties of Medicine, Science, and Engineering.

This Arts caucus was trying to push one of its own men into a vacant Chair when an outstanding man from Camford had presented himself. Well, they would hear both sides, of course, but these Arts people must be kept in their place at all costs — and a good man from Camford was not to be sneezed at.

In the Senate, Livewire's supporters had one great advantage — namely, that on all reports of committees the Vice-Chancellor had the right to speak first. And the Vice-Chancellor, nettled, it would seem, at the reception given to his plea by the Faculty Board, made a much longer and fuller statement, quoting freely from the letters of the external experts and from letters he had himself received which threw the two candidates even more sharply into contrast than before.[128]

There was no chance for sentimentality to rear its head till the Vice-Chancellor had finished. The issues were laid down fairly and squarely: scholarship and administration. When the case was put — the Committee's case, not the Faculty Board's, for the Vice-Chancellor was moving that the Committee's report be approved and the Board's recommendation disregarded — it seemed for a moment as though it were going to be carried *nem. con.* Wormwood, once more, sat with head in hands; Inaccessible was doodling; Eagles was absent;[129] the Dean was turning over his papers. It must have been a full minute before anyone stirred.

'Well', enquired the Vice-Chancellor, encouragingly, 'if no one wishes to discuss my proposal, we can proceed to a vote'.

---

128 Sir Archie Blake, it will be remembered, is probably modelled on both Adami and Hetherington (see above, pp. 333-34, note 11). As Peers points out in the first narrative, Adami was undeniably an opponent of the 'New Testament' (see '[E.A.P.] *Auto*', ch. 6, p. 164). So too was Hetherington, who, when he succeeded Adami in 1927, was determined not to stand any nonsense from the remnants of the 'New Testament'. His measures provoked protests from one of its number, Garmon Jones, Dean of the Faculty of Arts: 'Haff you heard what Bloody Hector iss up to now?' (quoted in Adrian Allan and Ann L. Mackenzie, *[A Descriptive and Analytical Catalogue of] Redbrick Revisited: The University of Liverpool 1920-1952. An Exhibition* [University of Liverpool, 1994], 19).

129 Another indication that Eagles might indeed be Eggli; for Eggli left for Paris before the question of Peers' appointment to the Gilmour Chair was considered by Council (see his letter, dated 27 June 1922, to Mr Garmon Jones — cited in Appendix I, p. 428).

That broke the spell. Three professors rose at the same moment.

'May I say, sir,...?' began the Dean.

'May I be allowed...?' enquired Professor Wormwood.

'Ah reckon...' observed Professor Loaf, who held the Chair of Zoology.[130]

'Professor Loaf', said the Vice-Chancellor, pleasantly.

'Ah reckon', repeated Loaf, who in his youth came from behind the plough and boasted a heavy Drabshire[131] accent but was a shrewd judge of men, as well as an eminent Zoologist. 'Ah reckon there's been some foonny business yer. Ah yer woon of ah colleagues has been accusing th'yoong Camford man of appropriating oother people's discooveries. Ah reckon th' Senate ought to yer soomthing abaht that'.

'Really, sir', exclaimed Wormwood, 'I must protest at that insinuation. It's perfectly true that I inadvertently misinterpreted an action of the candidate concerned, but I apologized and withdrew immediately I discovered my mistake and since then I have taken no further part in the discussions'.

'Quite true', observed the Vice-Chancellor, soothingly. 'It was a pure misapprehension, Professor Loaf, and Professor Wormwood has made all the amends in his power'.

'None the less, sir', went on Wormwood, 'I am still strongly of the opinion that Mr Livewire is an unsuitable person to hold the Chair. His narrowness, his inexperience, his personal traits, his lack of understanding of our peculiar problems...[132] But I was about to ask you, sir, if you would instruct the clerk to read one of the letters presented to the Committee which you yourself did not read. It is written, from close knowledge both of Mr Livewire and of this University, by one who for many years

---

130 Could the figure of Professor Loaf, Professor of Zoology, be modelled on John Share Jones (Professor of Veterinary Anatomy, 1920-38), who was present at the meeting? P. G. H. Boswell recalled that Share Jones was '...generally known as Ploughshare Jones, because of his bucolic appearance... hardly of University type... His persistence and style of oratory... was typically Welsh...' (Boswell's unpublished autobiography, p. 141).

131 Peers has an enviable capacity for inventing wittily evocative words. Since, in this narrative, Drabtown is Liverpool, Drabshire must be Lancashire.

132 These charges are similar to some of those levelled against Allison Peers by Professor Fitzmaurice-Kelly and Dr Henry Thomas.

was an honoured member of our body, who was listened to with the deepest respect as one of our wisest counsellors — in short, from our former Professor of Poetry, Emeritus-Professor Upright'.

The Vice-Chancellor inclined his head, whereupon the Dean, at a sign from Wormwood, passed the letter to the clerk to the Senate, who read it aloud.

I had forgotten about this letter, which, after Wormwood had read it in part, had been laid upon the table, collected with the rest of the papers by the Dean and forgotten. But, as it was read, I gasped, both at its barefaced effrontery and at its unspeakable pettiness.[133] It began by saying that the writer was continually in Camford, had exceptional opportunities of studying life there and had not only met Mr Livewire but had heard a good deal about him. He had been a young man of exceptional precocity, was a bright and interesting personality, but had published too much too soon[134] and was unlikely to make a solid reputation. So much, he said, was common knowledge. What was less generally known was that this young man was quick-tempered, intolerant and conceited and if he went to Redbrick would only create discord there.[135]

---

133 This description could accurately be applied to either of Fitzmaurice-Kelly's letters dated 14 and 16 February 1920 (reproduced in Appendix I), the confidential contents of which must have been privately revealed to Peers (by one of his supporters on the Committee?). Words which Truscot uses below to condemn the terms of Upright's letter, might likewise be applied without reservation to Fitzmaurice-Kelly's communications about Peers: 'mean, uncharitable, and, above all, totally uncalled-for'.

134 In the 'Redbrick' books, Peers is scathingly critical of those who seek to excuse their poor record of research by insisting on the supposed dangers of rushing into print: the principle that 'there must be no premature publication' is part of 'the Oxbridge tradition' which, unfortunately, has become generally accepted in Redbrick also. Peers notes also that there are professors at both ancient and modern institutions who find it convenient to encourage others falsely to believe that they have 'the uncompleted manuscripts of epoch-making works secreted somewhere' (see *Redbrick University*, 118, *Redbrick and these Vital Days*, 97-98). We may recall here the case of Professor Slocombe who had written 'nothing of importance for something like a quarter of a century' but created the legend —believed implicitly by undergraduates — that 'his study harboured some vast unfinished masterpiece' (see above, ch. III, p. 292).

135 Peers' 'pushful' arrogance is particularly deplored by Fitzmaurice-Kelly (see letter of 14 February 1920 — Appendix I). See above, pp. 353-55,

Those were the main lines. If the S.A. had set out to compile a malicious letter they could hardly have beaten this.

'Was he always like that?' whispered Bletherley to me, as the clerk sat down.

I shook my head, rather bitterly. The last grain of respect that I had had for my one-time hero was dispelled by this letter — mean, uncharitable, and, above all, totally uncalled-for, in which a scholar of international repute, save the mask, attempted to foil the career of another only half his age.[136]

However, the very violence of the tirade did nothing but harm to its cause.

'Ah reckon', remarked Professor Loaf, 'the man that wrote that letter, however eminent, was no gentleman. Ah move that the Senate proceed to vote'.

So we voted — not by show of hands, but by nominal roll, as is the custom of the Redbrick Senate. The succession of deep-voiced 'Ayes' was the sweetest music I had heard for years. Livewire was elected by forty-two votes to five, two abstaining.[137]

'The next report', said the Vice-Chancellor, 'is from the Committee on the Readership in Obstetrics and Gynaecology...'

The bickerings of the Arts Faculty were forgotten.[138]

---

'I thought you'd like to hear the end of it', said Dusty, with a chuckle.

He had invited Bletherley and me to dine with him on the last night of term, and I suspected that the omission of our ladies from the invitation meant that it was a 'shop'-dinner.

'But surely we *saw* the end of it?' I exclaimed. 'Livewire was elected by the Senate, and the Senate has the last voice on

---

and notes 67, 69. Also *cf.* p. 363, note 86; p. 366, and note 94.

136 *Cf.* 'B.T.', ch. III, the passage in which Truscot describes the change in Upright, when Truscot expressed his interest in being Upright's successor, and the mask of gracious benevolence slipped: 'he became someone new to me... from that moment I was dealing with a different person' (pp. 311-12).

137 Peers was elected to the Gilmour Chair of Spanish by the Senate by nineteen votes to twelve (and by nineteen votes to eight as the substantive resolution).

138 Peers indicates the need for a 'space' here, to mark the end of that part of the controversy.

THE CHAIR OF ENGLISH LITERATURE 385

matters that are purely academic'.

'Quite right, according to the book', agreed Dusty, 'but when the S.A. is faced with extinction it grasps at a straw. They actually put old Inaccessible up to one last move. He went to see the President of the Council'.[139]

'What could he hope for from him?' enquired Bletherley.

'Oh, what you might expect. Not an academic matter. Livewire's scholarship not contested (You bet it isn't — *now*). But sharp division of opinion on Selection Committee and Faculty Board. Parlous state of English Literature Department. Need for everyone to pull together. Excellent man already in virtual charge. Man with uncertain temper will cause disruption. Etcetera, Etcetera'.

'And what did he want the President to do?' I asked.

'Keep the job open for twelve months, put *you* in charge of the Department and finally re-advertise', replied Dusty, and burst out laughing at my dismay.

'That would have been nice for me', I said. 'And the S.A. is nothing if not fertile in expedients. What sort of answer did he get?'

'What you might expect. You know the old President's pompous manner. "But, my dear Professor, you are surely not suggesting that the Council, a lay body, should take upon itself to override the jealously guarded academic prerogatives of the Senate?" And he went on, so I'm told, to read him a magnificent lecture on the subject. The poor chap got greener and greener'.

'The Sea-Green Inaccessible',[140] I murmured.

---

139 The University Council took the final decision to appoint Peers to the Chair, as Peers himself explains in the other autobiography (see '[E.A.P.] *Auto*', ch. 6, p. 165). The Council set up a special Committee to consider the matter before reaching a decision. For their deliberations see, in 'A Chronology of the Filling of the Gilmour Chair', the entries of 20 June—4 July 1922, Appendix I, pp. 426-28.

140 A witty corruption of Thomas Carlyle's famous description of Robespierre, the 'seagreen Incorruptible' (Carlyle's *History of the French Revolution*, II). Perhaps Allison Peers observed with regret in Dr John Sampson — 'Professor Inaccessible' — an example, like Robespierre, of integrity corrupted. As a specialist in the culture and history of nineteenth-century Europe, Peers was evidently reminded of the Reign of Terror in France, in observing the reign of the 'New Testament' at Liverpool University. It is certainly true that the 'New Testamentarians', like Robespierre and other extremists of the French Revolution, protected their

'And eventually went back to the Arts Tower to report to his fellow-intriguers that their last shot was fired, their last card played, their last fangs drawn, or however you like to put it'.

'After which', I hazarded, 'they were seen no more, but a dull explosion was heard and the Arts Tower went up in smoke from which there issued a foul stench of burning sulphur?'

'Not exactly', retorted Dusty. 'They're still alive. But no longer kicking. In fact, I sat next to Eagles in the refectory yesterday, and I couldn't resist asking how the S.A. was taking it. And he shrugged his shoulders and said "It's finished". So that's that!'

'Good', I said. 'And now we must see that it's never started again under another name. No more of that back-stair intrigue while I can fight it'.

'Agreed', said Dusty. 'But don't you think we might ask Inaccessible to record its activities in a book? They deserve to be had in remembrance'.

'As a warning', growled Bletherley. 'But why ask old Inaccessible?'

'Well, after all', remarked Dusty, with a disarming smile, 'isn't he our Professor of Ancient History?'[141]

---

influence and power through intrigue, conspiracy and secret denunciation.

141 The final words of Bruce Truscot's narrative confirm Peers' good reason for publishing, and publicizing, through both autobiographies, the conflict over his appointment to the Gilmour Chair, the defeat of the 'New Testament' and the disappearance of that body into 'Ancient History'. Peers was concerned to ensure that no such society of secret intriguers should ever again dominate and corrupt the academic business of the Faculty of Arts at Liverpool University. Equally, he hoped that his book would serve as 'a warning' to right-minded colleagues in other institutions. They should resist with determination the formation of secretly self-interested groups capable of diminishing or destroying academic freedom and justice.

# POSTSCRIPT

In *The Autobiography of 'Bruce Truscot'*, upon his election to the Trevor Professorship of Poetry at Redbrick University, Truscot predicts that 'a professor at thirty-five, I had exactly thirty years of pleasurable activity stretching before me'.[1] Ironically, without realizing it, when he wrote these words Truscot's creator foretold the exact extent of his own career at the University of Liverpool as holder of the Gilmour Chair of Spanish. From his appointment as Fitzmaurice-Kelly's successor in 1922, Allison Peers continued to occupy the Gilmour Chair until his death, aged sixty-one, thirty years later. During that period he engaged indefatigably in the 'pleasurable activity' of advancing the development of teaching and research within the area of his chosen discipline: the extensive, but still extensively uncultivated, field of Hispanic Studies. Scarcely five years after the defeat of the 'New Testament' and the election of Peers to the Gilmour Chair of Spanish, the Acting Vice-Chancellor, Professor L. R. Wilberforce described with admiration the 'conspicuous success' which Allison Peers had already achieved at Liverpool during his tenure of that professorship. In a letter dated 10 May 1927, Wilberforce praised Peers' 'powers of arousing interest in Spanish Studies... his vigour and enthusiasm as a scholar, his popularity as a teacher, his competence as an administrator, and his reasonableness and trustworthiness as a colleague'.[2] By the time of Peers' death, twenty-five years later, his national and international reputation as a Hispanist was outstanding beyond question. In marked contrast to the attitudes taken by the Faculty Committee which had opposed Peers' appointment some three decades previously, not surprisingly, the Committee of Faculty made responsible in 1953 for the filling of the vacant

---

1   See *The Autobiography of 'Bruce Truscot'*, ch. III, p. 330.
2   A copy of this letter is preserved in the University Archives, Liverpool — see the *Vice-Chancellor's Letter Book*, S. 2363, p. 919.

Gilmour Chair at Liverpool University expressed highly favourable opinions as to the merits and accomplishments of Allison Peers:

> During the past thirty years the work of Allison Peers was devoted to the building-up and the widening of Hispanic Studies in Liverpool: the School of Hispanic Studies, as at present constituted, is concerned not only with the teaching of the Spanish Language and its Literature, but also includes as an integral part of the course of studies for Honours candidates: — Portuguese, Catalan and Spanish-American Studies. The high reputation of the School has been achieved by Allison Peers and the other members of his staff in establishing contacts with Schools not only on Merseyside but over a wide area of the country, in maintaining links with Spain — her people and her ideas — through the Liverpool Summer School, and by a ceaseless flow of publications on a wide range of topics of interest to scholars and students of Spanish institutions.
> (Extract from the 'REPORT of the CHAIRS COMMITTEE OF FACULTY on the Vacancy in the GILMOUR CHAIR OF SPANISH', January, 1953)[3]

'A man who has research in his blood', in the opinion of Sir Archibald Blake, Vice-Chancellor of Redbrick University, 'is like a man who has teaching in his blood: he will do it under any conditions, good or bad'.[4] A man with research and teaching in his blood in almost equally generous quantities, Allison Peers would have been extraordinarily productive as scholar and educator irrespective of the character and location of the higher institution of learning in which he had worked. Nevertheless, there is no doubt that Peers — despite, at the outset, the machinations of the 'New Testament', and, in later years, various frustrations, tensions and rivalries — felt himself to be in his best personal and professional element at the University and in the City of Liverpool. The urgent vitality which supplied his intellect and personality drew energy from an academic and civic environment that was charged, as he quickly recognized, with a closely related quality. Truscot describes for us Drabtown and Redbrick in terms which confirm the profound

---

3 Document preserved in the University Archives, Liverpool (ref. Faculty of Arts Report Book, vol. 10, p. 144).
4 See *The Autobiography of 'Bruce Truscot'*, ch. IV, p. 377.

sense of affinity Peers soon felt for Liverpool once his surface-preconceptions disappeared:

> Once you got used to the hideous tiles, the cramped and sordid surroundings, the Drabtown accent, and the indifference of the material you often had to work upon, there was a vitality, a sense of urgency, a tang of real life about Redbrick which Oxbridge, with all its amenities, had never provided. As yet I had penetrated very little into the inner workings of Redbrick, nor had I investigated more than a few of the inspiring possibilities of life in a civic university. But I had seen something of its Extension work..., visited some of Drabtown's large municipal schools and held the attention of a thousand boys and girls — some of them my undergraduates of the future — ...I was faced with the possibility of returning to the comfortable, easy-going life of an ancient university, and I realized that, in spite of its advantages, *I did not want to go.*[5]

Years before Peers, as Truscot, wrote these words, many others, students as well as staff, had been influenced, and energized, by the same vital quality in the place and institution, as this verse from the *Liverpool Students' Songbook* (1906) reveals:

> Not ours the groves of Academe,
> Where learned pedants drowse and dream;
> Not ours the cloistered calm retreat,
> Around us roars the city street,
> Whose surging tides of ceaseless strife
> Sound like a bugle call to life.

In Peers' case the strong bond of attraction which he inwardly formed with 'Our Alma Mater on the Hill',[6] was to endure to keep him there throughout his university career as teacher and researcher.

Peers' qualities as dedicated educator of his own students at the University of Liverpool are among the most noteworthy but generally least publicized aspects of his career. He maintained the 'ceaseless flow of publications'[7] that brought him

---

5   See *The Autobiography of 'Bruce Truscot'*, ch. III, pp. 324-25.

6   For the words of this song by N. L. Robinson (with music by R. J. Harvey Gibson), see the *Liverpool Students' Song Book* (Liverpool: The University Press of Liverpool/London: Williams & Norgate, 1906), pp. 34-35.

7   A Bibliography of Peers' publications on Hispanic subjects was compiled by H. B. Hall, and published in the *Memorial Number* of the *Bulletin of Hispanic Studies*, XXX (1953), no. 117, 12-20.

international fame; he gave talks and lectures to promote his subject in numerous schools and universities throughout Great Britain; he repeatedly organized Summer Schools and Vacation Courses in Spain. He made so many visits to colleges and institutions overseas that in the decade between 1929 to 1939, according to his own calculations, he had lectured at more than fifty different American universities.[8] Notwithstanding, during three decades, through tuition and intuition, he never neglected to fulfil the interests and needs, both academic and individual, of the undergraduates at Liverpool within the Department of Hispanic Studies. Peers was always a firm believer that 'you can lecture with the tongue of men and of angels, but if you only reproduce what is in books your audience will see through you'.[9] So in his classes he exploited fully the full reserves of his own knowledge and experience as critic and researcher in order to train even the least experienced of his students how to develop their individual capacities for scholarly analysis and investigation. As an educator Peers displayed that 'mysterious virtue' which he had so much admired in the great Spanish scholar Menéndez Pidal: the virtue that 'inspires you to inspire others'.[10] Many of Peers' Honours graduates went on to be Hispanists themselves, in schools, colleges or universities. But whether they became academics or took up wholly different occupations, having trained them, he did not abandon them, as he had been abandoned, upon graduation, by his tutors at Cambridge University. Like Truscot's students at Redbrick University, the graduates from Peers' Department at the University of Liverpool were, and felt themselves to be,

---

8  See Peers' farewell letter to the University of the South, Sewanee, published in *The Sewanee Purple*, 9 March 1939. On a visit to that University in 1978, thanks to information supplied by Professor Eric Naylor, I discovered, to my surprise, that Allison Peers had spent three weeks at the University of the South during the momentous year 1939, as part of a lecturing tour organized — ironically, as we might think now — 'under the auspices of the Carnegie Endowment for International Peace'.
9  See Bruce Truscot, *Redbrick University*, 143-44.
10  For this comment borrowed from a speech by Henri Mérimée, see Peers' essay on 'Ramón Menéndez Pidal', published in the series 'Hispanists Past and Present', in *Bulletin of Spanish Studies*, V (1928), no. 19, 127-31, at 131.

intellectually, and personally, related to him 'for life'.[11] The continuing extent of his positive involvement in the development of their careers and individual lives may be verified through reading any copy of the *University of Liverpool Hispanic Honour Society Newsletter*, which Peers founded, edited and regularly compiled. Sent out to his graduates while their lives and careers were still being disrupted by the Second World War, the twenty-fifth Number begins with characteristically authentic enthusiasm as follows:

> AT LAST!
> At last I am able to send out the sort of newsletter I have always dreamed of sending. News has been pouring in — real, thrilling news, of which I hope there will be another instalment in our next issue. *But it all depends on you.*
> E.A.P.

The same Newsletter contains, among other material, news of 'Two Double-Hispanic Marriages', extracts from letters received from graduates involved in D—Day, stationed in Italy, confined in an internment camp in Germany etc. The final section describes Peers' own activities within the Department of Hispanic Studies and elsewhere in the country, revealing his undiminished commitment to promote the development of his subject:

> The last Vacation Course of the Hispanic Council had to be postponed because of the flying bombs and we are holding it after Christmas instead — at the Regent St Polytechnic, as before. I am getting about a good deal among schools this winter — as far north as Edinburgh and as far south as Lewes. There seems to be a good deal of interest in Spanish but till the supply of teachers is normal it isn't practicable for many fresh schools to take it up. However, I hope to see the numbers multiplied at least tenfold yet.
> E.A.P.

October 21, 1944.[12]

---

11  *Cf.* Truscot's declaration: 'My own graduates know that they are mine for life, and that they can come to me at any time for whatever I am capable of giving them.' (*The Autobiography of 'Bruce Truscot'*, ch. I, p. 216).

12  Thanks to Mrs Elizabeth Hall, widow of Professor H. B. [Harold] Hall (see p. 474), a copy of this twenty-fifth Number of the *University of*

Though he was not one of Peers' graduates, William C. Atkinson, Stevenson Professor of Spanish at the University of Glasgow, did not omit to describe with insight in the obituary which he published in 1953 the unique qualities which the Second Holder of the Gilmour Chair of Spanish had utilized in educating at Liverpool successive groups of Honours students in Hispanic Studies:

> To these he gave without stint of his best, and of his interest, with a generosity that seemed scarcely compatible with the range of his other activities. He knew them individually much better than they realized, laboured as few professors do to keep in touch with them, and to keep them in touch with their university, after they had gone out into the world, and had his particular reward in the number of those who found their careers by treading in his footsteps.[13]

The recollections recorded below, written by three among Peers' remarkable band of graduates who 'treading in his footsteps' successfully 'found their careers' as university teachers and scholars, confirm the truthful profundity of Atkinson's observations.[14]

---

*Liverpool Hispanic Honour Society Newsletter* has been lodged in the Archives of the University of Liverpool.

13 See Atkinson, 'In Memoriam', *Bulletin of Hispanic Studies*, XXX (1953), no. 117, 4.

14 Atkinson's good knowledge of Peers' special gifts as a teacher might well have been derived from Ivy L. McClelland, who was for many years a colleague of Atkinson in the Department of Hispanic Studies at the University of Glasgow (*cf.* note *, p. 397).

# I

## Professor E. Allison Peers[*]

Your obituary notice on Professor E. Allison Peers mentioned one aspect of his life and work which may perhaps be amplified. He combined to an extraordinary degree the role of international Hispanist with that of teacher and trainer of the relatively small group who were fortunate enough to be his pupils in the School of Hispanic Studies of the University of Liverpool. He was completely free of that remoteness usually associated with the scholar, and he brought to every type of teaching the same qualities of enthusiasm, technical resource and sensitivity to the reaction of the taught. He was, in fact, that rarest thing among university dons, a born teacher. The miracle is that he managed to harmonize the demands this made on his time and energy with the needs of his research, which were never allowed to go neglected. But his energy was in itself extraordinary: lectures, organization, creative activity, seemed not to tire him, but to refresh him for these more personal contacts with undergraduates which were probably the most memorable part of their student days. He excelled in small groups, in seminar classes and advanced Honours work, directing each student individually and drawing from each capabilities and a capacity for work that he or she had never realized they possessed. To a small inner group of Honours undergraduates he was a powerful formative influence, which these men and women, university teachers themselves now, are

---

[*] Probably sent to the Acting Editor (William C. Atkinson) of the *Bulletin of Hispanic Studies* following publication of the 'Memorial Number' of the journal (*BHS*, XXX [1953], no. 117), which contained several tributes, including Atkinson's own obituary. After Peers' death, it was Atkinson who assumed, anonymously, responsibility for the *Bulletin of Hispanic Studies* until the appointment as editor, in 1953, of Albert Sloman, Peers' successor in the Gilmour Chair of Spanish. The author of this unsigned tribute was clearly a former student of Peers at Liverpool University, who, went on, with his encouragement, to a career as a university teacher in Hispanic Studies. This appreciation is among papers lodged in the University Archives, Liverpool (ref. D.265).

acutely grateful for having assimilated. Over twenty years he never lost touch with any of these, and each one of them knew that at any moment of intellectual or professional crisis his far-sighted and judicious advice was at their disposal, together with a degree of effort on their behalf that only his combination of affectionate interest and energetic activity could provide. With their own increasing maturity they came all the more to realize the extraordinary, even paradoxical qualities of his mind — exactness combined with a creative, imaginative grasp, a care for detail that accompanied a wide breadth of vision, profundity and wideness of range. And above all, they were able to appreciate a scholarship integrated and humanized by the whole personality with all the power of attraction and communication that that implies. For those who knew him closely as teacher and colleague his influence and spirit are a living force: this will help to assuage the bitter sense of loss which they must feel now.

## II

## Allison Peers as a University Teacher
## Recollections of a Former Student in his Department

IVY L. McCLELLAND*

*University of Glasgow*

Our first meeting as students with our Professor whom then, and afterwards, we regarded with pleasurable awe and lively interest was in a relatively informal seminar-group. And our first form of instruction was concerned with academic methods. We were not to assume, he told us, that a mere five or so lectures or tutorials per week indicated extensive opportunity for enjoying extensive freedom from academic demands. To our academic world we ought to give, he said, not less than eight hours each day for at least five days each week. The long summer vacation, he insisted, with particular emphasis, was not intended for use as holiday-time. Some two weeks resting and playing, would be considered permissible, he thought. But the rest of the time must be devoted to work — whether based in Britain or abroad. We must extend our knowledge, we were sternly informed, of the whole periods, historical and literary, in

---

\* Upon graduation from Peers' Department at Liverpool University in 1930, Dr McClelland was appointed to a post within the Department of Hispanic Studies at the University of Glasgow, where she spent her entire career as a university teacher and scholar. Though she retired in 1973, Dr McClelland continues to hold an honorary appointment at Glasgow University as Senior Research Fellow. The University of Glasgow in 1989 awarded her the honorary degree of Doctor of Letters, and in 1995 created a Chair with her name — The Ivy McClelland Research Chair of Spanish. These honours were bestowed in recognition of her outstanding career within the University and of her influential contribution, through numerous internationally acclaimed books, to scholarly understanding of the eighteenth century in Spain. For further details of Dr McClelland's career, see Ann L. Mackenzie's Introduction to *The Eighteenth Century in Spain. Essays in Honour of I. L. McClelland* (cited above, p. 11, note 21).

Dr McClelland's essay on Allison Peers was written in 1990-91, by invitation of the editors, for inclusion in this book.

which our 'special subjects' or 'set books' were located. We must not assume that an Honours course was an easy course. We must be prepared for hard, exacting work. Since he spoke in a quiet if firm tone of understanding, and with an accompanying smile of encouragement, we felt inspired by our agreeable challenge.

Nor during the years of our Degree course did this initially expressed principle, about full-time work and interest in the whole panorama of our Spanish study, decline in emphasis. The reality of Spain, historically and actually, engaged our steady attention. Influenced by one who visited Spain regularly and viewed it in practical detail, we learned to appreciate the complex structure and expression of Spanish identity.

When I was a student our Professor of Spanish was already a scholar of international fame, a revered author of Spanish and Catalan literature and history, a popular lecturer on Hispanic life and letters both in Britain and abroad. But I like to remember him best as a quietly inspiring director of our seminar-tutorials. His method was to choose a subject related to our study of particular texts or literary or historical periods. He required each student to contribute a written, preparatory assessment of each subject programmed for discussion, with importance given to philosophical and verbal analysis: a valuable gaining in detective perception. Then each contribution was read aloud and taken into general consideration. To my mind a notable feature of his reaction to our individual efforts in this respect was his quiet air of receptivity. Some teachers attempt to urge students on to a better or more elaborate or detailed explanation of their views by urgent tones of prompting or lively commentary: a method which seems socially agreeable but which can increase nervousness or tension in many students. Rather it was his way to listen in respectful silence, and late proffer comments or questions in a tone of quiet friendliness. In other words we were encouraged to develop our thinking without the popular aid of pedagogic shock-tactics or excited persuasion. The method served us well when later we entered the vast silent reaches of research. That method was imaginatively suggestive rather than domineering. As a man of musical talent — he was a good pianist — he was sensitive to the subtleties of sound-effect. He was an excellent lecturer in informative matter and in manner and voice. He firmly, if unobtrusively, exacted high standards. But when he entered into tutorials he was on comfortably equal terms with his students.

It was characteristic of our Professor to interest himself in the future careers of all his Honours students and to give practical advice, encouragement and help whenever possible. Many of his graduates, especially teachers in schools, attended his Summer Schools in Spain and remained on social terms with him. Those whom he considered suitable for academic careers were guided into research with a friendly critical interest on his part which helped the graduate to develop self-criticism energetically and to practise objectivity. At the appropriate stage of these graduates' attainments Allison Peers was untiring in his efforts to give them practical help and support in their applications for University Lectureships. He was a Professor aware of each student's individuality, therefore able to promote each student's natural ability. He was, in fact, a good psychologist, a quality which contributed to his instinctive understanding of Spain's national mentality.

## III

## E.A.P.
## Remembered

### AUDREY LUMSDEN-KOUVEL*
*University of Illinois, Chicago*

When I joined the staff of the Department of Hispanic Studies at Liverpool University in 1943 I was far from ignorant of its activities, which revolved round the personality of its head, E. Allison Peers, generally known, at least behind his back, as E.A.P. In fact, my first contact had been six years earlier, before the start of my undergraduate career, and that contact illustrates what I believe to be one of the dominant impulses which drove his extraordinarily motivated life and career — his sense of an educational and proselytizing mission.

I was a student at one of the Liverpool high schools and had taken up Spanish somewhat as a side-interest, my intention being to specialize at university for a degree in French. Allison Peers had been appointed to the Chair of Spanish at Liverpool some fifteen years earlier and had used his tenure to promote the study of Spanish — or, I should say, Peninsular studies, for his was never a narrow view — on both a local and a national level. Spanish at that time was relegated to an inferior position, a subject perhaps useful in the commercial area, one that might be mastered by students unable to cope with the challenge of Greek, Latin or French. His predecessor, James Fitzmaurice-Kelly, had written a well-known history of Spanish

---

\* An undergraduate then a postgraduate in Peers' Department, Audrey Lumsden was subsequently appointed (in 1943) to a lectureship in Hispanic Studies at the University of Liverpool. Thereafter, she was a lecturer at the University of Leeds before leaving Great Britain for the United States upon her marriage to the physicist, Professor Jim Kouvel. As Professor and scholar of the Golden Age in Spain, Audrey Lumsden-Kouvel has pursued a distinguished career at the University of Illinois, Chicago.

Professor Lumsden-Kouvel wrote this appreciation of Allison Peers in 1990-91, by invitation of the editors, for inclusion in this book.

literature, but would have quailed at the thought of visiting high schools to develop the kind of interest that could feed a university department. But the new Head made it his business to capture the attention of potential Spanish graduates. His own enthusiasm was the magnet that attracted me to this fresh field and I found myself being interviewed for entry into the Hispanic Honours programme at Liverpool University in spite of the offer of an exhibition at Oxford.

I found the atmosphere within the circle of Honours students — a small competitive group — a constant challenge. But Peers was responsible for the most important step in my intellectual development in his conduct of the special seminars which were the core of the programme. The reading out and discussion of papers before a critical audience, his searching yet sympathetic interventions, awakened in me a sense of the excitement of discovery. He treated all of us as if we were potential scholars and required of us the disciplines that this view demanded.

Another aspect of his missionary zeal was the Summer School he organized in Spain — the only foreign school there at that time. It was normally held in Santander, though my first experience of it, which was in the year after the end of the Spanish Civil War, was in the untypical environment of St Jean de Luz. But Peers' real skills were only fully apparent to me several years later, when I was associated with him as assistant director of the School during my time as lecturer in the Department of Hispanic Studies at Liverpool. The Summer School was located in San Sebastián, and I shall never forget the extra-academic stratagems that were required to lodge and feed our students in a ravaged post-war Spain. Allison Peers' ability to make contacts with the civil authorities was extraordinary: he negotiated special rations for families who boarded those who attended, and managed to maintain a useful relationship with the Civil Governor of the province while cultivating a genuinely cordial interaction with the prickly local Basques. We enjoyed the amenities of the Yacht Club overlooking the Concha and there was a memorable visit to one of the area's *Sociedades gastronómicas*.

The *viajes de estudios* which he organized in conjunction with the Summer School exploited in greater depth his knowledge of Spain and its culture, as well as the breadth of his personal contacts. From the Prior of the Carthusian Monastery of Miraflores, P. Edmund Gurdon, with whom he had close personal and professional ties, to a rustic mayor of Old Castile, who treated the group to an unforgettable taste of the local vintage, the students profited at every point from some unique insight. He knew everybody: Dámaso Alonso and the Café Gijón group in Madrid, the leaders of Catalan culture when this was a semi-secret activity, scholars in Valencia and Seville. And he brought many of them to Liverpool, as visiting professors, or, in the case of younger scholars, as the *lectores* who added so much to the undergraduates' background in contemporary Spanish affairs.

My five-year period in the Department of Hispanic Studies at Liverpool University drew, then, as I have indicated, on a previous background of undergraduate and graduate years. The transition was made easier by a capacity on the part of the Head to regard younger colleagues as fellow workers in the academic vineyard. Their contribution was severely but fairly assessed in a variety of contexts. The educational mission was always evident, whether in the meticulous supervision of teaching assignments, always accompanied by a helpful practical critique of one's performance, or in the painful initiation into the rigours of proof-reading. This discipline was accepted and profited from. But Allison Peers was always most generous in providing opportunities for growth: new and challenging courses to teach, encouragement and assistance in developing areas of research, looking out for the neophyte's professional advancement.

Throughout this period he was involved in the scrutiny of the university system which culminated in the pseudonymous *Redbrick University* publications. It is no secret, nowadays, that Bruce Truscot voiced the opinions of Allison Peers on the deficiencies of some of his own colleagues at Liverpool University. While he was the most merciless critic of laziness and inattention to the demands of teaching and research in some of those professors around him, his real message was a positive one: what a university community could and should be. Knowledge must always return as power, as Coleridge had said, and the conviction that scholars and teachers have the obligation to bring about change is perhaps what provides the clue to the unity of Allison Peers' diverse interests, extending from mysticism to the Spanish Civil War, from cloistered research to public speaking. No detail was too mundane to be neglected in the total effort, for, in the words which he so often quoted from Saint Teresa: 'Dios anda entre los pucheros' ('God moves among the pots and pans').

\* \* \* \* \*

In 1921, in his testimonial written to support Peers' application, Rudmose Brown had predicted that Peers

> would fill the Gilmour Chair of Spanish with honour to himself and to the University, and do much to carry on and add to the reputation which Liverpool University already possesses as the cradle of Spanish Studies in Great Britain.[15]

That confident prediction was comprehensively fulfilled. By 1952 Liverpool had acquired the reputation which, as Geoffrey Ribbans has commented, it still enjoys 'throughout the world among humanists and modern linguists for its preeminence in Hispanic Studies'. Peers' former Department is renowned 'as the birth-place of the prime Hispanic journal [the *Bulletin of Hispanic Studies*] of the country and of a teaching and research school of continued excellence'.[16] Moreover, by 1952 nearly every major university in Britain was endowed with a Department of Spanish or Hispanic Studies, to answer the largely increased demand for degree courses in that discipline. That demand came from numerous students who had first learned Spanish in numerous schools which had first been persuaded to teach the language by Allison Peers. 'It is doubtful if, before 1914, there were more than a dozen [schools]

---

15 For the full text of this testimonial, see below, Appendix I, p. 444.

16 See Geoffrey Ribbans, 'E. Allison Peers: A Centenary Reappraisal', Fifth E. Allison Peers Lecture. Delivered at the University of Liverpool, 10 June 1994, this lecture is published in *Spain and its Literature. Essays in Memory of E. Allison Peers*, edited by Ann L. Mackenzie (Liverpool: Liverpool U. P./London: Modern Humanities Research Association, 1996).

in the whole country'[17] that offered Spanish. No sooner had Peers begun his career at Liverpool, and his activities as teacher and publicist, than the number of such schools significantly rose, indeed rapidly multiplied. By the 1950s many departments of Spanish at Britain's universities were staffed by Peers' own graduates, or by the graduates of his graduates. Nowadays in Britain, numerous Hispanists hold Chairs and other posts, not only in Spanish but also in Portuguese, Catalan and Latin American Studies. They would not occupy these positions, for their posts would not have existed, had it not been for the work of Allison Peers. Which fact is not always remembered or sufficiently acknowledged. And not only within this country but throughout the world Peers' many important books and researches expansively influenced numerous scholars concerned to evaluate the essential contributions which Spain, Portugal and their former empires have made to the developing cultures and civilizations of mankind.

Nor was it simply through his Hispanic Studies and researches that Peers promoted change and advancement in the world of higher learning. Even in the early years of the twentieth century the Ancient Universities of Oxford and Cambridge still regarded with little interest and less respect those languages and literatures within the 'Modern Humanities'. Peers recollects in 1943, in *Redbrick University*, that only forty years previously Cambridge 'had no English Tripos, and no professorships of French, Italian, Spanish or English Literature', and in 1917 there were still those who regarded the teaching of modern languages as 'futile'.[18] As founder and first Secretary of the Modern Humanities Research Association,[19] from 1918 Peers exerted, with his fellow-members, an enduring and decisive influence upon universities and academics to disperse such prejudice. The high position of

---

17 I borrow from Peers' own words in *Spanish — Now* (London: Methuen, 1944), 82.

18 See *Redbrick University*, 32-33; *cf.* 'B.T.', ch. I, p. 200, and note 101. See also Brooke, *A History of the University of Cambridge*, Vol. IV *1870-1990*, 432-34. Brooke describes the rise of modern languages in the 1920s and 30s at Cambridge as reflecting 'a movement on the national stage' (435).

19 See '(E.A.P.) *Auto*', ch. 3, p. 104, and note 75.

importance justifiably given nowadays, in British institutions, to the Modern Humanities — which is in large measure owed to the work of Allison Peers — still continues to be protected and enhanced by the internationally esteemed Association that Peers established.

*'We need a higher standard and more efficient work in the Universities'.* Allison Peers made this still relevant and wholly topical observation at the University of Liverpool[20] nearly a decade before he explained in detail in *Redbrick University* how to achieve the improvements in standard and efficiency required. Rightly judged by Hector Hetherington, in 1944, to be 'one of the most valuable contributions to the discussion of a vitally important University problem which have yet appeared',[21] *Redbrick University* and its sequels, as we have shown, exerted a noteworthy influence upon academic attitudes and changing structures and policies within British universities during the post-war period of reorganization and reassessment. Geoffrey Ribbans recently defined the character and effect of Truscot's work as follows:

> In his creation of an image of Redbrick University, striving for academic and social prestige against the composite ancient university tradition of Oxbridge, he contributed substantially to a new confidence in institutions like Liverpool University which we have since come to take for granted.[22]

Fifty years after his books were written, Truscot's most original ideas for improving universities, ancient and modern — the proposals advanced for change that his contemporaries found daring — still strike us as bold, relevant and, strangely, modern. Even Truscot's views about the oppositions and prejudices which traditionally separate Oxbridge from Redbrick are by no means wholly outmoded or inapplicable. The 'Oxbridge if I can and Redbrick if I can't' mentality[23] — though no longer, we hope, prevailing — is still in evidence, as a recent

---

20 Peers made this comment during his address given at Liverpool in 1934, to inaugurate the Institute of Hispanic Studies. See *Bulletin of Spanish Studies*, XI (1934), no. 44, 186-200, 188 (his italics).

21 See Hetherington's letter to Bruce Truscot, dated 15 September 1944, reproduced in Appendix III, pp. 473-74.

22 See Ribbans, 'E. Allison Peers: A Centenary Reappraisal', *ed. cit.*

23 See *Redbrick University*, 36.

article in *The Times Higher Education Supplement*, about The Oxbridge Reject Society, confirms:

> 'There is something distinctive about being rejected from Oxbridge', says society treasurer Murray Buesst. 'Being rejected by Leicester or Nottingham does not have the same cachet'.[24]

Nowadays, admittedly, the major 'Battle of the Ancients and the Moderns' is not the same one that Truscot described. The topical conflict of oppositions is that which is being waged — over status and eminence, criteria and standards — between, on the one side, the established institutions of learning at Oxbridge, Camford, Glasburgh, Redbrick and Nottincester, and, on the other, the numerous former polytechnics which have changed their names, if not always their natures, into universities.

Especially demonstrative of the continued relevance of Peers' chief opinions about higher education is the definition he gives in Truscot's books of the higher purposes which universities must strive to fulfil. In *Redbrick and these Vital Days* he emphasizes that

> the aims of a university must be, primarily, the pursuit, and secondarily, the dissemination, of knowledge. Those two aims should be at once its soul and its inspiration; they should lie at the heart of its activities and be the source of its life.[25]

These are the same aims one finds in *Redbrick University*, already clearly formulated as follows:

> (1) *research* — patient and unremitting — including the cultivation of the spirit of research in even the youngest; (2) *teaching* — systematic and methodical, but also rich, stimulating and thought-provoking, so much so that again and again one finds the two aims merging and becoming temporarily indistinguishable one from the other.[26]

Given the importance which Peers insistently attaches to research as the primary function of universities, we may reasonably assume that he would have approved, in principle, of recently introduced measures such as the Research Assessment

---

24 See Claire Sanders, 'Oxbridge Rejects Guard Cachet', *The Times Higher Education Supplement*, 2 September 1994, 3.
25 See *Redbrick and these Vital Days*, 106.
26 See *Redbrick University*, 49.

Exercises, designed to facilitate selective funding policies and to stimulate, through reward, productivity in research. Doubtless he would have approved also, in principle, of official decisions recently taken to monitor and assess, nationally and systematically, the quality of teaching within the universities. Equally, he would have welcomed, in principle, the general implementation of the Scheme for Appraisal of University Staff, since he was outspokenly a believer that the performance of professors and others appointed to academic posts should regularly be subjected to review. On the other hand, he would have deplored the increased load of administrative work that the new policies of review and appraisal have imposed upon university staff and departments, with results disadvantageous and discouraging to the very activities — of teaching and research — which these policies have been formulated to encourage and improve. Assessment exercises, methods of appraisal, systems for monitoring courses, criteria for examining the criteria of examiners... have aggravated, in the 1990s, the main flaw that during the 1940s Peers observed in the newer British institutions: they have made still more cumbersome the 'cumbrous' 'Organization of a Modern University'.[27]

The treatment and standing of women in universities, both as students and members of staff — which major problem, understandably, preoccupies many academics and educationists nowadays — is a subject which Truscot considers incidentally and, therefore, for present-day readers, less than adequately. Nevertheless, his opinions, when he gives them, are invariably enlightened, and some are strikingly advanced. Thus, for instance, several decades before the measure that he advocated to equalize opportunities was put generally into practice, Truscot recommended that 'universities advertising posts in teaching and research... state: "Women are eligible for this post equally with men." '[28]

Interestingly, in a review-article published in the *Oxford Magazine* as recently as 1993, David Palfreyman discussed a number of Truscot's favoured opinions, and, quoting several

---

27 See *Redbrick University*, ch. 3, 'The Organization of a Modern University', especially p. 57.
28 See *Redbrick and these Vital Days*, 85.

passages at length from the 'Redbrick' books, illustrated their continuing relevance. Palfreyman reminds us, for instance, that Truscot drew attention to 'the issue of publication quantity rather than quality' (an issue 'so recently rediscovered'). This same critic recalls also what was Truscot's extreme, and extremely controversial, solution to the problem posed by 'Professor Deadwood', 'the leisured professor' who, once given his life-appointment, did little or no research. That solution was 'the abolition of tenure (a solution recently rediscovered by the Government)'.[29] Almost as interesting as Palfreyman's awareness of the topicality of Truscot's opinions, is the critic's apparent ignorance of the true identity of the author of *Redbrick University*. Which ignorance is evidently shared by the compilers of the *Oxford English Dictionary*, who, quoting from that book, simply give credit for coining the term 'Redbrick' to 'Bruce Truscot', without supplying the name of Truscot's creator. Given the persistent trouble taken during his lifetime to ensure that 'Truscot [would] remain Truscot until the whole of his work [was] done',[30] we may confidently assume that the author would have derived enjoyment, not displeasure, from the fact that, half a century after *Redbrick University* was first published, the invented figure of Bruce Truscot is better known among non-Hispanic circles of academics, intellectuals and educationists than is the person of the real Professor E. Allison Peers.

At the University of Liverpool, particularly during the past two years, important events have taken place and publications have appeared which have celebrated distinctive aspects of the varied life and diverse achievements of E. Allison Peers. Events have included a special lecture by Geoffrey Ribbans, delivered appropriately in the University's Victoria Building — the edifice whose appearance originally suggested the name and inspired the concept of *Redbrick University*. The subject of Professor Ribbans' lecture was equally appropriate: 'E. Allison Peers. A Centenary Reappraisal'. A Special Number of the *Bulletin of Hispanic Studies*, financed by the Gulbenkian Foundation, marked the seventieth birthday of the research journal Peers

---

29  See David Palfreyman, 'A Second View', *Oxford Magazine*, Eighth Week, Trinity Term, 1993, 3-5.

30  See Preface, *Redbrick and these Vital Days*, 15.

had founded (*Bulletin of Hispanic Studies* 1923-1993), and recognized Peers' pioneering work to develop in Britain the serious study of Portuguese and of *Portugal: Its Culture, Influence and Civilization*.[31] Liverpool University Press collaborated with the Modern Humanities Research Association to publish *Spain and its Literature*, a Volume of *Essays in Memory of E. Allison Peers*.[32] To commemorate publication of *Redbrick University* fifty years previously, an Exhibition was mounted in the University's Art Gallery. Financed from the Vice-Chancellor's Development Fund and by the Friends of the University, the Exhibition, of which an analytical and descriptive Catalogue was printed, illuminated the career of Allison Peers at 'The University of Liverpool: 1920-1952'. *Redbrick University* was again *Revisited*, thanks to a subvention from the University of Liverpool, through publication in this book of the autobiographies of Allison Peers and Bruce Truscot. Celebrations are planned to continue into 1997, when *Redbrick University* and *Redbrick and these Vital Days* will be republished in a one-volume edition, which will contain a Foreword written by Graeme Davies, and an Introductory Essay by Harold Silver, evaluating Truscot's ideas and their influence upon post-war developments in Britain's universities. Scheduled to follow the reappearance of Truscot's books, a Conference will take place at an appropriate location, during which, some 'Fifty Years after *Redbrick University*', eminent scholars, educationists and university administrators will discuss, and, it is to be expected, advance 'Research and Developments in Higher Education since 1945'. The Proceedings will be issued as a volume in the series E. Allison Peers Publications, for clearly more published research on this important subject is needed. In *The Times Higher Education Supplement* in 1991, Alison Utley reported upon 'Redbrick's Footnote on History' while describing the work of researchers engaged in 'A Case Study of the University of Birmingham'.

---

31 See *Portugal: Its Culture, Influence and Civilization*, edited, with an Introduction, by Ann L. Mackenzie, *Bulletin of Hispanic Studies*, LXXI, no. 1 (Liverpool: Liverpool U. P., 1994); see especially pp. 2-25.

32 Contributions published in this Volume include, as previously mentioned, Geoffrey Ribbans, 'E. Allison Peers: A Centenary Reappraisal' (*cf*. above, note 16).

Their investigations into 'Higher Education and Society' suggest that, since Bruce Truscot produced the first detailed discussion of the problems of a modern university, 'relatively little attention has been paid to the history of university development in England and Wales'.[33]

Perhaps after still forthcoming events and publications have been accomplished a book-length study might finally be undertaken, which would evaluate the character and achievements of Allison Peers as thoroughly as did Charles Illingworth the work and personality of Hector Hetherington, 'University Statesman'.[34] Certainly a full biography is justified, objectively to assess the contributions made by Peers to the advancement of human learning; and to place on final record 'all the mature wisdom of a fine scholar and an accomplished teacher' and 'the broad humanity and understanding sympathy of E. Allison Peers'. These are qualities — perceived by James Mountford in *First Year at the University* —[35] which we have observed throughout *Redbrick University Revisited: The Autobiography of 'Bruce Truscot'*.

Ann L. Mackenzie

*University of Liverpool, 1995.*

---

33 See *The Times Higher Education Supplement*, 11 January 1991. The researchers in question were Roy Lowe and Eric Ives; and their Project was funded by the Leverhulme Trust.

34 See Sir Charles Illingworth, *University Statesman: Sir Hector Hetherington* (Glasgow: Outram, 1971).

Research is currently being conducted (e.g., by Puri Gómez i Casademont, University of Sheffield) into Allison Peers' contribution to cultural and intellectual relations between Britain and Spain.

35 See Mountford, 'Bruce Truscot', *Memorial Number, Bulletin of Hispanic Studies*, XXX (1953), no. 117, 11.

# APPENDIX I

A     **A Chronology of the Filling of the Gilmour Chair of Spanish, University of Liverpool, 1919-1922**

Records concerning the Gilmour Chair of Spanish, 1908-09, and 1919-22, are contained in a box file of papers at the University Archives, Liverpool (ref. A.145). The papers relating to 1919-22 comprise mainly the following:

(a) Applications together with testimonials (in several cases several copies) submitted by the applicants for the Chair in 1919: these cover all twenty-three persons listed as applicants (30 October 1919).

(b) Correspondence of the successive Deans of the Faculty of Arts (Mr W. Garmon Jones, Dean, 1916-20; Professor A. Bruce Boswell, Dean, 1920-23) and of the Faculty's Chairman with members of the Chair Selection Committee, with applicants for the Chair and with applicants' referees, etc., 1919-22, together with a copy of the particulars of the Chair as advertised (May 1919). Letters from referees concern notably Peers, Madariaga and Sanín Cano.

(c) Brief notes taken [by the Dean] at the meetings of the Selection Committee, together with copies of reports submitted to the Faculty of Arts and the Senate, and related papers, 1921-22.

To assist the reader, information extracted from these records, and from other material in the University Archives, Liverpool, has been set out chronologically below. The names of the two principal persons involved in the debates and controversies are emphasized in bold type: **Edgar Allison Peers** and **James Fitzmaurice-Kelly**.

**1919**  5 March  Faculty of Arts accepts the report of a Committee which recommends that applications for the Chair be invited by advertisement in specified British, French, Spanish and South American journals. Report amended by Faculty to state that the Professor should be responsible for the 'organization and direction of research' as well as for lectures and classes, etc.

26 March  Letter of this date is received from Professor W. R. Halliday, Rathbone Professor of Ancient History at Liverpool, (writing from Glasgow) to Professor Bosanquet (who forwards it to Mr Garmon Jones) about Salvador de Madariaga. The latter worked in the Ministry of Information under Halliday's father-in-law, Professor Dixon, and made a considerable impression as a man of wide interests and intelligence and as a very attractive colleague. Halliday comments that Madariaga has an English wife who is remarkable on the intellectual as well as the aesthetic side; it would be worth trying to ensure Madariaga sees the advertisement 'unless **Fitz[maurice-Kelly]** has some swell up his sleeve'.

9 April  Letter of this date is received from Mr Thomas Jones, Offices of the War Cabinet, London, to Professor Roxby (Professor of Geography), stating that he has heard that the University may shortly proceed to the appointment of a Professor of Spanish and mentioning a friend of his, Salvador de Madariaga, who has been working for the British Government for the last couple of years and 'is a man of most unusual ability'; Madariaga's wife, who was a Miss Constance Archibald, a brilliant Glasgow student and translator of Gide's 'Political Economy' was an old pupil of Mr Jones.*

---

\* Mr Thomas Jones, C. H., 1870-1955, was a University Assistant in Political Economy at the University of Glasgow, 1899-1909; he was First Assistant Secretary, later

**1919**

[*c*.7] May — Chair is advertised in the press; applications with names of three referees and (if applicant so desires) twelve copies of testimonials to be sent to the Registrar by 30 June. Stipend £800 p.a.

14 May — Terms and conditions of the Chair are made available (to applicants).

28 May — Faculty of Arts appoints Committee to report on qualifications of candidates. Its members are: the Vice-Chancellor, officers of the Faculty (Mr W. Garmon Jones, Dean, and Professor R. C. Bosanquet, Chairman), Professors Case, Postgate and Terracher, Messrs J. Montgomery (Principal of the City School of Commerce, and Lecturer in Commercial Theory and Practice at the University) and Charles Booth, Miss Holt, and Dr P. Rébora (Senior Lecturer in Italian); amendment to add **Professor Fitzmaurice-Kelly** to the Committee is lost on division, but it is agreed that the Committee be empowered to consult the latter about the qualifications of the candidates.

25 June — Faculty of Arts agrees that (a) consideration of the applications for the Chair be deferred until the Autumn Term and (b) the Vice-Chancellor and the officers of the Faculty together with Mr Montgomery be empowered to make temporary arrangements for the teaching of Spanish in the Autumn Term; total number of applications for the Chair is not recorded at this date.

25 June — Letter of this date from **Mr E. Allison Peers**, The Old School House, Felsted, Essex, to the Electors of the Chair presenting himself as a candidate. **Peers** encloses three testimonials and names three referees.

14 October — Faculty of Arts adds Professors Collinson, Mair, and Bruce Boswell to the Committee to report on the Chair.

17 October — Memorandum from Professor Elton is sent to [?Dean of the Faculty] asking him to add 'this... a

---

Deputy Secretary of the Cabinet, 1916-30. See *Dictionary of National Biography*.

| | |
|---|---|
| **1919** | remarkable paper' to his *Spanish* file: Madariaga seems to have been setting his friends to work as he has been approached by two or three; forgets if he has already given him letters of Powicke* and [D. S.] MacColl (Keeper of the Wallace Collection, London) about Madariaga. |
| 29 October | Faculty of Arts agree to appoint Señor J. V. Varela to conduct the Intermediate and Final classes in Spanish. |
| 30 October | List of the applicants for the Chair is produced: a total of twenty-three persons, including two who had applied for the Chair in 1908. |
| [*c*.November] | Faculty Committee meets. Those present: Professors Postgate, Case, Bruce Boswell, and Collinson, Mr Alsop, Dr Rébora, and the Dean (Mr Garmon Jones). According to the notes of the meeting, they appear to have decided to omit **Peers**, [Dr C.] Pitollet, and [Dr J. M.] Villasante from further consideration, and to consider Salvador de Madariaga, José de Santiago, and J. [Jean] Saroïhandy. |
| 3-4 November | Letters of these dates provide references for Salvador de Madariaga. These are:<br>(a) from [Dr] D. S. MacColl, [Keeper of] The Wallace Collection, London, to Bruce Boswell.<br>(b) from Professor A. E. Zimmern, University College of Wales, Aberystwyth, to Mr Garmon Jones.<br>(c) from Mr Thomas Jones, Offices of the War Cabinet, London, to Mr Garmon Jones.<br>(d) from Professor W. Macneile Dixon, University of Glasgow, to an unnamed gentleman.<br>(e) from Professor F. M. Powicke, Manchester, to Professor Mair. |
| 4 November | Letter of this date from **Professor Fitzmaurice-Kelly**, London, to Professor Mair: requests copy of application of José de Santiago (whose work he |

---

\* Sir (Frederick) Maurice Powicke, F.B.A. (1879-1963) (knighted in 1946) was at the time Professor of Mediaeval History at the University of Manchester; later, 1928-47, he held the Regius Chair of Modern History at the University of Oxford. In 1905-06, he had been Assistant Lecturer in Modern History at the University of Liverpool.

| | | |
|---|---|---|
| **1919** | | does not know) and in the meantime would support a Spanish applicant, Madariaga for choice. |
| | 8 November | Dean of the Faculty of Arts sends **Professor Fitzmaurice-Kelly** the applications of Madariaga, Santiago, and Saroïhandy for his opinion. |
| | 13 November | Letter of this date from **Professor Fitzmaurice-Kelly** to the Dean of the Faculty of Arts: the former thinks that Madariaga is the best candidate of the three but suggests that Sanín Cano (from whom an application had not been received) 'would be a most excellent one, if it were at all possible'. |
| | 24 November | Faculty Committee meets. Present are: Professors Bosanquet, Mair, Case, Collinson, and Postgate, Dr Rébora, and Mr Montgomery. In light of **Fitzmaurice-Kelly**'s letter, they agree to enquire about Sanín Cano, and to seek **Fitzmaurice-Kelly**'s opinion of Mr Milton Buchanan (University of Toronto) and M. De Haan (Bryn Mawr College), neither of whom has applied, and to compare his opinions of Sanín Cano, Buchanan and De Haan. |
| | 26 November | Letter from **Professor Fitzmaurice-Kelly** to the Dean of the Faculty (in response to letter communicating the deliberations of the Committee): in his opinion, De Haan and Buchanan are much superior to anybody on the list of applicants; but he suspects neither would accept an invitation; he advocates the case of Sanín Cano. |
| | [30 November] | [**E. Allison Peers** interviewed by the Dean of the Faculty of Arts for the post of temporary lecturer 'to take charge of the Department of Spanish, and to give assistance in the Department of French for the Lent Term, 1920, at a salary of £200'.] |
| | [?3-4 December] | Faculty Committee meets. Present are: Professors Mair, Case, Postgate, Boswell, and Collinson, Dr Rébora, and Mr Garmon Jones. In view of **Professor Fitzmaurice-Kelly**'s letter, it is agreed that the Dean should write to Sanín Cano, inviting him to make a formal application (since perhaps the advertisement had not 'come under his notice'). |

| | | |
|---|---|---|
| **1919** | 5 December | Dean of the Faculty of Arts writes to Mr Sanín Cano inviting him to apply for the Chair, requesting a statement of his career and publications and the names of two or three scholars to whom reference might be made, and adding that he did not think 'we need trouble you for testimonials'. |
| | 8 December | Letter of this date received from Professor W. P. Ker, All Souls College, Oxford, to Professor Elton offering his opinion that Madariaga 'would very probably make a success of it [the Chair]'; he has twice heard him lecture. |
| | 16 December | University Council approved the recommendation of the Senate that **Peers** be appointed 'to take charge of the Department of Spanish, and to give assistance in the Department of French for the Lent Term, 1920, at a salary of £200'. |
| | 20 December | Letter of this date from Sanín Cano sent to the University Registrar offering himself as a candidate for the Chair, giving details of his career and the names of three referees (see under 26 January 1920). |
| **1920** | 8 January | Lent Term commenced. |
| | 26 January | Faculty Committee meets (no record of those present), and considers Sanín Cano in the light of letters received from three referees (**Professor Fitzmaurice-Kelly**; Dr C. Hagberg Wright of the London Library, who has been assisted by Sanín Cano; and [**Fitzmaurice-Kelly**'s friend and former colleague at Liverpool] Emeritus Professor J. M. Mackay). Committee decides to interview Cano, **Peers**, and Madariaga and to ask Cano to send any of his publications; Professor Postgate is 'to write to Richmond', and also to Sacolea, and to ask permission of **Fitzmaurice-Kelly** 'to use [him] for contacts'. |
| | 5 February | Letter of this date is sent by Professor H. J. C. Grierson, Edinburgh, to Shields Nicholson about Sanín Cano (who came to Edinburgh on **Fitzmaurice-Kelly**'s strong recommendation). Grierson praises Sanín Cano for his scholarship and as a man he would trust absolutely: he is strong and does an extraordinary amount of work. |

## APPENDIX I 417

| | | |
|---|---|---|
| **1920** | 9 February | Faculty Committee meets at 2.30 p.m. in the Dean's room to interview **Peers** (2.30 p.m.), Madariaga (3.00 p.m.), and Sanín Cano (3.30 p.m.). Members of the Committee present: Dr G. S. Veitch (Chairman of the Faculty), Professors Case, Boswell, Collinson, and Postgate, Dr Rébora, the Dean (Mr W. Garmon Jones) and Mr Montgomery. According to a letter sent by Dr Veitch (Chairman of the Faculty) to **Professor Fitzmaurice-Kelly**, on 14 February, seeking his advice, the Committee decided, after the interviews: that Cano ruled himself out through his other commitments; that Madariaga had no teaching experience — so that they doubted whether he could carry on, with any thoroughness, the work of an Honours School or undertake to direct higher work or research; and that **Peers** was not 'yet ripe enough for a big Chair' though 'some members of the Committee' were coming round to the view that he might be the safest man to appoint. He (Veitch) and Garmon Jones were not sure that **Peers** was yet strong enough for the post. Professor Collinson later reported to Professor J. G. Robertson that Madariaga made a 'splash' while **Peers** made a diffident impression on the Committee. |
| | 12 February | Letter of this date is sent from Professor J. G. Robertson, London, to Professor Collinson (in response to a letter from the latter about the three candidates for the Chair). Robertson declares that he knows Sanín Cano as an occasional contributor to the *Modern Language Review* and that he is a man of scholarly attainment. He does not know who Madariaga is. What he can say of **Peers** does not concern his Spanish scholarship, but Robertson praises his edition of De Vigny, has a high opinion of him personally ('he has shown quite marvellous energy and ability in organising The Mod. Lang. Research Association; he has the right ideals...') and is surprised to hear he made a diffident impression at his interview by the Committee. A year or two ago he had advised **Peers** to devote himself to Spanish and to visit Madrid and take up some field of special investigation in Spanish literature. Though at the time this plan was impossible to realise on practical grounds, he (**Peers**) is most anxious to realise it and if appointed to the Chair, Robertson is confident he |

**1920**

                        will do so. Robertson concedes that it is dangerous to appoint a man whose claims to a professorship rest to some extent on promises but **Peers** has the interests of higher modern languages study so much at heart that he is to be trusted.

14 February        Letter of this date is sent from **Professor Fitzmaurice-Kelly** to Professor Mair about the three candidates interviewed, dismissing Peers as not 'even a *possible* appointment', rejecting Madariaga, and hoping that Sanín Cano's work for *La Nación* will not stand in the way of his appointment to the Chair.

16 February        Letter of this date is sent from **Professor Fitzmaurice-Kelly** to Dr Veitch suggesting the appointment of Sanín Cano for five years; commenting that Madariaga 'is not a scholar' and that Peers 'is not a serious candidate'; and doubting the chances of attracting either De Haan or Buchanan, the former of whom he believes to be superior to the latter.

[16-21 February]     Faculty Committee meets during this week and considers **Professor Fitzmaurice-Kelly**'s letter; and Professor Mair proposes, and Professor Collinson seconds, that in the event of Sanín Cano being able to devote his whole time to the post, he be recommended for appointment. It is agreed that Peers 'goes' (from further consideration); that Madariaga 'be removed' (Dr Rébora and Mr Montgomery voting against); and that, before proceeding further, Sanín Cano should be written to and asked whether he would devote his full time to the work of the Chair as a professor resident in Liverpool, or whether he adheres to his statement that it will be necessary to make arrangements to allow him to continue his work in London. The Committee, practically unanimously, believes that, with the great influx of students and the closer relations of the City and University, a resident professor devoting substantially all his time and energies to the post is necessary.

APPENDIX I 419

| | | |
|---|---|---|
| **1920** | 27 February | Letter of this date is sent from Sanín Cano to the Dean of the Faculty stating that he cannot sever his connection with *La Nación* and would have to ask for time off to do this work in London. |
| | [?10]March | Faculty Committee meets. Present: Dr Veitch, Professors Postgate, Collinson, Boswell and Mair, Dr Rébora, and Mr Garmon Jones. The Committee agrees to report that they cannot recommend a candidate for the Chair. They should proceed, after enquiry, by invitation and should seek permission to offer, if necessary, an increased salary of £1,000 p.a. (Faculty, Senate and Council agrees to this report and its recommendations.) |
| | 29 March | Dean of the Faculty writes to Professor Milton Buchanan, University of Toronto, enquiring in a confidential, unofficial way (having consulted the Vice-Chancellor) whether he would accept the Chair if invited, and expressing confidence that professorial salaries will soon be increased to £1,000, and stating that the work 'at present is quite light but there are prospects of the School being considerably developed'. |
| | 10 May | Letter is sent from Professor Buchanan to the Dean stating that 'circumstances prevent my entertaining the thought of leaving my present position'. |
| | 16 June | Letter is sent from the Dean of the Faculty to Dr H. Thomas, British Museum, at the request of the Faculty Committee, enclosing a report on the applicants and inviting him to submit names and suggest any possible lines of enquiry — 'as we seem to have exhausted our resources'. |
| | 21 June | Letter is sent from Dr Thomas to the Dean of the Faculty suggesting that it would be simpler, and perhaps better, if he could make suggestions over a lunch-table to a member of the Faculty Committee who might intend to be in London. |
| | 24 June | Letter is sent from the Dean of the Faculty to Dr Thomas stating that he hopes to be in London sometime in the summer and will write again to suggest possible dates for a meeting. |

| | | |
|---|---|---|
| **1921** | 19 October | Faculty of Arts appoints Committee to consider and report upon the qualifications of candidates for the Chair. Members are the Vice-Chancellor, Officers of the Faculty (the Dean, Professor Bruce Boswell, and the Chairman, Professor Collinson), Professors Case, Eggli, Elton, Mair, and Slater, Dr Rébora, Messrs W. Garmon Jones, H. Wade Deacon, and J. Arthur Smith. (Wade Deacon and Smith are Vice-President of the University Council and a member of the University Council respectively.) |
| | 28 October | Faculty Committee meets (all members being present except Mr Smith) to review the situation. Reference is made to the three interviewed candidates, Sanín Cano, Madariaga, and **Peers**, and to Dr Thomas and [Mr G. A.] Kolkhorst).* It is decided to seek confirmation of Council's authorization to fill the Chair; and to seek authorization to increase the salary to the minimum of £900 p.a. attached to all full-time Chairs. |
| | 1 November | University Council agrees to the recommendation that Señor D. Nicolás González Ruiz be appointed temporary Lecturer in Spanish for Session 1921-22 — to assist **E. Allison Peers**. |
| | 15 November | University Council authorizes the Senate and the Faculty of Arts to proceed with their enquiries as to the possibility of filling the Chair, and agrees to a salary of £900 p.a. if a suitable candidate is found. |
| | 21 November | Faculty Committee meets (all members being present except the Vice-Chancellor and Messrs H. Wade Deacon and J. A. Smith). They agree that: Professor Mair would interview Dr Thomas as to whether he would himself stand on a short list; the Chairman is to write to Professor Robertson for details of Spanish scholars who might be approached; Professor Eggli is to make enquiries in France; the Dean is to write to Professor Buchanan seeking possible candidates in America who would be accessible to the Committee in Britain, and |

---

\* G. A. Kolkhorst (d. 1958) was Taylorian Lecturer in Spanish from 1921, and later, 1931-58, Reader in Spanish at the University of Oxford. John Betjeman, in his tribute to Kolkhorst (*The Times*, 17 September 1958), described him as 'one of the most beloved Oxford figures', who 'had no tolerance for pedantic research'. Kolkhorst was out of sympathy with modern literary scholarship and published little.

| | | |
|---|---|---|
| 1921 | | asking his opinion of the qualifications of **Mr Peers**, and particularly of his published work. The Dean is to ask **Mr Peers** whether he is willing to submit his name for consideration; and is to invite him to submit any additional material or more recent testimonials. |
| | 23 November | Letter of this date is sent from Professor J. G. Robertson, London, to Professor Collinson stating that he knows none of the Spanish Lecturers at any of the universities. When appointments have been made (if he has heard about them) the usual cry is that there are so few candidates who can even be considered; Edinburgh University in filling their lectureship ended by taking a young man from Oxford who had only just graduated. If **Peers** had not withdrawn he believes he would have been certain of this appointment. At King's College London they could not fill the Cervantes Chair [which had been vacated by **Fitzmaurice-Kelly** in 1920] and ultimately appointed a Reader who was really a jurist and not a Spanish scholar at all; but there were complications and cross-currents there. |
| | 28 November | Letter of this date is sent from Professor Mair to Professor Boswell stating that he had had an interview with Dr Henry Thomas about the possibility of becoming a candidate for the Chair and that the latter had asked for time for fuller consideration. Professor Mair had indicated that a decisive reply would be appreciated within a week. |
| | 30 November | **Mr Peers** writes to the Dean of the Faculty submitting a statement of his work since his first appointment at Liverpool and enclosing copies of original work (books and articles) and testimonials from eight persons in support of his candidature. |
| | 6 December | Letter of this date from Professor Buchanan to Mr Garmon Jones in strong support of the candidature of **Mr Peers**, mentioning his organization of the Modern Humanities Research Association, his publications, and his teaching. |

| | | |
|---|---|---|
| **1921** | 12 December | Letter of this date from Professor Buchanan to Professor Bruce Boswell (Dean of the Faculty of Arts), in response to the latter's letter of 22 November, in support of **Peers** as a scholar, teacher, and 'a man of extraordinary energy and with fine endowments for investigation and criticism', and stating that he knows of no teacher at present in Canada and the USA who would be accessible to the Committee (the study of Spanish having had such an extraordinary development in both countries). |
| **1922** | 9 January | Letter of this date from Professor Campagnac to the Dean of the Faculty enclosing a letter to the former from Professor Peter Sandiford, Ontario College of Education, passing on Professor Buchanan's opinion that Liverpool should give **Peers** the Chair. |
| | 16 February | Letter of this date from Professor Elton to the Dean of the Faculty stating that he will be unable to attend the Committee meeting tomorrow but admitting that there would seem to be a strong *prima facie* case for **Peers** being, not necessarily the best, but a worthy occupant of the Chair, subject to reassurances from the Spanish scholars who wrote about **Peers** in 1920, adding that his opinion is without prejudice to other candidates who may come forward. |
| | 17 February | Faculty Committee meets. Present are: the Dean, the Chairman, Professors Case, Eggli, and Slater, and Mr Garmon Jones); 'letters [are] read', and it is agreed that the Dean should write to **Professor Fitzmaurice-Kelly** asking whether he wishes to modify his previous statement of 16 February 1920 in light of **Mr Peers'** subsequent work (enclosing a copy of his statement etc.) or to give a fresh opinion. |
| | 20 February | Letter of this date is sent from **Professor Fitzmaurice-Kelly** [in the handwriting of his wife] to [the Dean] stating he has nothing to add to his 1920 statement. He comments that **Peers**, will have 'doubtless acquired a certain fluency in the use of the Spanish language'; but states that several of the chief witnesses cited by **Peers** are not particularly strong in Spanish and that the American professors' knowledge of him is naturally limited. |

APPENDIX I 423

| | | |
|---|---|---|
| **1922** | 24 February | Faculty Committee meets (all present except the Vice-Chancellor, Dr Rébora, and Messrs Wade Deacon and Smith). Letters from Buchanan [? of 12 December 1921] and **Fitzmaurice-Kelly** [of 20 February] are read, and Professor Mair reports on Dr Thomas. They decide to ask **Professor Fitzmaurice-Kelly** to examine [unpublished] material submitted by **Peers** and to provide a comparative estimate of the claims of **Peers** and Dr Thomas. They decide also to ask Professor W. P. Ker for his opinion on the situation as a whole, and on **Peers** and Dr Thomas. |
| | 25 February | Letter is sent from [the Dean of the Faculty] to Dr Thomas mentioning that for some months Professor Mair has been in touch with him about his becoming a candidate for the Chair and asking for his final decision during the week ending 4 March. |
| | 28 February | The Dean of the Faculty speaks to **Mr Peers** and the latter confirms in writing his willingness for his unpublished work, with the Committee, to be sent to **Professor Fitzmaurice-Kelly** for his opinion. |
| | '23'[?28]February | Letter of this date is sent from Professor Ker to the Dean of the Faculty stating that he knows nothing against **Mr Peers** 'except that he made me work for the Modern Languages Research Association — and I don't bear him a grudge for this' and asking 'why did you not elect Salvador Madariaga? You might have made a scholar of him'. |
| | 22 March | Letter is sent from the Dean of the Faculty (on behalf of the Committee) to Ramón Menéndez Pidal, Madrid, requesting his opinion of the scholarship and ability for research displayed by **Mr Peers**' work, forwarding him a copy of the application in which is listed **Peers**' work already published, and offering to show him the unpublished MSS. in addition if desired. |
| | 27 March | Letter of this date is sent from **Professor Fitzmaurice-Kelly** [in the handwriting of his wife] to the Dean of the Faculty, explaining that bad weather and illness have delayed his response about **Peers**' work which the Dean had sent. He cannot criticize the printed papers without this seeming to reflect on their various editors but as |

**1922**

regards the paper on the Duque de Rivas, **Peers** seems to follow Díaz almost too rigidly and omits reference to various mistakes of Díaz, which prevent one taking the English life of Rivas too seriously.

12 April
Letter is sent from [the Dean of the Faculty] to Dr Thomas conveying the Committee's regret that he has finally decided not to submit his name for consideration by the Committee and asking for his opinion on the field in general and on the claims of **Mr Peers**, the only candidate now being considered by the Committee.

2 May
Letter of this date is sent by Dr Thomas to [the Dean of the Faculty] stating that no one of the requisite training and standing is available in these islands; and that it is most unlikely that any foreign scholar of established reputation could be induced to come to England. Thomas comments that **Mr Peers** has produced Spanish school books since 1917, beginning with a grammar from which his reputation may in time recover (though its adoption as a medium of instruction at Liverpool does not hasten this end); he undertakes tasks for which his scholarship is unequal, and he has not developed the self-correction necessary to supplement an inadequate training. If an appointment cannot be postponed, Thomas suggests re-consideration of Madariaga, whom he has written to, failing which the Committee might enquire into Mr G. A. Kolkhorst (Exeter College), Lecturer in the University of Oxford, and Mr. W. Starkie[*] (Trinity College, Dublin), Lecturer in that college, both being young men 'of the type that one could confidently recommend for a lectureship, with the assurance that in a few years they would earn their promotion'. He suggests the Committee might take the risk of nominating one of them to a provisional post.

---

[*] Walter Starkie (1894-1976), Professor of Spanish, Trinity College, Dublin (1926-47), and Director of the British Institute in Madrid (1940-54), author of *Spanish Raggle Taggle* (1934) and other works, was appointed by Peers in 1949 to the newly formed Editorial Board of the *Bulletin of Hispanic Studies*. He contributed an appreciation of Peers to the *Memorial Number* of the journal (1953).

APPENDIX I 425

**1922**  4 May  Letter of this date is sent by Dr Thomas to the Dean of the Faculty stating that Madariaga has informed him that he is no longer available as he is contracted to the League of Nations; there is little prospect of finding a suitable Spaniard. He, therefore, advises the Committee 'to secure in some way the Englishman who promises best', favouring 'the Oxford man' [Mr Kolkhorst].

10 May  Letter of this date is sent by Ramón Menéndez Pidal to the Dean of the Faculty (in response to a letter of 6 May which enclosed a copy of the Dean's original letter of 22 March) stating that **Peers'** research which is known to him has 'been fruitful' and that in his *A Phonetic Spanish Reader* (1920) he shows 'an adequate understanding of the Spanish language, providing through it a useful tool for the teaching of an aspect of this language...'.*

16 May  Faculty Committee meets (all members being present except Messrs Wade Deacon and Smith). Letters are read from Professors Ker and **Fitzmaurice-Kelly**, Dr Thomas, and Ramón Menéndez Pidal. There is no record of the discussion.

22 May  Faculty Committee meets for its final discussion (all members present except Messrs Wade Deacon and Smith). Professors Slater and Collinson propose that in **Mr Peers** there is a candidate whom the Committee can recommend for the Chair, but an amendment (proposed by Professor Elton [?and Mr Garmon Jones]) to recommend the appointment of **Peers** to a Senior Lectureship for three years is carried by seven votes to three. The latter motion, with a £700 p.a. stipend, was then proposed as a substantive motion, to which Professors Slater and Collinson put an amendment (which was lost by three votes to seven) proposing **Peers'** appointment to the Chair for five years. The Report as thus agreed was then supported by seven members, and opposed by two; one did not vote, and two members were absent. The Report of the Faculty Committee states that, after long and thorough investigations, the members had the

---

\* The letter, in Spanish, from this eminent scholar, supporting **Peers**, is reproduced in facsimile on p. 158; a translation into English is provided in this Appendix (see p. 448).

**1922**  name of only one candidate before them. In view of the marked division of testimony as to the scholarship of **Mr Peers**, the Committee advise against any recommendation for appointment to the Chair but are strongly of the opinion that there is good and sufficient evidence as to **Mr Peers'** merits as a scholar and a teacher to justify proposing his appointment as Senior Lecturer in Spanish (Grade I) at a stipend of £700 p.a. for three years. The report quotes extracts from testimonials received from Professors Robertson, Churchman, and Buchanan, Señor Artigas, and Señor Menéndez Pidal.

7 June  Faculty of Arts receives the report of the Committee on the applications for the Chair:
(a) An amendment, moved by Professor Webster and seconded, to appoint **E.A. Peers** to the Chair, at a salary of £900 p.a., is lost by 13 votes to 14.
(b) An amendment is then moved by Professor Mair, seconded and carried, that the words 'Lecturer in charge of the Department of Spanish' be substituted for the words 'Senior Lecturer in Spanish, Grade I'.
(c) The report as amended is then carried by eighteen votes to two and forwarded to Senate and Council.

14 June  Senate receives the report of the Faculty of Arts:—
(a) An amendment is carried by nineteen votes to twelve that **Mr Peers** be appointed to the Chair for a period of five years as from 1 October 1922.
(b) This amendment is then adopted as the substantive resolution by nineteen votes to eight.

20 June  Council refers Senate's report on the Chair, for consideration and report, to a Committee composed of the following: the President, Pro-Chancellor Caton, the Vice-Chancellor, the Treasurer, Emeritus Professor Sir William Herdman, Lieut.-Col. J. J. Shute, Mr G. A. Solly, and Mr J. Carlton Stitt. (Members of the Council present at this meeting of Council included Professor Mair and Mr Garmon Jones.)

| | | |
|---|---|---|
| **1922** | 21 June | Faculty of Arts receives the report on the meeting of the Council held on 20 June, and the Dean states that the Council's Committee would be pleased to hear any member of Faculty who might wish to give evidence.<br><br>The Dean of the Faculty of Arts writes to the Registrar, in answer to his request, listing the Committee members and the final voting figures. The Dean encloses **Mr Peers'** applications of 1919 and 1921 and his testimonials, together with the letters received from Professors **Fitzmaurice-Kelly** (16 Feb. 1920, 20 Feb. & 27 March 1922) and Buchanan (6 & 12 Dec. 1921), Dr Thomas (2 & 4 May 1922) and Sr Menéndez Pidal (10 May 1922). Also enclosed are copies of the Report approved by the Faculty. |
| | 26 June | Meeting of the Committee of the Council. Those present are: the President (Mr H. R. Rathbone), the Treasurer (Mr C. Sydney Jones), the Vice-Chancellor (Dr J. G. Adami), Sir Wm Herdman, and Lieut.-Col. Shute).<br>The Dean of the Faculty of Arts (Professor Bruce Boswell) provides details of the voting in the Faculty Committee. It appears that the Faculty Committee Report was supported at 22 May meeting by the Vice-Chancellor, Professors Collinson, Eggli, Elton and Slater and two others, and opposed by two [? Professor Mair and ?], with one member not voting. The Dean refers to **Fitzmaurice-Kelly**'s letters ('their sweeping statements and unfortunate language'), Dr Thomas' condemnation of the phonetic Spanish reader, and **Peers**' record at Liverpool. He mentions opinions of 'B.B.' [Bruce Boswell]: '[**Peers**] is an admirable organiser and a first-class teacher'. The Dean states that the Faculty Committee was instructed that Dr Thomas be approached to advise about the field, and that the 'Committee had to discount **F.-Kelly**'s evidence'. Professor Collinson, as Chairman of the Faculty, evidently also appears before the Committee of the Council to give evidence. |
| | 27 June | Letter (in French) of this date is sent by Professor Eggli to Mr Garmon Jones, to whom he has spoken that morning, stating that he has to depart for |

**1922**  Paris tomorrow and so writes to advise on **Peers'** candidature as follows: Mérimée's testimonial for **Peers** appears to be voluntarily reserved; he [Eggli] does not personally approve of **Peers'** method of work, tackling large subjects with insufficient preparation (singling out his *Origins of French Romanticism*). Therefore, Eggli supports the Faculty Committee's recommendation, but he still hopes that **Mr Peers** can be assured of a stable and satisfying situation which will allow him to pursue work with much calm, without the preoccupations of an immediate candidature. It is advisable to reserve his [appointment to the Chair] until the time when the unfavourable judgements to which he has sometimes given rise may be clearly revised.

4 July  Council, (attended by twenty members, including Mr Garmon Jones and Professor Mair) rejects, by twelve votes to six, an amendment to the recommendation of the Special Committee of Council, that 'in accordance with the recommendation of the Faculty of Arts' **Mr Peers** be appointed Lecturer in charge of the Department of Spanish for a period of three years at a salary of £700 p.a., and approves, instead, the motion (which is the recommendation of the Special Committee of Council) that he be appointed to the Chair for a period of five years as from 1 October 1922 at a salary of £800 p.a.

4 July  The University Registrar writes to **Professor Peers**, St Winifred's, Cambridge Road, Worthing (the home of his parents), communicating the Council's decision to appoint **Peers** to the Gilmour Chair.

## B  Applications by E. Allison Peers for the Gilmour Chair of Spanish, University of Liverpool, 1919 and 1921

(i) Application of **Edgar Allison Peers**, M.A. for the Gilmour Chair of Spanish in the University of Liverpool, 1919.*

The Old School House,<br>
Felsted,<br>
Essex.<br>
25 June, 1919.

To the Electors to the Gilmour Chair of Spanish, The University, Liverpool.

Gentlemen,

I beg leave hereby to present myself as a Candidate for the vacant Gilmour Chair of Spanish in the University of Liverpool.

I am a Master of Arts of Cambridge and London Universities. From 1909 to 1913 I was a Scholar of Christ's College, Cambridge, and won during those years the Skeat and Calverley Prizes and the Porteous** Medal. In open competition in the University I won the Winchester Prize (1912), the Harness Prize (1913) and the Members' Prize (1914). In 1912 I was *proxime accessit* for the Charles Oldham Shakespeare Scholarship. In the same year I graduated, taking First Class Honours, with distinction, in the Mediaeval and Modern Languages Tripos. In 1915 I took the degree of Master of Arts at the University of London.

After taking my first degree I remained for a time at Cambridge, obtained a First Class with double distinction in the Examination for the Teachers' Diploma, and was entrusted by my College with the tuition of a number of pupils. In May, 1914 I entered for a Taylorian Lectureship in French at Oxford University, and was placed, out of sixty candidates, on a selected list of three.

Almost immediately afterwards, the War broke out, and as I was physically unfit for active service (my War record is given on another page) I accepted a Modern Language Mastership at Felsted School, where I was able to use in the O.T.C. the military knowledge gained during five years of O.T.C. training at school and university. At Felsted I have taught French and Spanish, together with some German, and

---

\* The information about his early life, experiences and qualifications which Peers provides in this letter of application confirms the accuracy of his account given in *The Autobiography of E. Allison Peers*.

\*\* In fact, the Porteus Medal, named after a Bishop of London, Beilby Porteus (d. 1808), who provided the funds to endow the Medal (*cf.* above, ch. 2, p. 82, note 23).

have organised the Modern Language Course throughout.

My interest in Spanish dates from my boyhood. When I was at Cambridge there was little encouragement to read it for a degree, but since the War began I have taken an active part, as my referees will testify, in the development of Spanish teaching and study in this country. For the last three years I have spared no efforts to secure to Spanish a more important place in the University syllabus and the school curriculum; at Felsted I was entirely responsible for the introduction of the language into the school; I am engaged upon a doctorate thesis dealing with Spanish literary relations; I have published a *Skeleton Spanish Grammar* which has been taken up very widely in the British Isles; I am an active member of the Spanish Sub-Committee of the Modern Language Association, continuously, since its inception; and I have recently undertaken the general Editorship of a series of Advanced Spanish Texts to be issued by the Manchester University Press.

My interests, however, are by no means solely academic. I speak Spanish with fluency and correctness, and desire in a practical way to promote closer relations with Spain, and no less with Spanish America, where I have family connections. I feel very keenly the paramount importance of the relations between Modern Languages and Commerce and if elected to the Chair should do my utmost to further them. Last March I made a special journey to Madrid and other intellectual centres of Northern Spain with the object of investigating at first hand the possibilities of approximation between England and Spain in the immediate future. On my return from this visit, His Excellency the Spanish Ambassador, to whom I am personally known, invited me to attend a Conference of the Anglo-Spanish Society with other corporations for the purpose of setting on foot new movements to further an intercourse with Spain, and at that meeting nominated me as one of the original members of the Anglo-Spanish Council.

My experience of organisation has been considerably widened since the foundation of the Modern Language Research Association,[*] a body designed to encourage and stimulate advanced study in Modern Languages and Literatures, which at the end of its first year numbered more than three hundred members, drawn both from this country and abroad. I am entirely responsible for the organisation of the Association — of which I am Honorary General Secretary and Honorary Organiser of the Spanish Group — and I trust that in a new sphere I may now be able to make use of the experience which I have gained in this.

I am competent and shall be willing to teach Portuguese as well as Spanish, if required.

I have a good general knowledge of European languages and literatures other than Spanish and Portuguese. I speak and write French very fluently, and have a ready command of German and Italian,

---

[*] Now called the Modern Humanities Research Association (see Peers' account of the establishment of the Association, in *The Autobiography of E. Allison Peers*, ch. 3, pp. 103-11).

besides a reading knowledge of Dutch and Russian. The latter language I studied in 1915 when I hoped that my medical category would not debar me from an interpretership abroad. I have published, besides my Spanish Grammar and some articles contributed to English and American learned reviews, an Essay entitled *Elizabethan Drama and its Mad Folk*, (1914); have edited Alfred de Vigny's Poems, with a critical introduction, for the Manchester University Press (1918), and have now in the Press a volume (written in collaboration) on early nineteenth-century literature.*

Testimonials are enclosed with this application from:—

    (1) Dr A. E. Shipley, Master of Christ's College and Vice-Chancellor of the University of Cambridge.
    (2) Norman McLean, Esq., Senior Tutor of Christ's College, Cambridge.
    (3) Dr E. G. W. Braunholtz, Reader in Romance in the University of Cambridge.

The following Scholars, to all of whom I am personally well known, allow me to name them as referees in connection with this post:

    (1) Professor Ernest Mérimée, Professor of Spanish, University of Toulouse, France.
    (2) Professor L. E. Kastner, Professor of French, University of Manchester.
    (3) Professor J. G. Robertson, Professor of German, University of London; Editor of the *Modern Language Review*.

In conclusion, I would say that I fully appreciate the importance of the post for which I now apply, and the great responsibilities which it entails. I am willing and anxious to devote my life and energies to the task of promoting the study of a country, language and literature, to which I have always been attached — as well by practical activities as by teaching and research. If elected to this Chair I should do my utmost for the welfare of the University of Liverpool, both generally and in connection with the immediate duties of the Professorship.

    I have the honour to remain,
        Gentlemen,
            Your obedient servant,

                [signed] Edgar Allison Peers.

---

    * See below (p. 437) in his second application for the Chair (1921), his mention of his book, with M. B. Finch, on the *Origins of French Romanticism*. See also *The Autobiography of E. Allison Peers*, ch. 4, p. 127 and note 10.

**WAR STATEMENT**

(Instructions § 7.)

On August 5th, 1914, I applied through the Cambridge University Officers' Training Corps for a Commission in the Army, having previously served in this Corps and taken the War Office Certificate A. But being physically unfit (through a lung weakness and a defect in one eye) for active service, I received a Commission in the Territorial Force and was attached to the Felsted School contingent of the Officers' Training Corps. This Commission I still hold. On several occasions I have applied to go abroad as an Interpreter, but even here I have been unsuccessful. During Vacations I have attended Military instructional courses and done clerical and other War work, and I have been responsible in the Corps at Felsted for most of the Military preparation of Candidates for Woolwich and Sandhurst.

[signed] E. Allison Peers.

25 June, 1919.

## Testimonials of E. Allison Peers, M.A. (Cambridge and London)

Christ's College Lodge,
Cambridge.

MR. E. ALLISON PEERS was a student of this College from 1909 to 1912. He is a man of wide culture, and, in his way, exceptional learning. His conduct has been exemplary. He is a man with a sense of responsibility, and is thoroughly trustworthy. I have great confidence in recommending him for a post as a University Teacher.

[signed] A. E. SHIPLEY,
Master of Christ's College, Cambridge,
Vice-Chancellor of Cambridge University.

10th April, 1919.

# APPENDIX I 433

Christ's College,
Cambridge.

I have pleasure in testifying to the excellent qualifications of my friend and pupil, E. Allison Peers, M.A., for a teaching post or Lectureship in Modern Languages. Mr. Peers proved himself during his four years' course at Cambridge one of the ablest students and hardest workers in this college. He is a man of wide interests and reading and is particularly strong in his knowledge of English and French literatures.

His degree was an excellent one. He obtained Second Class Honours in English in the Mediaeval and Modern Languages Tripos at the end of his second year, and First Class Honours in French in the same Tripos at the end of his third year.

In October 1911, he was awarded the Skeat Prize at this College for English Literature and Philology, and in 1912, the Calverley Prize for an English Essay. He also obtained the Winchester Reading Prize and Members' Prize in the University, and, at this College, the Porteus Medal for reading in Chapel. He was *proxime accessit* in 1912 for the Charles Oldham University Shakespeare Scholarship.

In 1913, he was awarded the (University) Harness Prize for an essay published in 1914 as *Elizabethan Drama and its Mad Folk*, an able work on an exceedingly elusive subject. His *Skeleton Spanish Grammar* (1917) shows him alive to the needs of the moment, his introduction to and edition of *Vigny: Poèmes Choisis* (1918) as thoroughly abreast with the latest critical thought and able to take a wide and profound view of literature. In the summer of 1918, he founded the Modern Language Research Association, of which he is Secretary, and its initial success is entirely due to his enthusiasm and organizing ability.

I will only add that Mr. Peers is a man of the highest character and principle, and in every way a gentleman.

[signed] Norman McLean,
Fellow and Senior Tutor of Christ's College.

24th March, 1919.


Goslar,
Adams Road,
Cambridge,

20th March, 1919.

I have much pleasure in expressing the very high opinion I have formed of Mr. E. Allison Peers's capacities, acquirements, zeal, energy, and organizing power, and in warmly supporting his application for appointment as a University Teacher. Having known Mr. Peers since his undergraduate days I can testify to his marked success as a student of French language and literature, and as a candidate for the Tripos in that subject. I know that since leaving Cambridge he has, in addition to his work as a Modern Language Master, been indefatigably active in extending his knowledge of Romance languages and literatures and in pursuing research, particularly in the field of French literature. It is largely to his enthusiasm for research, his initiative and efficiency as an organiser, that we owe the foundation of the Modern Language Research Association, of which he is the Honorary Secretary.

I have no doubt whatever that Mr. Peers is particularly well-fitted for the work of an academic teacher and that by appointing him any University will make a valuable addition to its staff.

[signed] E. G. W. Braunholtz, M.A., Ph.D.,
University Reader in Romance.

(ii) Application of **Edgar Allison Peers**, M.A. for the Gilmour Chair of Spanish in the University of Liverpool, 1921.*

The University,
Liverpool,
November 30 1921

The Dean of the
    Faculty of Arts.

Dear Sir,
    In reply to your letter of the 21st I beg leave herewith to present myself as a candidate for the Gilmour Chair of Spanish. As the Committee will be aware, I have been appointed Lecturer and Head of the Department of Spanish since January 1920, twice for periods of one term concurrently with a post in the Department of French, and twice for periods of one year. During the last two years I have done my utmost to further the best interests of the Department and of the University, by teaching, organisation, and personal study and research. I should be glad if besides the original work and the testimonials which I send with this letter I might be allowed to submit to the Committee a brief statement of my work here since my first appointment.

---

* The length and content of the second application demonstrate the extraordinary progress and productivity which, in little more than two years, Peers achieved, as scholar, teacher and publicist of Spanish language, literature and civilization.

I   **DEPARTMENTAL WORK**

**Within the Department**:

In January 1920 there were in the Department fifteen students, only two or three of whom had done any Spanish before. In June 1920 there were 29. In October 1920 there were 54. There are now 75. Careful segregation of the better students and intensive work with them from the first, together with a large increase in the number of students who come to us having done some Spanish already, has been responsible for so marked an improvement in the standard of work that as far as my information goes our standard in Spanish is not below that of any other University in the kingdom. There are now nine courses, and three additional tutorial classes. An Honours School of Spanish has been established, and the first examination will be held in June 1923.

I have also endeavoured to bring the Department into close touch with:

(a) **The city and district**:

This has been attempted mainly by the foundation of the Society of Spanish Studies in September 1920. The Society numbers at present over 100 members, practically all living in or near Liverpool, and is steadily growing. Lectures (mainly in Spanish) are given; circles for the reading of Spanish literature and for conversation in Spanish have been established; together with a small lending library.

(b) **The Schools of the district**:

I have visited, by invitation, a number of secondary day schools in the Liverpool and Manchester areas, and got into touch with, I believe, practically all teachers of Spanish within a wide radius. In order to be in touch also with the evening schools of the country, and see something of the adult classes of others, I have accepted an invitation from the Board of Education to act as Occasional Inspector in Spanish, and have inspected evening schools, in term or vacation, in many centres in the country.

(c) **Universities and other Institutions in Spain**:

In order to establish a connection between this University, the University of Madrid, and the important Spanish Government Education Committee known as the Junta para Ampliación de Estudios,[*] a letter

---

[*] A government body then under the direction of Menéndez Pidal who provided an excellent reference in support of Peers' candidacy for the Gilmour Chair (see pp. 158, 448).

was recently sent by the Vice-Chancellor to the latter body making suggestions for co-operation in exchange of students and teachers etc., in the future,* and these suggestions I was able to follow up by an interview with representatives of the Junta in Madrid last April. Sr. Castillejo, its secretary, came to England on a mission in June, and spent a day at Liverpool, going over various of our Departments and examining the work which we have done in the Department of Spanish. The first result of this co-operation has already been seen in the personal help which Sr. Castillejo gave us during the vacation in the selection of a candidate for the recently filled post of Temporary Lecturer in the Department.

My principal activities, however, outside purely departmental work and personal research, have been connected with the foundation of a Summer School of Spanish, which was held at the University for the first time in August 1920, and attended by some 65 students. The School was repeated in August 1921, when over 80 students attended, and at the conclusion of the School I took a party of 14 of those who had taken this course to Santander, where a continuation course of one month was held, and arrangements were made to repeat it with 30 students in 1922. The chief aims of the School are:— (1) to raise the standard of work in the Department, and particularly to supply its greatest need, — an intensive pre-Matriculation course which together with Courses A and B will enable a capable student having learned no Spanish at school to compete successfully with others who have done so; (2) to attract promising students to the University to read for the new Honours School of Spanish or for the School of Modern Languages with Spanish as one language; (3) to encourage and promote the study of Spanish in Liverpool and district; (4) to set on foot active measures of co-operation between the University and Spanish Universities and institutions, in view of possible future developments. In this connection it is worthy of note that at each of the Summer Schools native teachers have come to Liverpool from the University of Madrid or associated schools of higher education there to give lessons and at the same time to improve their own English.

## II  RESEARCH WORK

My principal pre-occupation during the last two years, however, has been with the research work which for most of the period of the War circumstances prevented me from undertaking. From January to June 1920 the work of the Department, together with the claims of the Pass and Honours students in French, left me little time for study. At the end

---

\* A copy of this letter, from J. G. Adami, the Vice-Chancellor, is in the University's Archives [14 November 1920] (see the *Vice-Chancellor's Letter Book*, vol. 28, 495). Extracts from this letter are quoted in '(E.A.P.) *Auto*', ch. 4, p. 127, note 11.

APPENDIX I 437

of that time were published my *Phonetic Spanish Reader*, and also my *Origins of French Romanticism* (with M. B. Finch) (the latter of which was delivered to the publishers in 1916) and since the heavy mechanical work connected with these was completed I have been able to work steadily at various subjects the results of which work I set out below.

(1) *The Poems of Manuel de Cabanyes*

This edition, in book form, is completed in MS. and is submitted herewith. I propose to include it in the series of Spanish Texts for Universities published by the Manchester University Press of which I was asked to become General Editor in 1918 and of which three volumes have already appeared. Manuel de Cabanyes' complete poems are contained only in the posthumous edition of 1858 which has been for many years out of print. He is one of the most interesting figures of Spanish pre-Romanticism, for reasons set out in the preface to this edition, and in preparing a new edition I have had the co-operation of the poet's descendants and of the Director of the Biblioteca-Museo Balaguer at Villanueva y Geltrú, Cabanyes' birthplace. This town I have twice visited in order to examine all the family documents available and to compile a bibliography of the poet which the Catalan authorities whom I have consulted believe to be complete.

This edition was completed only a month ago, and is now ready for press after a final revision has been made.

(2) A Book entitled 'Angel Saavedra, Duque de Rivas, and his place in the evolution of Spanish Romanticism'.

Although the Duque de Rivas has a claim to be considered as the greatest of Spanish Romantics no full-length study of his life and works has yet been written. The book of which a portion is now submitted attempts to fill this gap, discussing both the evolution of the Romanticism of Rivas and the place which he fills in the history of the movement in Spain. The estimated size of the book when completed is of 600 MS quarto pages; about 400 of these have already been written, and are in various stages of progress. The whole can be submitted if desired.

The biographical part of this essay is drawn from various sources, the existing biographical sketches being incomplete or unreliable. Neither this chapter nor those on the Romances and *Don Alvaro* are in their final form, as will be seen from the MS.

The general scheme of the book is as follows:-
Chapter I: Biographical. Chapter II: The nature of Spanish Romanticism. Chapter III: The Romanticism of Angel de Saavedra, — War, Peace and Exile. Chapter IV: The *Moro*

*Expósito*. Chapter V: *Don Alvaro*. Chapter VI: The Romanticism of the Duque de Rivas: Romances and later lyrics. Chapter VII: The latest dramas. Chapter VIII: Conclusion.

There will be three appendices, which are ready:
(1) A comparative study of the editions of Rivas' works; (2) Fourteen poems not before reprinted from the very rare first edition of the juvenilia of the poet (This edition I visited the University of Sevilla to see); (3) Some hitherto unpublished letters of the Duque de Rivas bearing on his later dramas (In the library of the Sociedad Menéndez Pelayo, Santander, and to be reproduced by permission of the Society).

(3) ARTICLES

The following articles, like the two books, bear upon the general subject of Spanish Romanticism, which I have made my ground of research, and upon which I hope ultimately to write at greater length than as yet I have done. They are based upon the examination of Spanish journals from 1800 to 1850, which seems to be a necessary preliminary to a full study of the period, as they are both numerous and important. Up to the present time I have examined some two hundred volumes, making three visits to Spain for that purpose, and having worked while there in the libraries of Madrid (three), Barcelona (two), Santander, Cadiz, Sevilla, Granada, Valencia, Zaragoza, and Villanueva. A list of these articles follows, and several of them are submitted herewith, the remainder being in the hands of editors.

Articles published:

1. Some provincial periodicals in Spain during the Romantic Movement (Modern Language Review, July 1920)
2. Sidelights on Byronism in Spain (Revue Hispanique, Dec. 1920)
3. Some Spanish Conceptions of Romanticism (Modern Language Review, July 1921)
4. The earliest notice of Byron in Spain (Revue de littérature comparée, Jan 1922, — in type but not yet out.)

Articles accepted:

5. By Revue Hispanique: The Influence of Sir Walter Scott in Spain (With Philip H. Churchman, who is responsible mainly for the bibliographical portion).
6. For Homenaje a Menéndez Pidal: Spanish *emigrados* in England during the formative period of Spanish R'cism.

APPENDIX I  439

7. By Bulletin Hispanique: The periodical contributions of Sevilla to Spanish Romanticism.
8. By Studies in Philology: The Sources of *El Moro Expósito*.
9. By Modern Language Notes: The influence of Lamartine in Spain.

Articles of which MS is completed but not published:

10. (Offered* to the Romanic Review): The sources of *Don Alvaro*.
11. (To be offered to the Revista de Filología Española): Periodical contributions of Cádiz to Spanish Romanticism.
12. (The Boletín Menéndez Pelayo has also accepted in advance an article which will be based upon material available in manuscript in the Santander library, and will be entitled 'Algunas Observaciones sobre *El Desengaño en un Sueño*.)

This list, apart from my *Skeleton Spanish Grammar*, a number of general articles and some texts and editions for class use in schools and universities, represents the work which I have actually accomplished in Spanish.

I am, dear Sir,
Yours faithfully,

[signed] E. Allison Peers.


1. From Dr E. G. W. Braunholtz, Reader in Romance in the University of Cambridge.

7 September, 1920.

I have much pleasure in expressing the very high opinion I have formed of Mr. E. Allison Peers' capacities, acquirements, zeal, energy and organising power, and in warmly supporting his application for appointment as a University teacher. Having known Mr Peers since his undergraduate days I can testify to his marked success as a student of French language and literature, and as a candidate for the Tripos in that subject. I know that since leaving Cambridge he has, in addition to his work as a Modern Language Master, been indefatigably active in extending his knowledge of Romance languages and literatures, and in pursuing research, particularly on the beginnings and the history of Romanticism in France and Spain. I understand that he is at present

---

\* In a handwritten alteration Peers indicates that this article has been 'accepted' and should be listed accordingly.

engaged in preparing for publication several books and articles on subjects connected with the literature of Romanticism in Spain (an edition of Cabanyes, a study of the beginnings of Spanish Romanticism, articles on Scott's influence and on Byronism in Spain). It is largely to his enthusiasm for research, his initiative and efficiency as an organiser, that we owe the foundation of the Modern Humanities Research Association, of which he is the Honorary Secretary.

I have no doubt whatever that Mr Peers is particularly well fitted for the work of an academic teacher and that by appointing him any University will make a valuable addition to its staff.*

[signed] E. G. W. Braunholtz, M.A., Ph.D.,
University Reader in Romance.

Goslar,
Adams Road,
Cambridge.

2. From M. Ernest Mérimée, late Professor of Spanish in the University of Toulouse, and Dean of the Faculty of Letters; Director of the French Institute in Spain, Madrid.

7 Septembre, 1920.

Le Professeur soussigné a l'honneur de déclarer à qui de droit, et à toutes fins utiles, qu'il a été, à plusieurs reprises, en relations personnelles en Espagne avec M. E. Allison Peers, actuellement professeur à l'Université de Liverpool, qu'il a pu constater la connaissance sérieuse de la langue espagnole et de la littérature correspondante; que cette connaissance est attestée par les divers travaux déjà publiés par lui, et qu'elle le sera davantage encore par les ouvrages qu'il a en préparation, tels qu'une édition critique des Oeuvres de Manuel de Cabanyes, ou une Etude sur le Duc de Rivas et les Origines de Romantisme Espagnol.

M. Allison Peers connaît directement et pratiquement les principales bibliothèques d'Espagne, et je ne doute pas qu'il n'en tire de précieux éléments pour ses travaux.

[signed] E. Mérimée.
Professeur à l'Université de Toulouse,
Directeur de l'Institut Français en Espagne, Madrid.

Marqués de la Ensenada, 10,
Madrid.

---

\* This reference is only a slightly revised version of that written by Braunholtz in 1919 (*cf.* above, pp. 433-34).

3. From Professor J. G. Robertson, M.A., Ph.D., Professor of German in the University of London and Editor of the *Modern Language Review*.

11 November, 1921.

I have pleasure in supporting the candidature of Mr. E. Allison Peers for the Chair of Spanish in Liverpool. While unable to speak of Mr. Peers' Spanish work from the point of view of a specialist, I have been impressed by the excellence of his publications: they seem to me to be based on solid, scholarly methods, convincing in their conclusions, and presented in an attractive form. His investigations into the development of Spanish Romanticism have the benefit of his wide knowledge of the Romantic Movement in other literatures, and give promise of placing the Spanish movement in a more 'European' perspective than I find, as far as my reading goes, in the work of his predecessors in Spain and America. This would be, in the eyes of those who, like myself, are interested in the problem of Romanticism as a European phenomenon, an important advance.

Mr. Peers seems to me to stand alone among the younger generation of Spanish scholars in England. I know of no other who is making so determined an effort to maintain the standard of Spanish scholarship, and to win respect for English research in the subject in Spain.

[signed] J. G. Robertson.

University College,
Gower Street, W.C. 1.


4. From J. N. Birch, Esq., B.A., Hughes Lecturer in Spanish in the University of Sheffield.

17 November, 1921.

Mr. E. Allison Peers has asked me to write in support of his candidature for the Chair of Spanish in the University of Liverpool.

I have much pleasure in doing so. I have known Mr. Peers for a considerable time, and have formed a high opinion of his ability as an organiser and of his scholarship. During the past two years Mr. Peers has given undoubted evidence of this latter so far as the Spanish language and literature are concerned by the work he has already published. His articles on Spanish Romanticism evince a sound knowledge of Spanish literature of the nineteenth century as well as considerable acquaintance with the modern methods of research.

Mr. Peers has also in hand two works which should prove of very considerable value to all who are interested in Spanish Literature.

His ability as an organiser I regard as quite exceptional, and from this point of view a department under his charge would be assured of success.

I consider Mr. Peers fitted on all grounds to fill successfully the Chair of Spanish for which he is a candidate, and have no misgivings in strongly recommending him to the electors.

[signed] Jas. N. Birch.
Hughes Lecturer in Spanish, University of Sheffield.

The University,
Sheffield.

5. From Sr. D. Miguel Artigas, Director of the Biblioteca Menéndez Pelayo, Santander, and Editor of the Boletín de la Biblioteca Menéndez Pelayo.

**Translation**

Santander
16 November, 1921.

Your (latest) articles please me very much. Having had the opportunity of knowing you personally and of seeing your work in this library I am in no way surprised at the first-hand knowledge which these articles display, at the keenness of your judgments, nor at the extent of your bibliographical survey.

All your work on this interesting period of our literary history is filling a gap (and for once this phrase represents what is indeed a reality) which had been felt for a long time, viz., that of closely examining the influence which foreign writers — principally English, exerted on that movement. The path which you are taking — and which your collaborator, Mr. Churchman, took before you, — is moreover the right one. The detailed study and examination of the periodical publications of the time will throw very much light on this question, as on all those relating to influences in the last years of the eighteenth and early years of the nineteenth century. Another satisfactory step is that you have paid special attention to Catalan Romanticism, and the work of the editors of the Europeo, for in general the few and not very notable works which have appeared on this subject in Spain have either neglected it entirely or have, at the least, not given it its due importance. See, for example, Alonso Cortes' recent book on Zorrilla.

I am greatly looking forward to the publication of your book on the Duque de Rivas, and I hope then to write fully in the Boletín de la Biblioteca Menéndez Pelayo — which is edited as you know by the Master's principal followers and has a considerable position among Spanish reviews — both of this book and of your work in general. I want this work to be known not only by those of us who read foreign reviews — for we know it already — but by the many who are interested in Spanish literature without being specialists. So both for this reason and for the sake of the Boletín it would be good of you if you would send us one or two of the various pieces of work which you have in manuscript and which you spoke to me of last summer. Quadrado's unpublished works are being published bit by bit, but you can see the manuscripts when next you are here. I congratulate you on your recent work, and hope soon to see some further results of your mastery of Spanish Literature, and your excellent and well-considered researches.

[signed] Miguel Artigas.

6. From Professor Philip H. Churchman, Professor of Romance Languages at Clark University, Worcester, Mass., U.S.A., and author of *Byron and Espronceda, The Beginnings of Byronism in Spain*, etc.

8 November, 1921

TO WHOM IT MAY CONCERN.

It is a genuine pleasure for me to offer my testimony concerning the quality of the research work of Mr. E. Allison Peers in the field of Spanish literature and linguistics.

His *Phonetic Spanish Reader*, besides being a well-edited and intelligently selected series of texts, gives, in my opinion, evidence of a thorough understanding of the difficult science of phonetics, applied with a wise mingling of conservative accuracy with originality.

The brief studies of the long-hidden periodical, *El Europeo*, and of *Byronism in Spain* bear testimony to a spirit of patient investigation, together with intelligent handling of the material brought to light, both of which I have had occasion to see at closer range in the course of several months' collaboration upon a study of the influence of Sir Walter Scott in Spain. In this work I have seen the same enthusiasm for truth, the same patient search for all the facts, and the same intelligent control of the material, conjointly with the wider knowledge of the general field, the technical linguistic knowledge, and the true researcher's instinct which go to make the successful scholar.

[signed] Philip H. Churchman.
Professor of Romance Languages in Clark University.

7. From Professor T. B. Rudmose Brown, Professor of the Romance Languages in the University of Dublin, Examiner in Spanish and Italian in the University of Dublin, Occasional Examiner in Spanish in the National University of Ireland.

21 November, 1921

I consider Mr. E. Allison Peers to be a most suitable candidate for the Gilmour Chair of Spanish in the University of Liverpool. I have the highest opinion of his scholarly attainments; and his work, both published and in the press, which I have been privileged to read, appears to me to be most scholarly and thorough, and worthy of the great traditions of the Gilmour Chair. Mr. Peers' particular sphere of research is the Spanish Romantic Movement. His 'Survey of the Influence of Sir Walter Scott in Spain', his edition of Cabanyes, his 'Sidelights on Byronism in Spain', his 'Some Spanish Conceptions of Romanticism', his work on the Duque de Rivas, and a number of other papers and works show profound and careful research and a scholarly attitude and habit of mind. I know no other of our younger Spanish scholars who has so considerable and so excellent a record of research work to his name. Mr. Peers' work is not popular: he disdains merely showy work. It is all the work of a real scholar.

I should like to add my very high opinion of his work in the field of French Romanticism. His edition of Vigny, his work on the origins of French Romanticism, in collaboration with Miss Finch, and other contributions of his to French scholarship are notable productions. But I feel that Mr. Peers is before all things a Spanish scholar who has equipped himself for his task by mastering the other Romance languages as well, particularly French and Italian which are so deeply interwoven with Spanish during the period, above all, which he has made his own.

Mr. Peers has, in addition, produced some very sound school texts, well up to the best standard of this type of work. He has a clear mind, and has, I believe, the gift of clear and accurate expression. His work in organising the Modern Humanities Research Association has been ample proof of his patience, tact, and administrative abilities. I have the greatest pleasure in recommending Mr. Peers as a sound scholar and gentleman of culture, as well as an Englishman of the best tradition who would fill the Gilmour Chair of Spanish with honour to himself and to the University, and do much to carry on and add to the reputation which Liverpool University already possesses as the cradle of Spanish studies in Great Britain.

[signed] T. B. Rudmose Brown

8  From Sr. D. Fernando González, Director of the Biblioteca-Museo Balaguer, Villanueva y Geltrú.

**Translation**

Villanueva y Geltrú,
6 December, 1921.

I first made the acquaintance of the able Hispanic scholar and teacher, Mr. E. Allison Peers, in the year 1920, when he came to Spain for the purpose of making an exhaustive study of the poet Manuel de Cabanyes. From that time onwards I have followed the work which Mr Peers has done step by step, and I can honestly say that his biographical study is the completest of all which have been published up to the present time. His dates have been verified by references to the family documents, and various points have been cleared up which previous biographers had passed over. Mr Peers' critical study of the poetical works contains much sound judgment and no one who wishes to delve deeply into the works of Cabanyes and to study his peculiar qualities of mind will be able to neglect it. The family papers having been now investigated, it may safely be affirmed that no single composition remains unpublished. Finally the bibliography of Cabanyes' life and works, in which I have had the honour to collaborate, is complete to date; we have made researches in the principal libraries of Madrid and Barcelona and have scrupulously examined all the material which is available in this library.

These facts justify my saying that, thanks to Mr. Peers' valuable researches, Spanish literary criticism will shortly be enriched by the definitive edition, and a finished study, never likely to be surpassed, of the works of that ill-fated genius of whom the illustrious scholar Menéndez y Pelayo said 'Roma y Atenas le hubieran prohijado'.

[signed]  Fernando González.


9. From Professor Milton A. Buchanan, M.A., Ph.D., Department of Italian and Spanish, University of Toronto, Canada.

6 December 1921

My dear Sir:

I take the liberty of addressing you on behalf of Mr. Allison Peers who is, as he informs me, a candidate for the Chair of Spanish in your University. Mr. Peers first attracted the attention of scholars by organizing the Modern Humanities Research Association which now, thanks chiefly to his untiring efforts, includes scholars from all civilized countries. In scholarly work of the nature of research Mr. Peers has to his credit several studies on Romanticism which he knows thoroughly, not only as regards Spanish literature but in its international aspects as well. For the teaching of Spanish Mr. Peers has an indispensable foundation, namely, a thorough knowledge of phonetics. His 'Phonetic Reader of Spanish' is the standard work on the subject and has been favourably reviewed by authorities like Navarro Tomás.

Mr. Peers is a man whom I commend most highly to your consideration. I feel sure that Spanish scholars would be glad to see one so well qualified given a Chair which offers such opportunities for scholarly work.

Yours truly,

[signed]   Milton A. Buchanan*

## C   Selected correspondence with referees relating to Peers' candidacy for the Gilmour Chair, 1919-22

(i)   The eminent Hispanist, Ramón Menéndez Pidal, writes, in reply to requests from the Dean of the Faculty of Arts for his opinion of **E. Allison Peers**.

(a)

22nd March, 1922

Dear Sir,

I take the liberty of approaching you to ask if you would be so kind as to give your valuable assistance in the following matter, to the Committee approved by the Faculty of Arts of this University to consider and report upon the qualifications of candidates for the Gilmour Chair of Spanish.

---

\*   Professor Buchanan sent this letter of testimonial to Mr Garmon Jones. He had ceased to be Dean of the Faculty of Arts at the close of the Session of 1919-20; but he served as Chairman of the Faculty for the Session of 1920-21. As the Faculty's representative on the University Council, in 1921, he continued to wield considerable influence in University affairs. Though it was not one of the eight testimonials which Peers submitted with his application, this letter from Buchanan was received by the Faculty's Committee and was quoted in their report to the Faculty, June 1922.

Mr. E. Allison Peers, who is at present lecturer in charge of the Spanish Department, has sent in an application for the above chair, and, in doing so, has submitted published and unpublished material. As the Committee would gladly have the benefit of the opinion of those best qualified to form a judgment, I would ask if you would kindly express yourself as to the scholarship and ability for research displayed by Mr. Peers' work. The Articles and Books already published are set forth in the application which is herewith forwarded for your guidance. Should you desire to see the unpublished MSS. in addition, the Committee will be glad to let you have them.

Assuring you of the gratitude of the Committee for any assistance you can give us.

I am
    Yours very truly,

[A. Bruce Boswell, Dean]

Sr. Don Ramón Menéndez Pidal,
Almagro 26,
Madrid.

(b)

May 6, 1922

Dear Sir,

On the 22nd of March I wrote you a letter on behalf of the Committee which is considering the appointment to the Gilmour Chair of Spanish in this University, asking your advice and assistance. As I have received no reply from you it is possible that my letter has not reached you. I, therefore, enclose a copy of my letter, and reiterate my request that you will be so kind as to help my Committee in this matter.

Believe me to be
    Yours faithfully,

[A. Bruce Boswell, Dean]

Sr. Don Ramón Menéndez Pidal,
Almagro 26,
Madrid.

(c)

Ministerio de Instrucción Pública
Junta para Ampliación de Estudios
Almagro 26-Hotel-Madrid

10 de Mayo de 1922

Mr A. Bruce Boswell.

**Translation**\*

Dear Sir

I have received your second letter of 6 of this current month (the first one having gone astray), and I hasten to reply to your question concerning Mr. Peers, candidate for the Chair of Spanish within the Faculty of Arts of the University of Liverpool.

I am acquainted with several of the works published by Mr. Peers, which prove that their author has studied in detail the Romantic Movement in Spain. Mr. Peers' careful researches into the periodicals\*\* of this period not only those of Madrid but even the least known ones of the provinces and his studies [conducted] in private and provincial libraries above all in Barcelona and Cadiz, have been fruitful, for they clarify and rectify many hitherto confused and incorrect points about this period of Spanish literature.

In his book of phonetic readings,\*\*\* Mr. Peers shows an adequate understanding of the Spanish language, providing through it a useful tool for the teaching of an aspect of this language, for which there is an almost complete lack of bibliography and available materials. I rely upon the authoritative opinion of Mr. Navarro Tomás, set forth in the *REVISTA DE FILOLOGÍA ESPAÑOLA*, vol. VII, page 392, who praises the fine qualities of Mr. Peers' work.

I am most pleased to make this known to you, and I am, Sir,

Yours truly,

[signed] R. Menéndez Pidal.

---

\*     Menéndez Pidal's original letter is reproduced in facsimile at p. 158.
\*\*    The corresponding word in the original letter is 'periódos' but this word is evidently typed in mistake for 'periódicos' (periodicals).
\*\*\*   *A Phonetic Spanish Reader* (Manchester: Manchester U. P./Longmans Green & Co., 1920).

(ii) The letters, five in number, which **Professor J. Fitzmaurice-Kelly**, wrote to the Dean, etc., 1919-20, are exceptionally difficult to decipher; and the following transcripts, made by Adrian Allan, may not be wholly accurate. It should be noted that later letters from **Fitzmaurice-Kelly** are also amongst the papers but are in the (much more legible) hand of his wife.

1, Longton Avenue,<br>
Sydenham,<br>
London, S.E.26.<br>
4. xi. '19

My dear Mair:

As I should like to deal fully and fairly with all the candidates, and as I am not acquainted with Santiago's work, I am going to take advantage of your offer and ask you to have his dossier registered to me at the above address. Till I receive it, I must be content to give a general impression respecting the candidates whose names you mention. I do not know Saroïhandy personally, but have no hesitation in saying that he is the best *scholar* on the list. Is he a Pole? I cannot say. I do not know Pitollet either. He is not a bad scholar of the high and dry type; but I understand that he is very cantankerous and hard to work with. He used to write in the *Bulletin Hispanique*. But Morel-Fatio and Mérimée* were obliged to get rid of him there. Similarly, August was compelled to close the doors of the *livre germanique* on him. I am afraid that you would all find him very hard to get on with, and I should not recommend you to try. This practically reduces your list to Spaniards. I think I can explain why Villasante does not mention me, and why Madariaga does. The latter called on me at King's and Villasante came into the room. He of course guessed at once that Madariaga had come to solicit some 'academic' support which should stand instead of experience in teaching. Of experience Villasante has no lack, and I have good reason to think that he did not refer to me from reasons of delicacy. Apart from overwhelming conceit — a characteristic of Spaniards — Villasante is not a bad person, and I should be sorry to lose him, if he were appointed. Whether he would be a good head of a department is another matter. Madariaga speaks a better type of Spanish than

---

\* Alfred Morel-Fatio (1850-1924) and Ernest Mérimée (1846-1924). Their involvement with the *Bulletin Hispanique* is mentioned in *Chaire Ernest Mérimée, Toulouse 1886-1986*, at p. 30 (for more information on E. Mérimée see '[E.A.P.] *Auto*', ch. 6, p. 160 and note 27).

Villasante and, though he is (I think) quite wrong about Shelley and
Calderón, has a more ingenious mind. Until I see Santiago's *dossier* I
cannot be sure, but my inclination at present is to vote for a Spaniard:
Madariaga for choice. Kuno's* death was, as you say, tragic. Probably I
should never have heard from him again, but I feel his loss.

    Kindest regards to all your household.
Yours ever:

        [signed]  Jas. Fitzmaurice-Kelly.


                1, Longton Avenue,
                    Sydenham,
                      London, S.E.26
                        13. xi. '19

Dear Mr Dean:
    Herewith I return (registered) the three applications which you were
good enough to forward to me.
    What I said about the remaining candidates holds good. I need not
repeat what I said in my letter to Mair.
    If the Committee has, as I imagine, determined to elect a Spanish-
speaking person, its decision is (I think) a wise one. Thus the
Committee [?]accepts at least one very vital point: a thorough knowledge
of Spanish on the part of the successful candidate. All three men comply
with this condition. Saroïhandy, as a Basque, would perhaps not incline
to stress his Spanish origin as a rule. Still, he *is* a Spaniard in spite of
himself. He is not a very distinguished scholar, it is true. But he *is* a
scholar; his knowledge is quite adequate; he has experience at his back,
and he is better trained in philology than either of the other candidates.
He states emphatically that, during his first year in England, it would be
necessary for him to go over to Paris twice a month from December 1.
This is unlucky, but I do not know that it need be a fatal obstacle, if you
thought him satisfactory in other respects. I believe he is not interested
purely in literature.
    Madariaga, whom I happen to know, is not interested in philology.
Yet I am disposed to think him the best candidate of the three. He has
no experience and his publications are somewhat few and amateurish.
But he is intelligent, enthusiastic, and would be able to lecture at once in
English which he speaks well. Santiago says he can speak English, but
this is a case of self-deception, I should think. His book on Galician
philology is not good.
    I am surprised that no application was, apparently, sent in by Sanín
Cano. Your advertisement cannot have been seen by him, I imagine. I

---

    *    Kuno Meyer (see '[E.A.P.] *Auto*', ch. 5, p. 147, and note 23).

have the highest opinion of him, both as a scholar and a teacher. I have edited an *Elementary Spanish Grammar* of his for the Clarendon Press and formed an exceptionally high estimate of his abilities as a philologist, and of his wide and deep knowledge of Spanish literature. Whether he is now available I cannot say. He gave a lecture at Edinburgh some time ago on my recommendation. On the strength of this, he was at once snapped up by Edinburgh University as teacher of Spanish there. He is a Colombian, and consequently speaks Spanish of the Latin-American type. This is not an insuperable objection, though I happen to prefer the native Spanish method of articulation. You may happen to remember his being External examiner at Liverpool. Still, I cannot distinctly recall introducing him to anybody but Kuno Meyer (who seemed struck by him). However all this is in the air. I have no means of knowing whether the omission to apply is not fatal to Sanín Cano's chances, or of finding out off-hand what Sanín Cano's personal inclinations are. His appointment would be a most excellent one, if it were at all possible.

Yours very sincerely:

[signed] Jas. Fitzmaurice-Kelly.

1, Longton Avenue,<br>Sydenham,<br>London, S.E.26<br>26. xi. '19

Dear Mr Dean:

It would have been unbecoming for me to declare bluntly that the claims of the applicants are weak; but, since the Committee has reached that conclusion on its own account, there can be no harm in saying that I share the Committee's view on this point.

Fonger de Haan[*] is a Dutchman who has been at Bryn Mawr for a very long while. He is an excellent Spanish scholar — the best, I think, on the North-American continent. Buchanan is also a very good Spanish scholar: he is particularly well versed in the bibliography of the drama.

Both these gentlemen are much superior to anybody on your list, and you would be justified in asking either of them if he would consider an invitation to the Chair of Spanish at Liverpool.

I can just say that I have met De Haan for a few minutes at Bryn

---

[*] Dr Fonger de Haan (?1859-1930). On the staff at Johns Hopkins University (1893-97), latterly as Associate in Romance Languages (1896-97), he moved to Bryn Mawr College in 1897, where ultimately (1907-24) he was Professor of Spanish (see Caroline B. Bourland, 'Dr. Fonger De Haan', *Bryn Mawr College Alumnae Bulletin* [March 1931], 25-26; records on Fonger De Haan, Bryn Mawr College Archives).

Mawr: not enough to judge what he is like personally. He was said to be embittered at not being re-elected at Johns Hopkins University; I saw no sign of this, of course, in our short conversation. I have not seen Buchanan, as I was in Spain when he was last in Europe.

I do not know whether De Haan or Buchanan would be inclined to accept an invitation. I should have guessed *not*. De Haan has been so long at Bryn Mawr that he may be regarded as a fixture there. Buchanan is now the head of the Romance Department at Toronto. As he married a few years ago, domestic reasons might prevent his accepting an offer. I do not know whether he would gain financially by the exchange. As I understand, he would be bound to take this factor into account. I do not much like the idea of the Liverpool Chair of Spanish being hawked up and down.

I have not felt at liberty to mention the subject to Sanín Cano: so cannot say whether he would care to consider an offer if it came in his way. Nor could I easily do so, as he is teaching in Edinburgh. True, he often spends the week-end in London on business, but business does not bring him out so far as this.

As he is comparatively new to University work, he has not published much that is of a purely didactic character. But what he *has* written of that kind is very good. I have always been glad to print his contributions in the *Modern Language Review* and have regretted that there were not more of them. Two of the contributions stand out in my mind. One is philological — *The Spanish ch*: in this he describes phonetic experiments made by him with reference to this baffling sound. The other is a literary estimate of the poems of Rafael Paulo. Paulo was a countryman of his, but Sanín Cano showed that he knew how to deal faithfully with a friend. This struck me as being much above the ordinary informed review as regards style and knowledge and impartiality. Sanín Cano has also edited (at Paris) the poems of Valencia and of the late J. A. Silva. Both are very good.

Sanín Cano is a man of exceptionally wide cultivation. He is as strong as a horse, is capable of any amount of hard work and is very conscientious. Spanish is, of course, his native language. In this respect he has an advantage over both De Haan and Buchanan. He knows English well, can grasp the difficulties which English students are likely to find in Spanish, and can seize delicate shades of meaning. Of this I became convinced when he did my *Cervantes* into Spanish. In going over the text with him, I had ample opportunities of noting his ample knowledge, his quickness of mind and his intellectual force. He is (more or less) on the spot and is, as I can vouch for it, a good fellow. Were I on the Committee, I should certainly support him.

Yours very sincerely:

[signed] Jas. Fitzmaurice-Kelly.

1, Longton Avenue,
Sydenham,
London, S.E.26
14. ii. '20

My dear A. M.*

Thank you for your letter. What I had to say on the candidates for the Spanish Chair has been said. My excuse for returning to the matter is that I want to clear up some doubtful points. Let me take those who were interviewed in (what I think to be) the inverse order of merit.

Not much need be said of A. P. [**Allison Peers**]. His appointment is unthinkable and would cover the University with ridicule. He has precisely the same qualifications as my wife: a First Class with distinction in *French* at Cambridge. That does not help with Spanish. He has written a *Spanish Grammar* which we tried at King's. It had to be dropped as not up to the mark. It was a dangerous thing to appoint him *locum tenens*. He is not up to a University standard at all, being of about the level of a queerish school. I have come across him in connexion with the *Modern Language Review*; he was full of proposals for improving the bibliographies. So far as I could make out, his proposals would have increased the work being done by other people; moreover, they were quite unpractical. A. P. seems to be very 'pushful'. I see he applied to be appointed at London University in *both* French and Spanish. He was not, apparently, thought well of by either the French or the Spaniards. I was not able to be present at the discussion; but heard about it from the Spaniards who were foaming at the mouth because of his assurance in coming forward. But I need not say any more; I do not regard A. P. as even a *possible* appointment.

M. [Madariaga] at least knows some Spanish and that is a pall over A. P. Clearly he does not know any philology (he made that clear in the *Times* some weeks ago), and he can scarcely begin now. I had imagined that M. was definitively rejected already. Manifestly I was wrong. Probably he knows as much philology now as he ever did. Evidently something new has cropped up to cause his case to be reconsidered. He may have read more Spanish than A. P. and, as he is quite intelligent, he would read attentively. But he has not a *critical* mind, cannot tell the difference between a first-class thing and a second-class thing, praises too indiscriminately, and thinks it his mission to exaggerate the value of Spain's contribution to art and thought. I look on that as a needless curse, but I can understand that anybody might take the contrary view.

You will observe that I have carefully abstained from expressing any opinion as to M.'s qualities as a human being. That abstention is significant enough, I dare say. I do not intend to depart from it now, especially as you tell me that M. made a good impression personally.

---

\*   Alexander Mair.

It takes me much aback to learn that S. C. [Sanín Cano] was thought to be *dull*. This is either a mistaken impression or is due to the fact that S. C. was very shy and nervous. I heard from him just before he started and could see that he *was* exceedingly nervous. The Committee saw him for an hour or two. I have known him for many years and can vouch for it that his dulness is non-existent. He is a particularly bright person who often masks his brightness under a veil of solemnity.

Of course, his engagement to *La Nación* is a drawback. It occurred to me that Liverpool could do what Edinburgh did. S. C. *at my advice* mentioned the circumstances to the Committee. I told him it might be fatal to his election but that the Committee had a right to know about this. He was evidently even better than his word, and in his nervousness seems to have exaggerated the amount of his [?]advance. You will have noticed that, however well a man speaks a language, his complete command of it diminishes under the [?]stress of audition. I am rather pleased to know that S. C. exaggerated, instead of minimizing, the case against himself. As I understand it, his work for *La Nación* (a larger and more important paper than the *Times*) is not permanent, and will not take up much time. Anyhow, I do not see any way towards advising him to give up *La Nación*. If this stands in his way, I shall be sorry: for S. C. is one of the rare spirits who are really interested in teaching. Literary and philological problems seem to have an irresistible attraction for him. It will be regrettable if he has no chance of displaying his powers at Liverpool. The loss will be Liverpool's, and, much as I should lament that loss, I had rather that happened than that S. C. should prove unworthy of the confidence I place in him. One would be a temporary disappointment: the other would be a [?]noted blemish in his character.

I am sorry you did not see him; for I should have been curious to see if you had shared in the Committee's personal estimate of S. C. I am not blaming the Committee: members are obviously in a difficult position in having, as the result of one brief interview held in unedifying haste, to form a personal impression. One would need years to be certain that one's impressions are even approximately correct.

I heard from H. C. W.\* that he had just missed Southampton. For his sake, as he wanted to succeed, I was sorry. And here again I am glad that he stuck to his guns and rejected victory, if victory was only to be won by diluting the true doctrine. I am not at all sure that H. C. W. has lost much really. Southampton with its night classes does not sound as if it were made for him. Beware of night classes: the existence of such horrors at King's was unknown to me, or I should not have moved to London.

In a small way, I am proving a benefactor. After — perhaps because of — my resignation, the long-promised 'rise' to £800 has been passed by the London Senate. So that the rest are gainers. It is of course a

---

\* Henry Cecil Kennedy Wyld, Baines Professor of English Language and Philology at Liverpool, 1904-20. See also '(E.A.P.) *Auto*', ch. 5, p. 147 and note 24.

nuisance about the pension & c. But that cannot be helped now. In any case, as I began so late the pension would have been a very insignificant sum: scarcely enough to be disturbed about. I don't at all regret having retired. Perhaps it was a mistake to join the professorial ranks. If so, *felix culpa*: for I owe to that step the acquisition of some admirable friendships among which few are more precious to me than yours:
Believe me to be yours ever:

[signed] J.F.-K.


1 Longton Avenue,
Sydenham,
London, S.E.26
February 16. 1920

Confidential

Dear Veitch:
Thank you for your kind letter of the 14th inst. and for its good wishes. I hasten to acknowledge it, though — since I have said nearly all that I had to say about the candidates — I do not think that I can add much which is likely to help you in your difficulties. These are real enough. Though I foresaw that Sanín Cano's statement would stand in his way, I advised him to make it, so that I am in some sense responsible. It struck me that a policy of absolute candour was advisable and perhaps I imagined that Liverpool would be able to do what has been done at Edinburgh. However, I understand this to be impossible, and though it means losing so good a man as Sanín Cano — with a recognized reputation in literature, a sound equipment in philology, a good record of teaching experience, and a fund of independent judgement (an important point) — I try to see the situation as it presents itself to the Committee. I should have guessed that Sanín Cano's engagement with *La Nación* — a larger and better paper than the *Times* — would have been a point in his favour, inasmuch as it would help to make the Chair known in South America. But I gather that this is not the view of the Council and that the Committee will have to follow that view.

Madariaga assuredly knows no philology. On the other hand, he knows Spanish (though not of the purest type for I observe Galicianisms in his speech). He speaks English well, and lectures fluently, gliding over difficulties in a journalistic fashion. This is what you might expect. Madariaga is not a scholar and has not a critical mind. He is, I think, a capable journalist of the Spanish school.

Peers is not a serious candidate. His appointment would be absurd: it would imply a complete unacquaintance with relative values and a definite break with the high standard of Liverpool's tradition in these matters. Peers might do for a school. He is not of university calibre and I understand (for I was not able to attend) that he was recently rejected as Examiner in French and Examiner in Spanish by the University of London. His appointment I regard as inconceivable: it would amount to a serious slight on learning.

You ask me to advise the Committee in its difficulties. Of course it might be possible to get the Americans to compete. But this would mean delay, and you tell me that delay might be dangerous. However, it would almost certainly mean more money being offered, and even so the chances of success are doubtful. Only two American names have been mentioned, those of De Haan and Buchanan, both good men. But De Haan has been so long at Bryn Mawr that he might be indisposed to move (apart from pension difficulties). And Buchanan married some while ago: he might, for obvious domestic reasons, be almost equally difficult to transplant from one side of the Atlantic to the other. I ought to say that I do not know Buchanan personally, and that what I say of him is in the nature of conjecture. He does not strike me as equal to De Haan. I know his work, of course; and agree with Terracher* in thinking that its chief merit is bibliographical.

How would it do to recommend, in the circumstances, the appointment of Sanín Cano for five years? He would have to retire in seven or eight years anyhow, and by then, England may have raised a crop of Spanish scholars of its own. If Sanín Cano did not give satisfaction, you could sack him. If he *did* prove satisfactory, you could confirm him in his chair. Hitherto Spanish has been cultivated in England by only a few persons who were exceptionally favoured by fortune. There will probably be a steady supply of good scholars, if there are posts for them to fill: that seems likely to happen before 1927 or 1928. At any rate, I hope so. I am afraid that I have not helped you much: but I have done my best. And my proposal has a precedent: in Terracher's case.

Yours very truly:

[signed] Jas. Fitzmaurice-Kelly.

---

\* James Barrow Professor of French, University of Liverpool, 1913-19. See also '(E.A.P.) *Auto*', ch. 3, p. 109 and note 96.

The 'New Testament' (*c*.1914-1917)

An oil painting by Albert Lipczinski
(Art Collections, University of Liverpool)

Reproduced, courtesy of the University, by the
Central Photographic Service, University of Liverpool

# APPENDIX II

## The 'New Testament'

(i) Albert Lipczinski's painting, begun in 1914 and completed in 1917 (see photograph opposite), which is, appropriately, now housed in the Faculty of Arts, University of Liverpool, shows Professor John Macdonald Mackay, Rathbone Professor of History and founder of the group, addressing fellow members of the 'New Testament'.

Seated at the table are, left to right: Dr John Sampson (University Librarian) (Professor Inaccessible, in the 'Bruce Truscot' narrative). Sampson was 'a much finer scholar, and a greater man than any of the rest [of the "N.T."]', in the opinion of Allison Peers; Professor H. Cecil K. Wyld (English Language); Professor J. Fitzmaurice-Kelly (Spanish) (Professor Upright in the 'Bruce Truscot' text); Professor Bernard Pares (Russian) was 'another most able man, who had left before I came', Peers recollects; and Professor Oliver Elton (English Literature). Elton (Professor Slocombe in the 'Bruce Truscot' autobiography), 'was in his sixtieth year when I first met him', recalls Peers, '[and] had built up a reputation largely on personality and a "Survey" of English literature, of which only a small part had then been produced'.

In the background may be seen, left to right: Professor Charles H. Reilly (Architecture). He 'was an organizer', says Peers, 'who would have made no claim to be heard on matters of scholarship'; Professor R. H. Case (English Literature) (probably Anstruther in the 'Bruce Truscot' text), was 'a delightful but unproductive person', according to Peers, 'who late in life was given a Professorship which lapsed on his retirement');* Professor P. E. Newberry (Egyptology); Professor R. C. Bosanquet (Classical Archaeology); and Mr Norman Wyld (Secretary of the University Extension Board).**

(ii) In 1938 Oliver Elton (King Alfred Professor of English Literature, 1901-25) wrote the following poem*** (here published in its entirety for the first time) in honour of those members of the 'New Testament' portrayed in Lipczinski's painting:

### KAINE DIATHEKE****

BERNARD,[1] what though my style be rotten?
I tell you, and in Pushkin's rhyme,
A story that is long forgotten
Save by some few. The sands of time
Too soon may call for computation;
And so, perchance, a brief narration
May entertain both you and me.
I chronicle the Great *N.T.*
What now remains thereof? some pages
In dusty calendars betray

---

\*   Quotations are from '(E.A.P.) *Auto*', ch. 5, The 'New Testament'.

\*\*  From the evidence of an x-ray there was originally the head and shoulders of another figure in the painting. According to Collinson, that figure was Robert Petsch, Professor of German, 1911-14. Collinson states that Petsch (his predecessor in the Chair of German) 'should have stood in the top right hand corner next to Norman Wyld, but Lipczinski with his anti-Prussian bias had made such a grotesque caricature of him that Petsch's colleagues made him paint it out' (Collinson, 'Portraits from the Past', 1).

\*\*\* The late Mrs Boswell, widow of Professor A. Bruce Boswell (who succeeded Bernard Pares in the Bowes Chair of Russian History, Language and Literature in 1919), kindly made available a photocopy of the text of this poem (University Archives, Liverpool, ref. D.174).

\*\*\*\* Greek for 'New Testament'.

1   Bernard Pares, Bowes Professor of Russian History, Language and Literature, 1908-17 (see '[E.A.P.] *Auto*', ch. 5, p. 143, and note 10).

The blackened embers of the fray;
Our triumphs, disappointments, rages
On that contracted battlefield
Are there, by legal phrase, concealed.

There is a room, where men forgather
For morning coffee; and they gaze
Upon a pictured group, with rather
Vacant expressions of amaze,
And query, of each painted figure
That sits or stands in gloomy rigour,
'Who wert thou?' and one answers: — Why,
He in the centre was MACKAY,[2]
A man, they say, much loved, much hated,
Part crazed, and more than half inspired,
And with a holy passion fired,
Too easily by 'joltheads' baited;
Historian, who never wrote;
The theme of many an anecdote, —

Of how in Councils he exploded,
In Faculties and Senates; how
*O.T.*s with contumely he loaded.
His simple creed he would avow,
'Whate'er they do, is *Wrong!*' He meant it,
And let them curse him, and resent it.
And some good-naturedly forgave
The Highlander, and 'let him rave';
While other, sourer spirits hoarded
Their animosities, their fume,
And let it smoke beyond the tomb.
Historic truth must be recorded, —
Our dear MACKAY, 'less strong was he
In tactics, than in strategy'.[3]

He loved his friends, and yet would choose them
Chiefly as God's own instruments
Entrusted to MACKAY, to use them;
And seldom counted their expense,
But in the sacred war enlisted
Them all, — and few of them resisted;

---

2  For Peers on Mackay, see ch. 5, pp. 142-43; see also ch. 5, notes 8-9.
3  Said, reputedly, by Sir Walter A. Raleigh (1861-1922). Raleigh held the King Alfred Chair of Modern Literature and English Language at University College Liverpool, 1890-1900.

And for long years he waged it well,
And bade his foes to go to hell;
And so, by dogged resolution
And genius, though often scarred
And often tripped when off his guard,
Achieved a decent Constitution,
And fought, with changeable success,
For Learning — he did not profess.

His talk at times was Ossianic,
And swathed in mist from some far hill;
At times fuliginous, volcanic;
Then, on a sudden, he would thrill
Our ears with some strange divination
Of mother-wit — not calculation;
From sources far within it welled,
And fears of wavering souls dispelled.
Of contradictions he was fashioned:
We all *supposed* we knew MACKAY;
And yet he baffled us — and why?
Because the fellow, so impassioned,
Was of simplicity immense —
— was one of God's own innocents!

There too, inscrutably, reposes
Our Doctor, ironist, and droll,
Who to the Gentile world discloses
The Gypsy speech, the Gypsy soul.
Ah, now his pagan dust is blowing
O'er Cymric hills, the turf bestrewing!
That vagrant spirit roams the sky,
JOHN SAMPSON, our majestic RAI;[4]
A lover of the wild and lawless,
Autolycus[5] he much preferred
To all the office-hunting herd,
To dons, domestically flawless,
To bourgeois smug, who could not breathe,
Like him, the *Wind upon the Heath*.[6]

---

4 'Rai' was the name which the gypsies gave to Sampson (*cf.* above '[E.A.P.] *Auto*', ch. 5, p. 144, note 12).

5 In mythology, Autolycus, maternal grandfather of Odysseus, surpassed all men in thievery and swearing.

6 Title of John Sampson's Gypsy anthology, *The Wind on the Heath*, published by Chatto and Windus in 1930.

There sits FITZMAURICE,[7] lightest-handed
Of pundits, famed through all the Spains,
Who joined the warrior-brethren banded
And lavished precious hours and brains
Upon their cause. Well trimmed and burning
He kept his shaded lamp of learning;
Yet, though he shunned the vulgar mob,
Could scent an unobtrusive job
Swiftly, and pin it on the table.
FITZ of himself would rarely speak;
A touch of *l'esprit catholique*
Remained with him, and he was able
To veil his heart; yet well we knew
Him for *hidalgo* brave and true.[8]

From straight-backed Huguenots descended,
Northumbrian-bred and Eton-trained,
Athenian with Spartan blended,
Scholar and humanist ingrained;
With trophies from the East arriving,
The lore of excavations hiving,
And schooled in all the arts of Greece;
Most fiery, though a man of peace;
A witty, frank, and friendly creature,
While something of a martinet,
— And Quakerish too — CARR BOSANQUET[9]
Was Liberal by race and nature:
A smiling, faithful vote gave he
To our mad, motley, fierce *N. T.*

For NORMAN WYLD[10] we still are grieving,
A fertile, subtly-ranging mind;
Who in the race, and naught achieving
In the world's eye, was left behind;

---

7   James Fitzmaurice-Kelly, Gilmour Professor of Spanish, 1909-1916 (see '[E.A.P.] *Auto*', ch. 5, pp. 143-44, and note 11).

8   *Cf.* Fitz-Gerald's eulogy of Fitzmaurice-Kelly, in which he describes him as 'the perfect knight' (quoted in 'B.T.', ch. III, pp. 314-15, note 136). For Elton's own memoir of Fitzmaurice-Kelly, see *Revue Hispanique*, LX (1924), 1-11.

9   Bosanquet, Professor of Classical Archaeology, was, indeed, 'Northumbrian-bred' (*cf.* '[E.A.P.] *Auto*', ch. 5, p. 147, note 21).

10  If Norman Wyld is William Edward Norman Wyld of Middlesex (which is possible, but not certain), then he died in 1936. *Cf.* '(E.A.P.) *Auto*', ch. 5, p. 147, note 22.

A soul of generous composition,
Too proud to be a politician
Or to the cockpit to descend,
And ever flawless as a friend.
We see him as he smokes and muses
By rushing Thames, in Lechlade mead;
From piles of office-papers freed,
A silent comfort he diffuses,
Whilst aproned, philosophic SCOTT[11]
Intently scours the cooking-pot.

All these are gone; but sundry others
There by LIP[C]ZINSKI'S brush are limned;
But that surviving band of brothers
Are scarce in these rude verses hymned.
Not yet their bell is rung; they cherish
The memories, so quick to perish,
Of those their fellows in the fray,
And their own deeds in the melée.
— See CASE, the deep Elizabethan;[12]
And NEWBERRY,[13] of scarab lore;
And PARES, believer to the core;
And ELTON,[14] unrepenting heathen;
Keen generous REILLY,[15] Eire's child;
Bold, loyal HENRY CECIL WYLD.[16]

---

11 We have been unable to identify 'Scott' (a friend of N. Wyld?) with certainty. Scott might be the writer Dixon Scott, with whom Norman Wyld was, indeed, friendly (see Reilly, *Scaffolding in the Sky*, 145, 244). More probably, however, Elton is alluding to the composer, pianist and writer, Cyril Scott (1879-1970). As Ramsay Muir mentions in his autobiography (*op. cit.*, 49) Cyril Scott was a frequenter of the University Club. In his own autobiography Cyril Scott refers to the University Club and, for instance, to J. M. Mackay. But there is no mention of Norman Wyld (see *My Years of Indiscretion* [London: Mills & Boon Ltd, 1924]).

12 Robert Hope Case began his career at Liverpool University as Lecturer in Elizabethan Literature (*cf.* '[E.A.P.] *Auto*', ch. 5, pp. 146-47, note 19).

13 Percy Edward Newberry was Professor of Egyptology (see '[E.A.P.] *Auto*', ch. 5, p. 147, note 20).

14 On Oliver Elton see '(E.A.P.) *Auto*', ch. 5, p. 145, note 13.

15 For Charles H. Reilly see '(E.A.P.) *Auto*', ch. 5, pp. 145-46, note 16.

16 Elton, possibly with deliberate irony, praises the loyalty of Henry Cecil Kennedy Wyld, Professor of English Language and Philology. As Peers explains, Wyld 'left the N.T.' (see '[E.A.P.] *Auto*', ch. 5, pp. 147-48, and note 24).

These are the braves commemorated
By LIPPY;[17] but a host beside
For our *N. T.* had fought, orated,
Manoeuvred, prayed, or testified.
Yet one, not least beloved, I may not
Pass over — and will then delay not
To end: — that brain and spirit rare,
Our brindled ALEXANDER MAIR.[18]
I hear him some discussion hectic
To truth and decency recall
From crooked pleas sophistical
With lofty-worded dialectic.
A fair conclusion to the list
Is that high-souled psychologist.

---

17 The painter, Albert Lipczinski.
18 See '(E.A.P.) *Auto*', ch. 5, p. 145, and note 14. Elton's opinion of the Professor of Philosophy at Liverpool, 1920-27, contrasts notably with that of Peers.

# APPENDIX III

## The 'Redbrick' Books: Selected Correspondence from and to 'Bruce Truscot' *

(i) Allison Peers replies to Faber and Faber, following their letter of agreement to publish *Redbrick University*.

N.B. The text of Peers' first letter offering Faber and Faber, his manuscript, which already emphasizes the importance of keeping secret his true identity, is reproduced, in facsimile, at p. 1 of the Introduction.**

12, Eddisbury Road,<br>
West Kirby,<br>
Cheshire.***

Hoylake 1145. December 7 1942

Dear Mr Faber,

Thank you for your letter of December 4. I am glad you like my book well enough to publish it. The terms you suggest are a good deal lower than I should expect for a book published under

---

\* These letters (some typed, others handwritten) have been selected for publication from a larger body of correspondence about the 'Redbrick' books and their author, which is located in the Archives of the University of Liverpool. The letters form part of a collection (D.265) which includes also press-cuttings and reviews of the 'Redbrick' books, together with other cuttings, kept by Peers, relating to higher education in Britain.

\*\* We are deeply indebted to Faber and Faber Ltd, London, for permission to reproduce the texts of both letters, the originals of which are housed in their archives.

\*\*\* In the original, handwritten letter Peers has ringed his address, and has written above it, to stress his concern for secrecy, the following words: 'Please use this address now for all correspondence about "Red Brick University"'.

my own name, but I quite realize that, by writing under a pseudonym, I am voluntarily becoming an 'unknown author' again, so that I accept your offer (including the payment of advance on signature of contract) gratefully. I know something of the difficulties of book production and the dates you suggest are quite satisfactory to me.

My chief concern at this stage is about the preservation of secrecy as to the authorship. As I said in my former letter, my position here would become impossible if this should get known and I have still quite a long time to go before retirement. (Originally I had intended to write the book after retiring, but the hope that it might play its part in the post-War shake-up spurred me to do it now). In writing, I carefully omitted most of the things that I could remember having said or written on the subject and I have been through the typescript again and cut out anything that might be revelatory. My experience has been (in publishing two other pseudonymous things) that if you use an *obvious* pseudonym everybody starts discussing the authorship, whereas if you adopt a perfectly normal name people for the most part assume that it is that of someone whom they just happen not to have heard of. I have therefore adopted the second expedient and I want to ask you if you will say as little as possible (in advance notices, on the wrapper, etc.) about its being a pseudonym at all. If etiquette permits, I should prefer the fact not to be mentioned but about this you will know best.

The press copy of the typescript is enclosed — I hope and believe it is as nearly correction-proof as possible. I imagine the analytical contents will make an index unnecessary. When you are sending the contract would you please return the carbon of the typescript for my convenience.

Yours sincerely,

[signed] E. Allison Peers.

(ii) Letters to or from 'Bruce Truscot' and 'Amelia Truscot' concerning the 'Redbrick' books.

**1943** letter from Bruce Truscot to Geoffrey Tillotson,* reviewer of *Redbrick University*, and Tillotson's reply.

27.12.43

Dear Sir,
   I am greatly honoured by, and deeply interested in, your very kind review of my book, but will you not please tell me what I have said that is 30 years out of date? And having told me, will you please forgive me, because it is nearer 40 years ago than 30 that I took First Class Honours in English. I must admit I have always had more to do with English Language than English Literature** but I did think the familiar quotations that I scattered through the book would have concealed that fact; and like many people of my age I had not realized I was such a Back Number.
   Far from thinking it is lucky to have me,*** my own particular Redbrick thinks I am what the Rajah of Rukh decided that Mrs Crespin would have been.**** So I am afraid your first paragraph was rather far out. But, unlike the majority of my other reviewers, you have seen clearly that what I really care about is research. My great quarrel with Redbrick is the calm way most of its professors and senior lecturers do absolutely none — and with

---

   \* Professor Geoffrey Tillotson, F.B.A. (1905-1969), was, at the time of writing, Reader in English Literature, University College London; in 1944 he became Professor of English Literature in the University of London (*Who Was Who, 1961-1970*). Tillotson's review of *Redbrick University* appeared in *English. The Magazine of the English Association*, IV (1943), no. 24, 199-200.
   \*\* Like much of the information about himself given to his correspondents, this observation is inaccurate, and made with the deliberate intention of providing false clues to the author's identity.
   \*\*\* *Cf*. Tillotson's remark that 'wherever he is now settled, brooding and working in his right name, the place is lucky to have him and must know it' (199).
   \*\*\*\* Our efforts to identify this literary allusion have proved vain. At the suggestion of Professor Kenneth Muir, we wrote to Professor Kathleen Tillotson, widow of Geoffrey Tillotson. In reply (8 November 1994) she comments that Peers' Rajah of Rukh is 'clearly not a real Rajah, and probably somewhere in the comic verse of late 19th/early 20th c. — but unless someone else spots it, will have to be given up'. We give up, and invite readers to try to spot it. Other possible sources — so experts tell us — are Kipling, Thackeray or Trollope.

such complacency that it has never even occurred to them to look for their portraits in my pages.* I hope you younger people will see to it that post-war universities insist that their teachers shall research as well as teach and sack them if they don't.

Yours, in a not over-Christmassy spirit, I am afraid,

Bruce True Scot. **

Dictated by B.T.S. and copied by his secretary. ***

---

Tel. Hampstead 5639.

23 Tanza Road,<br>Hampstead, N.W.3.<br>29 Dec. 1943

Dear Bruce True-Scot

I was delighted to have a letter from my admired author — and so was my wife who has read your book with an enthusiasm equal to my own. (By the way I specially asked Faber's and the editor of *English* to let me review the book, having liked it already. And my wife and I are responsible for the sale of quite a few copies, having sent choice colleagues haring to a bookseller by our glowing assurances).

When an author chooses to publish anonymously, he invites, I think, the maximum frankness and freedom of response. I had nothing to go on, when it came to guessing your identity, except the stuff of the book: and I guessed you were a historian (which is a great compliment!). I am proud to think I was wrong and that a 'member of my own subject' was capable of writing so widely intelligent and progressive a book. The remark which led me away from your being a lecturer in Engl. lit. was your mentioning

---

\* *Cf.* above, Introduction, p. 4.

\*\* Some academics believed that the pseudonym chosen by the author of *Redbrick University* indicated a Scottish nationality (see the Preface to *Redbrick and these Vital Days*, 11). Peers evidently enjoyed, as he does here through the misspelling of Truscot, fostering this false assumption.

\*\*\* The original letter handwritten by Peers is preserved in the University Archives. As the postscript reveals, what Tillotson received was a copy written by Truscot's secretary. This copy still exists — in the possession of Professor Kathleen Tillotson. Elizabeth Hall served obligingly as Truscot's secretary, to preserve the secret of the true author of *Redbrick University* (for more information on Mrs Hall's role, see below, p. 474).

Dowden* as a textbook likely to be in the hands of a young student of the present day.

Yours with best New Year wishes,

[signed] Geoffrey Tillotson.

**1944** letter to Bruce Truscot from Margaret and Jocelyn Toynbee.

22, Park Town  Newnham College
Oxford  Cambridge

11 April 1944

Dear Sir,

We had been meaning, for some time, to read your *Red Brick University*; for, although domiciled in 'Ox-' and now working in 'Ox-' and '-bridge' respectively, we have both had experience of modern universities, one of us as a research student in History for two years at Manchester University, the other as 'Grade II' Classical lecturer at Reading University for three years. But when we saw the passage on p. 49 of your book quoted in the article 'Universities after the War' in the issue of *The Times* for 3 April, we went out and bought the book at once. After reading it we feel that we must write to tell you how astonished and delighted we were to find there expressed precisely the views which we ourselves hold as to the paramount importance of research in university life. From our respective experiences as university teachers at 'Ox-' and '-bridge' we must regretfully bear testimony to the deplorable rarity of these views among our colleagues, nearly all of whom lay all the emphasis on teaching and on personal, social relations with their students.

We should like to see your book in the hands of every university teacher. Might we, in all diffidence, suggest that Chapters II, IV, and V in particular might be printed as separate pamphlets at a moderate cost so that they could be widely disseminated among

---

\* We are indebted to Professor Kathleen Tillotson for explaining that the reference to Dowden (see *Redbrick University*, 98) is to: 'Edward Dowden, *Shakespeare, a Critical Study of his Mind and Art*, 1875... In 1943 this would have seemed out of date in comparison with A. C. Bradley's book' (Kathleen Tillotson's letter to Ann Mackenzie, dated 2 November 1994).

students also. No student should enter a university without having read them. For, in spite of its title, your book seems to us to apply no less vitally to intending Oxbridge undergraduates, male and female, than to students of Red Brick.

There are only two points on which we venture to differ from you. (1). We have the greatest sympathy with Red Brick and the happiest memories of our sojourn there; but we cannot help feeling that you tend to underrate the historical traditions of Oxbridge and its external setting of art and nature which Red Brick, whatever its attractions, can never hope to rival. (2). We think that in Chapter V you overemphasize the value of organized student activities, such as societies, newspapers etc. In our experience, both at Oxbridge and Red Brick, it is just the excessive attention to such things which cuts across the primary duty of university students, namely concentration on scholarship.

We feel that all university teachers and students are deeply indebted to you for your outspoken words, recalling them to their true vocation. If they do not return to it, productive scholarship will be entirely in the hands of scholars who do not hold university appointments.

Yours very truly

[signed] Margaret R. Toynbee*

M.A. (Oxon), Ph.D. (Manchester), F.R.Hist. S.
formerly Lecturer in Modern History, St Hilda's College, Oxford.

[signed] Jocelyn M.C. Toynbee**

M.A. (Cantab), D.Phil. (Oxon), F.S.A.
Fellow, one-time Research Fellow, Director of Studies, Lecturer in Classics, Newnham College, Cambridge; Lecturer in Faculty of Classics, University of Cambridge.

---

\* Dr Margaret Toynbee (1900-1988) was part-time Lecturer in Modern History at St Hilda's College, 1924-42. She was Sub-Editor of the *Dictionary of National Biography*, 1923-50. An obituary of Dr Toynbee was published in *The Antiquaries Journal*, LXIX (1989), part II, 413.

\*\* Professor Jocelyn Toynbee, F.B.A. (1897-1985) was Fellow and Director of Studies in Classics at Newnham College, 1927-51; she was Laurence Professor of Classical Archaeology, University of Cambridge, 1951-62. Among the honours conferred on her was an honorary Litt.D., University of Liverpool, 1968.

(Dr Arnold J. Toynbee, C.H., F.B.A. (1889-1975), distinguished author, scholar and historian, was the brother of Jocelyn and Margaret Toynbee.)

**1944** exchange of letters between 'Bruce Truscot' and Sir Hector Hetherington, Principal and Vice-Chancellor, University of Glasgow.

c/o Messrs Faber and Faber,<br>24, Russell Square,<br>London, W.C.<br>7th September 1944

Sir Hector Hetherington,
The University,
Glasgow.

Dear Vice-Chancellor,
You have probably never heard of me but I am the author of a book called *Red Brick University* and last December I gave a talk in the B.B.C. African service following one by you on the Universities and the Public. At that time Miss Treadgold kindly sent me the script of your talk to see and I liked it so much that I want to ask you if I may quote about twelve lines in my forthcoming book *Redbrick and these Vital Days*. As the talk has not been published I don't think I ought to quote it without your permission, which I should be extremely grateful if you would give me.
Believe me to be,

Yours faithfully,


From The Principal.  The University
Glasgow, W.2

15th September, 1944

Dear Mr Truscot,
I imagine there are few people in the British University world who have not heard of you! I certainly read 'Red Brick University' with very great interest and admiration. I don't agree with all of it, but I thought it one of the most valuable contributions to the discussion of a vitally important University problem which have yet appeared.

If there is anything in my West African script which you think worth quoting, by all means annex it.

     Yours faithfully,

    [signed] H. J. W. Hetherington.

Bruce Truscot, Esq.,
 c/o Messrs. Faber & Faber,
  24, Russell Square,
   London, W.C.


**1945** letters between Professor Bonamy Dobrée,* University of Leeds, and Bruce Truscot and his wife, Amelia. These letters are of special interest, for a number of reasons, one of which is the information given by 'Amelia Truscot' that her husband intends to start his autobiography 'after his vacation' which will, however, not be published 'until he retires'. Peers composed himself the letters supposedly from Mrs Truscot. But they were typed and signed 'Amelia Truscot' by Elizabeth Hall (*née* Colquhoun), who was a postgraduate student in Peers' Department. She and her husband, the late Professor Harold Hall, a colleague and ex-student of Peers, and later holder of the Gilmour Chair (1978-81), were among the very few people at this time who knew the real identity of Bruce Truscot.


11th June '45

           Southbank,
           Collingham,
           Nr. Leeds.

Dear Truscot,
 (I take it that, seeing what we are, I can drop the honorific, even with a pseudonym.) You cover me with shame; for before I have had the grace to acknowledge your amusing squib in The

---

  * Lt.-Col. Bonamy Dobrée, O.B.E. (1891-1974), was Professor of English Literature, University of Leeds, 1936-55; he was also a member of the Central Advisory Council for Education (England), 1944-53. In his *Who's Who* entry he listed his recreation as gardening.

Universities' Review,* you overwhelm me with your very much appreciated gift of Redbrick and these Vital Days. So far I have read only the highly entertaining Preface, and just had a first taste of the rest. What enormous fun you must have had over your pseudonymity. Of course, if I had cared to apply my critical faculties to your style, I should instantly have discovered who you are; but I respected your desire for seclusion! (Stylistic analysis is a very amusing game, and perhaps a good sharpening exercise: but when we solemnly call it 'Research' and publish our results — well, look at the Shakesperean disintegrators!)

From what I have seen of your book I know I shall like it very much. That is a splendid attack of yours on the authorities for not letting the Arts people come to Universities. That policy** shows how much we still need educating as a nation. And thank you very much for your most kind remarks about my Earl Grey cup of tea; they make me feel very curmudgeonly, as I never lose a chance of attacking you on the points where I differ from you. Ultimately, of course, we are on the same side; at least we see that these are vital days, and that we have to put our house in order. I feel that the Arts Faculties especially must look to what they are doing, and my quarrel with you is that you seem to think that if we go on doing what we have been doing for the last fifty years, only more energetically, all will be well. I think that we need something more radical than that. But I won't embark on an essay just now.

For me, what matters in research, is where you direct your research. Don't your ideas lead us straight to the breeding of what Livingstone Lowes called 'diligent coral-insects rather than adventurous and constructive minds'? Deadwood, I agree, is a pest (he is not to be found in the Arts Faculties alone), yet I confess to using his argument that every lecture he gives is the result of research, or ought to be, that is, a reconsideration of his matter in the light of his, and his students' recent experience. Shutting himself up and discovering something which no one has yet discovered because no one has yet been ass enough to think it worth while, and then publishing the result,+ seems to me far worse escapism, and indeed idleness, than keeping himself really alert while he re-reads the matter for his lectures. However, if we ever meet, as I hope we shall, we can thresh these matters out.

---

\* 'A Redbrick Tea-party', *The Universities Review*, XVII (May 1945), no. 2, 38-40.

\*\* Fifty years later this same policy is still a topical and controversial issue — another indication of the enduring relevance of much of the critical and analytical thought-content of *Redbrick University*.

All success to your book, and with renewed thanks for sending it me,

      Yours sincerely,

      [signed] Bonamy Dobrée.

What I really resent is your jeering at Professors who garden! Gardening is the only thing which keeps me sane.

+See any volume of The Year's Work in English Studies.*

      As from:
      24 Russell Square,
      London, W.C.1.

      23rd June, 1945

Dear Professor Dobrée,

 Please forgive my husband for not answering you himself. He is very busy putting footnotes into a new book of his, because he says that if you don't put in footnotes nobody will call it Research, and we all want our work to be called Research, don't we? He thanks you for your friendly mode of greeting but says that if he gets too friendly he will certainly make a mistake one day and sign the wrong name; he very nearly gave himself away last time he saw you but just stopped in time.

 Bruce says that he doesn't in the least want to breed coral-insects and is all out for adventurous and constructive minds. He thinks you ought to have deduced this from Red Brick University. But at Redbrick, if not at Leeds, there are masses of lecturers, and professors too, who merely do six or eight hours' work a week, attend a few meetings and call that a full-time occupation. A long list of reappointments at increased salaries is made every year and the professors who pass it know perfectly well that many of the people concerned are not producing anything, but they naturally say nothing, because few of them are producing anything either. Nobody worth his salt would prepare lectures in any other than the way you describe, but that is not enough, except for people who are content with a 15 or 20 hours' week in a year with 22 weeks' vacation. What you want to do is to clear the

---

 * Added by Dobrée, in his own handwriting, to his typed letter.

drones out from the universities and put in adventurous and constructive minds instead.

We have been thinking of founding a Bruce Truscot Club, with not more than three members from any one university, all pledged to putting new life into the Arts Faculties and incidentally to keeping Bruce's identity a secret. He would visit each branch at intervals to devise and disseminate plans. It was my idea and he is very keen about it, but I am inclined now to think it a little dangerous. What do you think?

Meanwhile Bruce has written a little book for freshmen called First Year at the University, to be published next spring or summer and after his holiday he is going to begin on his autobiography. But that will not be published until he retires, which, unfortunately as I expect you have discovered with all your critical faculties, is going to be quite soon.* You wouldn't think he was such an old man, would you? Or am I prejudiced?

Yours sincerely,


P.S. Bruce likes gardening, too. He only jeers at the people who call it research.


22 Aug. 45

           Southbank,
           Collingham,
           Nr. Leeds.
        Collingham Bridge 262.

Dear Mrs Truscot,

Thank you very much for your letter of — Heavens! how long ago! Please forgive me for not answering it sooner. I offer no excuses: there obviously are none.

First of all I want to say that I welcome the idea of a Bruce Truscot Club. I think we could scrape up three people here to form the Leeds Branch. I think we would pledge ourselves to keep up the secret, and succeed fairly successfully. Do let me know if you are going on with the idea.

---

  * It will be remembered that Bruce Truscot (born in 1885) is six years older than Allison Peers.

Now to a little argument. Agreed that your husband and I both want to breed adventurous and constructive minds, and despise the coral insects. Agreed that there are a number of people who don't pull their weight (not in the Arts Faculties alone, by the way!) To take the second point first: I think this is a price you have to pay if you are to get people to feel really free. And between the first point and the second, there are a great many people who do a lot of reading and thinking, and give it all out again to their students. Why on earth publish? Aren't there enough second and third rate books published as it is? and do you expect every university lecturer to be able to produce first-rate stuff? Give me the lecturer who will produce students' plays, attend debates, talk privately, drink in pubs with students — and you can take all the lecturers who produce stuffy little papers in stuffy little journals. And then call themselves scholars!

What I am really afraid of in all this forced publication, this research — a bastard offshoot of the sciences, all analysis and no intuition, is that it will kill what little creative capacity there is on our staffs. Let them live a bit more and read a bit less, and only take up their pens when they feel they have something to say that they must say. But all this, I see, needs arguing at length, not in the scope of a letter.

I hope I shall hear soon about the formation of this club.

Yours sincerely,

[signed] Bonamy Dobrée

P.S. I should never dream of calling my gardening 'research'. I have far too much respect for gardening. It is creative.

## APPENDIX III

**1945** letter to Professor Field.* Two very long handwritten letters (the first received by Peers on 6 September, and the second dated 25 September 1945) about the 'Redbrick' books, sent to Bruce Truscot from Professor G. C. Field, of the University of Bristol (then President of the Association of University Teachers), together with Truscot's very much shorter answers (18 September and 11 October 1945) are in the University Archives, Liverpool (ref. D.265). Truscot's second letter, since it mentions his intention, when he retires, to publish his autobiography, is reproduced below.

24 Russell Square,<br>
London, W.C.1.

October 11th, 1945

Dear Professor Field,

Thank you for your second letter. I am glad I was wrong in thinking that my criticisms had hurt your feelings: that was how your letter sounded to me, and I was sorry, because, though I have had to be outspoken, I have always tried to be as objective as possible and to weigh both sides of every controversial question.

The only other point I want to clear up is about my correspondent from Bristol. Several people from Bristol (and from most other universities) have written to me; but the one I referred to wrote specifically to endorse what I had said about the neglect of research. Therefore we are evidently thinking of two different persons.

---

\* Professor G. C. Field, F.B.A. (1887-1955) was Professor of Philosophy, University of Bristol, 1926-52. During the period 1919-26 he was on the staff of the University of Liverpool (in other words when Peers was also a member of staff), as Lecturer in Philosophy, 1919-25, and Associate Professor of Philosophy, 1925-26; he served as Dean of the Faculty of Arts, 1923-26. As his letters reveal, Field had entertained the suspicion that he and Truscot might at some time have been colleagues. However Peers, concerned to protect Truscot's secret, in his replies, deftly, humorously, wholly misled Field into accepting that this could not have been the case. In a letter (dated 18 September 1945) Peers writes to Field: 'as you seem to think I am a person associated with you in some way, let me say quite definitely that I am not and that I do not even know you by sight'.

Your point that if the system of terminable professorial appointments were adopted it might become a formality is, I think, an important one, and it may be that you are right. My creator says that we keep renewing the appointments of numerous lecturers, whom we could get rid of, and who are not pulling their weight, so what chance is there that we should be strong-minded enough to get rid of an idle professor? He will not associate himself, therefore, with my proposed remedy, and says I am a hopeless idealist. My reply is that, if there is a better remedy, I should like to see it tried. What I have done is to draw attention to the abuse and am glad to find I have aroused a considerable number of people to its seriousness. Once this is generally recognized, something will be done about it, I have no doubt, though I may not live to see it.

Of course, I realize that we have a great deal in common and I hope you will like my next book, First Year at the University — a guide to freshmen, to be published next spring — better than the other two. When I retire, I hope to publish my autobiography, which will perhaps make it clear that my failure to show professors proper respect is founded on experience.

Yours sincerely,

# APPENDIX IV

## An Autobiographical Essay by 'Bruce Truscot'

Preserved in the University Archives,[1] Liverpool, there is a hitherto unpublished manuscript in Peers' tiny hand, which is described by him, in a note at the top left hand corner of its first page, as an 'Introductory essay of sorts'. Written by 'Bruce Truscot', and autobiographical in character, 'Any Faculty Board' is dated 21 June 1945. Only two days afterwards, on 23 June 1945 — Truscot's sixtieth birthday —, Peers began work on *The Autobiography of 'Bruce Truscot'*.[2]

Several of the characters described in 'Any Faculty Board' are also involved in *The Autobiography of 'Bruce Truscot'*. Inaccessible, the Professor of Ancient History, Active, the Professor of International Affairs, Jim Livewire, Professor of English Literature, and Bruce Truscot himself. Nevertheless, the meeting of the Faculty of Arts which the essay amusingly and satirically describes evidently 'took place' at Redbrick University some twenty years or more after the events chronicled in Bruce Truscot's autobiography. For young Livewire, it will be remembered, was appointed to his Chair only at the end of that autobiography, whereas at 'Any Faculty Board', he is, clearly, shown to be an experienced senior member of Faculty and well established as Professor of English Literature. Moreover, not only is there is no mention of the clique known as the 'Salvation Army', but Professors Livewire, Active and Truscot have formed themselves into a differently intentioned, progressive group of activists within the Faculty. Which group 'has come to be known as "Hell Corner" ' — presumably because its members like to stir things up and give

---

    1    Archives, University of Liverpool, ref. D.265.
    2    This date, 23 June 1945, is written at the beginning of Chapter I of the 'Truscot' autobiography. See above 'B.T.', ch. I, p. 173, and note 1.

their more reactionary colleagues hell, in the good interests of higher education and learning.

'Any Faculty Board' is almost like a companion piece to the published essay 'A Redbrick Tea-party' which, as 'Bruce Truscot', Peers also wrote in 1945.[3] Some of the characters are the same: Jim Livewire, Dusty, etc. There is a significant difference, however, in that 'A Redbrick Tea-party' has few autobiographical pretensions, consisting mainly of a discussion by his colleagues, and in his absence, of Bruce Truscot and his book *Redbrick University*. In contrast, this essay is Truscot's account, in the first person, of his experiences as a member of 'Any Faculty Board' at Redbrick University.

Not the least interesting feature of 'Any Faculty Board' is that 'Bruce Truscot' gives the impression of being engaged not simply in writing a briefly 'autobiographical' essay, but of being occupied in a much longer composition — as 'the author of this book' about his experiences at Redbrick University. Could it be possible that as early as 1945, and before completing the work we have just edited, Peers had already conceived the idea of writing a book-length sequel to the early life and career of Bruce Truscot? Was 'Any Faculty Board' to provide for this sequel an 'Introductory essay of sorts'? Peers was a sufficiently productive writer to have worked in this way.

There is, admittedly, another explanation. In a letter to Faber and Faber, written on 7 June 1947, Peers suggested possibly composing as 'the next Truscot', *A Descriptive Book on Redbrick*, which would contain 'a number of *sketches and narratives*, each complete in itself'.[4] Peers, as he says in this same letter, liked 'to plan well in advance'. It is possible that in 1945 Peers wrote 'Any Faculty Board' and 'A Redbrick Tea-party' with the intention of incorporating both essays, in due course, into a book of Truscot's 'sketches' or 'narratives' about Redbrick University — which book, regrettably, was never accomplished.

---

3 A 'Redbrick Tea-party' appeared in *The Universities Review*, XVII (May 1945), no. 2, 38-40 (*cf*. 'B.T.', ch. III, pp. 312-13, note 132).

4 My italics. *Cf*. Editorial Commentary, pp. 39-40, and notes 13 and 15.

The 'Introductory essay of sorts' is worth printing because of the additional light it helpfully casts, for readers of the 'Truscot' autobiography, on the activities of 'Bob' Truscot, Jim Livewire and their colleagues — we 'know them all, of course' — in the Faculty of Arts at Redbrick University, Drabtown. But the essay also stands well unaccompanied as a logically developed, stylishly structured, acutely witty description of 'Any Faculty Board' meeting. Derived from Peers' experiences of meetings of the Faculty of Arts at Liverpool University, the essay could be said aptly to describe **any** meeting of the Arts Faculty at **any** Redbrick University in Britain during the 1940s. Moreover, fifty years later, university teachers of the present day will recognize in the members of the Faculty Board that Peers describes attitudes, motives and manoeuvres strikingly similar to those which they have personally experienced at meetings of their own Faculties of Arts in ancient, Victorian, postwar and contemporary institutions of higher learning throughout the land.[5]

A.M.

---

5  It is worth recording that among papers deposited in the University Archives, Liverpool by Professor Kenneth Muir, King Alfred Professor of English Literature, 1951-74, is the typescript of *A Courteous Caveat, or A Short View of the Faculty of Arts in a Technological Age with Some Modest Suggestions for Reform* by Jeremy Longstaffe, gent. [i.e. Professor Muir], n.d. [post March 1959, pre 1970], 90 pp. (ref. D. 80/6).

## ANY FACULTY BOARD

You know them all, of course — the group of eighteen seated round the long, polished table in the Faculty of Arts Board Room. Well, in case any of them should be strangers, let me just introduce them as they sit there, waiting for the clock to strike three.

Come and stand behind the grey-haired Dean, for the last twenty years our professor of Geography,[6] who sits in the centre of the long side of the table, and, with his secretary on his right, is waiting to wield the gavel and begin the business of the afternoon. The Dean, at Redbrick, is not, as at some places, a glorified secretary, but one of the senior members of the Faculty, who holds office for five years at a time, has a secretary, two clerks and an office-boy and, as representing the senior Faculty, walks in university processions next to the Vice-Chancellor.[7]

On the left of the Dean is Crusty, Professor of English Language[8] and, by virtue of being Father of the Faculty, the Board's Deputy-President. The left-hand near corner of the table is occupied by three professors who are so apt to be lively in debate that their group has come to be known as 'Hell Corner'.[9] One of them is Livewire, Professor of English

---

6 Percy M. Roxby, John Rankin Professor of Geography at Liverpool University, 1917-44, was never Dean of the Faculty of Arts.

7 The Vice-Chancellor of Liverpool University from 1945-1963 was Sir James Mountford (Professor of Latin, 1932-45 and Dean of the Faculty of Arts, 1941-45).

8 In the 'Bruce Truscot' autobiography the principal model for Crusty, Professor of English Language, appears to be David Slater, Professor of Latin at Liverpool University. But in some parts of that narrative one perceives in Crusty certain elements of W. E. Collinson, Professor of German (see especially B.T., ch. III, pp. 298-99, note 99). For a suggested connection between Crusty and J. P. Postgate, Professor of Latin, see 'B.T.', ch. IV, p. 349, note 55).

9 This group of 'hell-raising' professors, with their good aims and admirable principles, have acquired a title as ironically inappropriate as the name given to the ill-intentioned and unprincipled band of academics — the 'Salvation Army' — that Truscot and his friends had helped to destroy.

Literature;[10] the second is Active, Professor of International Relations;[11] and the third — well, I am afraid the third is the author of this book.[12]

Down the left-hand short side of the table sit our three modern language professors, sometimes referred to as the Monkey House, though, far from chattering, they sit in perfect silence through the most heated debate. Our French Professor — a Frenchman by nationality —[13] is the Board's champion doodler, his speciality being caricatures of the flags of every nation, with which he must have covered reams of paper since he came here. The German professor,[14] who sits next to him, is British-born of British parentage, but from some remote ancestor he has inherited a Prussian neck and German patronymic, while his speech has frequent reminiscences of the glottal stop. The Italian professor, Ratti,[15] is a dark, explosive little man who frightens any intending students and seldom presents any candidates for examinations. In fact, the undergraduate story is that Ratti has only once had a student, and that student was an Italian — and bigger than himself!

The far left-hand corner is generally unoccupied, and at the long side, facing the Dean, are sitting only three people — the

---

10 Jim Livewire, as indicated previously, is another impersonation of Allison Peers (see 'B.T.', ch. IV, p. 346, and especially note 48).

11 The figure of Professor Active, as we have shown, is based on Charles K. Webster, Professor of Modern History at Liverpool University (*cf.* 'B.T.', ch. III, p. 301, and note 106; see also below, p. 490, and note 27).

12 That is, Bruce Truscot, Professor of Poetry at Redbrick University.

13 Perhaps a reference to André, Professor of French at Redbrick University in *The Autobiography of Bruce Truscot*. André is based (at least partly) on Professor L. A. Terracher. But Peers might here also have had in mind Terracher's successor, Professor J. E. Eggli, who was by no means an ally of Peers. Both Terracher and Eggli were Frenchmen (see Introduction, p. 6; 'B.T.', ch. IV, p. 373, note 111).

14 The Professor of German at Liverpool University throughout Peers' career was W. E. Collinson. But at Redbrick University in the early 1920s the German-born Professor of German was Eberhard — which name certainly conforms to the 'German patronymic' mentioned here. The figure of Eberhard might be loosely based on J. E. Eggli (see 'B.T.', ch. IV, p. 338, and note 27).

15 The figure of Ratti is based on either, or both, of the following lecturers in Italian at Liverpool University: Piero Rébora, Mario Praz. Peers has given Ratti a name to suit his 'explosive' nature ('ratty', in schoolboyish slang, meaning 'irritable'). See 'B.T.', ch, IV, p. 338, and notes 26 and 28.

youthful Professor of Economics,[16] who comes from Camford but wears an eyeglass and an Oxford manner; his lecturer, Miss Riley, the Board's only woman; and Anstruther, a middle-aged lecturer in English Literature,[17] who will sit silently through half a meeting, then jump up to shoot a query with the force of a machine gun, before relapsing into somnolence for the rest of the afternoon.[18] The far right-hand corner is also unoccupied, though usually — ah, yes, here he is, at the very last moment: our professor of Mediaeval History, Cuthbert Deadwood.[19] Ever since he came here he has occupied that corner nearest the door; and at every Board meeting there comes a point at which, when discussion on some subject is absorbing the attention of all, Professor Deadwood half-rises and makes a noiseless exit.

You will have noticed how our members group themselves together by subjects — and all the seats round that table, by the way, are sacrosanct: nobody ever dares to place-crash and newcomers are always told where to go.[20] Next to Deadwood

---

16  In the *Autobiography of 'Bruce Truscot'*, the Professor of Economics at Redbrick University is Eagles, a character possibly derived from J. E. Eggli (see 'B.T.', ch. IV, p. 373, note 111).

17  Anstruther, who is modelled principally on Robert Hope Case, Professor of English Literature, Liverpool University, was, it will be remembered, Jim Livewire's unsuccessful competitor for the Chair of English Literature (see 'B.T.', ch. III, pp. 294-98, and note 94; ch. IV, pp. 350, 359-62). Anstruther was thirty-two when, in 1924, he was a candidate for the Chair vacated by Slocombe (see 'B.T.', ch. IV, p. 344). In 1945, therefore, he would be fifty-three — that is, 'middle-aged', or, at any rate, not yet elderly.

18  For Anstruther's conduct at Faculty meetings, as similarly described in *The Autobiography of 'Bruce Truscot'*, see above, ch. IV, p. 344.

19  In creating Cuthbert Deadwood, the professor made famous by Truscot's *Redbrick and these Vital Days*, Peers might, or might not, have had in mind Alexander Mair, the Professor of Philosophy, who figures as Wormwood in Truscot's autobiography. See above, our comments in 'B.T.', ch. III, p. 308, note 120.

20  This observation is one of many which illustrate the continuing relevance of Truscot's writings about British academics and their institutions. In 1993, nearly fifty years after Peers wrote 'Any Faculty Board', Professor Sir Graeme Davies, then Chief Executive of the Higher Education Funding Council for England, delivered a speech at the University of Liverpool. In the speech, which was made in honour of Sir Albert Sloman, the recipient of a special *Festschrift*-Volume of the *Bulletin of Hispanic Studies*, Graeme Davies included an anecdote which reveals that, just as at 'Any Faculty Board' of Redbrick University, at meetings, in our more modern times, of the Committee of Vice-Chancellors and Principals all the seats are

comes his Modern History colleague who today happens to be absent. And there, down the right-hand side and at the near right-hand corner, are the representatives of the Ancient Humanities, linked with History by the Professor of Ancient History, Inaccessible, a professor of the Old School — or shall we say a professor of fiction? — if there ever was one.[21]

Next to him sits Lovewit,[22] our Philosopher, a typical Greats man and a cynic who gives us some of our finest moments. Then comes Vapid,[23] also a Classic, our Professor of Education,

---

'sacrosanct', for 'nobody ever dares to place-crash and newcomers are always told where to go'. Graeme Davies recalled an incident when, as a recently appointed Vice-Chancellor (University of Liverpool, 1986), that is, as a 'new boy', he had attended a meeting of the CVCP and 'had nearly made the embarrassing mistake of occupying a chair traditionally reserved for another university leader of longer service. Fortunately, Albert Sloman tactfully intervened in time to prevent a chain-, or chair-, reaction. Aware of the disruption of general order and goodwill which such "out-of-place" conduct might have occasioned, he discreetly located for Davies a seat likely to be less uncomfortable, because its usual occupant was "no longer with us" '. This anecdote is included in Ann L. Mackenzie's article entitled 'Haec Otia Studia [Hispana] Fovent', published [wrongly attributed to Dorothy S. Severin] in *Precinct* (University of Liverpool, August 1993), no. 11, p. 6.

21 Inaccessible, Professor of Ancient History, a character with a key-role in *The Autobiography of 'Bruce Truscot'*, as previously noted, is modelled on John Sampson, who was University Librarian at Liverpool University. 'Professors of fiction' is the name which Peers gives to those academics in fact who keep themselves inaccessible to their students and aloof from the realities of life at university (see 'B.T.', ch. III, pp. 284 and 308; and note 121).

22 We may assume that Lovewit is another pseudonym for Alexander Mair, Professor of Philosophy at Liverpool University — who is Wormwood in *The Autobiography of 'Bruce Truscot'* (*cf.* above, note 19). That Mair (Wormwood) was a lover of wit (Lovewit), when he spoke at meetings of Faculty, is clear from Truscot's allusions to Wormwood's 'graceful flourish of words rounded off with an epigram' and to the Professor of Philosophy's 'mordant wit' (see 'B.T.', ch. IV, pp. 341, 343).

23 Vapid might be another name for the character known as Bletherley in *The Autobiography of 'Bruce Truscot'*. Professor of Education at Redbrick, Bletherley, it will be remembered, had a curious 'half-vacant smile', which is also described as 'vapid'. His smile could mislead people to underestimate the strength and profundity of his true character (see 'B.T.', ch. IV, pp. 352, 367). The real-life professor usually and mainly represented by Bletherley, is W. E. Collinson, Professor of German, who was an opponent of the 'New Testament' and one of Peers' most effective supporters. However, Bletherley sometimes also represented David A. Slater. Professor of Latin at Liverpool University, Slater was another supporter whom Peers greatly admired.

about whom I hope to write a great deal some day.[24] And at the corner are Dusty,[25] another of our seniors, an energetic but rather hide-bound professor of Latin, and a much younger, and rather colourless, professor of Greek. And as the latter's neighbour is the Dean's secretary, the wheel has come full oblong, and —

*The clock strikes three.* Conversation stops, and, as not a sound can be heard behind the hermetically sealed windows, it is an absolute silence which is broken by the Dean's gavel.

'I call upon the Secretary to read the minutes.'

The minutes are read. To the most insignificant word and to the bitter end. Any committee of business men, to whom time is money, would have the minutes typed and circulated, or, at worst, would take three-quarters or more of the dreary stuff as read. But, at Redbrick, time is not money, and nobody minds wasting it. So the gist of every letter read at the last meeting goes on to the minutes; the name of every member of every committee appointed is read with the minutes; even the title of every set-book in every subject is read with the minutes — and in English Literature alone there are forty of them. The only thing ever 'taken as read' is an unpronounceable name — the

---

Slater was wrongly believed, by members of the 'New Testament', to be ineffectual — 'a harmless nonentity' (see '[E.A.P.] *Auto*', ch. 6, p. 154). Another possibility might be that Vapid corresponds to E. T. Campagnac, Professor of Education, who, as we have seen, played a chief role at Liverpool University in the downfall of the 'New Testament' and in Peers' election to the Gilmour Chair of Spanish. But in this essay, as in *The Autobiography of 'Bruce Truscot'*, Campagnac is probably represented by Dusty, Professor of Latin. *Cf.* 'B.T.', ch. III, pp. 298-99, note 99.

24 'Any Faculty Board' is dated 21 June 1945 — a date only two days before Peers began work upon *The Autobiography of 'Bruce Truscot'*. So this comment might allude to his intention — fulfilled in that narrative — to describe the chief role of Collinson (Bletherley; ?Crusty), of Slater (Crusty; ?Bletherley), or of Campagnac (Dusty) in the downfall of the 'New Testament' (the 'Salvation Army'). Alternatively, the author might be expressing his intention to write 'a great deal some day' about Vapid (Collinson, Slater or Campagnac) in a further volume of memoirs or essays about Redbrick University — which Peers did not live long enough to compose (*cf.* above, p. 482, and note 4).

25 Dusty, 'another of our seniors', is probably E. T. Campagnac, who, in fact, retired in 1938 (*cf.* above, note 23; and see 'B.T.', ch. III, especially pp. 298-305, and note 99; and ch. IV, pp. 348-49, note 55).

names of Polish or Czech students or of set books in Russian or Assyriology — and even then it is a point of honour that the Secretary shall attempt to pronounce each name before he gives it up with a smile and goes on to the next.

The minutes are over at last. The time is a quarter-past three.

'Correspondence', says the Dean.

The Secretary rises again, clutching a mass of letters. Livewire and Active groan; Deadwood yawns; the Professor of Philosophy looks philosophical; the Professor of French lays aside his first sheet of flags, about eighty per cent of which seem to be tricolours, and sets to work on the flag of Guatemala.

The letters are numerous. Every body in the University, and a good many people outside it, seem to have written to the Dean since the Board last met. The Vice-Chancellor has written; the Registrar has written; the Clerk of the Senate has written; the Bursar has written; even the Housekeeper has penned a few lines on the proposed addition of an extra penny to the cost of a cup of tea. The Registrars of other universities have written; the Secretary of the Committee of Vice-Chancellors and Principals has written; the Secretary of the Oxbridge and Camford Examinations Board has written ...

And that is only a small part of the correspondence. After he has read through the four- and five-page letters detailing new regulations or enumerating business sent forward to the higher bodies and passed by them, he comes to the domestic correspondence — some of it too trivial to need reading at all, but some, more provocative of discussion than anything which has been read yet. The widow of Livewire's recently deceased predecessor, the late Professor Miope,[26] wishes to thank the Dean for forwarding the Board's kind message of sympathy — and, in doing so, recalls in leisurely fashion various incidents of his long professoriate. It all has to be read. The Headmaster of Princes Road Modern School, Mudborough, covers various

---

26 Professor Miope is evidently another name for Professor Slocombe, Livewire's predecessor in *The Autobiography of 'Bruce Truscot'*. As previously indicated, George Slocombe is modelled on Oliver Elton, Professor of English Literature at Liverpool University (see 'B.T.', ch. III, pp. 279, 290-93, and note 49; *cf.* also 'B.T.', ch. I, pp. 185-86, note 52). Oliver Elton died on 4 June 1945, the same month and year in which Truscot wrote 'Any Faculty Board'.

sheets in protesting against the compulsoriness of Latin in the Arts Faculty: letters of that kind are received two or three times a year, but they all have to be read. The Chairman of the Student Appeals Committee reports seventeen of the Committee's decisions, the most vital of which seems to be that Patricia Risborough, an undergraduate beginning her second year, is to be allowed to take Mediaeval History as a three-year subject and German as a two-year subject, instead of German as a three-year subject and Mediaeval History as a two-year subject, notwithstanding Regulation 72, Section 3 (a) which declares this procedure to be illegal.

Then comes the tit-bits of the correspondence. Professor Active writes to say that he proposes to ask the Council for leave of absence in order to give some series of lectures at International Forums throughout the country.[27] Some support the idea because they think it a good one. Others support it because they will be glad to see less of Professor Active. Some oppose it because they consider the Department insufficiently staffed to stand the strain. Others oppose it on principle because they think such work should be done in the vacations. Some support it because they propose to ask for similar leave and this will constitute a valuable (others would say a dangerous) precedent. So currents and cross-currents intermingle; the debate grows lively — though never heated, for hardly anybody is saying all that is in his mind; and members are forgetting that the business on the agenda-paper has not yet begun, when —

*The clock strikes four.*

By a quarter-past four, Deadwood has made his usual inconspicuous exit and the Board has got to work on the appointment of committees. As it is the first meeting of the term, there are a good many of them. Newcomers to Redbrick

---

27 In *Redbrick and these Vital Days* Professor Active was refused permission to give lectures in another institution — a refusal which Peers, of course, deplored (see *op. cit.*, 75; and *cf.* 'B.T.', ch. IV, p. 339, note 30). Peers, as we have seen, was a confirmed believer in developing public and academic interest in the wider study of one's subject through repeated visits to schools, and through regular lectures given at universities, and to learned, and not so learned, societies throughout the land.

often wonder why its committees are so ridiculously bloated. Few committees need number more than five; many might consist of three.[28] The reason why they often run to twelve or fifteen is not merely that nobody minds wasting time and many people feel that somehow they are pulling their weight in the place if they sit on plenty of committees. The reason is that anybody can propose anybody and nobody ever says 'No'. This is how it worked out at the meeting we are describing now.

The Committee in question is required to fill a vacancy in the Department of Education caused by the unexpected resignation of the lecturer on method in the teaching of history. The appointment is a matter of urgency and the two people obviously qualified to make it are the Professor of Education and the Professor of Modern History: the Dean would make the third and last member to hold the balance between the other two. In any business-like community, it would be understood that, save for exceptional reasons, a committee charged with making a minor appointment should be of this type.

But not at Redbrick. No. Committees of three, even of five, are unheard of. In fact, the Dean sets the ball rolling by nominating five: the three obvious ones, plus the Professors of Ancient and Mediaeval History — these last, presumably, in the interests of inclusiveness.

'Any more names?' says the Dean, encouragingly.

He has not to wait. 'I propose Professor Crusty', comes from one corner. 'I propose Professor Lovewit', from another.

(There is not the slightest point in proposing these more than anyone else, but they have the name of being 'Committee men' and find themselves on about 75 per cent of all committees for no other reason whatever.)

'Any further names?' beams the Dean.

'Professor Livewire', ejaculates Vapid — and adds, in a whisper behind his hand, to Lovewit:

'Good fellow on Committees, Livewire, I always think.'

For a moment there is a pause. Then someone says:

'Don't you think we ought to have Miss Riley? After all, we *might* want to appoint a woman!'

---

28 *Cf*. Truscot's comment that 'the best Committee for appointments other than to Chairs and Readerships is one of three' (*Redbrick and these Vital Days*, 43).

The Dean refrains from observing that, as women are eligible for appointment to any office in the Faculty, the unfortunate Miss Riley ought to find herself, by that reasoning, on every one of the Board's appointment committees. But he contents himself with remarking blandly:

'That makes nine members. Do we want any more?'

It would have been more to the point to say:

'That makes very nearly half the Board. Why not have a few less?'

But the fifth Committee has yet to be appointed and it is twenty-past four. We must — unlike the Faculty Board — hurry on.

Somewhere about a quarter to five the assembly begins to experience a feeling of unrest. Five o'clock is the traditional hour of adjournment for tea, though if the meeting is nearly over this is sometimes postponed. The business before the Board is now changes in regulations, and Hell Corner begins to propose referring some of the knottier points to a standing committee. This is one of Hell Corner's favourite gambits, and, if the afternoon is yet young, the Classicists across the table start protesting vehemently. But to-day they observe that there are still twelve more items on the agenda and raise no protest.

*The clock strikes five.* Hardly has the last stroke died away than someone rises and suggests tea — an interpolation never, at five or any time after, ruled out of order. Everyone knows the game: all those not particularly interested in the after-tea agenda indulge in a hasty gulp and gobble, and, while the others are still standing at the buffet, leave for home. And nearly everyone approves the procedure, for it is remarkable how quickly the remaining business is disposed of when the members of the Board have been divided by two. In fact, if you have a motion which you know will prove highly controversial, the most practical manoeuvre is to get it into a position where it is bound to be postponed till after tea.[29]

---

[29] A manoeuvre, the usefulness of which is still well appreciated by present-day deans of faculties and heads of departments. It is instructive to compare the conduct of the members of 'Any Faculty Board' with that of the 'Salvation Army' at meetings of the Faculty at Redbrick University (see 'B.T.', ch. IV, especially pp. 340-42).

So at ten minutes past five we adjourn for tea and twenty minutes later the Dean, seeing the dispersal beginning, returns to the table, raps hastily with his gavel and calls out in a meaning voice:

'Are we a quorum?'

The intention is no doubt to recall some of the escapists. If so, it fails, for everybody knows that the Regulations specify no quorum for any Faculty Board at all. When the survivors are re-assembled, they number, alas, only seven. And there are still twelve items...

And they get through them! Oh, how they get through them! No quibbling, no amendments now. For the first time we sense urgency. Before tea, we were yawning, as well we might, in the air fetid with pipe-smoke[30] and unfreshened by a breath of Drabtown's[31] substitute for oxygen. But now we race through reports: Discipline Committee, Boards of Study... Through the arrangements for the Joint Conference of ___

*The clock strikes six.* Only three items are left.

Then up rises Professor Inaccessible, remote and statuesque, the genuine Professor of fiction.

'I do not want', he says, 'to take up the Board's time at this late hour. But — would any member object if I were to open a window?'[32]

Bruce Truscot

---

30 *Cf.* the reference to 'the smoke-haze of many pipes' during the meetings of the Faculty Board at Redbrick University, as described in *The Autobiography of 'Bruce Truscot'* (ch. IV, p. 341).

31 Liverpool. *Cf.* above 'B.T.', ch. III, p. 264, and see note 11; *Redbrick University*, 20-22; *Redbrick and these Vital Days*, pp. 29, 36 and 112-13.

32 With characteristic humour and deliberate irony, the author chooses Inaccessible (*cf.* above note 21) to make this request. The Professor of Ancient History was notorious for keeping his academic attitudes hermetically sealed against the disturbingly fresh air of change.

# BIBLIOGRAPHY

## I  Publications of E. Allison Peers*

### A  'Redbrick' books and related articles

Peers, E. Allison, 'First Impressions of 'Varsity Life', *The Dartfordian*, VI (Christmas 1909), no. 1, 15.

Truscot, Bruce, *Redbrick [Red Brick] University* (London: Faber and Faber, 1943).

Truscot, Bruce, 'The University and its Region', *The Political Quarterly*, XV (1944), 298-309.

Truscot, Bruce, 'A Redbrick Tea-party', *The Universities Review*, XVII (May 1945), no. 2, 38-40.

Truscot, Bruce, 'The Modern Universities' (lecture [?unpublished] broadcast, in Spanish and Portuguese, in the series 'The Pattern of English Life', on BBC Radio [Latin American Service], 23-26 August 1945).

Truscot, Bruce, *Redbrick and these Vital Days* (London: Faber and Faber, 1945).

Truscot, Bruce, *First Year at the University (a Freshman's Guide)* (London: Faber and Faber, 1946). Revised Edition by James Blackie and Brian Gowenlock (London: Faber and Faber, 1964).

Truscot, Bruce, 'Redbrick and the Future of British Universities', *Grand Perspective: A Contact Book* (London: Contact Publications Ltd/Wells, Gardner, Darton & Co., 1947), 61-63.

Truscot, Bruce, 'The Newest Universities' ([?] unpublished article written for the Central Office of Information, n.d. [?c.1950]).

---

\*  Only those works mentioned in *Redbrick University Revisited* are listed.

## B Hispanic and literary studies

Peers, E. Allison, *Elizabethan Drama and its Mad Folk: The Harness Prize Essay for 1913* (Cambridge: W. Heffer & Sons, 1914).

Peers, E. Allison, *The Beginnings of French Prose Fiction (down to 'L'Astrée') 1608 [sic]* (M.A. thesis, University of London, 1915).

Peers, E. Allison, *A Skeleton Spanish Grammar* (London: Blackie & Son, 1917).

Vigny, Alfred de, *Poèmes choisis*, ed., with critical introduction, by E. A. Peers, Modern Language Texts (Manchester: Manchester U. P./London: Longmans Green & Co., 1918).

Finch, M. B. and Peers, E. Allison, *The Origins of French Romanticism* (London: Constable, 1920).

Peers, E. Allison, *A Phonetic Spanish Reader* (Manchester: Manchester U. P./London: Longmans Green & Co., 1920).

Peers, E. Allison, 'Some Provincial Periodicals in Spain during the Romantic Movement', *Modern Language Review*, XV (1920), 374-91.

Peers, E. Allison, 'Some Spanish Conceptions of Romanticism', *Modern Language Review*, XVI (1921), 281-96.

Peers, E. Allison, 'The Fortunes of Lamartine in Spain', *Modern Language Notes*, XXXVII (1922), 458-65.

Churchman, Philip H. and Peers, E. Allison, 'A Survey of the Influence of Sir Walter Scott in Spain', *Revue Hispanique*, LV (1922), 227-310.

Peers, E. Allison, *Ángel de Saavedra, Duque de Rivas. A Critical Study* (*Revue Hispanique* [LVIII]: New York and Paris, 1923).

Peers, E. Allison, *Rivas and Romanticism in Spain* (Liverpool: Liverpool U. P., 1923).

Peers, E. Allison, 'The "Pessimism" of Manuel de Cabanyes', *Modern Philology*, XXI (1923), 49-52.

*The Poems of Manuel de Cabanyes*, ed. E. A. Peers, with critical introduction, notes and bibliography (Manchester: Manchester U. P./London: Longmans Green & Co., 1923).

Peers, E. Allison, 'The Influence of Ossian in Spain', *Philological Quarterly*, IV (1925), 121-38.

Peers, E. Allison, 'Homenaje a Don Ramón Menéndez Pidal', *Bulletin of Spanish Studies*, III (1926), no. 11, 105-11.
Peers, E. Allison, *Studies of the Spanish Mystics*, Vol. I (London: Sheldon Press, 1927; 2nd revised edition, London: S.P.C.K., 1951).
Peers, E. Allison, 'Hispanists Past and Present III. Ramón Menéndez Pidal', *Bulletin of Spanish Studies*, V (1928), no. 19, 127-31.
*Spain: A Companion to Spanish Studies*, ed. (and contrib.) E. Allison Peers (London: Methuen, 1929; 4th, revised, ed., 1948).
Peers, E. Allison, *Studies of the Spanish Mystics*, Vol. II (London: Sheldon Press, 1930).
Peers, E. Allison, ['Preliminary Remarks' to] 'The Study of Spanish Romanticism. The Presidential Address for 1932', *M.H.R.A. Annual Bulletin of the Modern Humanities Research Association* (December 1932), no. 11, 1-16, especially 1-3.
Peers, E. Allison, 'Inaugural Address', Publications of the Institute of Hispanic Studies, Lectures and Addresses, No. 1 (Liverpool: Institute of Hispanic Studies, 1934). Printed also in *Bulletin of Spanish Studies*, XI (1934), 186-200.
Peers, E. Allison, *The Complete Works of St John of the Cross* (translated and edited), 3 vols (London: Burns, Oates & Washbourne, 1934-35; 3rd, revised, edition, 1953).
Peers, E. Allison, *The Spanish Tragedy 1930-1936: Dictatorship, Republic, Chaos* (London: Methuen, 1936).
Peers, E. Allison, *Catalonia Infelix* (London: Methuen, 1937).
Peers, E. Allison, *Spain, the Church and the Orders* (London: Eyre & Spottiswoode, 1939).
Peers, E. Allison, *A History of the Romantic Movement in Spain*, 2 vols (Cambridge: Cambridge U. P., 1940).
Peers, E. Allison, *The Spanish Dilemma* (London: Methuen, 1940).
Peers, E. Allison, *Spain in Eclipse 1937-1943* (London: Methuen, 1943).
Peers, E. Allison, *Spirit of Flame* (London: S.C.M. Press, 1943).
Peers, E. Allison, *Spanish — Now* (London: Methuen, 1944).
Peers, E. Allison, 'How Can We Introduce Spanish?', *Bulletin of Spanish Studies*, XXII (1945), no. 87, 113-38.

Peers, E. Allison, *Mother of Carmel* (London: S.C.M. Press, 1945).
Peers, E. Allison, 'Diary: Spain, March-April 1950' (unpublished manuscript; copy in the Archives, University of Liverpool).
Peers, E. Allison, *Studies of the Spanish Mystics*, Vol. III, ed. I. L. McClelland (London: S.P.C.K., 1960).

## II Other Sources

Allan, Adrian, and Mackenzie, Ann L., *[A Descriptive and Analytical Catalogue of] Redbrick Revisited: The University of Liverpool 1920-1952. An Exhibition* (Liverpool: Univ. of Liverpool, 1994).
Alsop, Constance, *The Life of James W. Alsop, LL.D., B.A.* (Liverpool: Liverpool U. P., 1926).
Atkinson, William C., 'In Memoriam [E. Allison Peers]', *Memorial Number, Bulletin of Hispanic Studies*, XXX (1953), no. 117, 1-5.
Beloff, Max, 'Outside Oxbridge' [Review of *Redbrick University*], *Time and Tide* (11 September 1943).
Beloff, Max, 'More about Redbrick' [Review of *Redbrick and these Vital Days*], *Time and Tide* (7 July 1945).
Boswell, P. G. H., *[Autobiography]* (unpublished, n.d. [1942-c.1948]; University Archives, Liverpool, D.4/1/).
Bradbury, Malcolm, 'Introduction' to *Professor Lapping Sends his Apologies. The Best of Laurie Taylor* (Trentham, Stoke-on-Trent: Trentham Books, 1986), 1-5.
Brett-James, Norman G., *The History of Mill Hill School 1807-1923* (Reigate: Thomas Malcomson, The Surrey Fine Art Press, n.d. [1923]).
Brooke, Christopher N. L., *A History of Gonville and Caius College* (Woodbridge: The Boydell Press, 1985).
Brooke, Christopher N. L., *A History of the University of Cambridge*, Vol. IV *1870-1990* (Cambridge: Cambridge U. P., 1993).
Burmeister, W., [Review of *Redbrick and these Vital Days*], *Adult Education*, XVIII (March 1946), no. 3, 145-57.

*The Cambridge University Calendar 1911-12; 1914-15* (Cambridge: Univ. of Cambridge).
Clark, G. N., 'Sir Charles Kingsley Webster', *Dictionary of National Biography 1961-1970* (Oxford: Oxford U. P., 1981), 1064-65.
Collinson, W. E., 'Portraits from the Past' (unpublished essay, n.d. [post-1946]; University Archives, Liverpool, D.5/3/).
*Cousins' Chronicle: An Account of the Lives of the Grandchildren of Charles Allison and Susanna Bellamy Morris*, ed. Ralph Allison (1976).
Craze, Michael, *A History of Felsted School 1564-1947* (Ipswich: Cowell, 1955).
Cunningham, Colin, and Waterhouse, Prudence, *Alfred Waterhouse 1830-1905: Biography of a Practice* (Oxford: Clarendon Press, 1992).
Dobrée, Bonamy, [Review of *Redbrick University*], *Adult Education*, XVI (December 1943), no. 2, 96-98.
Dumbell, Stanley, *The University of Liverpool 1903-1953. A Jubilee Book* (Liverpool: Univ. of Liverpool, 1953).
Ellis, Walter, *The Oxbridge Conspiracy: How the Ancient Universities Have Kept their Stranglehold on the Establishment* (London: Michael Joseph, 1994).
Elton, Oliver, 'James Fitzmaurice-Kelly', *Revue Hispanique*, LX (1924), 1-11.
Fitz-Gerald, John D., 'Hispanists Past and Present X. James Fitzmaurice-Kelly', *Bulletin of Spanish Studies*, VII (1930), no. 27, 129-35.
Fletcher, B. A., 'The Future of Redbrick University' [Review of *Redbrick and these Vital Days*], *The Journal of Education* (August 1945), 416.
Flexner, Abraham, *Universities: American, English, German* (New York/London/Toronto: Oxford U. P., 1930).
*Gore's Directory of Liverpool and its Environs* (1920 and 1921).
Hampden-Cook, Ernest, *The Register of Mill Hill School 1807-1926* (London: Mill Hill School, 1926).
Harrop, Sylvia, *Decade of Change. The University of Liverpool 1981-1991* (Liverpool: Liverpool U. P., 1994).
Herklots, H. G. G., *The New Universities: An External Examination* (London: Ernest Benn, 1928).

*The History of the University of Oxford*, Vol. V *The Eighteenth Century*, ed. L. S. Sutherland and L. G. Mitchell (Oxford: Clarendon Press, 1986).
Hudson, Ronald L., *History of Dartford Grammar School* (Dartford: Dimond & Co. Ltd, 1966).
Illingworth, Sir Charles, *University Statesman: Sir Hector Hetherington* (Glasgow: Outram, 1971).
Johnson, Gordon, 'The Dreaming Conspirers' [Review of Walter Ellis, *The Oxbridge Conspiracy*], *The Times Higher Education Supplement* (30 September 1994), 20.
Johnson, Gordon, *University Politics. F. M. Cornford's Cambridge and his Advice to a Young Academic Politician* (Cambridge: Cambridge U. P., 1994).
Kelly, Thomas, *For Advancement of Learning. The University of Liverpool 1881-1981* (Liverpool: Liverpool U. P., 1981).
*The Life of a Modern University*, ed. Hugh Martin (London: Student Christian Movement Press, 1930).
*Liverpool Students' Song Book* (Liverpool: Univ. Press of Liverpool/London: Williams & Norgate, 1906).
Lúing, Seán Ó., *Kuno Meyer 1858-1919, a Biography* (Dublin: Geography Publications, 1991).
Mackenzie, Ann L., 'Introduction' to *Hispanic Studies in Honour of Geoffrey Ribbans, Bulletin of Hispanic Studies Special Homage Volume* (1992) (Liverpool: Liverpool U. P., 1992), 1-16.
Mackenzie, Ann L., 'Introduction' to *The 'Comedia' in the Age of Calderón. Studies in Honour of Albert Sloman, Bulletin of Hispanic Studies*, LXX (1993), no. 1, 1-15.
[Mackenzie, Ann L.], 'Haec Otia Studia [Hispana] Fovent', *Precinct* (University of Liverpool, August 1993), no. 11, 6.
[Mackenzie, Ann L.], 'Redbrick University Revisited', *Precinct* (University of Liverpool, April 1994), no. 19, 3-4.
Mackenzie, Ann L., 'Introduction' to *Portugal: Its Culture, Influence and Civilization, Bulletin of Hispanic Studies*, LXXI (1994), no. 1, 2-25.
Mackenzie, Norman, 'The Universities and the Future' [Review of *Redbrick University*], *New Statesman* (30 October 1943).
Marenbon, John, 'Echoes in the Studious Cloister' [review of *The History of the University of Oxford, II. Late Medieval Oxford*, ed. J. I. Catto and T. A. R. Evans; C. N. L. Brooke, *A History*

*of the University of Cambridge, IV 1870-1990], The Times,* 11 February 1993, 34.

Mitchell, S. J. D., *Perse, A History of the Perse School 1615-1976* (Cambridge: Oleander Press, 1976).

Mountford, J. F., 'Bruce Truscot', *Memorial Number, Bulletin of Hispanic Studies,* XXX (1953), no. 117, 10-11.

Muir, Ramsay, *Ramsay Muir: An Autobiography and Some Essays,* ed. Stuart Hodgson (London: Lund Humphries & Co. Ltd, 1943).

Murray, A. V., [Review of *Redbrick University*], *The Cambridge Review* (5 February 1944).

Murray, A. V., [Review of *Redbrick and these Vital Days*], *The Cambridge Review* (9 March 1946).

Newsome, David, *A History of Wellington College 1859-1959* (London: John Murray, 1959).

Palfreyman, David, 'A Second View' [review of Conrad Russell, *Academic Freedom*], *Oxford Magazine,* Eighth Week, Trinity Term (1993), 3-5.

Peile, John, *Biographical Register of Christ's College 1505-1905..., Vol. II: 1666-1905* (Cambridge: Cambridge U. P., 1913).

Pevsner, Nikolaus, *The Buildings of England: Essex,* revised by Enid Radcliffe (Harmondsworth: Penguin Books, 1965).

Pevsner, Nikolaus, *The Buildings of England: Lancashire. I: The Industrial and Commercial North* (Harmondsworth: Penguin Books, 1969).

Pevsner, Nikolaus, and Hubbard, Edward, *The Buildings of England: Cheshire* (Harmondsworth: Penguin Books, 1971).

Reilly, C. H., *Scaffolding in the Sky: A Semi-architectural Autobiography* (London: George Routledge & Sons, 1938).

*Resources of Merseyside, The,* ed. William T. S. Gould and Alan G. Hodgkiss (Liverpool: Liverpool U. P., 1982).

Ribbans, Geoffrey W., 'Preamble' to *Reality Plain or Fancy? Some Reflections on Galdós' Concept of Realism,* E. Allison Peers Lectures 1 (Liverpool: Liverpool U. P., 1986), 1-4.

Ribbans, Geoffrey W., 'El centenari d'Edgar Allison Peers (1891-1952)', *Serra d'Or,* XXXIII (Setembre 1991), núm. 381, 25-26.

Ribbans, Geoffrey W., 'E. Allison Peers: A Centenary Reappraisal' [Fifth E. Allison Peers Lecture], published in *Spain and its Literature. Essays in Memory of E. Allison Peers*, ed. Ann L. Mackenzie (Liverpool: Liverpool U. P./ London: Modern Humanities Research Association, 1996).

Robertson, Sir Charles Grant, [Review of *Redbrick University*], *Manchester Guardian* (13 August 1943).

Robertson, Sir Charles Grant, *The British Universities* (London: Methuen & Co., 1944).

Rosenhead, Louis, *When I Look Back 1933-1973* (Liverpool: Univ. of Liverpool, n.d. [1975]).

Round, Nicholas G., 'The Politics of Hispanism Reconstrued', *Journal of Hispanic Research*, I (1992), no. 1, 134-47.

Saville, Henry, [Review of *Redbrick University*], *Sheffield Telegraph* (7 August 1943).

Saville, Henry, '"Redbrick Varsity" Criticized' [Review], *Newcastle Journal* (7 August 1943).

Searby, Peter, *The Training of Teachers in Cambridge University: The First Sixty Years, 1879-1939* (Cambridge: Department of Education, Cambridge University, 1982).

Sencourt, Robert, 'Edgar Allison Peers. A Tribute', *The Tablet* (10 January 1953), 29.

Share Jones, John, 'University Vet' (unpublished autobiography, University Archives, Liverpool, D.161).

Sloman, Albert E., *A University in the Making* [The University of Essex], The Reith Lectures 1963 (London: The British Broadcasting Corporation, 1964).

Strachan, Hew, *History of the Cambridge University Officers Training Corps* (Tunbridge Wells: Midas Books, 1976).

Talboys, R. St C., *A Victorian School being the Story of Wellington College* (Oxford: Blackwell, 1943).

*Talking across the World. The Love Letters of Olaf Stapledon and Agnes Miller, 1913-1919*, ed. Robert Crossley (Hanover and London: Univ. Press of New England, 1987).

Taylor, A. J. P., [Review of *Redbrick University*], *Oxford Magazine* (10 February 1944).

*The University of Liverpool. A Photographic Portrait: Yesterday and Today* (Liverpool: Liverpool U. P./Ingram Publishing Ltd, 1989).

*The University of Liverpool Calendar 1903-04; 1919-20; 1920-21; 1938-39; 1946-47* (Liverpool: Univ. of Liverpool).

*The University of Liverpool Students' Handbook 1910-11; 1915-16; 1918-19; 1920-21* through to *1933-34* (Liverpool: Univ. of Liverpool).

Tillotson, Geoffrey, [Review of *Redbrick University*], *English. The Magazine of the English Association*, IV (1943), no. 24, 199-200.

Woods, Rex Salisbury, *Cambridge Doctor* (London: Robert Hale, 1962).

Wright, Myles, *Lord Leverhulme's Unknown Venture: The Lever Chair and the Beginnings of Town and Regional Planning 1908-48* (London: Hutchinson Benham, 1982).

# INDEX

Abercrombie, Lascelles, 52, 294, 372
Aberdeen, University of, 65, 300
Active, Professor [?Charles K. Webster], 2, 55, 301, 339, 481, 485, 489-90
Adami, John George (Vice-Chancellor, University of Liverpool, 1919-26), 14, 27, 52, 113, 121-22, 127-28, 160, 164, 331-34, 348, 361, 375-76, 379-81, 413, 419-20, 423, 426-27, 436; see also Sir Archibald Blake
*Adult Education*, 3
*Affair, The* (C. P. Snow), 15
Algeciras Conference, 244
*Alice's Adventures in Wonderland* (L. Carroll), 204
Allan, Adrian R., 21-25, 449
Allison, Charles, 62
Allison, Jessie Dale see Jessie Peers
Allison, Sydney Pennington, 73
Allott, Kenneth, 147
Alonso, Dámaso, 402
Alonso Cortés, Narciso, 442
Alsop, Constance, 378
Alsop, James, 378, 414
André [?L. A. Terracher; ?J. E. Eggli], 52, 54, 338, 348, 485, 489

Anglo-Spanish Society, 142-43
Anstruther, Robert [?Robert Hope Case; ?Leonard C. Martin], 14, 52-53, 294-98, 332, 343-45, 350, 354-55, 359-60, 362, 365-66, 371-72, 374-80, 459, 486
'Any Faculty Board' (B. Truscot), 22, 37, 40, 186, 279, 290, 299, 301, 308, 322, 338, 340-42, 346, 364-66, 376, 481-93
Appleton, R. B., 88
Archibald, Constance, 42
Arteaga, F. de, 113
Artigas, Miguel, 157, 159, 426, 442-43
Arts Tower, (Redbrick University) [The Victoria Building (Liverpool University)], 2, 45, 51, 277, 324, 343, 386
Asquith, H. H., 244
*L'Astrée* (Honoré d'Urfé), 105
Atkinson, Frank,
Atkinson, William C., 22, 394, 396
*Autobiography of 'Bruce Truscot', The* (E. Allison Peers), 15-17, 24, 26, 35-38, 40, 44, 46, 48, 162, 164, 173-386, 389, 391, 393, 459, 481-83, 485-89, *passim*

*Autobiography of E. Allison Peers, The*, 16, 35-36, 39, 46, 48, 61-167, 429, *passim*
Autolycus, 462
Azurdia, J., 121

Baker, A. T., 107-08
Ballads, 207, 310, 337, 339, 437-38
Beaumont, Francis, 91
Belfast, University of, 109, 156
Beloff, Max, 1-2
*Beowulf*, 77, 201
Berceo, Gonzalo de, 155
Berthon, H. E., 97
Betjeman, John, 420
Biblioteca Nacional, Madrid, 159
Bibliothèque Nationale, 95
Birch, J. N., 157, 441-42
Birkenhead, 120
Birmingham, University of, 409
Black, Dora Winifred, 103-04
Black, Sir Frederick, 103
Blackie, James, 44, 196
Blake, Sir Archibald (Vice-Chancellor, Redbrick University) [?Sir Hector Hetherington; and ?John George Adami], 14, 27-28, 52-53, 164, 326, 332-35, 343, 348, 365, 369, 371, 375-77, 380-84, 390, 489
Blake, William, 144
Blandford, F. G., 89, 221
Bletherley [W. E. Collinson; ?D. A. Slater], 52, 54, 299, 348, 351-53, 355, 357-58, 363, 365-70, 377, 384-85, 487-88
Bloxsidge, Robin, 25

Boas, Frederick Samuel, 111
Bonnier, Charles, 113, 320
Booth, Charles, 348, 361, 413
Bordeaux, University of, 109
Bosanquet, Robert Carr, 52, 147, 349, 413, 415, 460, 463
Boswell, A. Bruce, 52, 157, 160, 356, 371-73, 379, 411, 413-16, 419-25, 427, 447, 460; see also Fanshawe
Boswell, P. G. H., 150, 358, 361, 382
Bradbury, Malcolm, 15-16
Bradley, Andrew Cecil, 141, 471
Braunholtz, E. G. W., 78, 104, 106, 114, 157, 200, 431, 434, 439-40
Breul, K. H., 212
Bristol, University of, 9, 372, 479
British Museum / British Museum Reading Room, 55, 101, 117, 157, 182, 234, 313, 351-55, 419
Brooke, Christopher N. L., 17
Brownlow Hill, Liverpool, 130-32, 136, 272-74, 277, 285, 305, 309; see also Paradise Street, Drabtown
'Bruski' [Bruce Truscot], 43
Bryant, H. E., 67, 181, 183-84
Buchanan, M. A., 113, 150, 160-61, 349, 370, 415, 419-23, 426-27, 445-46, 452, 456
*Bulletin Hispanique*, 507
*Bulletin of Hispanic Studies*, 8, 26, 395, 403, 408-09, 424, 486
Bullough, Edward, 79-80, 85, 203

Bumpkin, Betty, 293
Burmeister, W., 1, 3
Burns, Robert, 310, 366
Burton-on-Trent, 64-65, 176, 179
Butler, K. T., 104
Byrne, Ceri, 24
Byron (George Gordon), Lord, 198, 440, 443-44

Cabanyes, Manuel de, 126, 161, 437, 440, 444-45
Calderón, Pedro, 204, 450
Cambridge, University of, 2, 12, 15, 17, 21-22, 51, 54-55, 69-70, 75-83, 85-87, 89, 91-92, 94, 97, 106-07, 108, 111, 114, 128, 153, 163, 182, 189, 197, 200, 206, 208, 210, 221-22, 224, 226, 233, 252, 256, 263-64, 270, 278, 297, 350, 392, 404, 406, 429-31, 439, 471-72
'Camford', 1, 9, 182, 231-32, 257, 263-64, 324, 350
Camford Grammar School [The Perse School], 51, 220-23, 229, 346
Camford University [University of Cambridge], 13-14, 17, 51, 54-55, 182, 184, 189-90, 196-217, 220-21, 224-26, 229-30, 232-33, 245, 248-49, 252, 256-57, 263, 269, 278, 284-85, 324, 327, 329, 347, 350, 353-54, 357, 361, 366-68, 374-76, 381-83, 406, 486, 489
Camford University Training College, 219-24
Campagnac, Ernest Trafford, 13, 52, 122, 137, 144, 146-47, 150-52, 163, 166, 298-302, 304, 320, 349, 358, 372-73, 378-80, 422, 488; see also Dusty; Vapid
*Canterbury Tales, The* (Chaucer), 202
Carey, Edward, 136-37, 262
Carlyle, Thomas, 385
Carroll, Lewis, 204
Cartmell, J. W., 75, 79, 202
Case, Robert Hope, 14, 52, 146, 149, 165, 294-95, 349, 372, 413-16, 420, 422, 459, 464, 486; see also Anstruther
Castillejo, J., 128, 436
Catalan, 390, 398, 402, 404, 442
Caton, Richard, 426
Cervantes, Miguel de, 29, 41-42, 204, 306, 313, 452
Cervantes Chair of Spanish Language and Literature (King's College London), 12-13, 112, 121, 143-44, 155, 205, 267, 421
Champkins, Clara, 62
Charlton, H. B., 107
Chaucer, Geoffrey, 76-77, 202, 223
Chatstone Grammar School [Dartford Grammar School], 44, 51, 180-86, 188-90, 197, 199, 205-06, 219, 225
Chouville, Léon, 78-79, 88, 104, 222-23
Christ's College, Cambridge, 51, 75-83, 87, 103-04, 106, 114, 196, 198-99, 204, 211, 224, 245, 251, 253, 257, 429; see also Trinity College, Camford
'Chronology of the Filling of the Gilmour Chair of

Spanish, 1919-1922', A, (A. R. Allan), 25
Churchman, P. H., 157, 160, 370-71, 426, 438, 442-43
Clackmarras School, 63-64, 175
Cockerell, C. R., 120
Coleridge, Samuel T., 402
Collinson, William Edward, 13, 52, 108, 120, 122, 139, 143-45, 147, 152-53, 163, 165-67, 299-300, 306, 338, 348-49, 351-52, 363, 372, 379, 413-15, 417, 419-21, 425, 427, 460, 484-85, 487-88; see also Bletherley; Crusty; Vapid
Committee of Vice-Chancellors and Principals, 487
Cook, H. C., 222-23
Corneille, P., 78, 200
Coulton, G. G., 110
'Courteous Caveat, or a Short View of the Faculty of Arts in a Technological Age with Some Modest Suggestions for Reform', A (Jeremy Longstaffe [Kenneth Muir]), 483
Craigie, W. A., 108
Cranstead School [Felsted School], 51, 53, 55, 102, 197, 226-50, 253, 262, 269, 283, 297, 347
Crusty [D. A. Slater; ?W. E. Collinson; ?J. P. Postgate], 52, 54, 298-300, 302, 323, 343, 348, 359, 484, 488, 491

Dale, Sir Alfred W. W. (Principal, University College, Liverpool [1900-03], Vice-Chancellor, University of Liverpool [1903-19]), 121, 130, 146, 318, 333, 375, 413
Dartford, 65-66, 179, 185, 199
Dartford Grammar School, 44, 51, 66-70, 180, 186, 188, 197, 205-06, 219, 246; see also Chatstone Grammar School
*Dartfordian, The*, 69-70, 209-10
Davies, Graeme J. (Vice-Chancellor, University of Liverpool, 1986-91), 26-28, 409, 486-87
Davies, J. G., 142
Davies, Josiah, 180, 184
Deacon, H. Wade, 361, 420, 423, 425
Deadwood, Professor, 2, 15, 308, 408, 486, 489-90
Dekker, Thomas, 91, 347, 364
[*Descriptive Book on Redbrick, A*], 39-40, 482
Dewsnup, Ernest Ritson, 372, 378-80
Dickens, Charles, 264
Disraeli, Benjamin, 286
Dixon, W. Macneile, 412, 414
Dobie, Dr (Dean of Arts, Redbrick University) [?W. Garmon Jones], 53, 268, 270, 278-79, 319, 326-28
Dobrée, Bonamy, 1, 3, 9, 22, 36, 40, 234, 474-78
*Don Álvaro* (Duque de Rivas), 437
*Don Quijote de la Mancha* (M. de Cervantes), 29, 41, 306
Doolittle, Beatrice, 293, 299
Dowden, Edward, 471
Downs, Brian Westerdale, 103-04, 213-14

Downside, Dr (Headmaster, Cranstead School) [J. D. McClure; W. W. Vaughan], 53, 55, 231-34, 239, 241-43, 247-50
Drabtown [Liverpool], 51, 264-66, 268, 272-74, 285-89, 303, 305, 315, 324-25, 382, 390-91,483, 493
Drake [A. W. Verrall], 55, 200, 205
Droop, John Percival, 153, 372
Dryden, John, 198
Dumbell, Stanley, 18, 27, 333
Dusty [E. T. Campagnac; ?E. Allison Peers], 37, 52, 54, 298-309, 311-23, 326, 328-29, 340, 342-43, 348-49, 358-59, 365, 367-69, 371-73, 384-86, 482, 488

Eagles, [?J. E. Eggli], 52, 308-09, 321, 341-42, 372-74, 381, 386, 486
Eberhard [?J. E. Eggli], 52, 338, 485
Edinburgh, University of, 109, 156, 421, 451-52, 454
Eggli, Jean Edmond, 6, 52, 153, 338, 348, 372-73, 379-80, 381, 420, 422, 427-28, 485-86; see also André, Eagles and Eberhard
*Elizabethan Drama and its Mad Folk* (E. Allison Peers), 91-92, 96, 226, 347, 356, 363, 431, 433
Elmes, Harvey Lonsdale, 120
Elton, Oliver, 29-30, 53, 113, 139, 145, 165, 186, 205, 279, 291-92, 295, 309, 316, 320, 323-24, 339, 344, 359, 372, 378, 413, 416, 420, 422, 427, 459-60, 464-65, 489; see also Slocombe; Miope
Engledow, Frank L., 67
*English*, 470
English Literature, Chair of (Redbrick University), 14, 47, 134, 185, 280, 299, 324, 328, 343, 346-47, 354, 361, 363, 373-74, 381, 486
Espronceda, José de, 443
*Europeo, El*, 442-43

Faber and Faber Ltd, 6, 39-40, 196, 467, 482
Faber, Geoffrey, 39, 467
'Fair Rosamond', 207
Fanshawe (Dean of Arts, Redbrick University) [?W. Garmon Jones; ?A. Bruce Boswell], 52-53, 341-42, 348, 358-59, 362, 365, 369-72, 377-83
Felsted School, 12, 51, 97-103, 114, 117, 129, 190, 197, 227-28, 234-35, 246, 252, 254, 270, 336, 429-30; see also Cranstead School
Fiedler, H. G., 108
Field, G. C., 9, 22, 36, 372, 479
Finch, Margery B., 104, 127, 161, 431, 437
*First Year at the University* (B. Truscot), 1, 8, 23, 37, 39, 44, 196, 199, 255, 410, 479
Fisher, H. A. L., 114
Fitzmaurice-Kelly, James, 12-13, 53, 112-14, 121, 135, 137, 141-45, 147, 150, 155-57, 163, 166, 204-08, 233, 261, 263-64, 267, 280,

283, 304-07, 313-18, 320, 328-29, 348, 350, 354-58, 366-67, 382-84, 389, 400, 412-18, 421-23, 425, 427, 449-56, 459, 463; see also G. C. Upright
Fitzmaurice-Kelly, Mrs Julia (*née* Sanders), 144, 305, 307
Fletcher, John, 91, 221
Fletcher, S. S. F., 89
*For Advancement of Learning. The University of Liverpool 1881-1981* (T. Kelly), 5-6, 18
Forbridge [West Kirby], 51, 288-89, 302, 314, 335
Ford, John, 91
Fouquet, M., 186-88
Fox, C., 89, 221
Frazer, Sir J., 371

Gabbitas, Thring & Co. (Education Agents), 93, 97, 116, 227
Garabedian, Dikran, 97
García de los Ríos Pedraja, L., 113
Gardner, E. G., 108
Garmon Jones, William, 53, 119-22, 136, 146, 160, 165, 279, 295, 322, 342, 346, 348-49, 358, 371-73, 379-81, 411-17, 419-20, 422, 425-28, 446, 450-51; see also Dr Dobie and Fanshawe
Garstang, John, 320
'Gentle river, Gentle river' ('Río verde, río verde'), 207
George VI, King, 332
George, Lloyd, 244
Gibberd, Sir Frederick, 132

Gide, Charles, 412
Gilkes, Maurice Webster [?Frank Renfield or Rönnfeld], 212-14, 280, 357, 368-69
Gilmour, Captain George, 53, 112, 312-13, 315-16, 318-19, 326; see also John Austin Trevor
Gilmour Chair of Spanish (University of Liverpool), 3, 10, 12, 14, 30, 38-40, 43, 51, 78, 81, 100, 105, 112-16, 121-22, 127-28, 133-36, 143, 149-67, 174, 178, 188, 205, 234, 261-62, 267, 312-13, 315-18, 320, 326, 328-30, 335, 337, 346, 348-50, 354, 357, 360-61, 363, 367, 369-73, 377-79, 381, 384-86, 389-90, 394-95, 400, 403, 411-56, 474; see also Trevor Professorship of Poetry
Gladstone, W. E., 286
Glasgow, University of, 9-10, 27-28, 43, 327, 333, 394, 397, 473
Glehn, Louis (Camille) de, 53, 78, 87-88, 90, 102, 221-23, 234; see also Hopewell
Gonner, Sir Edward C. K., 342
González, F., 157, 445
González Ruiz, Nicolás, 420
Gowenlock, Brian, 44, 196
Grace, Gordon, 104
*Graded Passages for Translation from English* (E. Allison Peers), 19
Grant, Alexander, 64-65, 175
Green, Julius [?Lascelles Abercrombie], 52, 294
Grierson, H. J. C., 109, 416

Gurdon,, Edmund, 402
Gurrey, Percival, 67

Haan, Fonger De, 415, 451-52, 456
Hall, Elizabeth (*née* Colquhoun), 24, 116, 393, 470, 474; see also Amelia Truscot,
Hall, Harold Baxter, 22, 116, 393, 474
Halliday, Sir William Reginald, 152, 372, 379-80, 412
Harchester [fictitious public school], 51, 230, 262-63
*Hard Times* (C. Dickens), 264, 353
Harmer, Thomas B., 62
Harness Prize, 82, 91, 225-26, 347, 429, 433
Harrison, Jane E., 107
Hayes, B. J., 104
'Hell Corner', 481, 484, 492
Henley, William E., 181
Herdman, Sir William, 427
Hetherington, Sir Hector (Vice-Chancellor, University of Liverpool, 1927-36), 9, 14, 22, 27-28, 53, 164, 333-34, 375, 381, 405, 410, 473-74; see also Sir Archibald Blake
Higher Education Funding Council for England, 26, 148
Hines, C. P., 184, 205
'Hispanic Scholar, A', 45
Hispanic Studies, 5, 11, 20, 37, 39, 105, 113, 116, 126, 136, 140, 144, 155-56, 161, 225, 307, 314, 325, 335-37, 346, 356, 389-90, 392-400, 403, 417, 443-45, 451

*History Man, The* (M. Bradbury), 15-16
*History of Elizabethan Poetry* (G. C. Upright), 205-06
*History of English Poetry* (G. C. Upright), 306, 309, 329, 339
*History of Spanish Literature, A* (J. Fitzmaurice-Kelly), 112, 205, 306
*History of the Romantic Movement in Spain, A* (E. Allison Peers), 5, 19, 126
*History of the University of Cambridge, A* (C. N. L. Brooke), 17
Hoare-Laval agreement, 245
Holt, Emma G., 348, 361, 413
Hopewell [L. (C.) de Glehn], 52, 221-24, 229, 233-34
Howden, Marjorie P. (Mrs M. P. Roxby), 294
Hume, Martin, 113
*Hunting of the Snark, The* (L. Carroll), 204

Ibsen, Henrik, 80, 103, 203
Illingworth, Sir Charles, 410
Inaccessible [John Sampson], 2, 4, 13, 15, 54, 308-09, 321, 341, 343-44, 348-49, 362, 364, 366, 369, 371, 374, 376-77, 385-86, 459, 487, 493
Institute of Hispanic Studies, Liverpool, 20, 405
Ives, Eric, 410

Jackson, Revd H. L., 104, 110
Jackson, K., 147
*Jealous Old Man of Extremadura, The (El celoso extremeño)* (M. de Cervantes), 42

Jennings, S. J., 184
John of the Cross, Saint, 7, 71, 254, 337
Jones, Dorothy C., 293
Jones, Sir C. Sydney, 334, 426-27
Jones, Thomas, 412, 414
Jones, W. H. S., 88
Jonson, Ben, 91
Jopson, N. B., 85
*Julius Caesar* (Shakespeare), 69
Junta para Ampliación de Estudios, 435

'Kaine Diatheke' (O. Elton), 29-30, 139, 359, 460-65
Kastner, L. E., 107, 115, 118-19
Kelly, R. E., 139
Kelly, Thomas, 5-6, 18
Ker, W. P., 416, 423, 425
King's College London, 13
Kipling, R., 469
Kolkhorst, G. A., 420, 424-25

Lamartine, Alphonse de, 439
Lamb, Norman J., 24, 197, 234
Langland, William, 76, 202
[*Last Year at the University*], 39, 44
Latin America, 5, 112, 390, 404, 412, 430, 451
Lee, Sir Sidney, 105, 110-11
Leeds, University of, 2-3, 265, 400, 476-77
Legouis, Émile, 223
Legouis, Pierre, 223
Leighton Buzzard, 62, 173
[*Letters of Bruce Truscot, The*], 39
*Lettres Provinciales* (B. Pascal), 78

Lewis, C. S., 308
Lipczinski, Albert, 139, 143, 458-60, 464-65
*Listener, The*, 2
Liverpool, city of, 45, 51, 119-20, 129-32, 264, 273-74, 286-88, 305, 315, 324, 358, 390, 418; see also Drabtown
Liverpool, University of, 2-7, 9-12, 14, 17-23, 26-30, 35, 38-40, 47-48, 51-55, 61, 100-01, 109, 112, 114, 116, 118-20, 122, 125-67, 179, 188, 197, 234, 256, 261, 264-68, 270-71, 276-78, 284-85, 290, 294, 297, 300, 306, 309, 312, 316-19, 324-25, 327, 330, 331-34, 336-37, 340, 345, 351, 356-57, 359-61, 372, 375, 378-80, 385-86, 389-92, 395, 397, 400-03, 405, 408-09, 411-29, 434-36, 440-41, 444-48, 451-53, 455, 458-60, 479, 483, 487, 489 and *passim*; see also Redbrick University
*Liverpool Students' Songbook* (1906), 391
Liverpool University Press, 25, 409
Livewire, Jim [E. Allison Peers], 2, 4, 14, 54, 134, 185, 280, 301, 328-29, 346-48, 350, 354, 356, 359-60, 362-67, 369-71, 373-74, 376-85, 481-86, 489, 491
Loaf [?John Share Jones], 54, 361, 382, 384
Lockhart, John G., 310
Lodge, Sir Oliver, 141
Lomax, D. W., 116

London, University of, 70, 105-06, 109, 112, 115-16, 151, 154, 162, 180, 182, 190, 198, 256-57, 300, 354, 429, 454, 456
Longmorn, nr Elgin, 63
Longstaffe, Jeremy [Kenneth Muir], 483
Lovewit [?Alexander Mair], 308, 487, 491
Lowe, Roy, 410
Lowes, Livingstone, 475
Lumsden-Kouvel, Audrey, 11, 24, 400-03
Lutyens, Sir Edwin, 132

Macaulay, G. C., 77, 91, 202
MacColl, D. S., 142, 414
Maccoll Lectures, The (Cambridge University), 51, 204, 233, 266; see also The Snark Lectures
Mackay, J. M., 120, 136, 139, 142-43, 150, 152, 156, 320, 358-59, 378, 459, 461-62, 464
Mackenzie, Ann L., 35, 116, 471
Mackenzie, D., 180
Madariaga, Salvador de, 135, 350, 411-12, 414-18, 420, 423-25, 449-50, 453, 455
'Mad Tea-party', A (L. Carroll), 204
Mair, Alexander, 12-13, 52, 113, 145, 156-57, 161-65, 301, 308, 314, 320, 322, 346, 348, 353-54, 356-57, 366, 370, 372, 379, 413-15, 418-21, 423, 426-28, 449, 453, 465, 486-87; see also Wormwood

Manchester, University of, 2, 107, 115, 118, 156, 319, 327, 471
Mansford, Charles John Jodrell, 66-69, 180-81, 184-89, 215
Marden, Charles Carroll, 155-56
Martin, Leonard C., 53, 291, 294-95; see also Anstruther
Massinger, Philip, 91, 347, 356, 364, 367-68, 370
*Masters, The* (C. P. Snow), 15
Mawer, Sir Allen, 109, 154, 372
McClelland, Ivy L., 11, 20, 24, 26, 43-44, 394, 397-99
McClure, Sir John David (Headmaster, Mill Hill School), 53, 93-96, 101, 103, 112, 228, 230-32, 241-43, 250; see also Dr Downside
McLean, Norman, 81, 83, 91-92, 114, 212-13, 215-16, 432-33
'Meaty', (?C. P. Hines), 184, 205
Menéndez Pidal, Ramón, 157-59, 392, 423, 425-27, 435, 438, 446-48
Menéndez y Pelayo, M., 113, 159, 445
Mérimée, E., 114, 159-60, 428, 431, 440, 449
Mérimée, H., 392
Merry del Val, Alfonso, 127
Meyer, Kuno, 113, 137, 142, 147, 312, 320, 450-51
Middleton, Thomas, 91
Mill Hill School, 53, 93-97, 102, 117, 190, 227-30, 233, 241, 336

Milton, John, 198
Miope, Professor [?Oliver Elton], 185-86, 279, 489
Modern Humanities Research Association, 22, 78-79, 100, 103-11, 118, 127-28, 143-44, 159-60, 313-14, 404, 409, 423, 430, 433-34, 440, 444-45, 417, 421
*Modern Language Review*, 111, 144, 243, 282, 314, 417, 452-53
Molière, 78, 200
Montague Summers, Revd A. J.-M. A., 110
Montgomery, J., 136, 413, 415, 417-18
Moore, B., 148
Moore-Smith, G. C., 91, 107
Morel-Fatio, Alfred, 449
Moreno, E. M., 113
*Moro Expósito, El* (Duque de Rivas), 437-39
*Mother of Carmel* [Saint Teresa of Ávila] (E. Allison Peers), 7, 72
Mountford, Sir James (Vice-Chancellor, Liverpool University, 1945-63), 3-4, 6, 8, 334, 410, 484
*Mr Perrin and Mr Traill* (H. S. Walpole), 239
Muir, Kenneth, 3, 469, 483; see also Jeremy Longstaffe
Muir, Ramsay, 113, 130, 139, 142, 278, 320, 464
Murray, A. V., 1
Myres, J. L., 137
*Mysticism and Modern Christianity* (E. Allison Peers), 255
Mystics of Spain, 44, 71, 337

*Nación, La*, 418, 454-55
Navarro Tomás, T., 113, 157, 448
Newberry, Percy Edward, 147, 150, 460, 464
Newcastle, University of, 3, 109
Newnham College, Cambridge, 106
'New Testament', The, 10, 12-13, 17-18, 21, 23, 29-30, 43, 51, 100, 113, 136-37, 139-50, 152-54, 156, 161-66, 284, 305, 308-09, 320-22, 328, 337-38, 348-49, 358-59, 364-65, 367, 371, 373, 378, 381, 385-86, 389-90, 458-65, 487-88; see also the 'Salvation Army'
Nicholson, Shields, 416

Oberlé, L. J., 67, 182-83, 186, 199
Odysseus, 462
*Origins of French Romanticism, The* (E. Allison Peers), 127, 161, 428, 431, 437, 440
Ormerod, H. A., 378-79
Ossian, 462
'Our Alma Mater on the Hill', 391
Owens, Andrea, 24
'Oxbridge', 1-2, 9, 45, 182-83, 202, 210, 231, 266, 405-06, 472, 486
Oxbridge University (University of Oxford), 13, 37, 45, 51, 182-83, 197, 199, 200, 204, 217, 229-30, 248-57, 262-65, 267-71,

273, 278, 281-84, 290, 293, 301, 303, 310, 324, 326, 329, 347, 349-50, 357-58, 383, 391, 406, 471, 489
Oxford, University of, 2, 51, 83, 94, 97, 108, 116, 135-36, 153, 163, 182, 210, 249, 252, 256, 267, 270, 278, 350, 404, 406, 421, 425, 472, 486; see also Oxbridge University
*Oxford Magazine*, 407

Palfreyman, David, 407-08
Paradise Street, Drabtown [Brownlow Hill, Liverpool], 272, 288-89, 302, 304, 326
Pares, Sir Bernard, 143, 150, 337, 459-60, 464
Pascal, Blaise, 77
Paues, Anna C., 106-07
Paulo, Rafael, 452
Pearson, Alfred Chilton, 153-54, 379
Peers, Edgar Allison, 1, 3-27, 29-30, 35-48, 50-51, 53-54, 61-167, 173-386, 389-456, 459-61, 464-65, 467-68, 477, 479, 479, 481, 483, 487-88, 490, *passim*; see also Bruce Truscot; Jim Livewire; Dusty
Peers, Jessie, 62, 71-73, 174, 192-93, 214, 247
Peers, John Thomas, 61-66, 69, 71-74, 174-77, 179, 192-96, 198-99, 214-15, 239, 247, 269
Peers, Robert, 61, 192
Peers, Winifred Dale, 62-63, 65, 71-72, 179, 192

Peet [W. W. Skeat], 54, 201-02
Peet, Thomas Eric, 153, 360, 372
Peile, J., 81, 211
Percy, Bishop Thomas, 207, 310
Pérez de Ayala, Ramón, 113
Perse School, 51, 53, 78, 86-88, 90, 92, 94, 220-23; see also Camford Grammar School
Petsch, Robert, 460
Phillips, W. Alison, 379
*Phonetic Spanish Reader, A* (E. A. Peers), 89, 161, 425, 437, 443, 448
Picton, Aenid, 294
*Piers Plowman* (W. Langland), 202
Pitollet, C., 113, 414, 449
*Poèmes choisis* (A. de Vigny; ed. E. A. Peers), 81, 126, 431, 433
Pole, W. L. A., 113
*Political Economy* (C. Gide), 412
Portugal / Portuguese, 5, 112, 204, 390, 404, 409, 430
Postgate, J. P., 54, 349, 379, 413-17, 419, 484; see also Crusty
Powicke, Sir (Frederick) Maurice, 414
Praz, Mario, 54, 338, 485; see also Ratti
Prior, O. H. P., 106
*Professor Lapping Sends his Apologies* (Laurie Taylor), 15-16
Prudhomme, René F. (Sully Prudhomme), 181

Pushkin, Alexander S., 460

Quadrado, J. M., 443
Quiller-Couch, A. (T.), 92, 200-01, 251

Rackham, H., 79, 81
Raleigh, Sir Walter, 141, 295, 461
Randall, Ellen M., 132, 287
Rathbone, H. R., 426-27
Ratti [?Piero Rébora; ?Mario Praz], 54, 338, 485
Rébora, Piero, 54, 338, 348, 413-15, 417-20, 423, 485; see also Ratti
'Redbrick', 1-3, 6-7, 9-11, 17, 20, 22, 24, 42-43, 130, 178, 182, 346, 350-51, 383, 405, 467, 469, 472, 479
*Redbrick and these Vital Days* (B. Truscot), 1-4, 7-8, 10, 16, 20, 23, 37, 43-44, 190-91, 230, 248, 255, 264-65, 269, 273, 284, 293, 297, 299, 301, 308, 325, 330, 339, 345-46, 350-51, 360, 364, 372, 375, 378, 383, 406-09, 467, 470, 473, 475, 479, 486, 490-91, 493
[*Redbrick, a Portrait*; *Redbrick as it is*], 39
'Redbrick Tea-party', A (B. Truscot), 37, 40, 204, 267, 308, 313, 346, 475, 482
Redbrick University [University of Liverpool], 2, 5, 12-16, 23-25, 27-28, 37-42, 44-45, 47-48, 51-55, 130, 134, 164-65, 178, 185, 197, 204-05, 257, 261-330, 360, 369, 373-75, 383, 389-92, 405-06, 409, 467, 469, 472, 476, 481-93
*Redbrick University* (B. Truscot), 1-4, 6-10, 13, 20, 22-23, 25, 29, 37, 41, 71, 92, 139, 143, 165, 180, 182, 188-89, 199-200, 202, 208, 210, 216-17, 221, 225-26, 235, 249, 252, 255, 257, 264-66, 270, 273, 278, 285, 290, 293, 299, 308, 311, 325, 330, 337, 345, 350-51, 360, 372, 375, 383, 392, 402, 404-09, 467, 469-73, 475, 479, 482, 493
*Redbrick University Calendar*, 311
*Redbrick University Revisited: The Autobiography of 'Bruce Truscot'* (E. Allison Peers), 19, 21, 25-28, 48, 51, 409-10, *passim*
Reilly, Charles H., 18, 130, 137, 139, 141, 143, 145, 147-48, 164-65, 308, 320, 322, 346, 372, 459, 464
*Reliques of Ancient English Poetry* (Bishop Thomas Percy), 207, 310
Renfield (or Rönnfeldt), Frank, 85, 212-13, 224, 468; see also M. W. Gilkes
Renwick, W. L., 295
Ribbans, Geoffrey W., 204, 403, 405, 408-09
Ricketts, A. N., 144
Riley, Miss, 486, 491-92
Rippon, Josiah [?Sir Henry Thomas], 55, 353-58, 368-69, 380
Rivas, Ángel de Saavedra, Duque de, 126, 161, 424, 437-38, 440, 444

Robertson, C. Grant, 1
Robertson, John G., 111-12, 115, 152, 161, 417-18, 420-21, 426, 431, 441
Robespierre, 385
Robson, Revd E. I., 101, 253-54
Romanticism/Romantic Movement in Spain, 112, 126, 306, 310, 336-37, 339, 356, 437-42, 444-45, 448
Rosenhead, Louis, 131
Round, Nicholas G., 20
Rouse, William H. D., 87-90, 220, 222-24, 346
Routledge, F. J., 6, 29, 373
Roxby, Percy Maude, 412, 484
Rudler, G., 108-09
Rudmose Brown, T. B., 157, 403, 444
Rugby School, 86, 106, 117-18, 220
Ruiz Pastor, A., 144
Russell, Bertrand, 103-04
Russian Revolution, 99

Saintsbury, G. E. B., 109-10
'Salvation Army', The [The 'New Testament'], 13-15, 42, 51, 284, 305, 308-09, 320-23, 330, 340-42, 344, 346, 348, 354-55, 357-59, 364-65, 371-72, 377-78, 380-81, 383, 385, 481, 484, 488, 492
Sampson, John, 13, 54, 144, 165, 308, 320, 349, 372, 459, 462, 487; see also Inaccessible
Sandiford, Peter, 424
Sanín Cano, Baldomero, 135, 350, 358, 411, 415-20, 450-52, 454-56

Santiago, José de, 414-15, 449-50
Saroïhandy, Jean, 414-15, 449-50
Savile, Henry, 41
Savory, D. (L.), 109
*Scaffolding in the Sky: A Semi-architectural Autobiography* (C. Reilly), 18
Scott, Cyril, 464
Scott, Dixon, 464
Scott, Sir Walter, 160, 310, 370, 438, 443-44
*Screwtape Letters, The* (C. S. Lewis), 308
'Senate in Laputa' (1934-35) (F. J. Routledge), 6, 29, 373
Shakespeare, William, 69, 77, 82, 91, 202, 213, 429, 433, 475
Share Jones, John, 54, 333-34, 382; see also Loaf,
Sheffield, University [University College] of, 2, 91, 108, 114
*Sheffield Telegraph*, 41
Shelley, Percy Bysshe, 450
*Shelley and Calderon* (S. de Madariaga), 135, 450
Shipley, Sir Arthur Everett, 81-82, 92, 103, 112, 114, 211-12, 215-16, 246, 280-81, 431-32
Shoebridge, 262-66, 270, 310
Shute, J. J., 426-27
Silva, J. A., 452
Silver, Harold, 409
Simmins, C. M., 104
Sing (Synge), Revd E. J., 211
Skeat, Walter William, 54, 76, 85, 111, 201-02, 251; see also Peet

*Skeleton Spanish Grammar, A* (E. A. Peers), 81, 100, 356, 424, 430-31, 433, 439, 453

Slater, David Ansell, 54, 154, 162, 298-300, 302, 349, 351-53, 373, 420, 422, 425, 484, 487-88; see also Crusty; Bletherley

Slocombe, George [Oliver Elton], 53, 186, 279, 283, 290-94, 296, 304, 322-24, 339, 344, 348, 350, 354, 360, 362, 365-66, 459, 486, 489

Sloman, Sir Albert, 395, 486-87

Smellie, Dr Janet, 6

Smith, J. Arthur, 361, 420, 423, 425

Smuts, Jan C., 82

Snark Lectures, The (Camford University) [The Maccoll Lectures (Cambridge University)], 51, 204-05, 233, 266

Snow, C. P., 15

Solly, G. A., 426

Southey, Robert, 310

Spain, 5, 7, 23, 37-38, 83, 105, 112-13, 115-16, 127, 132, 142, 204, 206-07, 310, 331, 339, 392, 398-400, 410, 423, 430, 437-41, 443, 445, 448, 462

*Spain in Eclipse 1934-1943* (E. Allison Peers), 4, 245

*Spain, the Church and the Orders* (E. Allison Peers), 5

Spanish, 5, 13-14, 39, 65-66, 75-76, 100, 102, 105, 112-16, 118-19, 121-22, 125-28, 136, 141, 149, 155-56, 160, 206-07, 244, 268, 325, 327, 335-36, 354, 371, 390, 393, 398, 400, 403-04, 412, 414-15, 417, 420, 422, 424-26, 428-30, 434-36, 438, 445, 447, 449-52, 456

Spanish Civil War, 19, 37, 115-16, 245, 401, 403

*Spanish Dilemma, The* (E. Allison Peers), 5

*Spanish Tragedy 1930-1936, The* (E. Allison Peers), 5, 245

*Sphinx, The*, 131, 144, 333

*Spirit of Flame* [St John of the Cross] (E. Allison Peers), 7

Starkie, W., 424

Steele Smith, Miss, 104

Stephenson, Revd Frank, 97-100, 115

Stewart, Revd H. F., 77-78, 104, 106, 108, 111, 200

Stinson, C. B., 67, 180-83

Stitt, J. Carlton, 426

Stockley, V., 104

Strachey, J. P., 104

Strasbourg, University of, 119

*Studies of the Spanish Mystics* (E. Allison Peers), 5, 20

Summer School of Spanish, 127-28, 136, 188, 390, 392, 399, 401, 436

*Survey of English Literature* (O. Elton), 145, 291

Swinburne, Algernon C., 181


Tankard, Allan P., 276

Tapias Navarro, A., 113

Taylor, A. J. P., 1

Taylor, Laurie, 15-16

INDEX 519

Tennyson, Alfred Lord, 198
Teresa of Ávila, Saint, 7, 71, 254, 403
Terracher, Louis Adolphe, 54, 109, 119, 121, 338, 348, 361, 413, 456; see also André
Thackeray, W. M., 1, 182, 198, 469, 485
Thomas, Sir Henry, 55, 156-57, 162, 204, 353-54, 356-57, 382, 419-21, 423-25, 427; see also Josiah Rippon
Tilley, Arthur Augustus, 78, 106, 108, 200
Tillotson, Geoffrey, 4, 469-71
Tillotson, Kathleen, 469-71
*Times, The*, 357, 453-55, 471
*Times Educational Supplement, The*, 262
*Times Higher Education Supplement, The*, 15, 240, 406, 409-10
Toller, T. N., 107
Toulouse, University of, 115
Toynbee, A. J., 472
Toynbee, Jocelyn M.C., 471-72
Toynbee, Margaret R., 471-72
Toynbee, P. J., 109-10
Trenery, Grace R., 293
Trevor, John Austin [Captain George Gilmour], 53, 312, 315-18, 326, 344
Trevor Professorship of Poetry (Redbrick University) [Gilmour Chair of Spanish (Liverpool University)], 13-14, 37, 40, 51, 204-05, 267-68, 270-71, 312-13, 315, 317-19, 323, 326-29, 336, 343, 346, 357, 361, 367, 383, 389, 485

Trinity College, Camford [Christ's College, Cambridge], 51, 75, 196, 198-99, 206, 211-13, 216-17, 219, 224-25, 235, 245, 249, 255-56, 266, 280-81, 310, 346-47, 357, 368
Trollope, A., 469
Troyes, Chrétien de, 78. 200
Truscot, Amelia [Elizabeth Hall], 9, 36, 40, 234, 469, 474, 476-77
Truscot, Bruce [E. Allison Peers], 1-5, 7-17, 19-20, 22-24, 26, 29, 35-48, 51, 53, 102, 165, 173-386, 389-93, 402, 405-10, 459, 467, 469-71, 473-74, 476-93, *passim*

University Club (Liverpool), 109, 136-37, 144, 149, 320, 358
University College, Liverpool, 130, 333
*University Gazette* (Camford), 204-05
*University of Liverpool. A Photographic Portrait: Yesterday and Today, The*, 26
*University of Liverpool Hispanic Honour Society Newsletter*, 216, 393-94
University Training College, Cambridge, 86-87, 219
Upright, George Charles [James Fitzmaurice-Kelly], 13-14, 37, 53, 141, 204-08, 222, 233, 261, 263-68, 279-84, 292, 301, 303-23, 326-30, 339, 341, 343-44, 348-49, 357, 362, 365-68, 383-84, 459

Upright, James see George Charles Upright
Urfé, Honoré d', 105
Utley, Alison, 409

Valencia, G., 452
Valentine-Richards, Alfred Valentine, 80-81, 211-12, 215
Vapid [?W. E. Collinson; ?D. A. Slater; ?E. T. Campagnac], 299, 487-88, 491
Varela, J. V., 121, 414
Vaughan, William Wyamar (Master, Wellington College), 42, 55, 117-19, 121-22, 133, 233, 250; see also Dr Downside
Veitch, G. S., 372, 379, 417-19, 455
Verrall, Arthur Woolgar, 55, 92, 200; see also Drake
Victoria Building, (Liverpool University), 2, 51, 130, 271, 276-77, 285, 309, 324, 340, 364, 408; see also Arts Tower (Redbrick University)
Vigny, Alfred de, 81, 126-27, 181, 417, 431, 433, 444
Villasante, Julián Martínez, 414, 449-50

Walpole, H. S., 239
Walsh, A., 104
War, First World (1914-18), 17, 21, 93, 98-103, 114, 139, 142, 144, 153, 155, 174, 210, 234, 238, 243-49, 252, 255, 278, 303, 331-32, 347, 429-30, 432
War, Second World (1939-45), 35, 37-40, 115, 216, 331-32, 393, 469-71

Warren, T. (H.), 108
Waterhouse, Alfred, 129-30, 276-77
Waterhouse, Paul, 129
Waters, E. G. R., 97
Webster, Sir Charles Kingsley, 55, 151, 301, 372, 426, 485; see also Active
Wellington College, 42, 55, 116-19, 129, 133, 190, 233, 250, 252, 268, 270
West Kirby, 51, 133, 288-89; see also Forbridge
Whitman, Walt, 92
Wilberforce, L. R., 389
Williams, R. A., 109
Wiltshire, 65, 69, 94, 179, 229
*Wind on the Heath, The* (J. Sampson), 462
Woodall, S. J. 183
Wootton, H. A., 223
Wordsworth, William, 280
Wormwood [Alexander Mair], 13-14, 53, 301, 308-09, 321-23, 341-44, 348, 353-55, 357-59, 362, 364, 366-71, 373-74, 380, 382-83, 486-87, 489
Wright, Hagbert, 416
Wyatt, A. J., 77, 202
Wyld, Henry Cecil Kennedy, 147, 150, 283, 306, 379, 454, 459-60, 464
Wyld, Norman, 147, 320, 460, 463-64

*Year's Work in English Studies, The*, 243, 476
Young, Marion (Mrs Marion Peers), 287, 335

Zimmern, A. E., 414
Zorrilla, José, 442